Copy #1

D0531923

Copy #1

FOCAL GROUP PSYCHOTHERAPY

Edited by Matthew McKay, Ph.D.
and Kim Paleg, Ph.D.

NEW HARBINGER PUBLICATIONS, INC.

Publisher's Note

This publication is designed to provide accurate and authoritative information in regard to the subject matter covered. It is sold with the understanding that the publisher is not engaged in rendering psychological, financial, legal, or other professional services. If expert assistance or counseling is needed, the services of a competent professional should be sought.

Distributed in the U.S.A. by Publishers Group West; in Canada by Raincoast Books; in Great Britain by Airlift Book Company, Ltd.; in South Africa by Real Books, Ltd.; in Australia by Boobook; and in New Zealand by Tandem Press.

FOCAL GROUP PSYCHOTHERAPY

ISBN: 1-879237-18-0 Hardcover

Library of Congress Catalog Card Number: 92-054160

Copyright © 1992 by New Harbinger Publications, Inc.
5674 Shattuck Avenue
Oakland, CA 94609

All rights reserved.

Printed in the United States of America using recycled paper.

00   99   98

10   9   8   7   6   5

For Pat Fanning, a friend like a brother.
—M.M.

For Tom Boyd and Devon, with all my love.
— K.P.

We wish to gratefully acknowledge three people whose efforts significantly contributed to this book. Barbara Quick for her close, developmental editing, Mary McCormick for copy editing and proofreading, and Gayle Zanca for book design.

Contents

Introduction

Among the many varieties of group psychotherapy, there is enormous diversity in terms of format, goals, and the role of the leader. Many authors have comprehensively addressed the conceptual and theoretical aspects of the more traditional group psychotherapies — for example, Irvin D. Yalom in his *Theory and Practice of Group Psychotherapy* (1975).

Surprisingly, there has been no similar undertaking with respect to specific focal groups. *Focal Group Psychotherapy* attempts to fill this clinical gap. Each chapter in the book describes the group process as it relates to a particular focal problem, providing concise, step-by-step directions for starting, structuring, and leading such a group.

Focal Groups and the Traditional Groups Therapy Model

The Tavistock and transference-focused groups, as well as the Gestalt and "encounter" groups, all have notable elements in common that set them apart from focal group psychotherapy. They have tended to treat a heterogeneous population — individuals with diverse problems — by promoting some form of affective sharing, reality testing, and a process designed to reexperience and examine maladaptive behavior patterns.

In contrast to these more traditional models, the last decade has seen the flourishing of homogeneous groups focused on specific client populations. These focal groups have addressed the treatment of a wide range of issues, such as spouse battering, incest (survivors and perpetrators), shyness, depression, post-traumatic stress disorder (PTSD), and codependency. Although formats, approaches, and styles for these groups certainly differ, they usually have about half a dozen general qualities in common. Focal groups tend to

- Have a high degree of structure

- Have a specific and limited target issue

- Be strongly goal-oriented

- Place a high value on efficiency (homework and structured exercises designed to promote rapid change)

- Have a high educational function

- Discourage attention to transference issues

It can be argued that focal groups afford clients less opportunity to explore process, reality test, and evaluate affective and behavioral responses than would be offered in more traditional groups. However, focal groups do create several important advantages. First, they promote greater group identification and faster cohesion because everyone presents with the same problem. A number of studies have supported the link between high cohesion and successful outcomes (Maxmen, 1978; Budman, 1981; Marcovitz and Smith, 1983). A second advantage is that focal groups are more effective, at least superficially, in reducing client distress. A body of evidence is beginning to show that focal groups provide greater symptomatic relief than traditional heterogeneous group models. After reviewing the literature, Klein (1985) suggests that "homogeneous group treatment may be the treatment of choice for symptom relief, and for situations in which time, expense, and patient resources are limited" (p 317). A third advantage, implied by Klein's conclusion, is that focal groups tend to offer a brief and concentrated therapeutic experience. Group members often show more rapid improvment because the high degree of group structure rivets attention on a single problem area. Because many focal groups are time-limited, clients may push themselves to learn and practice new behaviors in the short period available.

The issue of efficiency is worthy of special note. If therapy is to be brief, as well as successful, it may be focused. Burlingame and Fuhriman (1990), after reviewing the literature on time-limited group therapy, concluded the following: "No other dimension reaches such consensus among the writers as does the importance of focusing treatment objectives and processes.... There is substantial agreement that a focus needs to be taken by the clients, the therapist, and the total group" (p 105).

Advantages of Focal Groups Over Individual Therapy for Specific Target Populations

At a time when government-funded mental health resources are diminishing, HMOs are proliferating, and insurance companies are restricting mental health coverage, group therapy has emerged as an extremely cost-effective alternative to individual therapy.

Davies (1975) points out that, for most people, interaction in groups is the norm — at home, in the workplace, and in social situations. One-on-one pedagogic or emotional encounters are relatively rare in our society. This can make individual therapy extremely uncomfortable for certain individuals, and can even deter them from pursuing help.

Further, in a group setting, the difficulties clients have in their lives can be reproduced directly rather than symbolically, and thus can be dealt with more effectively. In groups, participants are encouraged to share their resources in coping with similar issues. They can develop new self-perceptions along the way, experiencing themselves, for example, as helpful, sympathetic, or supportive. It's also sometimes easier for clients to accept help or insight offered by their peers, rather than by a therapist in an authoritatian position.

Addressing the need for cost-effective treatment, Budman et al. (1988) compared time-limited individual therapy with time-limited groups. Clients rated themselves on various scales, and were also rated by the therapist, an independent evaluator, and their spouse or significant other. "Before" and "after" measures were used. Budman et al. concluded that there was significant improvement in both treatment conditions, and that, for the most part, subjects appeared to do equally well in the group and in individual therapy.

Research by Rose et al. (1986) showed no significant differences in outcome for groups that addressed issues of stress management versus individual therapy focused on the same topic. Clients in both treatment modalities felt that they'd benefited, and were pleased not to have been in the alternate modality. Rose and his colleagues also confirmed that the cost of group treatment was dramatically lower than the cost of individual therapy.

Toseland and Siporin reviewed the literature in 1986, finding 32 studies comparing individual and group treatment (these studies met the classical experimental criteria of random assignment of clients to individual and group modalities, with comparisons made across the two modalities). In 24 of the 32 studies — 75 percent — no significant differences in effectiveness were found between the two treatment modalities: group treatment was as effective as individual treatment. In the remaining eight studies (25 percent), group treatment was found to be significantly more effective than individual treatment. In no case was individual treatment found to be more effective than group therapy. Not only was group therapy more efficacious than individual therapy, but the dropout rate was also lower for the groups than for the cases involving individual treatment. While no clear pattern emerged indicating the particular presenting problems or characteristics of clients who would benefit most from group treatment, successful group treatments were reviewed for depression, agoraphobia, assertiveness, parenting, and incest, among others.

In a commentary on Toseland and Siporin's literature review, Mackenzie (1986) suggests that the group format is a powerful method for overcoming low motivation. In support of his observation, he reiterates the lower dropout rate in groups than among participants in individual therapy, and notes the success of group treatment with difficult client populations, such as substance abusers. Mackenzie also points out that the use of group therapy for treating aggressive clients has a lengthy and distinguished history in the therapeutic community. He concludes that "by far the most difficult challenge lies in overcoming professional and institutional resistance to the sensible application of group modalities" (p 210).

The Use of Focal Groups as an Adjunct to Individual Therapy

As noted above, research supports the advantages of focal group therapy over individual therapy, not only on the basis of cost effectiveness, but also with respect to outcome. However, it's also important to acknowledge that group interaction can be a powerful trigger for emotions and memories. Clients may need to have the additional support of individual therapy throughout the group process. This is especially true for clients whose clinical issues may require long-term treatment — for example, character disorders, abuse survivors, and so on. Such clients can nonetheless derive significant benefits from participating in a short-term focal group. The added support of individual therapy may also help prevent the attrition of certain difficult clients in group therapy.

Many clients will not accept group therapy as their sole treatment modality. In their 1986 study, Toseland and Siporin also found that when given a choice between individual and group therapy, many clients opted for a one-on-one therapeutic relationship. Budman et al. (1988) found a similar trend among their clients. Despite nearly identical effects within the two treatment modalities, clients subjectively perceived individual therapy to be more beneficial. Such client biases limit group therapy to an adjunctive role for many individuals. Nonetheless, as MacKenzie argued in 1986, as profesional resistance to group therapy decreases and a corresponding shift in "therapeutic atmosphere" occurs, client attitudes will shift accordingly.

Until such a shift occurs, group therapy can still serve as an important adjunct to individual therapy for those clients who do not wish to rely on the group process alone. Participants derive enormous hope and support from a group in which others are all struggling with similar issues. Group members are exposed to peer-generated problem solving in an atmosphere of learning and exploration: this can expedite the progress of individual therapy.

Peer pressure is a strong motivator for change in the group setting. Behaviors and skills developed in individual therapy can be rehearsed within the group; clients also learn from the work and progress of other group members.

The confrontation of denial provided by members in a group often speeds the progress of individual therapy. Similarly, the interpersonal patterns of individuals are more readily exposed in a group than in a one-on-one setting. This provides the group therapist with an array of projective patterns that may not be fully observable in individual transference relationships.

How To Use This Book

In composing these chapters, the authors have assumed a certain level of therapeutic expertise among their readers. Aspiring group therapists — whether graduate students or practicing professionals — should acquire not only basic therapy skills, but familiarity as well with the particular client group being addressed. It would be a mistake to attempt to run a focal group on the basis of one of these chapters alone, without a working knowledge of the clinical population in question.

Each chapter in *Focal Group Psychotherapy* follows the same organizational structure. Regardless of theoretical perspective, or the type and style of interventions, all chapters use a consistent format so that you can easily find the specific information you need. It isn't necessary to read every word of the shyness groups chapter, for example, to locate basic ground rules or main concepts and skills. For each type of group, this information appears in clearly marked sections.

Every chapter begins with an *Introduction* that gives an overview of the relevant problem area. This section may include research findings on the scope of the disorder, as well as commentaries on the effectiveness of specific treatments in the group setting. The *Selection and Screening* section provides criteria for determining who should and should not be in the group. In many chapters, this section includes screening techniques and even specific questions to ask prospective group members. The *Time and Duration* section makes recommendations about the ideal number of weeks the group should run, and the length of each group session. In some chapters, two alternate formats are provided for longer- and shorter-term groups.

The section *Structure* focuses on basic framework issues: whether the group should be open or closed, how many clients to accept, and so on. The *Goals* section describes appropriate client goals for amelioration of the target problem. There may also be group goals for providing education and information about the target problem, as well as creating opportunities for the acquisition of skills. *Ground Rules* provides recommendations for how the therapist should establish group rules about confidentiality, feedback, interruption, attendance, homework, and so on. Often this section is written in the form of a script, providing you with a model for introducing these issues to the group. Of course, every script in the book is subject to your individual revision. *Starting the Group* gives instructions for handling the first 15 to 30 minutes of the initial group session — again, this is in many cases presented as a script. The emphasis is on methods of introduction, ice-breaking techniques, and an overview statement to clearly establish the goals, ground rules, and format of the group.

The *Main Concepts and Skills* section provides concise summaries of didactic material that you can present at appropriate points throughout the group. *Concepts and Skills* are listed in an alphabetical outline format. For example: *A. Concept: Development of Agoraphobia; B. Concept: The Agoraphobic Personality Profile; C. Concept: The Causes of Agoraphobia; D. Concept: Relaxation; E. Skill: Abdominal Breathing; F. Skill: Progressive Muscle Relaxation.* Most of the information here is written in the first person, just as you might present it to group members. No one of these sections is meant to be exhaustive or universal: you will probably wish to modify the didactic material to better fit your particular group of clients and your own therapeutic approach.

As you read, you will notice that concepts are frequently followed by related skills (for example, *R. Concept: Knowing Your Boundaries*, followed by *S. Skill: Setting Limits*). The skill usually consists of a set of new behaviors that are at first described didactically, and later practiced in a series of experiential exercises for your members.

The *Main Interventions* section offers a week-by-week outline of how to blend content and process for each particular focal group. A given weekly session usually consists of some kind of opening process, such as discussing the previous week's homework, followed by the introduction of one or more concepts and skills. These match the outline format of the *Concepts and Skills* section so that you can refer back and forth between the two. While the *Concepts and Skills* section gives an example of how to present a topic didactically, the interventions allow you to experientially explore and teach a particular concept or skill.

You will notice that, in most chapters, the interventions are numbered. This is a time-saving device. It allows you to assume that each time you see Intervention 5 — Dyad Exercise, for example, this is essentially the same technique as previously described in the chapter. The instructions, therefore, don't have to be repeated.

Many of the interventions contain sample transcripts to show how a particular process can be played out in a group, and how you might deal with typical problems and client responses. The transcripts also model the therapist's function in this type of group.

As you read through the week-by-week outline in the *Main Interventions* section, keep in mind that this is a generic formula, subject at every step to the modifications that will make it function better for your particular client population. You may want to change the structure, type, and sequence of interventions, as well as the tone or individual style of the didactic sections.

Because focal groups are directed at specific target problems, there is a strong emphasis on behavior change. For this reason, most chapters include a section describing the criteria for measuring change. You will also find sections at the end of each chapter on problems specific to that particular focal group, relapse prevention, and strategies for coping with resistance.

References

Budman, S.H. "Significant treatment factors in short-term group psychotherapy." *Group*, 1981, 5, 25-31.

Budman, S.H.; Demby, A.; Redondo, J.P.; Hannan, M., Feldstein, M.; Ringer, J.; and Springer, T. "Comparative outcomes in time-limited individual and group psychotherapy." *International Journal of Group Psychotherapy*, 1988, *38*(1), 63-86.

Burlingame, G.M., and Fuhriman, A. "Time-limited group therapy." *The Counseling Psycholigist*, 1990, *18*, 93-118.

Davies, B. *The Use of Groups in Social Work Practice*, London and Boston: Routledge and Kegan Paul Ltd., 1975.

Klein, R.H. "Some principles of short-term group therapy." *International Journal of Group Psychotherapy*, 1985, *35*, 309-329.

Mackenzie, K.R. "Commentory: When to recommend group treatment." *International Journal of Group Psychotherapy*, 1986, *36*(2), 207-210.

Marcovitz, R.J., and Smith, J.E. "Patients' perception of curative factors in short-term group psychotherapy." *This Journal*, 1983, *33*, 21-39.

Maxmen, J.S. "An educative model for inpatient group psychotherapy." *This Journal*, 1978, *28*, 321-338.

Rose, S.; Tallant, D.; Tolman, R.; and Subramanian, K. "A multimethod group approach: Program development research." *Social Work With Groups*, 1986, *9*(3). 71-88.

Toseland, R.W., and Siporin, M. "When to recommend group treatment: A review of the clinical and the research literature." *International Journal of Group Psychotherapy*, 1986, *36*(2), 171-201.

Chapter 1

Co-Dependency Groups

Ani Amerslav, M.A., M.F.C.C.

Introduction

Co-dependency affects the lives of many people. It can be defined as "a specific condition that is characterized by preoccupation and extreme dependence (emotionally, socially, and sometimes physically) on a person or object. Eventually, this dependence on another person becomes a pathological condition that affects the co-dependent in all other relationships." (Wegscheider-Cruse, 1985) Co-dependency hinders marriages, friendships and healthy family functioning. It destroys trust and the ability to have honest and open communication. It blunts a person's feelings and impedes his or her judgment about reality. These things happen because co-dependents put their own needs aside, aren't assertive, often attempt to control others and outcomes of events, and are often unaware of their feelings.

One of the most effective ways of treating codependence is with group therapy (Cermak, 1986). Through the group process, a co-dependent's interactional problems are triggered; at the same time, peer validation, feedback, modeling of new behaviors, and healing can occur.

Twelve-step groups such as Al-Anon and Co-Dependents Anonymous (CoDA) are important adjuncts to a co-dependency group. Although there are big differences between a 12-step program and a psychotherapy group, a 12-step program offers invaluable ongoing support long after the therapy group has terminated.

As Cermak (1986) points out, co-dependency can be approached in three different ways: as a didactic tool, a psychological concept, and a disease entity. Utilizing these three views, in addition to the adjunct of a 12-step program, creates a dynamic framework within which group psychotherapy can be highly effective.

Selection and Screening

Several characteristics create a secure foundation for the group and help ensure success. The following issues are best screened for in an individual pre-group interview:

- Consistent attendance is of utmost importance. Potential absences are best discussed ahead of time, so group cohesion is not affected and the individual has an opportunity to explore the double message "I want to be in group and I can't come to group."

- This group is designed for beginners, people who have had little exposure to the clinical issues of co-dependency and have not been in long-term therapy groups focused on co-dependency. This group would be too basic for individuals who have had such experience and exposure.

- It's best to limit the group to adults, although mature older teens can fit in well. In such a case, assess whether the teen will be able to relate to adults in a group milieu. Most co-dependent teens relate easily to adults, but this is not always so.

It's also important to rule out clients with the following characteristics:

- Those who are actively chemically dependent. If needed, numerous evaluation instruments are available, including AA's "Twenty Questions" and the Michigan Alcoholism Screening Test. Recovery of at least one year is advisable for chemical dependents before pursuing a group such as this.

- Those who are actively psychotic or on heavy psychotropic medications.

- Those who have little insight into their own motivations and behavior and are unwilling to develop introspective skills.

- Individuals who are related or in a significant relationship with one another.

Keeping in mind the above considerations, meet with each potential group member individually. Explain the scope of the group, its goals, the expectations, and the cost. Be clear and concise. Being open to questions and concerns is very important. During this session, identify and rule out people with hostile, aggressive, or serious borderline characteristics. Careful selection in the beginning saves much aggravation and disruption later. This material, although it sounds simple, is very charged. Witnessing a group member decompensate or become verbally abusive is an experience other group members (and you) don't need to have.

Time and Duration

The group runs for 12 weeks and is 1½ hours long.

Structure

This group is designed to be a closed group. Group members develop skills and insights in a cumulative manner from week to week. For this reason, attendance of all 12 sessions is essential. Of course, if a client is ill or an emergency arises, all is not lost. However, the returning client may feel out of sync with the group and have a feeling of having "missed out."

The optimal size for the group is eight to ten people. It can be run alone or with a co-therapist. Pay attention to the room in which the group meets. Chairs should be placed in a circle so that everyone has a clear view of everyone else. Gently invite members to "join us in the group" if they are hiding behind others outside the circle, behind posts, or in doorways. A room with adequate ventilation and satisfactory lighting is also important, since many co-dependents have anxiety symptoms.

It's important to start and stop on time and to have a good understanding of the material being covered. Having these things under control, in addition to being relaxed and emotionally present, gives group members a sense of security. Members often enter group feeling anxious, fearful, and full of anticipation, wondering how they will be required to carry conversations, take care of others, or monitor you. A demonstration of good boundaries on your part, aptly modeled from the beginning, is necessary. A thorough discussion of boundaries can be found in Vannicelli (1989).

Goals

The goals are very straightforward:

1. Help clients understand what exactly co-dependency is and how it negatively affects them.

2. Improve boundaries for clients by helping individuals own their feelings and identify their own needs and wants.

3. Increase self-esteem as manifested by better assertiveness, more self-nurturing behavior, and a decrease in self-critical thoughts.

4. Help the client identify and begin to appropriately express feelings.

The behavioral skills taught during the group address the above goals. This in turn reduces the discomfort, fear, and depression with which co-dependents present. As they see that they are not alone, their problem is not unique, and that there is an ongoing outside support (peers, 12-step groups, and so on), a sense of relief and healthy control develops. This allows clients to make healthier choices in their lives and choose more appropriate outlets for their feelings.

Such group experiences can be the catalyst for existential awakenings, or what 12-step programs term "spiritual awakenings." AA literature goes into this phenomenon very adequately, as do the writings of Victor Frankl and many others. If you don't feel comfortable with this concept, it's imperative not to invalidate what a client reports, but to refer the person to someone well versed in this area.

Ground Rules

Confidentiality, timeliness, and attendance are mentioned in the first session, in addition to issues of no dating or sex with other group members. People with poor boundaries may confuse frank, open talk with sexual availability. This issue must be brought up. Don't reserve this information just for mixed-sex groups; it pertains to all-male and all-female groups, too. Also mention mandatory child and elder abuse reporting laws.

These are somber issues. To balance the heaviness, approach the group with an attitude of hopefulness and a sense of "this is the place where healing occurs." Modeling honesty and openness is imperative.

Description of Group Process

Each session begins with a brief check-in (except the first session, in which each client makes a brief introduction). Next, the didactic material scheduled for that week is presented. Lastly, the group processes that material and begins incorporating it into the body of knowledge each member is accumulating. Specific exercises are suggested for this portion of the group.

Starting the Group

You might begin in the following way:

"Hello everyone! I'd like to welcome you to our 12-week group. As you all know, I'm _____. Let me begin by going over some ground rules so we all have the same understanding of what this group's about and how it's run.

"As we've talked about before, it's really important that you attend every group meeting. Each week builds on the previous week, and it's easier if we all go through this process together. Also, please be on time. Come a few minutes early, because I start at 7:00 p.m. sharp. Please be sitting down and ready to go at that time. Anyone have any questions about this? I'll be making sure that we not only start on time, but that we end promptly at 8:30, too.

"In order for the group to work we must honor everyone's confidentiality. In other words, what's said in this group stays in this group. This is so important. Does anyone have any questions about this? Do we all agree to honor this rule? The only exception is if I believe that you or someone in your life is in a potentially life-threatening or abusive situation.

"It's each person's responsibility to let me know when they'd like to have some group time—so please speak up. I can't always tell if you need to speak; it's up to you. Also, only one person talks at a time. Otherwise I can't clearly follow what's being said, and we all miss each person's contribution.

"Then there's the issue of relationships between people in this group. It probably sounds odd to you, but I must ask that you not date or have sex with any other member of this group. Of course, after our 12 weeks together are up, what you do is your own business; but in the meantime, let's just come together for group therapy and not muddy the waters with socializing and sex.

"Okay, enough about ground rules. Now, what are we here to do? We're going to look at co-dependency—not only the issue in general, but how it relates to you specifically. We're going to look at how to change situations or behaviors that don't benefit you anymore. Oh, I know they probably worked great at one time in your life; but as life progresses, things change—sometimes we're stuck with old behaviors in new situations and the end result is pain...or fear...or self-defeating behaviors...or problems in relationships.

"This is probably a good time to get started with introductions. You all know me already. [*Note*: you may *briefly* self-disclose your interest and history with co-dependency at this point if you wish. This is optional.] Maybe each of you can take two or three minutes to tell us your name and then say what brings you to a co-dependency group."

Don't allow people to go over their time limit. Gently remind them that their time is up and that they will have opportunities later to talk in more depth.

Main Concept and Skills

A. Concept: How Co-Dependency Operates

"Co-dependency was first identified in work with alcoholic families. More recently it became clear that people can become co-dependent when no chemical addiction exists in the family. Some people believe that co-dependency is a disease, some that it's a personality disorder, and others claim it to be a spiritual deficit. What anyone believes really doesn't matter in this group. Let's just say that the condition of co-dependence develops from living in a dysfunctional, less-than-nurturing, or abusive family. John Bradshaw says, "Co-dependence is a loss of one's inner reality and an addiction to outer reality." (Bradshaw, 1988) Pia Mellody (1989) says that co-dependents have difficulty

1. Experiencing appropriate levels of self-esteem.

2. Setting functional boundaries.

3. Owning and expressing their own reality.

4. Taking care of their adult needs and wants.

5. Experiencing and expressing their reality *moderately*.

"Dysfunctional parenting can turn the natural characteristics of a child into co-dependent traits. This is not to say that your parents are bad or 'wrong-headed' people. In fact, they probably did the best they knew how. Co-dependency is transmitted from one generation to the next. Your parents passed on to you what was done to them."

B. Skill: Identifying Your Own Co-Dependency

"Codependence is passed on as long as there is no consciousness or awareness of it. As soon as you become aware, beginning to examine and question, the cycle is disrupted. So the first step in breaking the cycle is to become aware of your own co-dependent behaviors and thoughts.

C. Concept: Changing the Pattern That Maintains the Turmoil

"Constant and exclusive focus on another person or a behavior as the BIG PROBLEM keeps people stuck feeling anxious, worried, and powerless. Tensions rise, health suffers, relationships are hindered, and the BIG PROBLEM doesn't get better. Moreover, this focus gets in the way of appropriately and responsibly addressing one's own issues.

"Tensions are greatly reduced by taking the focus off the BIG PROBLEM and putting it on yourself. By broadening your perspective, you can begin to see how you and others in your life actually contribute to keeping turmoil going. Of course, you do this unwittingly; but, nonetheless, such behaviors as fighting, arguing, distancing, getting sick, and blaming keep tensions high.

"When you begin to focus on yourself, you automatically shift from a position of blaming others for your situation to one in which you take more responsibility. You can begin to be responsible for your health, mental well-being, and personal growth; you can then allow others to be responsible for themselves and their own issues. It's a form of detaching compassionately: disengaging from others' problems without simply cutting off; thinking about your needs and wants rather than reacting to theirs; and being assertive rather than passive or manipulative.

"As individuals begin taking better care of themselves, tensions in the system reduce and the system's overall health improves. The lower the levels of anxiety and tension in a system, the fewer living problems the members of the system are likely to experience.

Some achievable, moderate ways of putting the focus back on yourself are regular exercise, meditation, laughter, having meaningful friendships outside the primary relationship, and engaging in good communication."

D. Concept: Control

"When the focus is off the BIG PROBLEM and on you, several things become apparent:

- You really can't change anyone else.

- Trying to do so makes life difficult or unmanageable.

- Over the years, the need to control people's behavior, feelings, and thoughts, and the outcomes of situations, has become important — even though it doesn't work.

"The negative effects of attempting to control others are twofold. Attention to your inner reality is lost. When you're attempting to control others, your focus is on the outside: what others do, say, or think; the effect you're trying to make; the way events turn out. You lose touch with your inner life. A major symptom of this is not being able to adequately process your feelings. They get denied, sidetracked, stuffed, or overexpressed (as in overreacting). The second negative effect is that you're trying to control something that is not controllable by you. This failure at successful contol becomes food for shame and increases the need to control. Your self-esteem begins to depend on your controlling behavior. It's a vicious cycle with a no-win ending.

"No matter how adept at controlling you are, something always goes awry. Someone is late, you burn the eggs, you forget an appointment, an emergency comes up. Life is unpredictable.

"Having some control is a good, recommendable thing. You are not being told to lie down and give up. It's trying to control things that are beyond your control and not your business that's negative. It's important to know what is in your range of control and what is not."

E. Skill: Differentiating Between What You Can and Can't Control

(Adapted from Hall and Cohn, Self-Esteem: Tools for Recovery)

"Problems fall into two categories: those that can be controlled and those that can't. As a first example, let's consider an incest survivor. She can't control this past event. It happened. However, she can try to change her feelings about it. She has two options: one, she can resist, wish it hadn't happened, and try to forget and ignore the physical and mental side effects of the experience. Of course, this option most likely leaves her feeling rotten about herself. The second option is to accept the fact that the incest happened. She can take steps to overcome the effects of this devastating event. By exploring more about the events, their impact on her life, her feelings about the abuser and herself, she can begin to feel better about herself and to heal.

"Now let's consider a man with an eating disorder. This is a problem that can be controlled. The man has three options. One, he can attempt change and seek help to tackle the eating disorder. Entering recovery helps a person feel good about himself. Two, he can resist change and simply wish things were different. He can find excuses to support not changing. This leads to poor self-esteem. The third option involves accepting that the problem can be changed but realizing that he's not quite ready to do so. The man can understand how his eating disorder serves him and can accept the consequences. The small steps involved in this acceptance can lead to his feeling better about himself, and can eventually lead to tackling the problem."

F. Concept: Compassionate Detachment Versus Caretaking

"Caretaking is another form of control. It means not only taking care of others but also taking responsibility for them (and from them). Caretaking implies getting so deeply involved in other people's lives that you prevent them from growing and experiencing the natural consequences of their behaviors. Many times caretaking begins with love and concern. An example of this is an overprotective mother who loves and cares for her son but is blind to his need for independence. He is always her "good boy" and she gives him all the money he needs. When he incurs drug debts, she rescues him by paying the debts, giving him a place to stay, and telling lies on the phone for him.

"Another example is a man who constantly monitors his mate's feelings. He is constantly worried about her reactions, carefully watches what he says, and 'walks on eggs.' He worries about whether she's happy or not, and carefully controls his own actions in an attempt to ensure her happiness.

"Compassionate detachment means detaching from the problem, but not cutting yourself off from the person. Detaching in this way involves not controlling another's life yet remaining emotionally present to him or her. It means being there as a friend, listening and responding. It does not mean giving solutions, fixing the problem yourself, criticizing, or judging.

"All individuals have the right to be free, to have and to solve their own problems. When you don't allow others their personal freedom of choice, then you are being possessive. Solving their problems or being responsible for their feelings is also a form of possessiveness. Possessiveness is not love. Compassionate detachment allows us to love our friends and ourselves."

G. Skill: Identifying Feelings

"One of the major problems of co-dependency is not being in touch with your feelings. Most dysfunctional families either overtly deny your right to your feelings or covertly denigrate them. As you grow up, you teach yourself to either override, become numb, or overreact to your feelings. The exact method depends on what you had to do to survive in your family.

"This may have worked in your family of origin, but it can cause problems in adulthood and stand in the way of healthy relationships.

"Feelings are very important. We all have the potential to experience a wide variety of feelings. When they remain unexpressed or are stuffed down, they begin to cause emotional or physical trouble for us. They can show themselves inappropriately, become overwhelming or confusing, or become transformed into physical symptoms like high blood pressure and ulcers.

"A good way to start identifying your feelings is by using a very basic list:

Mad	Hurt
Sad	Ashamed
Glad	Afraid

Of course there are many more feelings than this, but the list is a good starting place.

"Remember, feelings are just feelings. Accepting them as they are is the key. You are experiencing the feelings you are experiencing. This doesn't mean you have to act on them. It doesn't mean you're good or bad because you have them. Feelings are not concrete facts in the outer world. Once you identify a feeling, then you have the choice to act on it or not."

H. Skill: Communicating Feelings

"Learning to talk about your feelings is the next step. It sounds so simple, yet in reality can be quite difficult, especially when you've been taught that your feelings are inappropriate. However, expressing feelings can enhance trust, improve your self-esteem, deepen intimacy, and reduce the need to control.

"A good way to start is to use this formula:

I feel _____(your feeling)

when you _____(an action)

because _____(your reason).

I. Skill: Dealing With Difficult Feelings — Fear, Shame, and Resentment

"Fear, shame, and resentment are very powerful emotions. Not dealing with them can keep you trapped.

Fear

"It is often said that fear is a lack of faith. Instead of a higher power running the universe, you feel as if you're personally in charge. Therefore, control plays a big part in struggling with fear. You may attempt to control people or outcomes rather than looking at the underlying, or root, causes of your fear.

"Root causes of fear may be rejection, abuse, the need for approval, hurt, suppressed anger, or ignorance about taking risks or knowing how to change. These things elicit fear because they seem overwhelming. You haven't learned how to address these feelings. Possibly your family of origin punished you in some way for having these feelings. As a result, you have a feeling, you don't know how to deal with it, and it turns into fear. It's easier to project fear outside of yourself than to see that it springs from your not knowing how to deal with a feeling or situation in a healthy way. And how do you deal with fear that is projected onto someone or something else? By controlling that person or thing. This is a vicious cycle that never addresses the underlying cause of fear.

"This, of course, doesn't refer to reality-based fears, such as being afraid of a mugger with a gun; or afraid of abandoned, dark alleys; or riding with a drunk driver. Such reality-based fears are matters of survival and protection. They keep us out of trouble."

Shame

"Shame and good self-esteem are never found together. Shame is used in dysfunctional families to control people and keep secrets. Guilt differs from shame in that whereas guilt implies that your behavior was not okay, shame implies that *you* are not okay. 'Shame on you!' means not only 'What you did isn't okay,' it also says, 'Who you are isn't okay, and nothing you do will change that.' (Beattie, 1989)

"Shame implies that what you did is a direct reflection of who you are. We become ashamed of our bodies, sexuality, feelings, mistakes, and even our thoughts."

Resentment

"Resentment is commonly identified with anger. However, the roots of the word mean to 're-feel.' Resentment can involve the re-feeling of most feelings: anger, hurt, grief, jealousy, fear, shame, and so on.

"As long as you feel resentment, you hold on to a feeling. This feeling grows and changes. It causes physical side effects. Pretty soon the original event or feeling is obscured by out-of-proportion resentment.

"The cure for resentment, as for fear and shame, is to look at the underlying cause and address it. In time, talking about the initial event or feeling and the resulting feelings and difficulties can alleviate the resentment. Acceptance starts to creep in and resentment diminishes."

J. Concept: Boundaries

"Boundary problems are common in co-dependency. Boundaries refer roughly to where you end and someone else starts. A boundary is a matter of knowledge, an internal line that marks off *me*. There is a sense of respect for 'me' and 'my space.' Only selected people are invited in. Boundaries have to do with what you feel comfortable doing and with whom.

"Boundaries are developed in your family of origin. Parents who have poor boundaries can be intrusive and disrespectful of their children's boundaries. They teach children how to have unhealthy boundaries. This is done by shaming, abusing, and controlling. When your boundaries aren't clear and healthy, you don't know where your responsibilities begin and someone else's end. The same goes for your feelings and even your life. You feel mixed up with other people.

"When you have poor boundaries in a relationship, you often end up taking on someone else's life at the expense of your own. A current joke asks what the co-dependent person sees as she's drowning. The answer is that someone else's life flashes before her eyes. Of course, such focus can seem like love or caring. But this obviously leads to controlling and, ultimately, trouble. At the other extreme, if you've walled yourself off (a form of poor boundary definition called rigid boundaries), relationships are very difficult to have because you can't let someone get close enough to be intimate.

"The ideal is flexible boundaries. To be able to give support and accept it. To respect your own and others' feelings, needs and wants, and to be clear about their separateness. To be able to talk and have fun with each other, while allowing each person to be responsible for herself or himself.

"As our boundaries become defined, our self-esteem improves. Melody Beattie (1989) sites the following facts about boundaries:

- Setting boundaries means learning to take care of ourselves.

- Defining what we deserve means developing boundaries.

- Knowing what our needs, wants, and likes are helps boundaries develop.

- Boundaries develop as we define our personal rights, and define who we are.

- Boundaries emerge as we honor and value ourselves."

K. Skill: Setting Limits

"Limit setting builds on what you learned to do with 'feeling scripts' (I feel _____
_____ when you _____ because _____.) by adding two important additional components:

1. *Your limit*. This should be stated specifically and behaviorally: 'I don't want you to shout at me when you're upset.' Or 'I don't want to have to do the dishes every night; I'd like us to do them on alternate nights.'

2. *Consequences of noncompliance*. This is your plan for how you will take care of yourself if the other person doesn't accept your limit. Don't make it sound attacking or punishing, just matter-of-fact. 'If you shout, I'll leave immediately and we'll talk about it only after you've calmed down.' Or 'If you won't do the dishes, I'm planning to start eating on paper plates.'

"Here's how to put it all together:

> I feel frightened and hurt when you shout during our conflicts because it reminds me of growing up with my family. I don't want you to shout at me when you're upset (limit). If you shout, I'll leave immediately and we'll talk about it only after you've calmed down (consequence). I feel frustrated and irritated, Sis, when I come to pick you up and you're not ready. I get concerned about rushing through traffic and being late to work. Please be ready when I get here (limit). I'm afraid I'll have to stop carpooling with you if this isn't possible (consequence)."

L. Concept: Honesty, Openness, and Willingness — "HOW" To Recover

"Recovery is about change. Changing the way we are inappropriately involved in others' lives. Changing the way we handle our feelings. Improving our communication and feeling better about ourselves.

"Three things that help keep recovery going are honesty, openness, and willingness."

Honesty

"Honesty is simply a matter of being truthful about your feelings, your needs, or whatever is going on for you. Many co-dependents lie. Honesty is an act of honoring yourself. Because you honor your feelings, you don't lie about them. They deserve to be valued."

Openness

"Openness refers to being emotionally present and available. You are able to put aside preconceived notions and feelings and really listen and hear what another person is saying. Openness means being flexible instead of rigid with demands and expectations. You are able to hear what is being said to you and reflect back. You are open to new options or different ways of approaching things."

Willingness

"Are you willing to do things another way? Hearing and being open is the first step, being willing is the next. Are you willing to actually try different approaches to living? Willingness takes great personal courage. It also opens the doors to change."

M. Skill: Congruity

"Congruity means that the way you look, the message you are giving, and the way you feel all match up. Incongruity is common in codependence. How many times have you asked a glassy-eyed, disheveled, exhausted woman how she is and received the response, 'Oh, just fine!' Or how about the man with fire in his eyes, clenched jaw, and red face exclaiming, 'I am NOT mad!'

"We learn to be incongruent in families in which having feelings is not okay. Some families cannot tolerate anger, so the children learn to cover up and deny their feelings. Some families cannot tolerate grief, so the children learn never to cry or show sadness. Those feelings are pushed down. Unfortunately, feelings don't just go away because they're ignored. Usually they are revealed nonverbally in body language, leading to the kind of incongruity just described."

N. Concept: Self-Esteem

"Mellody (1989) says this about self-esteem:

Healthy self-esteem is the internal experience of one's own precious-ness and value as a person. It comes from inside a person and is reflected outward into relationships. Healthy people know that they are valuable and precious even when they make a mistake, are confronted by an angry person, are cheated or lied to or are rejected by a lover, friend, parent, child, or boss…. Healthy individuals may feel other emotions such as guilt, fear, anger, and pain in these circumstances, but the sense of self-esteem remains intact.'

Self-esteem is about honoring your internal reality. Externally based self-esteem means your worth is dependent on who you are married to, how much money you make, what kind of fancy clothes you wear, the car you drive, where you go to be seen, and the kind of job you have. You value yourself only as you are reflected by external circumstances.

This kind of self-worth is very vulnerable because at any time these things can be taken away. It becomes important to try and control things that maintain your sense of worth and, as mentioned before, the world doesn't always function by your plans. When you lose something, your self-worth goes down.

Honoring your inner self is achieved by: focusing on yourself, con-trolling only that which is controllable, being compassionately detached, honoring and talking about your feelings, having healthy and flexible boundaries, being honest and open, and being congruent.

Healthy self-esteem can be manifested by actively working on ac-cepting yourself as you are rather than constantly criticizing or berating yourself, responsibly taking care of yourself rather than putting your own needs and wants aside in favor of another's, and honoring your value as a unique individual on this earth, rather than trying to mold yourself to be like someone else.

O. Skill: Examining Your Self-Esteem

"How do you feel about yourself? This is an important question. You can't change until you know where you're starting from. With a starting point in mind, you can then set goals for yourself."

P. Skill: Assessing Wants and Needs

"Co-dependents are notorious for not taking proper care of themselves. One way this is seen is through the tendency to overindulge oneself. The person who does this has poor self-esteem but attempts to mask it with extravagance, little regard for others, and what seems to be a self-serving lifestyle.

"Another way of not taking proper care of oneself is more blatant. It's demonstrated by the person in obviously poor physical condition and shaky mental condition, who eats poorly and doesn't get proper medical care. She has 'friends' who all take and don't give; her intimate relationships are in trouble or nonexistent. She may dress poorly and doesn't have time or energy to have fun. This person doesn't know what she needs or wants, and therefore rarely asserts herself.

"It is nearly impossible to have a healthy relationship with someone like this. Because they're so out of touch with their needs and wants, they can't be emotionally present in a relationship.

"Pia Mellody (1989) lists four categories of difficulty in meeting wants and needs. They include:

1. *Being too dependent*. You know your needs and wants, but don't meet them because you expect others to do so.

2. *Being antidependent*. You know your needs and wants, but insist on trying to meet them yourself. You're unable to accept help, and feel too vulnerable to ask.

3. *Being needless and wantless*. You are unaware of having any needs or wants.

4. *Needs and wants are confused*. You know what you want and you get it, but you don't know what you need. For example, you buy everything you want and you use this to 'cure' needs that aren't being met (maybe you're not even aware of them).

"Needs as opposed to wants, are necessities. Some examples of human needs are food, shelter, love, affection, nurturance, a sense of belonging, and medical care.

"Wants are things we'd like to have or do. They might include such things as: wanting to own a Corvette, wanting to go to Hawaii, wanting to learn to windsurf, wanting to get married, wanting to call a friend."

Q. Skill: Expressing Wants and Needs

"You can express wants or needs by using a very simple assertive script. It has three basic parts:

1. *The situation*. Just describe the facts—no blaming, no attacking, no pejorative language. Be as careful as you can to be objective and straightforward.

2. *Your feelings*. Use I-statements. This means you say 'I feel hurt' or 'I feel scared' or 'I feel overwhelmed'; not 'You hurt me' or 'You're scaring me' or 'You're overwhelming me.' Those are you-statements. They convey blame. They make people feel attacked and defensive, and less likely to respond to your needs.

3. *Your wants*. Be specific — what, when, and where. People have trouble remembering or responding to general requests. Ask for behavioral rather than attitudinal change. People can alter what they do a lot more effectively than change their beliefs.

"Here's how you can put the three parts together into a coherent assertive statement. Let's say, for example, that your best friend keeps borrowing money — $5 here, $10 there — but never pays it back.

"'Two or three times a week you borrow money for lunch or cabfare. But you often forget to pay it back [situation]. I feel irritated and frustrated sometimes when I don't get the money back [feelings]. I would like you to keep track of the tab and try to pay me back by the end of each week [wants].'

"Notice that the situation is described without using aggressive language, the feelings are I-statements, and the last part asks for a specific behavior change."

R. Skill: Self-Care

"You're learning to identify your needs and wants. The next step is to put them into practice and live in a self-caring way. To be self-caring means to honor and value yourself, your needs, and your wants. It means to live for you, not for others. You may — and hopefully will — choose to have others in your life; but they're not the sole reason for your living or dying.

"Self-care means moderation. Too much or too little involves denying your needs. For instance, impoverishment is a mask just as much as excess is.

"Self-care means self-discipline. You are like a flower garden that needs to be tended, watered, and cared for on an ongoing basis, a little every day. It's easy to start something and give up in a few days or weeks. Loving yourself enough to follow through and commit a bit of time *just for you* is a mark of good self-esteem.

"Self-care means that the focus is on you. Learning to control the things you can rather than trying to control what you can't. The focus is off the other person, place, or thing.

"Self-care means acceptance, accepting that you need to care for yourself. It means accepting yourself just as you are now and working with this body and soul to keep them running well.

"Self-care also means thoughtfulness. You have to contemplate your needs and wants and then determine how you can best care for yourself."

S. Concept: Tying It All Together

"Maybe you've noticed that all the issues we've covered in this group are somehow interrelated. For example, controllers have boundary problems and they have trouble detaching. People who are confused about their boundaries don't know how they feel, nor can they communicate well. They don't take good care of themselves, reflecting their poor self-esteem.

"Recovery from codependence begins with becoming conscious of what you're doing. Your focus must be redirected onto yourself.

"Learning to live with yourself in mind is the first step toward increasing your self-esteem. You cannot feel high self-esteem and shame at the same time. Honoring and valuing yourself means accepting yourself as you are in reality. You must take responsibility for yourself and work toward positive change. This is what recovery is — one day at a time."

Main Interventions

Week 1

Introduction

See Getting Started.

A. Concept: How Co-Dependency Operates

Intervention 1: Didactic Presentation (See Concepts and Skills section)

Intervention 2: Mini-Evaluation

After the didactic presentation, evaluate quickly how group members are responding to the material. The reason for this is

1. To determine which issues can be addressed during the group process

2. To quickly assess how individual group members are coping with the material

Sometimes the pulse of the group is calm, at other times a few clients might be upset, confused, or angry. Make a mental note of how various individuals are reacting, and weave this into later group process work if at all possible.

The best way to do a mini-evaluation is to briefly entertain questions (no more than 5 to 10 minutes) after the didactic part of the session. Observe each person and note the sorts of questions being asked.

> *Example*
>
> Leader: Okay, are there any questions about the way co-dependency operates?
>
> Chris: (*agitated*) I don't know. This sure seems like laying all the blame on my parents. I'm an adult. I came from a nice family.
>
> Leader: Yeah, it's difficult to understand this at first. We're not blaming your parents. Co-dependency is multigenerational and it happens to lots of nice families who just aren't aware of it. [Explain "multigenerational" if necessary.] But you're aware now, and because of your courage, the pattern won't have to repeat itself.

Note that Chris is experiencing difficulty admitting and accepting that his family of origin was dysfunctional. Consider focusing on or highlighting denial as a defense during an appropriate portion of the group process.

B. Skill: Identifying Your Own Co-Dependency

Intervention 1: Didactic Presentation (See Concepts and Skills section)

Intervention 3: Soliciting Examples From Clients

Clients often have trouble in the beginning verbalizing their symptoms. Trust has not yet been extablished within the group; this is also a new behavior. Gently guide clients along.

> *Example*
>
> Leader: I'd like to take a minute or two and see if you can identify any of your own co-dependent behaviors or thoughts. Let's go around the room and have everyone give at least one example.
>
> Dale: Well, I know that at times I just can't say no.

Leader:	To whom, Dale? Can you give an example?
Dale:	Oh, sure. My daughter. I just love her so much that when she's in trouble and seems to be really sorry, I just give in.
Leader:	So that's an example of a boundary issue. Thanks, Dale. Anyone else?
Sandy:	I can't come up with anything.
Leader:	Think about why you came to group.
Sandy:	I'm very unhappy at home. My life has been going down the tubes since all my kids left home.
Leader:	It sounds like your focus — whether you know it or not — has been on your kids more than it's been on you. Maybe your own needs aren't being met. What do you think?
Sandy:	I never thought that I focused too much on my kids, but I guess I did.

Intervention 4: Group Process

After everyone has given examples, engage the group members in a discussion concerning their co-dependent behaviors, how they feel about these, and what it's like hearing others talk about their co-dependency.

Homework

At the end of group, hand out the "Coping With Turmoil" worksheet located at the end of this chapter. Have clients bring these to group next week.

Week 2

Check-in

C. Concept: Changing the Pattern That Maintains the Turmoil

Intervention 1: Didactic Presentation (See Concepts and Skills section)
Share homework.

Intervention 2: Mini-Evaluation
Briefly entertain questions.

Intervention 5: Family Sculpting

The goal of family sculpting is to give clients a transformational experience of what it looks and feels like to be caught in a turbulent situation. Since it's often difficult for clients to verbalize family turmoil, sculpting allows them to reveal their private views of invisible but meaningful boundaries, alliances, triangles, roles, and so on. Clients do this by translating their thoughts and feelings about family into physical positions in space. You then are able to simply comment on or point out the dynamics in the sculpture.

Instruct individuals in the group to imagine their family as if they were going to pose them for a three-dimensional family portrait. This can show any stage of the family's life together. The important thing is that this pose be representational of the client's example of family turmoil from the previous week's homework assignment. A client chooses other individuals in the group to represent family members. The client positions each person and explains who he or she is playing. The whole sculpture is then observed by the group. The "sculptors" are asked to explain their creations. People representing parts of the sculpture may be called upon to comment on how they feel being in their specific stance.

Once the ice has been broken with the first sculpture, other clients are usually more than enthusiastic about having their turn at sculpting. For complete information regarding family sculpture, refer to Satir (1972) and Duhl, Kantor, and Duhl (1973).

Make sure there's time to process everyone's feelings before group ends.

Intervention 4: Group Process

Homework

At the end of group, hand out the "Control Within the Family System" worksheet found at the end of this chapter. Have clients complete the worksheet and bring it to group next week.

Week 3

Check-in

D. Concept: Control

Intervention 1: Didactic Presentation (See Concepts and Skills section)

E. Skill: Differentiating Between What You Can and Can't Control

Intervention 1: Didactic Presentation (See Concepts and Skills section)

Intervention 3: Soliciting Examples From Clients (Use homework)

   Example

Leader: I'd like everyone to look at their homework — the worksheet I passed out last week. I'd like everyone to share one example of what you can control and another example of something you can't. [*Note*: When they get to the latter example, ask them if their manner in attempting control is passive, aggressive, destructive, or some other style.]

Frank: My first example is that I can do something about my mental health — I'm going to therapy and this group. I can't control my wife's personality. She loves to travel; and every time she talks about it, I worry that she's unhappy here in our home.

Leader: So what do you do?

Frank: Sometimes I just keep it in and then get overly mad about something else. Sometimes I get on her case for not being happy at home. It eats me up.

Leader: Does that work?

Frank: No! She just gets mad at me and we end up fighting. It never works.

Leader: It sounds like neither the passive nor the aggressive approach works. Now, I'd like to talk about the last statement on the sheet: ways in which feelings aren't dealt with adequately. When we don't adequately address our feelings, then we tend to get into controlling behaviors. Would some-one like to share an example?

Loren: I've always had trouble with hurt. I just push it down and hope it goes away. Then I get resentful at the person who hurt me, and I avoid him. I've drunk a lot because of hurt.

Week 4

Check-in

F. Concept: Compassionate Detachment Versus Caretaking

Intervention 1: Didactic Presentation (See Concepts and Skills section)

Intervention 2: Mini-Evaluation

Briefly entertain questions.

Intervention 3: Soliciting Examples From Clients

At this juncture, tie in the concept of detaching with that of letting go of control. Point out that detachment does not mean cutting someone or something out; it's not a rigid reaction. The key is to tie the skill of differentiating what can and can't be controlled (Concept E) to the concept of detachment (Concept F). Have everyone come up with an example of caretaking from his or own life.

Intervention 6: Problem Solving

This intervention focuses on how clients are failing to fulfill their needs. When faced with a problem, they handle it in old ways that are no longer adequate. After this process is clarified, clients can then formulate new options that serve them and the problem better.

Example

Leader: Let's take a look at this caretaking behavior and see if you can't come up with some different options, behaviors based on compassionate detach-ment: letting others be responsible for their own problems, you for yours.

Alexis: I used to make excuses for my partner's drinking. I'd minimize how much he drank; I'd say he was under pressure. Down deep inside I didn't believe it — but I wanted to.

Leader: What might be a way of compassionately detaching?

Alexis: Next time I'm not going to make excuses for him. He has to be respon-sible for his own drinking. I love him, but next time someone says some-thing to me, I'm not going to bad-mouth him; but I won't cover up for him or excuse him either. Maybe I'll just shrug in agreement.

Leader: How do you feel about changing your behavior this way?

Alexis: Well, it's kinda scary. What if I can't do it?

Leader: If you don't succeed, don't give up. Just try it again the next time the situation comes up. Changing a way of responding is difficult, particularly when it involves letting someone you care about cope with their own problems — and floundering sometimes.

Intervention 4: Group Process

Week 5

Check-in

G. Skill: Identifying Feelings

Intervention 1: Didactic Presentation (See Concepts and Skills section)
Intervention 2: Mini-Evaluation
Briefly entertain questions.

H. Skills: Communicating Feelings

Intervention 1: Didactic Presentation (See Concepts and Skills section)
Intervention 3: Soliciting Examples From Clients

Use the formula given in the Concepts and Skills section (I feel_____, etc.). Have clients think of something that happened recently and have them fill in the formula with the appropriate feelings, actions, and reasons.

Then have group members recall an incident in which they were in a caretaking role with someone. Have them reflect on their feelings about the person's behavior, and then use the formula to express themselves. This is an introduction to the idea that expressing feelings is a healthy alternative to controlling or co-dependent behavior.

> *Example 1*
>
> Leader: Who would like to give an example using the feeling formula?
> Luke: I feel sad when I come to group because I hear all these things I identify with, and it makes me remember lots of things from the past that I had forgotten.
> Leader: Okay. Now can someone use the formula at a time when you've been in a caretaking role?
> Stacy: This one is for my boyfriend Roger. "I feel angry when you don't show up when you say you will, because I get all worried and obsessed with where you are. I go looking for you all over town. I guess I feel like you don't care about me and that I must be pretty worthless."

Intervention 4: Group Process

Homework

"Prepare at least three 'feeling scripts' (I feel_____ when you_____ because_____) regarding people you care about. Attempt to say at least one of them out loud."

Week 6

Check-in

Have group members give examples from their homework.

I. Skill: Dealing With Difficult Feelings — Fear, Shame, and Resentment

Intervention 1: Didactic Presentation (See Concepts and Skills section)

Intervention 2: Mini-Evaluation

Briefly entertain questions.

Intervention 4: Group Process

Group process at this juncture should focus on people's experiences of fear, shame, and resentment. Keep these three goals in mind:

1. Have them use the feeling formula for expressing these three feelings.

2. Whenever appropriate, point out how these feelings keep people stuck (not growing emotionally and psychologically).

3. Aid clients in searching for and examining underlying feelings and past events.

Intervention 6: Problem Solving

Group members have discussed how fear, shame, and resentment get in their way and how they don't adequately deal with these feelings. Now have them brainstorm new ways of coping.

Homework

"Keeping in mind what you said and heard in the group, think of one way in which you can deal differently with fear, shame, or resentment."

Week 7

Check-in

Explore group members' plans to cope differently with fear, shame, or resentment.

J. Concept: Boundaries

Intervention 1: Didactic Presentation (See Concepts and Skills section)

Intervention 2: Mini-Evaluation

Briefly entertain questions.

Intervention 5: Family Sculpting

"Boundaries help you to be in a relationship by defining who you are. That way you can always be with someone without losing the sense of who you are, what you like, and what you need. This sense of self is necessary for intimacy.

"Overcloseness or enmeshment is not intimacy. You are so entangled with someone that neither of you can stand on your own. Leaning on that other person is so much a part of you that if he or she leaves, then your balance is thrown off. With good boundaries, two people stand side by side, connected by mutual desire but each firmly balanced on his or her own.

"With this in mind, let's sculpt some enmeshed relationships. Let's use examples from your own life." As clients sculpt enmeshment, have them get a good feel for, and view of, the entanglements.

"Next, let's have some sculpting examples of relationships with good, healthy boundaries." Healthy boundaries are quickly sculpted.

K. Skill: Setting Limits

Intervention 1: Didactic Presentation (See Concepts and Skills section)

Intervention 7: Role-playing

Role-playing is used to help clients practice setting boundaries in an enmeshed situation. You can use the situations illustrated by their sculptures.

Example

Leader:	(*after observing Nell's sculpture*) I see you're feeling trapped and dragged down by your husband. You were talking earlier about his resistance to your working. Do you have any ideas what it would sound like for you to set some boundaries?
Nell:	No.
Leader:	John, play Nell's husband and tell her you don't like her working. Nell, verbalize to your husband how you feel. Use the script: "I feel____when you____ because____."
John:	(*playing husband*) Nell, I want you home with the kids. I need you to be here with us. You're my wife and that's your role.
Nell:	John, I feel humiliated when you order me around like that because it makes me into a helpless child.
John:	But I love you. I know what's best for you!
Leader:	(*coaching*) Okay, Nell—now's the time to set some limits.
Nell:	Well, John, you may love me and I love you—but it's my life and the decision to go to work part time is mine. That's what I'm doing.
John:	But the kids! Me! We need you.
Nell:	I'm not turning my back on you. I'm not leaving my family. I need to do this for me so I can be happier here at home.
Leader:	Good job, Nell. How did that feel?
Nell:	Wow! Really different! I feel as if I can stand up tall and breathe!

Repeat this process with a number of enmeshed situations. Be sure to practice asserting consequences where appropriate.

Intervention 4: Group Process

If there's time, you may want to process what this brings up for group members. This intervention is optional, depending mainly on how much time is left.

Homework

"Identify at least one situation in which you need to protect your boundaries with someone close to you. Prepare a limit-setting statement. You can either practice setting the limit or get support from the group next week to do so.

Week 8

Check-in

Discuss limit-setting homework.

L. Concept: Honesty, Openness, and Willingness: "HOW" To Recover

Intervention 1: Didactic Presentation (See Concepts and Skills section)

The concept of willingness to trust in a Higher Power may be added here. Given that some people have difficulty accepting this concept, it's best presented as an optional resource. For example, "Many people find the concept of a Higher Power useful in their path to recovery. This concept involves the notion that there is a power greater than you in the universe. This power, not you, runs the universe. In order to live by this concept, you must be willing to let go of control and then be open to and accepting of whatever happens."

M. Skill: Congruity

Intervention 1: Didactic Presentation (See Concepts and Skills section)

Intervention 3: Soliciting Examples From Clients

"Let's go around the room and have each of you give an example of congruent behavior." Clients do so. "And now, can you think of a time recently when you behaved in an incongruent manner?" Have clients give examples. Those who are stuck can get help from other group members who have possibly noticed their incongruent behavior in the group, or might remind them of incongruent behavior they've reported.

Intervention 4: Group Process

Process should assimilate concepts of HOW (honesty, openness, willingness) and congruity.

Week 9

Check-in

N. Concept: Self-Esteem

Intervention 1: Didactic Presentation (See Concepts and Skills section)

Intervention 2: Mini-Evaluation

O. Skill: Examining Your Self-Esteem

Intervention 1: Didactic Presentation (See Concepts and Skills section)

Intervention 4: Group Process

Have each group member list five strengths. Then have them list three weaknesses. The next step is to tie the weaknesses to their strengths.

Example

Bob:	My strengths are that I'm strong, hard-working, insightful, sensitive, and caring. My weaknesses are that I overwork, I get easily disappointed, and I'm impatient.
Leader:	Can you relate your weaknesses to the strengths you have, even those strengths that you haven't mentioned?
Bob:	My overworking comes from my being a hard worker! I get disappointed easily because I'm sensitive, and my impatience comes from my ability to see the big picture and from my intelligence.

Spend the rest of the group session processing this material and any other related issues that may come up.

Week 10

Check-in

P. Skill: Assessing Wants and Needs

Intervention 1: Didactic Presentation (See Concepts and Skills section)

Make sure that everyone understands the difference between wants and needs. Also go over the four categories of difficulty in meeting wants and needs. Writing them on a board may be helpful. Refer to Mellody (1989) for a complete explanation.

Also mention that moderation is an important issue here. In co-dependency, we tend toward too much or too little. Moderation needs to be cultivated.

Intervention 6: Problem Solving

Divide everyone into groups of two or three. The assignment is for each person to talk about his or her wants. Then each person is to identify his or her needs. If a client gets stuck, the others are to help. Advise group members to jot down their personal lists. These will be used later.

Intervention 4: Group Process

Example

Leader:	What did you discover about your wants and needs?
Carmen:	I had a very hard time with my needs. I know what I want, but I've never thought about what I need.
Luke:	I had the opposite problem — hat do I want? I know my needs.
Leader:	What did you come up with?
Luke:	I'll have to think some more, but I'm pretty sure that I want a mate. I'm so independent and I have lots of friends; but I think I'd like to get married. Also, I'd like to branch out in my consulting business, take advantage of my Navy background. Do something different in my work.
Carmen:	Safety in my home. I realize how unsafe I feel where I live. I also want to have more fun. My life is so serious!

At this point, discussing moderation may be in order. Use a group discussion format if necessary.

Homework

"Continue working on a complete list of wants and needs."

Week 11

Check-in

Q. Skill: Expressing Wants and Needs

Intervention 1: Didactic Presentation (See Concepts and Skills section)
Intervention 7: Role-playing
Here the emphasis is on practicing a brief assertive script.

> *Example*

Leader:	Think of something that you want in relation to someone you know pretty well. How could you express your desire, using the three-part assertive script: situation, feeling, want?
Miranda:	My mother's always calling me up and giving me advice on how to take care of my kids. I end up feeling incredibly criticized.
Leader:	Okay, what do you want in the situation?
Miranda:	Support, not criticism.
Leader:	Fine, but try to be more concrete about what you mean by support. How could your mother act supportively?
Miranda:	Just say what she appreciates about what I'm doing as a parent. And if she's worried about something, fine. But also tell me what I'm doing right.
Leader:	How does her advice or criticism make you feel?
Miranda:	Stupid, a failure, angry.
Leader:	Can you try putting it together into an assertive script?
Miranda:	"Mom, often you point out problems and give me advice with the kids. But I don't hear what you appreciate about me as a mother. I end up feeling stupid, like I'm not doing it right. And sometimes angry at you. Could you talk more about the things I do as a parent that you appreciate? About what I do right? And balance the advice out with what you see that you like?
Leader:	That really worked. The situation, feelings, and wants were very clearly expressed.

Try to role-play one assertive request with each person in the group. Emphasize that the situation should be described in nonblaming terms. Feelings should be expressed in terms of I-Statements. Wants should be specific rather than general, and behavioral rather than attitudinal.

R. Skill: Self-Care

Intervention 1: Didactic Presentation (See Concepts and Skills section)
Intervention 3: Soliciting Examples From Clients
Have group members give examples of self-care. As with last week, include the concept of moderation when necessary.

Intervention 4: Group Process

Homework

Using your list of wants and needs from last week, come up with a list of ways to care for yourself. Try and expand on your current repertoire of self-care behaviors. In addition, practice expressing a want or need to at least one person, using the three-part assertive script.

Week 12

Check-in

Homework review.

S. Concept: Tying It All Together

Intervention 1: Didactic Presentation (See Concepts and Skills section)

Intervention 4: Group Process

Start group with Robert Schuller's quote, "The 'I am' determines the 'I can.'" The leader can use this quote to emphasize how self-esteem ("I am") underlies everything we do. The better you feel about yourself, the more you believe you can achieve, and therefore do achieve. This group integrates all the information covered in weeks 1 through 11. Ask group members to briefly review what they've gotten from the group. Finally, bid everyone farewell and good luck. Don't be surprised if you get requests for another group.

Criteria for Measuring Change

The main criteria for measuring change are

1. A growing understanding of co-dependency terminology and concepts, as indicated by correct usage of terms during group and self-report of change in co-dependent behavior.

2. An increase in the ability to identify and communicate feelings.

3. An increase in self-esteem as manifested by improved assertiveness, more self-nurturing behavior, improved boundaries, and an increase in self-acceptance.

4. An understanding and improvement in boundary issues, such as knowing likes and dislikes, and an identifying of unacceptable behaviors.

5. The development of trust among group members.

Problems Specific to the Group

Nonparticipation is more prevalent during the first few sessions. This can be addressed by gently saying, "We haven't heard from all the group members. How about someone else contributing?" If someone is particularly silent, it's advisable to comment on it: "George, you've been so quiet tonight. What's going on for you? Could you share some of it with us?"

Another problem can be caused by one member who tends to dominate the group. Usually the signs of this tendency are visible early. The best strategy is to address the imbalance as soon as possible, before it becomes a chronic pattern. For example, "Thanks for being so open. I'm going to have to ask that we let someone else have their turn now. It's great that you can talk so freely—but with only an hour and a half for group, we have to make sure there's time for others to share as well."

Relapse Prevention

Since this is a beginning group, relapse simply means returning to a previous level of problematic functioning. Once clients are educated on the topic of co-dependency, a return to ignorance is impossible. Relapse behavior usually means that the client chooses to return to old behaviors for one reason or another. It's a conscious choice. Therefore, the only prevention is to predict in the group that such behavior is possible. The choice ultimately belongs to the client.

Resistance

Resistance is not usually a problem. Sometimes a certain topic is difficult for clients to accept or begin acting on. This is not resistance; it's usually fear. Work from the fear perspective and the trouble eventually dissolves, because you have aligned with your clients and they feel supported and understood in their trouble.

References

Beattie, M. *Beyond Co-dependency.* San Francisco: Harper and Row, 1989.

Bradshaw, J. *Bradshaw On: The Family.* Deerfield Beach, Florida: Health Communications, Inc., 1988.

Cermak, T. *Diagnosing and Treating Co-Dependence.* Minneapolis: Johnson Institute Books, 1986.

Duhl, F.J.; Kantor, D.; and Duhl, B.S. "Learning, space and action in family therapy: A primer of sculpture." In *Techniques of Family Psychotherapy: A Primer.* Edited by D.A. Bloch. New York: Grune & Stratton, 1973.

Hall, L., and Cohn, L. *Self-Esteem: Tools for Recovery.* Carlsbad, California: Gurze Books, 1991.

Mellody, P. *Facing Codependence: What It Is, Where It Comes From, How It Sabbotages Our Lives.* San Francisco: Harper Collins Publishers, 1989.

Satir, V. *Peoplemaking.* Palo Alto, California: Science and Behavior Books, Inc., 1972.

Vannicelli, M. *Group Psychotherapy with Adult Children of Alcoholics.* New York: The Guilford Press, 1989.

Wegscheider-Cruse, S. *Choicemaking.* Pompano Beach, Florida: Health Communications Inc., 1985.

Coping With Turmoil

1. What situation of unrest can I identify in my life or family?

2. How have I reacted to this unrest?

3. How has my way of reacting affected my emotional health? Physical health? Work situations?

4. What are some modest, thoughtful options for me to take?

Control Within the Family System

1. Define control. Give an example of a situation requiring control within your life or family.

2. Who has the most control in your life or family? The least control?

3. Do you want more control? If so, how can you gain it?

4. Is your manner of exercising control passive or aggressive? It is effective?

5. Is your manner of exercising control healthy or destructive? Give examples of each.

6. Give examples of ways in which you don't adequately deal with anger.

   • resentment

   • envy

   • fear

   • grief

   • shame

   • guilt

   • hurt

Chapter 2

Shyness Groups

Lynne Henderson, M.S., M.F.C.C.

Introduction

Current interest in psychotherapy for shyness began when Phil Zimbardo designed a research study utilizing a simulated prison. He discovered that normal students pretending to be guards and prisoners took on the characteristics of real guards and prisoners in a shocking way. Students eventually gave up basic human rights when they were punished for rebellion, acquiescing to coercive tactics and capricious rules. Zimbardo noticed that these rules and tactics no only inhibited spontaneous behavior, but the students also agreed to do things that were clearly incongruent with their values or even their welfare. He further noticed that they behaved like shy people (Zimbardo, 1986).

This research provoked Zimbardo's interest in shyness. He and his students developed a questionnaire called the Stanford Shyness Survey, which they administered to 400 other students. When 40 percent of these students reported being shy, Zimbardo revised the questionnaire, turning it into a checklist. It was eventually administered to thousands of people, cross-culturally as well as in the United States (ibid., item 4). A startling 93 percent of the population acknowledges feeling shy at some point in their lives.

People for whom shyness is an ongoing problem don't take advantage of social situations, date less, are less expressive verbally and nonverbally, and show less interest in other people than those who are not shy (Jones & Carpenter, 1986). Although shy people are perceived as being less friendly and assertive than others (Cheek & Buss, 1981; Pilkonis, 1977), they are not viewed as negatively as they fear (Curran, Wallander, & Fischetti, 1980; Smith & Sarason, 1975). Shy people simply remember negative feedback better than less socially anxious people do (O'Banion & Arkowitz, 1977) and remember negative self-descriptions better than positive self-descriptions (Breck & Smith, 1983). They overestimate the likelihood of unpleasantness in social interaction (Lucock & Salkoviskis, 1988), and are sensitizers — that is, they deal with threat by rumination and worry (Bell & Byrne, 1978; Schmitt & Kurdek, 1984). They underestimate their own ability to cope with social situations (Edelmann, 1985; Trower & Gilbert, 1989) and are pessimistic about social situations in general, failing to expect favorable responses even when their behavior is appropriate

(Maddux, Norton, & Leary, 1988). Shyness thus becomes a self-handicapping strategy — a reason or excuse for possible social failure (Snyder, Smith, Augelli, & Ingram, 1985; Snyder & Smith, 1986).

Cognitive factors are tremendously important in dealing with shy clients, because cognitive biases about social interaction and the self inhibit social performance even when appropriate social skills are available. In fact, clients who show the most cognitive change are less likely to relapse or need further treatment (Trower & Gilbert, 1989). In some cases, however, behavioral change may precede cognitive and affective change. Hammerlie and Montgomery (1986) studied shy males who, without any other intervention, participated in positively biased social interactions with friendly, facilitative confederates. Follow-up after six months showed increased dating frequency and long-term reduction in heterosexual anxiety.

Because the majority of shy people appear to lack self-confidence (Crozier, 1982) and have a negatively biased self-concept (Franzoi, 1983), they need to learn new ways of thinking about social interaction and themselves. It's important to teach shy clients self-assertion and self-expression through planning, rehearsal, and the organization of ideas in advance (Phillips, 1986). Because self-consciousness and negative evaluation interfere with shy people's ability to pay attention to social cues and the needs of others, they must also learn to actively observe other people and to attend to others' wants and needs. This facilitates social interaction and reduces anxiety (Alden & Cappe, 1986; Trower, 1989).

Ten to twenty percent of shy individuals are not only painfully shy but also lack social skills (Arnkoff, Glass , McKain, Shea, & Greenberg, 1984; Glass & Furlong, 1984). These people must be prompted, pushed gently into role-plays, and helped to practice, practice, practice.

The therapist in a shyness group must be more active, self-directed, and goal-oriented than in the usual psychotherapy group. For instance, you will find yourself frequently asking group members, "What do you want from the group? From the situation? From yourself? What do you want from others? How do you want to be?" Shy people view themselves as reactors, without agendas. But we all have agendas and wants and needs. Shy people need help in recognizing their needs and agendas and in acting on them.

The therapist must also be aware of an important affect in shyness — shame. I learned this the hard way in 1982 when I was struggling with my first shyness group. My shy clients seldom mentioned feeling guilty, as did clients in the psychotherapy groups I had been running for ten years. Nevertheless, around the third month of the group, they began to experience tremendous pain in relation to the self. Group members resisted their homework, became furious at me when they weren't making progress, felt stuck, and refused to do the most obvious things to make themselves feel better, like checking out other group members' reactions to them, paying a compliment, or telling about their hurt feelings at another's real or imagined slight. They were touchy, angry, hurting, and unempathic with each other. They wanted my approval and pushed me away at the same time.

I finally realized that these shy clients were feeling shame — an affect that can lead to intense cognitive interference and behavioral inhibition and to the sense that the self is worthless and devalued, by oneself and by others (Tomkins, 1987; Izard, 1971; Lewis, 1979). Group members began to talk about these feelings, discussing how difficult it was to make progress when they felt hopeless about improving. They talked about their fear of being unable to control their own destinies and their fear of expressing themselves and having no one listen.

Clients also discussed their secret feelings of superiority and their fantasies of appearing powerful and perfect. These discussions helped members begin to deal with their feelings of helplessness, powerlessness, and secret grandiosity and perfectionism. They began to experiment and find that they were not in fact helpless, that their immediate goals could become more aligned with current reality, and that they could reach them.

Selection and Screening

Candidates for a shyness group may exhibit one or all of these problems in social situations: anxiety and unpleasant somatic arousal, worry and cognitive interference, and behavioral inhibition. Occasionally clients have other psychological problems, such as a thought disorder that is extremely disruptive, borderline issues that involve acting out and an intense involvement with the therapist, or a high degree of sociopathy. You may choose to refer these clients elsewhere or work with them if they are currently in individual psychotherapy and you can consult with the therapist on an ongoing basis.

Testing

Candidates spend at least three to four hours taking tests. Because shy people fear negative evaluation, they frequently "overthink" their responses to test items or are intimidated by the testing process. Explain that there are no right answers, that the purpose of the testing is to clarify goals. You may also point out that there is homework in the structured groups, and the willingness to take tests may be an indicator of motivation to do the homework.

You may wish to use a social anxiety questionnaire (Cheek & Buss, 1981; Cheek, 1983; Jones, Briggs, & Smith, 1984), the Stanford Shyness Survey (Zimbardo, 1977), a depression inventory like Beck's, a self-esteem inventory (either Rosenberg's or Coopersmith's), the Fear of Negative Evaluation Scale and the Social Avoidance and Distress Scale (Watson & Friend, 1969). Any of these measures can be used for screening and for pre- and post-testing.

The MMPI (Minnesota Multiphasic Personality Inventory) or Millon will assess for characterological information and confounding pathology. Many clients, by the time they reach the Shyness Clinic, have psychological problems in addition to shyness and may find individual psychotherapy helpful in addition to the shyness group. A life history questionnaire of your choosing will also help to focus on problems that may not appear in the screening sessions.

A ten-item shame/guilt questionnaire called the Personal Feelings Questionnaire (Harder & Lewis, 1986) is useful because some of the most intense resistance in shy people, in terms of refusal to take risks, express feelings, and accept group support, revolves around issues of shame.

Screening Sessions

In addition to the tests, there are two screening session. Because shy clients may have difficulty talking in the first session, it's helpful to use a shyness situation questionnaire with a Likert-style response format. Ask the questions and have the clients respond with the numbers corresponding to the answers. "On a scale of one to five, how much distress or discomfort do you feel when you are at a party? Saying hello to someone of the same sex? Saying hello to someone of the opposite sex?" Develop your own questionnaire, using the most common situations that elicit shyness (social gatherings, classroom situations, dealing with an authority figure, talking on the telephone, asking for a date, and so on).

Use this first session also to explore the onset and development of a client's shyness and to define goals. "How old were you when you first noticed that you were shy? What is your earliest memory of being shy? What situations elicited shyness? How would you describe your early relationships with your mother and father?" Here you are looking for parental criticism and "too much" attention to the child's behavior in social situations. Parental scrutiny is frequently the breeding ground for the self-consciousness and intense self-criticism so common to the shy person. Shy people think they are too fat or too thin, don't like the way they talk, don't like their noses. You name it, and they don't like it. But they are often very attractive people.

"What were your relationships with your siblings?" Here you look for bullying or teasing by a sibling. "Were you ever hospitalized or separated from your parents at an early age or later?" Often shy people have experienced early separations or losses, which contribute heavily to their current insecurity and fear in relationships. They are afraid of rejection and abandonment, as well as criticism.

"What part did your shyness play in your experiences in elementary school?" Progress through junior high school, senior high school, and college, if appropriate. "Did you have friends? What were your friendships like? Did you date? How often? Have you ever had a steady girlfriend/boyfriend? Have any of your relationships been sexual? How did your relationships start? How did they end?" You are looking for traumatic or upsetting experiences that have provided the base for fears and biased perceptions about relationships, and for continuous and supportive relationships that can be used as positive examples when the client feels insecure and hopeless.

Your next task is to determine current social functioning. "What brought you to the Shyness Clinic just now? What are your current relationships with your family like? Do you have friends? Can you express yourself freely to them? How about a boyfriend/girlfriend? How do you like your work situation? How would you say your shyness affects you at work? What is it like for you when you meet people socially?" This line of questioning is very important because it provides information about the current support system and about appropriate homework — whether you will encourage assignments such as established eye contact and starting conversations first, rather than joining clubs or finding places to meet the opposite sex. Also ask what the client has done to deal with shyness and what has helped in the past.

Next, explore past and present experiences with psychotherapy. When was the client in therapy and for how long? Has therapy helped and if so, how? Clients will often say that nothing has helped. This may indicate a passive style and/or suggest the necessity for placing behavioral techniques and an *active* orientation first.

These questions should take you through the first screening session and perhaps into the second. Use the remainder of the second session to complete the history and explain the structure and activities of shyness groups. I do short-term and long-term groups. A long-term group is psychodynamic and involves here-and-now interactions within the group. A major focus is on issues relating to attachment (Bowlby, 1988), because insecurity and self-doubt in relationships are based on early separation anxiety and fears of abandonment. Fear of evaluation and rejection, with concomitant feelings of shame, again related to early family relationships, are other major concerns of group members. Short-term groups are highly structured and didactic. They involve weekly reading, homework, daily behavioral assignments, recordkeeping, relaxation practice, and cognitive and/or behavioral exercises during each group session.

At the end of the second screening session, have the client list three goals. These goals will have to do with changing unpleasant physiological arousal or painful emotions, persistent negative thoughts and worries, and inhibited or inappropriate behavior. Goals must be specific and measurable. Ask, "How will you and I be able to tell that you have made progress toward this goal?" "Because you will say fewer negative things to yourself during a given day," or "Because you will initiate at least one conversation with another person besides your family each day." Arrange goals in a hierarchy from most to least important. Clients usually tackle the easiest goal first, rather than the most important; but their most important goal will be the motivator for long-term change, and both you and the client need to stay focused on it.

Finally, ask clients to pick up four books: *How to Start a Conversation and Make Friends* by Don Gabor, *Feeling Good, the New Mood Therapy* by David Burns, Phil Zimbardo's *Shyness: What It Is, What To Do About It*, and David Johnson's *Reaching Out: Interpersonal Effectiveness and Self-Actualization*. Have them read Don Gabor's book in its entirety because it is used during the first session. Also suggest that clients get a notebook they can carry with them to record their shyness homework.

Time and Duration

Groups meet weekly for an hour and a half. Members may come 15 minutes early to discuss their homework with each other after the group has been meeting for a few sessions.

Although the group described here is 12 weeks long, it is sometimes necessary to be more flexible. Short-term groups meet anywhere from 6 to 20 weeks, depending on the needs of the group and the participants' ability to tolerate the stress of group interaction. Because shy people are highly sensitive to criticism and are afraid of hurting others, the expression of thoughts and feelings can be a highly stressful process. If members of a group seem fragile, we contract for 6 weeks and then decide whether to continue at the end of that time. Groups usually last for at least 12 weeks, but can run up to 20 weeks.

Most shy individuals completing work in a short-term group need additional practice in developing intimate relationships. Many want to go on to a long-term group — an experience lasting a year or more — while others find opportunities in the community to continue developing their social skills. Political action groups, service groups, and volunteer groups can be wonderfully helpful after a shy client has "kick-started" himself or herself with a structured group.

Structure

Short-term groups are closed and have three to five members, depending on clients' level of functioning and the availability of people who are ready to begin therapy. Shy people find more than four other people at a time difficult to manage.

Long-term groups are open and can involve up to eight members. When a client is added to the group, give two weeks' notice and plenty of group time for members to explore their feelings before the new person arrives. Clients are usually afraid that a new person will be critical, because they remember how critical they were when they first arrived and how much they feared criticism.

They are also usually angry at the therapist for bringing in someone new. Because shy people often see themselves as "losers," they may think that new people are being added because the group is not good enough as it is. Eventually, though, established members of the group usually acknowledge that they are curious and even excited about having a new viewpoint and a new source of feedback in the group.

Commitment

Creating commitment is crucial for behavior change in both short- and long-term shyness groups. Shy people frequently have histories of being passive, feeling ineffectual, and waiting to be directed. Explain to clients that if change is to occur, they must have an active orientation, pay their fees, do their homework, and make their commitment to group a top priority in their lives. Otherwise they will waste their time and set themselves up for the failure that shy people expect in interpersonal situations.

Shy people tend to believe that they will not be missed if they are absent from the group. Explain that they must not miss sessions, because they are depending on each other and no one is able to take anyone else's place. Ask them to think about their feelings when someone else is absent; and to recognize that their own absence will spark these feelings in others. Constancy and commitment are of the utmost importance. Help clients take responsibility for the group by confronting each other about absences and lack of participation. By fulfilling their responsibilities, they can improve their self-esteem and enhance their feelings of self-efficacy. There are times, of course, when someone does miss a session. If a member does this to take advantage of an important opportunity socially or at work, the group is usually pleased.

The collection of fees is the same in both long-term, unstructured groups and in the short-term groups. If someone "forgets" to pay more than once or habitually pays late, treat it as a therapeutic issue. Is the person ambivalent about group? Does he or she feel a lack of support in the group? Is it hard for the person to take responsibility for him- or herself in this manner? Is it difficult to see him or herself as a full-fledged member of the group? Does he or she want to be special or exceptional — in other words, above the routine obligations of everyday life?

Often shy children are overprotected in their families, and not enough is expected of them in terms of contribution to group life. Treat nonpayment as the kind of behavior everyone feels like engaging in now and again, stressing that it's important to fulfill responsibilities and explore the feelings and reasons behind the behavior. Talking about these feelings in safety can function as an effective agent for change, because shy people often don't understand why they feel resentful at the expectations of others.

Goals

Individual goals in shyness groups include improved social skills, better interpersonal communication, reduced physiological arousal, cognitive restructuring of social situations including the shy person's role in social situations, and cognitive restructuring of the shy person's self-concept. Cognitive restructuring means identifying negative, illogical cognitive distortions and substituting more adaptive cognitions.

Short-Term Groups

The function of the structured short-term group is to provide instruction and opportunities for practice in social interaction through role-plays, behavioral rehearsal, and games. The short-term group also provides *in vivo* desensitization in and outside the group in the form of exercises and homework. Time set aside for spontaneous sharing builds group cohesiveness and individual self-esteem, and counteracts shame, helping members learn to express their feelings and to listen to themselves and others.

Long-Term Groups

Long-term groups are the place to practice techniques, to develop spontaneous expression of thoughts and feelings, to become a full participating member, and to assume leadership roles. The model is that of a collaborative problem-solving group. The goal for the individual is to feel safe and productive, to take risks and receive constructive feedback. Group is a playground for hypothesis testing in the development of skilled interpersonal behavior. Clients share with new members what they have learned, and in peer tutoring, become more expert themselves.

In a long-term group, members work to build a culture free of destructive evaluation, a culture where shame arises only in small doses, occurring when clients are not pleased with their own behavior and have the immediate opportunity to try something different. Group becomes an environment for the emergence of stifled talents and self-expression, a phase that is highly rewarding for the therapist.

Group Process

As you read about the specific skills and exercises, remember that you may be flexible in your introduction of specific skills. Timing will vary, depending on the group. Each group is structured so that homework reporting and discussion come first, the concept to be learned and the exercise accompanying it next, and further discussion and conversation last. Clients design their own homework each week, continuing some tasks for several weeks and/or adding pieces as they go (for example, eye contact, then initiating conversations, continuing conversations, and so on).

Ground Rules

Confidentiality issues are among the most important in a shyness group. Assure members that you do not discuss the group process outside of group, except for purposes of consultation. Then explain that their commitment to confidentiality is essential for group function, because shy people are especially afraid of self-disclosure. Trust will be the most important aspect of their group life. Ask individuals whether they will be able to keep this agreement with other members. You, as a therapist, are bound by ethics and the law, but clients must make a choice and promise one another to maintain confidentiality.

There are few other ground rules except, of course, for ones forbidding behavior like hitting (unlikely in a shyness group!). Interruptions are tolerated in a shyness group because they indicate that members are becoming less self-conscious and more spontaneous. When necessary, prompt and encourage them to speak up. Discuss the danger of wanting to play "therapist" to gain approval and avoid risk.

Explain that this is their laboratory in which they can take risks and try new behaviors.

Starting the Group

A shyness group has a natural starting place — getting acquainted. After the new members give their names and before they begin interacting, use a short relaxation exercise. They will be using relaxation techniques throughout the group and this gives them practice, as well as help in beginning to interact in a relatively relaxed state.

In the exercise, have the group visualize a room and furnish it to make it safe and comfortable. Ask members to choose floor coverings — carpets, hardwood floors, oriental rugs, and so on. Ask: "What do you want to put on the walls? Your favorite painting? Wall hangings? Posters?" Tell the group that the room faces the ocean and has a huge window spanning most of one wall. Ask them to imagine a window treatment for the room. "Do you want curtains? Shades? Blinds? Shutters? Or do you want to leave the windows uncurtained and open to the view?" Then ask: "Do you want a piano or your favorite musical instrument in the room? Your computer? Your VCR? A sofa with thick down cushions that seem to melt underneath you? How about a rich wooden coffee table with a bowl of fruit? A desk, so you can write? Bookcases with your favorite books? What kind of art objects do you like?"

Use your judgment about how specific you will be. The point is that the room should be comfortable and, if clients like, luxurious — but mainly a place where they can be completely safe and at home and where they can meet their needs for peace and solitude.

Next, introduce SOFTEN — an acronym taken from *How to Start a Conversation and Make Friends* (Gabor, 1983). The acronym stands for smiling, open posture, forward lean, touch, eye contact, and nodding, behaviors that indicate that someone is receptive to contact with others. Have members write the words on the board, along with the goal of the behavior. This gets them moving around and focused on the behaviors they will use in the first exercise. Then briefly discuss the book and their reactions to it.

Next, have members break into dyads and use the information on the board to guide their behavior. "I'll give you ten minutes for this exercise, essentially five minutes a person. I want you to get acquainted. Ask each other where you were born, what it was like when you were a child, what work your parents did, what work you do now, what hobbies and interests you enjoy, etc. You can take five-minute turns, or you can ask each other questions as you go along so that you share the ten minutes. But be sure you find out what you'd like to know about each other. I'm going to leave the room, and when I come back I will ask you to introduce each other to the group."

Although this exercise seems a little difficult for shy people, they handle it well. If they leave anything out when introducing their partners, simply ask partners to fill in the information. There is no evaluation or feedback — just practice, exposure, and support and appreciation for their efforts.

After partners introduce each other to the group, ask individuals additional questions about their childhoods. Use information from your individual interviews to guide the questions so that clients become better acquainted with one another and see the commonalities in the development of shyness.

Main Concepts and Skills

A. Concept: Fear Reduction, New Thinking Styles, and Self-Acceptance Are Important in Dealing With Shyness

"Although many shy people do have social skills, they become anxious in social situations because they are deathly afraid of negative evaluation and rejection. Be cause of early family experiences with negative evaluation of themselves as social beings, and sometimes because of bullying by an older sibling or teasing in elementary school, shy people often have a shame-based self-concept. They've been criticized and devalued. Some have been physically abused, but most have suffered the emotional abuse that produces shame.

"As a result, either a feeling of shame triggered unconsciously, or a thought related to a shame-producing situation, can initiate a vicious cycle of thoughts and painful emotions that makes the shy person experience routine social situations as intensely painful and frightening.

"Shy people feel vulnerable, and they are. But they are mainly vulnerable to themselves and to their negatively biased accounts of social situations — situations in which they seem always to fail and remain helpless to do anything about it.

"The average person has what is called a self-enhancement bias — a bias that shy people reverse in interpersonal situations. The average person blames the situation when something goes wrong and takes credit when things go well. But shy people blame themselves when the outcome of an interpersonal situation isn't what they had hoped and give credit for a successful social outcome to the situation or to luck. It will take active effort for you to interrupt your negative thoughts about yourselves and to substitute positive thoughts instead. However, it *is* possible, and you *can* learn to control your anxiety through relaxation training and practice."

B. Concept: Self-Expression and Accurate Empathy Are Essential to Help Shy People Experience Social Interaction in New Ways

"In this group, you will learn to listen accurately to yourself and others. You will also learn to check with yourself to determine whether you have said what you really think and feel or simply what you thought the group wanted to hear."

C. Concept: Appropriate Self-Assertion and Negotiation Are Essential to Maintain Behavioral and Cognitive Gains

"It's important to learn to resolve conflict situations. Shy people are sometimes surprised to learn that these situations can be resolved by means other than passive accommodation or fearful compliance. Because their families have used domination and manipulation, shy people often think that they must either comply with others' wishes or dominate by force and/or manipulation. One way to learn conflict resolution is by practicing ways of handling criticism. Assertiveness training and negotiating techniques give you the confidence to handle criticism and decide for yourselves what you want to change. This will lessen any tendency you have toward hyper-sensitivity."

D. Skill: Social Skills

Social skills refers to the ability to initiate and maintain a conversation and to deal effectively with others. This also includes giving and accepting compliments, meeting people, and taking leave of them.

E. Skill: Relaxation Training

"Tension in the stomach, shaking, sweating, breathing difficulty, the urge to ur-inate, and dizziness are all symptoms of anxiety. Anxiety is distracting, causing you problems in social situations and in the group.

"Research shows that others do not notice these physical symptoms as much as you think they do. Nevertheless, such symptoms are uncomfortable. Exercises in-volving the tensing and relaxing of muscles will help make you aware of your bodies and better able to control your arousal level.

"Relaxation training leads not to loss of control but to increased control of the body and a sense of mental clarity. Furthermore, you remain in control of the pro-cess, able to interrupt it at any time. Some of you may leave your eyes open during the initial phases but close them after you realize that this facilitates relaxation. If your minds wander during relaxation, allow any thought to simply pass through before you go back to relaxing. It is not necessary to strain.

"A good way to estimate how tense you are is to use what we call the SUDS level, which stands for the Subjective Units of Distress Scale. This has a range from 0 to 100, with 0 representing extreme relaxation and 100 extreme tension. You may feel little change in tension the first time, which is fine; relaxation will develop na-turally with practice.

"Begin the relaxation by making yourself comfortable. Close you eyes, relax into your chair [or the floor], and feel yourself heavy, sinking into the chair. Develop an awareness of your breathing. Notice it getting deeper and deeper. Allow yourself to let your breath all the way out, feeling yourself relax more deeply with each exhalation. I will direct your attention to sensations in your body and show you how to reduce those sensations. First, direct your attention to your left arm. Clench your fist tight and notice the tension in your hand and forearm [five seconds]. Now relax your arm and let it rest comfortably. Notice the difference between the tension and the relaxation [ten seconds]. Now let's do the same with the right hand. Clench your fist tight and a little tighter. Note the tension in your hand and in your forearm [five seconds]. Now let go — relax your arm, and let your fingers relax, too. Notice the difference between muscular tension and muscular relaxation [ten seconds].

"Now bend both hands back at the wrists, tensing the muscles in the back of the hand and in the forearm. Point your fingers toward the ceiling. Study the ten-sion [five seconds]. Now relax [ten seconds]. Enjoy the difference between tension and relaxation. Notice your muscles beginning to loosen.

"Now clench both your hands into fists and bring them toward the shoulders, tightening your biceps in your upper arms. Feel the tension in the muscles [five seconds]. Now relax — let your arms drop down to your sides, and notice the dif-ference between the tension and the relaxation [ten seconds]. Your relaxation feels deeper and deeper. Just keep letting go.

"Now direct your attention to your shoulder area. Shrugging your shoulders, bring both shoulders up toward your ears. Notice the tension in your neck and shoulders. Hold it, study it [five seconds], and now let go. Let your shoulders relax, noting the difference between the tension and the relaxation [ten seconds]. Keep letting go, deeper and deeper.

"Wrinkle up your forehead and brow until you feel your forehead furrowed and tight [five seconds]. Now let go, and smooth out the forehead. Feel the muscles relaxing, loosening, and again notice the difference between the tension and the relaxation [ten seconds]. Feel the relaxation spread.

"Close your eyes tight. Feel the tension around your eyes as you squint them tightly, and hold the tension [five seconds]. Now relax, and let go of the tension. Notice the contrast between the tension and the relaxation [ten seconds], leaving your eyes comfortably closed.

"Now clench your jaws, biting your teeth together." (If the client wears dentures or has tooth pain, suggest that he or she press the tongue against the roof of the mouth instead.) "Study the tension in your jaws, and hold it [five seconds]. Now relax your jaws, and note the difference between the tension and relaxation in your jaw area.

"Now press your lips together as tightly as you can, and feel the tension all around your mouth [five seconds]. Now let go, and allow the muscles around your mouth to become loose and relaxed. Let your chin rest comfortably [ten seconds]. Let go of the muscles more and more. Notice how you are becoming more deeply relaxed. "Direct your attention to your neck, and press it back into the chair [or into the floor]. Feel the tension in the back of your neck and your upper back [five seconds]. Hold the tension. Now relax, and let your head rest comfortably, enjoying the difference between the tension and the relaxation [ten seconds].

"Now try to bury your chin in your chest. Feel the tension in the front of your neck, and study it [five seconds]. Now let go, becoming more and more relaxed [ten seconds].

"Direct your attention again to the muscles in your upper back. Arch your back, sticking out your chest and stomach [clients with back problems may simply stiffen the muscles of the upper back], feeling the tension in your upper back [five seconds]. Hold the tension. Now relax, letting your body relax, sinking into the chair. Notice the contrast between the tension and the relaxation, letting your muscles go. Continue to let your body feel looser and looser [ten seconds].

"Now take a deep breath, fill your lungs, and hold it, studying the tension in your chest and your stomach [five seconds]. Study the tension, and now relax. Notice again the difference between the tension and the relaxation [ten seconds].

"Tighten the muscles in your stomach. Make the stomach muscles tense and hard. Hold the tension [five seconds]. Now let go, allowing the muscles to relax more and more, loosening the tension. Notice the difference between tension and relaxation [ten seconds].

"Stretch both legs straight out in front of you. Feel the tension in your thighs as you stretch them way, way out [five seconds]. Now relax. Notice the difference between the tension in the thigh muscles and the relaxation you feel now [ten seconds]. Let your muscles go loose, get rid of the tension, relax more and more deeply.

"Now point your toes toward your head, tensing your calf muscles. You can feel the pulling, tightening sensations, the contraction in your caves and thighs. Hold the tension [five seconds]. Now let go, noticing again the difference between tension and relaxation [ten seconds].

"Now I am going to go through the muscle groups with you one more time so that you can continue to notice the difference between tension and relaxation. You will learn to notice tension in your muscles and learn to let go of the tension, direct ing your muscles to relax." (Go through the muscle groups again.)

"As you sit in the chair [lie on the floor] relaxing, I am going to review the muscle groups with you. As I name each group, notice any remaining tension in those muscles. If you notice tension, allow the muscles to relax. Develop the image of the tension rushing away from the area, slipping away from your body [five seconds]. Relax the muscles in your feet, ankles, and calves [five seconds]. Relax the muscles in your shins, knees, and thighs [five seconds]. Allow the muscles of your lower torso and hips to relax [five seconds]. Relax your stomach, waist, and lower back [five seconds]. Relax your upper back, chest, and shoulders [five seconds]. Relax your arms, upper arms, forearms, and hands, to the tips of your fingers [five seconds]. Loosen the muscles of your throat and neck [five seconds]. Relax your jaw and all the facial muscles, feeling your face go slack and loose [five seconds]. Allow all the muscles of your body to relax and loosen, until you are more and more deeply relaxed. Now sit quietly with your eyes closed for a couple of minutes [two minutes].

"Place yourself on the SUDS scale, from 0, complete relaxation, to 100, extreme tension. Write the number down in your notebook when you open your eyes and feel refreshed and wide awake. One...two...three...four...five. Open your eyes."

F. Skill: Developing Affirmations

"An affirmation is a short, powerful, positive emotional statement about the self. It may be said or written 20 or 30 times a day. Examples are 'I love myself the way I am,' 'I am a good person,' 'I share freely and receive freely.'

G. Skill: Systematic Desensitization

"Systematic desensitization is a technique for gaining some control over anxiety-producing situations. It consists of two parts. The first part requires developing a hierarchy of situations, ranked according to how much anxiety they provoke, from the least to the most anxiety-provoking. The second part involves using muscle relaxation and visualization to decrease the physiological arousal (anxiety) associated with each situation."

H. Skill: Behavioral Rehearsal

"Social interaction is like physical fitness. Even natural athletes have to stay in shape in order to perform at peak ability. It's possible to be out of shape socially, too, especially if you have withdrawn from social situations. That's why it's important to stay out there socially, exercising every day, or at least several times a week. If you do this, you will feel fit and happy, and both your performance and comfort level will steadily improve. With practice, social exercise becomes an enjoyable game or pastime.

"If you feel hesitant, remember that shyness is a self-handicapping strategy. Research shows that shy people use shyness as an excuse for possible negative outcomes in order to protect themselves from a sense of failure. This tactic protects self-esteem but it also makes you believe that you are not in control of thoughts and behavior related to shyness. You then continue to avoid social situations."

I. Skill: Cognitive Restructuring

"Aaron Beck (1976) indicates that it is the fear of the consequences of a given situation, not the situation itself, that causes people to avoid situations. You may fear you'll perform in a substandard fashion in a social situation and be judged negatively. The negative thoughts generated by this fear interfere with adequate social performance, are illogical, and lead to self-defeating behavior such as not attempting activities that are well within your competence. Negative, illogical thoughts can be changed, and positive, constructive thoughts substituted, leading to positive mood change and increasingly effective behavior.

"In David Burns' book, *Feeling Good, the New Mood Therapy* (1980), the author defines ten common cognitive distortions: all-or-nothing thinking, jumping to conclusions, mental filter, disqualifying the positive, magnification and minimization, emotional reasoning, should statements, labeling and mislabeling, overgeneralization, and personalization.

1. "*All-or-nothing thinking* refers to the tendency to think in black-and-white terms — 'If I'm not perfect, them I'm worthless.'

2. "*Jumping to conclusions* occurs in the absence of any facts to justify the conclusions. 'They think I'm stupid.' The thinker is so certain of the conclusion that it's not checked out to test for validity.

3. "*Mental filter* involves focusing on the negative details, no matter how small, and ignoring anything positive.

4. "*Disqualifying the positive* is the tendency to take positive experiences and not just ignore them but turn them into negative ones. For example, responding to a compliment with the statement, 'They must want something.'

5. "*Magnification and minimization* refers to the tendency to exaggerate the importance of your errors and fears while minimizing the value of your positive characteristics.

6. "*Emotional reasoning* is the backwards process of inferring reality from your emotions. 'I feel nervous' translates into 'Therefore I must be incompetent.' A more accurate reflection of reality is 'I feel nervous because I'm telling myself how incompetent I am.'

7. "*Should statements* are attempts to motivate yourself that result in guilt, frustration, and resentment.

8. "*Labeling and mislabeling* refers to the tendency to label yourself based on a particular mistake, making that mistake the sum total of who you are. 'I forgot her birthday; what a thoughtless, selfish person I am.'

9. "*Overgeneralization* is the tendency to assume that if you erred once, you will always err; if a bad thing happened to you once, it will always happen.

10. "*Personalization* involves assuming personal responsibility for a negative event in the absence of any valid basis for doing so.

"Burns, who worked with Beck, has a clear, informal writing style, and includes numerous useful exercises, such as the triple column technique, for changing negative thought patterns. The exercises will improve your mood as well as reduce social anxiety."

J. Skill: Trust Building

"Shy people anticipate criticism. They seldom feel safe and secure enough to take the risks that are necessary to build satisfying relationships. They also often view trust as a gift some people have rather than as a response that people learn and work to achieve. Because shy people frequently don't recognize their own impact on others, they don't realize that they need to earn the trust of others and that others are willing to work to earn their trust. Furthermore, they need to learn to trust themselves, to be able to count on themselves to take care of themselves, to support themselves when they fail, to persist in spite of failure, and to keep their commitments to themselves and others."

Johnson (1972) describes the elements of trust as openness, sharing, acceptance, support, and cooperativeness. In order to be willing to risk sharing thoughts and feelings, group members need to feel accepted and supported. In order to be considered trustworthy, group members must demonstrate acceptance, support, and cooperativeness. Shy clients may violate each other's trust by being judgmental, silent, or laughing nervously when someone self-discloses. They are not aware that they prevent the intimacy they crave.

Trust is a gradual, developing process. Self-disclosing too much too early may be overwhelming to another person and leave the discloser feeling vulnerable and exposed. It's important to disclose only in situations where the other person is not exploitive.

"Trust is also a self-fulling prophecy. If people trust each other and behave in a trustworthy manner, it increases the chances trust will be reciprocal. We will still sometimes get hurt, because that is the nature of relationships. People have conflicting needs and sometimes make mistakes or inadvertently hurt each other. But we will get hurt less often if we trust, and our experiences with people will be more enjoyable if we spend energy on trust building rather than on suspicion and guardedness."

K. Skill: Active Listening

"Active listening is the process of listening to both the verbal and nonverbal content of a person's communication. It involves listening without judgment, interpretation, or advice with the intent to understand fully the message being communicated. Active listening also involves confirming the accuracy of the message received by a process called paraphrasing. To paraphrase, the listener restates the sender's message, including feelings and meanings, using his or her own words.

"For example, in response to someone saying, 'I'm sick and tired of cleaning up after Jim,' a paraphrase might be 'you sound frustrated and angry at Jim for not cleaning up after himself.' Alternatively, in response to 'Oh god! What if I make a fool of myself and they think I'm an idiot?' A paraphrase might be 'you seem really nervous about your performance and how you'll be judged.'"

L. Skill: Perception Checks

"Because communication is complex, human beings cannot respond to everything, and people usually pay more attention to one part of a message that to others. Needs, expectations, and beliefs influence what is attended to and heard. If negative evaluation and rejection is expected, it will be heard, and messages that do not confirm beliefs may be misperceived or not perceived at all.

"Shy people remember negative feedback better than other people, and remember negative self-descriptions better than positive self-descriptions. It's important to check your perceptions to make sure you don't misinterpret what others are saying an doing, especially when you feel negatively evaluated or rejected."

M. Skill: *I*-Statements and Relationship Statements

"It's important to make I-statements. If you take responsibility for your own thoughts and feelings, you will be a strong communicator and avoid misinterpretation.

"The opposite of an *I*-statement is a *you*-statement. *You*-statements are usually perceived as blaming or attacking and tend to provoke defensive responses. Whereas 'I was worried when you didn't call me last night' takes responsibility for the anxiety experience, 'You never call when you say you will' simply blames. Be careful that *you*-statements don't get disguised as *I*-statements: 'I feel that you never....'

"Relationship statements are also useful either when conflicts arise or when relationships are going particularly well. For example, 'I really appreciate how well we are getting along, and the easy give-and-take I experience with you lately.' Or 'You seemed angry when I told you I didn't want to go to a movie last night, that I preferred to stay home. Is something wrong? Are you satisfied with the amount of time we spend going out?'"

N. Skill: Perspective Taking

"It's important to understand another person's perspective, because no two people have exactly the same perspective. You've all grown up in different families, and even members of the same family have different perspectives, such as that of parent or child. And men and women, youngest and oldest children, do not view the world in quite the same way. A person may also react differently at different times. Teasing may be funny at one time and hurtful at another, particularly if you are feeling vulnerable or have just been disappointed."

O. Skill: Expression of Feelings

"Because the sharing of feelings is the 'glue' that holds relationships together and provides intensity and meaning, it is one of the most important experiences in the life of the group. Feelings are internal states and are difficult to express when we fear rejection or disapproval. Fear of rejection and evaluation is constant for shy people, who habitually ignore their feelings and are frequently even unaware of them."

P. Skill: Self-Esteem and Self-Concept Restructuring

"You can improve your sense of self-efficacy by rewarding yourselves for doing your homework, using poker chips representing money, or by rewarding yourself with high-probability behaviors — that is, behaviors you like, such as taking walks, relaxing in hot baths, listening to music, and so on. That way, you reward yourself for your own behavior, rather than letting the outcome of a given situation determine your evaluation of your behavior.

"Using attributions in a deliberate and positive manner can also improve your self-esteem. Attributions can be distinguished according to whether they are internal or external, global or specific, and stable or transient (and of course positive or negative!). An internal attribution is 'I did well on the test because I studied effectively,' while an external attribution would be 'I did well on the test because it was easy.' A global attribution is 'I fall to pieces under pressure,' whereas a specific attribution might be 'I got really anxious about that presentation yesterday.' A stable attribution is 'I'm a thoughtful person,' while a transient attribution would be 'sometimes I think about other's feelings.'

"Giving yourself credit for success by using positive stable, internal attributions increases your motivation and makes you perform better. These kinds of attributions improve your self-image and change your self-concept to one including characteristics of maturity and self-confidence. When you hear yourself using a negative adjective that is internal, global, and stable to describe yourself, you must substitute a positive adjective or at least use one that is specific and transient. For instance, 'I am inadequate. If I introduce myself to this woman, she will see that I am inferior, that I cannot assert myself, that I lack something that others seem to have. It is no use.' This attribution is internal, global, and stable because it implies a permanent personal trait that is all-encompassing. You may substitute 'I am *nervous at the moment* (specific and transient), but I am also excited to meet this woman. I sometimes perform less well socially than I would like, but facilitative social behavior is a learned skill, and I am practicing. I feel deficient sometimes, but that is simply a cognitive label for a feeling state in which I feel a little sad and hopeless. I can choose to be optimistic and hopeful and can reinforce myself with each step I take toward self-confidence and friendly behavior. I can use meeting this woman as a learning experience. Here goes. 'Hi, I'm Andrew, I saw you at the meeting earlier about Saving the Bay. I wondered what you thought of the speaker.' Finally, use your affirmations daily to build self-esteem."

Q. Skill: Expression of Anger

"Do you ever send nonverbal messages through silence, 'forgotten' appointments, looks of boredom, gaze aversion, body tension, physical distance, or a 'spacey' demeanor? If so, you are probably angry. If you become aware of your anger, you can begin to recognize the feelings and/or frustrated needs underlying it, express these feelings and needs, and begin to negotiate with other people to get your needs met. Many shy people harbor a kind of seething resentment toward people around them because they have not learned to be assertive and to negotiate to get their needs met.

"Confrontation involves clear communication regarding one's thoughts and feelings about a situation or conflict. It can be defined as an attempt to meet the needs of the participants in a conflict by clarifying the issues involved: it's a collaboration in creative problem solving. Confrontation is most likely to result in successful negotiation when there is adequate time, when you can communicate openly with minimal threat and fully understand the other's perspective, and when you do not demand but rather request change. Requesting change acknowledges that the other person has a choice and does not trigger a control struggle that inevitably leaves at least one person feeling like a 'loser.' As with good communication in general, use

I-statements; express feelings about the situation and the other person; use behavioral descriptions only; acknowledge the other person's feelings and thoughts; use perception checks, practice nonthreatening feedback skills; and use statements that describe the effect of the other person's behavior on the receiver. The last item is particularly important because the intent of the sender and the message heard by the receiver are frequently different." (Adapted from Johnson, 1972.)

R. Skill: Responding to Criticism

"Do you expect criticism, fear it, avoid it, and tend to become silent or defensive when you encounter it? In this group the only being who may truly know what is right and wrong is God, who is not available for comment. Therefore group members who criticize each other are expressing their own preferences in terms of right and wrong. Each of you may define for yourself what is right and wrong, as well as decide whom you wish to please and whom you do not care about pleasing."

Fogging

"There is a good chapter on dealing with criticism in Manuel Smith's book, *When I Say No I Feel Guilty* (1975). Smith calls the primary verbal skills he uses 'Fogging,' 'Negative Inquiry,' and 'Negative Assertion.' The first skill you will learn and practice is Fogging, which simply involves refusing to offer resistance to manipulative criticism. Criticism can be agreed to 'in truth,' in 'principle,' or one can simply 'agree with the odds.' It's possible to agree with criticism and assertively state one's intentions at the same time.

"For example, a frequent criticism of the shy person is, 'You ought to get over this shyness. Just get out there and make friends. It isn't hard; it's all in your mind.' This advice of course comes from an extroverted friend who cannot understand what all the fuss is about. The shy person may feel embarrassed, ashamed of being shy, and agree that shyness is a disgraceful, but trivial, problem. A shy person usually becomes tongue-tied or stammers through some kind of defense — 'It's easy for you to say....'

"Instead you can substitute, 'I agree with you that I am shy and that it is a problem for me. I can see how it may not be hard to make friends; most people do seem friendly. I also agree that it is in my mind that I experience discomfort. I am working on my social skills and on the way I talk to myself in social situations. I intend to make friends at my own pace, using the skills I am learning.' These simple techniques are surprisingly powerful. People are often surprised at their own sense of personal power in social situations as they practice these strategies."

Negative Inquiry

"Negative Inquiry simply involves asking the critic exactly what it is about one's behavior that the critic finds objectionable or offensive. 'There you go off to that stupid Shyness Group again. Why don't you just get up the nerve to ask someone out on your own? This could go on forever!' The responder replies: 'What exactly is it about my going to a Shyness Group that bothers you? Tell me what it would mean to you if 'I did it on my own?' If it does take me some time to ask someone out, what about that bothers you?' This response is usually sufficient to quiet the critic. Critics don't usually analyze why they are bothered or upset but prefer to analyze others. If a critic is honestly concerned, he or she will respond to the negative inquiry. If the critic is simply manipulative, he or she usually doesn't answer, and the conversation is over. If the critic persists, the responder continues the negative inquiry."

Negative Assertion

"Negative Assertion involves agreeing honestly with someone who has criticized you about a shortcoming that you acknowledge and want to change. For example, 'You were very self-centered during our last conversation. You hardly listened to what I was saying; you didn't even look at me when I was talking.' The negative assertion in this case is simply, 'You're right; when I feel shy I become self-centered. I start criticizing myself and thinking how silly I look and sound, and I do lose track of what people are saying. I'm working on that and I appreciate your willingness to tell me how you felt about.'

"Shy people are usually surprised at how freeing it is simply to acknowledge a shortcoming. They may experience a good deal of shame and thus think that acknowledging a behavioral deficiency or excess is tantamount to acknowledging that they are inferior or bad people. You may be relieved to discover that you can simply acknowledge a behavior that you may change if you choose to do so. This discovery will help you view social situations as areas for experimentation and as places where you can learn from the consequences of your behavior and make choices as you go along."

Main Interventions

Week 1

Getting Acquainted, Getting Moving

See Starting the Group.

A. Concept: Fear Reduction, New Thinking Styles, and Self-Acceptance Are Important in Dealing With Shyness

Intervention 1: Didactic Presentation (See Concepts and Skills section)

B. Concept: Self-Expression and Accurate Empathy Are Essential to Help Shy People Experience Social Interaction in New Ways

Intervention 1: Didactic Presentation (See Concepts and Skills section)

It's important that social interactions become less an area for evaluating social performance and more simply an avenue to intellectual and emotional sharing, and growing self-expression.

C. Concept: Appropriate Self-Assertion and Negotiation Are Essential to Maintain Behavioral and Cognitive Gains

Intervention 1: Didactic Presentation (See Concepts and Skills section)

Be prepared for the ingenious passive aggressive techniques used by shy people, as well as the mind-reading games they play.

Shy people also seem "touchy" because they are hypersensitive to criticism and hypervigilant in recognizing even mildly negative evaluation in social situations. In other words, they take things personally and sometimes have a hard time processing even constructive feedback.

Homework

- "I want each of you to begin a social interaction diary in which you'll record each social interaction: what occurred, how you felt, what you said to yourself, and your physiological responses. Bring the diary next week and we'll discuss it.

- "Also finish *How to Start a Conversation and Make Friends* by Gabor (if you've not already done so), and Phil Zimbardo's chapter, "Developing Social Skills," in his book *Shyness: What Is It, What to Do About It* (1977).

- "Finally, begin reading at least one newspaper or weekly news magazine so you have topics of conversation at hand."

Week 2

Review Homework

Clients' awareness of their own interfering cognitions should be beginning to grow. These interfering thoughts can be used as examples of cognitions amenable to positive thought substitutions. Suggest that they begin using a thought-stoppage technique when they find themselves engaging in negative self-talk during social interactions. They simply yell "Stop!" to themselves whenever they hear themselves describing or labeling their behavior in a negative manner. Model the exercise for them, even slamming your hand down for emphasis. Stress the importance of doing the exercise consistently, every time negative self-talk occurs.

D. Skill: Social Skills

Intervention 2: Strategy Planning

Have clients strategize new behaviors to try. Refer back to the reading, and encourage them to share their strategies and rationales with one another. Emphasize their ability to choose to incorporate those strategies that make sense, and reject those that seem unworkable. Clients then learn that they can make their own decisions and do not have to look to others to tell them what to do.

For example, a client might say, "I don't like the way the author suggests that in the library, you approach so directly a person you don't know. I think I might stand next to them at the checkout desk for a few moments before I started a conversation. That would give the person time to get used to my presence." Shy people can often be quite considerate when they pay attention to others because they're sensitive to intrusion themselves and often approach people in a nonthreatening and gentle way.

Intervention 3: Exercise — Meeting People

"We're going to have a small 'party' in the waiting room. This will help you get further acquainted and give you practice in meeting people." Provide coffee, tea, soft drinks, and snacks so clients may practice juggling a glass, a napkin, and food while they interact. This exercise last 20 to 30 minutes, depending on how easily clients can keep conversations going.

Intervention 4: Discussion

Example

Fred: I didn't know what to say to Bob after I asked him how he was and he said "Fine." My heart started to pound, I heard myself saying what a stupid idiot I was that I couldn't even converse, and I felt myself blushing and just wanting to run out of the room.

Therapist: What happened then?

Fred: Well, we stood there a minute and I remembered I could just try anything, so I asked him about his job as a forest ranger. I was kind of interested in what he said about his job in the last meeting.

Talk about the rewards of continuing a conversation in spite of nervousness, the self-supportive feeling of being able to experiment socially, and the ease of picking up on free information (further information about the self that a person shares in the context of the current topic of conversation) to follow up in the next encounter. Often shy people are surprised at how well they recover when they don't allow themselves to bolt from a situation.

Homework

- "I want you to assign yourselves a behavioral task like making eye contact, initiating conversations, sustaining conversations, asking someone over for coffee, and so on. Do this behavioral task at least once a day and reward yourselves with tokens worth money, with food, or with activities you enjoy each time you do the homework. Record your performance in a homework notebook.

- "Second, read the rest of Zimbardo's book, *Shyness: What Is It, What to Do About It* (1977).

- "Third, write down 15 positive characteristics about yourself. You'll use these to begin practicing affirmations." (Although there is no exercise more cognitively simple than this one, this particular exercise illustrates clients' difficulty with self-esteem. They may not understand what is expected and may ask for an example. Or they want to know the definition of characteristics. If so, ask them to use 15 positive *adjectives* to describe themselves, explaining that if they have difficulty, they may ask family and friends for help.

- "Finally, list ten things you do well." (Interestingly, they do not usually ask questions about this exercise and are able to recite many things they do well.)

Week 3

Review Homework

Review behavioral homework including clients' cognitions associated with each performance, and their success with thought stoppage. Then review the 15 positive characteristics they have listed and the 10 things they do well. If they have fewer than the required number, help them add to their lists by sharing others' lists and by suggesting characteristics.

E. Skill: Relaxation Training

Intervention 1: Didactic Presentation (See Concepts and Skills section)

It's important to begin muscle relaxation by the third week, when many clients have begun to struggle with intense autonomic arousal. This arousal can distract them during ongoing social interaction and the group process. Group muscle relaxation training begins in a quiet room with relatively low lighting. (No one should have a light shining in his or her eyes.) Clients may sit in chairs or lie on the floor. They may want to remove contact lenses and loosen clothing. For a discussion of physical symptoms and how to cope with them, refer members to Johnathan Cheek's *Conquering Shyness* (1989).

Intervention 4: Discussion

Check to see whether clients are aware of the reasons for relaxation. Shy people fear a loss of control, particularly in situations that seem threatening.

Reassure clients who experience increased anxiety as they use relaxation techniques that they are simply becoming more aware of their anxiety and that it will dissipate with practice.

Intervention 3: Exercise — Letting-Go Induction

After a couple of weeks of practice or when clients begin to relax fairly easily (dropping to 20 or below on the SUDS scale), introduce a letting-go induction. Go through the muscle groups in the group session, simply suggesting relaxation, but not muscle tension. You may include suggestions to relax more and more deeply, further and further, heavier, looser, and calmer. You may want to provide tapes again for practice. When SUDS levels again drop to 20 or below, have clients begin to practice on their own before they turn on the tape.

Intervention 3: Exercise — Differential Relaxation

When clients have learned to relax consistently, add differential relaxation, in which you help them learn to relax muscles not in use at a given moment. When clients are engaging in role-plays, suggest that they become aware of the muscles they use to maintain a standing position. Then suggest they attempt to relax the muscles not needed at the moment, such as facial muscles. This kind of cueing during role-plays helps them become aware of the tension they hold during their daily activities and helps them remember to use their relaxation skills in other situations. Goldfried and Davison have an example of a letting-go induction and a differential relaxation procedure in their book, *Clinical Behavior Therapy* (1976).

F. Skill: Developing Affirmations

Intervention 1: Didactic Presentation (See Concepts and Skills section)

Affirmations practiced in the context of relationships often generate positive emotional states that carry over into social situations.

Intervention 3: Exercise — Writing Affirmations

"You may take your affirmations from the list of positive characteristics and the thing you do well that you wrote down in your notebooks for your homework exercise."

Intervention 3: Exercise — Relaxation With Affirmations

"As you practice relaxation, visualize yourself saying affirmations. Visualize your facial expressions in great detail as you remember your affirmations (about feeling loved, knowing you are good, sharing and receiving, and so on)."

Intervention 3: Exercise — Practicing Affirmations

Suggest to clients that they may also use their special room as a setting in which to practice their affirmations, visualizing themselves letting go of old negative self-descriptions and substituting positive self-descriptions. They may write their affirmations across the blue sky visible from the window of their special room. Or they may project themselves on the screen of a videotape monitor or home movie screen they keep in their special room On the screen, they may see themselves enjoying social interactions, looking self-confident and happy, socializing with people they want to know, and so on.

Homework

- Provide clients with audiotapes of the relaxation exercise. "Practice at home once or twice a day for up to 30 minutes in a quiet place. Use your notebooks to record your SUDS level before and after each session and to note any difficulties you notice in the session.

- "Practice your affirmations at the end of the relaxation practice session, while you're still in a relaxed state.

- "Finally, choose new behavioral homework, building on the skills you've already mastered, or continuing to work on the same tasks if you're having difficulty. One excellent piece of homework involves specifically focusing on aspects of the person you're interacting with. What color are their eyes, what is their facial expression? What are they feeling?" (They often have difficulty with this one: it is good practice in empathy training and taking the focus away from the self.) "Be sure that you're using your reward system. Reward your own behavior as soon as possible after the behavior occurs, or at least imagine the reward you'll give yourself immediately after the homework."

Week 4

Review Homework

G. Skill: Systematic Desensitization

Intervention 1: Didactic Presentation (See Concepts and Skills section)

Intervention 3: Exercise — Construction of a Hierarchy

Pass out 3-by-5-inch cards, and have clients describe in detail one anxiety-arousing situation on each card. If, for example, they are fearful of public speaking, have them write down items, or situations, leading up to the actual speaking experience, from least to most anxiety-producing. Situation 1 may, for example, involve receipt of an invitation to speak at an organizational meeting or a request to give an oral report at the next staff meeting at work. Situation 2 may involve sitting down to prepare the talk. Situation 3 may be practicing, with notes, in front of a mirror at home. Situation 4 may involve listening to a tape recording made of the talk; situation 5, listening to the introduction of the talk; situation 6, approaching the podium; situation 7, placing the notes on a table or podium and looking at the audience; and so on. Clients reshuffle the cards and add situations as they occur.

Some clients may choose to write down situations that are graduated in terms of arousal level but do not build to an eventual goal, like giving a talk or asking for a date. Instead, they write a series like this: 1) "Starting a conversation with another person of my own sex," 2) "Starting a conversation with someone of the opposite sex," 3) "Starting a conversation with someone I'm attracted to." What is important is that the hierarchy begin with items lower in anxiety arousal and build to items that are higher in arousal. Emphasize that clients should include the details of each situation; the finer the detail, the more effective the exercise.

Intervention 3: Exercise — Visualization

Have clients imagine their first, or least, anxiety-producing situation in fine visual detail, including colors. Also ask them to include sounds, body sensations, and even touch, taste, and smell. Ask them to rate their SUDS levels on a scale of 0 (no distress) to 100 (extreme distress).

When clients have reached SUDS levels of 60 or above, give them instructions to relax each muscle group according to the relaxation training described in the Concepts and Skills section. Do not include suggestions to tighten their muscles. They relax while they are visualizing the scene. When all clients' SUDS levels have come down to 30 or below, have them click off their scene from the hierarchy and relax, using a pleasant image if they wish. They may use a relaxation image (like that described in Starting the Group).

Homework

- "Because the next session will be devoted entirely to desensitization, continue working on your hierarchies at home. Continue practicing your affirmations as well, using your growing collection of relaxation techniques.

- "Choose another behavioral task for this week and remember to reward yourself as soon as possible following the performance of your desired behavior."

Week 5

Review Homework

Ask about experiences with affirmations as well as with the thought-stoppage technique. Ask clients to report one thing they felt proud of this week. Check to see that they are rewarding themselves for their behavioral homework.

Also check that clients have finished developing their hierarchies for the desensitization exercises.

G. Skill: Systematic Desensitization (continued)

Intervention 3: Exercise — Systematic Desensitization

Ask clients to visualize their first anxiety-arousing situation in careful detail. When they are aroused, at SUDS levels of 60 or above, have clients signal arousal by raising one finger. When the last person raises a finger, begin using relaxation suggestions, such as "You are now beginning to feel your muscles relax and loosen, your breathing deepen, your heart rate slow down, and your limbs and body becoming more and more deeply relaxed." Or you may use, from the relaxation training exercise in the Concepts and Skills section: "Feel your feet, ankles, and calves loosen; let the tension slip away from your shins, knees, and thighs...." Have clients proceed through their hierarchies, reporting their SUDS levels at the end of the exercise.

Intervention 4: Discussion

Encourage clients to discuss their experiences with reducing their levels of anxiety.

Homework

- Choose another behavioral task for this week.

- Have clients read Chapter 11, "Visualization," from McKay and Fanning's book, *Self-Esteem*. Ask clients to read the chapter and do the exercise where they visualize performing their chosen behavioral task, and then visualize their overall goals.

Week 6

Review Homework

By now, many clients should be asking someone to lunch or a movie, or calling a singles' group, attending meetings of volunteer organizations, and so on. Have clients brag about one thing they have done in the past week. Check that they are rewarding themselves consistently.

H. Skill: Behavioral Rehearsal

Intervention 1: Didactic Presentation (See Concepts and Skills section)

Intervention 5: Role-Plays

Once systematic desensitization is under way, clients may begin behavioral rehearsal of the situations they wish to master. Have members choose a situation from their hierarchy to rehearse, selecting another group member to role-play with them. The situation may be a conversation they would like to initiate with someone at work, a friend they would like to ask out for coffee, or a phone call to ask someone for a date. The clients describes the situation in detail, including what the other person might be likely to say and what it is that the clients would like to say and do. Ask the client to state the SUDS level as the interaction begins and when it is finished.

> *Example*
>
> Sam: Let's try an easy one first. I'll ask John to have coffee after our computer programming class this evening. I've started several conversations with him in the last two weeks, and he seems very friendly. We're both looking for jobs as technical writers, so we can talk about changing careers and job searches. Alan, will you please play John? We talked about job interviewing last week and I'll start the conversation there. Just act friendly and please say yes!"
>
> Alan: Okay, I'll play John. Is there a particular interview you talked about?

Sam:	Oh yes, I forgot. I told him I was interviewing at HiTech this week and that I would let him know how it turned out.
Alan:	*(as John)* Okay. Hi, Sam.
Sam:	Hi, John. Interesting class tonight.
Alan:	Yeah, I'll be sorry when the course is over.
Sam:	Me too. By the way, remember I told you I had the interview at HiTech this week? I've got some more thoughts about what companies are looking for in tech writers. Would you like to go out for coffee and kick some ideas around?
Alan:	Sure, Sam. That's uppermost on my mind now. Where would you like to go?
Sam:	I discovered a place just around around the corner last week that's pretty good. Let's go there.
Alan:	Great.

Stress that the purpose of initial role-plays is exposure and practice in learning to relax while interacting. If group members' SUDS levels are still high after a role-play or if they are dissatisfied with the interaction, they may do it again, several times if they wish. If they ask specifically for feedback, offer a suggestion, but do not focus on it; these first practice times are tough enough without fine-tuning. That can be done later during communication training. Give each member of the group at least one chance, and more if possible. Allow for more than one session, if necessary; but if the role-plays run a great deal longer than expected, break up the group and move around the room to help people who need it.

Intervention 3: Exercise — Paradoxical Intention

Ask each member to describe the symptom that is the most troublesome in social situations. It may be a physiological symptom, a behavioral pattern, or a thought pattern. For example, "My heart thumps faster and faster when I walk into a room filled with people"; "I begin to shake before a job interview"; "I blush when people look at me."

Ask each member to demonstrate and experience their pattern in front of the group. This task functions as an intervention using paradoxical intention. If the symptom is a fast heart rate, ask the member to exaggerate it to make the heart beat even faster. As the person concentrates on the task, the heartbeat, of course, begins to slow down. A client who usually becomes silent in a situation is asked to become silent sooner and stay silent longer. Most clients have trouble maintaining an even greater silence and begin to think of things they want to say. Discuss the experience afterward and allow some free interaction. Suggest that they also try this during the week.

This exercise shows clients that they have more control than they think they do, which is useful during behavioral rehearsal in the group and during *in vivo* desensitization outside the group in their behavioral homework exercise.

Homework

- "Read David Burns' book, *Feeling Good: The New Mood Therapy*.

- "Also, continue with your behavioral tasks [assigning themselves a new task as the previous one is mastered]."

Week 7

Review Homework

Ask clients to brag about one behavior they feel proud of. Check that they are rewarding themselves consistently. Stress the importance of control of one's own reinforcement.

I. Skill: Cognitive Restructuring

Intervention 1: Didactic Presentation (See Concepts and Skills section)

Intervention 6: Soliciting Individual Examples

While subjects are using behavioral rehearsal to continue desensitizing to threatening social situations, it's a good time to begin work with the cognitive distortions discovered by Aaron Beck in his pioneering work with depression (1979). David Burns' book includes numerous useful exercises for changing negative thought patterns. Shy people, by the time they come to a shyness clinic, are often depressed as well as socially anxious and avoidant, so that their cognitive distortions are typical of those of both depression and anxiety. Review cognitive distortions in the group session, and have group members write their automatic thoughts, cognitive distortions, and rational responses on the board. Have members help each other to identify common cognitive distortions and to come up with rational responses.

> *Example 1*
>
> | *Automatic thought:* | I'm making a total fool of myself. |
> | *Cognitive distortion:* | All-or-nothing thinking. |
> | *Substitutive thought:* | Even if I seem a little awkward, I can work on it, I can learn. |
>
> *Example 2*
>
> | *Automatic thought:* | I'm hopeless, I can *never* act right in social situations. |
> | *Cognitive distortion:* | Overgeneralization. |
> | *Substitutive thought:* | People are generally supportive, and no one is perfect. |

Homework

- "Use Burns' triple-column technique as homework for the next two-week period. (The mood of the group shifts perceptibly when members are faithful in doing this piece of homework.)

- "Read the chapters from Johnson's book *Reaching Out: Interpersonal Effectiveness and Self-Actualization* (1972) on trust, self-disclosure, and listening.

- "Continue working on behavioral tasks."

Week 8

Review Homework

Review progress on the continuing behavioral homework, as well as reading assignments. Have each member brag about one behavior this week. Review, in detail, examples of the triple-column technique, giving feedback on the examples. Answer questions.

J. Skill: Trust Building

Intervention 1: Didactic Presentation (See Concepts and Skills section)

Intervention 4: Discussion

Ask questions about the extent to which group members self-disclose, are honest with each other, are supportive, listen carefully, and so on. Ask members to discuss the ten most important things they can do to develop trust within the group.

Intervention 3: Exercise — Trust Walk

Have the group do an old-fashioned "trust walk," in which one person leads another "blind" person (eyes closed) on a brief excursion through the office and the waiting room. The person leading helps the "blind" person explore the surroundings by using all senses except sight. The "blind" person can touch furniture and books, listen to the office noises, smell fresh flowers, and the like. When group members discuss the experience, they usually discover how difficult it is for them to rely on another person, to relinquish their sense of control.

Intervention 3: Exercise — Self-Disclosure and Trust Building

Depending on the level of trust established, ask group members to pair up with the person they trust the least, share their thoughts about the reasons for the low trust level, and make suggestions for improvement. Have them be aware of the level of self-disclosure and the degree of acceptance and support. Next have them choose the person they trust the most and discuss why the trust level is high.

These exercises function to build awareness and to establish a context for interpersonal skills training. Because shy people are asked to do things that they find extremely frightening, they must be highly motivated and understand the rationale for the exercises in order to be willing to participate.

K. Skill: Active Listening

Intervention 1: Didactic Presentation (See Concepts and Skills section)

Intervention 4: Discussion

Have group members discuss the effect of childhood experiences on their communication patterns, and name one behavioral pattern involving listening that they want to change.

Intervention 3: Exercise — Paraphrasing

In dyads, have one partner make a statement (it needs to be personally meaningful) to the other and have the listener paraphrase the statement. The sender makes five statements which are paraphrased by the listener, and then the roles are reversed. After paraphrasing the first five statements, the original sender makes one more set of five statements, and then the roles are again reversed.

Example 1

Susan: The boss was uptight today and bugged me all day about a report that is due tomorrow.

Andrew: Sounds like your boss was stressed and made your life stressful today too.

Example 2

David: I'm attracted to a woman I work with but I avoid talking to her. It makes me nervous.

Sam: You like a woman at work but you feel nervous and scared about talking to her.

Following the exercise, group members discuss how they felt listening and being listened to, and whether they had difficulty paraphrasing without evaluation.

Intervention 3: Exercise — Listening for Meaning

On the board, list common problems in communication that interfere with attending to the meaning of the communication. These include lack of organization, too many or incomplete ideas on the part of the sender, thinking of your reply rather than the other person's message, evaluating, and excessive focusing on details.

Following a brief discussion of these communication problems, have members repeat the paraphrasing exercise, this time listening specifically for meaning. The sender makes a statement about himself or herself, about the receiver, or about the relationship. The receiver responds by saying, "I think you mean...." The sender agrees or corrects the receiver until they are in agreement. They each make five statements in all.

Intervention 4: Discussion

"What did you notice about your own communication and listening skills and about those of your partner?"

Homework

* "Continue to work on the cognitive restructuring assignment given at the end of Week 7.

* "Read communications skills chapters from Johnson's *Reaching Out: Interpersonal Effectiveness and Self-Actualization* (1972).

* "Continue with behavioral tasks."

Week 9

Review Homework

Review, in detail, examples of the cognitive restructuring homework. Review behavioral homework. Individual group members can add new homework assignments of increasing difficulty and risk level as their anxiety decreases and skill improve. If they have initiated more conversation during the week, they may extend them, ask more questions, and increase self-disclosure.

L. Skill: Perception Checks

Intervention 1: Didactic Presentation (See Concepts and Skills section)

Intervention 3: Exercise — Perception Checks

Have group members check perceptions of evaluation from each other and use examples from their lives.

Example

Alan: When I walked in the waiting room tonight and said hello to you, you looked angry.

Kathy: Oh really? What I was really feeling was nervous. I think I frown sometimes when I'm nervous.

M. Skill: *I*-Statements and Relationship Statements

Intervention 1: Didactic Presentation (See Concepts and Skills section)

Intervention 6: Soliciting Individual Examples

Have group members practice making personal statements (*I*-statements) about their strengths and weaknesses and their wants and needs.

Intervention 3: Exercise — Practicing Relationship Statements

Have group members practice relationship statements in dyads. For example, "I've been wondering how our relationship is going. You were quiet when we went out for coffee and you didn't return my last phone call. Have I done something that upsets you?" Or "I'm enjoying our relationship so much lately. Having a friend to talk to makes a big difference in my life."

N. Skill: Perspective Taking

Intervention 1: Didactic Presentation (See Concepts and Skills section)

Intervention 5: Role-Play

"We're going to role-play a communication exercise to different receivers. You have just successfully completed a shyness homework exercise that you've been working toward for weeks. There's a person in your pottery class that you're attracted to. You've been initiating conversations with him or her for a month and have finally extended an invitation to go out for coffee after class next week. The person has just accepted. Communicate this news to a) a fellow group member, b) your father, who is critical of your shyness, and c) a co-worker."

Intervention 4: Discussion

Have members discuss how they communicated differently with each person, depending on the perspective. Ask them to describe the perspectives of the group member, the father, and the co-worker.

Intervention 5: Role-Play

"We're going to role-play both senders and receivers in the following scenario. You're having difficulty completing a report at work because your boss expected you to complete several other important projects as well. You just haven't had sufficient time to put into the report, even though you worked until nine o'clock every night last week. You are also having difficulty getting some information you need from your counterpart in another department, who was directed by his or her manager to have it to you two weeks ago. Your boss calls and complains, your counterpart reminds you that you are well behind schedule, and your counterpart's manager asks you why the report hasn't appeared on his or her desk for next week's meeting. Consider, in each case, the role of the person, the nature of the relationship, and the possible consequences of communication." (Johnson, 1972)

Have group members discuss their thoughts and feelings, and describe the perspectives of each participant.

Intervention 5: Role-Play

Have group members practice real-life examples:

Sam: Mary, last week when you said I talked too much when I was nervous, I felt hurt and misunderstood. You don't seem to want to hear what I have to say and are accusing me of hogging attention.

Mary has an opportunity to hear how she affected Sam and to correct a misperception.

Mary: I'm sorry I hurt your feelings last week. I just meant that you seem to talk more and repeat yourself when you're nervous. I feel pushed away when you do that, but I do want to hear your feelings. You've said some things that have helped me a lot. I don't think you are hogging attention on purpose, but I want to have time to talk, too.

Sam can learn to repeat himself less (people in fact react negatively when he does, and he feels hurt) and Mary can refine her feedback skills.

O. Skill: Expression of Feelings

Intervention 1: Didactic Presentation (See Concepts and Skills section)

Intervention 5: Role-Play

Have group members role-play situations in which they express their feelings (angry, sad, hurt, happy, joyful, and afraid). Shy people, in an exercise where they simply tell another person they are scared of being judged or of being close, will often experience a transformational experience and say, "Gosh, that wasn't so bad! I've never told another human being that I'm scared of rejection or of being close! It doesn't seem so scary or so unsurmountable, or even so unusual. Actually, John said he was scared, too. I knew that I wouldn't purposefully hurt him, so what was I so scared of? He probably wouldn't intentionally try to hurt me either!"

Homework

*   "Continue using your relaxation technique in social situations.

*   "Finish reading Johnson's *Reaching Out: Interpersonal Effectiveness and Self-Actualization* (1972)."

*

Week 10

Review Homework

Check to see whether clients are rewarding themselves consistently for their behavioral homework. Have them brag about one behavior that week.

P. Skill: Self-Esteem and Self-Concept Restructuring

Intervention 1: Didactic Presentation (See Concepts and Skills section)

Shy clients sometimes have shame-based self-concepts that cause them to feel badly about themselves in a global way. They may believe that they are inadequate or inferior and that simply changing their behavior and thinking patterns will not be sufficient to change "who they really are." These kinds of thinking patterns are motivation killers. Some clients change, become more expressive and assertive, and still claim that they are not doing better or even that they are doing worse. Some will effectively role-play an assertiveness situation, demonstrating clearly to the group that they have the capacity and the know-how for effective interpersonal performance; and then shrink from praise and applause, reaffirming loudly that they could not possibly repeat their performance in real life, that they are really hopeless, and so on. Some of their strongest assertions will involve their insistence that they are indeed inadequate. In these situations, prod them gently to affirm their effective performances, to acknowledge themselves for good work, and to use positive adjectives to describe themselves and their behavior.

Intervention 6: Soliciting Individual Examples

Have each member practice restructuring his or her internal cognitions about the self with two examples from his or her own life. Also ask clients to brag for several minutes at a time about something that made them proud of themselves during the week. They may brag about completing homework, changing a thought pattern, finding good positive substitutes for negative thoughts, or gradually changing their attitudes. Ask them to stand up for emphasis or shout how proud they are of themselves and how pleased they are with their own behavior, their thoughts, or even their physiological well-being. They have been practicing this during homework review, which makes it a bit easier to do.

Intervention 4: Discussion

Have clients increase their self-esteem, as well as build a sense of expertise, by sharing their problem-solving techniques and coping mechanisms with each other.

Q. Skill: Expression of Anger

Intervention 1: Didactic Presentation (See Concepts and Skills section)

Intervention 5: Role-Play

Put a list of questions on the board. What do you want to achieve? On a scale from one to ten, how important is your goal to you? How important is this relationship to you? What is the best way to reach an agreement? What can you learn about your communication skills that you can use in the next conflict situation? Have you asked for feedback? Is this a situation in which an agreement can be reached? If not, what can you live with? Can you agree to disagree? Ask members to consult the board as they role-play, and hold a discussion after the exercises. In the discussion, group members may share strategies that worked and consult each other for additional ideas. You may make up vignettes that are relevant to group members' daily lives, or ask them to volunteer recent situations that are applicable.

For example: "I sense that you are angry at me for resisting going to the movie. Actually, I would rather stay home. I realize that I am angry at you because we have gone out at your suggestion the last three nights and you haven't asked me what I want to do. I would like to stay home tonight and perhaps go to the movie tomorrow. How do you feel about it?"

Homework

- "Read Chapters 5 and 7 of *Asserting Yourself* by Sharon and Gordon Bower (1976).

- "People profit from planning and organizing their thoughts before they encounter a situation that requires assertive behaviors and responses. Choose two real-life situations in which you want to be more assertive — one situation that is work- or school-related, and the other involving a more intimate relationship, either a friendship or a love relationship. Write scripts for these situations following the examples in *Asserting Yourself*, and plan to role-play them next week.

    "The Bowers use the acronym *DESC* to describe their scripts. Use this acronym, writing scripts that first *DESCRIBE* the problem, then *EXPRESS* your thoughts and feelings about it, next *SPECIFY* what you want, and finally that state the positive and/or negative *CONSEQUENCES* of getting or not getting what you want.

    "During desensitization training, you visualized scenes that evoked anxiety for you, and learned to use visual detail and all five senses to create anxiety-provoking scenes in your imagination. Use these same skills in writing your scripts in order to make them as lifelike as possible." The role plays that follow script-writing thus will serve as desensitization exercises as well as behavioral rehearsal for increased assertiveness.

Week 11

Review Homework

Have clients read their usual and revised attributions out loud. Give clients additional ideas and ask them to rehearse one or two adaptive attributions aloud in group. Ask them for examples of cognitive restructuring in relation to their self-concepts.

Homework

Role-play DESC situations that members have written. If you haven't done so previously, it's a good time to use a video camera to give members feedback and to build confidence. At the end of the role-play, have clients practice two or three affirmations in front of the camera.

Week 12

Review Homework

Ask about behavioral homework. Check to see if clients are using rewards.

R. Skill: Responding to Criticism

Intervention 1: Didactic Presentation — Fogging (See Concepts and Skills section)

Intervention 3: Exercise — Practicing Fogging

Have group members practice fogging, using situations from their own lives.

Intervention 3: Exercise — Responding to Continuing Criticism

As group members practice and become more confident, have them take part in an exercise in which there is continuing pressure. When they respond to the first criticism, come up with another. Criticize the way they respond at each moment as they continue the fogging response. At some point, the exercise usually becomes funny, and they begin to laugh at the absurdity of the underdog position.

Intervention 1: Didactic Presentation — Negative Inquiry (See Concepts and Skills section)

Intervention 3: Exercise — Practicing Negative Inquiry

Have group members role-play situations from their own lives and then role-play with the therapist (if they want a tougher critic) continuing their practice of negative inquiry for a longer time.

Intervention 1: Didactic Presentation — Negative Assertion (See Concepts and Skills section)

Intervention 3: Exercise — Practicing Negative Assertion

Allow as much group time as possible for role-playing these kinds of interactions, again taking examples, that are pertinent to shy people or using examples from group members' lives.

Intervention 4: Discussion

Ask group members what it was like to be criticized and to criticize others.

Termination Discussion

Hold a wrap-up discussion in which members express their feelings about leaving, talk about their original goals and the extent to which they met them, and discuss how they will continue on their own. Have them be specific about changes in thoughts, behaviors, and feelings. Ask for feedback about techniques that were helpful and those that were not. Encourage group members to express any negative feedback to you about the group. (This serves as further practice in giving negative feedback in general.)

Criteria for Measuring Change

Measurable behavioral goals were set in the second screening session. Criteria for measuring change are: reduced physiological arousal; new, more positive, and hopeful thinking patterns about social situations and the self; and new behaviors that were not evident previously. Increased self-esteem and self-expression are usually present.

Relapse

Shy clients relapse if they do not practice or keep themselves in social situations, just as people get out of shape physically if they don't exercise. Explain this phenomenon to the group. To prevent getting out of "social shape," recommend and encourage them to get into community groups, dating services, and church activities. If they do relapse, they can come back for individual booster sessions or another group experience without further screening.

Resistance

Shy people resist change in general more than most people — so you should expect a good deal of resistance in shyness groups. Clients will hesitate to try new behaviors in group, and resist doing their homework. This of course varies within the group, because shy people are also conscientious and want to please you. This counterforce aids them in carrying out their behavioral and cognitive assignments.

Passive aggression is the dominant style among shy people, who are highly creative in finding methods to defeat themselves and you. Shy clients can try your patience beyond anything you have experienced in working with other therapy groups. Confront group members about passive aggressive techniques, and share your feeling about these maneuvers. Confront their use of shyness as an excuse not to assume the ordinary risks and responsibilities of everyday living. Confront also the arrogance that assumes that everyone is watching and evaluating them, the shy people. They are shocked to discover the hidden arrogance in the shy position. They are surprised to find that they often expect to be treated as exceptions, as special. They expect others to initiate, contact, to seek them out, and to lead and take care of them. Acknowledging these aspects of themselves to the group, and working on them together, makes it less painful for clients to confront their attitudes. People do not feel singled out and can hear others acknowledge these tendencies in themselves.

The single biggest contributor to resistance in the Shyness Group is the affect of shame. Talk about it early on during the course of the group, describing shame and how it manifests itself in such cognitions as "I am inadequate and inferior." Feelings influence cognitions and cognitions influence feelings, often creating a vicious circle. Saying that "I am inadequate" simply creates additional feelings of shame. It's better to express the feelings themselves rather than the cognitions, because feelings pass and people can be comforted and reassured when they express them. Encourage group members to say aloud that they feel ashamed when these feelings come up. Encourage them to express the behaviors, thoughts, and feelings that cause shame. They find that others experience similar feelings and that they are not as unique or deficient as they thought they were. Shy people frequently are moralistic, perfectionistic, and naive about ordinary behavior, thoughts, and feelings because they have not had opportunities to share in an intimate way with other people. Sharing in this manner is one of the most powerful healing experiences in the life of a Shyness Group.

Group members will sometimes be absent because they are ashamed of the way they are feeling or behaving, or because they haven't done their homework. Respect their right to choose, but stress that it is only through taking the risk of acknowledging who they really are and through sharing and mutual support that they will change. The choice is theirs, but it is a choice, acknowledged or not.

Termination

Termination is an experience of separation, difficult for shy people because they feel insecure in interpersonal relationships. In long-term groups, ask members who are leaving to give the group three month's notice so that they can take the time to complete unfinished business and say goodbye. Group members explore their feelings about the termination and associate this loss with previous losses. The process is powerful. Group members recover forgotten experiences and connect the memories and feelings with their reluctance to become intimate with others as well as their reluctance to say goodbye to someone with whom they have become close.

Group members share whatever unexpressed thoughts and feelings they have toward the departing person, often finding the courage to say things they may not have dared to say before, such as how close they felt, how angry they were during an interaction, or that they were sexually attracted to the departing member.

In short-term structured groups, mention termination several weeks before the group is due to end. Encourage clients to use the impending termination to motivate themselves to take risks that they might not otherwise take and to allow their feelings about separation to emerge. Emphasize in shyness groups that clients may come back for booster sessions and that more work is not a sign of failure but is usually a sign of another growth spurt or of the readiness to tackle a new developmental task. They may also join another group later or a long-term group if they like, without further screening. Encourage them to check in, to let you know how things are going, and just to touch base if they like. These groups are springboards to increased association and intimacy with others, and you may become a bit of a home base for some of these people, who come back off and on for years. Sometimes they agree to continue seeing each other socially or to telephone each other when they need someone to talk to. These negotiations are best left to the individuals in the group.

References

Adler, R.B., and Towne, N. *Looking Out/Looking In.* New York: Holt, Rinehart, and Winston, 1970.

Alden, L., and Cappe, R. "Interpersonal process training for shy clients." In *Shyness: Perspectives on Research and Treatment.* Edited by W.H. Jones, J.M. Cheek, and S.R. Briggs. New York: Plenum Press, 1986, 343-356.

Anderson, C.A. "The causal structure of situations: The generation of plausible causal attributions as a function of type of event situation." *Journal of Experimental Social Psychology,* 1983, *19,* 185-203.

Arnkoff, D.B.; Glass, C.R.; McKain, T.; Shea, C.A.; and Greenberg, J.M. "Client predispositions to respond to cognitive and social skills treatments for shyness." In *Shyness: Personality Development, Social Behavior, and Treatment Approaches.* Symposium conducted at the meeting of the American Psychological Association, Toronto, 1984.

Beck, A.T.; Rush, A.J.; Shaw, B.F.; and Emery, G. *Cognitive Therapy of Depression.* New York: Guilford Press, 1979.

Bell, P.A., and Byrne, D. "Regression-sensitization." In *Dimensions of Personality.* Edited by H. London and J.E. Exner. New York: 1978, 449-485.

Bowlby, J. *A Secure Base*. New York: Basic Books Inc., 1988.

Bower, S.A., and Bower, G.H. *Asserting Yourself*. Menlo Park, California: Addison-Wesley, 1976.

Breck, B.E., and Smith, S.H. "Selective recall of self-descriptive traits by socially anxious and nonanxious females." *Social Behavior and Personality*, 1983, *11(2)*, 71-76.

Burns, D.D. *Feeling Good, the New Mood Therapy*. New York: New American Library, 1980.

Cheek, J.M. *Conquering Shyness*. New York: Basic Books, 1989.

_____. *The Revised Cheek and Buss Shyness Scale*. Unpublished manuscript, Wellesley College, 1983.

_____, and Buss, A.H. "Shyness and sociability." *Journal of Personality and Social Psychology*, 1981, *41*, 330-339.

_____; Carpentieri, A.M.; Smith, T.G.; Rierdan, J.; and Koff, E. "Adolescent shyness." In *Shyness: Perspectives on Research and Treatment*. Edited by W.H. Jones, J.M. Cheek, and S.R. Briggs. New York: Plenum Press, 1986, 105-115.

_____. *Emotional Disorder and Psychotherapy*. New York: Plenum Press, 113-131.

Crozier, W.R. "Explanations of social shyness." *Current Psychological Reviews*, 1982, *2*, 47-60.

Curran, J.P.; Wallander, J.L.; and Fischetti, M. "The importance of behavioral and cognitive factors in heterosexual-social anxiety." *Journal of Personality*, 1980, *43*, 285-292.

Edelmann, R.J. "Individual differences in embarrassment: Self-consciousness, self-monitoring, and embarrassibility. *Personality and Individual Differences*, 1985, *6(2)*, 223-230.

Franzoi, S.L. "Self-concept differences as a function of private self-consciousness and social anxiety." *Journal of Research in Personality*, 1983, *17*, 275-287.

Gabor, D. *How to Start a Conversation and Make Friends*. New York: Fireside Books, 1983.

Glass, C.R., and Furlong, M.R. "A comparison of behavioral, cognitive, and traditional group therapy approaches for shyness." In *Shyness: Personality Development, Social Behavior, and Treatment Approaches*. Symposium conducted at the meeting of the American Psychological Association, Toronto, August 1984.

Goldfried, M.R., and Davison, G.C. *Clinical Behavior Therapy*. York York: Holt, Rinehart, and Winston, 1976.

Hammerlie, F.M., and Montgomery, R.L. "Self-perception theory and the treatment of shyness." In *Shyness: Perspectives on Research and Treatment*. Edited by W.H. Jones, J.M. Cheek, and S.R. Briggs. New York: Plenum Press, 1986, 329-342.

Harder, D.W., and Lewis, S.J. "The assessment of shame and guilt." In *Advances in Personality Assessment, 6*. Edited by J. Butcher and C. Spielberger. Hillsdale, New Jersey: Lawrence Erlbaum, 1986.

Izard, C.E. *The Face of Emotion*. New York: Appleton-Century-Crofts, 1971.

Johnson, D.W. *Reaching Out: Interpersonal Effectiveness and Self-Actualization*. Englewood Cliffs, New Jersey: Prentice-Hall, 1972.

Jones, W.H.; Briggs, S.R.; and Smith, T.G. "Shyness: Conceptualization and measurement." *Journal of Personality and Social Psychology*, 1986, 51(3), 629-639.

_____, and Carpenter, B.N. "Shyness, social behavior, and relationships." In *Shyness: Perspectives on Research and Treatment*. Edited by W.H. Jones, J.M. Cheek, and S.R. Briggs. New York: Plenum Press, 1986, 329-342.

Kroger, W.S., and Fezler, W.D. *Hypnosis and Behavior Modification: Imagery Conditioning*. Philadelphia: J.B. Lippincott Company, 1976.

Lewis, H.B. *Shame and Guilt in Neurosis*. New York: International Universities Press, 1971.

_____. "Shame in depression and hysteria." In *Emotions in Personality and Psychopathology*. Edited by C.E. Izard. New York: Plenum Press, 1979, 371-398.

Lucock, M.P., and Salkoviskis, P. "Cognitive factors in social anxiety and its treatment." *Behavior Research and Therapy*, 1988, 26(4), 297-302.

Maddux, J.E.; Norton, L.W.; and Leary, M.L. "Cognitive components of social anxiety: An investigation of self-presentation theory and self-efficacy theory." *Journal of Social and Clinical Psychology*, 1988, 6(2), 180-190.

McEwan, K.L., and Devins, G.M. "Is increased arousal in social anxiety noticed by others?" *Journal of Abnormal Psychology*, 92, 417-421.

McKay, M., and Fanning, P. *Self-Esteem*. Oakland, California: New Harbinger Publications, 1987.

O'Banion, K., and Arkowitz, H. "Social anxiety and selective memory for affective information about the self." *Social Behavior and Personality*, 1977, 5, 321-328.

Phillips, G.M. "Rhetoritherapy: The principles of rhetoric in training shy people in speech effectiveness." In *Shyness: Perspectives on Research and Treatment*. Edited by W.H. Jones, J.M. Cheek, and S.R. Briggs. New York: Plenum Press, 1986, 357-374.

Pilkonis, P.A. "Shyness, public and private, and its relationship to other measures of social behavior." *Journal of Personality*, 1977a, 45, 585-595.

_____. "The behavioral consequences of shyness." *Journal of Personality*, 1977b, 45, 596-611.

Schmitt, J.P., and Kurdek, L.A. "Correlates of social anxiety in college students and homosexuals." *Journal of Personal Assessment*, 1984, 48(4), 403-409.

Schutz, W. *The Interpersonal Underworld*. Palo Alto, California: Science and Behavior Books, 1966.

Smith, M.J. *When I Say No I Feel Guilty*. New York: Bantam Books, 1975.

Smith, R.E., and Sarason, I.G. "Social anxiety and the evaluation of negative interpersonal feedback." *Journal of Consulting and Clinical Psychology*, 1975, 43, 429.

Smith, T.W.; Ingram, R.E.; and Brehm, S.S. "Social anxiety, anxious self-preoccupation and recall of self-referent information." *Journal of Personality and Social Psychology*, 1983, 44, 1276-1283.

Snyder, C.R., and Smith, T.W. "On being "shy like a fox": A self-handicapping analysis." In *Shyness: Perspectives on Research and Treatment*. Edited by W.H. Jones, J.M. Cheek, and S.R. Briggs. New York: Plenum Press, 1986, 161-172.

_____; Smith, T.W.; Augelli, R.W.; and Ingram, R.E. "On the self-serving function of social anxiety: Shyness as a self-handicapping strategy. *Journal of Personality and Social Psychology*, 1985, *48*, 970-980.

Tomkins, S.S. "Shame." In *The Many Faces of Shame*. Edited by D.L. Nathanson. New York: Guilford Press, 1987.

Trower, P., and Gilbert, P. "New theoretical conceptions of social anxiety and social phobia." *Clinical Psychology Review*, 1989, *9*, 19-35.

Watson, D., and Friend, R. "Measurement of social-evaluative anxiety." *Journal of Consulting and Clinical Psychology*, 1969, 33(4), 448-457.

Zimbardo, P.G. *Shyness: What It Is, What to Do About It*. Reading, Massachusetts: Addison-Wesley, 1977.

_____. "The Stanford shyness project." In *Shyness: Perspectives on Research and Treatment*. Edited by W.H. Jones, J.M. Cheek, and S.R. Briggs. New York: Plenum Press, 1986, 17-25.

Chapter 3

The Agoraphobia Treatment Group

Edmund J. Bourne, Ph.D.

Introduction

Agoraphobia is one of the most disabling of the anxiety disorders, affecting approximately 5 percent of the adult population in the United States. The term *agoraphobia* was originally coined by Westphal (1871) to describe a fear of walking in open spaces. However, the principal fear in agoraphobia involves apprehension about having a panic attack in situations where escape is perceived to be difficult. Common phobic situations include driving, stores and restaurants, elevators, planes and other public transportation, and being alone. Agoraphobia usually develops after an individual has been experiencing panic attacks and begins to avoid situations previously associated with panic or perceived as likely to bring on panic. The fear can, in some cases, progress to the point where a person is entirely housebound. Agoraphobia frequently involves dependency on a spouse, partner, or support person who must accompany the agoraphobic on forays away from their safe place. It also may involve depression: agoraphobics feel helpless and hopeless in avoidance of routine activities which they formerly accomplished easily. Some agoraphobics also experience obsessive, intrusive thoughts, warranting a dual diagnosis of agoraphobia and obsessive-compulsive disorder.

About 75 to 80 percent of agoraphobics are women, and the disorder typically begins in the early twenties. There is some evidence for a hereditary basis, as concordance rates for identical twins are three to four times higher than for fraternal twins (Torgersen, 1983; Slater & Shields, 1969). Predisposing family history factors are also involved: parents who are overly protective, overcritical and perfectionist, or phobic themselves may set the stage for their children to later develop agoraphobia or another anxiety disorder.

The most effective treatment for agoraphobia is *in vivo* exposure — a process in which the client directly but gradually confronts a phobic situation in small increments. Typically, the agoraphobic and a support person will go together to confront a situation, such as a grocery store, continuing to the point where anxiety becomes slightly unmanageable. The client temporarily retreats from the situation at that point, allowing the anxiety to subside. After doing some breathing and relaxation exercises, the client proceeds with the exposure and then reenters the situation until anxiety rises to a certain criterion level again. Frequently, the agoraphobic will have desensitization to the situation in imagination (following Wolpe's systematic desensitization techniques — see Wolpe, 1958, 1973) prior to undertaking *in vivo* exposure.

Recent research indicates that self-paced exposure, carried out over a longer period of time and utilizing a support person, is superior to intense exposure (also known as *flooding*) over a short period of time (Barlow & Waddell, 1985). It is also critical that clients receive extensive training in learning to cope with panic attacks prior to engaging in *in vivo* exposure (Barlow, 1988, Chapter 11, and Bourne, 1990, Chapter 6). Current treatment protocols emphasize training clients to control panic symptoms that are deliberately provoked during treatment sessions (Barlow & Craske, 1989).

Another critical area to address in treating agoraphobia is the client's anxious self-talk and underlying core beliefs or cognitive schemata that predispose this self-talk. Clients are taught to identify anxiety-provoking thinking patterns, as described by Beck (1979) and Beck & Emery (1985). They learn to rationally dispute distorted thoughts and replace them with more rational, supportive self-statements based on direct experience. Core beliefs that perpetuate anxiety are also identified. Their origins are explored in the context of the client's developmental history, and then the client learns to evaluate their validity and work with more rational, self-supportive affirmations.

Agoraphobia can be treated through individual therapy, or in a group format as described in this chapter. There are advantages to each approach. It is important, in initially evaluating a client, to explore his or her preferences as well as ability to be comfortable in a social situation (see next section). Groups can provide considerable *interpersonal support* for recovery as well as *incentive* to do homework and practice self-paced exposure between sessions. It may be asking a lot from individual therapy to be able to generate the same degree of support and motivation to practice that is possible within a group, although clients who prefer individual therapy tend to do better in that mode.

The approach to group treatment presented in this chapter draws considerably from TERRAP — a group treatment program for agoraphobia developed by Arthur Hardy more than 20 years ago. TERRAP (a contraction derived from "territorial apprehensiveness") currently offers treatment groups throughout the United States and is operated by TSC Corporation in Menlo Park, California. This chapter also draws heavily from *The Anxiety and Phobia Workbook* (Bourne, 1990), which is based on the author's clinical experience with individual and group therapy treatment approaches.

An adequate recovery program for agoraphobia can be achieved in ten weeks by a group covering the main treatment interventions described above, namely

- The Causes of Panic and Agoraphobia (Weeks 1 and 2)

- Relaxation Training (Week 3)

- Physical Exercise (Week 4)

- Coping with Panic Attacks (Week 5)

- Imagery Desensitization (Week 6)

- Real-Life Desensitization (Week 7)

- Field Trip 1 (to practice *in vivo* exposure) (Week 8)

- Self-Talk (Week 9)

- Mistaken Beliefs and Affirmations (Week 10)

These are core ingredients of recovery that constitute the main focus of this chapter and need to be addressed in any effective treatment program.

Additional treatment components that might be included in a more comprehensive program would include:

- Identifying and Expressing Feelings (one session)

- Assertiveness Training (two sessions)

- Self-Esteem Training (two sessions)

- Nutrition and the Use of Medication (one session)

- Anxiety and Life Meaning (Existential-Spiritual Perspective) (one session)

A longer, 18-week treatment format incorporating the above elements constitutes, in my opinion, an ideal program for recovery. Space limitations prohibit detailed discussion of these components in this chapter. Relevant chapters of *The Anxiety and Phobia Workbook* cover them in some depth, however.

Selection and Screening

A pre-group evaluation is necessary to determine the suitability of prospective clients for the group. Generally, only those clients who meet DSM-III-R criteria for Panic Disorder with Agoraphobia or Social Phobia are appropriate for inclusion. Since so much of the work of the group focuses on desensitization to phobias, clients presenting with other types of anxiety disorder — such as "pure" panic disorder, generalized anxiety disorder, or obsessive-compulsive disorder — are likely to feel misplaced. Individuals dealing with a simple phobia, for example, who are *only* fearful of freeways or flying, and who do not have panic attacks, can utilize the group, although they may find the section on coping with panic attacks to be irrelevant to their problem.

Clients who are motivated to overcome their difficulties and are willing to make a 10- to 18-week commitment are most likely to benefit from the group. It's important to ask clients about their motivation and commitment at the outset. A moderately to severely phobic person may have no conception of the discipline needed, nor the commitment it really takes, to recover. Many phobics say "yes" emphatically, that they are ready and willing to work toward recovery. Yet when it comes right down to doing the work required, they will rationalize and avoid to extremes.

Another issue is clients' social anxiety level. Certain individuals are so phobic about being in any group that they are likely to do better by completing a course of individual therapy focusing on communication skills such as self-disclosure and desensitization to social situations prior to entering a group. It is important to raise the issue of comfort level in a social situation with all prospective clients.

Two additional variables predict outcome in group treatment: depression and marital adjustment. Agoraphobic clients who concurrently meet DSM-III-R criteria for dysthymic disorder or major depression may be too depressed to do the homework necessary for recovery — in particular, real-life exposure to phobic situations. The moderate to severely depressed client is likely to gain support from the group, but may make little real progress until the depression abates. Individual psychotherapy helping a client to resolve life crises or interpersonal issues causing depression may be a necessary adjunct to effective group work. Sometimes these issues get resolved in the latter sessions of the extended group, which focus on feelings, assertiveness, and self-esteem.

Research has repeatedly demonstrated that clients with a spouse or partner tend to do very well when the partner is supportive of their recovery. (Munby & Johnston, 1980; Barlow, O'Brien & Lust, 1984) Conversely, when the partner is indifferent or in opposition to the treatment, the chances of success are significantly diminished. This is the reason for including clients' partners or support persons in the group during the first seven sessions and in subsequent sessions on assertiveness and communication. It is most useful at the stage of the pre-group evaluation to explore the possibility of collusions between client and partners against recovery.

Time and Duration

Groups can be run either for 10 or 18 weeks. The shorter version focuses on providing training in relaxation, panic-reduction, desensitization, and cognitive skills and includes one field trip where clients practice *in vivo* exposure. These are the "bare essentials" for beginning recovery. The longer version adds an emphasis on interpersonal skills (assertiveness and communication, self-esteem, nutrition, medications, and personal meaning). The advantage of the 18-week group lies not only in providing clients with additional relevant skills, but in giving them a longer period of time for practicing real-life desensitization within the structured context of the group. (A second field trip, where clients practice exposure during the regular time of the group meeting, is offered in this extended version).

Group sessions typically last between one-and-a-half and two hours.

Structure

The agoraphobia treatment group works best as a closed group consisting of eight to ten clients. When there are more than ten clients, group members don't have enough opportunity to share their experiences on a week-to-week basis. Partners or support persons of clients are included in the group during the first seven sessions to help make the group a "safe place." In the longer format, partners return for later sessions on assertiveness and communication to engage in role-plays with clients.

Attendance at all sessions is stressed. This is reinforced by having the client pay in advance for each month (or for each of three six-week segments) of the group. Clients sign agreements at the outset that they will pay for the groups at the beginning of each month or six-week segment.

The group leader takes responsibility for presenting the lesson for each week, handling clients' questions, stimulating discussion, and conducting exercises and role-plays. For the group to be successful, the leader must provide guidance and instruction to clients individually, confronting them when necessary. At the same time, he or she needs to create a supportive atmosphere, impart enthusiasm to the group, and inspire commitment in each group member to do the homework.

In addition to the leader, there is a group assistant who is preferably a recovered agoraphobic. The group assistant takes minutes of the meeting each week, reinforce the lesson discussed, and writes up a one- to two-page summary that is mailed out to clients a day or two after each meeting. The most important function of the group assistant is to be available to clients between group meetings. Clients are encouraged to call the assistant if they have any questions or concerns during the week.

If the assistant is unavailable or unable to answer the client's questions, the group leader may be contacted instead.

Goals

The goals of the agoraphobia treatment group are fourfold:

1. To provide clients with strategies and skills for coping with panic attacks — specifically, abdominal breathing, muscle relaxation, grounding skills such as physical exertion, and cognitive skills emphasizing the use of coping statements (sessions 3 and 5).

2. To provide clients with a knowledge of how to practice both imagery and real-life desensitization as a means to overcoming their phobias. In addition, clients are given support and encouragement to practice desensitization on a regular basis at home (sessions 6 and 7).

3. To assist clients in identifying and modifying unhelpful self-talk and mistaken beliefs that contribute to their anxiety on an ongoing basis (sessions 9 and 10).

4. To assist clients in increasing their self-esteem and overcoming the original insecurity, shame, and/or sense of inadequacy out of which their problems developed. Self-esteem is promoted by helping clients to: a) identify and express their feelings, b) master assertiveness skills, c) recognize their needs and learn how to meet them, and d) develop self-nurturing skills and an awareness of their relationship with their "inner child" (sessions 11-14).

Ground Rules

The following ground rules are presented to clients during the first week of the group:

1. Assigned homework is to be completed and turned in each week. Homework consists of a self-monitoring form on which clients check off whether they practiced relaxation, exercise, desensitization, and cognitive restructuring or affirmations on a daily basis. Additional written homework assignments relevant to each component of the program are given each week. Completed homework is turned in to the group assistant, who takes it home and provides written comments to the client. It is given back to the group leader prior to each group meeting and is reviewed by the leader at the outset of that meeting. Both the leader and assistant repeatedly emphasize to group members during the first few weeks that completing homework is *essential* to their progress toward recovery.

2. Clients are told that the door to the group room is always left open and that anyone who feels the need to leave can do so at any time. Clients are encouraged to leave the group only *temporarily* if they are feeling anxious, to allow themselves time to calm down and recover, and then to make every effort to return to the group, if possible, for the remainder of the session. However, it's OK to leave for the day and call the assistant afterwards if they feel that doing so is absolutely necessary.

3. Clients are encouraged to share with the group on a weekly basis what is going on in their life and any progress they're making in their recovery

program. However, they are asked *not* to talk about specific anxiety or panic symptoms (such as heart palpitations, sweaty hands, feeling dizzy, disoriented, out of control, or fearful of something terrible happening). Agoraphobics tend to be very suggestible and are susceptible to "swapping" symptoms.

4. Clients are told to avoid watching television programs or reading newspaper articles that focus on violent or fearful themes. This only serves to aggravate their proclivity to view the outside world as an unsafe place.

5. Each week after the second session, every client is to call one other person in the group. During the second week, clients are given a list of group members with their telephone numbers and are told to call a different person each week. When they call, they are to discuss how their week has been going and any progress they've made with their program, but to avoid talking about symptoms. If clients feel shy or awkward about calling someone, it's OK for them to share that they're feeling that way — or that they can't think of anything to talk about — and to stay on the phone for just a minute or two.

    The purpose of this exercise is to help clients give and receive support, reduce their social anxiety, and foster group cohesion.

6. It is emphasized from the outset that everything that goes on in the group is to be kept strictly confidential. If a client's partner or support person has participated in the group, it's OK to discuss the group's process with that particular person (even on weeks when they aren't in attendance), but with nobody else. Clients are permitted to record group sessions if they choose.

Starting the Group

The group needs to begin with the leader and group assistant introducing themselves. Then clients introducing themselves. I've found it helpful to have clients break up into dyads afterwards (not with their support person) for more extensive introductions. This begins the process of group members getting acquainted. Additional "get-acquainted" periods of five or ten minutes each during the first three weeks of the group, in which each client meets a new person each time, will help build an atmosphere of support and cohesiveness.

Following introductions, the ground rules mentioned in the previous section should be discussed. The leaders should acquaint clients with basic policies and procedures of the group, and distribute handouts describing ground rules, policies, and procedures.

It is very important when starting a group to emphasize the importance of doing the assigned homework. This is a good place to present anecdotal evidence that the most successful "graduates" of previous groups were the ones who consistently did homework and practiced real-life exposure.

Main Concepts and Skills

A. Concept: Development of Agoraphobia

"Agoraphobia is a complication that develops in some individuals who have experienced panic attacks. A panic attack is a sudden intense surge of anxiety that seems to be coming out of the blue, involving such symptoms as: 1) heart palpitations, 2) chest constriction and difficulty breathing, 3) dizziness or vertigo, 4) faintness, 5) sweating, 6) trembling, 7) feelings of unreality (sometimes called *depersonalization*), and 8) fears of imminent danger, such as dying, going crazy, or losing complete control. Panic attacks are so uncomfortable that when one has occurred, you may become fearful of ever again entering the situation that provided its context — especially if this is a situation you can't easily exit, such as driving on the freeway, being in an elevator, or standing in line at the checkout stand in the grocery store. Because you want to avoid future panic attacks, you start avoiding those situations in which you're afraid one might occur. It's this avoidance that really marks the beginning of agoraphobia. What you're *really* afraid of is not so much the specific situation — the grocery store or the freeway — but of having a panic attack in such situations.

"Agoraphobia can be mild, moderate, or severe, depending on the number of situations you avoid and the degree of restriction this imposes on you. In the most severe cases, you can become housebound altogether. All agoraphobics need a "safe person" and a "safe place" where they can feel at ease and free of fear about panic. In the most extreme case, an agoraphobic cannot leave this safe place at all without panicking. In many cases, though, there are a variety of situations and places you can still deal with outside your home, and you have only a few, select phobias.

"Two secondary problems that develop with agoraphobia are *dependency* and *depression*. Being with someone you can trust — your 'safe person' — enables you to engage in activities or go places you wouldn't try alone. So you become dependent on that person, typically to a greater degree than you'd like. Depression develops because of the feelings of helplessness you get from not being able to control your panic reactions — and especially from being unable to go places and do things you used to negotiate with ease. In recovering from agoraphobia, you will gain both a grater sense of self-sufficiency and a more optimistic, hopeful outlook toward life."

B. Concept: The Agoraphobic Personality Profile

"Agoraphobia affects one in every 20 people in the United States, or about 5 percent of the population. As an agoraphobic, you have a number of special personality characteristics, many of which are quite positive, that set you apart from the 'average' person:

- You're very sensitive. You are sensitive to environmental stimuli such as temperature, light, smells, and sounds. And you are also often sensitive to other people and their feelings. Many agoraphobics have a heightened sense of intuition — some are 'psychic.'

- You probably have an above-average IQ.

- You're creative. Being both intelligent and creative, you have the best of both worlds. Typically, you have a very rich and vivid imagination. In this group, you'll learn to use your imagination positively, instead of against yourself, by magnifying your fears.

- You have intense emotions and often a high degree of emotional reactivity. This is usually an inborn trait, and it makes your experience of life more vivid and poignant. In this group, again, you can learn to make this trait work for rather than against you.

"Many famous people have this profile of characteristics and have struggled with phobias, including Johnny Carson, Barbra Streisand, Carly Simon, Bob Dylan, and Vladimir Horowitz.

"Some of the *less* positive traits you may have include:

- A lot of negative thinking — particularly 'what-if' and 'should' thinking.

- A tendency to be compulsive (doing things compulsively) or obsessive (having recurring, repetitive thoughts).

- A tendency to be a perfectionist — you can become very upset if things don't work out exactly the way you'd like them to.

- A tendency to procrastinate — you put off things you don't want to deal with. You're also very adept at avoidance and have great skill at coming up with excuses for getting out of what you don't what to do.

- You're a 'people pleaser' — from an early age you have sought others' approval and often believe that pleasing others is more important than taking care of yourself. (The modern term for this characteristic is co-dependency.)

- You're secretive — it's often difficult for you to tell anyone else about your problem. You feel ashamed of your problem and fear that others will make fun of you or regard you as 'crazy' if you talk about it.

These less positive traits are 'learned' and can therefore be unlearned and replaced with more positive patterns of thought and behavior."

C. Concept: The Causes of Agoraphobia

"There are three *levels* of causes which contribute to developing agoraphobia:

1. Long-term, predisposition causes

2. Recent causes, such as the conditions and circumstances that trigger a first panic attack

3. Maintaining causes, conditions such as negative self-talk and withheld feelings that keep the problem going

"There are three types of long-term, predisposing causes: 1) heredity, 2) your childhood environment and upbringing, and 3) cumulative stress over time. Agoraphobia tends to run in families. About 20 percent of children of an agoraphobic parent develop panic attacks or agoraphobia, while the incidence of agoraphobia in the general population is about 5 percent. More compelling evidence for the role of heredity comes from the fact that if one identical twin has problems with phobias, the other twin is up to three times more likely to have problems as well than would be the case with a pair of fraternal twins. Researchers believe that you do not inherit agoraphobia *per se* but rather a volatile, reactive nervous system that is more easily sensitized to anxiety-provoking situations. The particular type of anxiety disorder you develop, given this personality, depends on other factors.

"Apart from heredity, there are several types of dysfunctional family circumstances that show up in the background of agoraphobics. The most common ones are as follows:

- *Your parents communicate an overly cautious view of the world.* Parents of agoraphobics — even when not explicitly phobic themselves — often are excessively concerned about potential danger to their children. They frequently attribute danger to normal childhood activities that aren't really dangerous.

The child of such parents, unfortunately, learns to regard the world outside the home as a dangerous place.

- *Your parents are overly critical and set excessively high standards.* A child growing up with critical, perfectionist parents is never quite sure of his or her acceptability. As an adult, such a person may be overly eager to please, look good, and be nice at the expense of his or her needs and feelings. Having grown up feeling insecure, you have a tendency as an adult to depend on a safe person or safe place and to restrict yourself from activities involving public, performance, or social situations where there is a possibility of losing face or 'looking bad.'

- *You've grown up with emotional insecurity and dependency.* There are many kinds of disfunctional family situations that can generate deep-seated insecurity. Loss of a parent due to death or divorce can precipitate strong fears of abandonment in a child. Neglect, rejection, physical or sexual abuse, or family alcoholism also leave a child feeling very insecure. When that child responds to this insecurity with excessive dependency, the stage is set for over-reliance on a safe person or place later in life. While agoraphobia isn't the only type of problem that can develop when a child has learned to be overly dependent, it's a common outcome.

"The third long-term, predisposing factor that contributes to the onset of panic and agoraphobia is cumulative stress. Stress can accumulate over months or years as a result of long-standing psychological problems. Or it can accumulate as the result of too many 'major life changes' (such as marriage or divorce, a change of jobs, geographical moves, health problems, a financial reversal, and so on) within a short period of time. [It's very helpful to have clients fill out the Homes-Rahe "Life Events Survey" at this point to get an estimate of their current level of cumulative stress — see Chapter 2 of *The Anxiety and Phobia Workbook*.]

"When stress isn't managed well, it tends to accumulate. The long-term effects of stress are varied. Some people develop chronic tension headaches, ulcers, or high blood pressure. Others become depressed. In those who have a genetic vulnerability to anxiety, panic attacks may be the outcome in place of a psychosomatic illness. An important implication of this is that good stress management — including relaxation, exercise, good nutrition, time management, social support, and adopting low-stress beliefs and attitudes toward life — should help reduce or eliminate your vulnerability to panic attacks."

Recent Causes

"A first panic attack is often triggered by some kind of stressful event or situation. This acts as a 'last straw,' since in most cases stress has been accumulating for many years beforehand. Among the most common precipitating events are

- *A significant personal loss* — This can be the loss of a significant person through death or divorce, the loss of employment, a financial loss, or the loss of physical health.

- *A significant life change* — Any turning point in your life cycle qualities, such as getting married, having a baby, going off to college, changing jobs, making a geographical move, and so on.

- *Stimulants or recreational drugs* — It's not uncommon for a first panic attack to develop after excessive ingestion of caffeine. Even more common is the appearance of panic attacks in people using cocaine. Amphetamines, LSD, high doses of marijuana, and withdrawal from sedatives and tranquilizers can also jolt a person into a first panic attack."

Maintaining Causes

"Maintaining causes operate in the here-and-now to keep panic attacks and agoraphobia going. Most of the skills you will be learning in this group will help you to deal with maintaining causes. The primary maintaining causes are

1. *Phobic Avoidance*

   "Continuing to avoid facing your phobia is what maintains its hold over you. Obviously, it's very rewarding to continue this avoidance; the reward is that you're saved from having to experience anxiety. Trying to think or reason your way out of a phobia won't work as long as you continue to avoid confronting it directly.

2. *Anxious Self-Talk*

   "Self-talk is what you say to yourself in your own mind. You engage in an internal monologue much of the time, although it may be so automatic and subtle that you don't notice it unless you step back and pay attention. Much of your anxiety is created by statements you make to yourself beginning with the words 'What if' — such as 'What if I have another panic attack?' 'What if I lose control of myself while driving?' 'What will people think if I get anxious while standing in line?' This type of self-talk *anticipates* the worst in advance. The more common term for this type of thinking is simply 'worry.' You can learn to recognize anxiety-provoking self-talk, stop it, and replace it with more supportive and calming statements to yourself.

3. *Withheld Feelings*

   "Holding in feelings of anger, frustration, sadness, or even excitement can contribute to a state of *free-floating* anxiety. Free-floating anxiety is when you feel vaguely anxious without knowing why.

   "You may have noticed that after you let out your angry feelings or have a good cry, you feel calmer and more at ease. Expressing feelings seems to have a distinct physiological effect that results in reduced levels of stress and anxiety.

4. *Lack of Assertiveness*

   "To express your feelings to other people, it's important that you develop an assertive style of communicating. Assertiveness, in a few words, is expressing yourself in a direct, forthright manner. It involves a healthy balance somewhere between submissiveness, where you are afraid to ask for what you want at all, and aggressiveness, where you demand what you want through coercion or threats. People who are prone to anxiety and phobias frequently tend to act submissively. They avoid asking directly for what they want and are afraid to express strong feelings, especially anger. Often they are afraid of imposing on others or of not maintaining their self-image as a pleasing and nice person. They may be afraid that assertive communication will alienate their safe person, on whom they feel dependent for their basic sense of security.

   "Learning to be assertive, and to directly communicate your needs and feeling, is essential to overcoming agoraphobia.

5. *Lack of Self-Nurturing Skills*

"Common to the background of many people with anxiety disorders is a pervasive sense of insecurity. This is especially apparent in agoraphobia, where the need to stay close to a safe place or safe person can be so strong. Such insecurity arises from a variety of conditions in childhood, including parental neglect, abandonment, abuse, overprotection, perfectionism, as well as from patterns of alcoholism or chemical dependency in the family. Since they never received consistent or reliable nurturing as children, adult survivors of these various forms of deprivation often lack the capability to properly take care of their own needs. Unaware of how to love and nurture themselves, they suffer from low self-esteem and may feel anxious or overwhelmed in the face of adult demands and responsibilities. This lack of self-nurturing skills only serves to perpetuate anxiety.

"The most lasting solution to parental abuse and deprivation is to become a good parent to yourself. In session 13 of this group, you will learn how to gain awareness of your needs and develop a nurturing relationship with your 'inner child.'" (It would be useful for ten-week group leaders to briefly discuss the relevance of self-esteem to recovery from agoraphobia and refer clients to Chapter 14 of *The Anxiety and Phobia Workbook*.)

6. *High-Stress Lifestyle*

"Managing your stress will help reduce your vulnerability to panic attacks and anxiety in general. Mastering the concepts and skills taught in this group in connection with relaxation, exercise, nutrition, self-talk, mistaken beliefs, feelings, and assertiveness will all contribute to helping you reduce the sources of stress in your life. Other stress management skills such as time management, delegating, and pacing are described in such books as *Life after Stress*, by Martin Shaffer, and *The Relaxation and Stress Reduction Workbook*, by Martha Davis, Matthew McKay, and Elizabeth Eshelman.

7. *Lack of Meaning or a Sense of Purpose*

"It has been my repeated experience that people experience relief from anxiety as well as phobias when they feel that their life has meaning, purpose, and a sense of direction. Until you discover something larger than personal self-gratification — something that gives your life a sense of purpose — you may be prone to feelings of boredom and a vague sense of confinement because you are not realizing all you can be. This sense of confinement can be a potent breeding ground for anxiety, phobias, and even panic attacks.

"We will explore various ways of creating meaning and a broader sense of life purpose in the next-to-last session of this group.

D. Concept: Relaxation

"Relaxation is one of the most powerful tools at your disposal for overcoming anxiety and a predisposition to panic. It is at the very foundation of any program undertaken to overcome agoraphobia. The type of relaxation that really makes a difference is the *regular daily* practice of some form of *deep* relaxation. Deep relaxation refers to a distinct physiological state that is the exact opposite of the way your body reacts under stress or during a panic attack. This state was originally described by Herbert Benson (1975) as the 'relaxation response.' It involves a number of physiological changes, including:

- a decrease in heart rate
- a decease in respiratory rate
- a decrease in blood pressure
- a decrease in skeletal muscle tension
- a decrease in metabolic rate and oxygen consumption
- a decrease in analytical thinking
- an increase in alpha-wave activity in the brain

"If you are willing to practice deep relaxation for 20 to 30 minutes per day on a regular basis, a *generalization* of the state of relaxation to the rest of your life will occur. After several weeks of practicing deep relaxation on a regular basis, you will feel more relaxed all of the time.

"Some of the more common forms of deep relaxation include: abdominal breathing, progressive muscle relaxation, visualizing a peaceful scene, medication, autogenic training, guided imagery, biofeedback, and sensory deprivation. For the purposes of this group, we'll be focusing on the first three."

E. Skill: Abdominal Breathing

"Abdominal breathing means breathing fully from your abdomen or from the bottom of your lungs. It is exactly the reverse of the way you breathe when you're anxious or tense, which is typically shallow and high in your chest. If you're breathing from your abdomen, you can place your hand on your stomach and see it actually *rise* each time you inhale. To practice abdominal breathing, observe the following steps:

1. Place one hand on your abdomen right beneath your rib cage.

2. Inhale slowly and deeply through your nose into the bottom of your lungs (the lowest point down in your lungs you can reach). Your chest should move only slightly, while your stomach rises, pushing your hand up.

3. When you've inhaled fully, pause for a moment and then exhale fully through your mouth. As you exhale, just let yourself go and imagine your entire body going loose and limp.

4. In order to fully relax, take and release ten abdominal breaths. Try to keep your breathing *smooth* and *regular* throughout, without gulping in a big breath or exhaling suddenly. You might count each breath on the exhale, as follows:

   Slow inhale — Pause — Slow exhale (count 1)

   Slow inhale — Pause — Slow exhale (count 2) — and so on

   If you start to feel light-headed while practicing abdominal breathing, stop for 30 seconds and then start up again.

"You'll find that abdominal breathing will help to slow you down any time you feel symptoms of anxiety or panic coming on. Three or more minutes of abdominal breathing can abort a panic attack if you initiate it before the panic has gained momentum. Abdominal breathing will also counteract hyperventilation symptoms, which can be mistaken for symptoms of panic." (*Note*: An explanation of hyperventilation and how it can contribute to panic attacks may be in order here.)

F. Skill: Progressive Muscle Relaxation

"Progressive muscle relaxation is a time-honored relaxation technique that is very helpful in reducing skeletal muscle tension, which is one of the principal contributing causes of anxiety. To best utilize it, practice the technique

- for at least 20 minutes
- at a regular time
- preferably before or one hour after a meal
- in a quiet setting
- with your head supported

"While practicing, make a decision to let go of your worries and concerns. Refrain from judging your performance or the results of the exercise. Follow these steps:

1. Clench your fists tightly. Hold them clenched for 7 to 10 seconds. You may want to count one-thousand-one, one-thousand-two, and so on, to mark off seconds.

2. Concentrate on what's happening. Feel the buildup of tension in the muscles of your hands. It may be helpful to visualize the muscles tensing.

3. After 7 to 10 seconds, release the muscles in your hands abruptly, imagining them going loose and limp. Allow relaxation to develop for at least 10 to 20 seconds before proceeding. Use the same time intervals for all the other muscle groups in your body.

4. Tighten your biceps by drawing your forearms up toward your shoulder and "making a muscle" with both arms. Hold for 10 second, then relax for 15 to 20 seconds.

5. Tighten your triceps (the muscles on the undersides of your upper arms) by extending your arms out straight and locking your elbows. Hold and then relax.

6. Tense up the muscles in your forehead by raising your eyebrows up as far as you can. Hold...and then relax. Imagine your forehead muscles becoming smooth and limp as they relax.

7. Tense up the muscles around your eyes by clenching them tightly shut. Hold ...and then relax. Imagine sensations of deep relaxation spreading all around the area of your eyes.

8. Tighten your jaw by opening your mouth so wide that you stretch the muscles around the hinges of your jaw. Hold...and then relax. Let your lips part and allow your jaw to hang loose.

9. Tighten the muscles in the back of your neck by pulling your head way back, as if you were going to touch your head to your back. Focus only on tensing the muscles in your neck. Hold...and then relax. Since this area is often especially tight, it is good to do the tense-relax cycle twice.

10. Tighten your shoulders by raising them up as if you were going to touch your ears. Hold...and then relax.

11. Tighten the muscles around your shoulder blades by pushing your shoulder blades back, as if you were going to touch them together. Hold the tension in your shoulder blades...and then relax. Since this area is often extra tense, you might repeat the tense-relax sequence twice.

12. Tighten the muscles of your chest by taking in a deep breath. Hold for up to 10 seconds...and then relax slowly. Imagine any excess tension in your chest flowing away with the exhalation.

13. Tighten your stomach muscles by sucking your stomach in. Hold...and then release. Imagine a wave of relaxation spreading through your abdomen.

14. Tighten your lower back by arching it up. You can omit this exercise if you have lower back pain. Hold...and then relax.

15. Tighten your buttocks by pulling them together. Hold...and then relax. Imagine the muscles in your hips going loose and limp.

16. Squeeze the muscles in your thighs all the way down to your knees. You will probably have to tighten your hips along with your thighs, since the thigh muscles attach at the pelvis. Hold...and then relax. Feel your thigh muscles smoothing out and relaxing completely.

17. Tighten your calf muscles by pulling your toes toward you. Hold...and then relax.

18. Tighten your feet by curling your toes downward. Hold...and then relax.

"The entire progressive muscle relaxation sequence should take you about 20 to 30 minutes the first time. With practice, you may decrease the time needed to as little as 15 to 20 minutes."

G. Skill: Visualizing a Peaceful Scene

"While progressive muscle relaxation is useful for relaxing your muscles, visualizing a peaceful scene will help you to relax you mind. Any scene that feels very calming to you will do. It could be a remote beach, a mountain stream, a calm lake, or an indoor scene such as a cozy fireplace or your own bedroom. It's very important in visualizing a peaceful scene to take time to see it in as much detail as possible. Focus on all the objects you can see — their colors, shapes, and sizes. Also be aware of any sounds, smells, or things in the situation you can touch." A suggested script for visualizing a peaceful scene is as follows:

> Close your eyes and imagine you're in a very peaceful, comfortable setting. It can be outdoors or indoors. It can be realistic or imaginary. You find that you feel very safe and supported there...this is a safe place. (Pause) Now look all about you and notice the colors of everything in this particular scene. (Pause) You might focus on one color in particular ...and you find this color to be very relaxing. As you feel more and more relaxed, take notice of any sounds that you can hear in this special place. (Pause) You might now focus on one sound in particular, and you find this sound to be very relaxing. Now become aware of anything that you're touching on the ground or elsewhere. How does it feel? Let these tactile sensations help to relax you still more. Just continue allowing yourself to settle in, feeling very relaxed and at peace in this wonderful place. You're feeling very safe, secure, and at ease.

Remember that the more you picture yourself in this peaceful scene, the easier it will be to return there whenever you like. You can learn, after a while, to retreat to your own special scene — the safe place in your mind — whenever you're feeling anxious or tense.

H. Concept: Physical Exercise

"A program of regular physical exercise will help you to reduce your vulnerability to panic attacks and anxiety in general. Exercise provides a natural outlet for the excess adrenalin and physiological arousal that accompany anxiety states. It also releases muscle tension and stimulates production of endorphins in the brain, resulting in a state of increased calmness and well-being. There is some evidence that regular exercise helps to correct some of the neurophysiological imbalances associated with panic attacks.

"To optimize the anxiety-reducing effects of exercise, it is best to do an *aerobic* form of exercise at least *four times per week* for *at least 20 to 30 minutes*. Aerobic exercises include brisk walking, jogging, aerobic dancing, bicycling or riding a stationary bike, swimming, jumping rope, running in place, and ice or roller skating. If you do brisk walking, you'll want to double the minimum time, for example, from 20 to 40 minutes, to obtain the best results.

"If you haven't been doing any type of exercise for some time, it is best to start with walking for only very short periods (from 5 to 10 minutes) of more vigorous exercise. If you have any medical conditions that might limit exercise, and experience such symptoms as high blood pressure, diabetes, chest pains, fainting spells, or joint stress — or if you are forty or older — be sure to consult with your doctor before undertaking an exercise program.

"Some people avoid exercise because they fear it will aggravate a panic attack. The state of physiological arousal accompanying vigorous exercise reminds them of the symptoms of panic. If this applies to you, you might want to do 40 to 60 minutes of walking on a daily basis; or you can very gradually build up to a more vigorous level of exercise.

"Many people find it helpful to vary the type of exercise they do. This can help reduce boredom, as well as give you the chance to exercise different body parts. Popular combinations include doing an aerobic type of exercise such as jogging or cycling three to four times per week, and a socializing exercise such as tennis, volleyball, or bodybuilding exercise twice per week.

"If you're starting an exercise program or are otherwise not used to vigorous exercise, observe the following guidelines:

1. Approach exercise gradually. Start out by exerting only 10 minutes (or to the point of being winded) every other day for the first week. Add 5 minutes to your workout time each successive week until you reach 30 minutes.

2. Give yourself a one-month trial period. Make a commitment to stay with your program for at least a month despite aches, pains, inertia, or resistance. By the end of a month, you may find exercise to be sufficiently rewarding so that you will want to continue.

3. Expect some discomfort initially. Aches and pains are normal when you start out, but disappear as you gain strength and endurance.

4. Find ways to reward yourself for maintaining a commitment to your exercise program.

5. Warm up before exercising by doing some toe-touches and jumping jacks. When you're finished with vigorous exercise, cool down by walking around for 2 or 3 minutes.

6. Avoid exercising within 90 minutes of a meal or when you feel overstressed.

7. Stop exercising if you experience any sudden, unexplainable body pains or other symptoms.

8. If you find yourself getting bored with exercise, find a partner to go with you or a form of exercise requiring a partner.

9. Exercise more than once per week. It's stressful to your body to exert vigorously then fall out of shape before you exert again.

10. Work toward the goal of doing aerobic exercise four to five days per week for 20 to 30 minutes each session."

I. Concept: The Panic Cycle

"A panic attack is a sudden surge of mounting physiological arousal that can occur out of the blue or in response to encountering — or merely thinking about — a phobic situation. Physical symptoms include: heart palpitations, tightening in the chest, shortness of breath, dizziness, faintness, sweating, trembling, shaking, or tingling in the hands and feet. Psychological reactions that accompany these bodily changes include: intense desire to run away, feelings of unreality, and fears of having a heart attack, going crazy, or doing something uncontrollable.

"The panic cycle involves a reciprocal interaction between bodily symptoms of panic and fearful thoughts. The cycle looks like this:

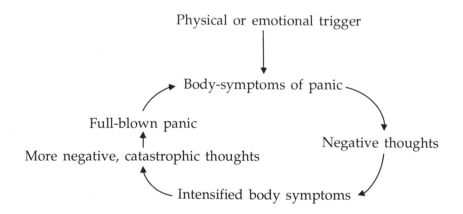

"Hyperventilation may, in some cases, be added to the loop. Rapid, shallow breathing during early stages of panic may produce hyperventilation symptoms such as tingling in the hands and feet, dizziness, disorientation, and feelings of unreality. Be aware, however, that panic attacks can produce these symptoms in the absence of hyperventilation."

The following concepts are very useful for learning to cope with panic attacks:

J. Concept: Panic Attacks Are Not Dangerous

"Recognize that a panic attack is nothing more than the well-known fight-or-flight response occurring out of context. This is a natural bodily response that enables you (and all other mammals) to be alerted to and quickly flee a truly life-threatening situation. What makes a panic attack hard to cope with is that this intense reaction occurs *in the absence of any immediate or apparent danger*. Or, in the case of agoraphobia, it occurs in situations that have no immediate life-threatening potential (standing in line at the grocery store or being at home alone). Because there is no apparent, external danger in a panic attack, you tend to *invent or attribute danger* to the intense bodily symptoms you're going through. Your mind can very quickly go through the process: 'If I feel this bad, I must be in some danger. If there is no apparent external danger, the danger must be inside of me.'

"In short, you may imagine that heart palpitations will lead to a heart attack, that your constricted breathing will lead to suffocation, that dizzy sensations will result in fainting, or that you will lose control and 'go crazy.' In fact, none of these ever occurs. You can't have a heart attack from a panic attack. Your heart is made of very strong and dense muscle fibers. According to Dr. Claire Weekes, a noted authority on panic, a healthy heart can beat 200 beats per minute for days — even weeks — without sustaining any damage. Electrocardiogram tracings of panic attacks show rapid heartbeat, but none of the types of abnormalities seen in individuals with heart conditions. By the same token, you can't suffocate from a panic attack. Your brain has a built-in reflex mechanism that will *force* you to breathe if you're not getting enough oxygen. Feelings of faintness or dizziness may come on because of reduced circulation to the brain during panic, but you won't faint. These sensations can be relieved by slow, abdominal breathing. It's also important to know that agoraphobics *never* lose control or 'act crazy.' It's unheard of.

"The upshot of all this is that a panic attack is not dangerous. If you can convince yourself of this at the time panic occurs, you may significantly reduce the intensity of your reaction."

K. Concept: Don't Fight Panic

"It's important to avoid fighting a panic attack, for example, tensing up against panic symptoms or trying to 'make' them go away. This only creates more muscle tension, which is one of the contributing causes of panic. In her books, *Hope and Help for Your Nerves* and *Peace from Nervous Suffering*, Claire Weekes describes a four-step process that many people have found very helpful:

1. *Face panic symptoms* rather than running from them. Instead of telling yourself, 'I can't handle this,' you might say, 'This will pass...I've handled it before and I'll manage it this time, too.'

2. *Accept* what your body is going through. Again, don't fight panic. Work on adopting an attitude of acceptance. Ideally, learn to *observe* your body's state of physiological arousal, no matter how uncomfortable it may be, instead of reacting to it.

3. *Float* with the 'wave' of a panic attack, instead of forcing your way through it. You might imagine that you are literally riding a wave, moving with the upsurge and gradual fading out of panic. Realize that it takes only a few minutes for most of the adrenalin produced by panic to be reabsorbed, so that the worst will be over quickly.

4. *Allow time to pass.* Realize that reactions you're going through are time-limited. Say to yourself, 'This will pass,' and engage in some distracting activity such as conversation, moving around, abdominal breathing, or repeating positive statements until the reaction subsides."

L. Concept: Separate First From Second Fear

"Claire Weekes makes a distinction between first fear and second fear. First fear consists of the physiological reactions underlying panic; second fear involves making yourself afraid of these reactions by saying such scary things to yourself as: 'I can't stand this!' 'I'm going to have a heart attack!' 'I've got to get out of here right now!' Try to keep this distinction in mind when panic symptoms come on. Instead of scaring yourself (second fear) about your body's reactions, you can move with them and make such reassuring statements as: 'These are just exaggerated bodily symptoms. I can go with them until they pass' or 'I've handled this before, and I can do so now.'" A list of positive coping statements that clients can use to help them float through a panic attack is on the next page. This can be used as a handout.

M. Skill: Learn To Distinguish the Early Stages
of Panic — The Anxiety Scale

"With practice you can learn to identify the preliminary signs in yourself that a panic attack may be imminent. For some people this may be signaled by a sudden increase in heartbeat. For others it might be a tightening in the chest, sweaty palms, or queasiness in the stomach. Most people experience some type of preliminary symptoms before a 'point of no return' is reached beyond which a significant panic attack is inevitable.

"It's possible to distinguish different levels or degrees of anxiety by using a ten-point scale:

The Anxiety Scale*

7-10 *Major Panic Attack*	All of the symptoms in Level six exaggerated; terror; fear of going crazy or dying; compulsion to escape
6 *Moderate Panic Attack*	Palpitations; difficulty breathing; feeling disoriented or detached (feeling of unreality); panic in response to perceived loss of control
5 *Early Panic*	Heart pounding or beating irregularly; constricted breathing; spaciness or dizziness; definite fear of losing control; compulsion to escape
4 *Marked Anxiety*	Feeling uncomfortable or "spacey"; heart beating fast; muscles tight; beginning to wonder about maintaining control
3 *Moderate Anxiety*	Feeling uncomfortable but still in control; heart starting to beat faster; fast breathing; sweaty palms
2 *Mild Anxiety*	Butterflies in stomach; muscle tension; definitely nervous
1 *Slight Anxiety*	Passing 'twinge' of anxiety; feeling slightly nervous
0 *Relaxation*	Calm, a feeling of being undistracted and at peace

---

*This scale was adapted from a similar one developed by Dr. Arthur Hardy in the TERRAP Program Manual, page 5. Menlo Park, California: TSC Publications, 1986.

Coping Statements

Use any or all of the following positive statements to help you cultivate attitudes of acceptance, "float," and allow time to pass during a panic attack. You may find it helpful to repeat a single statement over and over again — in conjunction with deep, abdominal breathing — during the first minute or two when you feel panic symptoms coming on. If one statement gets tiresome or seems to stop working, try another.

This feeling isn't comfortable or pleasant, but I can accept it.

I can be anxious and still deal with this situation.

I can handle these symptoms or sensations.

This is not an emergency. It's okay to think slowly about what I need to do.

This is not the worst thing that could happen.

I'm going to go with this and wait for my anxiety to decrease.

This is an opportunity for me to learn to cope with my fears.

I'll just let my body do its thing. This will pass.

I'll ride this through — I don't need to let this get to me.

I deserve to feel okay right now.

I can take all the time I need to let go and relax.

I can always leave if I need to.

There is no need to push myself. I can take as small a step forward as I choose.

I've survived this before and I'll survive this time, too.

I can do what I have to do in spite of anxiety.

This anxiety won't hurt me — it just doesn't feel good.

This is just anxiety — it won't hurt me.

This is just anxiety — I'm not going to let it get to me.

Nothing serious is going to happen to me.

Fighting and resisting this isn't going to help — so I'll just let it pass.

These are just thoughts — not reality.

I don't need these thoughts — I can choose to think differently.

This is not dangerous.

So what.

"Although the level of symptoms at the various levels of this scale are typical, they may not correspond exactly to the specific symptoms that you experience. The important thing is to identify what constitutes a Level 4 for you. This is the point where — whatever symptoms you're experiencing — you feel that your control over your reaction is beginning to drop out. Up to and through Level 3, you may be feeling very anxious and uncomfortable, but you still feel that you're managing what's going on. Starting at Level 4, you begin to wonder whether you can control what's happening, which leads you to panic even further. With practice you can learn to catch yourself — to abort a panic reaction — before it reaches this point of no return. The better you become at recognizing the early warning signs of panic — up through Level 4 on the scale, the more control you will gain over your panic reactions."

N. Skill: Learning To Retreat

"When your anxiety reaches Level 4 on the Anxiety Scale and you associate that anxiety with a particular situation, *retreat* from the situation. Staying in a situation when anxiety begins to get out of control (Level 4 or above) will *sensitize* you to that situation. If you aren't phobic toward the situation, you could become so. If you already have a phobia about the situation, that phobia will be reinforced. *Retreating is not escaping*. Retreat simply means that you temporarily withdraw from a situation, allow your anxiety to subside down to Level 1 on the Anxiety Scale, and then *return* to the situation. If your anxiety reaches Level 4 while driving, retreat by pulling off the road as soon as you can, getting out of your car, and walking around. If your anxiety reaches Level 4 while standing in line at the grocery store, put your groceries down and retreat outside until you feel better, then return. Work on letting go of concerns about what other people will think about your actions.

"Learning to retreat is *essential* to your recovery from agoraphobia. You will use this skill again and again when you start practicing real-life desensitization."

O. Skill: Using Diversion Techniques
To Reduce Panic

"Any technique that helps to redirect your attention away from bodily symptoms as well as from fear-evoking thoughts during the early stages of panic will stop the reaction from gaining momentum. Many people have found that the following techniques will abort a panic attack before it reaches Level 4 or 5 on the Anxiety Scale:

- Talk to another person

- Move around or engage in physical activity

- Engage in a simple, repetitive activity (in a grocery store, for example, count the number of cans on the shelf or count the money in your wallet)

- Do something requiring concentration (read a magazine, solve puzzles, knit or sew, calculate or compute, or play a musical instrument)

- Express angry feelings (pound a pillow or hit your bed with a plastic bat — do *not* vent anger on people)

- Experience something immediately pleasurable (for example, receive a hug, have sex, soak in your bathtub)

- Practice thought stopping. Shout 'stop' several times and/or visualize a large stop sign. This will help disrupt a chain of negative thoughts. Follow this by repeating a positive affirmation."

P. Skill: Use Abdominal Breathing To Reduce Panic

"When panic symptoms come up to Level 4 on the Anxiety Scale, use the abdominal breathing skill previously described. Continue with slow, regular abdominal breathing — inhaling through your nose and exhaling through your mouth — for two to three minutes. This practice alone will help reduce the intensity of your physiological reactions. At Level 4, it's also helpful to use progressive muscle relaxation techniques, but confined to the arms, head, neck, and shoulders only. Focus on the areas that hold the most tension."

Q. Skill: Use Coping Statements To Reduce Panic

"Negative self-talk always aggravates panic, creating the 'second fear' that was described earlier. If you can learn to replace negative self-talk with positive coping statements, you will eliminate or at least diminish the severity of your panic reactions. Select three or four coping statements from the list in Section L. Write these down on a 3 by 5 card and keep it in your purse or wallet. When symptoms come on, pull out the card and repeat one of the coping statements again and again. It may be necessary to do this for three or four minutes — but with practice, you'll find the technique to be effective.

"You may want to combine this skill with the abdominal breathing skill previously described."

R. Concept: Desensitization

"Sensitization and desensitization are important concepts in understanding phobias. *Sensitization* is a conditioning process in which you learn to associate anxiety with a particular situation (or with an internal thought, sensation, feeling, or memory). For example, if you were to panic while sitting in an airplane or in a restaurant, you might acquire a strong association between being in these situations and being anxious. Thereafter, being in, near, or perhaps just thinking about the particular situation might trigger your anxiety again. An automatic connection between the situation and a strong anxiety response is established — a connection that is seemingly beyond your control. To avoid experiencing anxiety, you also avoid the situation to which you've become sensitized: and so a phobia is established.

"*Desensitization* is the process of unlearning an unwanted connection between anxiety and a particular situation (or object, animal, person, and so on). For desensitization to occur, you need to experience a different kind of response to a situation that initially causes you to feel phobic, a response that is *incompatible* with anxiety. One such response is *relaxation*. If you can experience relaxation (or a relative state of relaxation) in the presence of a situation or object that typically elicits anxiety for you, you will *unlearn* your anxiety response and replace it with another. This response can simply involve having *no* adverse reactions; or may be characterized by a relative degree of relaxation.

"There are two kinds of desensitization: *imagery desensitization* and *real-life desensitization*. In imagery desensitization, you *visualize* while you're deeply relaxed being in a situation that makes you feel phobic. Should any anxiety arise, you retreat from the phobic scene in your mind and imagine yourself in a peaceful scene instead. When you're fully relaxed, you return in your imagination to the phobic scene. In real-life desensitization, you confront a phobic situation directly, but retreat to a safe place if your anxiety exceeds Level 4 on The Anxiety Scale. Other terms for real-life desensitization are *in vivo desensitization, exposure therapy,* or simply *exposure.* In both types of desensitization, the idea is to: 1) unlearn the connection between a particular situation and an anxiety response, and 2) reassociate feelings of calmness and relaxation with that situation.

"It's generally a good idea to practice imagery desensitization first with a particular phobia before undertaking real-life desensitization. Much of your anxiety about a phobia is attached to internal thoughts and fantasies about the situation anyway; desensitizing in fantasy initially will help make it easier for you to confront the situation in real life. Also, there are some phobic situations (such as airplane travel or taking a professional exam) for which it would be inconvenient or expensive to practice your desensitization in real life."

S. Concept: The Phobia Hierarchy — Facing What You Fear in Small Increments

"You can construct a series of scenes (or real-life situations) relating to your phobia which are graduated as a hierarchy, ranging from scenes that are mildly anxiety-provoking to those that produce full-blown panic. The hierarchy makes the task of facing a phobia much easier by breaking it down into many small steps. You begin by facing a very mild instance of your phobia, and do not proceed to confront the next step up in the hierarchy until you're completely comfortable with step one. Continue this process of getting used to each step in the hierarchy, all the way up to the most anxiety-producing step at the top. This is *incremental desensitization.* Two examples of hierarchies follow. Note that a good hierarchy contains at least 8, and as many as 20 steps.

"Phobia About Driving on Freeways

Visualize:

1. Watching cars on the freeway from a distance.

2. Riding in a car on the freeway with someone else driving. (This could be broken into several steps, varying the distance or time on the freeway.)

3. Driving on the freeway for the distance of one exit with a friend in the car at a time when there is little traffic.

4. Driving for the distance of one exit with a friend when the freeway is busier (but not at rush hour).

5. Repeat Step 3 alone.

6. Repeat Step 4 alone.

7. Driving for the distance of two exits with a friend when there is little traffic.

8. Driving for the distance of two exits with a friend when there is moderate traffic.

9. Repeat Step 7 alone.

10. Repeat Step 8 alone.

"In steps above Level 10, you would increase the distance you drive and also include driving during rush-hour conditions.

"Phobia About Getting Injections

Visualize:

1. Watching a movie in which a minor character gets a shot.

2. A friend talking about her flu shot.

3. Making a routine doctor's appointment.

4. Driving to a medical center.

5. Parking your car in the medical center parking lot.

6. Thinking about shots in the doctor's waiting room.

7. A woman coming out of the treatment room rubbing her arm.

8. A nurse with a tray of syringes walking past.

9. Entering an examination room.

10. The doctor entering the room and asking you about your symptoms.

11. The doctor saying that you need an injection.

12. The nurse entering the room with injection materials.

13. The nurse filling a syringe.

14. Alcohol being applied to a cotton ball.

15. Seeing the hypodermic poised in the doctor's hand.

16. Receiving a penicillin shot in the buttocks.

17. Receiving a flu shot in the arm.

18. Having a large blood sample taken."

T. Skill: Constructing an Appropriate Phobia Hierarchy

"A well-constructed hierarchy allows you to approach a phobic situation gradually and incrementally. Use these guidelines:

1. Choose the particular phobic situation you want to work on — for example, going to the grocery store, driving on the freeway, giving a talk in front of a a group.

2. Imagine a very mild instance of having to deal with this situation, one that hardly bothers you at all. You can create a mild instance by imagining yourself somewhat removed in space or time from full exposure to the situation — for example, parking in front of the grocery store without going in, or imagining that it is one month before you have to give a presentation. Or you can diminish the difficulty of the situation by visualizing yourself with a supportive

person. Try to create a very mild instance of your phobia and designate it as the first step in your hierarchy.

3. Now imagine what would be the strongest or most challenging scenario relating to your phobia and place it at the opposite extreme — the highest step in your hierarchy. For example, if you're phobic about grocery stores, your highest step might be waiting in a long line at the checkout counter by yourself. For air travel, such a step might be taking off on a transcontinental flight, or encountering severe air turbulence midflight. For public speaking, you might imagine giving a presentation to a *large crowd,* giving a *long presentation,* or speaking on a very *demanding topic.* See if you can identify what specific parameters of your phobia make you more or less anxious, and use them to develop scenarios of varying intensity.

4. Now take some time to imagine six or more other scenes of varying anxiety-provoking potential relating to your phobia. Place these in ascending order between the two extremes you've already defined. Use the sample hierarchies to assist you.

5. Generally, 8 to 12 steps in a hierarchy are sufficient, although in some cases you may want to include as many as 20. Having fewer than 8 steps is usually insufficient.

6. Sometimes you may find it difficult to go from one step to the next in your hierarchy. You may be able to relax within the scene you placed at Step 5; but become very anxious when you visualize Step 6. In this instance you need to construct an *intermediate* scene (at 5½) that can serve as a bridge between the two original scenes.

7. If you have difficulty getting over anxiety in reaction to the initial scene in your hierarchy, you need to create a still less anxiety-provoking scene to start out with."

U. Skill: Practicing Imagery Desensitization

"Success with imagery desensitization depends on four things: 1) your ability to enter into a deep state of relaxation, 2) the vividness and detail with which you visualize phobic scenes as well as your peaceful scene, 3) having enough steps — or small enough increments — in your hierarchy, and 4) your willingness to practice on a regular basis.

"In practicing imagery desensitization, follow these steps:

1. *Relax.* Spend 10 to 15 minutes getting very relaxed. Use progressive muscle relaxation or any other relaxation technique that works for you.

2. *Visualize yourself in your peaceful scene.* Get comfortable in the peaceful scene you learned to visualize in the previous session on relaxation.

3. *Visualize yourself in the first scene in your phobia hierarchy.* Stay there for 30 seconds to 1 minute, trying to picture everything with as much vividness and detail as possible, as if you were 'right there.' If you feel little or no anxiety (below Level 2 on the Anxiety Scale), proceed to the next scene up in your hierarchy.

4. If you experience *mild to moderate* anxiety — a Level 2 or 3 on the Anxiety Scale — spend 30 seconds to 1 minute in the scene, allowing yourself to relax

within it. You can do this by breathing away any anxious sensations in your body or by repeating a soothing affirmation such as 'I am calm and at ease.' Picture yourself handling the situation in a calm and confident manner.

5. After about a minute of exposure, retreat from the phobic scene to your peaceful scene. Spend about 1 minute in your peaceful scene or long enough to get fully relaxed. Then *repeat* your visualization of the same phobic scene as in Step 4. Keep alternating between a given phobic scene and your peaceful scene (about 1 minute each) until the phobic scene loses its power to elicit any (or more than very mild) anxiety. You are then ready to proceed to the next step up in your hierarchy.

6. If visualizing a particular scene causes you strong anxiety, Level 4 or above on the Anxiety Scale, do not spend more than 10 seconds there. Retreat immediately to your peaceful scene. Accustom yourself gradually to the difficult scene, alternating short intervals of exposure with retreat to your peaceful scene. If a particular step in your hierarchy continues to cause difficulty, you probably need to add an additional step, one that is intermediate in difficulty, between the last step you completed successfully and the one that is troublesome.

7. Continue progressing up your hierarchy step by step in imagination. Generally, it will take a minimum of two exposures to a scene to reduce your anxiety within it. Keep in mind that it's important not to proceed to a more advanced step until you're completely comfortable with the step before. Practice 15 to 20 minutes each day, and begin your practice *not* with a new step, but with the last step that you successfully negotiated. Then proceed to a new step."

V. Skill: Practicing Real-Life Desensitization

"In practicing real-life desensitization, observe the following steps:

1. *Use the hierarchy you developed for imagery desensitization.* Note that it may be necessary to add some additional intermediate steps in your hierarchy when exposing yourself to a phobia in real life.

2. *Enter and/or stay in your phobic situation* (whatever step in your hierarchy you're on) *up to the point where your anxiety reaches Level 4* on the Anxiety Scale — the point where your anxiety *first begins to feel a little unmanageable.* Even if you are uncomfortable in the situation, *stay with it* as long as your anxiety does not go beyond Level 3.

3. *Retreat* from the situation at the point where your anxiety reaches Level 4. Retreat means *temporarily* leaving the situation until you feel better, and then *returning.* Retreat is *not* escaping or avoiding the situation. It is designed to prevent you from 'flooding' and risking the possibility of resensitizing yourself to the situation.

4. *Recover.* After you have temporarily pulled back from your phobic situation wait until your anxiety goes back down to Level 1 or 2 on the Anxiety Scale.

5. *Repeat.* After recovering, reenter your phobic situation and 1) keep going into it or 2) stay with it up to the point where your anxiety once again reaches Level 4. If you are able to go further or stay longer in the situation than you did before, fine. If not — or if you can't even go as far as you did the first

time — that's fine, too. Progression and regression in terms of what you can tolerate are all part of the exposure therapy.

6. Continue going through the above cycle — Expose — Retreat – Recover — Repeat — until you begin to feel tired, then stop for the day. Your daily practice session can take from 30 minutes to 2 hours. The limit as to how far you go in any practice session can be determined by the point where your anxiety reaches Level 4 on the Anxiety Scale."

W. Concept: Utilize a Support Person

"It's often very helpful to rely on a person you trust (spouse, partner, friend, helping professional) to accompany you into the phobic situation when you first begin *in vivo* work. The purpose of the support person is to provide 1) reassurance and safety, 2) distraction (the person usually is talking with you), 3) encouragement to persist with practice, and 4) praise for small successes.

"Your support person should *not* push you. It's good for him or her to encourage you to enter a phobic situation without running away. Yet it is up to you to decide on the amount of exposure you want to undergo, and when you have reached Level 4. Your support person should not criticize your practice or tell you to try harder. Yet it is good if he or she can recognize any resistance on your part and help you ask yourself whether any resistance is present. Mainly the support person's job is to provide encouragement and support without judging your performance." Guidelines for the support person can be found in Section CC.

X. Concept: Dealing With Resistance

"Undertaking exposure to a situation you have been avoiding may bring up resistance. Notice if you start procrastinating or putting off getting started with your exposure sessions by saying, 'I'll do it later.' The mere thought of actually going into a phobic situation may elicit strong anxiety, a fear of being trapped, or self-defeating statements to yourself such as: 'I'll never be able to do it,' or 'This is hopeless.' Instead of getting stuck in resistance, regard it as a major therapeutic opportunity to learn about yourself and to work through long-standing avoidance patterns or excuse-making that has held up your life."

Y. Concept: Tolerating Some Discomfort

"Facing situations that you have been avoiding for a long time is not particularly comfortable or pleasant. It is inevitable that you will experience some anxiety. In fact, it's common to feel *worse initially* when undertaking exposure therapy before you feel better. Recognize that feeling worse is *not* an indication of regression, but rather that exposure is really *working*. Feeling worse means that you are laying the foundation to feel better. As you gain more skill in handling symptoms of anxiety when they come up during exposure, your practice sessions will become easier, and you'll gain more confidence about following through to completion."

Z. Concept: Reward Yourself for Small Successes

"People going through *in vivo* exposure often fear that they're not moving fast enough. There is no standard or 'correct' speed for progress. What's important is to consistently reward yourself for small successes. For example, being able to go into a phobic situation slightly further than the day before is worthy of giving yourself a reward such as a new piece of clothing or dinner out. So is being able to stay in the situation a few moments longer — or being able to tolerate anxious feelings a few moments longer. Rewarding yourself for small successes will help substantially to maintain your motivation to keep practicing."

AA. Concept: Practice Regularly

"Regular practice — rather than hurrying or pressuring yourself — will produce the most time-efficient results. Optimally, it is good to go out and practice three to five times per week. Longer practice sessions, with several trials of exposure to your phobic situation, tend to produce more rapid results than shorter sessions. As long as you retreat when appropriate, it's impossible to practice too much exposure in a given session (the worst that can happen is that you might end up somewhat tired or exhausted).

"The *regularity* of your practice will determine the rate of your recovery. If you're not practicing regularly, notice the excuses you're making to yourself and sit down with someone else to discuss their legitimacy. Regular practice of exposure is *the key* to a full and lasting recovery."

BB. Concept: Expect and Know How To Handle Setbacks

"Having a setback — in other words, not being able to tolerate as much exposure to a situation as you did in a previous session — is a *normal* part of recovery. Recovery simply doesn't proceed in an upward linear fashion — there are plateaus and regressions, as well as times of moving forward. It's very important not to let a setback discourage you from further practice. Simply chalk it up to a bad day or bad week and learn from it. Appreciate that nothing can take away the progress you've made up to the point of the setback. You can use each setback as a learning experience that will tell you more about how to best proceed in mastering a particular phobic situation. A setback can be a good learning experience. It only means you went too far, too fast."

CC. Skill: Support Person Skills

The following skills are taught by the group assistant to clients' support persons during Week 7. In this session, support persons split off from the rest of the group.

1. "Before practicing, communicate clearly about what the phobic expects of you during practice. Does she want you to talk a lot to her? Stay right with her? Follow behind her? Wait outside? Hold her hand?

2. Let your phobic partner pick the goal she wishes to work on during a practice session — not the goal you're interested in.

3. Be familiar with the phobic's early warning signs of anxiety. Encourage her to verbalize when she's becoming anxious. Be willing to ask her from time to time how she's doing.

4. Don't allow your partner's distress to rattle you. Remember that reason isn't always present when someone panics. If your partner panics, quietly lead her to safety, end the practice session for the day, and go home with her. Above all, don't leave her alone.

5. Be where you say you're going to be during a practice session. Don't move to another location because you want to test your partner. It can be very frightening for the phobic to return to a prearranged meeting place to find you gone.

6. Don't push a phobic person! She knows what is going on in her body and may panic if pushed further than she's ready to go at the moment.

7. On the other hand, encourage your partner to make the most out of practice. It's better to attempt to enter a situation and have to retreat than not to try at all. If you feel that your partner's resistance is preventing her from undertaking practice or from making progress with practice, ask: 'Do you think something is getting in the way of your progress?' Assist her in identifying and exploring any resistance.

8. Let the phobic have responsibility for her own recovery. Be supportive and encouraging, but avoid trying to step in and do it all for her. This will only undermine her confidence.

9. Try to see things from the phobic's point of view. Things that seem insignificant to others, such as walking down a street or eating in a restaurant, may involve a great deal of work and courage for the phobic to achieve for even a short period of time. These accomplishments, and the efforts leading to them, should be recognized.

10. Phobics generally are very sensitive and need a great deal of praise for every step they take. Be sure to give your partner recognition for small achievements. Praise her for whatever she accomplishes and be understanding and accepting when she regresses.

11. Encourage practice with rewards. For example, you might say: 'When you can handle restaurants, let's have lunch together somewhere special.'

12. Accept the phobic's bad days and reinforce the idea that she can't have a perfect day every time. It's natural that there will be times of backsliding.

13. It may be necessary to readjust you own schedule in order to facilitate your partner's practice. Be sure that you are willing to make a commitment to work with your partner regularly over a sustained period of time before offering to be a support person.

14. Know your own limits. If your capacity to be supportive has been stretched to the limit, take a break. Avoid expecting yourself to be perfect."

DD. Concept: Self-Talk and Anxiety

"*What we say to ourselves* in response to any particular situation is what mainly determines our mood and feelings. Imagine two individuals sitting in stop-and-go traffic at rush hour. One perceives himself as trapped and says such things to himself as 'I can't stand this,' 'I've got to get out of here,' 'Why did I ever get myself into this commute?' He feels anxiety, anger, and frustration. The other perceives the situation as an opportunity to lay back, relax, and put on a new tape. He says such things to himself as 'I might as well go with the flow,' or 'I can unwind by doing some deep breathing.' What he feels is a sense of calmness and acceptance. In both cases, the situation is exactly the same, but the feelings in response to that situation are vastly different.

"What you tell yourself happens so quickly and automatically that you don't even notice it, and so you get the impression that the external situation 'makes' you feel the way you do. But it's really your judgments and thoughts about what is happening that lead to your feelings. This sequence can be represented as

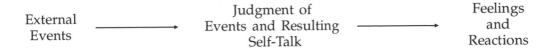

External Events ⟶ Judgment of Events and Resulting Self-Talk ⟶ Feelings and Reactions

"In short, you are largely responsible for how you feel. This is a profound and very important truth — one that it takes many individuals a long time to fully grasp. It's often much easier to blame the way you feel on something or someone else than to take responsibility for your reactions. Yet, it is precisely through your willingness to accept that responsibility that you will be able to take charge and have mastery over your life.

"People who have phobias, panic attacks, and general anxiety (or depression) are especially prone to engage in negative self-talk. Anxiety can be generated on the spur of the moment by repeatedly making statements to yourself by repeatedly making statements to yourself that begin with the two words 'What if.' Whenever you experience anxiety in advance of confronting a difficult situation, it's likely that you have 'what-ifed' yourself into it. If you finally decide to avoid a situation, it may be because you've asked yourself 'What if I panic?' 'What if I can't handle it?' or 'What will other people think?' Just noticing when you fall into 'What if' thinking is a first step in the direction of gaining control over negative self-talk. The real change occurs when you begin to *counter* and *replace* negative 'What if' statements with positive, self-supportive statements such as 'So what,' 'These are just thoughts,' 'This is just scare talk,' 'I can handle this,' 'I can breathe, let go and relax,' and so on. There are several basic points about self-talk to keep in mind:

1. Self-talk is usually so *automatic* and *subtle* that you don't notice it or the effect it has on your moods and feelings. You react without noticing what you told yourself right before you reacted.

2. Self-talk often *appears in telegraphic form*. One short word or image contains a whole series of thoughts, memories, or associations.

3. Self-talk is typically *irrational but almost always believed*. For example, anxious 'what if' thinking leads you expect the worst possible outcome, one that is highly unlikely to happen. Yet, because it occurs so quickly, it goes unchallenged and unquestioned.

4. Self-talk *perpetuates avoidance*. You tell yourself that a situation such as the freeway is dangerous, and so you avoid it. By continuing to avoid it, you reinforce the thought that it is dangerous.

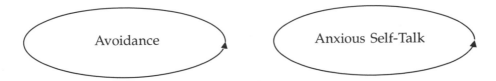

Avoidance   Anxious Self-Talk

5. Negative self-talk is a *series of bad habits*. You aren't born with a predisposition to fearful self-talk — *you learn it*. Just as you can replace unhealthy *behavioral* habits, such as smoking or drinking excess coffee, with more positive, health-promoting behavior, so can you replace unhealthy thinking with more positive, supportive mental habits."

EE. Concept: Self-Talk Subpersonalities

"Not all negative self-talk is the same. Human beings are complex, with different aspects or facets that are sometimes referred to as 'subpersonalities.' These different voices or parts of yourself can defeat you with different types of negative inner dialogue. Four of the more common subpersonalities that are prominent in anxiety-prone people include: the *Worrier*, the *Critic*, the *Victim*, the *Perfectionist*.

1. **The Worrier** (promotes anxiety)
   "Often this is the strongest subpersonality in people who are prone to anxiety. Playing a greater role in directly generating anxiety than the critic, victim, or perfectionist described below. The Worrier's dominant tendencies include: a) anticipating the worst, b) fearing the future, and c) creating grandiose images of potential failure or catastrophe. The Worrier is always vigilant, watching with uneasy apprehension for any small symptoms or signs of trouble.
   "By far the favorite expression of the Worrier is 'What if....'"

2. **The Critic** (promotes low self-esteem)
   "The Critic is that part of you that is constantly judging and evaluating your behavior. It tends to point out your flaws and limitations whenever possible. It jumps on any mistake you make to remind you that you're a failure. It likes to compare you with others, and usually sees them coming out favorably.
   "The Critic's favorite expressions include: 'You stupid....' 'Can't you ever get it right?' 'Why am I always this way?' 'Look at how capable _____ is.' 'You could have done better.' 'You'd better do it over.'"

3. **The Victim** (promotes depression)
   "The Victim is that part of you that feels helpless or hopeless, and plays a major role in depression. It has a tendency to believe that there is something inherently wrong with you — you are in some way deprived, defective, or unworthy. The Victim always perceives insurmountable obstacles between you and your goals. Characteristically, it bemoans, complains, and regrets things as they are at present.
   "The Victim's favorite expressions include: 'I can't.' 'It's useless.' 'I'll never be able to.' 'Why bother?' 'I don't care anymore.'"

4. **The Perfectionist** (promotes chronic stress and burnout)
   "The perfectionist is a close cousin of the critic, and may make self-critical remarks. However, its concern is less to put you down than to push and goad you to do better. It is the hard-driving part of you that wants to be best, and is intolerant of mistakes or setbacks. It has a tendency to try to convince you that your self-worth, rather than being inherent, is dependent on external qualities such as: a) vocational achievement, b) money and status, c) being accepted by others, d) being pleasing and nice to others. It is common for the Perfectionist to push you into stress, exhaustion, and burnout, despite warning signals from your body.
   "Some of the Perfectionist's favorite expressions include: 'I should.' 'I have to.' 'I must.' 'If you can't do it right, don't do it at all.'"

FF. Skill: Identifying and Countering the Self-Talk of Subpersonalities

"Take some time to reflect on how each of the subpersonalities plays a role in your thinking, feelings, and behavior. Which of the four is strongest and which is weakest for you? What does each characteristically say to you? How might you begin to counter the negative statements used by each against you?

"To get started, here are some examples of positive counterstatements that you can use with each of your subpersonalities:

The Worrier

"Instead of 'What if ...,' you can say:

'So what.'

'I can handle this.'

'I can be anxious and still do this.'

'This may be scary, but I can tolerate a little anxiety, knowing that it will pass.'

'I'll get used to this with practice.'

'I can retreat if necessary.'"

The Critic

"Instead of putting yourself down, you can say:

'I'm okay the way I am.'

'I'm lovable and capable.'

'I'm a unique and creative person.'

'I deserve the good things in life as much as anyone else.'

'I accept and believe in myself.'

'I'm worthy of others' respect.'"

The Victim

"Instead of feeling hopeless, you can say:

'I don't have to be all better tomorrow.'

'I can continue to make progress one step at a time.'

'I acknowledge the progress that I've made and will continue to improve.'

'It's never too late to change.'

'I'm willing to see the glass as half-full rather than half-empty.'"

The Perfectionist

"Instead of demanding perfection, you can say:

'It's okay to make mistakes.'

'Life is too short to be taken so seriously.'

'Setbacks are part of the process and a necessary learning experience.'

'I don't have to always be _____.'

'My needs and feelings are at least as important as anyone else's.'"

GG. Concept: Cognitive Distortions

"Anxious people actually think in distorted, unrealistic, or illogical ways, in the same manner as people who are depressed. Cognitive therapists such as Aaron Beck and David Burns have described in considerable detail these distorted modes of thinking and their effect on mood and behavior. All of these distortions tend to skew the way you perceive and evaluate yourself, others, and innumerable situations in everyday life. This distortion is responsible for creating and *sustaining* much of the anxiety, depression, guilt, and self-criticism that you experience. Learning to recognize and counter these distorted modes of thinking with more rational, positive affirmations will go a long way to help you view yourself and life in a more balanced, objective fashion. And this, in turn, will significantly reduce the amount of anxiety, depression, and stress you experience. I will describe seven cognitive distortions that have special relevance for people dealing with anxiety disorders:

1. *"All-or-Nothing Thinking:* The hallmark of this distortion is an insistence on black-or-white choices. You tend to perceive everything in terms of extremes, with very little consideration of the middle ground. Either the day was terrific, or it was the worst day of your life. Either he loves you or he hates you. If you can't be brilliant, you're stupid.

2. *"Ignoring the Positive:* When you're anxious or depressed, you have a tendency to overlook all indications of your ability to cope successfully. You forget positive experiences and accomplishments of the past, and anticipate insurmountable problems in the future. You focus on the problem rather than considering steps toward a solution.

3. *"Catastrophizing:* When you think about something that is somewhat challenging or risky, you perceive total disaster as the probable outcome. For example, you've been making progress and then have a setback. Instead of seeing the setback as inconvenient and a normal part of recovery, you feel as though you're back at the beginning. Or you anticipate the very worst even when it is highly improbable. In short, you project a catastrophe.

4. *"Overgeneralizing:* One negative experience, such as being turned down for a promotion, will be translated into a law governing your entire existence — 'I'll never get anywhere in life' or 'I just can't make the grade.' Or one stranger is rude to you and you conclude that all strangers are unkind. Or you have a problem in one store, therefore all stores should be avoided. Overgeneralizing is betrayed by *absolute statements* such as 'I'll *never* be able to trust anyone again,' or 'No one would remain my friend if they really knew me.'

5. *"Personalizing (taking things personally):* This is a tendency to relate everything to yourself, thinking that everything people do or say is some kind of reaction to you. A stranger frowns at you, thus you have done something wrong. Your spouse snaps at you, so you reason that it must be your fault. You enter a room and conversation ceases: they must have been talking about you. When you personalize, you fail to recognize that other people's negative behavior probably reflects *their* mood. Instead, you imagine it as a personal reaction to you.

6. *"Emotional Reasoning:* You believe that you are what you feel. If you feel stupid, then you must *be* stupid. If you feel like a loser, then you must be a

loser. If you feel guilty, then you must have done something wrong. The problem with emotional reasoning is that emotions by themselves have no validity as definitions of who you are.

7. "'Should' Statements: You try to motivate yourself by insisting on what you *should* do or be, without reference to what you actually want to do or be. The word 'should' is a telltale sign of the Perfectionist subpersonality described earlier. 'Should' can be part of a healthy ethical concern. But it can also reflect self-imposed standards that are excessively high or unrealistic."

HH. Skill: Identifying and Countering Cognitive Distortions

1. "'Catch yourself in the act' of negative self-talk. Be aware of situations that are likely to be preceded or accompanied by negative self-talk. For example:

   • Any occasion when you're feeling anxious, upset, or depressed

   • Occasions when you've made some kind of mistake or have failed to meet your own expectations

   • Situations in which you feel under scrutiny or criticized

   • Occasions when you're angry at yourself or others

2. "Ask yourself, 'What have I been telling myself that led me to feel this way?' 'Do I really want to do this to myself?'
   "If you're feeling too upset to undertake the task of identifying and countering self-talk, at least give yourself the opportunity to acknowledge and release your feelings. When you've calmed down and are ready to relax, you can proceed with the steps below. (See Chapter 12 of *The Anxiety and Phobia Workbook* for ideas and guidelines for expressing feelings.)

3. "*Relax* or *distract* yourself. *Disrupt* the train of negative thoughts by taking some deep abdominal breaths or using some method of distraction. The point is to *slow yourself down and relax.* Negative self-talk is so rapid, automatic, and subtle that it can escape detection if you're feeling tense, speeded up, or unable to slow down. In extreme cases, it may take 15 to 20 minutes of deep relaxation, using breathing, progressive muscle relaxation, or meditation, to slow yourself down sufficiently to be able to identify your self-talk. If you're not excessively wound up, you can probably do this step in a minute or two.

4. "*Write down* the distorted self-talk or inner dialogue that led you to feel anxious, upset, or depressed. It's often difficult to decipher what you're telling yourself by merely reflecting on it. It can be confusing to try to think about what you've just been thinking. The act of writing your thoughts down will help to clarify the specific statements you made to yourself.
   "This is the step that may take some practice to learn. It's important in identifying self-talk to be able to disentangle thoughts from feelings. One way to do this is to write down just the feelings first and then deduce the thoughts which led to them. For example, the statement 'I feel stupid and irresponsible' is one where thoughts and feelings are still entangled. It can be broken down into a particular feeling — 'I feel upset' or 'I feel disappointed in myself' — and the thought (self-talk) that logically produces such a feeling — 'I am

stupid' or 'I am irresponsible.' As another example, the statement 'I'm too scared to undertake this' mixes a feeling of fear with one or more thoughts. It can be broken down into the feeling 'I'm scared,' which arises from the negative self-statement 'This is unmanageable' or 'I can't undertake this.' You can ask yourself first, 'What was I feeling?' Then ask yourself, 'What thoughts went through my mind to make me feel this way?'

5. "*Challenge* your distorted self-talk with questions that ask for evidence or proof of their validity. Good questions to ask might be:

- What is the evidence for this?

- Is this always true?

- Has this been true in the past?

- Am I looking at all sides of this — the whole picture?

- Am I being fully objective?

- What's the very worst that could happen? Would that be so very bad?

6. "*Counter* your distorted self-talk with positive, supportive affirmations. Write these down in a column next to the distorted self-statements. Your positive affirmations should be believable and feel 'right' to you (avoid mere positive thinking that you don't really believe in)."

Two examples follow of the process of challenging distorted thinking and writing counterstatements:

Example 1

Catastrophizing:	"People will think I'm weird or crazy if I start to panic during the meeting."
Questioning:	"How often has this happened in the past?" (Answer: Probably never.) "What are the odds of this really happening?" (Answer: Very unlikely.)
Counterstatement:	"If I start to feel panicky in the meeting, I can excuse myself, saying that I have to go to the bathroom. Even if people do see me panicking, it's much more likely that they'll express concern than that they'll think I'm crazy or weird."

Example 2

Overgeneralization:	"That panic attack I had on the freeway yesterday was so bad that I'll *never* be able to drive on freeways again."
Questioning:	"What are the odds of this being really true?" "Has this been true in the past?"
Counterstatement:	"I may need to lay off driving freeways for a while. After some time has passed, I'll feel good enough to try it again, and I believe I can succeed if I break the task down into small enough steps. After all, I was able to drive freeways in the past, so I know I can do it again."

II. Concept: Rules for Writing Positive Counterstatements

1. "Avoid negatives in writing your counterstatements. Instead of saying 'I'm not going to panic when I board the plane,' try 'I am confident and calm about boarding the plane.' Telling yourself something will *not* happen is more likely to create anxiety than giving yourself a direct affirmation.

2. "Keep counterstatements in the present tense. 'I can breathe and let these feelings pass' is preferable to 'I will feel better in a few minutes.' Since much of your negative self-talk is in the here-and-now, it needs to be countered by statements in the present tense.

3. "Whenever possible, keep your statements in the first person. Begin them with 'I' or refer to 'I' somewhere in the statement. It's okay to write a sentence or two explaining the basis for your counterstatement, but try to end with an I-statement.

4. "It's important that you have some belief in your positive self-talk. Don't write something down just because it's positive if you don't actually believe it."

JJ. Skill: Working With Positive Counterstatements

1. "Read through your lists of positive counterstatements slowly and carefully for a few minutes each day for at least two weeks. This will help you integrate them more deeply into your awareness.

2. "Make copies of your worksheets and post them in a conspicuous place. Take time once a day to read through your positive counterstatements.

3. "Put your counterstatements on tape, leaving a pause of about 5 seconds after each one, so that it has time to 'sink in.' You can significantly enhance the effect of such a tape by giving yourself 15 minutes to become very relaxed before listening to it.

4. "If you're having a problem with a particular phobia, you might want to work with positive counterstatements that are *specific just to that phobia*. For example, if you're afraid of speaking before groups, make a list of all your fears ('What-ifs') about what could happen, and develop positive statements to counter each fear. Then read through your list of counterstatements carefully each day for two weeks or make a short tape, as previously described."

KK. Concept: Mistaken Beliefs

"Where does negative self-talk come from? In most cases, it's possible to trace negative thinking back to deeper-lying beliefs, attitudes, or assumptions about ourselves, others, and life in general. These basic assumptions have been variously called 'scripts,' 'core beliefs,' 'life decisions,' 'fallacious beliefs,' or 'mistaken beliefs.' We learned them from our parents, teachers, and peers, as well as from the larger society around us while growing up. These beliefs are typically so basic to our thinking and feeling that we do not recognize them as *beliefs* at all — we just take them for granted as 'the true nature of reality.' Examples of mistaken beliefs might be: 'I'm powerless,' 'Life is a struggle,' or 'I should always look good and act nice, no matter how I feel.'

"Mistaken beliefs are at the root of much of the anxiety you experience. Underlying your anxious patterns of self-talk are basic destructive assumptions about yourself and the 'way life is.' You could spare yourself quite a bit of worrying, for example, by letting go of the basic assumption, 'If I worry about this problem enough, it will go away.' Similarly, you would feel more confident and secure if you would let go of the mistaken beliefs, 'I'm nothing unless I succeed' and 'I'm nothing unless others love and approve of me.' Once again, life would be less stressful if you would let go of the belief, 'Either do it perfectly or don't bother.' You can go a long way toward creating a less anxious way of life by working on changing the basic assumptions that tend to perpetuate anxiety."

LL. Skill: Identifying Mistaken Beliefs

"*Recognizing* your own particular mistaken beliefs is the first and most important step toward letting go of them.

"The following questionnaire will help you to identify some of your own unconstructive beliefs. Rate each statement on a 1-to-4 scale according to how much you think it influences your feelings and behavior. Then go back and work with the beliefs that you rated 3 or 4." (This questionnaire can be used as a handout.)

MM. Skill: Countering Mistaken Beliefs
With Affirmations

"Attempt to come up with a positive affirmation to counter each of the unproductive beliefs you rated 3 or 4 on the Mistaken Beliefs Questionnaire.

"Use the following guidelines for constructing affirmations:

1. An affirmation should be *short, simple,* and *direct*. 'I believe in myself' is preferred to 'There are a lot of good qualities I have that I believe in.'

2. Keep affirmations in the *present tense* ('I'm prosperous') or *present progressive tense* ('I am becoming prosperous').

3. Try to *avoid negatives*. Instead of saying 'I'm no longer afraid of public speaking,' try 'I'm free of fear about public speaking' or 'I'm becoming free of fear about public speaking.' Similarly, instead of the negative statement 'I'm not perfect,' try 'It's okay to be less than perfect' or 'It's okay to make mistakes.'

4. Start with a direct declaration of a positive change you want to make in your life ('I'm making more time for myself every day.'). If this feels a little too strong for you at first, try changing it to, 'I'm willing to make more time for myself.' *Willingness* to change is the most important first step you need to take toward achieving substantial change in your life. A second alternative to a direct declaration is to affirm that you are *becoming* something or *learning* to do something ('I'm learning to make more time for myself.').

5. It's important that you have *some* belief in — or at least a willingness to believe — your affirmations. It's by no means necessary, however, to believe in an affirmation 100 percent when you first start out. The whole point is to shift your beliefs and attitudes in the direction of the affirmation."

Mistaken Beliefs Questionnaire

How much does each of these unconstructive beliefs influence your feelings and behavior? Take your time to reflect about each item.

1 – Not At All
2 – Somewhat/Sometimes
3 – Strongly/Frequently
4 – *Very* Strongly

Place the appropriate number in the box by each statement:

☐ I feel powerless or helpless.

☐ Often I feel like a victim of outside circumstances.

☐ I don't have the money to do what I really want.

☐ There is seldom enough time to do what I want.

☐ Life is very difficult — it's a struggle.

☐ If things are going well, watch out!

☐ I feel unworthy. I feel I'm not good enough.

☐ Often I feel that I don't deserve to be successful or happy.

☐ Often I feel that it's useless to bother.

☐ My condition seems hopeless.

☐ There is something fundamentally wrong with me.

☐ I feel ashamed of my condition.

☐ If I take risks to get better, I'm afraid I'll fail.

☐ If I take risks to get better, I'm afraid I'll succeed.

☐ If I recovered fully, I might have to deal with realities I'd rather not face.

☐ I feel like I'm nothing (or I can't make it) unless I'm loved.

☐ I can't stand being separated from others.

☐ It's very hard to be alone.

☐ What others think of me is very important.

☐ I feel personally threatened when criticized.

☐ It's important to please others.

☐ People won't like me if they see who I really am.

☐ I need to keep up a front or others will see my weaknesses.

☐ I have to achieve or produce something significant in order to feel okay about myself.

☐ My accomplishments at work/school are extremely important.

☐ Success is everything.

☐ I have to be the best at what I do.

☐ I have to be somebody — somebody outstanding.

☐ To fail is terrible.

☐ I can't rely on others for help.

☐ I can't receive from others.

☐ If I let someone get too close, I'm afraid of being controlled.

☐ I can't tolerate being out of control.

☐ I'm the only one who can solve my problems.

☐ I should always be generous and unselfish.

☐ I should be the perfect: (rate each)
    ☐ employee   ☐ professional
    ☐ spouse   ☐ parent
    ☐ lover   ☐ friend
    ☐ student   ☐ _____

☐ I should be able to endure any hardship.

☐ I should be able to find a quick solution to every problem.

☐ I should never feel tired or lazy.

☐ I should always be efficient.

☐ I should always be competent.

☐ I should never be angry or irritable.

☐ I should always be pleasant or nice no matter how I feel.

☐ I often feel: (rate each)
    ☐ ugly   ☐ slow-witted
    ☐ inferior or defective ☐ guilty or ashamed

☐ I'm just the way I am — I can't really change.

☐ The world outside is a dangerous place.

☐ Unless you worry about a problem, it just gets worse.

☐ It's risky to trust people.

☐ My problems will go away on their own with time.

NN. Skill: Ways To Work With Affirmations

"Once you've made a list of affirmations, decide on a few that you would like to work with. In general, it's a good idea to work on only two or three at a time, unless you choose to make a tape containing all of them. Some of the more helpful ways you can utilize affirmations are to

1. Write an affirmation repetitively, about five or ten times every day for a week or two. Each time you doubt you can believe it, write down your doubt on the reverse side of the paper. As you continue to write an affirmation over and over, giving yourself the opportunity to express any doubt, you'll find that your degree of belief in it increases.

2. Write your affirmation in giant letters with a magic marker on a blank 8-1/2- by- 11-inch or larger sheet of paper. The words should be visible from at least 20 feet away. Then affix it to your bathroom mirror, your refrigerator, or some other conspicuous place in your home.

3. Put a series of affirmations on tape. If you develop 20 or so affirmations to counter statements on the Mistaken Beliefs Questionnaire, you may wish to put all of them on tape. You can use either your own voice or have someone else make the recording. Make sure that the affirmations are in the first person, and that you allow about 10 seconds between them so that each one has time to 'sink in.' Listening to the tape once a day for 30 days will lead to a major shift in your thinking and the way you feel about yourself. It's okay to play the tape any time, even while cleaning the house or driving in your car. However, you can expedite the process by giving the tape your full attention in a very relaxed state when you've slowed yourself down enough to deeply feel each affirmation."

For the sake of brevity, concepts and skills utilized during Weeks 11 through 18 of the agoraphobia treatment group are not presented separately here. See the discussion of interventions for each of these weeks in the following section. Also refer to the appropriate chapters in *The Anxiety and Phobia Workbook* for detailed presentations of relevant concepts and skills.

Main Interventions

Because the main interventions used in the agoraphobia treatment group consist of didactic presentation and group discussion, these interventions are not specifically labeled each time they appear. All other interventions are listed as exercises.

Week 1: Introduction

Procedures

Begin with the group leader's and group assistant's personal introductions. Let the group know about how you got involved in working with agoraphobia. Explain to group members how they can get in touch with you and the assistant.

Have group members introduce each other. They can pair up for five minutes to get acquainted; then each member of a dyad introduces the other. Many agoraphobics actually find this process less threatening than introducing themselves.

Go over the basic ground rules of the group, as specified in the previous section on ground rules. To help reduce anxiety, emphasize that clients are free to bring support persons during the first five weeks of the group and that each group member is free to leave the room at any time. Explain that homework will be required each week and that keeping up with it is essential to making progress toward recovery.

Concepts A and B: The Development of Agoraphobia

The Agoraphobic Personality Profile

Present and discuss the material in the Concepts and Skills section. Make sure that clients understand the causal sequence between panic attacks and subsequent development of phobic avoidance, dependency, and depression. When discussing the personality profile, have group members share about the specific traits with which they identify.

Procedures

If the group runs two hours, introduce a ten-minute break in the middle. Many agoraphobics prefer not having to sit still for long periods of time. (Do this in all subsequent sessions.) During the break, group members are encouraged to spend time getting to know each other.

Emphasize before the group is over that clients are not to put themselves into unnecessarily anxiety-provoking situations. Briefly explain the concept of desensitization (to be covered in detail in Week 6) and instruct clients not to enter phobic situations, unless they have to, for the time being. They need to master skills of relaxation, exercise, and coping strategies for minimizing panic before they undertake exposure to phobic situations.

Have clients fill out the self-evaluation form that can be found in the subsequent section of this chapter, Measuring Change. They will complete it a second time at the end of the group to track their progress.

Homework

- Clients should read Chapter 2 of *The Anxiety and Phobia Workbook*.

- Hand out the reading list of popular books on panic attacks and agoraphobia (see References at the end of this chapter) and encourage clients to read at least two books of their choice during the course of the group. *The Anxiety and Phobia Workbook* is required reading for the group; assignments from various chapters will be given in subsequent weeks.

- Group members should write out their personal goals for the group. These should include specific phobias they would like to overcome and any other behaviorally defined goals (such as fewer panic attacks, finding gainful employment, upgrading communication with their spouse, driving, coping with medical appointments).

- Clients are to make a list of their questions about the program and bring them in for discussion the following week.

Week 2: The Causes of Panic and Agoraphobia

Homework Review

Review homework from the preceding week, beginning with a discussion of clients' questions about the group. Encourage clients to call the group assistant or leader as questions arise during the course of the program.

Have clients share, for no more than three minutes each, their personal goals for the group.

Concept C: The Causes of Agoraphobia

Present and discuss material in the Concepts and Skills section. Emphasize the distinction between predisposing, short-term, and maintaining causes of panic/ agoraphobia. Reassure clients who are concerned about panic attacks being hereditary or physically caused that these links do not compromise recovery.

Procedures

At this point, clients often raise issues about medication — both whether they should be taking drugs and what drugs to take. Indicate that the two criteria for deciding to take medication are: a) *severity of symptoms* — in other words, the more severe, frequent, and disabling panics attacks are, the more appropriate it is to consider medication, and b) *personal values* — the client's individual views and feelings about medication ultimately determine the choice about whether to utilize them. A discussion of the pros and cons of the two major classes of drugs used to treat panic disorder — antidepressant medications and minor tranquilizers — is in order here. See Chapter 16 of *The Anxiety and Phobia Workbook* for a detailed discussion of these issues.

Pass out a list of group members' phone numbers. Each member of the group should call a different person on the list every week. The purpose of this assignment is to foster an atmosphere of support and interpersonal closeness in the group. Each client starts by calling the person below her or his name on the list and advances one name each week. Calls should focus on getting acquainted and discussing what individuals have been doing to work on recovery — not on a discussion of symptoms. (Symptoms and other problems can be discussed with the group assistant.) If a client has difficulty coming up with something to say, it's OK to share that fact and keep the phone call brief. (For example, "Hi, I'm just calling to say hello. I can't talk any longer, though, because this is hard for me now.") Emphasize the importance of making each call each week, because group members can tend to feel rejected if they don't receive a call.

Homework

- Chapter 4 of *The Anxiety and Phobia Workbook* is the assigned reading.

- Clients should list any additional questions they have about the program and bring them in the following week.

- Have clients cut pictures out of magazines that remind them of their phobia or otherwise produce anxiety, and bring them in as well.

- Clients are to call another member of the group, as discussed above under Procedures.

Week 3: Relaxation Training

Homework Review

Go over clients' questions from the homework. Ask about whether everyone received a phone call from someone in the group. Spend 10 to 15 minutes having clients share and talk about pictures from magazines that remind them of their phobias.

Concept D: Relaxation

Present and discuss the material in the Concepts and Skill section. Emphasize that relaxation is at the foundation of everything else clients will be doing toward their recovery. Distinguish deep relaxation techniques such as abdominal breathing, progressive muscle relaxation, and meditation from more passive forms of relaxation such as watching TV, stressing that the former are more effective in achieving the "relaxation response." A daily commitment to practice some form of deep relaxation will greatly expedite recovery.

Skill E: Abdominal Breathing

Explain that even though abdominal breathing may feel unusual at first, it's the natural way that babies, small children, and relaxed adults breathe. Have clients hold their right hand over their stomach as they practice. Their hand should rise if they are doing abdominal breathing correctly. Emphasize that a minute or two of abdominal breathing is an efficient way to diminish anxiety or the early symptoms of panic on the spur of the moment.

Skill F: Progressive Muscle Relaxation

After 5 minutes of practice with abdominal breathing, introduce progressive muscle relaxation. Turn down the lights in the room, have clients remove uncomfortable outer clothing and remain seated (they may lie on the floor if they prefer). Model tensing and relaxing the 15 muscle groups in sequence with clients watching, so that they will have a good idea of how to do each muscle-tensing exercise. Before starting progressive muscle relaxation, explain to clients that occasionally during relaxation, fears of falling or losing control may come up. Emphasize that neither of these outcomes is in fact possible, and that if anyone feels uncomfortable, it's okay to stop doing the exercise. Sometimes it's necessary for some clients to desensitize to relaxation. Now read the script for progressive muscle relaxation contained in the Concepts and Skills section. Clients should receive a copy of this script for home practice, or, even better, a tape of recorded instructions.

Skill G: Visualizing a Peaceful Scene

Instruct clients to create in their mind a peaceful scene of their own choosing. Use the script provided in the Concepts and Skills section or devise your own script. At the end of the exercise, bring clients back to an alert state by counting from 1 up to 5. On the count of 5, suggest that they will feel awake and alert.

It's important that clients relax sufficiently to experience their peaceful scene in detail, using all of their senses. Afterwords, ask group members to individually describe their scene and any problems they might have had visualizing it. If someone doesn't have a scene, it's part of their homework for next week to develop one. If some group members have difficulty visualizing, instruct them to ask themselves such questions as "What are the main objects in the scene?" "What colors are visible?" "What sounds are present?" "What time of day is it?" "What is the temperature?" and so on. (A handout listing questions designed to evoke multisensory imagery might be helpful.) Mention that developing a reliable peaceful scene — a sort of "safe place" in the mind — is a prerequisite for imagery desensitization, a skill for overcoming phobias that you will teach to the group 3 weeks later. Also indicate that regular practice will improve group members' ability to visualize.

Homework

- Chapter 5 of *The Anxiety and Phobia Workbook* is assigned reading.

- Clients are to practice abdominal breathing for at least 5 minutes each day. They are also to try practicing this form of breathing at times when they feel anxiety or the early symptoms of panic coming on.

- Clients should practice the complete progressive muscle relaxation sequence, which will take from 20 to 30 minutes, at least once (preferably twice) each day, seven days per week. They should find a quiet place to practice where they won't be distracted. During practice, they should be free of uncomfortable clothing with their head supported. Practice should be avoided on a full stomach — the best times for practice are upon awakening in the morning, during lunch break, after getting home from work, or before retiring. It's best to maintain a regular practice time each day.

- After completing progressive muscle relaxation, clients are to visualize going to their peaceful scene and stay there for a least 3 minutes. If they have problems identifying a peaceful scene or visualizing it, they are to call the group assistant.

- *Note:* Clients who find active progressive muscle relaxation uncomfortable or otherwise objectionable may substitute passive muscle relaxation or a guided visualization for their daily deep-relaxation practice. Scripts for these alternative forms of relaxation may be found in Chapter 11 of *The Anxiety and Phobia Workbook*.

- Starting with this week, clients will fill out the Weekly Practice Record (from Chapter 3 of *The Anxiety and Phobia Workbook*) to monitor their practice of skills and competencies taught in the program. (For Week 4, they should check off Used Deep Breathing Technique and Used Deep Relaxation Technique Monday through Sunday.) Clients turn in their Weekly Practice Record, along with any other assigned homework, at the beginning of each group meeting.

Week 4: Physical Exercise

Homework Review

Collect homework.

Procedures

Ask clients about their experiences with practicing progressive muscle relaxation (or alternative) and visualizing their peaceful scene. Were they able to practice each day? If not, what types of barriers got in the way? Have a discussion about the types of self-talk and excuses that people can use to talk themselves out of activities promoting their recovery. In the case of practicing relaxation, ask clients whether they can identify with any of the excuses listed under Some Common Obstacles To Implementing a Daily Program of Deep Relaxation at the end of Chapter 4 of *The Anxiety and Phobia Workbook*. Reiterate the importance of practicing all three relaxation skills — abdominal breathing, active or passive deep-muscle relaxation, and visualizing a peaceful scene — on a daily basis.

Ask how phone calls are going. If calls aren't being made, this is the time to explore reasons why and to mildly confront group members who are remiss.

Present and discuss the concept of physical exercise as a means of reducing vulnerability to panic and anxiety. Explain how physical exercise reduces anxiety through release of muscle tension, metabolism of excess adrenalin, production of endorphins, and so on.

Have clients determine their level of fitness, using the worksheet in Chapter 5 of *The Anxiety and Phobia Workbook*. Also have them take their resting pulse rate. They can use both indices as a measure of their fitness level.

Concept H: Exercise

Discuss material presented in the Concepts and Skills section. Ask clients what types of exercise, if any, they are doing and how often. For those who aren't exercising, what forms would they consider? For clients who are housebound, emphasize that there are several forms of aerobic exercise that will meet their needs, such as stationary cycling, jumping on a rebounder, or aerobic workouts on video.

By the end of this discussion, each client who is not already exercising regularly should have made a commitment — before the group — to undertake an exercise program. "Commitment" means exercising a minimum of 4 times per week for a minimum duration of 20 minutes.

Go over the guidelines in the section Getting Started from Chapter 5 of *The Anxiety and Phobia Workbook* for the benefit of any clients who are contemplating beginning an exercise program. Emphasize the importance of starting off gradually. Clients who have not exercised in a while and are over forty should consult with their physicians before undertaking any exercise program.

Some clients may be phobic about exercise; the increased heart and respiratory rate associated with exercise may seem all too much like a panic attack. Encourage these clients to begin by walking 30 to 45 minutes per day or to do a milder form of aerobic exercise, such as swimming (using the breaststroke) or light jogging. An exercise program can progress gradually: clients can begin with very short sessions (as little as 5 minutes per day for several days) and then increase the duration by 2-minute increments.

Homework

- Chapter 6 of *The Anxiety and Phobia Workbook* is assigned reading.

- Clients should continue practicing relaxation techniques learned the preceding week and monitor their practice on the Weekly Practice Record.

- All group members should engage in physical exercise — either brisk walking or a more vigorous, preferably aerobic, exercise — on at least 4 days of the following week. They can track their practice on the Weekly Practice Record.

Week 5: Coping With Panic Attacks

Homework Review

Collect homework from the preceding week and ask clients how they did with exercise. For those who've just begun exercising, did they find a form they can enjoy? How many times did they do exercise during the week? It's likely that some clients will resist getting started with exercise — so this is a good time to explore self-talk and excuses that maintain their resistance. Go over the common types of excuses for not exercising listed in the section Obstacles To Implementing an Exercise Program in Chapter 5 of *The Anxiety and Phobia Workbook*. (Spend no more than 15 to 20 minutes on this, as there are several concepts to be presented this week.)

Procedures

Introduce and discuss the following concepts:

Concept I: The Panic Cycle

Concept J: Panic Attacks Are Not Dangerous

Concept K: Don't Fight Panic

Concept L: Separate First Fear From Second Fear

It's important to emphasize that panic is nothing other than the "fight-or-flight" response — a response necessary to our survival — that simply occurs in the absence of any life-threatening situation. Because panic makes you feel like you do when there's real danger, you imagine danger where there isn't any. Go over the various illusory dangers commonly associated with panic (heart attack, suffocation, and so on) and present scientific data to refute each danger.

In discussing Claire Weekes's four attitudes for managing panic, emphasize the importance of learning to observe and go with bodily symptoms rather than fighting or reacting to them. When presenting the distinction between first and second fear, ask clients to come up with their own examples of self-talk that could instigate or aggravate panic. Then pass out copies of the list of coping statements (see Concept L in the previous section) and instruct clients to find a few statements they like. They should practice rehearsing those when they feel symptoms of panic coming on.

Skills M and N: Distinguishing Early Forms of Panic and Learning To Retreat

Introduce and discuss the material in the Concepts and Skills section. Hand out a copy of the Anxiety Scale (presented in Section M) to the group, pointing out that the symptoms described on various levels of the scale are not universal. Each individual will in fact have her or his own unique set of symptoms that define the point where a sense of control starts to diminish. This point where control first seems to drop out is defined as Level 4. Panic can usually be aborted if action is taken at this level. Ask clients in the group each to try to define what would constitute a level 2, 3, or 4 *for them*. Those clients who haven't thought this through are asked to do it as homework for the following week.

Distinguish three basic skills for coping with panic:

Skill O: Distraction Techniques

Skill P: Abdominal Breathing and Muscle Relaxation

Skill Q: Replacing Self-Talk With Positive Coping Statements

Discuss the material in the respective Concepts and Skills section. Take a survey of the group, asking people what techniques they've used in the past to counter an oncoming panic attack, and how well those techniques have worked. Then present skills associated with the use of distraction, breathing, muscle relaxation (progressive muscle relaxation exercises involving arms, head, neck, and shoulders only), and coping statements. Have clients rehearse three minutes of breathing or muscle relaxation in combination with the use of one coping statement. They should practice this same combination for a few minutes each day during the following week.

Discuss options for dealing with panic attacks *above* Level 4 in intensity on the Anxiety Scale. These include: a) retreating from the situation if possible, b) walking about or engaging in some simple physical activity, c) calling someone if a phone is available (some clients who have difficulty driving like to have a cellular phone in their cars), d) continuing slow abdominal breathing and inhaling through the nose (to stop hyperventilation), e) breathing into a paper bag (also to stop hyperventilation), f) "floating past" the panic (see Concept K), g) "grounding" by touching the floor or physical objects in the surrounding environment, h) crying or screaming into a pillow to discharge arousal, or i) with the approval of their doctor, taking an extra dose of a minor tranquilizer (sometimes the mere act of doing this will offset panic). Ask clients which strategies they would consider trying should they experience above a Level 4 during the next few weeks.

Homework

- Clients are to continue practicing deep relaxation (progressive or passive muscle relaxation) for 20 minutes every day and to engage in vigorous exercise at least 4 times per week.

- During the following week, clients should keep a log of their panic attacks, where they note:

    – The date and time when panic occurred

    – Any antecedents or triggers that might have brought on panic

    – The maximum intensity of panic on the Anxiety Scale

    – Coping technique(s) used to abort or limit the panic reaction

    This log will be turned in the following week.

- Clients should rehearse the combination of abdominal breathing (or progressive muscle relaxation) and repeating a coping statement for 3 minutes each day. They are to use this combination when actual symptoms of panic arise.

- Chapter 7 of *The Anxiety and Phobia Workbook* is the assigned reading.

Week 6: Imagery Desensitization

Homework Review

Collect clients' logs monitoring panic reaction during the preceding week and have the group discuss different types of antecedents that may instigate panic. Clients often gain insights from each other about various factors (such as lack of sleep, too much caffeine, failure to act assertively) that can predispose them to a panic reaction.

Procedures

Ask clients to share what coping statements they've been using to reframe their response to the bodily symptoms of panic. Encourage them to continue practicing the combination of abdominal breathing and repetition of a coping statement every time they feel the onset of panic symptoms.

Concept R: Desensitization

Present and discuss the material in the Concepts and Skills section. Contrast desensitization with the notion of sensitization. Clarify the distinction between imagery and real-life desensitization and how the former provides a good preparation for the latter.

Concept S and Skill T: The Phobia Hierarchy

Discuss the material from S and T of the Concepts and Skills section. The process of confronting a phobic situation is made easier by breaking it down into small steps. Here it is helpful to have clients give examples of their phobias and actually write out 2 or 3 hierarchies on a blackboard. Teach them the skill of constructing a proper hierarchy, defining extremes at the low and high ends of the continuum first, and then filling in 7 or 8 intermediate steps of varying difficulty.

Skill U: Practicing Imagery Desensitization

Introduce and discuss the material from the Concepts and Skills section. I've found it useful to have a prerecorded tape that leads clients through the process — alternately asking them to visualize a phobic scene and then retreating to their peaceful scene. It's essential that everyone has a good grasp of the Anxiety Scale presented the week before and understands the importance of "switching off" a phobic scene if it causes anxiety to rise above Level 4. Otherwise, they are to stay with the phobic scene for about one minute and imagine breathing away any anxiety and/or repeat a calming affirmation. It also helps to instruct clients, while visualizing a phobic scene, to see themselves in the scene handing it with composure and confidence. Finally, make sure group members understand that they are not to advance to the next scene in a hierarchy until the preceding scene has lost its capacity to elicit anxiety above Level 1 on the Anxiety Scale.

Emphasize that success with imagery desensitization depends on the ability to relax and to visualize both phobic scenes and a peaceful scene or safe place in multisensory detail. It's useful here, if you haven't already, to give clients a handout with a list of questions they can ask themselves to evoke more detailed imagery.

Remind clients not to be concerned if they do *not* feel any anxiety while doing imagery desensitization. You might make the comparison between their brain and a tape recorder and emphasize that they are rerecording positive images over an old negative image. Clients often feel they have failed to do imagery desensitization correctly unless phobic scenes evoke anxiety. Reinforce the importance of practicing desensitization in fantasy over the next few weeks, whether or not clients experience any anxiety with the procedure.

Instruct clients that they are to practice *only* imagery desensitization during the subsequent week and not to begin real-life exposure. If they have any questions about details of the imagery desensitization process, they are to contact the group assistant. (Here again, a prerecorded tape leading clients through imagery desensitization can be quite helpful.)

Homework

- Clients continue exercising, having a daily session of deep relaxation, and using their preferred coping strategies to deal with panic reactions.

- Have clients construct hierarchies for three phobias they wish to work on. They should turn in copies of these the following week. Refer group members to Appendix 3 of *The Anxiety and Phobia Workbook* for several examples of hierarchies.

- Following each daily session of deep relaxation, clients are to practice 15 to

  20 minutes of imagery desensitization, beginning with the first step of their hierarchy. They should work with only one phobia (one hierarchy) at a time. If they feel no anxiety with the first step, they are to expose themselves to it twice and then proceed to the next step, exposing twice to this scene and progressing to any scenes further up in their hierarchy in a similar fashion until they reach a scene that causes mild anxiety. They should practice imagery desensitization with this last scene until it no longer elicits anxiety, then stop. During any given practice session, individuals are to work with no more than two scenes at a time if these scenes are eliciting anxiety.

- Chapter 8 of *The Anxiety and Phobia Workbook* is assigned reading for the following week.

Week 7: Real-Life Desensitization

Homework Review

Collect clients' hierarchies assigned from the previous week and point out examples of properly and improperly constructed hierarchies. Make sure that everybody understands at this point how to construct a hierarchy.

Procedures

Have clients share how imagery desensitization practice went during the past week. Did anyone encounter resistance to practicing? Did anyone have problems getting sufficiently relaxed? Were there problems with visualization? Reassure clients that even though they may feel like they're not getting much out of the process (especially if phobic scenes don't elicit anxiety), continuing to practice over the next few weeks will make it easier for them to undertake real-life desensitization.

Skill V: Practicing Real-Life Desensitization

Present and discuss the material in the Concepts and Skills section. Emphasize that real-life exposure is the single most important component of a recovery program, but that it is effective only if practiced properly.

Go over the notion of retreating from exposure when anxiety reaches or exceeds Level 4 on the Anxiety Scale (Skill M). This concept needs special attention because clients are typically not used to the idea of retreating and tend to take an all-or-nothing approach to dealing with phobias. Either they have to "tough it out" and deal with a situation no matter how anxious they feel, or else avoid the situation altogether. Emphasize that neither approach works. Excessive or too rapid exposure will only increase their sensitization to a given phobia. Continued avoidance will only keep them from dealing with the problem. Get across the idea that retreating is not "cowardly" — it is the most efficient way possible to succeed with real-life exposure to any phobic situation. Also emphasize the distinction between retreating and escaping. Escaping or running away from a phobia only serves to reinforce it, while retreating and then returning to the same situation after anxiety has subsided accomplishes desensitization. [*Note:* Clients who are highly anxious much of the time — near Level 4 on the Anxiety Scale even when not engaged in exposure — should be taught initially to retreat to the first increment of anxiety they feel when confronting a phobic situation.]

Concept W: The Support Person

Discuss the importance of having a support person along when first undertaking real-life desensitization. The support person provides a sense of safety, encouragement, and also a distraction from bodily symptoms of anxiety. It's best to have the support person go along for the first few exposures to a given step in a hierarchy and then to try the step out alone (or with the support person at a distance). Alternatively, the support person can accompany the client through most or all of a hierarchy before the client tries any of the steps alone.

During this session, the group assistant usually meets with support people in a separate room for about half an hour and discusses guidelines for working with their phobic partners (as described in Section CC: Support Person Skills).

Concepts X and Y: Dealing With Resistance and Tolerating Discomfort During Real-Life Exposure

Present and discuss the material in the Concepts and Skills section. It's important that clients fully understand and are prepared to accept the reality that exposure is hard work and seldom comfortable in the early stages. It will not be intolerably uncomfortable if retreating is handled properly. These ideas should be reiterated several times during subsequent weeks.

Expect clients to offer considerable resistance to practicing real-life desensitization. They will need frequent exhortations to practice and in many cases individual attention on the part of the group leader to assist them in overcoming long-standing avoidance patterns. I recommend an individual session — or at least a phone call to each group member at the end of the first eight to nine weeks — to explore feelings and resistance around the practice of *in vivo* exposure.

Concept Z: Reward Yourself for Small Successes

Explain the material from the Concepts and Skills section.

Concept AA: Practice Regularly

Emphasize that success with real-life desensitization is fostered by regular practice, at least three times per week. One practice session per week is not enough.

Homework

- Clients are to continue practicing exercise, relaxation, and imagery desensitization four to seven times per week.

- For the coming week, clients should select one phobia for practicing real-life desensitization. They can use the same hierarchy for real-life exposure that they constructed for imagery desensitization, but in some cases they may want to add some extra steps. Very small steps are often necessary for real-life desensitization. Individuals should practice at least three times, approximately one hour each time. If possible, they should work with a support person and be sure that they retreat whenever their anxiety reaches Level 4 on the Anxiety Scale. If they have any difficulties or questions in regard to the exposure process, they are to call the group assistant.

- Chapter 9 of *The Anxiety and Phobia Workbook* is assigned reading for the following week.

Week 8: Field Trip 1

Homework Review

Collect Weekly Progress Records and ask clients what progress they made with real-life exposure. At this point, simply have them share what progress (if any) they made toward a specific goal, rather than getting into a detailed discussion of resistance to exposure. It's necessary to dedicate most of this two-hour session to the field trip.

Procedures

Announce that the group will be taking a field trip today to a nearby shopping center or small shopping mall. The announcement needs to be a surprise in order to ensure attendance and to cut down on clients' anticipatory anxiety. Expect moans, groans, and other expressions of fear or not wanting to go. You and the group assistant need to encourage and reassure everybody that you will be available to help as much as they need help, and that no one will be forced to do anything they don't want to do. Insist that all clients go. Avoid spending more than a few minutes listening to complaints, as this will only increase the general anxiety level for the entire group.

Explain the purpose of the field trip as follows:

- To learn and practice, step-by-step, the real-life desensitization process discussed last week.

- To learn, in particular, how to retreat when anxiety reaches Level 4.

- To give clients an opportunity to go as a group and thus feel safer with each other.

Keep the trip short — no more than an hour in duration. The group can caravan in three or four cars to a pre-assigned spot in front of one of the stores in the shopping mall. Clients who are very phobic about riding in a car may be given the alternative of walking, with someone accompanying them, provided the shopping center is close by. When you arrive at the shopping center, divide into two groups — those who are ready to practice exposure *inside* a store and those who aren't yet ready to go inside. The leader and assistant each take a group. Clients ready to go into a store should start with a smaller store and progress toward a department store with several floors (exposure to elevators or escalators can be included, if appropriate). Throughout the field trip, the leader and assistant watch carefully and *ask* clients for indications that anxiety has risen to Level 4. When this happens, the client is exhorted to retreat, recover, and return to exposure only after anxiety has subsided to Level 1. The retreating client should leave the store with another group member for support. Have them remain outside until anxiety has reduced to Level 1, when they should again attempt exposure.

After one hour of practice, return to where the group meeting is regularly held and have clients discuss their experiences and reactions. If there is any time left, have them talk more about any resistance that came up during the field trip or during their weekly practice of *in vivo* desensitization. Emphasize that a willingness to take risks is *essential* to their recovery. Then add that the way risk-taking is made possible is by ensuring that risks are kept *small*.

Homework

- Clients are to continue practicing on a daily basis deep relaxation and imagery desensitization relevant to the phobias they're working on. All members of the group should be exercising at least four days per week. Clients track all of this in the Weekly Progress Record.

- *In vivo* exposure should be practiced at least three or four days per week, preferably with a support person. Clients will be asked during the remaining weeks of the group how they're doing with their *in vivo* goals.

- Clients should finish reading Chapter 9 of *The Anxiety and Phobia Workbook* for the following week (but shouldn't yet do the exercises).

Week 9: Self-Talk

Homework Review

Collect Weekly Progress Records.

Procedures

Ask how *in vivo* exposure has been going. Go around the group and make sure that everyone has gotten started with exposure practice. This is the time to review clients' reasons for resisting practice. Clients need to understand that exposure isn't necessarily a comfortable process. Feeling uncomfortable and wanting to resist are a *normal* part of the process. If they weren't feeling *any* discomfort, you would have doubts about whether they were really practicing exposure. In short, exposure is not always supposed to feel good. Next, ask clients whether they've all identified Level 4 for themselves and are retreating when anxiety begins to reach this point. Letting anxiety get too high during exposure will defeat the purpose. Reemphasize the importance of rewarding themselves every time they go out and practice, even if progress is nominal. This will increase the likelihood of their continuing to practice.

Concept BB: Expect and Know How To Handle Setbacks

Emphasize that setbacks are a *normal* part of the process. All phobics have their good and bad days. On good days, they'll make great strides with exposure — on bad days, they may be unable to do what they did two weeks ago. Ups and downs during recovery are expected. Over the long-term (it takes, on the average, six months to two years to recover) they will experience *gradual* progress.

Concept DD: Self-Talk and Anxiety

Present and discuss the concept of self-talk and its role in perpetuating anxiety (see the Concepts and Skills section). Clients should already be somewhat familiar with the concept from the previous discussion, in Week 5, of self-talk and panic attacks. Make sure that everyone understands that self-talk frequently is so automatic and subtle that it goes unnoticed if there is not a deliberate effort to identify it.

Concept EE and Skill FF: Identifying and Countering Subpersonalities

As described in the Concepts and Skills section, these are the Worrier, the Critic, the Victim, and the Perfectionist. Clients can use a blackboard to write down examples of typical statements made by the four subpersonalities. Have group members offer their own examples and share which subpersonalities they feel to be most dominant for them.

Allow 15 minutes during which clients try to identify and write down self-talk that served to aggravate an upsetting incident during the preceding week. This can be a time when they felt anxious, depressed, angry, self-critical, or guilty. Emphasize the importance of learning to distinguish *thoughts from feelings*. "This is frightening" is not a pure example of an internal thought, because it contains a feeling word — "fright." It is necessary to deduce from the feeling of fright the thoughts one had to instigate that fear, for example: "What if they see me start to panic while I'm standing here?" From this, follow the statement of feeling, "This is frightening." Both the instigating thought and the resulting feeling statement are a part of the negative self-talk, but only the former gets at the root of the problem. Go around the group and have each client share her or his examples of self-talk, correcting any cases where thoughts have not been differentiated from feelings.

Concept GG: Cognitive Distortions

If time permits, present the concept of cognitive distortions and the seven distortions that are particularly relevant to anxiety (from the Concepts and Skills section). Alternatively, clients can be instructed to review the section on distortions with examples in Chapter 9 of *The Anxiety and Phobia Workbook* and identify during the next week which ones are prominent in their own thinking. (Don't spend too much time on this segment, since learning to counter anxiety-provoking self-talk should be the exclusive focus of this week).

Present the various steps involved in countering self-talk:

Skill HH: Identifying and Counterin Cognitive Distortions

Concept II: Rules for Writing Positive Counterstatements

Skill JJ: Working With Positive Counterstatements

It's important here to take two or three examples of negative self-talk from clients, create a refutation, and have the client come up with oral counterstatements. It may also be helpful to write out Socratic questions to use in the refutation, and at least one of the resulting counterstatements, on a blackboard. A typical refutation might go like this:

Therapist: What did your worrier tell you that time?

Client: What if I had a heart attack from panicking while trying to learn to drive again?

Therapist: What is the evidence that panic attacks cause heart attacks?

Client: I don't know.

Therapist: Go back and read Chapter 6 of *The Anxiety and Phobia Workbook* where it explains that a panic attack can't cause a heart attack. There's simply no evidence for any relationship between cardiovascular disease and panic. Now, what would be a good counterstatement to your original 'What if' statement?

Client: A panic attack, however uncomfortable, is not dangerous to my heart. I can let panic rise, fall, and pass, and my heart will be fine.

An example of a refutation involving the cognitive distortion of catastrophizing might go as follows:

Client: What if I'm home alone and start to panic? That would be *terrible* — I don't think I could handle it.

Therapist: Is it really the case that panicking alone at home would be utterly terrible? What's the absolute worst that could happen? Would you actually die?

Client: No, of course I couldn't die. I'd just be very frightened.

Therapist: Is it absolutely true that there is nothing you could do? That you'd be completely helpless, without recourse?

Client: No, I guess not. I would try and call John or else my friend, Cindy. I could also call the group assistant. If no one was available, I could call the local crisis hotline.

Therapist: Would it help to make a list of people who you could contact if you ever find yourself panicking while alone?

Client: Probably, yes.

Therapist: So what would be a counterstatement to your original negative self-statement?

Client: *So what* if I did panic while I'm alone at home. I'd probably feel pretty uncomfortable for a while, but it's just not true that I couldn't handle it.

After illustrating the process of refutation and developing counterstatements, have the group break into dyads and repeat the process. Person A in the dyad finds an example of negative self-talk while Person B challenges the example and asks A to develop a counterstatement. Then the roles are reversed.

Go over the rules for writing positive counterstatements and suggest various alternatives for working with positive counterstatements described in II and JJ.

Homework

- Clients should continue to chart their practice of exercise, relaxation, imagery, and real-life desensitization, using the Weekly Progress Record.

- Hand out a copy of the Daily Record of Dysfunctional Thoughts (see Chapter 9 of *The Anxiety and Phobia Workbook*). Clients are to make 50 copies of it for future use. For next week, they should spend 15 to 20 minutes a day tracking, challenging, and countering instances of negative self-talk that arise. Although clients may mot be able to write out self-talk (and counterstatements) at the very time it occurs, they should try to do so within the same day. If possible, they are to indicate the subpersonality and any cognitive distortions involved in their negative self-statements. Completed worksheets should be turned in the following week. Clients should call the group assistant if they have any questions that come up during the week on any aspect of the process of identifying and countering self-talk.

- Clients should read Chapter 10 of *The Anxiety and Phobia Workbook*.

Week 10: Mistaken Beliefs

Procedures

Have clients share examples of countering anxiety-provoking self-talk. They can use the Daily Record of Dysfunctional Thoughts worksheets from the preceding week. Discuss examples and then have group members share about how they are doing with the process of countering unconstructive inner dialogues. Some individual attention may be necessary here to ensure that everyone understands the various steps of the process. Request that clients continue to write down everything on the Daily Record of Dysfunctional Thoughts for another week. Writing out self-talk and refutations will help them *internalize new habits* of noticing and countering the unhelpful things they tell themselves. Eventually, they will be able to do this automatically, without writing it all out.

Concept KK: Negative Beliefs

Present and discuss the concept of mistaken beliefs, including basic assumptions about self, others, and life in general that underlie negative self-talk.

Skill LL: Identifying Mistaken Beliefs

Hand out the Mistaken Beliefs Questionnaire presented under LL in the Concepts and Skills section, and tell group members to take their time in completing it. Give them from 10 to 15 minutes. Ask clients to share examples of mistaken beliefs they rated 3 or 4, then use these to illustrate how to counter mistaken beliefs and to develop constructive affirmations.

As in the preceding week, engage in dialogue with a few clients to challenge a mistaken belief, using Socratic questions. Then ask a client to come up with an affirmation to counter the mistaken belief. An affirmation is a short, terse statement that summarizes an entire belief or attitude, as distinguished from the positive self-talk that clients learned about last week.

In challenging mistaken beliefs, there are two additional questions — besides Socratic questions, which challenge the logical basis of such beliefs — that are very helpful:

- "Does this belief promote my well-being?"

- "Did I freely choose this belief, or did it develop out of my experiences in childhood?"

[Chapter 10 of *The Anxiety and Phobia Workbook* provides the rationale for these questions, and examples of dialogues using them. Be sure to use these questions in your dialogues designed to refute the mistaken beliefs of individual group member.]

Skills MM and NN: Countering Mistaken Beliefs With Affirmations and Ways To Work With Affirmation

Discuss the rules for writing affirmations presented under MM and NN of the Concepts and Skills section. Especially emphasize the importance of keeping affirmations in the present tense and avoiding negatives. If for any reason an affirmation causes an anxiety reaction, clients may need to use imagery desensitization before they can use the affirmation successfully.

Exercise

Now have clients break up into dyads. Rehearse the process of challenging mistaken beliefs and developing a positive affirmation in the same manner in which you worked with negative self-talk during the preceding week.

Finally, have group members share one or two affirmations that were particularly meaningful to them. Each clients should work with this affirmation during the following week, writing it down several times each day *or* meditating on it *or* writing it in big letters on a large piece of paper posted in a conspicuous place.

If this is the second-to-last session, encourage clients to share their feelings about the group coming to an end.

Homework

- Clients should continue their practice of exercise, relaxation, and imagery and *in vivo* exposure. They should also continue to use the Daily Record of Dysfunctional Thoughts to write out counterstatements to instances of negative self-talk.

- Instruct clients to write affirmations to counter any beliefs which they rated 3 or 4 on the Mistaken Beliefs Questionnaire. They should make a list of these affirmations and read through them slowly each day. Alternatively, they can make a tape, either in their own voice or someone else's, with the affirmations presented slowly at ten-second intervals. They can listen to the tape each day, following their deep relaxation session or before going to bed at night.

Week 11 (Shorter Program) or Week 18 (Longer Program)

Homework Review

Briefly discuss homework from the preceding week.

Procedures

This is the final group session for the shorter program. Plan to summarize everything that has been learned. Emphasize the importance of a multilevel approach to recovery. Tell clients that they will optimize their chances of making excellent progress by following up with all of the strategies learned during the group.

Ask clients to make an estimate of how much they've improved during the course of the group. What changes have they seen? Are they satisfied with their progress?

Have clients complete the Self-Evaluation form they filled out at the beginning of the group to track more specifically the progress they've made (see the section on Measuring Change under Week 18). Have group members discuss their findings.

Encourage clients to try, if they feel ready, to deliberately reach Level 10 on The Anxiety Scale in confronting phobic situations. This serves at least two purposes: a) if they do reach Level 10, they'll find out that they can go through it and still survive; b) taking conscious control by "willing" severe anxiety to come often stops the anxiety (this is the concept of paradoxical intention developed by Victor Frankel, Jay Haley, and others).

Discuss with clients their plans for continuing to work on recovery goals after the group has disbanded. Let them know that they can continue to call in with questions, concerns, or to talk about their progress.

Optional Activities

Follow up the last group meeting with a "graduation dinner" extending into the evening. Reframing the last meeting of the group as a festive occasion will help clients to deal better with feelings of loss and abandonment that will come up at this time. Encourage clients to maintain contact with each other after the group has ended.

Week 11: Feelings

Procedures

Tell clients that they can expect to have more feelings come up as they begin to confront phobic situations they've been avoiding for a long time. Emphasize that this is an expected part of their recovery, and that it's a sign that they're getting better.

Discuss reasons why phobic people have a tendency to suppress their feelings (see Chapter 12 of *The Anxiety and Phobia Workbook*). Have group members share characteristics of their parents or early family situations that might have contributed to the habit of withholding feelings.

Go over the list of symptoms of suppressed feelings described in Chapter 12 of *The Anxiety and Phobia Workbook* and have a discussion about how to recognize suppressed feelings.

Hand out the "Feeling List" from Chapter 12 of *The Anxiety and Phobia Workbook* and discuss its use in identifying feelings.

Discuss the guidelines for dealing with anger presented in Chapter 12 of *The Anxiety and Phobia Workbook*. Pay special attention to attitudes that prevent agoraphobics from acknowledging their anger, such as fear of losing control over themselves or fear of alienating their significant other.

Stress the importance of discharging angry energy by writing it out or physically releasing it onto inanimate objects. Group members need to do this *before* they communicate anger to the person they perceive as responsible for their feelings. It's also appropriate to express angry feelings to a neutral person first and then prepare to make an assertive request of the person with whom they feel angry. (This is a good point at which to introduce the distinction between aggressive and assertive communication. This will be elaborated on in the following week.)

Use the last 30 minutes to have group members write a letter communicating their feelings to a significant person in their life who, for whatever reason, is not available for a direct confrontation (see Exercise 5 at the end of Chapter 12 in *The Anxiety and Phobia Workbook*). Then have several clients share their letters. This process works very well to bring up feelings in the group.

Homework

- Have clients start keeping a feeling journal and give themselves the opportunity during the following week to share their feelings with a person they can trust (Exercises 3 and 4 at the end of Chapter 12 of *The Anxiety and Phobia Workbook*).

- Have clients read Chapter 13 of *The Anxiety and Phobia Workbook*.

Week 12: Assertiveness

Homework Review

Review homework on feelings from the preceding week. Suggest that clients continue to keep a feeling journal and/or set aside at least an hour and a half per week to share their deeper feelings with their partner or a friend they can trust (the latter person needs to listen carefully without interruption or judgment).

Procedures

Define the concept of assertiveness by contrasting it with various nonassertive styles of communication (for example, submissive, aggressive, passive-aggressive, manipulative). Have clients complete the What's Your Style questionnaire in Chapter 13 of *The Anxiety and Phobia Workbook* (allow about 10 minutes for this), to identify their characteristic styles).

Hand out a copy of the Personal Bill of Rights presented in Chapter 13 of *The Anxiety and Phobia Workbook*. Have clients talk about which rights are especially important to them.

Discuss the various facets of assertive communication:

- Developing nonverbal assertive behavior

- Recognizing your basic rights

- Being aware of your feelings and knowing what you want

- Making an assertive request

Give special emphasis to various elements of an assertive request, such as keeping it short and simple, being concrete and specific, using *I*-statements, objecting to behaviors rather than to personalities, not apologizing for your request, and not demanding or commanding.

Model assertive behavior in front of the group by having one of the group members role-play a situation that demands your assertive response. For example, one group member could play a salesperson who doesn't give up, or a retail clerk who wants to give a store credit rather than a refund.

Another example might involve a partner who won't cooperate with a particular household chore, or a parent who is being manipulative. Have clients share their reactions to the role play, then have them divide into dyads to give everybody the chance to practice. Person A plays the role of a mechanic who did extra, unsolicited work on Person B's car and demands that B pay for everything. When the roles are reversed, Person B plays the role of trying to persuade A to buy a product or engage in an activity that A isn't interested in. After both role-plays have transpired, the group reconvenes and discusses what happened.

Time permitting, discuss and illustrate some of the tactics for avoiding manipulation discussed in Chapter 13 of *The Anxiety and Phobia Workbook*: broken record, fogging, content-to-process shift, and so on.

Homework

- Clients should post the Personal Bill of Rights in a conspicuous place at home and read through it carefully every day during the following week.

- Everyone should complete the Assertiveness Exercises in Chapter 13 of *The Anxiety and Phobia Workbook* and turn them in the following week.

- Group members can practice being assertive with friends or close family members, using the skills learned in today's session. Warn them not to expect significant others to be entirely supportive of their assertive behavior if they aren't accustomed to it. The purpose of learning to be assertive is not to please others, but to gain increased confidence about expressing one's own feelings and needs.

- Clients should share with someone whom they haven't told before that they are agoraphobic, explaining their condition. This is a bold but essential step to recovery. They can use the Dear Person Letter at the end of Chapter 6 of *The Anxiety and Phobia Workbook* as a guide for doing this.

- Clients should begin reading Chapter 14 of *The Anxiety and Phobia Workbook* for the following week.

Week 13: Self-Esteem 1 — Taking Care of Yourself

Homework Review

Review the homework on assertiveness from the preceding week. Recommend that clients take a class or workshop on assertiveness (through the adult education programs at local colleges) so that they can continue practicing skills.

Procedures

Define the concept of self-esteem. It's often useful to derive a definition from the group's ideas about the meaning of self-esteem.

Discuss causes of low self-esteem in terms of the variety of dysfunctional family situations that can lead to feelings of insecurity, inferiority, or shame (as described in Chapter 14 of *The Anxiety and Phobia Workbook*).

Have clients identify (from the Needs list in Chapter 14 of *The Anxiety and Phobia Workbook*) those particular needs to which they would like to give more attention. What can they do specifically to better meet these needs?

Introduce the important concept of the inner child, defining it both as a source of playfulness and creativity, and the part of the individual which carries the pain and emotional trauma from childhood. Time permitting, lead clients through the inner child visualization presented in Chapter 14 of *The Anxiety and Phobia Workbook* (allow about 30 to 40 minutes for the visualization and for a discussion of feelings it brings up).

Homework

- Clients should select two or three needs from the needs list and take specific actions during the coming week to meet those needs. Everyone will report on this the following week.

- Have clients take specific actions to cultivate a relationship with their inner child, as suggested in Chapter 14 of *The Anxiety and Phobia Workbook* (for example, writing a letter to the child, carrying around a childhood photograph, or engaging in activities that give expression to the child).

- Clients should follow through with one item from the list of Self-Nurturing Activities in *The Anxiety and Phobia Workbook* (pp. 271-273) each day during the following week.

- Part III of Chapter 14 from *The Anxiety and Phobia Workbook* is assigned reading.

Week 14: Self-Esteem 2 — Personal Goals and Accomplishments

Homework Review

Review homework from the preceding week.

Procedures

Continue discussion from the preceding week about how to take care of the inner child. What will clients do over the next month to take better care of their needs and to cultivate a more intimate relationship with their inner child?

Talk about the relationship of goals and accomplishments to self-esteem, as discussed in Part III of Chapter 14 of *The Anxiety and Phobia Workbook*. What goals have clients accomplished in the group so far in terms of overcoming specific fears and phobias? After a discussion of recovery goals, have clients do a goals-clarification exercise for their life in general. They can complete the worksheet (My Most Important Personal Goals) in Chapter 14 of *The Anxiety and Phobia Workbook*. Allow 20 minutes to complete the worksheet, and then have clients share their goals before the group as a whole.

Time permitting, clients should also complete the worksheet at the end of Chapter 14 of *The Anxiety and Phobia Workbook*, listing previous accomplishments, and then share what they've written with the group. In most cases, it's best to do either this or the long-term goals list described above, rather than both, to allow time at the end for discussion. The other exercise is left as homework.

Homework

- Clients should complete either the worksheet on their most important personal goals or the list of previous accomplishments, to be turned in the following week. Hand out the list of self-esteem affirmations from Chapter 14 of *The Anxiety and Phobia Workbook*. Clients should select those affirmations that are most relevant or personally meaningful. Then they either: a) write these down on a list, which they'll read through each day, or b) put them on tape (allowing 10 seconds between each affirmation), which they'll listen to each day.

- Chapter 15 of *The Anxiety and Phobia Workbook* is assigned reading.

Week 15: Field Trip 2

The guidelines for Week 8 are applicable here. It's desirable at this point to go to a larger shopping mall than the one dealt with in Week 8, or else one that is farther away. Some clients may choose at this time to work on practicing driving — or perhaps on bridges or heights — with another person in the group accompanying them, rather than confronting phobias about stores or restaurants.

Week 16: Nutrition

Procedures

Have group members share about their use of caffeinated beverages and refined sugar. Then discuss the importance of avoiding both, as considered in Chapter 15 of *The Anxiety and Phobia Workbook*. It's useful to have clients complete the caffeine chart in Chapter 15 and then discuss the importance of reducing caffeine consumption to less than 100 mg a day. Also give some time to presenting the concept of hypoglycemia and its influence on anxiety and depression. Ask clients about whether they've noticed any symptoms of hypoglycemia (such as weakness, irritability, or spaciness three hours after a meal) and present dietary guidelines for stabilizing blood-sugar levels.

Review and discuss the Low Stress/Anxiety Dietary Guidelines presented in Chapter 15 of *The Anxiety and Phobia Workbook*. What steps toward meeting these guidelines are clients willing to take in the next month?

Talk about the role of vitamin supplements in increasing resistance to stress, with particular emphasis on B-vitamins, vitamin C, calcium, and magnesium. Good books for upgrading your knowledge about nutrition and supplements are *Diet and Nutrition*, by Rudolph Ballentine; and *Healing Nutrients*, by Patrick Quillin. Patricia Slagle's book, *The Way Up From Down*, is a good resource for the use of amino acids to treat depression.

Homework

- Have clients keep a food diary for one week, using the worksheet in Chapter 15 of *The Anxiety and Phobia Workbook*, to be turned in during the following week.

- Clients should start taking vitamin supplements. At the bare minimum, they should take a high potency multivitamin tablet once per day. Preferably they can begin taking B-complex, vitamin C, and calcium-magnesium at the doses suggested in *The Anxiety and Phobia Workbook*.

Week 17: Meaning, Purpose, and Spirituality

Homework Review

Review homework from the preceding week, going over clients' food diaries.

Procedures

Present and discuss the existential perspective on anxiety, pointing out the connection between a lack of personal meaning or life direction and a predisposition to anxiety. A good background book for this discussion is Rollo May's *The Meaning of Anxiety*.

Clients should complete the Life Purpose Questionnaire from Chapter 17 of *The Anxiety and Phobia Workbook* (allow 20 to 30 minutes) and then share their responses with the group. What are they willing to do in the next weeks and months to take steps toward realizing their identified life goals?

As an alternative to a discussion of the existential perspective, you may want to focus on the theme of spirituality. This, of course, requires very delicate handling because of probable differences in religious motivation and orientation among group members. Since the program is focused on recovery from agoraphobia — and is not a course on spiritual growth — a discussion of spirituality is left to the discretion of the group leader.

Have clients discuss their feelings about the group ending next week.

Homework

Beyond practicing basic skills of relaxation, exercise, desensitization, and countering self-talk, there is no specific homework assigned for this week. If clients feel that they need to spend more time on the Life Purpose Questionnaire, and/or ponder more deeply about what might give their life a greater dimension of meaning, they should do so.

Week 18: Conclusion

See the previous discussion under Week 11 (Shorter Program).

Criteria for Measuring Change

At the outset of the group, clients are given the Self-Evaluation form found at the end of this chapter and asked to rate their degree of confidence on a percentage basis for each relevant phobia at three times: 1) the beginning of the group, 2) the end of the group, and 3) six months after the group has ended.

Problems Specific to the Group

Noncompliance

Since recovery from agoraphobia depends on learning and integrating a variety of skills, the greatest obstacle to progress is the client's unwillingness to complete weekly homework assignments. Several things can be done to foster compliance. At the beginning of the group, the leaders must emphasize that clients are responsible for their own recovery, and that doing the homework is essential to their progress. While the group can provide support, guidance, and structure, it cannot do the work for them. Going over the homework at the beginning of each group session and asking clients how they did with the assignments will help emphasize the importance of daily homework. Clients are also told to set up reward systems, where they allow themselves pleasurable activities (such as calling friends or reading a favorite book), contingent on completion of homework. Part of the homework, in fact, is to develop a self-reward system and to report on it to the group. (It's especially useful to set up a reward system for practicing real-life desensitization.)

Since real-life desensitization (exposure therapy) is at the very heart of the treatment, clients are asked to share how their practice is going from time to time following the introduction to desensitization in Week 6. Resistance to practice is confronted through systematic inquiry instead of by pressuring, coercing, or otherwise embarrassing the client in front of the group. Relevant questions to ask might be: "What do you think is getting in the way of you practicing exposure?" "How do you feel about practicing?" "Is there anything that you feel might help make it easier for you to practice?"

Lack of Motivation

It's important to take notice of low motivation on the part of any client and to discuss it — preferably one-on-one, rather than in front of the group. Reasons for poor motivation are numerous, and can include clinical depression, secondary gains for remaining phobic (such as not having to go to work or remaining dependent on a spouse, unconscious collusion with partner/spouse to sabotage treatment, overt fear of real-life exposure, and diversion of a client's attention away from the program by situational stressors). Since unmotivated clients seldom say anything about their problems, it's incumbent upon the leader to deal with motivational issues as soon as they appear.

If the group as a whole appears to be unmotivated, the leader needs to examine his or her own leadership style and approach. Since many agoraphobic clients have a tendency to be depressed, a purely didactic style of conducting the group is usually inadequate. The leader must be able to create (and sustain) an atmosphere of enthusiasm, consistently providing encouragement that recovery is possible. Copious praise of group members for their successes will help. Fostering a feeling of support and strong cohesiveness among group members will also help. Cohesiveness can be built by leading dyadic exercises during the first few weeks to enable group members to get acquainted. It can be sustained by ensuring that clients make assigned phone calls to each other each week. Finally, the leader may ask for feedback from clients after the first few weeks.

Relapse Prevention

During the final session of the group, you should emphasize what it will take to maintain the gains acquired from the group and to continue making progress toward long-term goals for recovery. The following four skills need to be practiced by clients on a daily (or nearly daily) basis to ensure optimal immunity from a resurgence of generalized anxiety or panic attacks.

1. A deep relaxation technique

2. Physical exercise (if possible, aerobic)

3. Good nutritional habits, minimizing the use of stimulants, sugar, and processed foods

4. Stopping negative self-talk through the use of distraction, positive counter-statements, or affirmations

To overcome specific phobias, clients need to continue practicing imagery and real-life desensitization at least twice a week (and preferably more often). Clients must practice exposure until they are able to enter and comfortably deal with *all* of the situations they previously avoided. Harboring even one phobic situation that is never confronted can lead to avoiding other phobic situations and a general regression to old patterns of thought and behavior.

Resistance

Resistance to practicing real-life exposure to phobic situations is typically the greatest stumbling block for clients. Leaders should make group members aware of this problem during the sixth or seventh week by saying something like the following:

> Undertaking exposure to a situation you've been avoiding may bring up resistance. Notice any procrastination or delay in getting started with your exposure sessions: whether your attitude is "I'll do it later." The mere thought of actually going into a phobic situation may elicit strong anxiety, a fear of being trapped, or self-defeating statements to yourself such as: "I'll never be able to do it," or "This is hopeless." Instead of getting stuck in your resistance, you can see your situation as a major therapeutic opportunity to learn about yourself and work through long-standing patterns which have held your life up.

> Once you work through your initial resistance to real-life desensitization, the going gets easier. If you feel that you're having problems with resistance at any point, let me or the assistant know.

Clients also need to be told to expect some discomfort when they first confront situations they've long avoided. Some level of discomfort is actually a sign that exposure is working. You can tell clients:

> Facing situations that you've been avoiding for a long time is not particularly comfortable or pleasant. It's inevitable that you'll experience some anxiety. In fact, it's common during exposure therapy to feel *worse initially* before you feel better. Realize that feeling worse is *not* an indication of regression, but rather that exposure is really *working*. Feeling worse means that you are laying the foundation to feel better. As you gain more skill in handling symptoms of anxiety when they come up during exposure, your practice sessions will become easier and you'll gain more confidence about following through to completion.

The concept of "secondary gain" should also be explained at some point during the first ten weeks, for example:

> Any person, situation, or factor that consciously or unconsciously *rewards you for holding onto your phobias* will tend to undermine your motivation. For example, you may want to overcome your problem with being housebound. However, if consciously or unconsciously you don't want to deal with facing the outside world, getting a job, or earning an income, you'll tend to keep yourself confined. Consciously, you want to overcome agoraphobia, yet your motivation is not strong enough to overcome the unconscious "payoffs" for not recovering.

You should then ask clients to think about whether any secondary gains are impeding their progress. If so, they should write down what they feel their own secondary gains might be and submit this to the group assistant as part of the homework for the following week. Either the assistant or the leader then arranges a one-on-one conversation with the client, usually by phone, to explore those sources of resistance.

References

Barlow, D.H. *Anxiety and Its Disorders: The Nature and Treatment of Anxiety and Panic.* New York: Guilford Press, 1988.

_____, and Craske, M. *Mastery of Your Anxiety and Panic.* Albany, New York: Graywind Publications, 1989.

_____; O'Brien, G.T.; and Lust, C.G. "Couples treatment of agoraphobia." *Behavior Therapy*, 1984, *15*, 41-58.

_____, and Waddell, M.T. "Agoraphobia." In *Clinical Handbook of Psychological Disorders: A Step-by-Step Treatment Manual.* Edited by D.H. Barlow. New York: Guilford Press, 1985.

Beck, A.T. *Cognitive Therapy and Emotional Disorders.* New York: New American Library, 1979.

_____, and Emery, G. *Anxiety Disorders and Phobias: A Cognitive Perspective.* New York: Basic Books, 1985.

Benson, H. *The Relaxation Response.* New York: David Morrow & Co., 1975.

Bourne, E.J. *The Anxiety & Phobia Workbook.* Oakland, California: New Harbinger Publications, Inc. 1990.

Davis, M.; Eshelman, E.R.; and McKay, M. *The Relaxation and Stress Reduction Workbook.* Third Edition. Oakland, California: New Harbinger Publications, 1988.

Hardy, A.B. *TERRAP Program Manual.* Menlo Park, California: TSC Publications, 1986.

May, R. *The Meaning of Anxiety.* New York: W.W. Norton & Co., 1977.

Munby, J., and Johnston, D.W. "Agoraphobia: The long-term follow-up of behavioral treatment." *British Journal of Psychiatry,* 1980, *137,* 418-427.

Shaffer, M. *Life After Stress.* New York: Plenum Press, 1982.

Slater, E., and Shields, J. "Genetical aspects of anxiety." *British Journal of Psychiatry,* 1969, *3,* 62-71.

Torgersen, S. "Genetic factors in anxiety disorders." *Archives of General Psychiatry,* 1983, *40,* 1085-1089.

Westphal, C. Die Agoraphobia: Eine Neuropathische Eischeinung. *Archives für Psychiatrie und Nerven Krankheiten,* 1971, *3,* 384-412.

Wolpe, J. *Psychotherapy by Reciprocal Inhibition.* Stanford, California: Stanford University Press, 1958.

_____. *The Practice of Behavior Therapy.* Second Edition. New York: Permagon Press, 1973.

Popular Books Relevant to Agoraphobia

Greist, J.W.; Jefferson, J.W.; and Marks, I.M. *Anxiety and Its Treatment.* New York: Warner Books, 1986.

Handly, R., with Neff, P. *Anxiety and Panic Attacks: Their Cause and Cure.* New York: Rawson Associates, 1985.

Neuman, F. *Fighting Fear: The Eight-Week Program for Treating Your Phobias.* New York: Bantam Books, 1986.

Seagrave, A., and Covington, F. *Free From Fears.* New York: Pocket Books, 1987.

Sheehan, D. *The Anxiety Disease.* New York: Bantam Books, 1986.

Swede, S., and Jaffe, S. *The Panic Attack Recovery Book.* New York: New American Library, 1987.

Weekes, C. *Hope and Help for Your Nerves.* New York: Bantam Books, 1978.

_____. *Peace From Nervous Suffering.* New York: Bantam Books, 1978.

Wilson, R. Reid. *Don't Panic: Taking Control of Anxiety Attacks.* New York: Harper and Row, 1986.

Self-Evaluation*

This evaluation is designed to measure your own estimate of your ability to function in the situations mentioned below, and is an indication of your confidence in certain common situations both before starting the program, after finishing the program, and six months after the program. Using the scale below (10 to 100), please rate your ability and confidence level in each of the following areas.

10	20	30	40	50	60	70	80	90	100

almost impossible to handle; low confidence	able to handle sometimes; uncertain	usually able to handle; moderately confident	always able to handle; very self-confident

	Before	After	6 Months Later
1. Leaving safety of home in company of support person			
2. Functioning alone within your home			
3. Functioning alone outside your home			
4. Driving a car around your neighborhood with someone			
5. Driving a car around your neighborhood alone			
6. Driving a car on a freeway with someone			
7. Driving a car on a freeway alone			
8. Riding as a passenger in a car			
9. Being with small groups of people (*i.e.*, parties, etc.)			
10. Being in crowds (*i.e.*, football games, shopping malls)			
11. Air travel			
12. Crossing bridges			
13. Riding in elevators			
14. Heights (from inside)			
15. Heights (from outside)			

---

* Adapted from the TERRAP Program Manual (TSC Publications, Menlo Park, California) with the permission of Dr. Arthur B. Hardy.

	Before	After	6 Months Later
16. Eating in restaurants			
17. Signing name in public			
18. Shopping in supermarket			
19. Assertiveness			
20. Ability to relax when alone			
21. Ability to relax when in a group			
22. Ability to communicate your feelings			
23. Ability to accomplish goals you have set for yourself			
24. Ability to handle anxiety without drugs or alcohol			
25. Ability to handle changes in routine and/or new situations			
26. Ability to assess situations in terms of reality			
27. Ability to make decisions			
28. Self-image, in general			
29. Ability to set long-term goals for yourself			
30. Ability to take charge of your own life			

Name _____ Starting Date _____

Program Location _____ Ending Date _____

Chapter 4

Cognitive-Behavioral Group Treatment for Depression

Jeanne Miranda, Ph.D.,
Janice Schreckengost, Ph.D.,
& Linda Heine, M.S., R.N.

Introduction

Depression is one of the most prevalent psychiatric disorders in the United States (Myers et al., 1984). Using the Diagnostic and Statistical Manual III-Revised (American Psychiatric Association, 1987), at least 8 percent of the population will exhibit symptoms of major depression or dysthymia at some time during their lives (Weissman et al., 1988). Furthermore, depression has a high rate of recurrence, so that individuals who have had an episode of depression are more likely to have such episodes in the future.

Morbidity from depression includes decreased productivity, decreased quality of life, and job and family disruption. Depression is more debilitating than most chronic medical conditions (Wells et al., 1989), and is the major risk factor for suicide, which is one of the ten leading causes of death in the United States.

Numerous studies have demonstrated the effectiveness of cognitive-behavioral group therapy in reducing depressive symptoms and increasing functioning in depressed clients. The available evidence favors homogeneous group composition and structured, time-limited interventions (Beck, 1979). Covi and Lipman (1987) demonstrated a significant superiority of group cognitive-behavioral therapy alone or combined with the drug imipramine over traditional interpersonal group psychotherapy.

Selection and Screening

Group cognitive-behavioral therapy can provide effective treatment to clients with nonpsychotic, unipolar major depression. A clinical interview that includes a complete history is necessary before beginning therapy to ensure the inclusion of appropriate clients. The Beck Depression Inventory (BDI) (Beck et al., 1961) is a 21-item scale for measuring depressive symptomatology which can be used as a measure of the severity of depression. (Copies and permission to use this scale can be obtained by writing to the Center for Cognitive Therapy, Room 602, 133 South 36th Street, Philadelphia, PA 19104.)

Although group cognitive-behavioral therapy is effective for a broad range of depressed individuals, some clients should be excluded from the groups. Clients with active suicide plans, active psychotic symptoms, or bipolar disorders should be referred elsewhere. In addition, exclude clients who are currently abusing drugs or alcohol. They should be told that it's impossible to treat depression while they are abusing substances that contribute to the disorder. Clients may contract to begin cognitive-behavioral therapy after a month of abstinence from drugs or alcohol.

You should pay particular attention to signs of dementia in the patient during the intake. Encourage clients to consult with their medical practitioner to rule out underlying medical problems that can cause or contribute to depression. These include hormonal, nutritional, or endocrine abnormalities; drug effects; and the multiple physical consequences of systemic disease.

Exclude clients who are too hostile, asocial, or have such extensive difficulties in interpersonal relationships that interactions with other group members will be problematic. Those clients who won't accept others easily or, in turn, won't be understood by others should also be excluded. Clients who need long-term psychotherapy should be referred accordingly; although some dysthymics and dysphoric somatizers may benefit from this treatment. Concurrent individual therapy is often most appropriate for such clients.

Clients with "difficult" personality characteristics can be challenging in the group, but they often benefit from therapy. Sometimes these are the very clients whom Yalom (1970) recommends excluding from groups, such as obsessive-compulsive somatizers. Inclusion criteria should be as flexible as the goals for treatment. Clients with major depression and few other problems usually experience a full resolution of the depressive episode after therapy. Other clients with more complicated presentations often become less depressed as a result of the treatment but may need additional therapy to address some of their longer-term problems.

Time and Duration

This treatment for depression is both highly structured and time limited. Clients attend weekly two-hour sessions, for sixteen consecutive weeks. The program is divided into three four-week modules, focusing respectively on how mood is affected by thoughts, activities, and contacts with people. Clients repeat the first module during their last four weeks in the program. Repeating the initial module allows participants to reflect on their progress and to learn material they may have missed because of poor concentration early in the group. The two-hour group time permits sharing of current concerns, as well as presentation of didactic material and working through individuals' difficulties using cognitive-behavioral methods.

Modifications can be made for different clinical settings; however, 12 to 16 sessions are recommended to cover the content areas and provide sufficient time for symptom reduction. Some programs (for example, Lewinsohn et al., 1984) have used twice-weekly meetings for the first several weeks to provide additional support and more intensive initial intervention.

Structure

Groups consist of six to ten clients and two group leaders. New members are added into the group at the beginning of each four-week module. In addition to meeting the practical demands of the referral system, this structure allows "older" members to share their experiences with new group members and to act as role models. Older members acquire a greater sense of efficacy while modeling hope of recovery for newer members. Transitions of group members provide an opportunity for participants to deal with beginning and ending relationships in a supportive setting.

The treatment program may also be conducted as a closed 16-week group. A closed group may offer a more stable and cohesive environment. Begin with a large group to maintain sufficient group size even if members drop out.

Creating commitment to the group is particularly important with depressed clients. They may initially lack the energy to come to meetings or have little hope that they can be helped by the group. Some clients need practical assistance with clearing time away from family and work responsibilities, as well as permission to care for themselves by coming to treatment. These are therapeutic issues that are best dealt with in early sessions; they can provide powerful examples of how to alter dysfunctional thinking, to be assertive, to manage time creatively, and so on. Discussion of participants' hopes and fears about the group also provides a common ground upon which cohesion is built.

Commitment is also generated through discussion prior to acceptance into the group. Ground rules and expectations are discussed in pre-group orientation meetings held individually or in small groups of new members. Members are expected to commit to the entire 16-week program and to come each week. Although no penalties are imposed on poor attendance, an effort is made to discuss what is interfering with group attendance and to provide alternate referrals if the participant cannot attend regularly.

More formal rules for group attendance might also be appropriate in some settings or for inclusion in research protocols. If fees are collected, we recommend that a flat fee be assessed for the entire program (rather than payment per session), to reinforce the expectation that participants will attend each session for the duration of the group.

Goals (Conceptual and Behavioral)

The overall goals of this therapy are twofold: 1) to treat the current episode of major depression so that the client is no longer experiencing significant depressive symptoms, and 2) to teach the client skills that will help prevent relapse of the depression in the future. The goals should be circumscribed—that is, clients who have a myriad of problems apart from their depression may continue to experience those peripheral problems. The goals within the context of the group are specifically related to depression.

To meet the dual goals of treating current depression and preventing future depressions, you need to cover three topics. Within each topic area, specific goals are addressed in turn.

The first area is cognition. The goal here is to teach clients to identify and to change negative, dysfunctional cognitions that precipitate and maintain depression to more positive, health-enhancing cognitions. The second area of treatment involves activities. The goal in this area is to increase the number of pleasant activities in which the client participates. The final area of treatment involves improving interpersonal relationships. The goal is individualized for each client, and may include expanding friendship networks, improving relationships with others, becoming more assertive, or learning to value friendship.

The group functions on a teaching and participation model. Therapists work on the three goals identified above: 1) modifying dysfunctional thinking, 2) increasing pleasant activities, and 3) improving interpersonal relationships. However, clients are encouraged to bring their specific problems to the group. The therapists' goal is to integrate the clients' ongoing concerns with teaching materials relevant to the treatment of depression. Clients are encouraged to share their feelings with the group; therapists work to facilitate group support for individual members.

Ground Rules

Ground rules are discussed explicitly with clients in the orientation session and the first group meeting. Commitment to the group is discussed, as well as the expectation that clients will come each week, be on time for meetings, and complete homework assignments.

Group Process

Group process guidelines include being supportive, caring, constructive, and willing to give everyone a chance to participate. You should encourage clients to give constructive and practical feedback to one another, and to focus on positive solutions rather than dwelling on problems or negative thinking. Criticizing, confronting, pressuring, or telling others what they "should" do is discouraged. Finally, you should instruct clients to maintain confidentiality.

Homework is an essential part of the program. Clients are given the rationale that homework is a way to practice what they are learning. By practicing they will learn which methods are helpful for them, so they can continue to control feelings of depression after the group has ended. Difficulty completing assignments is discussed in the group; often other group members can provide examples of how they overcame similar difficulties or reluctance to complete assignments.

Starting the Group

The best way to begin the group is to talk about the goal of the group: the purpose of therapy is to treat depression by teaching ways to control mood. The therapy attempts to reach four goals related to the overall purpose: 1) to diminish feelings of depression, 2) to shorten the duration of depression, 3) to teach strategies to prevent future depressions, and 4) to help members feel more in control of their lives.

Next, give the members an overview of the first session. Tell them that during this first session, you will explain how the group therapy meetings will be run and discuss the ground rules for the group. Everyone will be introduced, and therapists will discuss a new way to think about depression.

Main Concepts and Skills

A. Concept: What Is Depression

The word *depression* is used in many ways. It can mean a feeling that lasts a few minutes, a mood that lasts a few hours or days, or a clinical condition that lasts at least two weeks and causes strong emotional pain, making it hard to carry out normal activities. This therapy group is intended to treat the clinical condition of depression. Clinical depression can be different for everyone, but most people suffer from some of the following symptoms:

- Feeling depressed or down nearly every day
- Not being interested in things, or being unable to enjoy things you used to enjoy
- Having appetite or weight changes (either increases or decreases)
- Experiencing changes in sleep patterns (sleeping less or sleeping more)
- Noticing changes in how fast you move
- Feeling tired all the time
- Feeling worthless or guilty
- Having trouble thinking, concentrating, or making decisions
- Thinking a lot about death, wishing to be dead, or thinking about hurting yourself

Group cohesion is often built as members acknowledge that they share a common set of symptoms comprising depression.

When symptoms are discussed, the issue of suicide is often raised. We suggest saying, "Some people can feel so bad that they don't feel like continuing to live. If any of you find yourself feeling this way, you should contact one of therapists immediately." At this time, therapists should provide all clients with emergency resources to deal with suicidal feelings as they occur. This might be a 24-hour emergency service or suicide prevention program.

B. Concept: Defining Cognitive-Behavioral Therapy

"The kind of therapy that we describe is called *cognitive-behavioral therapy*. Cognitive refers to *thoughts*. Behavioral refers to *actions*. Depression mostly has to do with *feelings*. By learning which thoughts and actions influence feelings, you can learn to get more control over your moods. Our treatment for depression focuses on what's going on in your life right now. The techniques you will learn in this group focus on how to control depression in practical ways that you can use now and in the future."

C. Skill: Monitoring Your Mood

An important part of therapy for depression involves teaching clients to pay attention to and monitor their moods. They need to learn what makes their mood worse and what makes their mood better. They may find that certain times of the day or certain activities or interactions with others influence how they feel. Some clients may maintain that they feel terrible at all time; but with exploration and monitoring, they will be able to track variations in their moods.

The Beck Depression Inventory is assigned weekly for the clients to monitor their depressive symptomatology. They are asked to complete the questionnaire prior to the session and bring the complete form to group. Among other things, therapists should always check item 9, which addresses suicidal ideation. If a group member indicates that he or she feels suicidal, therapists should keep the client after group to assess the need for interventions to help protect that individual's safety.

D. Concept: Thoughts That Cause and Maintain Depression

The first unit teaches clients to decrease their depression by influencing thoughts, particularly dysfunctional thoughts. Define thoughts as "things we tell ourselves. Thoughts are very powerful. Through thoughts, you tell yourself about everything that goes on around you. Some of your thoughts have been influenced by upbringing, others by culture, and others reflect your unique way of responding to the world. Thoughts are like someone whispering in your ear all the time, telling you how to respond to the world around you. These thoughts have an influence on many things: on your body, on your actions, and on your moods.

"Thoughts are very important in influencing feelings; they have a major impact on determining your mood. Certain types of thinking can lower your mood and maintain depression. These thoughts are 'trap thoughts' that keep people down. Learning to recognize and talk back to such thoughts can improve your mood.

"In everyday experience, things that happen around us seem to 'cause' bad moods. For example, a woman has a quarrel with her husband. She then feels sad during the following day. She may feel that having the fight with her husband made her sad.

"Perhaps she'll discover after a while a particular thought that made her feel sad: 'If my husband yells at me, it means that I'm an awful wife.'

"This thought is actually what made the woman feel sad, rather than the fight itself. She might learn to recognize such thoughts as a 'trap' for her. She can learn to replace trap thoughts with more positive and logical ones, such as: 'My husband is yelling at me because I don't do things exactly as he wants them done. Just because he yells at me doesn't mean that I'm not a good wife.' With this new thought, she is unlikely to feel so sad during the day following a quarrel.

"Some thoughts make it more likely that you'll become depressed and others make it less likely. Imagine that you have exactly one hour to get to an important meeting during rush hour. If you're sitting on the freeway saying to yourself, 'Oh, no, I'm going to be late. I can never get there on time. I'll look bad if I show up late. This might hurt my career!', you are likely to feel upset and anxious. If you are in the same situation but are saying to yourself, 'I really can't do anything about this traffic. I might as well use this time to relax, so that when I arrive at the meeting I'll feel as good as I possibly can. I'm going to turn on the radio and relax and enjoy this time!', you might manage to make yourself feel very calm and relaxed. This illustrates how important thoughts are in terms of influencing our moods."

Thoughts are ideas that we tell ourselves. Help clients learn to "tune in" to these thoughts. Ask them to pay attention to the thoughts that are going on inside their heads. For example, "What are the thoughts you're telling yourself right now? Some of you may be saying to yourselves, 'This isn't going to work for me. They don't understand my problems. Nothing is ever going to help me.' If you're telling yourself those things, you may have trouble using this therapy. Others among you may be saying to yourselves, 'I hope this works. I'm willing to try this in order to feel better.' If you're telling yourself to try, this therapy is more likely to help you." Practicing "tuning into" thoughts will help clients learn to listen to the tape that constantly plays in their heads.

E. Concept: Identifying Errors in Thinking

After clients learn to "tune into" the thoughts running through their minds, they must learn to identify those thoughts that cause them to feel depressed. This is often best done through the method of "working backwards." That is, ask clients to notice the times during the day or week when they feel the worst. Then have them notice what thoughts they are having during these times. Thus, they start with the feeling and work backwards to the thought.

Clients will learn to identify such errors in thinking as "all-or-nothing thinking" (believing that if you do one thing wrong, everything about you is wrong), "should" (believing that you or other people must behave in specific ways), or "over-generalization" (believing that one example of something negative means that everything will be negative). We recommend that clients read *Feeling Good: The New Mood Therapy*, by David D. Burns, M.D. Pages 31 through 47 identify typical errors in thinking and help clients to identify their own errors in thinking.

Clients who have difficulty learning to identify their dysfunctional thinking may be helped by Burns' downward arrow technique. To use this technique, the therapist asks the client to identify situations that are upsetting to him or her. The therapist then asks repeatedly, "Why is this situation upsetting to you? What does it mean to you?" After answering these questions for each situation, the client often arrives at the dysfunctional belief.

Depressed thinking is different from nondepressed thinking. These are some of the ways in which it differs:

Depressed Thinking

- Depressed thinking is *inflexible*. For example, a depressed person might think: "I'm always scared." Flexible thoughts that keep us from being depressed might be, "I'm scared sometime, but at other times I'm not."

- Depressed thinking is *judgmental*. A depressed person might think: "I am a terrible coward." The nonjudgmental thinker may say, "I am more afraid than most people I know, but that doesn't necessarily mean anything bad about me."

Nondepressed Thinking

- Nondepressed thinking is *reasonable* as well as *flexible*: "I am afraid in some situations sometimes." This contrasts with such depressed thinking as, "I always have been and always will be a coward."

- Nondepressed thinking looks at what you do, not who you are. Flexible and reasonable thinking says, "I have been acting in ways that are not working for me right now." Depressed thinking might say, "I am bad."

- Nondepressed thinking hopes for change: "Nothing I've tried yet has helped, but this is new and the time might be right for me to start feeling better." Depressed thinking is hopeless: you believe that nothing will help.

Teach clients to spot types of thinking that are traps for depression. Present the following three concepts:

1. *Constructive versus destructive thinking:* "Constructive thinking is the type of thinking that helps 'build yourself up' and 'put yourself together.' For example, the thought, 'I can learn to control my life to get more of what I want'

is constructive. Try to work toward more constructive thinking. Destructive thinking 'tears you apart.' For example, you might think 'I'm no go at all,' or 'I've made too many mistakes in my life.' Try to turn destructive thinking into constructive thinking."

2. *Necessary versus unnecessary thinking:* "Necessary thinking reminds us of the things that we have to do, such as 'I must remember to fill out the daily mood graph before I go to sleep tonight.' Unnecessary thinking simply is worry. Examples of unnecessary thinking are, 'This country is going to be ruined,' 'I'm going to get old and sick,' or 'My kids aren't going to turn out like they should.' Such unnecessary thinking can be a trap thought for making you feel bad. Try to reduce the amount of time you spend in unnecessary, negative thinking."

3. *Positive versus negative thinking:* "You know the saying about the cup being half empty or half full. Positive thinking helps you look at what you do have in a positive light instead of focusing on what you don't have or on negative things. Depressed thinking focuses on the negative. For example, a depressed person reported going for a walk on a beautiful fall day. She walked through a lovely park, but felt that her whole day was ruined because she had seen a dead bird beside the sidewalk. She focused exclusively on the one negative thing in the otherwise beautiful day.

   "Focusing on the positive can help lift depression. An example of positive thinking is, 'Things are rough right now, but at least I'm here doing something about them.' Negative thinking only makes you feel worse, like saying, 'It's just no use.' When you're depressed, you should work to focus on the positive to help improve your mood."

F. Skill: Increasing Thoughts That Improve Mood

Present clients with the following typed list of ways to increase thoughts that improve mood. Read each item and ask if anyone tried this and how it works for them.

1. "Simply increasing the number of positive thoughts you have can make you feel better. You might make a list of good thoughts that you've had about yourself and your life. Write these thoughts down and read them over every day.

2. "Giving yourself mental 'pats on the back' can increase your positive mood. Make yourself aware of what you really do every day. Most of the things we do are not really noticed by others. Notice the things that you do and give yourself credit for doing them.

3. "Sometimes it's most healthy to give yourself a break. Particularly if you are a worrier, you may need to learn to say to yourself, 'Hold everything!' This means to pause and give yourself a mental 'time out.' Let your mind simply relax for a moment. Pay attention to your body's ability to be at peace. Feeling at peace can give you energy. Do this several times a day.

4. "When you're feeling bad, time projection can be really helpful. That is, imagine moving forward in time when things will feel better. Imagine how you will feel about this bad time from the perspective of the future."

G. Skill: Decreasing Thoughts That Lower Mood

Present clients with the following typed list of ways to decrease thoughts that lower mood. Read each item and ask if anyone has tried the method.

1. "If you find that a particular thought is lowering your mood, try to stop that thought. Agree with yourself that you are not going to think about that right now. Move on to other thoughts.

2. "If you are a worrier, sometimes it's helpful to set up a 'worrying time' each day. That is, set aside 15 to 30 minutes each day to worry. Do your worrying during that time and leave the rest of the day open without feeling that you have to worry. If you find yourself worrying about something, write it down so that you can worry about it during your next worrying time.

3. "If you have a good sense of humor, sometimes you can make fun of your own problems by exaggerating them. For example, if you worry about whether everyone likes you, imagine that one person doesn't like you. Then blow up the worry by imagining that person carrying a placard that says she hates you. Keep blowing up the image until you can laugh at how silly your worries might be.

4. "Often, vague fears about what could happen make us more depressed than thinking things through and facing the worst possibilities. Remember that the worst that can happen is only one of many possibilities, and just because it's the worst, it's not the one most likely to happen.

5. "As you work on your depression, learn to become your own coach. This is just like helping someone else do something difficult. Give yourself instructions. Think of this as a time when you are *learning* to feel better."

H. Concept: The ABCD Method

Clients must learn to "talk back" to or modify their errors in thinking in order to control negative moods. We suggest teaching the ABCD Method (Ellis & Dryden, 1987) to develop skills for modifying errors in thinking. Using this method, the client learns to identify *A* (activating event that precedes negative feelings), *B* (belief about the event that causes the negative feelings), *C* (the consequence of the belief, often feeling sad, lonely, frightened, and so on), and *D* (a dispute for the belief). Clients use the skills developed earlier to identify the events, beliefs, and errors in the beliefs that underlie their depression. You can then encourage them to dispute the beliefs and replace them with thoughts that maintain or enhance more positive feelings.

For example, have one client in the group talk about a difficult time that she had in the past week. If she says that she felt sad all week because she expected her daughter to call on Wednesday and she did not, ask her what her thoughts were. She may say that she thought, "I am not a good mother because my daughter doesn't care enough about me to call me every week." On the board write "*A:* The activating event was that your daughter did not call you." Across from the *A* write "*B:* The belief is that you are not a good mother if your daughter doesn't call you every week." Below these, write "*C:* The consequence is depression." Next, ask the group to help generate alternative thoughts or beliefs. Other group members are likely to offer such alternatives as, "If your daughter doesn't call you, it's probably because she's busy — not because you aren't a good mother," or "Even if your daughter is mad at you and not calling you right now doesn't mean that you aren't a good mother. Maybe she's mad at you because she hasn't really grown up yet." Ask the client to read the alternative responses out loud. Then ask her how she feels after reading them.

Often patients aren't able to communicate clearly the dysfunctional beliefs they hold at the beginning of this exercise. They usually *are* able to describe the situation that is upsetting to them. Use of the downward arrow technique described in concept E can be helpful. In addition, generating alternative thoughts is a time to build cohesion in the group. Ask each group member to describe an alternative way of thinking about the situation.

I. Skill: Modifying Errors in Thinking

In order to best teach clients to talk back to their negative thoughts, present them with common dysfunctional thoughts. Have the group identify the error and suggest alternative thoughts. Below is a list that can be used:

1. "I should be loved and approved of by everyone." This is an example of one of the "shoulds." An alternative thought is, "It is nice to be loved and approved of, but no one is liked by everyone."

2. "I should always be able to do things well and work hard all of the time to feel good about myself." This is another example of the "shoulds." An alternative thought is, "Some things I do well and others I do less well. I can feel good about myself even when I don't succeed at something."

3. "Some people are bad and should be punished." This is an example of all-or-nothing thinking when we think in terms of the "shoulds." No one is all bad; and we get in trouble when we think in terms of "shoulds." An alternative thought is, "Some people do things that I don't approve of some of the time. People are different and see things differently."

4. "I will feel awful if things don't go the way I want them to go." This is an example of all-or-nothing thinking. If one thing goes wrong, everything isn't necessarily ruined. An alternative thought might be, "This is important to me, so I hope that some of the things I want will happen. I realize that other people think differently at times — so some things may not go as I want them to. I will enjoy as much as I can."

5. "Other people and things are what make me unhappy." This is an example of thinking that your problems are out of your control. You think that you need someone else to behave differently before you can be happy. An alternative thought would be, "I can't control what other people do, but I can learn to control my own mood. I can learn to make myself happy no matter what others do."

6. "I'm worried about bad things that could happen." This is an example of objectifying your mood. That is, when you're anxious, you begin to believe that something bad is going to happen. An alternative is, "I am anxious. When I'm anxious, I believe that something bad is going to happen. But my anxiety doesn't predict the future. I need to relax and then I won't believe that something bad is going to happen."

7. "I can never be happy if I don't have someone to love me." This is an example of overgeneralization. If you are not happy in one area of your life,

you assume that you will always be unhappy. An alternative thought is, "I can have lots of things going on in my life. Some will work out and some won't work out. I will be able to make myself happy with those things that do work out for me."

8. "I can't change the way that I am; I was born stubborn." This is an example of self-labeling. This doesn't look at your specific behavior, but labels you as bad. An alternative statement is, "Sometimes it's hard for me to change directions — but I can work to be more flexible."

9. "I must feel depressed because people I care about are having a bad time."

This is an example of the "shoulds" and all-or-nothing thinking. First, just because others are sad, you needn't be sad yourself. This thought focuses solely on the current sadness, rather than noticing anything positive. An alternative statement is, "When people I care about are feeling down, I feel bad for them. I know things will turn around for them, and they may benefit from seeing that I don't become depressed with them. I may be able to help them feel better in time. One of the things I can do is to take care of myself and stay happy so that I can be of some help to them."

10. "So-'n-so will be disappointed in me if I don't do the right thing." This is an example of mind reading (assuming you know what others think). An alternative thought is, "I am going to do my best and learn from my mistakes. The important thing is to try to please myself."

J. Concept: Increasing Pleasant Activities

The second unit focuses on pleasant activities. Depressed clients often have reduced their activity level. Increasing the number of events and activities they engage in can affect their mood. Depressed clients often don't feel like doing the kinds of activities that are likely to be a source of satisfaction for them. A "vicious cycle" ensues in which the more depressed people feel, the less active they are; and conversely, the less they do, the more depressed they feel. Generally, three kinds of activities are useful in combating depression: 1) those that involve clients in rewarding interactions with other people; 2) those that make them feel more competent, or give a sense of purpose; and 3) those associated with emotions of happiness and contentment.

In presenting pleasant events to clients, several things are important to consider. First, clients often need a rationale for having to put effort into finding enjoyable activities. One rationale is that most depressed clients have had losses that precipitated their depression. These losses, such as loss of a spouse, job, and so on, may also involve loss of pleasant activities. Therefore, the client may need to learn different ways to enjoy activities or learn to consider different activities. Second, pleasant activities don't have to be special. Many of them are ordinary, such as taking a bath or going for a walk. Often adding simple changes in daily routines can make activities enjoyable, such as taking a relaxing bubble bath instead of simply bathing. Third, people differ in the types of activities that they enjoy. Encourage all members of the group to share examples of what they enjoy. Often leader modeling is useful in beginning this process. Stress the point that identification of individual pleasant activities adds to self-knowledge. This self-knowledge is important for learning which activities affect mood on an individual level.

K. Skill: Identifying Pleasant Activities

Clients learn to assess the degree to which pleasant activities contribute to their mood. Because those who are depressed often have a low number of pleasant activities in their lives, the goal is to increase the number of enjoyable activities they participate in. In the groups, the Pleasant Events Schedule is used to identify activities they have enjoyed in the past and activities they would enjoy now. They monitor their daily activity level and gradually increase the number of pleasant events they engage in.

L. Skill: Pleasure Predicting

Often, when clients are planning activities for themselves, negative thinking can diminish the anticipated pleasure and keep the client from engaging in the activity. Teach clients to anticipate how much pleasure a certain activity will hold for them and to write their prediction down before they engage in the activity. After completion of the activity, they write down how pleasurable they actually found it to be. They are then encouraged to see the connection between anticipatory thoughts and their subsequent experience. Often clients find that they would have missed an enjoyable activity if they had relied on their "depressed thinking" to guide them.

M. Skill: Setting Goals

Clients learn to develop and implement a self-change plan aimed at increasing the number of, or frequency of their involvement in, enjoyable activities. Initially they learn to write a contract with themselves to engage in one new activity in the coming week and to name a reward to give themselves after completing the activity. Rewards increase the likelihood that clients will continue to implement their self-change plan. Constructing a "reward menu" — a list of events and things the client wants — can be useful. Be careful that clients don't include rewards that are dependent on someone else's behavior, unless they are sure they can count on that person's cooperation.

This skill progresses into the area of time management and planning. You will teach clients to prioritize the things they want to get done in a given week. Top-priority activities are plotted into their weekly schedule where they have time to accomplish them. Lower-priority items are plotted in last where there is room. You and the clients can scrutinize their weekly plans, to ensure a balance between responsibilities and pleasant activities.

Goals set to overcome depression must be reasonable and clear. Encourage clients to set realistic goals. A goal may be too big or unwieldy and may need to be broken down into smaller steps. For example, one woman who wanted to join some activities at the senior center made it her goal for the first week to go to the center and get the schedule of weekly activities. Goals must be clear and not so expansive that it's hard to formulate a plan. "I want to be less isolated" may have to be restructured into "This week I will call one friend and ask him to go for a walk." One additional benefit involved in setting goals may be to add structure to a client's day. For example, one woman who lost her job because of medical problems was faced with empty time, which she found overwhelming. Step by step she built her own structure with a daily walk, going out for coffee, taking adult education classes, and so on.

In planning for the future, help clients think of their lives in terms of manageable pieces of time. Setting personal goals involves organizing them into three categories:

1) short-term goals (to be realized within one or two months), 2) long-term goals (to be realized at some point in your life), and 3) life goals (your general philosophy of life or what matters most).

N. Concept: Improving Interpersonal Relationships

The third unit teaches the concept that depression is related to difficulties in interpersonal relationships and that improving contacts with people can affect one's mood. Work in this area is individualized for each client. It may include increasing one's network of friends, improving the quality of existing relationships, becoming more assertive and socially skilled, or changing one's attitude about relationships.

Clients are taught that higher levels of depression relate to 1) being with other people less, 2) feeling uncomfortable or awkward with people, 3) being less assertive, and 4) being more sensitive to being ignored, criticized, and rejected.

O. Skill: Increasing Social Activities

When clients feel depressed, they are less likely to socialize. By socializing less, they lose a good source of happiness and then become more depressed. This creates a vicious cycle of depression and isolation. In the group, clients learn that increasing social contact can reverse the cycle.

Discuss with clients the ways in which a supportive social network can be beneficial — for example, helping to cope with stress or providing involvement in meaningful and enjoyable activities. Clients may not be using the support that is available to them. It's helpful for clients to list the people in their support networks, including friends, family, neighbors, co-workers, or anyone else who is important to them. Clients who are isolated or have small networks are encouraged to enlarge their circle of contacts. Those who have an adequate network are encouraged to appreciate it and keep the relationships healthy. All clients learn to monitor their level of social activities, both positive and negative, and to set goals to initiate more pleasant social activities.

In the group, clients generate ideas for meeting others and maintaining contact with people. They are taught that a good way to meet people is to do something they really enjoy, in the company of other people. This helps to ensure that they are in a good mood and will meet people who share similar interests. Depressed clients often have difficulty initiating activities due to fears of rejection. It's important to practice asking others to do things and anticipating negative thoughts that might get in the way.

P. Skill: Increasing Assertiveness

Assertiveness is taught to help the client get greater enjoyment out of social interactions and reduce negative contact with people. Clients first identify problem areas in their interactions with people. Assertiveness skills are then learned and practiced in the group, using situations from the participants' lives. Between sessions, they first practice with covert rehearsal and imagining assertive responses, progressing to practice in real-life situations.

Assertiveness is defined as being able to comfortably express your feelings and reactions, both positive and negative. In the group, clients discuss the differences between passive, aggressive, and assertive responses. Depressed people are often quite passive; they may feel that others take advantage of them and that they are powerless to change things. The passive person is unlikely to get people to meet his or her needs and preferences; thus resentment toward others is likely to build. Such people may then brood or avoid social contacts altogether. The aggressive client is likely to respond to negative situations with excessive anger toward others. Aggressive responses tend to alienate others and reduce the chances of a positive outcome. Some depressed clients shift from extremely passive responses to aggressive responses — for example, letting an interpersonal problem go undiscussed until it reaches the breaking point, then reacting with anger. Clients may also have difficulty expressing positive thoughts or feelings; this produces discomfort around people and limits their attractiveness to others.

Assertiveness is presented as an alternative response: stating one's feelings honestly and attempting to work out difficulties as they occur. Clients learn assertiveness skills, such as focusing on how they feel ("*I*-statements"), rather than blaming or judging the other person. It's essential for clients to identify what they want from a person or a situation, and to learn to ask for this simply and directly. Finally, they learn how to follow through on their requests with appropriate consequences and rewards.

Assertiveness is often difficult to learn, thus you should encourage clients gradually to try more assertive responses and to keep trying if they don't succeed initially. They should first practice a response to the situation, imagining what they will say and how the person will react; when they feel ready, they can try out their assertive response in the actual situation. Encourage clients to get ideas by observing others whose style they like, and to get suggestions from friends on how to handle a given situation. In the group, role-plays and discussions assist clients in coming up with assertive responses to difficult situations.

Q. Skill: Enhancing Social Skills

Some depressed people are uncomfortable in social situations because they lack social skills or they believe themselves to be socially incompetent. Social skills are taught with an emphasis on how the client comes across to others. Group members provide one another with feedback on their appearance, facial expressions, and speaking style. Many clients also benefit from learning basic conversational skills, such as expressing interest in what others say and initiating topics of discussion. Finally, some clients may have adequate social skills but suffer from anxiety, which impedes them. These clients will benefit from learning and practicing relaxation in anxiety-provoking social situations.

R. Skill: Dysfunctional Thoughts About People

The quality of social interactions is often affected by dysfunctional beliefs about people. For example, the client who believes, "People don't really care about me, they're just out to take advantage of me," is likely to avoid close relationships and be constricted and suspicious during social interactions. Social situations are also powerful triggers for negative thoughts about oneself. The client who stumbles when speaking in public may believe, "I can't do anything right; everyone must think I'm stupid" — which then exacerbates depressed mood and makes withdrawal more likely.

Teach your clients to combat these dysfunctional beliefs and replace them with more adaptive attitudes about people. They can use the methods they learned in the "Thoughts" module (see sections E, H, and I in the Concepts and Skills section) — for example, they can use the ABCD method for generating alternative, nondysfunctional thoughts. In the second example above, the alternative thought might be, "I made a mistake in speaking, but others make mistakes too. I don't need to be perfect for people to like me."

Clients learn to identify which thoughts help them to be comfortable with people — for example, "I have ideas I can share with this person; he might enjoy being with me." Other thoughts get in the way — for example, "This person could take advantage of me; I'd better not reveal anything about myself." Encourage clients to think more positively and modify their negative thoughts.

S. Skill: Maintaining Relationships

The final skill emphasizes the importance of maintaining relationships over time. Teach clients that relationships with people are important for mood because they can a) help you have rewarding experiences, b) support the values you want to live by, c) provide companionship and a sense of stability, and d) reflect an important image of yourself. Several skills for maintaining relationships are helpful for depressed clients.

First, present the rationale that relationships are worth working on. It takes effort to maintain relationships and adapt to changes, but there are substantial long-term benefits. Second, help clients learn to set reasonable expectations for relationships. Expecting too much may lead to dissatisfaction, while expecting too little causes one to miss rewarding opportunities. Third, when relationships don't work, it doesn't help to think there is something wrong with you. Encourage clients to focus on constructive questions. For example, do both people want the same things from the relationship? Do they share interests? Can they tell each other what they think and feel clearly? Fourth, teach clients to practice listening and understanding what others say. Suggest that they try repeating back what they heard, to clarify if that is what the person meant. This technique can help avoid arguments and misunderstandings based on immediate emotional reactions. Finally, encourage clients to choose relationships and social environments that support their sense of self-worth and confidence, rather than those that hurt or demoralize them. Mention the group as an example of a supportive environment.

Main Interventions

Week 1

Introduction

Begin by introducing the purpose of the group and the purpose of this first meeting. Introduce the ground rules regarding how the group will run.

"The group meetings will be helpful in overcoming your depression. They will allow you time to share your concerns with other, to get support from others in the group, and to realize that you are not alone in having real problems and difficult times in your life.

"We're now going to introduce ourselves to one another. For now, we would like to know who you are apart from your depression; so try to introduce yourself without presenting the problems bothering you right now. It's important not to think about yourself only as a 'depressed person.' Tell us things such as where you grew up, who your family is, what kind of work you've done, your main interests, and things about yourself that you think are very important." Therapists may participate in this introduction as well.

A. Concept: What Is Depression

Intervention 1: Didactic Presentation (See Concepts and Skills section)

Intervention 2: Group Exercise

Ask group members to describe what depression is like for them. Therapists should write on the board the symptoms that clients have experienced. Ask what kinds of thoughts group members have when they feel down. What do they do when they're depressed? How do they feel when they're depressed? After listing the symptoms, say, "You all have similar symptoms that tell us that you're depressed. This group is intended to overcome your depression."

B. Concept: Defining Cognitive-Behavioral Therapy

Intervention 1: Didactic Presentation (See Concepts and Skills section)

C. Skill: Monitoring Your Mood

Intervention 1: Didactic Presentation (See Concepts and Skills section)

Intervention 2: Group Exercise

Begin by having each person consider his or her own current mood. Give the following instructions: "Let's each rate our mood." On the board, draw a scale from 9 to 0. "If a 9 represents the best mood you can ever imagine and 0 represents the worst mood you can imagine and 5 represents a typical mood for you when you are not depressed, where would you put yourself right now?" Have each group member assign a number to their current mood. Clients will perform a similar rating each day during the next week using the Daily Mood Graph.

Homework

The Daily Mood Graph and the Beck Depression Inventory. Have each member complete a daily chart of his or her mood just before going to bed and assign a number to that mood. For clients whose mood varies greatly, have them assign a worst and best rating for the day, using different colors.

Week 2

Introduction

Go over the Daily Mood Graph and the Beck Depression Inventory as clients come into the group. Ask if anyone was surprised by anything they learned when filling out the graph. Ask what it was like to fill out the graph every day. Often clients can learn about important factors that influence their mood simply by filling out the graph.

Explain the purpose of the homework again. It's important for clients to understand that the group occupies only two hours of their week and that to feel better may require more active participation during the rest of the week. Encourage people who did not complete homework to keep the mood graph during the following week.

Intervention 3: Group Demonstration

Choose one client's graph to put up on the board to illustrate how the graph works. Try to tie concepts of dysfunctional thinking, activities, and interactions with others to this person's mood. For example, if the client reports that his mood was worse on a day when he stayed inside and better on a day when he went out to buy groceries, point out that getting out of the house for activities may be an important factor in raising his mood. Similarly, if the client reports that her mood was worse on a day when her daughter failed to call her, ask what she was thinking. If she responds, "...that I am a failure as a mother," point out that this thought by itself might be making her feel down.

D. Concept: Thoughts That Cause and Maintain Depression

Intervention 1: Didactic Presentation (See Concepts and Skills section)

E. Concept: Identifying Errors in Thinking

Intervention 1: Didactic Presentation (See Concepts and Skills section)

Intervention 4: Soliciting Examples and Group Discussion

Ask a few clients to identify and share beliefs that have been keeping their mood low. Ask the group to identify errors in the thinking.

Homework

- Clients should fill out the Daily Mood Graph and the Beck Depression Inventory.

- For homework reading: David Burns, *Feeling Good: The New Mood Therapy*, William Morrow and Company, 1980, pp. 7-48.

Week 3

Introduction

Review the purpose of the treatment and how thoughts, activities, and interactions with others affect mood.

Review homework. Go over the daily mood scale. Discuss the errors in thinking studied during the past week. Ask if people noticed errors in their own thinking.

Teach the following: "Today we will focus on three things. First, we'll talk about increasing thoughts that make us feel better. Then we'll talk about decreasing thoughts that make us feel bad. Finally, we'll practice spotting errors in thinking and correcting them."

F. Skill: Increasing Thoughts That Improve Mood

Intervention 1: Didactic Presentation (See Concepts and Skills section)

G. Skill: Decreasing Thoughts That Lower Mood

Intervention 1: Didactic Presentation (See Concepts and Skills section)

H. Concept: The ABCD Method

Intervention 1: Didactic Presentation (See Concepts and Skills section)

Intervention 3: Group Demonstration

Have two or three clients work through their errors in thinking using the ABCD method on the board. A sample discussion follows below:

Naomi:	I felt very bad on Saturday when my back was hurting.
Therapist:	So the event that made you feel sad was back pain. Did you feel anything besides sad?
Naomi:	Yes, I felt defeated. I felt like I couldn't do anything that would be fun because I was sick.
Therapist:	What were you thinking when you noticed the back pain?
Naomi:	I thought that it means that I am sick again. When I am sick, I can't do anything that I like to do. It felt overwhelming, like I can never have a good time because I am always sick.
Therapist:	Can anyone in the group see any errors in the thoughts Naomi is having?
Norman:	Yes. She's saying never and always. I can see why she feels so bad when she is thinking she can never have any fun.
Naomi:	It feels that way when I have back pain.
Therapist:	I am sure that you do feel very sad when this happens to you. It might be that the thoughts you are having are what really make you feel so bad. Can anyone in the group think of an alternative thought that Naomi might have when she feels back pain that might not make her feel so sad.
JoAnn:	One thought might be that even though your back hurts there are some things that you can enjoy. Can you still enjoy visiting friends or watching a movie?
Bob:	She could say my back hurts now, but it's not always going to hurt. Tomorrow I may feel better and I can do something fun then.
Sara:	She could say that her back hurts but that a lot of her is still well. You know, like her mind is still okay and her stomach may still be fine. She's not totally disabled by her back pain.
Therapist:	Naomi, how would it feel to you if you had some of these thoughts instead?
Naomi:	When I am sick, I feel totally sick. I think I may have learned that when I was little. If I was sick and wanted to stay home from school, I was expected to be really sick! But you are right, there are many things that I can do and my back doesn't hurt all day every day. I think I would feel better if I remembered this when I have back pain.

Homework

- Clients should complete the Daily Mood Graph and the Beck Depression Inventory.

- Assign the ABCD method — for everyone to practice analyzing at least one thought that brings them down during the week.

Week 4

Introduction

Check on homework. Were clients able to complete the ABCD method during the week? Go over some examples on the board.

I. Skill: Modifying Errors in Thinking

Intervention 1: Didactic Presentation (See Concepts and Skills section)

Intervention 3: Group Demonstration

Use clients' homework to practice the ABCD method on the blackboard.

Homework

- Clients should complete the Daily Mood Graph and the Beck Depression Inventory.

- Continue working with the ABCD method.

Week 5

Introduction

Go over homework from the previous week and see if there are any further questions about the thoughts module. Introduce the next basic concept about how actions affect mood. Explain the material didactically, giving many examples and encouraging discussion of the clients' own experiences.

J. Concept: Increasing Pleasant Activities

Intervention 1: Didactic Presentation (See Concepts and Skills section)

K. Skill: Identifying Pleasant Activities

Intervention 1: Didactic Presentation (See Concepts and Skills section)

Intervention 2: Group Exercise

"Pleasant Events Schedule" (Lewinsohn, Munoz, Youngren, & Zeiss, 1986) is a list of 320 potentially pleasant activities generated by asking people to name 10 activities they find pleasant. You may want to adapt this model and scale the list down to 100 items that are most pertinent for your population. Leave room at the bottom for clients to write in activities that they find pleasant, but aren't on the list, such as motorcycle riding. Examples of activities on the list include: be outdoors (beach, country...), take a bath, visit friends, cook meals, and so on.

Pass out the adapted "List of Pleasant Activities" and have the group leaders and members take turns reading each item out loud. Instruct the clients to put a check mark next to each item that has been pleasurable to them in the past or that they think they might enjoy. Ignore or line through those items that are not pleasurable for that person — for example, "talk about sports." The group leaders should do this at least once themselves to share the experience with clients.

Encourage discussion at this point about what clients discovered about themselves in terms of the number of activities checked (which will vary widely), and how long ago they engaged in each activity. Stress that for now you just want them to keep track of their activities on a daily basis for a week, and not yet try to increase them. (The list is columned off for 14 days.)

Homework

- Clients should fill out the Daily Mood Graph and the Beck Depression Inventory.

- "Put a check mark next to each of the things you did in your list of pleasant activities at the end of each day. Write the number of checks per day at the end of the list, and at the bottom of the Daily Mood Graph."

- Clients should bring the graph and the list to the next week's session.

Week 6

Introduction

Go over the homework and explore any problems or questions about adapting the list of pleasant activities. Also inquire into any observations clients are making about activity level and their mood.

Intervention 3: Group Demonstration

Have one or two clients volunteer to share their homework with the group. One leader should draw a client's mood graph on a blackboard that's visible to all group members. Then list the number of activities completed under each day. Have the client talk about the week illustrated on the board, and show the connection between activity level and mood. Talk about how an adequate level of activities makes us feel healthy. Encourage discussion about the balance between things we "have to do"and those we "want to do."

Intervention 2: Group Exercise

Often a discussion about activities leads to the complaint that most pleasant activities cost too much money. Turn this into another group exercise to generate a list of free or low-cost pleasant activities. Other group members can be very helpful with this.

Intervention 2: Group Exercise

Anticipating obstacles: how might your thoughts interfere with engaging in pleasant activities? How can you use thoughts to help you plan and enjoy certain activities? It's often very helpful to put these ideas up on the blackboard as people suggest them and to encourage note-taking.

L. Skill: Pleasure Predicting

Intervention 1: Didactic Presentation (See Concepts and Skills section)

Homework

- Have clients make a personal contract to do a new activity from the pleasant activities list during the coming week. Have them specify in the contract that if they fulfill it they will reward themselves with _____ within two days. This is more powerful if it's written.

- Have clients anticipate how much pleasure an activity will give them. They should write this down before they engage in the activity. Afterwards, they should write how pleasurable the activity actually was and make comments about this. (Negative thinking can diminish the anticipated pleasure, and often inhibits trying.)

- Clients should fill out the Daily Mood Graph and the Beck Depression Inventory.

- Clients should go over the activities list.

Week 7

Introduction

Review all the homework and again use one or two examples up on the blackboard. Stress the lessons that can be learned from the personal contract and pleasure predicting. Point out that you don't have to wait until you feel like doing something to do it — in fact, it's better not to wait. Remind clients that they can choose to do something and it can be enjoyable even if they didn't predict it would be. They can influence their mood with their activities: the more practice they get, the more control they can achieve.

M. Skill: Setting Goals

Intervention 1: Didactic Presentation (See Concepts and Skills section)

Intervention 5: Individual Exercise

To assist with time management, have the group do the following: 1) Make a list of everything they want to accomplish this week and assign each item a priority member: "A" items have highest priority, "B" items are next, and "C" items have lowest priority. 2) Place an "A" item somewhere in their week on a particular day. If there's room to do more on that day, add other items. If not, have clients just do the "A" item. Make sure that they have made room for pleasant activities during their week.

Homework

- Clients should fill out the Daily Mood Graph and the Beck Depression Inventory.

- Clients should review the activities list.

- They should also carry out their specific planned activities for the week.

Week 8

Introduction

Go over the homework and let each client check in on how their plan for the week went. Be positive about attempts made and even small steps taken. Discourage any comparison or competitiveness in the group. Check for cognitive distortions about what is actually being accomplished.

Intervention 3: Group Demonstration

Repeat the blackboard exercise correlating a particular client's mood graph with his or her activity level. The more clients are able to associate their activity level with mood, the more they will feel able to control their moods.

Intervention 5: Individual Exercise

Each group member fills out an Individual Goals form. This form divides goals into three categories: 1) short-term (within one or two months, 2) long-term (at some point in your life), and 3) life goals (your general philosophy of life or what matters most). In addition to these three categories, the form can list Maslow's hierarchy of needs. Other goals to consider include: spiritual, economic, educational, recreational, and those for your level of physical activity. It's important that clients put down only the goals they believe to be important. Have them notice which goals they've already accomplished.

Homework

- Have clients fill out the Daily Mood Graph and the Beck Depression Inventory.

- Clients should review the list of activities.

Week 9

Introduction

Go over homework from the previous week and see if there are any further questions concerning the activities module. Introduce the new module, which focuses on relationships with people.

N. Concept: Improving Interpersonal Relationships

Intervention 1: Didactic Presentation (See Concepts and Skills section)
Intervention 6: Group Discussion of Concepts

O. Skill: Increasing Social Activities

Intervention 1: Didactic Presentation (See Concepts and Skills section)
Intervention 2: Group Exercise

Have clients come up with ideas of places or activities that present opportunities for meeting others. Ideas that come up frequently include adult education classes, health clubs, bingo games, outing groups, cultural or political events, and parks. Clients often have very good ideas for each other, and can gently confront one another's excuses. Have clients generate ideas for activities to which they can invite others: for example, going for a walk, shopping, coffee, dinner, movies, and so on. Have group members practice or role-play inviting someone out.

Homework

- Clients should complete the Daily Mood Graph and the Beck Depression Inventory.

- Clients should review the activities schedule and note their number of contacts with people, marking whether these were positive or negative

Week 10

Introduction

This session continues the work on contacts with people, focusing on the interrelation of thoughts, feelings, and behavior which have an impact on social contacts. You will introduce skills for assertive behavior and general social skills.

Begin by reviewing the homework, emphasizing connections between positive or negative social activities and daily mood. Encourage clients to continue to try out enjoyable activities with other people. Often clients will also bring up conflicts with people which caused their mood to drop. These negative interactions can be used as examples to demonstrate assertive behavior later in the session.

P. Skill: Increasing Assertiveness

Intervention 1: Didactic Presentation (See Concepts and Skills section)

Intervention 2: Group Exercise

Have group members practice role-playing assertive responses to situations, preferably using situations they are currently facing. For example, a client who feels that her son takes advantage of her by asking her to babysit on short notice might work on ways to tell him that she will need more advance notice so that she can make her own plans. Have group members take turns playing the assertive responder.

Q. Skill: Enhancing Social Skills

Intervention 2: Group Exercise

Have participants discuss how they appear to others. First, have them generate a list of what they consider to be socially skilled behaviors. Then have them assess their own behavior and ways in which they would like to improve. Encourage group members to be honest with one another about their positive and negative behaviors. They should consider the following questions: How do you act around others? Do you smile, make eye contact? Is your body slumped or tired-looking? Is your grooming and clothing appropriate? Is your speech too slow or soft? How are your conversation skills — do you show interest in what others say? Do you ignore them or act critical? Do you complain a lot? Can you say what you feel and think?

Intervention 3: Group Demonstration
Role-play actual listening skills with a volunteer from the group.

Intervention 2: Group Exercise
Divide the group into dyads and have one of the pair describe a problem in relationships while the other uses active listening. Have them switch roles. Ask members to provide feedback to each other.

Homework

*   Clients should complete the Daily Mood Graph and the Beck Depression Inventory.

*   Regarding the weekly activities schedule, clients should note the number of contacts with people, and mark whether these were positive or negative.

*   Clients should practice assertiveness with one positive and one negative situation.

Week 11

Introduction

In this session, continue to work on assertiveness and on thoughts and feelings about people. Review homework, again emphasizing connections between people's daily mood and their social interactions. Reinforce clients' efforts to expand their social network or increase social activities, assisting with any problems. Have them share their experiences with assertiveness practice. Encourage them to keep practicing; have group members help generate alternative responses to difficult situations. Try to label any dysfunctional thoughts that are interfering with relationships or assertiveness, then work on alternative thoughts in the session.

R. Skill: Modifying Dysfunctional Thoughts About People

Intervention 1: Didactic Presentation (See Concepts and Skills section)

Intervention 4: Soliciting Examples and Group Discussion

Use the session for open discussion and problem solving around important relationships, integrating the three skills presented in this module. Encourage the group to make a mini treatment plan for each problem discussed. Often parent-child or marital relationships present recurrent problems. For example, a client mentioned earlier felt very bad about her relationship with her adult daughter. She believed that her daughter didn't care about her, and waited each night for her to call, becoming more depressed when her daughter did not. In this case, we worked first on identifying the client's dysfunctional thought — "She doesn't care, she thinks I was a bad mother" — replacing it with "I did the best I could; I won't let her get me down." The client also adjusted her unreasonable expectation of daily calls. She realized that her own decrease in activities had made her expect more of her daughter. Finally, she identified more assertive behavior for herself, including initiating contact with her daughter and telling her daughter how she felt.

In discussing relationships, have participants consider the following areas:

1. What are your thoughts when you're around people?

2. How do you act with people?

3. What are your feelings when you're with others?

Use the group to practice solutions to problems in relationships or social situations currently being faced by participants. Have group members practice asking each other for advice and information. Each person should make a commitment to try to change an aspect of his or her thinking or behavior with people.

Homework

- Clients should fill out the Daily Mood Graph and the Beck Depression Inventory.

- Regarding the weekly activities schedule, clients should note the number of contacts with people, and mark whether these are positive or negative.

- Tell clients: "Practice thinking and behaving differently with someone in your life. Write down problems you would like the group to help with."

Week 12

Introduction

In this session, review concepts on social interaction. Continue the focus on relationships, emphasizing their value in one's life and adaptive ways of viewing difficulties in relationships.

Review homework, emphasizing connections between mood and social interactions. Have clients share their experiences of changing their thinking and behavior in current relationships.

S. Skill: Maintaining Relationships

Intervention 1: Didactic Presentation (See Concepts and Skills section)

Intervention 2: Group Exercise

Have group members share their thoughts about relationships, including feelings about one another or any group members who may be leaving the group. Emphasize what they have learned about relationships by being involved with other group members — for example, that others appreciate their sensitivity, sense of humor, and so on. Continue to practice relationship skills, such as active listening.

Homework

- Clients should fill out the Daily Mood Graph and the Beck Depression Inventory.

- They should also continue to notice pleasant and unpleasant interactions with people, and practice skills to improve relationships.

Criteria for Measuring Change

Several outcome measures are used to assess change. The Beck Depression Inventory, administered weekly, is plotted on an individual graph kept in the client's chart, giving a visual record of the client's progress. The weekly mood graphs completed by the client also demonstrate both a change in mood and an increase in skill utilization. Each client meets individually with a therapist following completion of the group series for a second diagnostic assessment, at which time it is expected that the client will no longer meet the criteria for major depression. Finally, the clients' own reports of a decrease in their depressive symptoms — for example, being able to sleep through the night — demonstrate significant change.

Noncooperation

Clients may have trouble adhering to the principles of the group early in treatment. An initial problem can be motivation to attend the group. We suggest tackling this problem aggressively early in the treatment. For example, at a group orientation session when describing the therapy, say: "Thoughts can keep some people from coming to treatment. Did anyone here have thoughts that almost kept them from coming today?" Work with any dysfunctional thought that might prevent attendance.

Emphasize early in treatment the importance of attendance. Outreach can be very helpful. If a client misses a group, call him or her and discuss the absence. Clients may need help problem solving situations that keep them from coming. This outreach can usually be stopped as soon as the client becomes attached to other group members.

Homework is frequently not completed early on in treatment. Two things are helpful in building an atmosphere that leads to completion of homework. First, the therapists should communicate that they consider the homework to be extremely important. Ask, "How did the homework go for you?" Spend time explaining assignments. Second, when clients do not complete homework, use the framework of therapy to investigate the causes. Ask such questions as, "What thoughts got in the way of your completing your assignment?" *Not* completing homework provides information that can help clients learn about themselves.

Finally, group cohesion is a very helpful tool for assuring adherence to rules. Emphasize that all group members are working to overcome a common problem: depression. This emphasis often helps build group cohesion and thus results in better adherence.

Resisting — Challenging the Therapist

Although many clients can be challenging in this type of therapy, general therapeutic skills are often successful in maintaining a positive atmosphere in the group. Clients who are particularly challenging to therapists often can be dealt within the framework of the therapy. For example, clients who use group time to complain and insist they cannot change can be shown that this thinking may be helping to maintain their depression. Similarly, some patients challenge therapists by suggesting that alternative ways of thinking are not "right." The therapists can emphasize that there are no right or wrong ways of thinking, but there *are* ways of thinking that lead to positive or negative moods. The therapy is not designed to help clients discern "reality," but rather to help them improve their moods.

Relapse

Relapse prevention is an integral part of cognitive-behavioral treatment of depression. In this group program we emphasize teaching clients to identify early symptoms of depression so that they can prevent recurrence of a depressive episode. Clients learn to achieve greater control over their mood by observing and modifying their thoughts, activities, and interactions with people, thus averting a sustained depressed mood. If symptoms begin to recur, clients are encouraged to seek assistance early. Some clients have repeated the program during periods of high vulnerability, for example, following major stresses such as losing a job or having a death in the family. We also currently have a support group consisting of graduates of the program. This group offers informal support and operates on a drop-in basis.

Conclusion

Group cognitive-behavioral treatment of depression offers a quick and effective method for treating depression and preventing recurrence of depressive episodes. Clients benefit both from the supportive environment of the group and from learning specific skills for controlling their moods. The group therapy offers an advantage over individual therapy for many clients by providing support, socialization, and an opportunity to practice new skills during the treatment.

References

Diagnostic and Statistical Manual of Mental Disorders. Second Edition. Washington, D.C.: American Psychiatric Association, 1987.

Beck, A.T.; Rush, A.J.; Shaw, B.F.; and Emery, G. *Cognitive Therapy and Depression.* New York: Guilford Press, 1979.

_____; Ward, C.H.; Mendelson, M.; Mock, J.; and Erbaugh, J. "An inventory for measuring depression." *Archives of General Psychiatry*, 1961, 4, 561-571.

Burns, D.D. *Feeling Good: The New Mood Therapy.* New York: David Morrow & Co., 1980.

Covi, L., and Lipman, R.S. "Cognitive behavioral group psychotherapy combined with Imipramine in major depression. *Psychopharmacology Bulletin*, 1987, 23, 173-176.

Ellis, A., and Dryden, W. *The Practice of Rational Emotive Therapy.* New York: Springer Publishing Co., 1987.

Lewinsohn, P.M.; Antonuccio, D.O.; Breckenridge, J.S.; and Teri, L. *The Coping with Depression Course: A Psychoeducational Intervention for Unipolar Depression.* Eugene, Oregon: Castalia, 1984.

_____; Munoz, R.F.; Youngren, M.A.; and Zeiss, A.M. *Control Your Depression.* New York: Prentice-Hall, 1986.

Myers, J.K.; Weissman, M.M.; Tischler, G.L.; Holzer, C.E.; Leaf, P.L.; Orvaschel, H.; Anthony, J.C.; Boyd, J.H.; Burke, J.B.; Kramer, M.; and Stolzman, R. "Six-month prevalence of psychiatric disorders in three communities." *Archives of General Psychiatry*, 1984, 41, 959-967.

Weissman, M.M.; Leaf, P.J.; Tischler, G.L.; Blazer, D.G.; Karno, M.; Bruce, M.L.; and Florio, L.P. "Affective disorders in five United States communities." *Psychological Medicine*, 1988, *18*, 141-153.

Wells, K.B.; Stewart, A.; Hays, R.D.; Burnam, A.; Rogers, W.; Daniels, M.; Berry, S.; Greenfield, S.; and Ware, J. "The functioning and well-being of depressed patients." *Journal of the American Medical Association*, 1989, *262*, 914-919.

Yalom, I.D. *The Theory and Practice of Group Psychotherapy*. New York: Basic Books, 1970.

Chapter 5

Anger Control Groups

Matthew McKay, Ph.D.

Introduction

Chronic anger is costly, both emotionally and physically. The relationship between hostility and heart disease has now been clearly established (Barefoot et al., 1983; Rosenman, 1985; Shekelle et al., 1983; Williams et al., 1980). Links have also been established between chronic anger and ulcers, gastritis, and colitis (Wolff & Wolf, 1967; Lewis & Lewis, 1972). Recent studies show that hostile individuals have higher death rates *from all causes* (Rosenman, 1985). And one study of chronic anger has shown a death rate as much as four times higher than that of nonhostile individuals (*New York Times*, 1989).

Chronic anger also leads to verbal and physical assault (Hazaleus & Deffenbacher, 1986; Rule & Nesdale, 1976), damage to interpersonal relationships (Hazaleus & Deffenbacher, 1986), loneliness (Jones et al., 1981), and loss of social support (Hansson et al., 1984).

The first major study of anger control strategies was done by Raymond Novaco in 1975. He used a cognitive restructuring technique called Stress Inoculation, in combination with specific relaxation coping skills. Novaco had clients imagine anger-generating scenes while attempting to relax and use more realistic appraisals of upsetting events. While Novaco found that the cognitive control measures had stronger anger-reducing effects than relaxation coping skills, other researchers have found the relaxation procedures to be equally effective (Deffenbacher et al., 1986; Hazaleus & Deffenbacher, 1986). Deffenbacher and others are now recommending that the cognitive and relaxation components be used together because 1) they are both highly effective and the effects remain at a one-year follow-up, 2) they are complementary skills that work in both interpersonal and noninterpersonal situations, and 3) the combined techniques generate greater client satisfaction and less resistance than cognitive control techniques used alone.

Other anger control researchers have emphasized social skills training (mainly assertiveness and behavioral rehearsal) as the proper vehicle for improving relationships and dealing with conflict situations (Moon & Eisler, 1983; Rimm et al., 1974). Social skills training allows clients to rehearse a new repertoire of healthier conflict resolution behaviors.

The anger control group model described here employs all three major anger control interventions: cognitive restructuring, relaxation coping skills, and social skills training. The social skills component is based on a technique called *response choice rehearsal* (McKay, Rogers, & McKay, 1989) that trains clients to use up to six adaptive responses when struggling with an anger-provoking situation.

Selection and Screening

A successful anger control group depends on appropriate selection. Pre-group interviews should be conducted. Ask questions about the duration and quality of relationships that would help you rule out personality disorders. Narcissistic or borderline personality disorders are rarely helped by cognitive and behavioral anger control measures. And they are often disruptive and time-consuming to group members. Ask questions to determine if the client enjoys his or her anger, nurtures it, relies on it, or is otherwise invested in maintaining an anger stance. Clients who experience their anger as rewarding and useful tend to have less success in anger control groups.

Perhaps the best predictor of a positive outcome is the willingness of a client to honestly examine and admit the consequences of poor anger control. Because anger control groups require a great deal of compliance in the form of homework and self-monitoring, you want people who are motivated. Desirable clients are those who recognize what anger has cost in terms of their relationships, health, work life, and so on.

Other types of individuals who should probably be excluded are people who are severely depressed and describe suicidal thoughts and impulses, people with a history of physical violence or who are themselves victims in an abusive relationship, people who have paranoid beliefs that influence their anger responses, and non-recovered alcohol or drug abusers.

If you wish to use an assessment instrument, the State Trait Anger Inventory (Spielberger et al., 1983) has been well researched and is very useful for clinical purposes.

Time and Duration

Groups can be designed to run for either six or twelve weeks. If you wish to confine yourself to the cognitive/relaxation components, six weeks should be sufficient. If you wish to also include the response choice rehearsal training component, expect to double the time commitment to twelve weeks. Sessions should last between one-and-a-half to two hours.

Structure

Clients should make a commitment in advance for the entire duration of the group. Ask clients to stick with it and give feedback about their dissatisfactions instead of dropping out. Because the group's focus in on developing skills, and because each new skill relies, to some extent, on what has previously been learned, it's inadvisable to add new clients during the course of the group.

Groups should consist of five to ten clients. Groups with more than ten members offer each client insufficient opportunities for role-playing, questions, and shared experiences.

Goals

There are two goals for each client. The first is to reduce levels of anger in provocative situations. The second is to learn effective coping behaviors to stop escalation and resolve conflicts.

The goal of the group is *not* to talk about each member's anger experience, to process anger, to understand the individuals' psychodynamics of anger, or to help people ventilate their anger. Because the primary focus of the group is education and skill acquisition, the leader must be highly directive. He or she will initiate most interactions with group members, and there will be typically much less member-to-member interaction than in process-oriented group therapies.

Here is a typical leader description of the group goals and ground rules:

> We have a lot to cover in this group. We're going to have some fun, but we're also going to have to work pretty hard. You can achieve two things here: you can learn to reduce angry feelings, even with difficult people. You can also learn to protect yourself and take care of your needs without anger. To really achieve these goals, you'll have to work at home as well as here. There will be homework to do, and you will begin practicing what you've learned in real situations. Most of our time in here will be spent learning new skills and then practicing them, both in imagination and by role-playing with each other. There's a lot for us to do. Let's see if we can roll up our sleeves and get started.

Starting the Group

The best way to begin is to let clients introduce themselves and describe what made them want to join an anger control group. You should emphasize that each person has a good reason for being in the group, and underscore the themes that are shared by several group members.

At this time, you should discuss the goals and ground rules mentioned in the previous section. This is also a good time to establish the group rules regarding confidentiality.

The last thing you need to explain is the anger log. The log is an indispensable tool for self-observation, facilitating change, and monitoring progress. An anger log entry should include the date and time, the situation, anger-triggering thoughts, emotional arousal (rated on a one-to-ten scale), and aggressive behavior (rated on a one-to-ten scale). Clients should have a separate piece of paper for each date of their log. The easiest thing is to give them handouts with the words *date and time, situation, trigger thoughts, emotional arousal,* and *aggressive behavior* printed across the wide part of an 8-1/2-by-11-inch sheet. Clients can then make their entries down the page.

Main Concepts and Skills

A. Concept: Anger Is a Two -Step Process

"Anger starts with the experience of pain. The pain can be physical or emotional: it can be a stomachache or fatigue, feelings of rejection or loss. The pain leads to arousal, a strong drive for discharge and stress reduction.

The second step in the production of anger occurs when people use *trigger thoughts*. These are attributions that blame and condemn others for the painful experience. Individuals use trigger thoughts to ignite feelings of anger and discharge some of their arousal. So, pain, stress, and arousal lead to blaming trigger thoughts, which lead to anger and more trigger thoughts and more anger in an escalating spiral. Thoughts and angry feelings become a feedback loop that can be self-perpetuating. It is often the feedback loop that keeps anger simmering for hours or even days without letup. It isn't possible to get angry without the presence of both painful arousal and trigger thoughts. That's why you will be taught to control both stress and blaming cognitions."

B. Concept: Ventilation Doesn't Work

"Psychotherapists used to encourage their clients to get angry. But anger is now better understood. New research shows that ventilation only makes you angrier, because you rehearse all the bad and nasty things that others have done to you. It solidifies, or "freezes," your beliefs about another's wrongness and your sense of being victimized. Ventilation not only serves to prolong anger, it also makes it easier to get angry in the future (it doesn't take much to remind you of what a jerk the other guy really is)."

C. Concept: Anger Is Different From Aggression

"Anger is an emotion. It's what happens when pain, stress, or arousal, and blaming trigger thoughts, combine to *create* feelings of anger. Aggression is *behavior*. It's something you do; it's a way of interacting with other people. Aggression can be in the form of either physical or verbal assault. You can be angry without being aggressive, and vice versa. Hit men are rarely angry when they pull the trigger; conversely, many angry people choose not to assault the target of their wrath."

D. Concept: Coping Is Better Than Blaming

"Every painful situation presents a choice. You can blame somebody for what happened or you can use cognitive and relaxation coping skills to reduce your feelings of being upset, and then assert your needs in a nonblaming way. If you tell a roommate that she is lazy for not doing her chores, it really feels good for a minute to get it off your chest. But things will likely escalate from there. You both may end up shouting; your relationship may descend into the deep freeze. In a few weeks, it will be possible to make another choice. You might decide to use some relaxation skills to lower your stress level, change some of your trigger thoughts, and talk to your roommate nonblamingly about the problem of the chores. Very soon that really will be a choice you can make."

Relaxation Skills

Mastery of basic relaxation skills is essential to anger management. Particularly during the early stages of anger arousal, relaxation training can be extremely helpful in reducing tension and promoting effective coping strategies.

E. Skill: Progressive Muscle Relaxation

"Make a fist with each hand and squeeze tight. Really concentrate on the feeling of tension in your fists and forearms. Hold for several seconds. Now relax. Feel the difference in your muscles. Notice a heaviness or warmth or tingling or whatever relaxation feels like for you. Now raise your arms and tighten them in a 'Charles Atlas' pose, flexing your biceps. Hold the tension for seven seconds, then let your arms fall limp by your sides. Once again notice feelings of relaxation, of warmth or heaviness spreading through your arms as you let them drop. Really notice the contrast between tension and relaxation in your arms.

"Now turn your attention to your upper face. Frown, squint your eyes shut as hard as you can, hold for seven seconds. Relax, and notice what it feels like to let go of tension in your upper face. Now tighten your jaw (not so hard that you'll crack a tooth) and push your tongue up against the roof of your mouth. Hold it for seven seconds. And relax. Notice what it feels like for your jaw to let go, to be really loose. Now tense your neck muscles by shrugging your shoulders upward as far as you can (but don't try to pull your neck in like a turkey). Wait a moment, and relax. Let the relaxation move from your shoulders and neck up to your jaw and all the way to your forehead.

"Now move your awareness to your chest and back. Take a deep breath and hold it. Tense your chest, shoulders, and upper back muscles, making your entire upper torso rigid. Take another deep breath. After seven seconds, let out the breath with a long, loud sigh, and let your torso go limp. Really melt down into the chair and focus on the difference between the tense and the relaxed states.

"Now move your attention downward — into your stomach, lower back, and pelvic regions. Tighten your stomach, lower back and buttocks carefully. After seven seconds, relax and melt again into the chair. Notice feelings of warmth or heaviness spreading throughout your abdomen.

"Now work on your legs. With your toes pointed straight out, like a ballerina, tense your thighs, your calves, and your feet. Hold this for seven seconds, then let your legs totally relax. Feel the heaviness and warmth flood into your legs as they go limp. Now tense your legs again, this time pulling your toes up toward your head. Hold for seven seconds and let the relaxation spread like a wave throughout your entire body, into your abdomen and your chest, into your arms, your neck, your face and forehead, until you feel totally relaxed. Take another deep breath."

F. Skill: Relaxation Without Tension

Take clients through the major muscle groups in exactly the same sequence as your progressive muscle relaxation script. But this time don't have them tighten anything. Instead, have them scan each muscle group for tension and *relax away* any tightness they may experience. The catch phrase *Notice and relax* should be used frequently throughout this exercise. Be sure to begin and end the *relaxation without tension* exercise with a deep breath.

"Take a deep breath. Focus on your arms and notice any tension you may feel there. Now relax away the tension. Just let it go. Notice and relax the tension. Feel the difference as you relax your arms.

"Now turn your attention to your upper face. Notice any tension and relax it away. Let it go. Notice and relax the tension. As you relax, really feel the difference in your upper face. Notice any tension in your jaw, and relax. Relax it away. Notice what it feels like for your jaw to let go, to be really loose...."

G. Skill: Special Place Visualization

"Think about a place where you've felt especially safe, relaxed, or content. It could be the beach, mountains, meadows, your childhood bedroom, or a remembered moment of deep relaxation and peace. It can be a real place, or you could just make one up. Close your eyes and try to see the shapes and colors of your place...hear the sounds of your place, hear birds, or waves or babbling water...feel the temperature of your place — is it cool or warm?...feel the textures of whatever you touch in your special place.

"Make sure that everything in your special place makes you feel relaxed and safe. Change anything that doesn't feel right. If you want to add some trees, put them in. If you want the sound of a waterfall, add it. If you want to be alone, take the people out of your scene. If you want your dog, put him in."

When group members are satisfied with their ability to visualize, say the following: "I'd like you to use your special place visualization quickly, almost like a reflex, when things get stressful. Go ahead and visualize your special place, construct the scene as quickly as you can, really get into it until you feel the peacefulness, the safety, the relaxation. [Pause one minute.] Now get ready to leave the scene. Open your eyes, look around. Notice the people in the group, our room, the environment. [Pause.] Now close your eyes again and return to your special place. See it, hear it, feel it, let it surround you and touch each of your senses. [Pause one minute.] Now, if you will, come back to the room and take a quick look at other group members. [Pause.] One last time go back to the special place. Get there as quickly as you can, let it bathe your senses, see its shapes and colors, hear the sounds, feel it in your skin. [Pause one minute.] Now come back to the room. You can go to your special place any time you need to relax, to get out of a situation that provokes or disturbs you."

H. Skill: Breathing-Cued Relaxation

"Start by putting one hand over your chest and the other over your abdomen, just above your belt line. Try taking a deep breath, way down into your belly. Really try to push your diaphragm down. As you breathe in, the hand on your abdomen should rise, while the hand on your chest remains relatively still. Focus all your attention on your belly — send your breath down, down, down to fill your belly. Let your breath slightly stretch, and relax your abdomen."

I. Skill: Cue-Controlled Relaxation

"Now it's time to select a word that will cue deep relaxation each time you repeat it. The word could be *relax* or *om* or *one*. It might be a color, such as *green*, or a feeling, such as *love*. One- or two-syllable words are best.

"With your cue word in mind, turn your attention again to your breathing. With each exhalation, say your cue word to yourself. Keep saying your cue word for the next ten breaths."

J. Skill: Combined Relaxation

Go through the entire progressive muscle relaxation procedure. At the end of this, ask clients to return to their special place imagery. After one minute, ask clients to come back into the room and take a series of three deep, abdominal breaths. Make sure that the abdominal hand is rising, while the chest hand remains relatively still. Then, for the next ten breaths, have clients repeat their cue word for relaxation. Remind them to say their special word with each exhalation.

Cognitive Control Concepts

K. Concept: ABC Cognitive Theory

"Imagine that you're working in an office where several co-workers play radios at their desks. The sound is low, but you nevertheless find it distracting. Really visualize the scene for a moment. Now imagine that you are saying to yourself how inconsiderate they are, how selfish, how uncaring of the needs of others. Imagine yourself thinking that they're doing this to you because they simply don't give a damn about anyone but themselves. Do you notice your feeling?" Elicit a discussion about group members' angry reactions. "Now let's imagine something else. You're in the same office, the same co-workers are playing their radios. But instead, you say to yourself: 'I can't think, I can't concentrate, I'm never going to get my work done. I'm never going to get this in on time. I'm not going to be able to function here. How can I keep my job if I can't do a simple task like this when there's a little noise?' What feeling comes up now?" Look for and reinforce any responses that have to do with anxiety. "Now let's go back to the same situation once more. The radios are playing and you think to yourself, 'I never fit in anywhere, things always bother me, and my colleagues will probably be resentful if I ask them to turn their radios down. I'm so rattlebrained that I can't even think with a little music in the background. I can't handle the slightest stress or problem.' What do you feel now?" Encourage a brief discussion about some of the depressed reactions.

Now explain Ellis' ABC model of emotion, where A (event) leads to B (thought, interpretation, assumption, appraisal), which in turn leads to C (emotion). "When you get angry, it feels as though the event is making you angry. It feels as though somebody is doing something to you and the only natural response is anger. What really happens is that the event starts you thinking. Like the person in the office, you can think different kinds of thoughts. You can think about dangerous or catastrophic consequences and get anxious, or you can think about your failures and inadequacies and get depressed. Or you can think blaming thoughts and label others as bad or selfish or stupid. Then you get angry.

"The same situation will produce different emotions, depending on what you think about it. That's where the trigger thoughts come in. You can't really get angry until you respond to the situation with trigger thoughts that get you hot. Right now, we have an opportunity to learn some thoughts that will cool down the anger response. These are thoughts that take away the sting of blame and help you look at things with a little more detachment.

"Imagine you were in that office with the radios and you said to yourself, 'This is no big deal. They're having a good time. They don't know they're bugging me. I'll find a diplomatic way to get them to turn the radios down.' Notice that these are cooling thoughts. The anger melts away as you stop blaming. You begin to feel that there's something you can do about it."

L. Concept: Trigger Thoughts

Shoulds

"Anger is heard often as a judgment based on a set of rules about how people should and should not act. People who behave according to the rules are right, and those who break the rules are wrong. Angry people think that others know and accept their rules, and deliberately choose to violate them. The first problem with shoulds, however, is that people with whom you feel angry rarely agree with you.

Their perception of the situation leaves them blameless and justified. Other people's rules always seem to exempt them from the judgments you think they deserve. The second problem with shoulds is that people *never* do what they should do. They only do what is reinforcing and rewarding for them to do. It turns out that shoulds are one person's values and needs imposed on someone else who has very different values and needs." Below are some coping responses to shoulds. You can go over these with your clients, or pass them around as a handout before going on with your explanation.

1. What needs influence him or her to act this way?

2. What problems, fears, or limitations influence this behavior?

3. What beliefs or values influence him or her to act this way?

4. Forget the shoulds, they only get me upset.

5. People do what *they* want to do, not what *I* think they should do.

"There are three special types of shoulds that are particularly upsetting. Let me describe, first of all, the entitlement fallacy."

Entitlement. "The entitlement fallacy is based on the simple belief that because you want something very much, you ought to have it. The degree of your need justifies the demand that someone else provide for it. The underlying feeling is that you are entitled to certain things in life, and if you don't get them, someone is deliberately or selfishly or maliciously depriving you.

"The problem with entitlement is that a person confuses desire with obligation. It feels as though wanting something very much somehow makes it unacceptable for others to say no. But entitlement can be very damaging to relationships. It requires that the other person give up his or her limits and boundaries for you. It says that your need and your pain must come first." Some relevant coping statements are listed below:

1. I am free to want, but he or she is free to say no.

2. I have my limits and you have your limits.

3. I have the right to say no, and so do you.

4. My desire doesn't obligate you to meet it.

Fairness. "The fallacy of fairness rests on the idea that there is some absolute standard of correct and fair behavior which people should understand and live up to. When you believe that the concept of fairness applies to relationships, you end up keeping an emotional ledger book that balances what you give against what you get in a relationship. The problem is that no two people agree on what fairness is, and in personal relationships, there is no court or arbiter to help them. What's fair becomes a totally subjective judgment, depending entirely on what each person expects, needs, or hopes for from the other. Since the standard of fairness is inevitably a measure of one's own beliefs and wants, people can literally call anything fair or unfair. Calling someone unfair just inflames the argument. It never convinces anyone or solves a conflict." You might suggest the following coping statements:

1. Our needs are equally important.

2. Each need is legitimate — we can negotiate.

Change. "The fallacy of change is based on the conviction that you can really make people different if you apply sufficient pressure. If you just appeal to them enough, or rag on them, or blame them enough, they will start doing what you want.

"The problem is that people only change when 1) change is reinforced and 2) they are capable of the change. In other words, people change when *they* want to, not when *you* want them to. And the sad part is, the angrier you get, the more people dig in and resist you. They get stubborn and immovable." Clients can use these coping statements:

1. People change only when change is reinforced and they are capable of changing.

2. People only change when they want to.

Blamers

"This is the feeling that *they did it to you*. Whatever pain you feel, whatever hurt or fear or deprivation, they did it to you. One problem with blaming is that it leaves you feeling helpless. Whatever is wrong, whatever is hurting you, it feels as though the power to solve the problem lies with others. When you get stuck in blaming, you forget that you can do something, that you have the ability to make the situation different. You forget that there are choices you can make, because your main concern is with the other person's behavior.

"The other problem with blaming is that people are mostly doing the best they can. We always choose the action that seems the most likely to meet our needs. Sometimes what we do disappoints or hurts others. But the main objective of any action is to take care of ourselves. When we blame others for what they're doing, we're blaming them for taking care of themselves in the best way they know how at the moment." The following pair of coping statements may be useful for your clients:

1. I may not like it, but they're doing the best they can.

2. I'm not helpless — I can take care of myself in this situation.

"There are three special categories of blamers that are frequent triggers for anger. The first one is assumed intent."

Assumed intent. "Assumed intent is really mind-reading. You assume that whatever has happened is the consequence of someone's deliberate effort to do you harm. A friend is late for dinner and you feel like he's deliberately trying to annoy you. You assume that your mother is trying to put you down when she asks where you got a certain piece of furniture. The problem with assuming that someone is trying deliberately to harm you is that you can never really know another person's true motives. *Assume* means that you think you know, but you never ask. An assumption of mind-reading is so often wrong, and yet it is probably the greatest source of anger." You can suggest the following coping statements:

1. Assume nothing, or else check out every assumption.

2. Don't second-guess the motives of others.

3. No one is a mind-reader.

Magnification. "Magnifying is the tendency to make things worse than they are. You anticipate that something awful is going to happen. You think of events as *terrible, awful, disgusting,* or *horrendous.* Or you overgeneralize by using words such as *always, all, every, never.* 'He's always as slow as molasses…She's awful with the whole support staff…He never helps…This is going to be a horrible mess next week.' These magnifications tend to crank up your sense of anxiety, and of being victimized. When you exaggerate the problem, you start to feel really deeply wronged. They're bad and you're innocent." Suggest that clients use these coping statements:

1. No more *always* or *never.*

2. Let the facts speak for themselves.

3. Accuracy, not exaggeration.

Global labeling. "Global labeling is the act of making sweeping negative judgments. You label people as bad, stupid, selfish, assholes, screw-ups, and so on. Global labels fuel your anger by turning the other person into someone who is totally bad and worthless. Instead of focusing on a particular behavior, you indict the entire person. You inflate one aspect of the person to fill the entire picture of who he or she is. Once you've made someone totally despicable, it's very easy to get angry." Clients can use these coping statements:

1. No one's bad — people do the best they can.

2. No mean labels.

3. Be specific.

You can use the following list of coping thoughts as a handout:

For trigger thoughts:

- Forget shoulds — they only upset me.

- People do what *they* want to do, not what *I* think they should do.

- I am free to want, but she is free to say no.

- I have the right to say no, and so do they.

- My desire doesn't obligate them to fulfill it.

- Our needs are equally important.

- Each need is legitimate — we can negotiate.

- People change only when change is reinforced and they are capable of changing.

- People only change when they want to.

- I may not like it, but they're doing the best they can.

- I'm not helpless — I can take care of myself in this situation.

- Don't second-guess the motives of others.

- Assume nothing, or else check out every assumption.

- No more *always* or *never.*

- Accuracy, not exaggeration.

- No one's bad, people do the best they can.
- No mean labels.

General coping thoughts and strategies:

- Take a deep breath and relax.
- Getting upset won't help.
- Just as long as I keep my cool, I'm in control.
- Easy does it — there's nothing to be gained in getting mad.
- I'm not going to let him get to me.
- I can't change her with anger; I'll just upset myself.
- I can find a way to say what I want to without anger.
- Stay calm — no sarcasm, no attacks.
- I can stay calm and relaxed.
- No one is right, no one is wrong. We just have different needs.
- Stay cool, make no judgments.
- No matter what is said, I know I'm a good person.
- I'll stay rational — anger won't solve anything.
- I don't like it, but he's using the best problem-solving strategy available to him right now.
- Her opinion isn't important — I won't be pushed into losing my cool.

Response Choice Rehearsal

M. Concept: Description of Response Choice Rehearsal (RCR)

"Response choice rehearsal is a method for handling conflict that has the advantage of requiring very little thought or preparation. You can do it when you're stressed and you don't have time to plan a response. You can still do it even when your buttons are pushed, you're getting angry, and you want to smash somebody. The bad news is that you'll have to memorize the six RCR responses (see RCR handout). But the good news is that they really will work to de-escalate some of your conflicts *while making room for real problem solving.*" The following list of *RCR opening lines* can be used as a handout:

Active Responses

1. *Ask for what you want:* I'm feeling [what's bothering me is] _____. And what I think I need [want/would like] in this situation is _____.

Passive Responses

4. *Get information:* What do you need in this situation? What concerns [worries] you in this situation? What's hurting [bothering] you in this situation?

2. *Negotiate:* What would you propose to solve this problem?

3. *Self-Care:* If [the problem] goes on, I'll have to [your self-care solution] in order to take care of myself.

5. *Acknowledge:* So what *you* want is _____. So what concerns [worries] *you* is _____. So what hurts [bothers] *you* is _____.

6. *Withdraw:* It feels like we're starting to get upset. I want to stop and cool off for a while.

Once clients have had an opportunity to examine the RCR handout, emphasize the following six points:

1. RCR consists of six prelearned strategies for adaptively coping with angry encounters.

2. Strategies are divided into active and passive responses.

3. RCR will help you to cope even when you are extremely angry.

4. RCR will enable you to learn adaptive reactions that help solve problems rather than escalate tension.

5. RCR will keep you from getting stuck with a response that isn't working, and will make it more likely that you'll find a response that will get you what you want.

6. RCR will help you experience anger as a signal to cope and try a new response rather than as a signal to escalate your angry feelings.

"When one RCR response doesn't work (because you're just too angry or things are still escalating), you simply choose another one. Eventually, you'll find a response that decreases tension and gives you enough emotional safety to start reaching for some kind of agreement.

"You'll notice that there are active and passive responses. Either kind can be effective. But the key to understanding how to use RCR is to keep in mind that no single response is likely to be the right one, the answer. The first thing you try might not have much impact on your anger or on the anger of the provoking person. Your second response still might not work. Even your third may be a complete miss. But taken together, a series of adaptive responses is highly likely to cool you down and eventually de-escalate the conflict. Sooner or later, you're going to find something that will turn the anger around, or at least get you out of the situation.

"In RCR, you use your anger as a red flag that signals you to switch to a new coping response. So instead of fueling more aggression, your anger is a sign to change tack, to shift your strategies. Anger is merely an indication that you're stuck: the current response isn't working, isn't solving the problem. When you're proficient at RCR, anger will just mean, 'I'd better try something new.'"

N. Skill: RCR Switching

The following rules will help clients learn how to shift successfully from one RCR response to another as they cope in a provocative situation.

1. All of the lines must be memorized to the point where they can be recalled without effort.

2. Whenever possible, rehearse in advance active response numbers one and three. Decide if you wish to include your feelings about the situation. Then formulate your request and your fallback position. Make sure it's behavioral and specific. Also try to generate a self-care response. Ask yourself how you can take care of the problem *without* the other person's cooperation.

3. Continued anger or escalation is your signal to *switch* responses. Don't get stuck if a response isn't working. Move on to what you feel, intuitively, is the next best option.

4. Don't be afraid to repeat responses. You may wish to return, several times, to questions that get more information. You may wish to acknowledge what you're learning about the other person's experience. And as the discussion progresses, you may wish to invite another round of negotiation.

5. If you don't know what to do next, try shifting from active to passive responses (or vice versa). If you've been focusing on getting information, try expressing your own needs. If you're stuck in fruitless negotiation, consider asking for information.

6. As a rule, start with active response one (ask for what you want) when you're angry or want something changed. Start with passive response four (get information) when the other person is angry and on the attack.

7. Keep shifting among responses until the problem feels resolved or further communication feels pointless. If you're still angry and stuck, go to one of the exit responses (either self-care or withdrawal).

Encourage clients to use the following two coping thoughts whenever a response isn't working and they need to switch:

1. Take a deep breath and relax.

2. I have a plan to cope with this. What's the next step?

Main Interventions

Week 1

Introduction

Now is the time to introduce didactically the four general concepts about anger described in the Concepts and Skills section:

A. Concept: Anger Is a Two-Step Process

B. Concept: Ventilation Doesn't Work

C. Concept: Anger Is Different From Aggression

D. Concept: Coping Is Better Than Blaming

Encourage discussions of each concept. Ask clients to share any doubts or objections that have come up in their minds.

E. Skill: Progressive Muscle Relaxation

Start by explaining that learning to relax can calm people down sufficiently in a provocative situation so that they can manage to think of better ways to handle the conflict. Then read the progressive relaxation script provided in the Concepts and Skills section.

F. Skill: Relaxation Without Tension

Instructions are in the Concepts and Skills section. Relaxation without tension can be substituted for progressive muscle relaxation when clients wish to use a quicker, less obvious technique. It can be used anywhere, without the potentially embarrassing ritual of progressive muscle relaxation.

G. Skill: Special Place Visualization

Help every group member identify his or her special relaxation image. Use the script provided in the Concepts and Skills section. Make sure that the major senses are involved. Group members should be able to see the shapes and colors, hear the sounds, feel the temperature and textures of their special place. If there are smells and tastes, include these also. Have individuals work carefully on constructing the image, developing as much detail as possible. Make sure that the image is capable of eliciting the emotion of contentment, safety, and calmness. Have several group members describe their scenes and discuss any problems they may have in image construction.

Homework

- "Daily monitoring through the anger log.
- "Practice progressive muscle relaxation, relaxation without tension, and imagining the special place at least once each day for the next week." Have clients put a *p* at the top of each day of the anger log when they have practiced.

Week 2

Introduction

Go over the homework. Explore any problems with the progressive muscle relaxation or the special place visualizations. Also explore any observations clients are making about their anger behavior as a result of self-monitoring.

H. Skill: Breathing-Cued Relaxation

Use the instructions contained in the Concepts and Skills section. Emphasize that this deep-breathing technique stretches the diaphragm and very quickly relaxes abdominal tension associated with anger. It's crucial that clients succeed in pushing the belly out with each intake of breath. Monitor each client to be certain that there is at least a rudimentary mastery of deep breathing.

I. Skill: Cue-Controlled Relaxation

See instructions in the Concepts and Skills section.

J. Skill: Combined Relaxation

See instructions in the Concepts and Skills section. This is the opportunity for clients to put all their relaxation skills together into one sequence. Go over the sequence at least twice. Emphasize that it should be practiced at home to the point where it is "overlearned" and automatic.

K. Concept: ABC Cognitive Theory

A didactic description of cognitive theory is offered in the Concepts and Skills section.

L. Concept: Trigger Thoughts

Give clients a handout describing the major trigger thoughts. After a didactic explanation of each trigger thought (see the Concepts and Skills section), discuss the coping rejoinders and ask the group for ideas about additional coping statements. Also ask for examples of when group members have used a particular trigger thought to ignite anger.

Homework

- Ask clients to go through the coping statement handout and mark the responses that seem most useful to them.

- "Continue self-monitoring in the anger log."

- Ask clients to select two low-anger (rated three to four on a ten-point scale) scenes to work with during the next week.

- "Practice the complete relaxation sequence of progressive muscle relaxation (or relaxation without tension), special place visualization, breathing-cued relaxation, and cue-controlled relaxation daily for the next week. Mark a p on the practice log for each day of relaxation practice completed."

Week 3

Introduction

Go over the homework. Discuss any problems with the relaxation practice. Explore what clients are discovering through self-monitoring. Some of the clients may have noticed changes at this point. Open a discussion about how changes in the experience of anger may be reflected in frequency, intensity, or duration of anger. Give feedback about changes in any of these three dimensions. It is particularly important to begin to emphasize situations in which clients are acting and coping differently, relaxing instead of blowing up, or perhaps using coping statements to replace anger-triggering thoughts.

Cognitive Control/Relaxation Training

It's now time to combine cognitive and stress-reduction techniques. The best way to achieve this is through the use of imagery.

Intervention: Coping Skill Rehearsal

Clients should come prepared with two anger scenes in the three-to-four range. Explore some of these scenes with certain group members and help them develop the sensory detail that will make the scenes come alive. Also, make sure that clients are including in the scene trigger thoughts and any physiological sensations of anger arousal. This process will help other group members add the necessary details to their scenes to evoke viscerally some angry feelings.

Now, using the same client scenes you've been discussing, ask group members to think of coping responses that might block or diminish some of the trigger thoughts. Individuals can use the coping statements handout for ideas, or develop their own creative coping responses.

This is a critical time for you as a group leader. You will need to strongly reinforce appropriate coping statements, and at the same time, show why some coping suggestions are inappropriate for the particular anger scene. The more active you are at this juncture, the more clients will learn about how to develop appropriate coping responses.

Therapist:	Jill, what's your anger scene?
Jill:	John's late picking up the kids again and the play-school people call. He's always late, it really ticks me off.
Therapist:	Okay, what kind of trigger thoughts did you use?
Jill:	I guess I'm saying he *should* be there. Also, I'm magnifying a bit — he's not *always* late.
Therapist:	How could you cope with the trigger thought — what could you say to yourself that would cool the anger:
Jill:	I guess I could remind myself that he's only late once in a while, and it's usually because he's harried.
Therapist:	Anything else that would help from the coping thoughts handout?
Jill:	He does the best he can.
Therapist:	Does that really help — do you believe that at all?
Jill:	Not really.
Therapist:	How about a more general coping statement that just reminds you to calm down, or that anger doesn't help?
Jill:	Yeah. "There's nothing gained in getting mad." That's true. I just get crazy for nothing.

It's time to begin *coping skill rehearsal*. Here's what you do.

1. Have clients go through their complete relaxation sequence: progressive muscle relaxation, relaxation without tension, special place visualization, breathing-cued relaxation, and cue-controlled relaxation. Have clients signal that they are fully relaxed by raising their hands.

2. Now ask them to visualize one of the anger scenes they chose during their previous week's homework. Encourage them to get involved in the scene as if it were really happening. Remind them to use their trigger thoughts and to

notice any feelings of arousal. Ask clients to signal, by raising their hands, that they have become angry.

3. When clients have experienced anger for approximately 30 seconds, ask them to erase the scene and return to some of their relaxation coping skills. Suggest that clients use several of the coping thoughts that might be helpful in the situation. Have them signal, by raising their hands, when they once again feel relaxed.

4. Repeat the entire sequence, using the second anger scene.

5. Have a group discussion about the coping statements that seem to work best. Particular attention should be paid to clients who have problems generating effective coping statements. Both group members and the group leader can help with the development of more effective coping responses.

So, Mary, it looks like the trigger thoughts you're using in the situation really kind of magnify your feeling that something bad or awful is going to happen, is that right? But your coping statements don't seem to work.... [Turning to the group] Are there coping statements we can develop that would change this into a problem or a hassle, but not an overwhelming nightmare? What could Mary say to herself that would demagnify her feelings in this situation?

When you're helping clients build an anger scene, be sure to pay attention to each element of the experience. Here is an example: "Okay, now that you're relaxed, I'm going to ask you to turn on one of your anger scenes. Really try to be there. Notice the setting, the details, the colors, and the shapes. Notice any sounds. Notice your physical sensations in the scene. Try to make it real. Remember your trigger thoughts — really let yourself go. Get into the blamers or the shoulds. Tell yourself you're entitled to better treatment, or they're being unfair. Tell yourself they're doing it to you. Label it bad or stupid or selfish. As your anger builds, notice what it feels like inside your body. Notice the arousal and growing tension. Where in your body does the tension grow first? As you notice the tension, try to let yourself get even angrier. Keep fanning the flames. What's the matter with them, anyway? Why do they keep doing this to you? Angrier. Angrier and angrier. Really feeling it in your body. Tell yourself how outrageous, how wrong, how unfair. Feel more and more anger."

Throughout the scene induction, clients will be raising their hands to signal that they have become angry. When everybody's hand has been up for at least 30 seconds, you can terminate the scene and return them to relaxation methods of their choice. After they've switched the scene off, remind them of some general coping statements they can make:

• Everyone makes the best choice possible.

• I can stay calm and relaxed.

• No one is right, no one is wrong. We just have different needs.

• Getting upset won't help.

• There's nothing to be gained in getting mad.

• I'm free to want things, but others are also free to say no.

Continue to repeat the relaxation/anger scene/relaxation sequence up to six times. After the first two sequences, ask clients to use relaxation without tension instead of progressive muscle relaxation. It saves time. Following each sequence, have group members describe their coping thoughts and discuss which ones are working and not working in a particular anger scene. Help them modify their coping thoughts or develop new ones. If you're having difficulty developing coping thoughts that help, go back to the trigger thoughts and get a clear sense of what the client is saying to ignite anger. Explore how the trigger thought may be unrealistic in the situation and help the client develop a more realistic appraisal of what is likely to be going on. Since the clients prepared two anger scenes as part of their past week's homework, make sure that they alternate scenes during repetitions. However, if one scene isn't working to generate real anger, have the client drop it and use the other.

Homework

- "Practice relaxation without tension daily, as well as other relaxation techniques." Remind clients to mark a *p* in the anger log for each day of completed practice.

- Now in the anger log have clients record their coping efforts under each anger situation. Have them note whether emotional arousal and/or aggression scores decreased after coping procedures.

- Have clients select two more anger scenes, this time in the five-to-six range, for use in the next week's group session.

Week 4

Introduction

Focus on the homework, the relaxation practice, and, in particular, on situations in which clients are beginning to use new coping skills. Make a big deal of this. Make detailed inquiries about the particular efforts clients are making and how those efforts affect arousal and aggression. Ask if there are clients whose coping statements are not working. Look at some of the situations in which coping skills have not worked and encourage group discussion about new attitudes or coping statements that might yield a better result.

Try to encourage discussion of a variety of anger situations: anger episodes that come from brooding long after the event, anger immediately following some highly charged event, anger in traffic, leftover anger from situations in which it was too scary to speak up, and so on.

More Coping Skills Rehearsal

Make sure that clients have selected two anger scenes in the five-to-six range. If they have not done their homework, ask them to recall scenes from their anger log that fall into this arousal range.

Now repeat exactly the coping skills rehearsal procedure outlined in Week 3. Make the same effort to ensure that scenes really come alive and generate authentic anger reactions.

Homework

- "Continue relaxation practice.

- Continue the anger log, with particular attention on the coping process in each anger situation." Make sure that clients rate any changes in emotional arousal and aggression following their coping response.

- "Generate two anger scenes in the seven-to-eight range that will be used during the next group session."

Week 5

Introduction

Now is the time to pay a lot of attention to what's working. Have clients discuss in detail situations in which relaxation or cognitive control measures reduced their anger response. Celebrate what works. Get excited about success. If clients describe less arousal but aren't quite sure why, try to help them identify new attitudes or ways of thinking that are helping them stay more relaxed.

Also, pay some attention to anger situations in which clients feel less in control. Do some digging to expose the trigger statements. "You're really expecting them to come through for you, aren't you?…That's kind of a big should, isn't it?…It really sounds like you're expecting disaster to strike if they don't do it your way…. It's when you use that word 'selfish' that you really seem to get incensed." Have the group discuss other ways of coping with the problematic situation.

Intervention: Coping Skills Rehearsal — Coping in the Scene

Have people identify, if they have not done their homework, the two anger scenes that they'll use in the seven-to-eight range. Spend some time having clients describe their scenes and facilitate group discussion about coping statements that might be helpful.

This week, the coping skills rehearsal will have a slightly different structure. From now on, clients will not leave the anger scene 30 seconds after they have experienced arousal. Instead, they'll be instructed to remain in the scene and practice their relaxation and cognitive coping skills *while the anger scene continues*. Here's what the instructions sound like:

> Really get into the anger scene — remember your trigger thoughts, really try to feel the growing tension on a physical level. Remind yourself of the unfairness, the wrongness, the outrageousness of the offense. [A few hands go up, signaling anger.] When you really feel the anger, start your coping responses. Keep pushing, keep pushing up the anger. [More hands.] But once you get there, once you're angry, start relaxing. Start breathing deeply. Recall your special place. Focus on your body; notice tension and relax it away. Talk back to the trigger thoughts. What can you say to cope? Try some coping statements and see which ones work. Do whatever works for you to cool down. Your hand should stay up until you've found a way to control anger. When you've controlled your anger, let your hand drop and terminate the scene. When you've relaxed away your anger, when you've talked back to your anger, when you've coped with your anger, let your hand drop and terminate the scene.

Clients are expected to keep working on the scene until they have mastered the anger. As soon as they are sufficiently aroused and have raised their hands, they switch immediately into the coping mode. Their hands remain raised until their anger feels controlled and they're beginning to relax. Once the scene is terminated, clients should continue the cognitive and relaxation coping efforts until the next anger scene is introduced. Continue this process for up to six repetitions. Always alternate between the two anger scenes.

After several cycles, initiate a discussion with the group about what's working and what's not working in controlling anger. Celebrate some successes. Pay a lot of attention to clients who are beginning to feel some mastery as they relax and talk away anger arousal in the scene. Clients who are having problems should also get attention. Examine carefully their coping procedures and generate group discussion about ways to modify the coping process. It's always appropriate to suggest new coping responses if clients are struggling with their current ones. If anger in a particular scene is very difficult to control, once again explore the trigger thoughts. Help the client develop more realistic appraisals in the problematic situation.

Therapist:	How are you doing with the scene, George?
George:	I get pissed off, but then I stay upset. The anger has a life of its own.
Therapist:	What are your trigger thoughts?
George:	That my girlfriend's selfish, that she doesn't care about me.
Therapist:	What have you tried to say to yourself to cope?
George:	That we each have different needs, that I shouldn't assume the worst about her.
Therapist:	But that doesn't work.
George:	Not a bit.
Therapist:	Ideas from the group?
Al:	How about just reminding yourself to stop judging her?
Sylvia:	Focus on asking for what you want and assume you'll both have to compromise.
Mark:	How 'bout just telling yourself to say what you want without anger?
Therapist:	Any of that helpful?
George:	I think just reminding myself to tell her what I want without anger.
Therapist:	Are you remembering to take a deep breath?
George:	I didn't really do that.
Therapist:	That will help, too. What makes your girlfriend so adamant at times? Do you know?
George:	She thinks I don't spend enough time with her.
Therapist:	Does that mean she's afraid you don't care about her, too?
George:	I guess that might be true.
Therapist:	So you could say to yourself, "We're both scared here, I'd better deal with this without anger."

Homework

- Continue relaxation practice.

- Continue self-monitoring, paying particular attention to the coping efforts in each anger situation. Continue to rate emotional arousal and aggression *after* the coping efforts.

- Develop two high-anger scenes, in the nine-to-ten range, for use in the next group session.

Week 6

Procedures are identical to Week 5.

At the end of the session, pass out the handout on Response Choice Rehearsal (RCR) *opening lines*.

Homework

- "Continue monitoring anger and coping in the anger log.

- Memorize RCR response 1."

Week 7

Introduction

Review homework from the previous week. Again, emphasize the positive. Review and celebrate coping successes.

Invite reactions to the RCR *opening lines* handout. There will be resistance, so accept this. Encourage people to reserve judgment until they have learned the whole package of responses and have begun testing them in real-life situations.

M. Concept: Description of Response choice Rehearsal (RCR)

Using the description contained in the Concepts and Skills section, go through each of the RCR responses. Emphasize that not all six of the responses will be appropriate for a given anger situation. Emphasize the concept of switching from one response to another to cope with growing anger or escalation. Although a single anger control strategy often fails during provocations, the ability to use a variety of strategies and responses in succession increases the likelihood of resolution.

The key attitude to convey to clients is problem solving rather than vengeance. This is a slightly different version of the earlier "cope-don't-blame" dichotomy. An avenger wants to punish and injure the offending party to the same degree that he or she has been hurt. Pain must be paid back. A problem solving attitude assumes that the problem is a matter of conflicting needs. There is no right or wrong about it; each person's needs are legitimate and important. The goal is to work toward agreement through discussion and compromise.

First RCR Response: Ask for What You Want

1. Memorize these opening lines:

"I'm feeling (what's bothering me is)_____.
And what I think I need (or want or would like in this situation) is _____
_____."

2. Rules.

   a. What is bothering you (your feeling) is optional. Include this if you think it's important information that will help the other person to be more responsive, or if the other person is an intimate who deserves to know your reactions.

   b. Ask for something behavioral, not attitudinal.

   c. Ask for something specific, limited to one or two things.

   d. Develop a fallback position — for instance, the minimum change that would be acceptable to you. This gives you room to negotiate.

3. Intervention: Therapist-client role-play.

Ask a group member to play the part of the provocateur in a recent anger situation. Find out what the client wanted or didn't want in the situation. While the client provokes you, model the first RCR response by asking for what you want. Make sure that the request is behavioral and specific. Present a fallback position. Emphasize the concept of voice control. Keep your voice low in volume without much inflection. So often voice tone and volume communicate anger, blame, contempt, sarcasm, and so on. Voice control guards against escalation that is triggered by hidden messages in your tone of voice.

Client: *(provocateur)* This is ridiculous, rushing like this. So damn compulsive. For Christ's sake, relax!

Therapist: I'm feeling really anxious that we're going to be late for the surprise party. What I want is to be at least thirty minutes early.

Client: *(provocateur)* Thirty minutes of just standing around waiting for things to start? Forget it! That's nuts!

Therapist: *(fallback position)* I'm feeling really anxious that we'll miss the surprise. Fifteen minutes early seems like the minimum margin we need.

Note: Stop at this point. Don't let the provocateur respond and defeat you.

4. Intervention: Client visualization.

   a. Clients visualize a scene from their anger logs which grew out of some unmet or frustrated need. Clients see themselves using the RCR response and having success.

   b. Ask clients to visualize a second scene. This time the initial RCR response is rebuffed, but they are successful in offering a fallback position.

5. Intervention: Group discussion.

Discuss visualized scenes and any problems that clients encounter in generating need statements. The therapist should give a lot of attention to clients who've had trouble generating statements and fallback positions. Use group discussion to generate specific behavioral need statements in the problematic situation. Some people may profess helplessness at this point. They'll argue that nothing they could ask for would have any chance for success. Acknowledge that this may indeed be the case, and that's why there are five other responses to choose from. You should also suggest that learning to articulate needs, in addition to a fallback position, is extremely helpful in many conflict situations. And whether or not clients expect much success, they should at least try to describe their needs in the visualized situation.

6. Intervention: Client role-play.

   One client describes a scene from his anger log, including what he wanted in the situation and how the event proceeded. He then plays the role of provocateur while a second client plays the first client practicing the RCR response. The therapist should coach both the provocateur and the client practicing RCR. Again, emphasize the importance of sticking to behavioral and specific requests. Remind clients to suggest the fallback position when the first request is rebuffed.

7. It's time to emphasize the importance of expressing wants and needs. Ask group members if there are concerns about what it's okay to ask for. Explore resistance and fears about asking. Exercise feelings of increased vulnerability and the opening of old wounds when needs are finally put into words.

Homework

- "Continue monitoring in the anger log.

- Pick three scenes from the log (low, medium, and high anger). Generate need statements and fallback positions for each one.

- Practice visualizing each scene, using RCR response 1 successfully. Start with the low-impact scene and progress to a high-impact scene." Ask clients to practice the visualization daily.

- "Memorize RCR responses 2 and 3."

Week 8

Introduction

Review successes from the anger log. Discuss visualization homework and any difficulty clients may have had in imagining asking for what they want. Remind clients that this is just the first of six RCR responses, and that it will be effective in only some of their anger situations. Again, return to the theme of asking for what you want, and emphasize the importance of putting needs into words.

Second RCR Response: Negotiate

1. Review opening line:

   "What would you propose to solve this problem?" (*Note*: If clients don't feel comfortable with the phrasing of the opening line, let them modify it so that it feels right to them.)

2. Rules.

   a. If you get resistance or a worthless proposal, offer your fallback position.

   b. If you hear a proposal that has possibilities, begin negotiation. Look for compromise. Examples of compromise options include:

      "Let's split the difference."
      "Try it my way for a week. If you don't like it, we'll go back to the old way."
      "My way when I'm doing it, your way when you're doing it."
      "We'll do this one my way, but we'll do _____ your way."

    c. Compromise can only be reached when the solution takes into account *both* people's needs.

3. Intervention: Therapist-client role play.

As in Week 7, a client plays provocateur in a situation growing out of his or her anger log. Before commencing the role-play, have the client first describe the situation, to make sure that it's appropriate for a compromise response. Again, emphasize voice control as you role-play negotiating with the provocateur.

Client:	*(provocateur)* Stop hassling me about my radio! You make enough noise blabbing all day to your friends. Music is the only way I can stand this job.
Therapist:	What would you propose to solve the problem?
Client:	For you to stop being so tight-assed.
Therapist:	*(fallback position)* I just can't think with it on. I'd like you at least to keep it off in the morning when I do most of my writing. How about that?

Note: Instruct provocateur that he or she should make some counter-proposal at this point.

Client:	Why don't you buy me a Walkman? That would solve your problem.
Therapist:	*(looking for compromise)* How about if I split the cost of a Walkman with you? How would that feel?

Note: Stop the role-play here before you get defeated.

4. Intervention: Client visualization.

Have clients select a scene from their anger log in which they feel there is room for negotiation and compromise. Have them imagine a successful resolution after they offer a compromise suggestion.

5. Intervention: Group discussion.

Discuss problems with the visualization. If a significant percentage of group members are having difficulty with the visualizations or report frustration in developing images and seeing the scenes evolve, you might consider dropping the visualization component for the remaining group meetings. Encourage group discussion of problems with developing compromise suggestions, phrasing the suggestions, and dealing with situations in which negotiation and compromise may be inappropriate.

6. Intervention: Client role-plays.

Proceed exactly as you did in Week 7. Again, be sure that the anger situation includes room for negotiation and compromise. Because negotiation skills are often very difficult to learn, it's important that you be an extremely active coach for this role-play. When a role-play bogs down, have the group make suggestions for new compromise options.

Third RCR Response: Self-Care

1. Review opening line:

"If [the problem] goes on, I'll have to [self-care solution] in order to take care of myself."

Explain that this is an exit response. If there continues to be no progress toward agreement, you can stop the discussion here.

2. Rules.

   a. The self-care solution should have as its main purpose the role of *meeting your needs*, not hurting the other person. This isn't something you do *to* the other person, it's something you do *for* yourself.

   b. Emphasize that this is your way of solving the problem yourself, not a pushy ultimatum, and not a punishment.

   c. Examples of self-care solutions:

      "I want to be on time, so if you're late, you'll have to go on your own."
      "If you can't help with laundry and housework, I'm going to hire a maid."
      "Jimmy, if your clothes aren't on when I'm ready to leave, you'll just have to go out in your underwear and get dressed in the car."
      "Okay, you really don't want to do anything tonight. If you're too tired to go out, I'll go with Jennifer."

3. Intervention: Therapist-client role-play.
   Same as Week 7. Be sure you understand the situation, and extract from the client some ideas about how he or she can initiate self-care in the situation before actually beginning the role-play.

4. Intervention: Client visualization.
   Again, make sure that group members select an appropriate scene and that they identify a self-care solution before beginning the visualization.

5. Intervention: Group discussion.
   Discuss problems with the visualization and any difficulties developing self-care solutions. Encourage the group to brainstorm self-care alternatives for a variety of provocative situations.

6. Intervention: Client role-play.
   Again, be certain that clients have identified the self-care solution before commencing the role-play.

Homework

* "Continue monitoring in the anger log."

* Clients should identify low-, medium-, and high-anger scenes, as well as appropriate self-care solutions for each.

* Clients should practice visualizing the negotiation of a compromise settlement, as well as imagine making a self-care statement for each scene. Emphasize that each visualized scene should end in success. Ideally, visualization practice should be done daily.

* "Memorize RCR response 4."

Week 9

Introduction

Review important problems in the anger log. Review RCR responses 2 and 3 and discuss any problems with the homework. Emphasize that responses 1-3 are "active" responses, while 4-6 are "passive" responses.

Fourth RCR Response: Get Information

1. Review these opening lines:

   "What do you need in this situation?"
   "What concerns (worries) you in this situation?"
   "What's hurting (bothering) you in this situation?"

   Whether a client asks about needs, worries, or hurts depends on the nature of the conflict and what information the client feels that he or she needs in the situation.

2. Rules.

   a. Use this response when someone is angry at you and there is something behind the anger that you don't understand.

   b. If you don't already know what the other person's need or worry is, the process of getting information is vitally important.

Repeat steps 3, 4, 5, and 6 as previously discussed.

Fifth RCR Response: Acknowledge

1. Memorize these opening lines:

   "So what you want is _____."
   "So what concerns (worries) you is _____."
   "So what hurts (bothers) you is _____."

   Emphasize that acknowledgment should always follow the information-gathering response. Hearing the other person's concern is an important step in de-escalation.

2. Rules.

   a. Use the fifth response when someone has given a clear message about his or her feelings.

   b. Expect the other person to correct or modify what you said if you didn't get it right. Then reacknowledge the new information.

   c. Acknowledgment is not just to let people know you hear them. It is a way to clarify and correct your misconceptions.

Repeat steps 3, 4, 5, and 6 as previously described.

Sixth RCR Response: Withdrawal

1. Memorize this opening line:

   "It feels like we're starting to get upset. I want to stop and cool off for a while."

   Explain to group members that this is an exit response. It means that they must be committed to immediately stopping the interaction at this juncture.

2. Rules.

   a. Keep repeating yourself, like a broken record, if you encounter resistance. Acknowledge the other person's desire to keep the discussion going, or acknowledge his or her general distress, but keep repeating your withdrawal statement.

b. Physically leave the situation. Don't just leave the immediate vicinity, really get away.

c. With intimates, give a specific time at which you will return to resume the discussion.

Repeat steps 3, 4, 5, and 6 as previously described.

Homework

*   "Continue the anger log.

*   Pick three scenes from the anger log (low, medium, and high) and visualize using RCR responses 4 and 5.

*   Visualize the same three responses, but now include RCR response 6 (withdrawal)." Encourage clients to do visualizations daily.

*   Ask group members to review the opening statements in responses 1-6 each day.

Week 10

Introduction

Review anger logs, problems, and successes. Review homework and discuss any problems. A number of clients will have done little or none of the visualization homework. At the very least, encourage them to memorize the responses, because the next week's homework will involve actually practicing RCR in real situations.

N. Skill: RCR Switching

Now it's time to emphasize the core principle of RCR switching to new adaptive responses if anger and conflict continue. The rules for switching are described in the *Main Concepts and Skills* section.

Intervention: Role-Play Triads

This is the time to do role-play switching. Break the group into triads. In each triad, one person will play the provocateur, one person will practice RCR coping responses, and one person will be the coach.

1. In each triad, have the person who will use RCR responses choose a low-rated anger situation from his or her log.

2. Make sure that the situation is described in enough detail so that the provocateur can role-play anger-evoking behavior with some degree of realism. If a role-play begins and the client playing the provocateur isn't getting it right, have the triad stop and discuss in more detail the provocateur's behavior in the actual situation.

3. The coach in each triad can facilitate coping by reminding the provoked client of the two key coping thoughts. He or she can also remind the coping client of opening lines for RCR responses, if these have been forgotten. The coach may also suggest switching to a new RCR response. The provoking client is coached to resist until at least three or four different RCR responses have been made.

4. The provoked client should use anger as a cue to switch. He or she is generally in charge of choosing which RCR response to try next.

5. Make sure the role-play ends with successful resolution.

6. Have the triad switch off so that each member gets to play all three parts.

7. The therapist should move from triad to triad, listening in, offering suggestions, and encouraging effective RCR responses.

Larry:	(provocateur) Why don't you spend more time with your kids and less time trying to raise money for all these big causes, all this political shit?
Sheila:	(trying response 1) You're my brother. I feel really put down and hurt when you say things like that. What I'd like is for you to ask me, if you don't approve, why I do things — not just pass judgment.
Larry:	It's all stupid, Sheila. You're wasting your time.
Coach:	Could you try your fallback position, Sheila?
Sheila:	Larry, could we just agree to say nothing then? Just leave it alone rather than hurt each other?
Larry:	You like to run away from the truth, Sheila.
Sheila:	(trying response 4) What's worrying you about my political activities?
Larry:	The kids look stressed, they're cranky. They seem a lot more aggressive than they used to be.
Coach:	Could you try acknowledging that?
Sheila:	So what's worrying you is that they need to see me more, that they aren't getting enough attention?
Larry:	Yeah. And it's affecting their behavior. Frankly, they're turning into brats.
Sheila:	(explosively) Brats?
Coach:	Remember to take a deep breath and relax.
Sheila:	Okay, this is what drives me nuts.
Coach:	Remind yourself that you have a plan for coping. What should you switch to next?
Sheila:	(trying response 1 again) I really feel hurt when you say that. What I'd like is to assure you that I'll think about what you've said. But I'd also like an acknowledgment from you that you know I care about my kids and that it's hard to balance parenting with trying to do something in the world.
Coach:	The request seems a little vague. How do you want Larry's behavior toward you to change?
Sheila:	I want to hear what he's noticing about my kids without the heavy judgment.
Coach:	How can you put that into a request?
Sheila:	I want to hear what you notice about the kids, but I'd like you to say it without judging the other stuff I do.
Larry:	But the "other stuff" is the problem, Sheila. You don't want to face that.
Sheila:	This is too much!
Coach:	A deep breath...maybe an exit response?
Sheila:	Like self-care?
Coach:	Have you thought out a self-care response yet?
Sheila:	I could tell him I don't want to discuss my work again. And if he brings it up, I'll simply stop the conversation and walk out.

Coach:	Try it.
Sheila:	I don't want to discuss my political work. Let's drop it. If we get into this again, I'm just going to take off.
Coach:	This is a good place to stop.

Intervention: Group Discussion

The role-play should be followed by a group discussion about problems experienced in switching. The group can be encouraged to brainstorm solutions to any difficulties that grew out of role-plays.

Homework

- Continue anger logs.

- Encourage clients to review all opening lines on a daily basis.

- *In vivo* homework:
  - Using the anger log, have clients pick a low-risk individual with whom they've had conflict. They should visualize using RCR with that person, and plan out a need statement, a fallback position, and a self-care solution.
  - Clients should seek an opportunity to engage in an RCR exchange with that person.
  - Results should be recorded in the anger log.

Weeks 11 and 12

You should continue the role-play switching exercise from Week 10. Always encourage clients to switch back to old responses that have already been tried. Individuals can acknowledge, negotiate, or ask for what they want more than once. As clients become more proficient at RCR, begin using medium-, then high-impact anger scenes from the logs.

During these weeks, it's time to reemphasize the relaxation and cognitive coping skills learned earlier. Check in and uncover how clients have adapted these skills for their own use.

Homework

Use the same homework assignment as in Week 10. But now make sure that clients are picking at least medium-risk individuals and situations as targets for their RCR practice. Clients should continue to record results in the anger log.

Criteria for Measuring Change

Change can be measured by the anger log ratings. During the final session, you can ask clients to compare their anger log ratings of frequency, and of degrees of arousal and aggression, during the first three weeks with ratings during Weeks 9, 10, and 11. For most group members, the average ratings will have decreased significantly.

Noncooperation

The most significant problem in any skills-oriented group is the difficulty in motivating clients to do homework, maintain log records, and integrate the new behavior they are learning into daily life. One sure way to encourage cooperation is to ask to see the logs at the beginning of each session. Emphasize that progress and change are directly related to the amount of practicing done at home. Encourage clients to develop reward systems for doing their homework. An evening visualization session can be followed by a pleasant soak in the tub, reading an enjoyable book, or telephoning friends. Clients should make the rewards *contingent* on successful completion of daily practice assignments.

Some clients will cooperate more during one segment of the group than during others. This is to be expected. The cognitive control and RCR segments of the group, in particular, may be difficult for some clients. Be supportive, and emphasize that each skill is important in achieving anger control. Clients who have trouble with rehearsal and visualization should, at the very least, be attempting to apply their new skills to provoking situations that come up during the week. Your work is to consistently encourage them to convert the concepts and skills they are learning into real-life behavior.

People who don't do their homework, yet continue to come in with stories of anger upsets, should be challenged. They shouldn't be allowed to take up group time with war stories if they are not attempting to implement their new skills.

Some clients will come in each week with a story about how they tried their new skill but it didn't work. Some of these people may be playing a version of Eric Berne's game, "Yes, but." Have this sort of client describe in detail what he or she did to cope with the situation. Ask group members to look for flaws or problems in the client's coping strategy. In some cases, clients will try methods that are obviously inappropriate for the particular situation. After you or the group have suggested a more appropriate coping strategy, you might delicately raise the question of how inappropriate anger-coping strategies may be an unconscious way of making sure nothing changes.

Relapse Prevention

It's important to emphasize in the final session what to do if anger reemerges as a problem in the client's life. Relapse usually means that the client has forgotten to implement some of what he or she has learned. If anger is reemerging, the client should:

1. Reestablish his or her relaxation and stress-reduction program.

2. Begin rehearsal by imagining the problem situation, including appropriate coping statements.

3. Identify any significant cognitive distortions that are triggering the anger, and develop appropriate responses or rebuttals.

4. Rehearse, in advance, any RCR responses that might be helpful in the situation.

Resistance

Resistance in the anger group can be traced to one of two causes. Either the client has strong fears about changing, or there are rewards and secondary gains for maintaining high levels of anger. Finding out what the resistant client fears is an extremely important step. For some, anger functions as a defense against feelings that are too painful to openly acknowledge. Merely getting clients to name these underlying feelings can be an important first step toward overcoming resistance. Some clients are afraid that no one will listen to them or acknowledge their needs if they express themselves *without* anger. These individuals should be encouraged to experiment with direct, nonblaming requests in situations in which they previously used anger. Additional group or individual work may also be indicated for developing assertiveness skills.

Some clients feel more powerful in the world and in their relationships because of anger. The secondary gain, particularly in an intimate relationship, may include certain forms of control, the ability to avoid unpleasant feedback, regulating the level of closeness, sexual stimulation, special concessions and favors, and so on. Some clients are willing to openly examine how they use anger to meet certain needs. Others are not.

Whether resistance stems from fear or secondary gain, it can be further addressed by encouraging clients to examine the personal costs of their anger. The leader can assign homework to the group as a whole that encourages members to identify how their anger harms relationships at work, with friends, with family, with lovers, and with children. Clients should be encouraged to explore the effects of anger not only in current relationships, but also in any significant past relationships as well. During the following week's session, the group leader can give special attention to resistant clients and the interpersonal costs of their expression of anger.

References

Barefoot, J.C.; Dahlstrom, W.G.; and Williams, R.B. "Hostility, CHD incidence, and total morbidity: A 25-year follow-up study of 255 physicians." *Psychosomatic Medicine*, 1983, 45, 59-63.

"Cynicism and mistrust linked to early death." *New York Times*. Thursday, January 17, 1989.

Deffenbacher, J.L.; Demm, P.M.; and Brandon, A.D. "High general anger: Correlates and treatments." *Behavior Research and Therapy*, 1986, 24, 481-489.

Hansson, R.D.; Jones, W.H.; and Carpenter, B. "Relational competence and social support." *Review of Personality and Social Psychology*, 1984, 5, 265-284.

Hazaleus, S., and Deffenbacher, J. "Relaxation and cognitive treatments of anger." *Journal of Consulting and Clinical Psychology*, 1986, 54, 222-226.

Jones, W.H.; Freeman, J.E.; and Gasewick, R.A. "The persistance of loneliness: Self and other determinants." *Journal of Personality*, 1981, 49, 27-48.

Lewis, H.K., and Lewis, M.E. *Psychosomatics: How Your Emotions Can Damage Your Health*. New York: Viking Press, 1972.

McKay, M.; Rogers, P.R.; and McKay, J. *When Anger Hurts*. Oakland, California: New Harbinger Publications, Inc., 1989.

Moon, J.R., and Eisler, R.M. "Anger control: An experimental comparison of three behavioral treatments." *Behavior Therapy*, 1983, 14, 493-505.

Novaco, R. *Anger Control: The Development and Evolution of an Experimental Treatment*. Lexington, Massachusetts: Heath, 1975.

Rimm, D.C.; Hill, G.A.; Brown, N.H.; and Stuart, J.E. "Group-assertive training in treatment of expression of inappropriate anger." *Psychological Reports*, 1974, *34*, 794-798.

Rosenman, R.H. "Health consequences of anger and implications for treatment." In *Anger and Hostility in Cardiovascular and Behavioral Disorders*. Edited by M.A. Chesney and R.H. Rosenman, Washington, D.C.: Hemisphere Publishing Co., 1985.

Rule, B.G., and Nesdale, A.R. "Emotional arousal and aggressive behavior." *Psychological Bulletin*, 1976, *83*, 851-863.

Shekelle, R.B.; Gale, M.; and Paul, D. "Hostility, risk of CHD, and mortality." *Psychosomatic Medicine*, 1983, *45*, 109-114.

Spielberger, C.D.; Jacobs, G.A.; Russell, S.; and Crane, R.S. "Assessment of anger: The state-trait anger scale." In *Advances in Personality, Vol. 2*. Edited by J.N. Butcher and C.D. Spielberger, Hillsdale, New Jersey: Erlbaum, 1983.

Williams, R.B.; Haney, T.L.; Lee, K.I.; Kong, Y.; Blumenthal, A.; and Walen, R.E. "Type A behavior, hostility, and coronary atherosclerosis," *Psychosomatic Medicine*, 1980, *42*, 539-549.

Wolff, H.S., and Wolf, S. "Stress and the gut." *Gastroenterology*, 1967, *52*, 2.

Chapter 6

Assertiveness Groups

Martha Davis, Ph.D.

Introduction

Assertiveness was originally described by Andrew Salter in the late 1940s as an innate personality trait. Wolpe (1958) and Lazarus (1966) redefined assertive behavior as "expressing personal rights and feelings." They determined that assertiveness was situationally specific: most people can be assertive in some situations, and yet be ineffectual in others. Assertiveness training expands the number of situations in which a person can choose to be assertive.

When a person is passive, opportunities are lost and unpleasant situations are tolerated. In time, bad feelings can build to a point where one more event can trigger an explosion of resentment that in turn provokes upsetting criticism or rejection. Stress-related physiological responses can be caused by excessive passivity or aggression. Behavior that masks unpleasant thoughts and feelings may occur, such as drinking, withdrawal, or obsessing with physical symptoms (Gambrill, 1978). Nonassertive behavior has been implicated in a wide range of presenting problems, including anxiety, depression, antisocial aggressive behavior, marital discord, and low self-esteem (Ruben, 1985).

Assertiveness training has been employed with a variety of populations, including grade school children, adolescents, college students, the elderly, psychiatric patients (both inpatient and outpatient), professional groups, women, alcoholics, drug addicts, and couples (Ruben, 1985).

The majority of assertiveness training groups focus on building assertive skills, using model presentation and rehearsal. The entire chain of behaviors, verbal and nonverbal, is presented, and the group members imitate it. Bandura (1969) has documented the effectiveness of model presentation in establishing new behaviors and reducing avoidance behaviors.

While some clients may lack an assertive skill altogether, rehearsal usually reveals that most clients possess many of the necessary components of a skill which can be further "shaped" by instruction, positive feedback, and prompting during subsequent rehearsal. Practicing new behaviors in a safe environment reduces discomfort, particularly when rehearsal closely resembles the actual problem situation. A study by Lawrence (1970) found significant effects after only 12 minutes of rehearsal. Kazdin (1975) determined that covert modeling, in which clients imagine themselves or someone else dealing effectively with social situations, was as effective as actual rehearsal.

Graduated homework assignments allow clients to apply their newly acquired assertive skills first to situations in which the likelihood of success is high and the degree of discomfort is minimal. Initial success tends to reduce anxiety, increase the probability that clients will generalize the new assertive behavior to other situations, and encourage assertive behavior in more challenging situations. Homework is reviewed at the next group session where successive approximations of the final behavior are reinforced, and instructions and additional homework assignments are given as necessary. As Gambrill (1978) suggests, this process offers clients a model of how to alter their own behavior: they identify small changes to be made, practice these, and praise themselves for improvements.

The assertiveness training model described here emphasizes the building of assertiveness skills, using model presentation, rehearsal, positive feedback, prompting, covert modeling, and homework assignments. Basic assumptions regarding one's assertive rights are made explicit, traditional assumptions and fears that inhibit assertive behavior are challenged, and the pros and cons of assertive and nonassertive behavior are explored.

Selection and Screening

Ideally, you should screen your clients in an individual session. If you are relying on referrals from other therapists or on self-referral to a publicly offered workshop or class, you may want to circulate a brief written statement that includes typical problems of nonassertive behavior, a definition of assertiveness, its benefits, and a list of the skills to be taught.

Assertiveness training is most useful for people who can identify social situations in which they have difficulty communicating assertively; and who lack certain assertiveness skills, or are not comfortable in certain situations using what assertiveness skills they do possess.

Do not accept clients into an assertiveness group who are in crisis, who are of potential danger to self or others, who are actively psychotic, or who have an untreated mood disorder. Likewise, do not accept clients who are primarily interested in talking about their problems and are not motivated to make significant behavioral changes.

Assertiveness training is highly structured so that many socially anxious people can tolerate the group setting; when they complete the group, they are likely to report a significant reduction in anxiety in general. Some people, however, are so anxious that they are unable to concentrate on new information in the presence of a group. Such people often suffer from performance anxiety and are hypersensitive to criticism. These people are best taught assertiveness techniques in a one-on-one setting with a therapist.

When conducting an individual screening interview, ask potential group members to think of a social situation in which they did not communicate their feelings, thoughts, or wishes in a way that allowed them to achieve their desired outcome. Tell them that you are going to ask them some questions about this situation to get a better understanding of their problem. Then ask the following questions:

1. "Describe briefly the setting and the person or persons with whom you were interacting.

2. "What did you actually say and do?

3. "What was the other person's response to your behavior?

4. "What did you say to yourself about the situation?" Determine whether clients believe they have a right to be assertive in this situation; whether they anticipate rejection, failure, or some other catastrophe if they're assertive; or if they're rewarded in some way for being nonassertive in this situation.

5. "What would you have liked to have said or done to achieve a more favorable outcome?" Determine whether their desired outcome can possibly be attained using assertive behavior.

6. "Have you been able to do that in any situation in the past?" Determine whether in the past or in other situations clients have been able to be assertive in the way they desire, or whether they lack a specific assertiveness skill.

7. "What do you think keeps you from doing this?" Determine whether they define their obstacles in terms of behavior they can change, such as their own nonassertive behavior, beliefs, or fears. This question will also elicit beliefs about the dangers of being assertive.

8. "Describe briefly other kinds of social situations in which you've had difficulty being assertive and have ended up with less than what you really wanted." Find out with whom they tend to have difficulty. If it is exclusively with their spouse, consider marriage counseling. If it is exclusively with their children, a parenting group may be more appropriate than an assertiveness group. If they have a significant problem with controlling their temper, they might benefit from an anger control group before participating in an assertiveness group. If their thought content is heavily loaded with cognitive distortions, they should first consider individual or group cognitive therapy before attempting assertiveness training.

Clients are appropriate for the group if they indicate that they understand that their nonassertive behavior is contributing to undesirable outcomes, that they can learn assertive behavior to achieve their objectives, and that it is worthwhile for them to meet the basic requirements of the assertiveness class to achieve their goals.

When clients agree to be in the group, instruct them to write down a brief description of five examples of social situations in which they have difficulty being assertive, and in which the outcomes are not to their liking. Tell them to bring their list to the first group meeting.

A heterogeneous group of people allows clients to rehearse with individuals who resemble the difficult people in their lives. It's particularly useful to have a mix of passive and aggressive clients in the same group. In addition to excellent role-playing possibilities, they give each other insight into the thoughts and feelings that lie behind passive or aggressive behavior. On the other hand, an advantage to working with a homogeneous group is that the leader can quickly focus in on common problem areas: group members can easily mimic, during role-play, difficult people familiar in their lives.

Time and Duration

Assertiveness groups range significantly in length. Some are one- or two-day workshops held on the weekend. Some are short-term groups or classes ranging from four to eight weekly sessions of one-and-a-half to two hours in duration. The group described in this chapter is designed to meet for eight consecutive weeks. Each session is two hours long, including a ten-minute intermission.

Structure

Give individual clients the following instructions: "Plan to attend all eight sessions. If you're having any problems with the group, discuss them with me during a break rather than dropping out. Since this is a skill-building group and each new skill relies, to some extent, on what has previously been learned, all members must start the group at the beginning."

Groups usually consist of eight to twelve members. As you become a more experienced leader, you will be able to manage much larger groups, if you so choose. It's helpful, though not essential, to have an even number of participants for the structured exercises.

Group Process

"Each meeting, except the first, will begin with a review of homework. I will then introduce new concepts and skills with a brief lecture, and demonstrate new skills to you before you practice them in group and then at home. You'll receive constructive feedback as you practice these new skills so that you will have a good chance of success when you apply them to real situations in your life."

Goals

"These are the goals of this group: You will learn what assertiveness is and how to distinguish it from aggressive and passive communication. You will find out about your assertive rights and compare them with certain mistaken traditional assumptions that discourage assertive behavior. You will be able to explore your fears about being assertive and decide whether it is worth it to you to be assertive in a given situation. You will learn how to respond assertively to five socially challenging situations that you identify as important to you. The purpose of the group is not to discuss at length your personal problems; rather the aim is to learn assertive communication skills that can be used in a variety of social settings to improve your relationships."

Ground Rules

1. "The group will begin and end on time.

2. "Everyone is encouraged to participate and to do homework assignments. Practicing new behavior requires some risk-taking and will invariably feel awkward at first. Nobody won any trophies for the high dive without a great deal of practice, moments of anxiety, and a number of mistakes.

3. "On the other hand, everyone has the assertive right to say 'no' to situations that are too uncomfortable. Setting limits is an important part of taking care of yourself.

4. "While you are free to share the concepts and skills presented in the group, I ask you to maintain confidentiality regarding the personal information of

other members of the group. Do you agree to this?" Be sure that everyone pledges their compliance.

5. "As group leader, I will break confidentiality and contact the appropriate authorities only if I learn that a client poses a danger to himself or others; or if a minor, elder, or handicapped person is being neglected or is in danger.

6. "There will be no verbal or physical abuse in this group.

7. "Everyone will take turns speaking."

Starting the Group

Begin by introducing yourself and the name of the group. Give information about your professional and/or personal background, particularly as it relates to assertiveness training. Describe the time, duration, structure, process, goals, and ground rules of the group. Invite questions about what you have said thus far.

Have clients introduce themselves by sharing something about their lives and why they want to be in an assertiveness group. Invite group members to ask questions of the speaker at the conclusion of his or her introduction before moving on to the next person. If a client is being too vague, ask for more specific communication or for concrete examples of problems and goals. If one member of the group is taking up too much time, thank him or her for sharing and suggest that it is time to move on to the next person. End this introductory phase by pointing out the themes that many of the group members share in common, and stressing that everyone there has a good reason for being in the group.

Main Concepts and Skills

A. Skill: Learning To Identify Your Own Behavior as Assertive, Aggressive, or Passive

Use this form (adapted from Davis, Eshelman & McKay, 1988) as a handout.

My Typical Responses to Problematic Social Situations

1. As you walk out of a supermarket, you realize that you have been short-changed a dollar.
   I would _____
   _____
   _____

2. You order a rare steak and it arrives medium-well.
   I would _____
   _____
   _____

3. A co-worker asks you to give him a lift to where his car is being repaired. It's not convenient for you to do this favor.
   I would _____
   _____
   _____

4. You are going to a movie with a friend who gets a phone call from an old school chum just as you are going out the door. The phone conversation goes on and on and you realize that you are going to be late if you don't leave right now.
   I would _____
   _____
   _____

5. You've been waiting in line for a movie for 30 minutes and somebody cuts in line ahead of you.
   I would _____
   _____
   _____

6. You are watching your favorite TV program when your spouse says, "I have to talk to you right now — it's really important."
   I would _____
   _____
   _____

7. Your boss criticizes you unfairly in front of your peers.
   I would _____
   _____
   _____

8. An acquaintance suggests that the two of you go to restaurant A and you very much prefer to go to restaurant B.
   I would _____
   _____
   _____

B. Concept: Three Modes of Communicating

Assertive Communication

"Assertive communication involves clearly stating your opinion, how you feel and what you want, without violating the rights of others. The underlying assumption in an assertive communication is: 'You and I may have our differences, but we are equally entitled to express ourselves respectfully to one another.' The major advantages of assertive communication include active participation in making important decisions, getting what you want without alienating others, the emotional and intellectual satisfaction of respectfully exchanging feelings and ideas, and high self-esteem.

"Assertive communicators speak in a calm, clear tone of voice. They make good eye contact. They have relaxed good posture. Let me demonstrate an assertive exchange between a supervisor and a software programmer:

Supervisor:	I notice that you haven't finished that program that was suppose to be done on Monday, and here it is Friday. I'm feeling really tense and up against a wall. The big boss wants this project completed by Monday so he can show it to the customer. I would very much appreciate you coming in on the weekend to finish it. If you do, you can have a day off next week. If you don't, we'll both be in hot water.
Programmer:	Yes, I'm behind on this program. It turned out to be more complicated than I anticipated. I'm not thrilled about working on it this weekend here at the office, but if you'll let me work on it at home on my own computer, I promise I'll have it done for you for the Monday meeting. A three-day weekend next weekend would certainly be welcome.
Supervisor:	That seems reasonable to me. Thanks.

"Assertiveness is a skill that can be learned, not a personality trait that some are born with and others not. Nobody is consistently assertive. For example, you may find it easy to be assertive with strangers, but have difficulty being assertive with your parents. You may choose to be assertive with your friends in one situation and passive or aggressive with them in another. Learning to be assertive means that you can choose when and where to assert yourself."

Aggressive Communication

"In aggressive communication, opinions, feelings, and wants are honestly stated, but at the expense of someone else's feelings. Aggressive communicators are usually loud and direct. They tend to have excellent posture and, if possible, tower over others. Sarcasm, rhetorical questions, threats, negative labels, profanity, you-statements, absolutes such as always and nobody, finger-pointing, table pounding, hands on hips, and glaring are a few of the weapons in their arsenal. I'll demonstrate an aggressive supervisor speaking to the software programmer:

Supervisor:	You idiot, there are so many bugs in this program that I should call an exterminator! I don't care if you have to stay here all weekend; get it fixed by Monday or you're fired. You're always missing your deadlines and you never do things right. You programmers are a bunch of worthless bums. It's because of lousy workers like you that America is losing its cutting edge on technology!

"The underlying message in an aggressive communication is: 'I'm superior and right and you're inferior and wrong.' The advantage of aggressive behavior is that people often give aggressors what they want just to get rid of them. The major disadvantages are that aggressiveness can cause others to retaliate in kind or get even in some devious way. Aggression tends to create uncooperative enemies with whom you'll have to deal in the future."

Passive Communication

"In passive communication, opinions, feelings, and wants are withheld altogether or expressed only partially or indirectly. The passive communicator tends to speak softly. Eye contact is often poor, and posture is frequently slouched yet tense, conveying a message of submission. I'll demonstrate a passive software programmer responding to an aggressive supervisor:

Programmer:	(under her breath) I don't get paid enough to have to take this kind of abuse from this jerk! (out loud, after a big sigh, with faint sarcasm) I'll get on it right away, boss.

C. Skill: Learning To Distinguish Between the Three Modes of Communication

Use this list (adapted from Davis, Eshelman & McKay, 1988) as a handout.

Six Problematic Social Scenes

Scene 1

A: Looks like somebody's been driving by the Braille system. Isn't that a new dent I see in the car?

B: Its not my fault and I don't want to talk about it now!

A: No way are we going to let this go. You always try to weasel out of your responsibilities.

B: Get off my case!

A: I want to take care of this right now.

B: No way!

A's behavior is ___ Assertive ___ Aggressive ___ Passive

Scene 2

A: Why didn't you call me last night? You know that I was feeling lonely because your Dad is away on a business trip.

B: I was busy.

A: Too busy to call your own mother?

B: Sorry, Mom, I just forgot.

A: Well, I think that you are very thoughtless.

B: Thanks a bunch, Mom.

A's behavior is ___ Assertive ___ Aggressive ___ Passive

Scene 3

A: I know that this will be a big inconvenience to you, but would you mind changing the time of our appointment on Thursday?

B: No can do.

A: Well, I hate to bother you, but could you at least look at your calendar to see if there might be some other time you can squeeze me in?

B: Look, I'm busy...get back to me later.

A: All right. Sorry for the interruption.

A's behavior is ___ Assertive ___ Aggressive ___ Passive

Scene 4

A: Susan called and asked if we could babysit Friday night so that she can have a little time alone with her husband. I think that it would be fun.

B: Fun? After working all week? You know I'm always dog-tired by Friday night!

A: I'd really like to help Susan out. Friday night is your night to play couch potato, Saturday we have plans, so how about Sunday?

B: Much better...I'd enjoy that.

A's behavior is ___ Assertive ___ Aggressive ___ Passive

Scene 5

B: Can I borrow your car tonight? I have to go to the library.

A: When?

B: Just from six until nine, when it closes.

A: That means you won't be back until nine-thirty.

B: So nine-thirty then...can I have it?

A: Will you put gas in it?

B: I can put a buck into it, if you like.

A: I don't think I can spare it tonight. I might need it to go out — the kids have bad colds. What if I had to take them to the hospital in an emergency?

B: Have Joe drive you — he's going to be here all evening.

A: Well, I guess you're right...Okay.

A's behavior is ___ Assertive ___ Aggressive ___ Passive

Scene 6

(Over lunch, *A* tells her girlfriends that she is a pro-lifer, and they criticize her for not being willing to leave the choice about whether to have an abortion up to the individual woman.)

A: You certainly have a right to your opinions, but I happen to believe that the unborn child has a right to live, and it depresses me to think that a child's life is snuffed out because it's inconvenient to the mother. I'd like to see stronger legislation to protect the unborn child's rights and support motherhood.

A's behavior is ___ Assertive ___ Aggressive ___ Passive

Answers:

Scene 1: *A* is aggressive. *A* uses sarcasm, rhetorical questions, *you*-messages, and absolutes. He does not take into account the feelings of *B*, who becomes immediately resentful and uncooperative in response to the accusations.

Scene 2: *A* is aggressive. The tone is accusing and blaming. *B* responds with reluctance and out of guilt.

Scene 3: *A* is passive. *A*'s timid requests, preceded by apologies, make it easy for busy *B* to say "no."

Scene 4: *A* is assertive. The request is specific, nonhostile, open to negotiation, and successful.

Scene 5: *A* is passive. *A* can't say "no" directly and instead asks a series of questions, hoping to discourage *B*. Finally *A* makes a lame excuse that *B* easily counters.

Scene 6: *A* is assertive. She calmly stands up to the prevailing opinion of the group and achieves a clear, nonthreatening statement of her position.

D. Skill: Defining Criteria for Measuring Change in Assertive Behavior

Use the following example and the blank form as a handout.

Assertiveness Problems and Goals

Instructions: rate situations on a 1 to 5 scale in terms of their importance and of the difficulty in achieving assertive behavior.

Five Social Situations in Which I Have Difficulty Being Assertive	Importance		Difficulty		Total

Examples:

1. *Problem*: I always say "yes" to my boss when he asks me to do overtime. (passive)

   Goal: I'd like to say "no" when I'm feeling burned out or have made plans for the night.

   2   x   3   =   6

2. *Problem*: I never ask my co-workers for help. (passive)

   Goal: I specifically want to ask for help when it's the end of the day, I still have several customers to help, and I don't know the answer to a customer's question.

   1   x   3   =   3

3. *Problem*: I rarely tell my parents what I think of what they're doing when I know it will start a fight, since we see things so differently. (passive)

   Goal: I want to tell my father that I think he has a drinking problem. I want to tell my mother that I disagree with her policy of cleaning up my father's messes when he gets drunk.

   5   x   5   =   25

4. *Problem*: I get tongue-tied when I try to express my positive feelings to my wife, so I don't do it. (passive)

   Goal: I want to tell her I love her and how much I appreciate her support.

   4   x   5   =   20

5. *Problem*: I tend to blow up at my son when he behaves like a smart aleck and doesn't do his chores. (aggressive)

   Goal: I would like to calmly restate what I want him to do and the consequences if he doesn't.

   3   x   4   =   12

Total: 66

Your Name:_____ Date:_____

Assertiveness Problems and Goals

Instructions: rate situations on a 1 to 5 scale in terms of their importance and of the difficulty in achieving assertive behavior.

| *Five Social Situations in Which I Have Difficulty Being Assertive* | *Importance* | *Difficulty* | *Total* |

Examples:

1. *Problem:*

   Goal: _____ x _____ =

2. *Problem:*

   Goal: _____ x _____ =

3. *Problem:*

   Goal: _____ x _____ =

4. *Problem:*

   Goal: _____ x _____ =

5. *Problem:*

   Goal: _____ x _____ =

                                        Total: _____

E. Concept: Basic Premises Underlying the Three Modes of Communication

"Assertive communication is based on the assumption that individuals are the best judge of their own thoughts, feelings, wants, and behavior. They are better informed than anyone else about their heredity, history, and current circumstances that shape them into unique human beings. Thus, the individual is best qualified to express his or her position on important issues. Since everyone is unique, there are many times when an individual will disagree with significant others. Rather than overpower the meek or give in to aggressors, individuals have the right to choose to express their position and try to negotiate their differences.

"Passive people tend to believe that their feelings, beliefs, and opinions are not as important or valid as those of other people (Jakubowski-Spector, 1973, and Alberti & Emmons, 1970). As children, they learned to seek validation and guidance from their elders, and to doubt their own perception and judgment. As adults, they haven't reexamined the traditional assumptions of their childhood, and therefore they tend to give in to or are easily led by others. When they encounter a conflict between what they truly want to do and what someone else expects of them, they tend to feel guilty, wrong, anxious, stupid, or one-down; and they often end up deferring to the other person.

"People who often lapse into the aggressive mode of communication seem to have an inflated sense of their own importance and feel entitled to whatever they want without considering the rights or sensitivities of others. Often buried under this layer of self-importance is a damaged ego. As children, aggressive people were often abused by their elders, and later adopted the aggressive mode of communication in favor of passive victimization. Other aggressive people learned to believe from their early childhood experiences that they are superior and therefore entitled to dominate others. Prejudice learned in childhood can lead to subtle as well as blatant aggression in adults. People who are aggressive need to consider the rights and feelings of others as well as their own."

F. Skill: Identifying Mistaken Traditional Assumptions and Countering Them With Assertive Rights

Use this list (adapted from Davis, Eshelman & McKay, 1988) as a handout.

Mistaken Traditional Assumptions	Your Assertive Rights
1. It's selfish to put your needs before others'.	You have the right to put yourself first sometimes.
2. It's shameful to make mistakes.	You have a right to make mistakes.
3. If you can't convince someone that your feelings are reasonable, then they must be wrong.	You have a right to be the final judge of your feelings and accept them as legitimate.
4. You should respect the views of others, especially if they are in a position of authority. Keep your differences of opinion to yourself. Listen and learn.	You have a right to express your own opinions and beliefs.

Mistaken Traditional Assumptions	Your Assertive Rights
5. You should always try to be logical and consistent.	You have the right to change your mind.
6. You should be flexible and adjust. Others have good reasons for their actions and it is impolite to question them.	You have a right to question what you don't like and to protest unfair treatment or criticism.
7. You should never interrupt people. Asking questions reveals your stupidity.	You have a right to interrupt to ask for clarification.
8. Things could get even worse; don't rock the boat.	You have a right to negotiate for change.
9. You shouldn't take up others' valuable time with your problems.	You have a right to ask for help or emotional support.
10. People don't want to hear that you feel bad, so keep it to yourself.	You have a right to feel and express pain.
11. When someone takes the time to give you advice, you should take it seriously.	You have the right to ignore the advice of others.
12. Knowing that you have something special or have done something well is its own reward. People don't like showoffs. Success is secretly disliked and envied. Be modest when complimented.	You have a right to receive formal recognition for your special qualities and talents and for your work and achievements.
13. You should always try to accommodate others. If you don't, they won't be there when you need them.	You have a right to say "no."
14. Don't be antisocial. People will think that you don't like them if you say that you would rather be alone than with them.	You have a right to be alone, even if others request your company.
15. You should always have a good reason for what you feel or do.	You have a right not to justify yourself to others.
16. When someone is in trouble, you should give help.	You have the right not to take responsibility for somebody else's problem.
17. You should be sensitive to the needs and wishes of others, even when they are unable to tell you what they want.	You have a right not to have to anticipate the needs and wishes of others.
18. It's always a good policy to stay on people's good side.	You have a right not to worry about the goodwill of others.
19. It's not nice to put people off. If questioned, give an answer.	You have the right to choose not to respond to a question or situation.
20. You should be able to answer all questions about a field of knowledge with which you are familiar.	You have the right to say "I don't know" or "I don't understand."

G. Skill: Broken Record Technique

Introduction

"The good news is that you have the assertive right to express what you think, feel, and want. The bad news is that most people in this world have not taken an assertiveness class, and many will try to ignore or distort your efforts to stand up for your rights. The *broken record technique* is one of seven assertive skills that will help you deal more effectively with uncooperative and manipulative people.

"When a record is broken, it repeats the same piece of music over and over again. The key to the broken record technique is persistent repetition in the face of adversity. You will need to remember your legitimate rights if you are not to be manipulated into giving in to individuals whose interests conflict with your own. Occasionally you encounter people — encyclopedia salesperson, children, or a stubborn friend — who will not take "no" for an answer. When you want to set limits and someone else is having difficulty getting your message, you need to take a stand and stick to it.

"This approach is also effective in telling people what you want when their own wishes are preventing them from seeing yours. Examples include when you want your five-year-old to finish his dinner and he wants to watch TV; when you want to go home and your boss wants you to work overtime for the fifth night in a row; when you want to return a defective item and get your money back from a sales clerk.

"Here are the five steps of the broken record technique:

1. "Decide exactly what you want or don't want. Review your thoughts about the situation, your feelings, and your rights.

2. "Create a brief, specific, easy-to-understand statement about what you want. One sentence is best. Give no excuses or explanations. Do not say 'I can't.' The other person will point out to you that this is just another excuse and show you how you can. It's much simpler and more truthful to say 'I don't want to.' Eliminate any loopholes in your brief statement which the other person could use to further his or her position.

3. "Use body language to support your statement: good posture, direct eye contact, and a calm, confident, and determined voice.

4. "Firmly repeat your brief statement as many times as necessary for the person to get your message and to realize that you won't change your mind. He or she will probably invent a number of excuses or simply say 'no.' Eventually even the most aggressive person will run out of no's and excuses, if you are persistent. Change your brief statement only if the other person finds a serious loophole in it.

5. "You may want to acknowledge the other person's opinions, feelings, or wants before returning to your broken record. But do not feel obligated to answer questions. Be careful not to be distracted from your goal."

H. Skill: Confronting Your Fears About Being Assertive

"Many people hesitate to behave assertively because they fear that something bad will happen to them. Three typical fears include: fear of rejection, fear of failure, and fear of making a fool of oneself. Some fears are more realistic than others. For example, it is likely that if you give a talk to a large group, expressing your own opinions, one or more people will disagree with you or ask a question that you can't answer. It is highly unlikely that your audience will get up and walk out on you, thinking that you are an idiot. If your fears tend to take on unrealistic, catastrophic proportions, it's essential that you reduce their negative power over you by replacing them with more realistic alternatives. Here are nine questions and hypothetical answers to guide you in examining your fears about being assertive and in deciding whether it is worth it to you to be assertive in a particular situation."

Use the following example as a handout and/or read it aloud.

Confronting My Fears About Being Assertive

1. If I am assertive in this situation with so-and-so, what is the worst thing that could happen?
(Example: If I ask Doug to the dance and he says "no," I will feel worthless.)

2. What beliefs do I have that would lend probability to this happening?
(Example: I'd have to believe that my worth hinges on Doug indicating his approval of me by accepting my invitation.)

3. Is there any evidence to support this belief?
(Example: Not really.)

4. What evidence is there to refute this belief?
(Example: I have value that is independent of Doug's opinion of me. I value myself as a person; I have a lot of good qualities and I am a good friend, student, musician, and daughter.)

5. What would be a more realistic negative outcome of my being assertive in this situation?
(Example: Doug could say "no," in which case I would be disappointed.)

6. How might I respond to or cope with this negative outcome?
(Example: I would feel disappointed for a while. I would remind myself of my value as a person and that one rejection doesn't destroy my worth. I would talk to my best girlfriend about it, and then ask someone else to the dance.)

7. What is the best thing that could happen?
(Example: Doug would accept my invitation and we would have a great time.)

8. What is going to happen if I continue to do what I have been doing?
(Example: I will spend Friday night at home alone.)

9. Is it worth it to me to be assertive in this situation? [Weigh your responses to questions 5-8 before answering.]
(Example: It is worth risking the disappointment of Doug turning down my invitation on the chance that I won't have to stay home Friday night but instead will have a date for the dance?)

Use the following form as a handout.

Confronting My Fears About Being Assertive

1. If I am assertive in this situation with so-and-so, what is the worst thing that could happen?

2. What beliefs do I have that would lend probability to this happening?

3. Is there any evidence to support this belief?

4. What evidence is there to refute this belief?

5. What would be a more realistic negative outcome of my being assertive in this situation?

6. How might I respond to or cope with this more realistic negative outcome?

7. What is the best thing that could happen?

8. What is going to happen if I continue to do what I have been doing?

9. Is it worth it to me to be assertive in this situation? [Weigh your responses to questions 5-8 before answering.]

I. Concept: Criticism as a Form of Manipulation

"Many people have difficulty dealing with criticism because they experience it as personal rejection. As a child, you faced criticism from a one-down position. When you made a mistake, your elders passed judgment on you: 'Stevie, you shouldn't have broken your sister's toy. Bad boy.' You were wrong therefore you were bad. Eventually you learned to feel ashamed whenever you were criticized. This is a very powerful form of manipulation used to teach children to conform. Less damaging ways of instructing children in how to behave include: 1) reinforcing appropriate behavior and ignoring unwanted behavior, 2) pointing out what is wrong with the behavior and suggesting a more desirable alternative behavior, and 3) modeling appropriate behavior.

"You probably developed special strategies to minimize the pain of criticism that have followed you into adulthood, such as blowing up, recalling the sins of your critic, or pretending you didn't hear the criticism yet still feeling miserable inside. These aggressive and passive strategies for dealing with criticism can damage your relationships and your self-esteem. You are about to learn seven assertive strategies for dealing with criticism which will help you keep your relationships and self-esteem intact. These strategies include acknowledgment, clouding, probing, the content-to-process shift, time out, slowing down, and the broken record technique."

J. Skill: Acknowledgment

"When someone offers constructive criticism, you can use this feedback to improve yourself. When you have made a mistake, having someone point it out to you can be helpful in preventing future errors.

"Whenever you receive criticism with which you agree, whether it is constructive or simply a reminder, acknowledge that the critic is right. Examples: 'Yes, I did manage to put on one navy and one black sock this morning. Thanks for pointing it out.' 'You're right, I *am* running 30 minutes late with my appointments today.' 'Thanks for letting me know that my voice is too soft for you to hear in the back of the room.'

"You do not need to give excuses or apologize for your behavior. When you were a child, you were asked such questions as 'Why did you spill the milk?' or 'Why were you ten minutes late?' You were expected to give reasonable answers, and you learned to manufacture reasonable excuses. As an adult, you can choose to give an explanation for your behavior, but you do not need to. Ask yourself if you really want to, or if you're just responding out of habit."

K. Skill: Clouding

"Nonconstructive, manipulative criticism with which you disagree deserves the assertive technique known as clouding. The manipulative critic takes a grain of truth and elaborates on it, using his or her ample imagination to put you down. For example: 'Williams, late with that report? You're always late. I can't imagine how you keep your job with your inadequate work habits. Why, if everybody in this company were as slow and lazy as you are, we'd have to hang a hammock in every office!'

"Manipulative critics are expert at name-calling and *you*-messages. They bring up old history. They use absolutes such as *always, never,* and *everyone.* If you are foolish enough to try to reason with them, you only give them more ammunition for their case. They are not interested in listening to you, even when they ask you a question. Their fragile egos require them to be right and to always win their point. When you're tempted to justify yourself or retaliate in kind to manipulative criticism, remind yourself that you will only feed a senseless argument which you cannot possibly win. If you are still unconvinced, reflect back on times you have tried to reason or get even with a manipulative critic. Why continue to waste your time doing something so unpleasant and unproductive? As an alternative, learn how to stop manipulative critics in their tracks.

"I'm going to teach you three ways to diffuse manipulative criticism."

Agree in Part

"The first way involves finding some part of the manipulative critic's statement that you think is true, and agreeing with it. Rephrase the critic's sentence so that you can honestly concur. Drop the absolutes. Ignore the rest of the message. In response to the example just stated, you might simply reply, 'You're right, I am late with this report.'

"The critic will usually try to force you into admitting further wrongdoing. But if you continue to find some part of what the critic is saying to agree with, he will soon tire of trying to prove that he is right and you are wrong. After all, it is not much of a challenge to argue with someone who keeps agreeing with you."

Agree in Probability

"Now I'm going to teach you a second form of clouding which you can use with a manipulative critic. Find something in what the manipulative critic is saying with which you can probably agree. You can think to yourself that the odds of his being right are one in a hundred as you reply, 'You're probably right that I'm often late.' Again, change the critic's wording slightly so that you do not compromise your integrity and agree with something you don't believe."

Agree in Principle

"The third and final form of clouding involves agreeing with the manipulative critic in principle. This requires simple logic: if X, then Y. 'If everyone in the company were as slow and lazy as you say I am, we would have to file for Chapter 11.'"

L. Skill: Probing

"Occasionally you will be uncertain about the critic's motivation. Is the critic trying to help you and merely going about it awkwardly? Is the critic actually trying to hurt you under the guise of being helpful? Are the critic's comments actually hiding unspoken beliefs, feelings, and desires? Especially if the critic is someone who matters to you, you may want to probe further into the criticism to answer these questions. This requires listening carefully — a major feat when someone is giving you criticism."

M. Skill: Content-to-Process Shift

"When your conversation with someone gets stymied because of strong feelings or because of a conflict of needs or wants, shift the focus of the discussion from the topic to an analysis of what is going on between the two of you.

"For example, you are assertively asking your spouse to talk to you more, and he responds with: 'You feel like I'm ignoring you? Why, I remember on our honeymoon you hardly spoke to me.' Rather than getting into a fruitless argument about the past, you reply: 'We're getting off the point now,' 'We've been derailed into talking about old issues,' or 'You appear to be angry with me.'

"Typical problems that you may have in practicing content-to-process shift for the first time include:

1. "Lapsing into an explanation of why the other person has gotten off the track, when the purpose of this tool is simply to point out that the conversation has been derailed so that it can be brought on track again.

2. "Being accused of psychoanalyzing the other party as a ploy to discount the content-to-process shift. A good response to this is, 'I'm simply stating my own opinion,' and then to return to the original topic.

3. "Being told that the process comment is wrong. Rather than getting into a debate, use acknowledgment or clouding, and then return to the original topic.

4. "Rigidly sticking to the original topic when the content-to-process shift comment has brought up something that would best be resolved before your

return to the original topic. This is particularly true when the other party has an agenda that is so important to him that it prevents him from recognizing yours."

N. Skill: Time Out

"When you reach an impasse in a discussion, you may want to postpone the conversation until another time. Time out is useful when the interaction is either too passive or too aggressive. One of you may be silent, crying, distracted, unready to make a decision, or agreeing with everything the other says. Or perhaps one of you is hitting below the belt by name-calling, bringing up ancient complaints, or being manipulatively critical. If you or the other person feels too pressured to communicate or think at the moment, give yourself time to cool off, reflect on what has been said, and return later with the positive intention of communicating instead of merely proving your point and winning. For example, in response to your teenager who is pouting, you assertively call a time out: 'This is not a good time to resolve our difference of opinion. Let's talk about it tomorrow.'"

O. Skill: Slowing Down

"Don't feel that you have to respond immediately to every situation. You don't have to produce an instant answer. Momentary delays allow you to

1. Be sure that you understand what the speaker has said.

2. Process what has been said.

3. Become aware of what you think, feel, and want in regard to what has been said.

4. Avoid saying things that you may regret later.

5. Consciously influence the situation toward the outcome you want."

"Typical statements that you can use to slow down an interaction include:

1. 'This is too important to race through...let's slow down.'

2. 'That's an interesting point...let me think about it for a moment.'

3. 'Wait a minute. I want to give you my honest answer.'

4. 'Is this what I hear you saying?' (Repeat what you think you heard while taking time to take it in and reflect on it.)

5. 'I'm not sure I understand...could you say that again?'"

P. Skill: Assertive Position Statement

"When you want to express yourself on a specific issue, use an assertive position statement. The issue may be a small one, such as where to have dinner with your mate, or a major one, such as explaining to your boss why you deserve a raise. In any event, you need to express your position clearly and fully, because partial communication can lead to misunderstandings and frustration.

"An assertive position statement includes four important elements:

1. Your perspective on the situation

2. Your feelings

3. Your wants

4. A reinforcement to motivate the other person to cooperate

"The first element is your definition of the problem, or how you see the situation. It's essential for focusing the discussion. Here is your opportunity to share your opinion and beliefs regarding the issue at hand. Try to be nonblaming. Use noninflamatory language that states the problem as *objectively* as possible. For example: 'It's time to make a decision about where we're going to eat tonight. I know you love Mexican food, but we've eaten at Tijuana Joe's the last three times we've gone out for dinner. We're in a bit of a rut!'

"The second element, your feelings, gives the other person a better understanding of how important an issue is to you. Do not substitute an opinion for a feeling ('I think that Mexican food should be abolished!'). An example of a feeling is, 'I hate Mexican food!' Once they are expressed, your feelings can often play a major role in helping you get what you want, especially when your opinion differs markedly from that of your listener. If nothing else, the listener may be able to relate to and understand your feelings about an issue, even when he or she totally disagrees with your perspective. When you share your feelings, you become less of an adversary. Expression of your feelings often makes possible either an agreement to disagree or a workable compromise. Unfortunately, feelings are often left out of communication.

"The third element, your wants, is best stated in a simple sentence or two. Instead of expecting others to read your mind and magically meet your needs, as in the case of the passive individual, you clearly state your wishes and needs. Try to be specific about what you want. Ask people to change behavior, not attitudes. Rather than assuming that you are always right and entitled to get your way, as an aggressive person might, state your wants as preferences rather than commands. For example, 'I would really like to go to a French restaurant tonight.'

"The fourth element is to motivate the other person to give you what you want by reinforcing his cooperation. Let the other person know how he will benefit by cooperating with you: 'We'll save money,' 'I'll be less tired and more fun to be with,' 'I'll make your favorite meal,' 'You'll have more time to....' If the other person is very resistant, positive reinforcement may not work. In such cases, state the negative consequences for failure to cooperate. When describing negative consequences, do not make threats such as this: 'If you don't pick up after yourself, I'm going to throw out every stitch of your clothing I find on the floor.' This only breeds defensiveness and hostility. Instead, say how you will take care of yourself if your wishes are not accommodated: 'If you won't help with the chores, I'll hire a maid with your allowance money.' 'If you drink, I'll drive.' 'If you don't go with me, I'll invite a friend to go instead.'

"Here are a few examples of the assertive position statement:

"'I've noticed that you've been late to our staff meeting several weeks running. We end up having to stop the meeting to fill you in. I'm really irritated when this meeting runs into the lunch hour, and I would appreciate your making a point of getting here on time. That way, we can break earlier for lunch.'

"'In talking with you this past hour, I'm impressed that we have so much in common. I sure have enjoyed getting acquainted with you. In fact, I haven't had such a good time in months! I'd like to invite you to dinner to continue our conversation.'

"'In reviewing your performance record over the last six months, I see that you haven't met your monthly quota once. We've talked about this before. I'm disappointed with your performance. I want you to reach your quota this month or quite frankly I'm going to ask you to leave.'

"Expressing your thoughts, feelings, and desires in an assertive position statement enhances the chance that the message you want to send will be the message the listener receives. Notice that these assertive position statements do not blame or use attacking labels. The listener is unlikely to become highly defensive, tune out what you are saying, and prepare a counterattack or retreat. The situation is described specifically and objectively without slipping into negative judgments. By using *I*-messages rather than *you*-messages, you own your opinions, feelings, and wants. When delivering an assertive position statement, use good posture, direct eye contact, and a calm voice.

"An assertive position statement is difficult to ignore or misunderstand. Just in case, check to be sure that your listener is following what you're saying. You can do this by periodically asking the listener to summarize what he or she heard you say. If the synopsis is accurate, you can safely proceed. Don't ask your listener, 'Do you understand?' Instead, you might say, 'I'd like to hear your version of what you heard me saying,' or 'Could you restate what I've just said, so I can be sure I'm making myself clear?'"

Hand out copies of the following form to your clients.

Individual Exercise: Assertive Position Statement

Instructions: Use this form to write assertive position statements for four situations in your life in which you would like to convey your position clearly.

Situation 1: (Describe) _____

    I think (your perspective) _____

_____

_____

    I feel _____

_____

_____

    I want _____

_____

_____

    If you_____

_____

_____

Situation 2: (Describe) _____

    I think (your perspective) _____

_____

_____

    I feel_____

_____

_____

I want_____

_____

_____

If you _____

_____

_____

Situation 3: (Describe)_____
I think_____

_____

_____

I feel _____

_____

_____

I want_____

_____

_____

If you _____

_____

_____

Situation 4: (Describe)_____
I think_____

_____

_____

I feel _____

_____

_____

I want_____

_____

_____

If you _____

_____

_____

Q. Skill: Assertive Listening

"In listening assertively, you focus your attention on the other person so that you can accurately hear the speaker's opinions, feelings, and wishes. Use the techniques of *slowing down* and *time out* when appropriate. Assertive listening involves three steps:

1. **Prepare**: Become aware of your own feelings and needs. Are you ready to listen? Are you sure that the other person is ready to speak?

2. **Listen**: Give your full attention to the other person: listen to the speaker's perspective, feelings, and wants. If you are uncertain about one of these three elements, ask the speaker for more information. Examples: 'I'm not quite sure how you view the situation...could you say more about it?' 'How do you feel about this?' 'I don't understand what you want...could be more specific?'

3. **Acknowledge**: Communicate to the other person that you heard his or her position, using reflective listening. For example, 'I hear you don't want to take on this new project because you're feeling overwhelmed with your current responsibilities and want to catch up.' Another way to acknowledge the other person's feelings is to share your own feelings about what has been said: 'I'm feeling overwhelmed, too, and I feel terrible about having to ask you to do more work.'"

R. Skill: Assertive Position Statement — Expressing and Listening

"When you are involved in a heated conflict with another person, the two of you can take turns using assertive expressing and listening. Many problems are resolved simply by stating clearly what each of you thinks, feels, and wants. This can frequently clear up misunderstandings or create unexpected solutions to problems. Opportunities for this type of communication abound between people who live or work together. Sometimes these opportunities occur spontaneously, but often you need to arrange a mutually convenient time and place to discuss the problem."

S. Skill: Workable Compromise

"When two people's interests are in direct conflict, a fair compromise that totally satisfies both parties is difficult, if not impossible, to achieve. Instead, you can look for a workable compromise you can both live with, at least for a while. Here are a few examples of workable compromises (Davis, Eshelman, & McKay, 1988).

- My way when I do it, your way when you do it.
- My way this time, your way next time.
- Part of what I want with part of what you want.
- If you'll do X for me, I'll do Y for you.
- We'll try my way this time; and if you don't like it, you can veto it next time.

"Although a compromise may naturally emerge in your discussion, you sometimes need a brainstorming session to come up with one. Brainstorming a workable compromise involves the following four steps:

1. Make a list of all the alternative solutions you can think of. Let your imaginations run wild while generating as many solutions to the problem as possible. Don't judge any of the suggestions at this stage of brainstorming.
2. Cross off the solutions that are not mutually acceptable.
3. Decide on a workable compromise that you can both live with.
4. Agree to review your compromise after a specific length of time (say, a month). At that time, you can examine the results of your changed behavior. If you aren't both sufficiently satisfied, you can then renegotiate. If your compromise seems to have adequately resolved the conflict, congratulate yourselves.

"Another approach to finding a workable compromise involves asking the other person to counter your proposal. If you find the counterproposal to be unacceptable, be sure that you understand the feelings and needs of the other person regarding the issue at hand, and then come up with another proposal of your own. Continue back and forth until you come up with a proposal you both can live with.

"A useful question to ask when you're having difficulty arriving at a compromise is: 'What would you need from me to feel okay about doing this my way?' The answer to this question may serve as the basis for a workable compromise."

Main Interventions

Week 1

Introduction: Starting the Group

A. Skill: Learning To Identify Your Own Behavior as Assertive, Aggressive, or Passive

Intervention 1: Individual Exercise — My Typical Responses to Problematic Social Situations

"Before we discuss what assertive communication is and how it differs from other forms of communication, I would like you to write down how you would typically respond in each of these eight problem situations. We will come back to your responses later in this session." Read aloud or hand out copies of My Typical Responses to Problematic Social Situations for group members to fill out.

B. Concept: Three Modes of Communicating

Intervention 2: Didactic Presentation (See Concepts and Skills section)

Intervention 3: Answer Questions and Invite Comments

C. Skill: Learning To Distinguish Between the Three Modes

Intervention 4: Large Group Exercise — Three Modes of Communication

Read aloud one problematic social scene at a time. Ask for volunteers from the group to label person *A*'s behavior as assertive, aggressive, or passive, and to explain their answers. Encourage discussion of the answers to clarify the three modes of communication. Refer to the answers at the end of the *Six Problematic Social Scenes*.

Intervention 1: Individual Exercise — My Typical Responses to Problematic Social Situations

Have your clients imagine that they are person *A* in the problematic situations. Ask them to label their responses to the situations as assertive, aggressive, or passive.

Intervention 5: Dyad Exercise

"Sit down with one other person and review each other's labels of typical responses to the problematic situations. Discuss any differences of opinion regarding the labels. If you are unable to agree on a label for a particular response, bring the example back to the larger group for discussion."

Intervention 3: Answer Questions and Invite Comments

D. Skill: Defining Criteria for Measuring Change in Assertive Behavior

Intervention 6: Demonstration

Hand out copies of the example and two blank versions of the form called Assertiveness Problems and Goals, from the Concepts and Skills section. Explain: "The purpose of this form is twofold: First, it helps you focus on those social situations in which you have difficulty being assertive and to define how specifically you would like to change your behavior. Second, at the end of the group, when you rescore the form, you will be able to see what progress you've made toward achieving your goals.

"Let's go through the examples as I explain to you how to fill out the form. On the left-hand side, under *Problem*, you briefly describe the situation in which you are having trouble being assertive. Include useful identifying information such as when, where, and with whom you are having the problem. Describe your current behavior. Label it as *passive* or *aggressive*. Then, under *Goal*, state specifically how you would like to change your behavior. Let's look at a few examples....

"In the second column, marked *Importance*, rank your five situations in relative order of importance to you, with 5 being the most important, and 1 being the least important.

"In the third column, marked *Difficulty*, rate how difficult you think it would be to be assertive in each of these situations (5 = very difficult, 4 = quite difficult, 3 = fairly difficult, 2 = somewhat difficult, and 1 = a little difficult).

"In the far right-hand column, marked *total*, multiply the number given importance by the number for difficulty for each item, then add up the five numbers in this column for a total number. Write this in the bottom right-hand corner.

"Hand in this sheet with your name on it so that I can make copies for you to use during the course of the group. At the end of the group, you will rescore the importance and difficulty level of each item, and compare your original and final scores to evaluate your relative progress. You may want to work on this at home —in which case, you should remember to give it to me at the beginning of our next session."

Intervention 1: Individual Exercise

Have clients fill out this form on their own as instructed. Walk around and answer questions individually; help out anyone who seems to be stuck or confused.

Homework Assignment

Tell your clients to finish this form for homework if necessary and return it the following session.

Week 2

Review Homework

Collect forms Assertiveness Problems and Goals, and make copies for group members to refer to in future sessions; keep the original for final measurement of change. Answer questions. Be sure that members' goals are specific, observable, and reasonably challenging, yet possible to achieve.

E. Concept: Basic Premises Underlying the Three Modes of Communication

Intervention 2: Didactic Presentation (See Concepts and Skills section)

F. Skill: Identifying Mistaken Traditional Assumptions and Countering Them With Assertive Rights

Intervention 2: Didactic Presentation (See Concepts and Skills section)

Intervention 1: Individual Exercise (combined with Intervention 2 above)

Hand out copies of the form called Mistaken Traditional Assumptions and Assertive Rights and then explain: "While children have no choice about the traditional assumptions they were taught to make, adults have the option of choosing whether or not they are going to hold on to beliefs that discourage assertive behavior and create stressful feelings. Each of the following mistaken assumptions violates a legitimate adult right (adapted from Davis, Eshelman, & McKay, 1988). As I elaborate on each of these, put a check mark by any of the *mistaken traditional assumptions* that you still believe in and by any of your *legitimate rights* that you have difficulty accepting. When I'm finished, you will have an opportunity to discuss your views."

"Here is an example of an elaboration on item 2 of the list: It is shameful to make mistakes. How many times as a child did you hear, 'Shame on you!' when you made a mistake? The implication was that if you did something incorrectly, it was bad, and you were bad for doing it. Your value as a person depended on your actions, so it became very important to do well and please others in order to feel good as a person. When self-worth becomes closely tied to performance, then shame is what you feel when you make a mistake. You would merely feel regret if you viewed your mistake as an error in performance and did not go on to equate performance with self-worth. Regret is a useful emotion in that it motivates you to correct your mistakes. Shame can serve the same function, but it also wears away at your self-esteem and contributes to compulsive overachieving. People who are prone to shame believe that only 100 percent is good enough.

"If you believe that it's shameful to make a mistake, you are likely to avoid taking risks, even if it means forfeiting your rights. People will use your fear and shame about making mistakes to take advantage of you. For example, when you ask for a raise, your boss responds with: 'I seem to recall that you forgot to call in when you were sick earlier this year. That's not the behavior of someone who deserves a raise.' And you back down because you agree with him. The association of mistakes with shame inhibits your assertive behavior.

"Now consider your assertive right to make mistakes. Just as a toddler learns to walk by falling down many times, you learn from your mistakes. Something worth doing right is worth doing wrong at first. Mistakes have the added benefit of keeping you humble. Only God is perfect; it is human to err. This assertive right does not free you from the consequences of your errors; you are still responsible for your actions. But it frees you from the shame of equating your actions with your self-worth. A healthy dose of regret is a sufficient motivator for you to minimize and correct your errors; you do not need shame.

"When you can simply acknowledge your mistakes and not feel ashamed of them, you become difficult to manipulate. For instance, when your boss points out that you failed to call in sick earlier this year, and uses this as the reason for not giving you a raise, you don't give up in shame. You respond with, 'You're right, I did make that one mistake for which I'm sorry. Now let's talk about what I've done right for the company this year.' Belief in the freedom to make mistakes allows you to learn, take risks, be spontaneous and creative. It supports your assertive behavior."

Intervention 6: Demonstration

After you have read aloud and expanded upon each of the *mistaken traditional assumptions* and *assertive rights*, ask for a volunteer who is still convinced that his mistaken traditional assumption is correct, or is having difficulty accepting one of his assertive rights, to explain why this is so. Assist him in exploring how he came to this way of thinking. Gently confront him with questions such as: "While this was true for you as a child, do these conditions exist for you as an adult?" "As an adult, do you have alternative ways of coping with these conditions?" "How does this traditional assumption interfere with your assertive behavior?" "How would exercising your assertive right free you to behave more assertively?"

For example, the group leader asks Sharon how she came to believe that it is selfish to put her own needs first. Sharon describes how she learned from her family, her church, and her teachers when she was growing up that it is selfish to think of her own needs before those of others. She was often scolded and spanked for being selfish. Consequently, as an adult, she thinks of others first; and she has a difficult time expressing her own needs. She volunteers that this is a problem in her marriage. The group leader asks her if there are people in her adult life who will scold and spank her if she expresses her needs as an adult. Sharon laughs and says, "Only in my head." The leader asks her what she can do to cope with these critical thoughts. She replies, "When I hear my mother's voice say, 'Don't be so selfish!' I could say to myself, 'I'm an adult now. I decide when I will put myself first and when I will put myself second or third. It's not selfish to put myself first sometimes.'" The group leader suggests that Sharon use this tactic whenever the old critical thoughts come up about being selfish.

Intervention 5: Dyad Exercise

With one other person, have your clients discuss *mistaken traditional assumptions* that they still believe and *legitimate rights* that they still question. To minimize debate, direct the discussion toward how they came to believe in a particular assumption. Have them explore whether the conditions in which they learned it are still true for them today. If not, do they want to continue to behave as though they do? For example, if they were slapped, yelled at, or given disapproving glares for interrupting their elders and asking questions as children, they need to ask whether this would happen to them as adults. If the answer is "yes," do they have any options open to them that they did not have as children? Other useful questions include, "How does your mistaken traditional assumption discourage assertive behavior?" and "How would exercising your assertive right as an adult free you to be assertive?"

Often clients state that they know intellectually that the assertive rights are correct, yet they still feel and act according to their mistaken traditional beliefs. Suggest to these individuals that they continue to explore on their own the origin of their mistaken beliefs as they have been doing in group today, as well as consider how their assertive rights support assertive behavior and their mistaken traditional assumptions do not. This is usually best done in writing. Recommend that they repeat daily their assertive rights, and feel and behave as though they believed them. Tell them to post their assertive rights in a place where they can read them often as an external reminder. With enough practice, they will eventually assimilate the knowledge of their assertive rights at more than the intellectual level.

G. Skill: Broken Record Technique

Intervention 2: Didactic Presentation (See Concepts and Skills section)
Intervention 6: Demonstration

Have your co-leader or a member of the group role-play the boss in the following example as you go through the steps of the broken record technique playing an assertive employee.

Step 1

| Assertive employee: | *(thinking to himself)* I've done overtime four days this week. I'm really sick and tired of all work and no play. I really don't want to stay late tonight. I'm afraid of what my boss will think of me if I say, "no," but I know that I have the right to say no and to put myself first sometimes. |

Step 2

| Assertive employee: | *(thinking to himself)* Let's see, what excuse could I give him? I could say I can't stay because I have to go to my mother's birthday party. No — he'd tell me I could go later. I'll just tell him that I won't do overtime tonight, and not give him a dumb excuse that he'll figure out a way to get around. |

Steps 3 and 4

Boss:	I hate to ask you to stay late again, but I have to because of our deadline.
Assertive employee:	I know the fiscal year ends next week, but I'm not going to work overtime tonight.
Boss:	I didn't think you were the kind of person who would let me down at a time like this. I really need your help.
Assertive employee:	I hear that you're disappointed with me for not staying late, but I'm not going to work overtime tonight.
Boss:	If you don't do the work tonight, when will you do it?
Assertive employee:	I know that the work has to get done, but I'm not going to work overtime tonight.
Boss:	Well, I can't force you to stay overtime...but I will certainly be interested in seeing how you get all your work done by the end of next week.
Assertive employee:	Me too.

Intervention 1: Individual Exercise

"Write down three situations in your life for which the broken record technique would be suitable. For example, you might write down: 'I want to return this dress to the store where I bought it and get my money back.' 'I want to tell my husband not to come in and change the channel when I'm watching a program on TV.' 'I want to tell my eighteen-year-old son that he must start paying room and board at the beginning of next month if he wants to continue living with me without going to school.'"

Intervention 6: Demonstration of Covert Modeling

"I'm going to demonstrate a way for you to begin practicing using the broken record technique in your mind — the technique of covert modeling. First, I'll select a situation in my life for which the broken record technique would be appropriate, and then I'll go through the first two steps of the technique. For example, I might decide to return a dress to the store where I recently bought it. I realize that it isn't really what I wanted. I know I have the right to change my mind. I settle on this broken record statement: 'I want to return this dress and get my money back.' I sit or lay down in a comfortable position, close my eyes, and relax.

"I imagine taking the dress up to the store clerk and waiting my turn to talk to her. I pay attention to the sights and sounds around me, and how I feel. I get her attention, hand her the receipt with the dress, and give my broken record statement. I imagine her response: 'We don't give cash on returned items. I can write you out a credit. Would you like to look around the store for something else?' I imagine my response: 'Thank you, no. I'm returning this dress that I bought here and I want my money back.' Her response: 'I told you our store policy: no cash refunds.' My response: 'I'm hearing your policy for the first time. I'm returning this dress and I want my money back.' Her response: 'I realize that we don't post our policy about returned items, but you could have asked about it when you bought the dress. Perhaps you should talk to the manager. Unfortunately, she's not here today. Maybe you could come back some other time.' My response: 'I bought this dress here and I want my money back.' Her response: 'I really can't help you.' My response: 'Yes you can. I'm returning this dress and I want my money back.' Her response: 'Well, perhaps I can make an exception in your case.' My response: 'I would appreciate that.' I imagine her giving me my money and my walking out of the store, feeling very satisfied with what just transpired."

Intervention 1: Individual Exercise on Covert Modeling

Instructions: "Starting with your easiest situation, go though the first two steps of the broken record technique. Write down your broken record statement. For instance, you might write, 'I'm returning this dress that I bought here and I want my money back.' You may choose to acknowledge what the other person said or briefly clarify a point, but don't let yourself be distracted from your statement.

"Close your eyes and relax. As in the demonstration I just went through, imagine using your broken record statement in a dialogue in which you also go over how the other person might respond. If you can't imagine yourself successfully using the broken record technique in a dialogue, imagine someone else doing it. You may want to write down the dialogue later as a script. Repeat this process for the other two situations in your life for which the broken record technique would be appropriate."

Intervention 6: Demonstration of a Role-Play of the Broken Record Technique, Constructive Feedback, and Prompts

"I would like two volunteers to demonstrate the broken record technique. Someone who is ready to practice his or her broken record statement — tell us what it is and to whom you want to say it. Give us some background information about the situation, if you think this is needed. To role-play the scene with you, pick a group member who most closely resembles the actual person with whom you would like to use this statement. Then give some examples of what that person would typically say in response to you. Now I'd like you two to role-play this scene, practicing the broken record technique."

When the dyad is through with the role-play, give them constructive feedback. For example, "Jim, I liked the convincing way you role-played Sally's stubborn four-year-old. Your whining tone of voice and insistent questions and complaints gave Sally lots of opportunities to practice her broken record statement." "Sally, you started off great using the broken record technique, then got side-tracked into explaining. Stick with your broken record statement; it's a good one. You have a beautiful smile, but it doesn't convey that you mean business the way the tone of your voice does. Make your facial expression congruent with that of your voice and words. Let's do this role-play one more time, and I'll give you a reminder to look stern when you start smiling by pointing to my lips like this." (Demonstrate gesture.)

After the second role-play, reinforce the good points and give constructive feedback for further improvements. Thank the two volunteers, and ask for two more volunteers to role-play another instance of the broken record. Have one of them go through a brief explanation of a situation and how the other person should typically respond. Ask for two more volunteers to coach the players.

Tell the coaches about their job: "At the end of the role-play, say what you think worked, positively reinforcing assertive verbal and nonverbal behavior. Suggest increasing particular assertive behaviors such as eye contact, voice volume, use of the broken record technique, and acknowledging the other person without being side-tracked. This shaping of appropriate behavior is a nonthreatening way of giving constructive feedback. If the player forgets to use the broken record — perhaps because she is manipulated into defending her position — point out how the role-play was working up to that point, and suggest that she try to stick with her original broken record statement or else modify it slightly if it seems flawed." Unless there are some questions, go ahead with the role-play, followed by constructive feedback from the coaches.

Stop the coaches if they give negative criticism. (For example, "You only used the broken record once before you started rationalizing why he should do what you want him to." "Your voice is too soft." "Your acknowledgment of what the other person said sounded phony.") Ask the coaches to restate their negative criticism as positive feedback. (For example, "You used the broken record once. You could continue to use it, instead of explaining why he should do what you want him to." "What you were saying was good. Try saying it even louder next time." "You acknowledged what the other person was saying; perhaps you could say the same thing with more sincerity." Encourage the coaches to be specific and give examples, if necessary, to clarify your point. For example, the term "sincerity" is vague; the coach who uses it might demonstrate what he means by role-playing a few "sincere" acknowledgments. Have the coaches suggest helpful visual prompts during the role-play to remind the person practicing being assertive to speak up (point to your throat), make eye contact (point to your eyes), or get back to the broken record (make a circle in the air with your finger).

Invite the entire group to give constructive feedback when the coaches are through. Add your own feedback at the end.

Assuming that the person practicing the broken record technique has room for improvement, she can repeat the same scene, incorporating the feedback that she has just received. At the end of the second role-play, again have the coaches give constructive feedback, with emphasis on what has improved and what can be further improved upon. Thank the volunteers.

Intervention 7: Exercise for Group of Four (if time permits)

"Form groups of four to practice your easiest broken record situation in the way just demonstrated. Two people will role-play a broken record scene while the other two will serve as coaches. Everyone should get to role-play his or her broken record twice. I'll be walking around, listening in, and answering questions."

Intervention 3: Answer Questions and Invite Comments

Homework on the Broken Record Technique

"Before I give you your homework, let me suggest that you keep a written record of your assignments, including my instructions and a brief description of what you actually do and when. Include any insights and questions that come to mind. This will increase the likelihood of successfully completing your homework.

"Here is your assignment for this week. Practice imagining successfully using the broken record technique in the situations you've identified. Other ways to practice at home include writing out the dialogue in script form, role-playing the dialogue in front of a mirror, or recording it on audio- or videotape. You can play both roles yourself, or enlist the help of a partner to play opposite you. Finally, use the broken record technique in real life. After your experiment, ask yourself what worked and what needed improvement. Remember to give yourself credit for practicing a new behavior, no matter what the outcome was."

Week 3

Review Homework

Return copies of Assertiveness Problems and Goals and suggest that clients bring them back each week to refer to when asked for examples of problem scenes to role-play.

Review the five steps of the broken record technique. Ask what group members did during the week with the technique and what questions and comments they have about their particular experiences.

Intervention 6: Demonstration

Have two volunteers role-play for the group a broken record situation with which one of them is having difficulty. Coach the dyad, modeling good coaching for the group. Review coaching skills, with emphasis on constructive feedback.

Intervention 3: Answer Questions and Invite Comments

Intervention 7: Exercise for Group of Four

Have all group members role-play a scene of their choice, using the broken record technique, in groups of four (see Week 2, Intervention 7).

H. Confronting Your Fears About Being Assertive

Intervention 2: Didactic Presentation (See Concepts and Skills section)

Intervention 6: Demonstration

Hand out copies of and/or go over the example of a young woman answering the nine questions under Confronting My Fears About Being Assertive (in Concepts and Skills section).

Intervention 1: Individual Exercise

Give your clients at least two copies of the form called Confronting My Fears About Being Assertive. Have them fill out a form for one problem situation as you just demonstrated. In answering question 2, you can suggest that they review their mistaken traditional assumptions and assertive rights.

Intervention 6: Demonstration

Have one person volunteer to go through his or her answers to the questions in Confronting My Fears About Being Assertive. Assist the volunteer with any of the questions that presented difficulties.

Intervention 3: Answer Questions and Invite Comments

Intervention 5: Dyad Exercise

"Get together with one other person to discuss your answers to the nine questions. Get feedback. Reverse roles. Bring any unanswered questions and comments back to the larger group when we reassemble."

Intervention 3: Answer Questions and Invite Comments

Reassemble the group and open the floor to questions and comments.

Homework Assignment

"For each of your five specific assertiveness problems and goals, answer the nine questions under Confronting My Fears About Being Assertive. Continue practicing broken record technique." Remind clients to keep a written record of their homework experiences."

Week 4

Review Homework

"What did you do with the broken record technique this past week?" Answer questions and listen to comments. "Who had a problem answering the nine questions under Confronting My Fears About Being Assertive for specific assertiveness problems and goals?" Ask for a volunteer to go through the nine answers, and give assistance as needed. Take questions and comments. Explain that the group will be returning to these nine questions as people work on their specific assertiveness problems and goals in later sessions.

I. Concept: Criticism as a Form of Manipulation

Intervention 2: Didactic Presentation (See Concepts and Skills section)

J. Skill: Acknowledgment

Intervention 2: Didactic Presentation (See Concepts and Skills section)
Intervention 4: Large Group Exercise

"I'm going to go around the room and criticize each person so that you will all have an opportunity to practice the assertive skill of acknowledging criticism. Be sure not to agree with something I say that down deep you think is incorrect. Try to rephrase my criticism in such a way that you can agree with it. For example, if I say, 'You were ten minutes late to group today,' and you know that you were late, but not exactly how late, you might say: 'You're right, I was late today.' If I say, 'Your hair is blown every which way,' you might respond with, 'Yes, I suppose it is.' If I say, 'Your shoes are scuffed up and need to be polished,' you might come back with, 'Yes, they sure are scuffed up and need to be polished.'"

Take care to give minor criticisms with which your clients are likely to agree without being embarrassed or hurt.

K. Skill: Clouding

Intervention 2: Didactic Presentation (See Concepts and Skills section: Agree in Part)

Intervention 4: Large Group Exercise

"I'm going to go around the room and criticize each one of you from the point of view of a nasty, manipulative critic. Remember that as a manipulative critic, I'm less interested in being objective than in putting you down any way I can. I want you to respond by agreeing with some part of what I have to say, and ignoring the rest. For example, if I say, 'You're always making a mess of our home; you never clean up. I always know where you've been by the trail of dirty clothes and dishes you leave behind. Why can't you be more considerate like your sister?' you might respond with, 'You're right, I don't always pick up after myself.'"

Intervention 2: Didactic Presentation (See Concepts and Skills section: Agree in Probability)

Intervention 4: Large Group Exercise

"I'm going to go around the room again and criticize you from the point of view of the manipulative critic, and I want you to respond by clouding with agreement in probability. For instance, if I say, 'You wear the strangest combination of clothes of anyone I have ever had in one of my groups. Why do you need to wear four shirts at one time? Aren't you being a little redundant? Make up your mind — pants or a skirt, not both. You look like a clown!' you might respond with, 'I probably am wearing the most unusual combination of clothes of anyone who has ever participated in one of your groups.' If I say, 'The dinner you made us was terrible. The vegetables were mush, the meat was burned, the rice was cold. The army serves better food that this,' you might respond with, 'The army may very well serve better food than this.'"

Intervention 2: Didactic Presentation (See Concepts and Skills section: Agree in Principle)

Intervention 4: Large Group Exercise

"I, your not-so-friendly, manipulative critic, will once again blast you with criticism. You will respond by clouding with agreement in principle. For instance, I might say, 'You did a lousy job washing my car. It still has bird doo-doo on it, for heaven's sake. You're a bunch of lazy half-wits. You're not going to be in business long with shoddy work like this!' You might respond with, 'You're right, we won't be in the car-washing business long if we leave bird doo-doo on a car.'"

Homework Assignment

Suggest that group members write down their assignment.

- "Continue practicing the broken record technique.

- "Begin practicing acknowledging and clouding when you're criticized. Review your experience afterwards, and ask yourself, 'What did I say that was effective? How can I improve on my response next time?' Since this may be an infrequent occurrence, take advantage of any criticism you hear directed at someone else, and imagine how you would respond with acknowledgment or clouding. You can even do this when listening to criticism on TV dramas. Take ten minutes to imagine past instances of being criticized, or occasions that are likely to occur in the future. Imagine successfully using acknowledging and clouding.

- "Practice giving constructive criticism, as you've been doing as coaches."

Week 5

Review Homework

"How did you handle criticism this week? What techniques did you use?" Review how to use clouding and acknowledgment.

Intervention 4: Large Group Exercise

Have two people volunteer to role-play a situation in which one of them is having difficulty using these two skills. Invite the group to give constructive feedback. Give pointers on constructive feedback as needed.

L. Skill: Probing

Intervention 2: Didactic Presentation (See Concepts and Skills section)

Intervention 6: Demonstration

With a co-leader or a client, role-play the following example of probing:

Critic:	Late again, I see. One of these days you'll arrive at work only to find that we've all gone home for the day.
You:	What is it about my being late that bothers you?
Critic:	There's no such thing as a free lunch. You've been getting away with working less than the rest of us, and I'm mad!
You:	What is it about my working less than you that makes you mad?
Critic:	I haven't had a vacation in over a year, and I work overtime every night. You waltz out of here every night at five o'clock and get away with it. It's just not fair.
You:	What do you think about this lack of fairness?
Critic:	Well, now that you've pinned me down, I guess I don't really believe that life is fair. I guess I feel pretty stupid for working so hard when you're living proof that I don't have to.

"In this example, probing the critic was useful for placing responsibility for the dissatisfaction where it belonged: with the critic. Often, the critic doesn't budge from his righteous position and isn't amenable to probing. When you've assured yourself that the criticism is manipulative, shift from probing to clouding. If you agree with the criticism, acknowledge it.

"Be careful when you probe that you do not either verbally or nonverbally give the message 'So what's bugging you now?' (which implies that you see the other person as a nag). If used properly, probing can turn a manipulative critic into an assertive person who directly expresses his or her thoughts, feelings, and wishes while also respecting yours."

Intervention 7: Exercise for Group of Four

"In groups of four, take turns practicing probing. Two people serve as coaches, while the third person plays the critic, and the forth person probes the criticism to determine if it is constructive or manipulative, or if the critic is willing to admit a hidden issue such as unmet needs, wishes, or hurt feelings. If it's apparent that the critic is just being manipulative, shift to clouding. If the prober agrees with the criticism, he or she can simply acknowledge it. For the purpose of this exercise, let's have the critic complain about the housework not getting done."

Intervention 3: Answer Questions and Invite Comments

M. Skill: Content-to-Process Shift

Intervention 2: Didactic Presentation (See Concepts and Skills section)

Intervention 6: Demonstration

Role-play this example with your co-leader or client.

Parent:	Okay, now that you've watched your favorite TV show, you have to do your homework.
Child:	Come on, just one more show. It's a special and only half an hour long.
Parent:	No, you have to do your homework now. (This is the broken record statement.)
Child:	You let Anna Lisa stay up for special programs. You're being unfair to me.
Parent:	You're getting us off the track by bringing up how I treat another person. You have to do your homework now. (Content-to-process shift and broken record.)
Child:	You always treat her better than me. You never give me a break. You're always on my case. I hate you.
Parent:	I hear that you're really angry at me, but you have to do your homework now. (Content-to-process shift and broken record.)
Child:	None of my friends' parents would do this to their kids. They love their kids and want them to be happy.
Parent:	You're changing the subject again. You have to do your homework now. (Content-to-process shift and broken record.)
Child:	I remember last weekend you let me stay up until after midnight watching a movie. There have been lots of week-nights when you've let me stay up late. Why not tonight?
Parent:	You're avoiding doing your homework by bringing up things that happened in the past. You have to do your homework now.
Child:	You sure are tough.

Intervention 7: Exercise for Group of Four

"Get into groups of four, with one person practicing content-to-process shift. This person can role-play a parent or boss who is trying to convince his child or employee that he should do his chores or work, using the broken record and content-to-process shift. The second person role-plays the child or employee who tries to derail the parent or boss. The other two people serve as coaches who give constructive feedback at the end of the role-play."

N. Skill: Time Out

Intervention 2: Didactic Presentation (See Concepts and Skills section)

O. Skill: Slowing Down

Intervention 2: Didactic Presentation (See Concepts and Skills section)

Homework Assignment

"You have now learned seven assertive skills for dealing with people who are manipulative and/or uncooperative: the broken record technique, acknowledgment, clouding, probing, content-to-process shift, time out, and slowing down. You must practice these skills so that you will remember to use them instead of reverting to your old habitual responses to manipulation. You can do this in your imagination, by writing out a script, and/or by role-playing alone or with a partner. After every real interaction with a manipulative or uncooperative person, review your response. In what ways were you effective in dealing with the manipulation? How might you improve your performance next time? Remember to give yourself credit for any improvement and build on it."

Week 6

Review Homework

"What did you do with the manipulative and/or uncooperative people in your life this week? How did you practice your seven assertive skills to deal with manipulative people?"

Intervention 4: Large Group Exercise

Have two volunteers role-play for the large group a problem situation of their own involving manipulative or uncooperative people. Invite constructive feedback from the group. Hold your own feedback until the group has responded. Repeat this exercise with other volunteers as needed and as time permits.

Intervention 3: Answer Questions and Invite Comments

P. Skill: Assertive Position Statement

Intervention 2: Didactic Presentation (See Concepts and Skills section)

Intervention 1: Individual Exercise

Give group members the handout shown in the Concepts and Skills section and have them fill it out.

Intervention 5: Dyad Exercise

"With one other person in the group, go over your Assertive Position Statement form and get constructive feedback. Rewrite your statements if necessary. Then reverse roles."

Q. Skill: Assertive Listening

Intervention 2: Didactic Presentation (See Concepts and Skills section)

R. Skill: Assertive Position Statement — Expressing and Listening

Intervention 2: Didactic Presentation (See Concepts and Skills section)

Intervention 6: Demonstration

Role-play the following with a co-leader or client:

Wife:	I'd like to talk to you about the toilet seat. Is this a good time?
Husband:	Not really. How about after the game...it should be over in ten minutes.
Wife:	*(after the game is over)* This may seem like a small thing to you, but it's been bothering me ever since we got married. I think that the correct position for the toilet seat is down. I'm sick and tired of having to put the toilet seat down when I have to use it or landing on the cold porcelain when I go to the bathroom at night. I get irritated with you for leaving the seat up.
Husband:	Well, I can understand your preference for having the seat down, and I can hear your anger. To be frank with you, I prefer the seat up. I'd rather not have to fiddle with the toilet seat every time I went to use it.
Wife:	I feel the same way — and I'm often in more of a hurry than you are!
Husband:	I think you're being self-centered. It's just as important for me to have the seat up as it is for you to have it down. Your demand seems unfair to me. I'd rather that you leave the seat in the up position for *me*."
Wife:	No way — but I see your point. I feel stuck. Even though I may be asking for something that you think is unfair, I still want my way on this.
Husband:	Look, if you'd be willing to put the seat up after you use it next month, I'll put it down after I use it this month.
Wife:	Okay — but lets talk again after the second month to see if we want to try working out another solution. Maybe we need to think about building another bathroom!
Husband:	I'm game — let's try the cheaper fix first!

Intervention 7: Exercise for Groups of Four

"Form into groups of four people. Two people will practice the assertive position statement using assertive expressing and listening. Here's a ready-made problem situation: Your plans for the weekend have fallen through. Each of you has a different alternative plan. Express and listen to your respective positions on this problem and see if a mutually acceptable compromise naturally emerges regarding how to spend your weekend together. If it doesn't, that's okay. We'll be discussing Workable Compromise next. The two remaining people will serve as coaches who give feedback at the completion of the role-play. Then the coaches can role-play this same problem situation while the first two people coach. I'll take questions and comments as I walk around and at the conclusion of the exercise."

Intervention 3: Answer Questions and Invite Comments

S. Skill: Workable Compromise

Intervention 2: Didactic Presentation (See Concepts and Skills section)

Intervention 6: Demonstration

Role-play this example with your co-leader or a client. "Here is an example of arriving at a workable compromise, using brainstorming:

Jack:	Okay, we've both clearly stated how we see the problem, how we feel about it, and what we want; yet no easy solution has emerged that we can both live with. You want to spend our vacation in the mountains, and I want to spend it by the sea. Let's brainstorm and see if we can come up with some new solutions that we both would enjoy and that we haven't thought of yet.
Cynthia:	That's okay with me. I'll do the writing. Here's one alternative that neither of us has thought of before: let's go to the desert!
Jack:	Forget that, I can't stand the heat.
Cynthia:	No judgments at this point. We just put down whatever comes to mind.
Jack:	Okay — sorry. Let's have a beach vacation this summer, and a mountain vacation next year. Or we could spend three days in the mountains and four days by the sea. Or we could find a mountain sticking out of the ocean.
Cynthia:	Let's go to Hawaii — lot's of ocean and mountains. Or we could go to Lake Tahoe...there's water *and* mountains.
Jack:	We could take separate vacations. We could stay home.
Cynthia:	We could go visit my family in Montana.
Jack:	We could go visit my family in Rhode Island.
Cynthia:	I'm ready to stop this stage of brainstorming; I've run out of creative ideas.
Jack:	Me too. Let's cross off the alternatives that aren't acceptable to either of us. I refuse to go to the desert for my vacation! I don't want to visit your family or mine just now. I don't want to take separate vacations or stay home. That covers my vetoes.
Cynthia:	I don't want to go on a beach vacation this time and postpone being in the mountains until next year. I don't want to split our time between the mountains and the sea...too much driving if we try to do that in this state. We don't have the money to fly to Hawaii...nice idea though.
Jack:	'Well, that leaves us with Lake Tahoe. Certainly not my first choice, but I can live with it.'
Cynthia:	'Great. Maybe we can afford Hawaii next year!'"

Intervention 5: Dyad Exercise

"In dyads, use brainstorming to arrive at a workable compromise regarding how to spend $10,000 that the two of you have just won in a contest. To make this more interesting, let's add that you can spend the money on only one thing."

Intervention 3: Answer Questions and Invite Comments

Homework Assignment

Instructions: "Practice assertive position statement, assertive listening, and workable compromise in your imagination, in role-plays, and in real life. Next week we'll practice putting these three skills together in different problem situations."

Week 7

Review Homework

"What did you do with the assertive position statement, assertive listening, and workable compromise?" Briefly review these three skills with the group.

Intervention 4: Large Group Exercise

Ask for volunteers to role-play problem situations in which one or more of these three assertive skills would be appropriate. Invite the group to coach the players with you.

Working on Assertiveness Problems and Goals

Intervention 1: Individual Exercise

Review your Assertiveness Problems and Goals list. You probably have at least a couple of problems or goals that you have not practiced yet in the group or at home. Go over these in your mind, and imagine role-playing them, using the skills you've learned in the group.

Intervention 4: Large Group Exercise

Have one client volunteer to role-play a situation from his list of assertiveness problems and goals. Have him briefly describe to the group the problem situation and his goal. If he has any fears or concerns about being assertive in this particular situation, ask the nine questions under Confronting Your Fears About Being Assertive in the Concepts and Skills section. Remind him of his assertive rights as needed. Ask him what assertive skills he imagines himself using. Suggest others, if appropriate. Have him select a volunteer to role-play the scene with him (this should be someone who most closely resembles the person with whom he'd be interacting in real life). Have him explain to the volunteer how this person would typically respond. After the role-play, ask the two volunteers to share what worked for them and what needed improvement, then ask the same question of the larger group. Have the volunteers repeat the role-play if necessary after receiving constructive feedback.

If your group is small enough, or if you believe that your clients need your close supervision, continue to work in this manner on other clients' assertiveness problems and goals. If your group is large, or if you believe that your clients can work effectively on their assertiveness problems and goals in smaller groups, break up your clients into groups of four. Circulate among the small groups to assist and answer questions.

Homework Assignment

"Continue practicing new assertiveness skills. Practice applying assertiveness techniques to your specific problem situations in your imagination, in role-plays, and in real life."

Week 8

Review Homework

Ask for questions and comments regarding homework.

Intervention 4: Large Group Exercise

Same as for Week 7, Skill T (Working on Assertiveness Problems and Goals, Intervention 4).

Intervention 7: Exercise for Group of Four

Use this intervention if your group is large or if you feel that your clients do not need your close supervision to work on their assertiveness problems and goals. Otherwise, continue with Intervention 4.

"I want you to break into groups of four now to role-play being assertive, using one of the five items on the form you filled out for assertiveness problems and goals. Present your problem and goal to your small group. If you have not satisfactorily completed the nine questions under Confronting Your Fears About Being Assertive for the situation you are about to role-play, or if you are not sure of your rights in this situation, ask your partners in the small group for assistance. If you're uncertain about which assertiveness skills would be best to use, ask the opinion of members of your group. When you're ready to role-play, ask one of the other three people to be your partner; the remaining two people can serve as coaches who will give you feedback at the conclusion of the role-play. I'll be circulating around the groups to provide assistance as needed. Repeat the role-play, incorporating the coaches' feedback if you feel that it would be helpful. Otherwise, move on to the next person who will present his or her assertiveness problem and goal for discussion and role-playing. Each person in the group should get a chance to work on at least one assertiveness problem and goal."

Intervention 1: Individual Exercise

Return copies of the Assertiveness Problems and Goals form to your clients with the original scores blanked out or folded over. Remind your clients how to score it. After they have completed the computations, have them compare their new score with their original score to evaluate their relative progress. Suggest that people who finish before others take a quiet individual break.

Intervention 4: Large Group Exercise

Ask all clients to share their initial and final scores on the Assertiveness Problems and Goals form, to talk briefly about what they've learned in the group, and what they still need to work on. As time permits, give clients feedback regarding your observations of their progress and work left to do. Also, as time permits, invite feedback from the group on each client's progress and unfinished work.

Relapse

Intervention 2: Didactic Presentation (See Relapse Prevention below)

Intervention 4: Large Group Exercise

Ask for feedback about the group and for any remaining questions or comments before ending the final session.

Relapse Prevention

Throughout the group you will be reinforcing a model for ongoing individualized assertiveness practice. You can mention its elements explicitly in your closing remarks:

"Replacing passive and aggressive communication with assertive communication requires a lifetime commitment. It's easy to revert to old patterns at times when you are under stress, such as when you're tired, hungry, afraid, angry, guilty, ashamed, or trying to do too much. As soon as you catch yourself — whether moments or hours later — review what happened. Ask yourself what was going on that prevented you from being assertive. Remember that you have a right to make mistakes: learn from them rather than dwelling on them. Review your assertive rights. Explore your fears to make sure that they're realistic, and ask yourself if it is worth it to you to be assertive in this situation. Focus on the constructive things you said or did that you can build on, so that the next time that situation comes up you'll be more assertive. Ask yourself what assertiveness skills you could use the next time you're in that situation. Role-play communicating assertively in that situation in your mind, in front of a mirror, on tape, or with a friend. Include what you think the other person would say. When you anticipate a difficult situation, mentally role-play communicating assertively including the other person's responses."

Noncooperation

Homework compliance is the major problem in an assertiveness training group. As a group leader, you can increase your clients' motivation to do homework in the following ways (adapted from Davis, 1989):

1. Explain clearly the purpose of the homework.

2. Describe the homework, using simple step-by-step instructions.

3. Demonstrate the homework.

4. Give clients an opportunity to practice any new technique in class and to ask questions before practicing it at home.

5. Have clients keep a written record of their homework progress, along with any comments and questions.

6. Review homework at the beginning of the next session, giving clients an opportunity to discuss their successes and problems and to ask questions.

Do not chastise clients who don't do their homework. People learn in different ways. Keep in mind that some clients will go through the entire group doing little or no homework and yet will appear to have benefited from the group. They seem to pick up what they need by attending the group and doing the exercises while there.

As the group leader, you are responsible only for *teaching* assertiveness skills; it is the clients' responsibility and option to use these skills as they see fit. Reiterate that they have the right to say "no" to any situation they find too uncomfortable.

Resistance

See the nine questions under Confronting Your Fears About Being Assertive in the Concepts and Skills section. Also look at the chapters in this book on anger and shyness.

References

Alberti, R. E., and Emmons, M. *Your Perfect Right*. Revised Edition San Luis Obispo, California: Impact Press, 1974.

Bandura, A. *Principles of Behavior Modification*. New York: Holt, Rinehart and Winston, 1969.

Bloom, L. Z.; Coburn, K.; and Pealman, J. *The New Assertive Woman*. New York: Addison-Wesley, 1976.

Davis, M., *Leader's Guide: The Relaxation & Stress Reduction Workbook*. Oakland, California: New Harbinger Publications, 1989.

_____; Eshelman, E.; and McKay, M. *The Relaxation & Stress Reduction Workbook*. Oakland, California: New Harbinger Publications, 1988.

Gambrill, E. D. *Behavior Modification: Handbook of Assessment, Intervention, and Evaluation*. San Francisco, California: Jossey-Bass Publishers, 1978.

Kazdin, A.E. "Covert modeling, imagery assessment and assertive behavior." *Journal of Consulting and Clinical Psychology*, 1975, 43, 716-724.

Jakubowski-Spector, P. "Facilitating the growth of women through assertive training." *The Counseling Psychologist*, 1973, 4, 75-86.

Lawrence, P.S. "The assessment and modification of assertive behavior." Doctoral dissertation, Arizona State University, 1970 (University Microfilms, 396-B, No. 70-11, 888).

Lazarus, A. "Behavior rehearsal vs. nondirective therapy vs. advice in effecting behavior change." *Behavioral Research and Therapy*, 1966, 4, 209-12.

Ruben, D. *Progress in Assertiveness. 1973-1983: An Analytical Bibliography*. Metuchen, New Jersey: The Scarecrow Press, Inc., 1985.

Smith, M. *When I Say No, I Feel Guilty*. New York: The Dial Press, 1975.

Wolpe, J. *Psychotherapy by Reciprocal Inhibition*. Stanford, California: Stanford University Press, 1958.

Chapter 7

Groups for Eating Disorders

Stephen S. Zimmer, C.S.W.

Introduction

The incidence of bulimia has reached epidemic proportions.

The overwhelming majority of people in treatment for bulimia are women. This is due to a variety of factors, including sex-role stereotypes and societal pressures on women to be thin. I suspect, however, that there are many more men suffering from this disorder than would be indicated by treatment records. The fact that bulimia is commonly thought of as a "women's disorder" probably inhibits men from acknowledging the problem in themselves or from seeking help.

The physical and psychological toll of binging and purging is great. Common physical consequences include dental enamel erosion (an irreversible condition), increased cavities, irregular menstrual cycles or none at all (amenorrhea), electrolyte imbalance leading to muscle cramping and weakness, dehydration manifested by dry skin and brittle hair and nails, cold intolerance, and digestive problems.

The range of psychological features includes depression; powerlessness; numbness; fear, anxiety, and anger; low self-esteem; hypersensitivity to approval and criticism; social preoccupation with food, weight, and appearance; social withdrawal and isolation.

Bulimia is a secret disorder. While the anorexic may receive overt and covert admiration for her self-starvation, the binge-purger is looked down upon. She "cheats" by regurgitating the food she has eaten. She's "gross" because she vomits or abuses laxatives. She receives little in the way of positive reinforcement from society.

Secrecy is the result of the tremendous shame and guilt that the bulimic feels about her "nasty habit." Low self-esteem often predates the bulimia and is a precondition of the disorder. Secrecy and isolation encapsulate both behaviors and the negative self-image, making it difficult for her to get help.

Group treatment can penetrate the "capsule." When bulimics sit face to face with each other and see that they are not alone, that "nice" people are bulimic, they have begun a process that reduces their isolation, their shame, and their guilt. This process is extremely valuable, as it creates an opportunity for the bulimic to begin working toward recovery.

Selection and Screening

The intake interview is your major screening tool. Be sure to use it! Here are some of the topics you will want to cover.

What is the client's overall capacity to function in a group? Find out by asking about her experiences in various groups throughout her life (such as Girl Scouts, sports teams, clubs, groups of friends, and so on).

How does she feel in group situations? Occasionally, you'll have someone apply to be in your group who is absolutely terrified of groups. Her choice to join the group might well be a self-destructive one. Be wary of including her — you might serve her better with a referral to individual psychotherapy.

Does the client identify herself as bulimic? You may be surprised at how helpful this identification with the symptom can be at the beginning of the group. Typically, at the beginning of her recovery, the bulimic feels connected and allied to those other group members whose food behaviors are like her own, while a client whose symptoms are alien to the group may find herself initially excluded from the group process.

Rule out psychosis and other psychological problems that result in severely impaired social functioning. Also be alert to any substantial alcohol or drug abuse. Substance abuse is a common concomitance to bulimia, and needs to be addressed before the bulimic enters group treatment.

Assess the client's motivation for being in the group. Poorly motivated clients tend to be bad risks, as they can demoralize other group members and may not get much out of the group themselves.

How effectively is the client able to sit and listen to another person? How able is she to control and limit what she has to say? "Monologuers" who seem to have *no* ability to sense the presence and needs of others don't belong in a group setting. However, people with this *tendency* can learn a great deal and change dramatically in a group that provides good feedback.

Remember — group member selection is not a scientific process and you are not going to do the screening for the group without making some mistakes. Trust your intuitions and err by being too conservative until you have actually conducted a few of these groups.

Bulimics tend to do best with other bulimics. Some compulsive overeaters who do not purge may fit at times. Emaciated and restrictive anorectics will probably not be accepted by the group. Slightly underweight anorectic types who purge may or may not be accepted by the other group members.

The bulk of your applicants will probably be in the twenty-one to twenty-eight year-old category. Difficulties can develop with some high school age clients and some over-forty clients who are at different life stages than the core group. However, since the group is symptom-focused and highly structured, less substantial age differences often are not a serious problem.

If you are in a situation in which you are receiving large numbers of referrals (30 to 50 or more), you might want to consider beginning two groups, one being an adolescent group or an over-thirty-five group, and the other including clients in the eighteen to thirty-five age range.

Time and Duration

Make the group roughly one and one-half hours long and start it on a weekday evening after regular business hours. The group generally is 12 weeks in duration. It can be compressed, however, to 10 sessions if necessary.

If you have the time and the scheduling flexibility, find out possible times from all the people you interview, and pick a time that works for the most people, including yourself.

If you don't have much flexibility in your schedule, select the time and day of the group before you begin your screening, and give that information to prospective members on the telephone. This will permit a self-selection process, eliminating clients who cannot attend at that time, before you schedule your intake interviews.

Structure

This is a closed group of approximately 12 weeks in duration. If you have trouble getting 8 to 9 clients for the group, you can admit new members through the second session. Don't start the group without at least 6 members.

When forming the group, you will probably need 15 to 20 phone inquiries about the group to lead to 10 to 15 scheduled intakes. This will likely give you the 8 or 9 members necessary for the optimal sized group. You will probably still lose 1 or 2 members over the 12 weeks.

Hand out the expectation sheet (see Handout 1: Short-Term Group Policies) for group members during the intake interview and have the clients sign it. The expectation sheet explains the requirements for group participation.

Be sure to collect the entire fee for all 12 sessions before the first group, or no later than during the first group session. Make exceptions to this rule at your own peril!

Goals

The most important goal of the group is to give group members a sense of hope about their future and their recovery. You will teach a series of psychosocial skills that will give the members alternatives to binging and purging. By establishing a therapeutic environment of trust, honesty, and acceptance, you will promote emotional healing. Finally, you will attempt to reduce the group members' isolation, shame, and guilt while enabling them to increase their self-esteem.

Description of Group Process

This group is a synthesis of support group, psychodynamic psychotherapy group, and cognitive-behavioral group therapy. It is a support group in the way it links people together in a helping network. It is psychodynamic in the way it helps members connect their acting-out behaviors to their feelings, while valuing the development of conscious awareness and acceptance of those feelings. It is cognitive-behavioral in the way it utilizes structured interventions to help the client learn what the triggers are to the binge-purge syndrome, and how to develop healthier alternatives.

For most of the group sessions outlined below, you will find that time has been set aside to review homework assignments, introduce new concepts and skills, practice these skills, and give new homework assignments. Treat this structure as a guide, not a prescription. Each group is a living thing with its own unique needs. Stick too closely to the structure and you can lose the purpose of the group. Strive for balance.

Starting the Group

Often these groups almost begin themselves, and the chances of a successful first meeting are quite good. As the new group members look around the room and size each other up, they are often startled at how "normal" and "attractive" most of them look. This is usually quite a relief, and they are anxious to hear each other's stories. They are delighted that *these* people share the same symptoms about which they are so embarrassed and ashamed.

You might begin the group by saying, "After meeting you all one by one over the course of the last six weeks, it is a real pleasure to be with you as a group. I want to take a moment to congratulate you all for making it here tonight. By taking the brave step of pursuing this group, you have already begun to ease the isolation, loneliness, and shame that are part of being bulimic.

"Let's go around the group now and each say your name and take a minute to explain what brings you here tonight. Susan, why don't you start...."

Give this initial "go-round" 20 to 30 minutes, leaving yourself an hour for the rest of the material to be presented. Quite often the group ends with everyone feeling happy and excited about their first group meeting.

Main Concepts and Skills

A. Concept: Bulimia "Works" for People

For the bulimic, binge-purge behaviors "work" for them in a variety of ways. Bulimia serves as an antidote to self-hate, guilt, stress, anxiety, boredom, depression, anger, and so on. Thus, it is important that group members understand the function of the behavior in their lives, and the need to develop new skills and abilities in order to be able to give up bulimia as a coping mechanism. A possible way to introduce this concept to group members is as follow:

"No one in this group is crazy or stupid, and everyone here is bulimic. You are bulimic because, on some level, bulimia works for you — by reducing tension and anxiety, extinguishing feelings you can't stand (including self-hatred, depression, boredom, and anxiety), by expressing your anger, getting your much-needed attention, removing you from an uncomfortable situation, and so on.

"Therefore, let's not treat this syndrome as though it were some disgusting thing to be gotten rid of. You will need to develop new skills and abilities that will enable you to solve the problems you're now using your bulimia to address. And this will take time. Don't try to give up your symptoms immediately. Remember that you are entitled to the time it takes you to recover."

B. Concept: Clarifying Expectations

Bulimic clients frequently set unrealistic goals and standards for themselves. In the group, this tendency appears as members set overly ambitious goals for change and growth. It is important to address this tendency and remind group members that the recovery process is one that will begin in the group but continues long after the group ends.

You might introduce this topic with:

"It's natural to come to the group feeling needy, hopeful, or hopeless. Bulimia develops over a long period of time, and many of you have been bulimic for a long time. Your problem is unlikely to disappear over night. What you *will* do a little later on in this group is work together to develop realistic and manageable short-term goals that may or may not be symptom-related."

C. Concept: Dieting Doesn't Work

Bulimics tend to be chronic dieters, and the deprivation caused by stringent dieting often contributes to binging behavior. In addition, bulimic clients often do not eat in response to physical hunger. Rather, they follow diet-determined eating patterns when restricting their intake. When they are off the diet, they often eat in response to nonphysiological triggers and cues such as the way they look in the mirror, how their clothes fit, how they're feeling emotionally, etc. Therefore, it is important to help group members understand that dieting does not usually result in long-term weight loss, and one of their tasks will be to learn to eat in response to physiological hunger cues. This concept can be introduced as follows:

"Studies indicate that 90 to 95 percent of dieters have gained all their weight back in five years. Because of a rebound effect, people often end up weighing more at the end than when they started dieting. Even if you can't imagine giving up dieting, understand that rigid dieting is not appropriate for bulimics who are trying to make some inroads into diminishing their symptoms. Dieting provokes severe hunger pangs as well as a more general sense of deprivation. You are having enough trouble coping with those feeling when you're eating normally. The stress of a diet intensifies these feelings to an intolerable extent, and leads to the next binge-purge episode."

D. Skill: Keeping a Food Journal

"A food journal is an important tool for beginning the process of recovery. The journal can be used to track eating patterns, identify binge triggers, and provide information that will be helpful in distinguishing between emotional and physical hunger.

"Each food journal entry can be organized in any convenient form, as long as it includes the information shown in the worksheet." See the sample food journal on the next page.

E. Skill: Distinguishing Between Physical and Psychological Hunger

Since bulimics tend to respond to emotional states with binge-purge behavior, their ability to learn to distinguish between emotional and physical "hunger" is important to the recovery process. Psychological "hunger" can be explained this way:

"Psychological feelings can actually feel like hunger and prompt you to eat. Such emotions as loneliness, sadness, emptiness, frustration, and even annoyance can create physical sensations similar to hunger, and trigger your desire to eat or binge, even when you're not hungry. Since learning to eat when you're physically hungry is part of the recovery process, learning to identify emotional hunger, as opposed to physiological hunger, is an important part of that process.

"If you learn to know what you're feeling, then you're more likely to be able to attend to particular feelings rather than eating in response to feelings in general. Keeping the food journal will facilitate this skill."

Food Journal

1. Date and time of day:

2. Location:

3. Were you alone or with other people? If so, with whom?

4. How physically hungry were you?*

5. What were you feeling before you ate?

6. What did you eat or drink?

7. How much did the food satisfy you?

8. If the eating evolved into a binge, what were you thinking just before your eating became a binge?

9. What were you thinking after you finished eating?

---

*On a scale of 1-5, with 1 being the least hungry.

F. Skill: Setting Realistic Short-Term Goals

Goal setting is a very delicate subject that demands particular sensitivity on the part of the group leader. It is all too easy for members to engage in an unspoken competition in which they see themselves as the loser. They can set themselves up to fail and then give up on themselves when they do. Conversely, they can "miraculously" give up a symptom or their need for the group.

Be sure to educate the group as to the purpose of this task. Prepare carefully for it yourself, and be aware of the risks involved. Remember, if this or any other of the tasks in this chapter seem not to be working, skip it and move on. Goal setting might be an extremely valuable project for group A, and almost meaningless to group B.

Not only should the goals be manageable in size, but they should also be as specific as possible. The more vague and general the goal, the more difficult it will be to know whether or not it has been accomplished. Also, the more specific the goal is, the easier it will be to assess its appropriateness for a particular group member. You can begin this education about goal setting by saying:

"Setting goals can be the single most powerful skill you learn in this group. You can easily set yourselves up to fail if your goals are too high. For example, setting a goal to stop binging and purging is much too difficult and abstract, but setting a goal of making Tuesday a binge-purge-free day might be manageable for some of you right now. Not only should goals be manageable in size, but they should also be as specific as possible. The more general the goal, the more difficult it will be to achieve."

G. Concept: Good and Bad Foods and Enough Versus Too Much Food

For many (if not most) bulimics, the gray area between enough and too much is almost nonexistent. Typically, as soon as they decide they've eaten one bite too much, they've "blown it" (their rigid diet) and might as well "go all the way" (binge) because they'll "have to purge anyway" (because they ate that one thing too many).

Typically, bulimics, as well as many other people, live with the idea that some foods are "good" (okay to eat) and others are "bad," forbidden, terribly fattening, things only a "gross" person would eat. This attitude toward food is another "setup" for binge-purge behavior. For instance, many bulimics think that if they consume any amount of bad food, they must purge. Also, in a more general way, bulimics see *themselves* as either good or bad, according to whether they've been eating good or bad foods.

Introduce this concept in the following way:

"I'm wondering if any of you tend to put the food you eat in good and bad categories." (Most members of the group give affirmative nods.) "Which foods tend to fall into which categories?" (A discussion ensues.) "How do you feel when you've eaten something you consider to be in the bad category? Does it affect your binge-purge behavior in any way? In a more general way, can eating a bad food affect the way you feel about yourself as a person?

"When you do your goal setting for the week, try moving one food out of the bad category: make this one of your goals if you can. Be careful not to bite off more than you can chew! Perhaps you can try a food that is marginally bad instead of a food that is totally bad. Remember that moving it out of the bad category means eating it and *keeping* it — not purging. *Don't* expect to do this and not feel anxious. Permitting and tolerating the anxiety is part of the recovery process."

H. Skill: Identifying Feelings — Taking a Feelings Inventory

"One way bulimics use the binge-purge syndrome is to avoid, diminish, or relieve uncomfortable feelings. Therefore, when you try to diminish the number of times you binge and purge, you feel very uncomfortable. You may be unable to identify this discomfort specifically. After extinguishing most of your strong emotions with the same tool for such a long time, you've impaired your ability to identify and differentiate between feelings.

"To begin to try to deal with your feelings in more specific and less self-destructive ways, you have to learn how to differentiate between them, and how to address each of your feelings more appropriately. This involves becoming aware of the possible range of feelings you can experience, identifying which situations are likely to stimulate which specific feelings, and learning to identify the particular physiological symptoms associated with different feelings."

I. Skill: Identifying the Internal Critic

"Binging and purging can be linked to specific feelings such as anxiety, self-hatred, anger, sadness, and so on. There are often critical thoughts that trigger those feelings. For example, "I can't do anything right," can lead to binge-purge behavior. So can, "I'm a fat, disgusting pig." In the first case, binging can provide an escape from the conviction that you are incompetent and helpless. In the second case, the self-hatred generated by the statement can serve as the trigger for the behavior.

"Part of the healing process includes identifying your internal critic, stopping its self-destructive voice, and replacing it with a healthier, more compassionate and objective response. Glancing in the mirror on the way out to lunch, you might say to yourself, "Boy, you look fat and ugly," giving your self-esteem another beating and perhaps triggering a lunch-time binge. Or you could say, "Well, okay, the color of this shirt really becomes you," which gives you a positive stroke rather then a dose of self-hatred.

Although a slow process, this will get easier with practice. Since negative feelings about yourself are almost always triggered by a critical thought, looking for that thought whenever you feel bad about yourself is a good place to start."

J. Skill: Developing Alternatives to Binging and Purging

"Once you're able to accurately identify your feelings and your inner critic, it's possible to develop more appropriate responses than binge-purge behavior. It's important to try and short-circuit the binge reflex as soon as you become aware of the trigger. When the trigger is a critical thought, shout "Stop!" inside your head as loudly as you can, and immediately remind yourself of something positive, more compassionate, and objective. For instance, "I'm doing the best I can — nobody's perfect" is a good replacement for "Here you go, eating *again*." When there seems to be no critical thought behind the feeling, contacting a friend, perhaps even a fellow group member, and talking it out is often an excellent alternative. Going to a 12-step group meeting, such as Overeaters Anonymous, will be effective for many people. Sometimes taking a walk or going to a movie helps. Staying out of the kitchen obviously helps! Predicting binge triggers and learning how to avoid them altogether are useful, too. It's much easier to avoid a predictable binge trigger than it is to interrupt a binge that has already begun.

"Sometimes you'll find a binge trigger about which you can do nothing. There's no critical thought that you can identify, your alternatives seem to have been exhausted. Now what?

"There's one alternative that's always available. That's the simple but quite difficult challenge of tolerating your uncomfortable feeling. At first it sounds almost silly: if you're angry, give yourself permission to be as angry as you are; if you're sad, be sad. Don't try to make the feeling go away. Remind yourself that you *can* tolerate your feelings.

"Eventually, this can become the most potent alternative of all. Meeting this challenge relies on nothing outside of yourself. It presupposes a high level of self-acceptance ("My feelings are okay with me."). It teaches a particular kind of self-confidence ("The worst feelings in the world will go away all by themselves if I just give them the time to disappear."). You can develop this skill in small increments. For some of you, it might be helpful to begin by extending the time that you're able to sit with your trigger feeling before binging. Only after you feel more comfortable tolerating the discomfort would you attempt to prevent the binge altogether, sitting through the entire cycle of tension and eventual relaxation."

K. Skill: Asking for Help

Bulimics tend to be poor negotiators when it comes to getting their own needs met. In order to be able to diminish binge-purge behavior, the individual must learn to become a skillful advocate for herself and her needs. Developing this skill helps the bulimic function more effectively in the world, thereby preventing many situations that might otherwise develop into binge episodes. Learning to ask for help is one important step in the process of developing assertiveness. To the group you might say:

"By applying for membership in this group, all of you went through the process of asking for help. Try to contemplate this particular aspect of beginning group therapy. Was it hard for you to do? How are you in general at asking for help?" Chances are that you will hear a lot of group members admitting to having difficulty asking for help. Explain to them that this is a skill that can be developed and that they will be working on this in the weeks to come.

L. Skill: Expressing Negative
Emotions — Saying "No"

Learning how to say no and express negative feelings is another important skill group members need to develop. Bulimics often come from families in which there were inadequate boundaries and limits. Their parents tend to be either overly permissive, overly strict, or inconsistent. In addition, it may have been unacceptable to express negative feelings appropriately, or to accept their expression by others. As a result, the bulimic usually lacks the skill necessary to maintain appropriate boundaries, set limits, and express negative emotions. In fact, one way to understand the binge-purge process is as a technique for maintaining internal boundaries. Knowing this, be careful not to pressure them to give up their symptoms prematurely. Give them the time to develop more sophisticated self-regulatory mechanisms first.

To the group, you might say:

"Many of you have already realized that a major binge trigger is activated when you feel compelled to say or do things that you aren't comfortable with or when you have to act as though you feel something that you *don't*. You don't feel able or confident about how *not* to do what is being asked of you, so you do it, feel terrible, and then binge and purge out of anger or frustration. Developing and refining your ability to say no directly can put you back in control of yourself, eliminating the need to binge and purge in these situations."

Week 1

Follow instructions in the section Starting the Group for help in breaking the ice so that members can begin to learn about each other and get more comfortable in the group.

A. Concept: Bulimia "Works" for People

Intervention 1: Didactic Presentation (See Concepts and Skills section)

B. Concept: Clarifying Expectations

Intervention 2: Group Discussion

Example

Therapist:	I'd like to take a little time here at the beginning of our work together for you to think out loud about some of the things you're hoping to get out of coming to these meetings. There are no right or wrong answers to this — please try not to leave out anything, even if you think it might be unreasonable. If they're your ideas, we want to hear them. Who'd like to go first?
Sue:	I think I've been hoping that maybe when I was finished with this group I wouldn't have to binge and vomit anymore. I'm really sick of it, but I don't have a clue about how to stop.
Therapist:	Thanks, Sue. That's just the kind of stuff I was asking about. Who's next?
Robin:	I'm afraid I'm worse off than Sue. I don't know how to stop either. But I've pretty well lost hope about ever stopping.
Therapist:	The longer you're bulimic, the more you tend to lose hope. That's natural. But think hard. What were you hoping to get by coming to the group?
Robin:	You know, I think I just realized one of the reasons I'm here. I think I had the idea that if I sat with other people who were trying to get better, maybe it would rub off a little…maybe I could hope again.
Therapist:	Nicely put, Robin.
Kathy:	Just this past year I realized that bulimia is my major coping mechanism in my life. Whenever anything is going wrong or even going *too* right, I binge and vomit. I want to relearn what people do to cope, without using food.
Jane:	My expectations feel more like dreams. It may sound silly, but I want to feel happy again. It's been so long since I really felt happy. I was a happy person once and I really would like to feel happy again. [She starts to cry a little.]
Sue:	Jane, I know just what you mean. It's been a long time for me, too.

Don't be put off by extremes of optimism or pessimism. That's normal. Remember that you will be able to return to these issues more productively in the fourth group meeting. For now, your goal is for group members to become conscious of the existence of their expectations so that they can begin to evaluate these themselves. The group is quite fragile at this early stage, so take special care that no one comes out of the discussion feeling as though she has been judged and found wanting in some way.

Intervention 1: Didactic Presentation (see Concepts and Skills section)

Week 2

Review of Previous Session —
Members' Comments

Have the group give feedback on the first group meeting. Keep your ears peeled for the "pink cloud" phenomenon that may last during the first few sessions — group members may express a sort of euphoria about their anticipated recovery without taking account of the hard work that will be involved or the inevitable setbacks they'll encounter along the way. Solicit negative as well as positive comments. Predict the disappearance of the pink cloud as things get a little rougher, as group members get to know each other a little better. Predicting this helps to cushion the eventual blow.

Carefully control and discourage major confrontational situations. Many people with eating disorders are extremely sensitive. Sometimes it feels as though you're working with people who have no psychological "skin": remarks that have any kind of an "edge" to them seem to cut these people to the bone. Consider reducing the intensity of your comments until you feel more familiar with this group of clients. Be prepared to limit heated exchanges between members for the same reason. It can happen that a group may appear to handle strong feelings well — and then only two out of nine members show up for the next meeting!

C. Concept: Dieting Doesn't Work

Intervention 1: Didactic Presentation (See Concepts and Skills section)

D. Skill: Keeping a Food Journal

Intervention 1: Didactic Presentation (See Concepts and Skills section)
Intervention 2: Group Discussion

Hand out the journal format, then ask for clients' reactions to it. For example:

Therapist:	When you look over this outline for the food journal, what kind of reactions do you have to it?
Annie:	I try *not* to think about the answers to most of those questions when I eat! It seems almost impossible to me.
Sharon:	I can think about those things alright, but I can't imagine sharing my writing with anyone! I feel really exposed just thinking about it.
Therapist:	Remember, this is not a test or a competition. However you do yours is fine, and no matter what you do, you're likely to learn something about

Erica:	yourself just by trying. You won't be forced to share your journal with anyone else if you don't want to. What you write is primarily for you.
Erica:	It doesn't matter what I'm thinking or feeling before I binge. I binge out of habit, no matter what. I'm afraid this might get me off on the wrong track.
Therapist:	You may be absolutely right. Sometimes binging becomes so much of a ritual that it's no longer directly connected to specific feelings. Before you decide, give this a chance. You may identify more feelings and thoughts than you imagined. If any of the questions really don't work for you, you can omit them or modify them, but first see if you can give them a try.
Nancy:	I'm afraid that if I start doing this, I'll become even more obsessive and compulsive about food than I already am. I'm trying to get all these food thoughts out of my mind. They're driving me nuts!
Therapist:	Some people can't do this because they turn it into one more obsession. Try not to let that happen. Don't get too hung up on all the details. Stick to the basics and keep it as simple as you can. If you find, after you've given the food journal a real try, that it's making things worse for you, stop the activity. It's not for everyone.

Homework

Assign the task for the coming week of keeping a food journal and bringing it to the next group meeting. Anticipate problems with completing the assignment and discuss members' feelings about the homework. Explain that everyone will bring their journals to group, but will not be required to read from them. Let clients know that they will at least talk about their journals with each other for a portion of each group session during the next three to four meetings.

Week 3

Review of Homework: Keeping a Food Journal (continued)

Keeping a food journal will be a difficult project for many group members. Encourage clients to share with one another the problems they encounter. Individual members may be able to offer helpful suggestions to one another.

Have members who are willing read from their journals. Permit discussion of people's journal material, but control and limit critical comments. Value clients' efforts and don't worry too much about the quality. The value of the food journal will largely be determined by the amount of attention given to the task in subsequent meetings. If you assign it but don't pay attention to the results, clients are much less likely to continue keeping a food journal. Give lots of strokes to those who are able to do the task, while being accepting and encouraging toward those clients who are not yet able to complete the assignment.

Let the group find its own way to discuss the experience of trying to keep a food journal. There are many questions you could ask (such as "What did you learn? How did it feel to pay such close attention? What did you think about possibly sharing your journal with the group?" and so on). But you should resist the impulse to be overly controlling. Group members are probably becoming interested in each other by now. This can afford an opportunity for individuals in the group to get to know each other better and for the group as a whole to develop trust.

E. Skill: Distinguishing Between Physical and Psychological Hunger

Intervention 1: Didactic Presentation (See Concepts and Skills section)

Intervention 2: Group Discussion

Journal material can be used as group members begin the process of learning to distinguish between physical and psychological hunger. Invite group members to share material from their journals that exemplifies situations in which feelings have been experienced and responded to as though they were hunger pangs. This is also a good time to have the group think about where in their bodies they *feel* real hunger. Different people will feel it in different places. Where in their bodies do they feel anger, sadness, tension, and so on? By having group members go through this exercise, they come a little closer to being able to distinguish their feelings from one another as they are happening. Also, your valuing this process helps the group members begin to value it themselves. If they learn to know what they are feeling, then they are more likely to be able to tend to that feeling specifically, rather than feeling like eating in response to most feelings.

Here is a sample discussion.

Therapist:	Who here is pretty sure she usually knows when she's feeling hungry? [No one says a word.] That's interesting — really *interesting*, and not a euphemism for bad, sick, or problematic. Does anyone have any ideas about why it is that no one in the group is all that clear about when she's hungry?
Cathy:	I don't know about everyone else, but I've either been on a strict diet or binging and purging for so long that I think I've lost track of what the feeling of hunger actually is. [A number of group members nod in agreement.]
Nancy:	Since I started coming to group, I've been thinking about how I eat. I'm beginning to realize that I eat in order to feel better. It's such a natural thing for me to do that I really hadn't noticed it before. If I'm hungry or upset or annoyed, I eat and I feel better, especially since I know I'll get rid of it soon.
Therapist:	Chronic dieting and eating to feel better will gradually cause people to lose their natural sense of physical hunger. Hunger becomes confused with a variety of other feelings; and they all get treated as a physical hunger for which food is perceived as the cure. Does anyone have any ideas about the appeal of relieving yourself of unpleasant feelings this way?
Joanne:	That seems pretty obvious. Why would anyone want to feel uncomfortable if they didn't have to?
Therapist:	Good point. But what I'm getting at is why choose the food solution as the method of making those feelings go away?
Joanne:	That's easy, too. The food I can do myself. If something is really bugging me and I binge and purge, it's gone and I go about my business.
Therapist:	Okay. The food solution gives you a way to make the feelings go away while not having to trust anyone but yourself. And that seems really attractive to you.
Joanne:	You bet!
Therapist:	One of the problems with this solution is that it's addictive. After a while

you're eating instead of feeling almost anything, or choosing instead to not eat at all.

If you can begin to separate your other reasons for eating and purging from your actual feelings of hunger, you will be able to consider at any given time whether you want to respond to a particular feeling or situation by eating. When you develop the habit of making your feelings go away, you no longer have a reason to distinguish one feeling from another. Different feelings are "melted down" into generalized anxiety: you eat to combat the chronic anxiety.

Intervention 3: Soliciting Individual Examples

Journal material can be used as group members begin the process of learning to distinguish between physical and psychological hunger. Invite individual members of the group to share material from their journals that exemplifies situations in which feelings have been experienced and responded to as though they were hunger pangs. This is also a good time to have group members think about where in their bodies they *feel* real hunger. Different people will feel it in different places. Where in their bodies do they feel anger, sadness, tension, and so on?

Homework

- "This week try to use your food journals to help you make the distinction between physical and psychological hunger. You may not be able to do anything about it right now, even when you learn to recognize the differences. But the issues will at least become clearer, and eventually this will help you to overcome your binge-purge behavior."

- Suggest that clients employ any useful modifications to the homework assignment that have come out of the group discussion.

Week 4

Review of Homework

Ask members to read aloud particular segments they want to share from their food journals. You might notice a tendency in many members to go for fairly long periods of time without eating by skipping a meal entirely, not eating meals at all, or only eating particular foods. Explain that starvation is different from normal hunger, and that it isn't good for them. Not letting themselves get too hungry helps maintain an emotional balance. Getting too hungry is a way to set themselves up for a binge. Encourage members to try to eat at least three meals a day (or more), and to try not to let themselves get too hungry.

Be sure to pick up on items from the food journals that refer back to last week's discussion on the difference between physical and psychological hunger. For example:

Therapist: Joanne, I noticed that you and a number of others in the group tend to binge and vomit before you go to sleep.

Joanne: Yes. I always get the munchies late at night.

Therapist: Try to think about last night, for instance. What were you doing before you went to bed?

Joanne: Well, I ate a good meal and I did my laundry and I watched TV and I folded clothes.

Therapist:	Can you remember anything about what you were thinking while you were folding clothes?
Joanne:	It's funny, I do remember — but it's kind of embarrassing.
Therapist:	Well, if it's a little embarrassing I hope you can still trust us with it. If it seems really embarrassing, maybe you should keep it to yourself for now.
Joanne:	No, it's alright. I was thinking that I'm sick of doing my laundry by myself." [A few members nod their heads sympathetically.]
Therapist:	Do you remember what feelings were connected with that thought?
Joanne:	I think I felt sort of empty inside. Empty and sad.
Therapist:	It sounds to me like you were feeling a little lonely. Tell me — when you were done binging and vomiting, how did you feel?
Joanne:	I felt spaced and tired. I really wanted to go to sleep.
Therapist:	You may have been feeling spacey, but it sounds as if binging and purging eased your feelings of loneliness.

F. Skill: Setting Realistic Short-Term Goals

Intervention 1: Didactic Presentation (See Concepts and Skills section)

Intervention 4: Exercise and Goal Setting

The process of learning how to set realistic goals is begun by having each member select a goal she would like to try to accomplish by the next group meeting (in other words, in one week). The goal doesn't have to be related to food, but it should have emotional significance for the individual (without being so difficult or complex as to be overwhelming). Help each member refine her goal into specific, manageable increments or portions. For example:

Cathy:	I want to try getting to work on time next week.
Therapist:	Could you be a little more specific, Cathy? What time do you want to get to work, and how many times next week?
Cathy:	I'd like to get to work by 8:45 a.m. every day.
Sue:	What time do you normally get there?
Cathy:	Well, usually it's closer to 9 a.m.
Therapist:	How many times in the past week or month have you gotten to work at 8:45 a.m?
Cathy:	Probably not more than once a week.
Therapist:	So what do you think about this goal in terms of it's manageability?
Jane:	I think it's too big.
Sue:	Maybe getting to work at 8:45 only three days next week would be more manageable.
Therapist:	What do you think, Cathy? Which days?
Cathy:	How about if I try to get to work at 8:45 on Monday, Wednesday, and Friday of next week?

Homework

"Try to accomplish the goal you've clarified this week. It's a difficult assignment, so just do the best you can with it."

You should predict for the group potential problems with completing this portion of the week's homework. Ask group members to imagine how they might feel if they are unable to meet their own goal. Anticipated negative reactions include 1) feeling like a failure, 2) binging and purging, 3) feeling inadequate, 4) self-loathing, and 5) feeling embarrassed.

"I'll be reviewing the journals with you for the last time next week, but you're welcome to continue the process on your own. You'll also evaluate the task for yourselves at our next meeting."

Week 5

This entire session focuses on the homework.

Review of Homework: Goal Setting

Intervention 3: Soliciting Individual Examples

Some people will have some genuine successes in the group. Let them tell their stories. This imparts an atmosphere of hope, and energizes the room. For example, one group member reported the following experience with a goal-setting assignment:

"I've been binging and vomiting one to five times a day for the last three years. I didn't even stop when I had the flu! This week I had my first two days without binging and vomiting. It's really amazing! I thought that I couldn't stop. I even told myself that I didn't want to stop, that it was *fine* for me. That was bullshit. Binging hasn't really been fun for me for years now. I was just addicted and I felt pretty hopeless about the whole thing — but not today. Today I feel more hopeful about my recovery than I have in a long, long time."

Successes such as this one are mixed blessings. On the up side, people really begin to *see* that their condition is subject to change. This can be a tremendous relief. Often the motivation of the successful individual makes the motivation of the group as a whole increase markedly. On the down side, the successful individual may become more focused on performance than on change. She might experience her improvement as a pressure, and feel compelled to "up the ante." She might grow frightened and, as a result, become even more symptomatic. The group can have negative as well as positive reactions to the success of one individual member. Typically, feelings of competition, envy, and despair can develop. If you keep the focus on process rather than performance, all of this will be simply grist for the mill. By helping group members become aware of their reactions and feelings, particularly if these threaten the group process, you will maintain a positive direction and maximize everyone's progress.

Intervention 2: Group Discussion

Begin by asking group members how they felt about the assignment. How anxious did it make them feel? How did it feel to accomplish their goals? How did it feel to fall short of their goals? Did anybody not try to meet her goals? What got in her way?

Because of the difficulty of the assignment, it's important for you to be supportive and interested in each client's experience, whatever the outcome. Tell them that it is brave of them to try, and that it's also understandable if they are too afraid just yet to try. Success will come. You can help those clients having the hardest time by helping them scale down their goal to something more manageable. For someone who is binging and purging three to five times daily, not purging during work hours on Mondays and Wednesdays might be a realistic goal. For another client, attending her first meeting of Overeaters Anonymous might be an appropriate goal. It's your job to help clients set goals that are realistic, productive, and manageable.

Review of Homework: Keeping a Food Journal (continued)

Intervention 3: Soliciting Individual Examples

   Example

Therapist:	Since this is the last time we'll be reviewing and discussing your food journals, I'd like to hear how this exercise worked for you.
Erica:	I think it worked for me on a couple of different levels. For years I had this gimmick where I would always make believe I was eating about 25 percent more calories than I really was. Then I would stop eating sooner, and lose weight! A year or two ago the whole system broke down and I couldn't stop overestimating even when I wanted to. Somehow doing the food journal made it okay for me to be honest again about how much I'm actually eating. For the first time in over six years, I really know just what I've eaten on a given day.

      Also, I learned something simple, but important, about when I binge. I thought it was just nights, but it's much more often than that. Mostly, I binge whenever I'm alone — my journal showed me that. It also showed me that I'm usually thinking pretty negative things about myself too, when I binge. I realize now that coping with being alone, being alone less, and being less critical of myself are things I really need help with!

Homework

Help members set new or revised specific and manageable goals for the next week.

Week 6

G. Concept: Good and Bad Food and Enough Versus Too Much Food

Intervention 1: Didactic Presentation (See Concepts and Skill section)

Intervention 2: Group Discussion

Ask group members to think about whether they think of different foods as "good" or "bad." Which foods fit into what categories for them? What about distinctions between enough and too much food? To what extent is their eating controlled by these ideas? How often are these notions used as catalysts for binge-purge behavior?

You might want to introduce this topic by immediately asking group members about the kind of distinctions they make, or fail to make, about food and eating patterns. This will initiate a discussion during which many of the points of your introductory presentation will be covered.

Review of Homework: Goal Setting

Intervention 3: Soliciting Individual Examples

Nancy: I had a really hard time with this. I knew I wasn't ready to cut back on the binging, but I tried to do it anyway and I couldn't do it at all. In fact, I binged more often than usual.

Therapist: Nancy didn't feel ready to cut back on her binging, yet she decided to try it anyway. I wonder if that sounds familiar to anyone else?

Susan: It does to me. I think I sometimes avoid the possibility of failing at something by setting it up so that my failure is guaranteed. That way I don't have to worry too much and it confirms all the negative things I think about myself already. It's a lot easier for me to see when Nancy does it than when I do it myself.

Cathy: I do the same sorts of things, but my reasons are different. For some reason, small achievements make me feel embarrassed, maybe even demeaned. As though I were settling for something so far beneath my potential that it's proof that I'm worthless and stupid. So I avoid all that by trying to achieve "major" things. Unfortunately, this often turns out for me like it did for Nancy.

Nancy: I thought *I* was the only one who did stuff like that! [Everybody laughs.]

Therapist: How did it go for the rest of you?

Sharon: Well, I've got some good news to report. My goal was to stop binging and purging on my lunch hour and to have a light lunch instead. I was able to do that four out of the last five days, and that's an improvement for me. I'm still doing plenty of binging and purging, but *after* work. It was really just a matter of time before someone would find out at my job and I would really hate that. So it feels like I actually was doing something constructive for myself rather than, my usual self-destructive number.

Therapist: That's great, Sharon. It must feel good to see yourself make a change like that.

Keep the floor open until everyone who wants to has shared. If one or two members are very quiet, see if you can engage them in discussion by speaking directly to them and asking constructive questions. In the process, be careful not to send the message that those who don't speak much are doing something wrong. Different people relate in groups differently and learn in different ways. The group — and you — should accept many different styles of relating as meaningful and valid.

Nancy: I'm afraid food journals just aren't for me. I have a tendency to get very compulsive with lists of any kind. I'm paranoid about leaving anything out, so I spend hours reviewing the journal, afraid that I've forgotten something important or cheated somehow. I knew in my head that I was getting too involved and should have been more moderate, but I couldn't help it. I stopped keeping the journal last week because it was just making me crazy!

Sharon: At least you tried it, Nancy. I couldn't get the first word down on paper. I never noticed how hard a time I have being told what to do. When I was a teenager, I would never listen to anything my parents said — but I thought I was over all that. All my bosses at work are men and I really haven't had this kind of problem with them. Maybe it has something to do with you [the therapist] being a woman? Anyway, I didn't keep the journal, and I didn't get a lot out of the exercise.

Barbara: I didn't always write in the journal, but when I did, it helped me feel more in control of the food, which is good for me. One surprise was noticing how often I could forget to do something that was really helping me not binge and purge. I was so sure I wanted to recover immediately; but I can tell from the way I've been avoiding this task that, in a way, I'm still avoiding getting better. The good news is that now I know it. I'm going to keep writing in the journal as often as I can.

Therapist: As you can see from what people have been saying, you didn't have to do this task perfectly in order to get something out of it. For those of you who found the exercise helpful, please continue keeping your journal. If it didn't work for you, then feel free to stop. Not all of the things we're going to do will be helpful for everyone; but by the time our group is over on the (specify date), I'll bet that each of you will have found a number of concrete things that will help you recover from your eating disorder.

Homework

Clients should set new or revised goals.

Week 7

Review of Homework: Goal Setting

Intervention 3: Soliciting Individual Examples

Intervention 2: Group Discussion

Focus this week's discussion of goal setting on the concepts of dieting, good and bad food, and "enough but not too much." What goals did people come up with that related to these issues? Did anyone break any food taboos during the week? What was it like for them? Did their goal setting this week teach them anything about the way in which their rigid thinking controls their behavior in annoying and destructive ways?

It may happen that the majority of the group avoided or didn't complete this assignment (or another assignment over the course of the group). It's probably counterproductive to get into a power struggle with the group about the issue of uncompleted homework assignments; yet this issue needs to be addressed in some way. Some groups tend to be extremely compliant, others are completely oppositional, while still others fall somewhere in between. Each extreme is problematic. In the case of overcompliancy, it's less likely that the leader will push the group to examine its tendency to be so passive. You should do so, however, since overly compliant behavior can breed the anger and resentment that, in turn, can trigger binge-purge behaviors. One group member told a particularly poignant story of how far her compliance could go:

"I'm terrified of the water. I always have been. I've never been able to learn how to swim and I have this fear of drowning that paralyzes me. Last week my boyfriend said he wanted to take me out on his dad's little boat with this tiny motor and no life preservers. I went with him. I didn't even ask about the life preservers and I was never so scared in my entire life. I wanted him to like me so much that I just hid the whole thing from him. I'm surprised I didn't vomit from the *fear!*"

When the group is oppositional in response to the assignments, point this out and enlist group members' involvement in trying to get to the root of their reaction.

Be optimistic that they eventually will be more cooperative. Often this will turn out to be the case. If group members still don't do their homework, continue to investigate the source of their resistance.

H. Skill: Identifying Feelings — Taking a Feelings Inventory

Intervention 1: Didactic Presentation (See Concepts and Skills section)

Intervention 3: Soliciting Individual Examples

One simple way to help clients develop the ability to identify and differentiate their feelings is to pay attention to the expression of particular feelings as they arise. During discussion of the homework, ask individuals to be more specific about their feelings. You can help them by offering alternatives. An example of this process follows below:

Therapist: Just then, Joanne, when you were describing that incident with your mother, you seemed to be having some feelings about it as well. Do you know what they were?

Joanne: No, I wasn't feeling anything.

Therapist: I could be wrong, Joanne — but take a second and just think about the incident you were telling me about. See if you can't find a feeling.

Joanne: *(she thinks for a moment with her eyes closed.)* Yes, I was feeling a little weird about that...

Therapist: Okay, great. You found it. Now let's think about "weird" a little bit. Any other word that might describe your feeling even more closely?

Joanne: Upset. I guess I was upset about that.

Therapist: Uh huh. That was an upsetting situation and you got upset; makes sense. Any other feelings beside being upset?

Joanne: No, that's it, upset....

Therapist: What about annoyed? I wondered if you might have been feeling a little annoyed with your mother. What do you think?

Joanne::   I think you might be making too big a deal over all this, but I guess it's true that I was a little annoyed with her. But what's the big deal? How come you're spending so much time on this?

Therapist: Because if you're going to learn how to handle your feelings in new, nonbulimic ways, you're going to have to get a lot more specific about them. The better you understand exactly what you're feeling, the easier it will be to figure out what you might want to try to do to ease that feeling.

Homework

Ask the group to take an inventory of their feelings during the week, making a list of all the feelings they experience. Suggest they try to make the list somewhere in the 25 to 40 word range.

This exercise can produce a wide range of valuable information. At one end of the spectrum, a group member may come to realize how inadequate her feeling vocabulary is, and how that handicaps her in the process of trying to understand her emotions. At the opposite extreme, another member may feel overwhelmed by the number and variety of her feelings, particularly negative ones. In either situation, recognizing feelings opens up the possibility of choosing alternative ways of dealing with them.

Week 8

Review of Homework: Identifying Feelings

Intervention 2: Group Discussion

Begin by asking group members how they felt about doing the feeling inventory. Expect that many members will have found it difficult, and some will have not done it at all. In this case, you can respond, "If this had been easy for all of you, it wouldn't have been an appropriate exercise."

Ask those who completed the assignment how they would feel about reading their lists out loud to the group. You shouldn't force anyone to do this; but you can encourage participation by stressing that the group gives useful feedback. Query whether individual group members learned anything about themselves while making their inventory. Is this a skill they feel they would like to sharpen? Can they appreciate the value of knowing more precisely what they're feeling?

One member of a group, Bob, shared the following list:

exhausted	angry	sad	depressed
edgy	irritable	tense	confused
satisfied	guilty	defensive	safe
frightened	anxious	worthless	confident
hopeless	unsure	warm	proud
superior	inferior	claustrophobic	desolate
despairing	desperate	weak	unworthy
serene	calm	bored	restless
closed	solicitous	lonely	neglected
excited	fraudulent	frustrated	unattractive
empty			

The group had a very strong reaction to this list. Everyone noticed how many negative emotions were on it. They guessed that Bob was much unhappier than he had ever let on in group meetings. The group's response to his list helped Bob take the inventory more seriously, rather than minimizing his emotions, as was his habit. His self-revelation in front of the group pushed Bob to face his feelings and accept that the words were accurate representations of emotions he often felt. The group's honesty and support were aids to Bob in his recovery.

I. Skill: Identifying the Internal Critic

Intervention 1: Didactic Presentation (see Concepts and Skills section)

Intervention 3: Soliciting Individual Examples

As members become better able to identify their feelings, individuals become aware of thoughts that trigger their feelings. During a discussion of the homework, you can help members identify their internal critic, as per the following example:

Cathy:	So I got home from visiting with my sister and headed straight for the refrigerator.
Therapist:	What were your feelings?
Cathy:	Really depressed; I felt like shit. I mean, she has this perfect life — a good job, great husband, two beautiful children.... I guess I was jealous.
Therapist:	What were you saying to yourself at that moment — what was your critic telling you?
Cathy:	Well, I remember thinking that I'd never have that kind of life, that in particular no man would even want me because I'm fat and disgusting.
Therapist:	I can imagine that if I said those things to myself, I'd feel pretty depressed, too. It's important to recognize when the internal critic is making generalizations (*no* man would *ever* want me) that are based on subjective opinions (I'm fat and disgusting). Then you can develop more rational, objective responses. The first step, though, is to identify the critic.

J. Skill: Developing Alternatives to Binging and Purging

Intervention 1: Didactic Presentation (See Concepts and Skills section)

Intervention 2: Group Discussion

Have the group pose problem feelings and ask for ways in which others have successfully dealt in the past with these emotions and the thoughts underlying them.

Example 1

Carol Ann:	One of my problem feelings is boredom. When I get bored or I feel like time is weighing heavy on me, I go straight to the kitchen and pig out. It's almost like it's my entertainment for the evening.
Therapist:	Has anyone ever been successful in not acting on the feeling of wanting to binge out of boredom?
Nancy:	Yes. Sometimes I feel myself getting ready to binge out of boredom, and that's when I know I have to get out of the house. I have a couple of friends who know what I'm going through, and I call them and *run* out the door.

In addition to alternative coping strategies, emphasize that some feelings need to be tolerated. Tell the group, "Feelings come like a wave and gradually pass." Look for examples that illustrate "riding out the wave of feeling."

You can help members develop healthier self-statements to replace their internal critic. Have the group continue to pose situations, or use examples from their homework.

Example 2

Building on the previous section, in which Cathy described returning from a visit with her sister feeling depressed and jealous:

Therapist:	So, Cathy, telling yourself that no man would ever want you because you're fat and disgusting left you feeling pretty depressed. What could you tell yourself that would be more objective and compassionate?
Cathy:	It's hard, because that voice *feels* like the truth.

Therapist:	But in reality "fat" and "disgusting" are simply value judgments. The critic thrives on value judgments. *(to the group:)* "What could Cathy tell herself as an alternative to listening to the critic?
Erica:	I know that if I try telling myself anything too positive, I just don't believe it. But what about something like "My life may not be exactly the way I'd like it, but I'm working on changing things and I'm doing the best I can." That helps me.
Therapist:	What do you think, Cathy?
Cathy:	That sounds like something I should tell myself a lot, in a whole variety of different circumstances.

Homework: Goal Setting

Explain that next week will be the last of your formal discussions on goal setting because the group needs time to cover new material. This does not suggest any assumption on your part that everyone is now successful at the goal-setting process. This will be everyone's ongoing, long-term project. Encourage clients to continue their work by recording reasonable and manageable goals in their journals. They can also write about their feelings connected to these goals, or can discuss their feelings with other members of the group or with spouses, partners, or friends.

Week 9

Preparing for Termination

Initially, most group members were probably comforted by the knowledge that the group would end in 12 sessions. They felt protected against becoming overly dependent on the group — which is a typical sort of fear among bulimics. Yet, as the group draws to its end, many group members will feel upset about the upcoming termination and separation. If you do not deal with these feelings, some members may individually or collectively leave the group prematurely in an attempt to make their uncomfortable feelings disappear. It's important to remember that bulimics are people who are particularly sensitive to feelings of rejection and abandonment, feelings that are likely to be evoked during the normal termination process. It's helpful, therefore, to explicitly raise this issue (even if members of the group don't) and give individuals the opportunity to confront it collectively. Predict some of the possible feelings that clients might have in reaction to the termination process, along with the potential to "act out" in response to those uncomfortable feelings.

Be clear about the possibilities that may or may not exist for the continuation of the group beyond 12 weeks. You should be prepared for the possibility that most members of the group may not want to prolong their participation at this time. This would not be unusual, and doesn't necessarily suggest that there was anything wrong with the group. Often people will choose to begin or resume individual therapy and/or a 12-step program. Some may want to reconvene the group at a later date. Don't continue the group with a paucity of members. If you and the group do decide to continue, you might want to contract for a certain number of sessions and to be paid in advance, rather that leaving the group's duration open-ended.

Pay attention if the group begins to dwindle in size as you near the final session; or if, when you try to raise the issue of termination, the group refuses to discuss it. These *could* be signs that the group is having trouble ending. In both cases, the situations need to be identified and discussed in the group. In the case of the "shrinking group" phenomenon, it may be too late to prevent its worst outcome, the attrition of group members. However, an opportunity to discuss these issues may encourage other clients to remain and work out their problems.

Review of Homework: Goal Setting

Intervention 1: Group Discussion

Follow up on some of the issues that have surfaced around the task of setting goals. Pursue themes that touch on identifying and differentiating feelings, identifying underlying critical thoughts, alternatives to binging and purging, good and bad foods, emotional versus physical hunger, and so on. End the goal-setting process clearly. Encourage group members to continue their work in setting goals if they have found it to be helpful so far.

Week 10

In weeks 10 and 11, two new and demanding topics are introduced. If group members have been responsive to the exercises and seem to want more, then by all means use them. If the group seems more focused on ending-and-process issues, don't force members to do the exercises. Use your clinical judgment about which issues seem most important for your group at this time.

K. Skill: Asking for Help

Intervention 1: Didactic Presentation (See Concepts and Skills section)

Intervention 5: Role-Play

Have everyone in the group think of a particular situation in which he or she has trouble asking for help. Working in pairs, group members should take turns reenacting their difficult situations. (If an extra person is needed, pair off with one of the group members yourself.) Have the one who is being asked for help give feedback to the other person about the effectiveness of the way in which he or she asked for help. Was the person asking for help direct, specific, clear, friendly, and so on? Then have this person describe what it felt like to ask for something. Clients should also describe how they felt their request was received.

Intervention 2: Group Discussion

Bring the group back into the circle and let members share their reactions to the role-play exercise. What did they learn from it? How does the inability to ask for what you want or need relate to binge-purge behavior? Discuss the role of assertiveness in setting and achieving goals.

Homework: Asking for Help

"During the week, I want you to ask three people for help with something that is of significance to you. Remember that even if your request is ultimately denied, you were still entitled to make it: whether or not you get the help is not what we're focusing on now. Write down what happens when you make your three requests so you can share your experience at the next meeting." Have group members discuss their reactions to the assignment; they might want to modify it somewhat. Consider all suggestions, and use them where it seems appropriate.

Review Termination

Intervention 2: Group Discussion

Discuss the feelings brought up for clients by the prospect of the group drawing to its close.

Week 11

Review of Homework: Asking for Help

As you listen, express your appreciation for any and all successes experienced by the group in doing the exercise. Also appreciate the efforts of clients who tried but were unsuccessful. Don't criticize those who had problems with the assignment, or those who couldn't do it.

You might notice that group members are just as interested (if not more) in each other's feedback as they are in yours. This is a normal and healthy part of group functioning.

Example

Therapist: I'm wondering if you were able to try the "asking for help" homework this week, and how it went for you?

Sharon: I got lost on the way to my sister's new place last Saturday, and I started to do my usual routine, which is to drive around until I find what I'm looking for. Sometimes I'm real good at that, but after about 20 minutes of driving aimlessly, I remembered the group and how much I avoid asking for help. So I thought, okay, here's my chance. Even though I hate to ask for directions, I did it anyway. I pulled into a gas station and asked how to get to 31 Gull Road. It was a good idea. I didn't realize just how lost I was, and it wasn't even hard to do. Funny — I really don't get why it's so hard for me to ask for directions.

Nancy: I assigned myself the task of asking my dance teacher for some special attention. I've been in the class for almost two years, and lots of people ask her for help, but I never could. I must have rehearsed my question a hundred times before I finally asked her, and you know what she did? She helped me! Simple as that. It makes me sad to think how many times I've missed out on stuff just because I was too afraid to ask.

Joanne: Nancy, I think I learned something even sadder this week. I decided not to do this exercise because I knew I didn't need to. Asking for help was not my problem, because I've made it a point not to need any help from anyone. I live alone, earn my own way, clean my own apartment, make my own food, I teach myself what I have to know for work. I even taught myself the piano!

But sitting with everyone tonight and hearing all of your battles as you try to get a little help, I think I'm finally understanding that I've never permitted myself to want help. To want it is to leave myself open to not getting it; and I decided that there was no point to that humiliation years and years ago. But you know what? That's very, very sad... *(starts to cry.)*

Therapist: Joanne, I'm really sorry that you had to cut yourself off from help completely for so long, but I'm really glad that you realized all of this today. You don't have to ask anyone for anything until you're ready; but maybe now you can think about it as a choice. There may be a time when it will seem worth it to you to make that choice.

Robin: I thought about asking my boss to explain a little more clearly what he wants me to do. He gives terrible instructions and then, when he doesn't get what he wants, he treats me like I'm and idiot and like it's my fault. But he's such a bastard that I couldn't bring myself to talk to him. Why should I? *He's* supposed to tell me what he wants. If he's so incompetent that he can't even do that, why should I bother to clue him in?

Therapist: Robin, that's a rough spot you're in, and I think most people would be furious with that boss of yours. But I want you to stop and think for a second. Who's suffering most as a result of your anger?

Robin: Well, if you put it that way, I guess I am.

Therapist: Great, you see that. After he's done yelling at you, you finally understand what he wants, and eventually he gets what he wants from you. But what are you getting from him?

Robin: I don't get a damn thing from him except trouble.

Therapist: Well, maybe it's time to consider changing that arrangement. If you keep in mind that asking him for help now is a way for you to protect yourself from unfair criticism and verbal abuse later on, then maybe it won't be so difficult for you.

L. Skill: Expressing Negative Emotion — Saying "No"

Intervention 1: Didactic Presentation (See Concepts and Skill section)

Intervention 3: Soliciting Individual Examples

Ask members to think about particular moments in the recent past when they would have loved to have said "no." Invite them to share these moments with each other.

Example

Sharon: (a new mother) I'm a little embarrassed to tell this, but I will. I've always given my close friends baked goods, made from scratch, for all their special occasions. I'd usually spend hours and hours baking for them, but I'd secretly feel trapped by the whole situation. I figured that by now they've come to expect it and would be hurt if I didn't bake for them. But I've also felt somewhat exploited, and that I don't really get back what I give. It all came to a head with the birth of the baby. Juggling my career, my marriage, and my baby was hard enough. When my friend John asked me to make the birthday cake for his wife's surprise party I got completely desperate. I was furious that he would ask me, but I felt unable to say no. I made the cake and was up until 3 a.m. doing it, even though I had to be up at 7:15 for work the next morning. I knew then that I had a problem saying "no."

As the group continues this discussion, you might notice that some members adopt a "what's done is done" attitude toward incidents they didn't handle as well as they might have. Explain that this is a mistake. "Often you can go back and 'fix' a situation by expressing your feelings to the person who was initially involved in the interaction. No one expects that you'll always express yourself perfectly the first time. Most people are willing to hear you out, even if it's about something that happened quite a while ago. You can achieve two benefits from doing this. First, you might very well resolve a conflict with someone and feel better about them and yourself. Second, by practicing going back and resolving old grievances, you will gradually develop the ability to confront issues as they happen.

Intervention 5: Role-Play

If the group was successful in using the role-playing exercise in which they asked for help, have members pair off again and practice saying "no" about something of significance in their lives.

Homework: Saying "No"

Assign the task of having clients say "no" on three separate occasions during the following week. Discuss their reactions to the assignment, and resolve any questions. Ask group members to keep a written record of their experiences in trying to say no, so that they can share them next week in group. Group members are likely to be quite apprehensive about the assignment whether or not they express their apprehension. Try to draw this out so that you can provide reassurance and encouragement.

Before ending, explain to clients that they will have an opportunity to evaluate their group experience in next week's session, which will be the final meeting.

Week 12

Review Homework: Saying "No"

Intervention 2: Group Discussion

Ask group members about their experiences saying "no." What did they learn about themselves in the process? How did others respond to their nay-saying? What do they imagine as their next step in this particular learning process?

Group members can also practice expressing uncomfortable emotions during your discussion about terminating the group. Ask them what kinds of feelings they are having as the group comes to an end? How is this ending either reminiscent of, or different from, other endings in the past? Can they tolerate their feelings without having to do anything about them? Can they share their feelings with one another?

Ask group members if they plan on continuing, in a formal way, the work begun in the group. Do they plan to keep in touch with any other group members? How would they describe their experience of being in the group?

Termination

Permit the group to devote most of its time to the closure process. Help participants find a thoughtful way of saying goodbye to one another and to the group itself. Include yourself in the process.

Hand out evaluation forms (see Handout 2). Give the group 10 to 15 minutes to fill them out before the end of the session (or else you won't get most of them back). Congratulate yourself for guiding the group through an arduous process. Summarize what you've learned from this group experience in writing, and use that information to make your *next* group more productive.

With a little luck (and I mean that), this will have been an emotionally satisfying experience for you as well as for the members of the group.

Criteria for Measuring Change

Bulimia is a symptom cluster that can occur in a heterogeneous group of people. This group consists of people with different character structures, psychopathologies, family backgrounds, class backgrounds, educational backgrounds, and so on. Symptomatology ranges from fairly mild to extremely severe. Therefore, one way to assess the changes that the group has produced in its members is to compare each group member with what he or she was like just before entering the group.

Symptom diminution and abatement is another way to assess change; but this is fraught with problems. If clients are given the message that "success" in the group is defined by a cessation of binging and purging, then they may lie about it; or they may simulate a "cure" and resume their bulimic behaviors as soon as the leader is no longer there to reward abstinence. Remember that symptom abatement, to be significant, must be accompanied by many of the changes outlined in this chapter. Recovery from bulimia can take years; sometimes, in successful treatments the symptoms are the last to go (much to the exasperation of everyone, including the therapist).

Try to use the group feedback forms as a way to get some data on your clients' own assessment of the changes they made while in the group. Since their recovery will ultimately be their own responsibility, their assessments are probably the most important ones. The individual's ability to appraise the progress of his or her own recovery and to respond appropriately is a key to long-term change. Self-deception is likely to undermine the recovery process.

Relapse Prevention

The disappearance of symptoms is not necessarily the hallmark of a successful or complete recovery from bulimia. This psychopathology typically indicates a developmental arrest; it is therefore progress in the maturational process that is the real goal. As a person matures emotionally, she develops healthier coping mechanisms that take the place of the eating disorder. Of course, this is not to say that a resumption or intensification of bulimic symptomatology is not problematic. Often it is. And there are things you can convey to group members to help them.

1. "Understand that by binging and purging again you've broken through a wall of your own creation that was protecting you. It's not nearly as strong as it was before you crashed through it; so be alert to the fact that you are much more likely to slip again, and will need to make an extra effort to remain abstinent.

2. "Contact people you trust (perhaps former group members) and let them know about your slip. Your honesty with them will help you be honest with yourself, and will promote your healing.

3. "Plan your eating more carefully. Be sure that you feel comfortable with what you're eating.

4. "Participate in self-help groups for compulsive eaters or for bulimics and share about your slip. Regular attendance at a self-help group can offer continued support for your abstinence."

References

Brownell, K., and Foreyt, J. *Handbook of Eating Disorders*. New York: Basic Books, Inc. 1986.

Center for the Study of Anorexia and Bulimia/Group Psychotherapy Division. *Group Psychotherapy with Bulimics*. New York: Center for the Study of Anorexia and Bulimia, 1984.

Johnson, C., and Connors, M. *The Etiology and Treatment of Bulimia Nervosa*. New York: Basic Books, Inc. 1987

O'Donnell, D. *Structural Interventions for Bulimics*. New York: Center for the Study of Anorexia and Bulimia. Unpublished manuscript.

Root, M.P.P.; Fallon, P.; and Friedrich, W.N. *Bulimia: A Systems Approach to Treatment*. New York: W.W. Norton & Co., Inc. 1986.

Siegel, M.; Brisman, J.; and Weinshel, M. *Surviving an Eating Disorder*. New York: Harper and Row, Inc. 1988.

Whitaker, L, and Davis, W. *The Bulimic College Student*. New York: The Haworth Press, 1988.

Acknowledgment

I wish to gratefully acknowledge Deborah O'Donnell, C.S.W., and Francis Hamburg, C.S.W., as well as the past and present members of the group treatment division of the Center for the Study of Anorexia and Bulimia, for developing many of the concepts articulated in this chapter.

Handout 1

Short-Term Group Policies

1. The fee for the entire short-term group is payable before the first group meeting. Group fees are nonrefundable.

2. Any group member missing more than two group sessions cannot continue in the group.

3. Group therapists may have occasion to contact a group member's individual therapist. Group members will be required to complete a release form at the time of their initial consultation authorizing communication between [yourself or your organization] and the therapist involved.

4. [Yourself/your organization] is not a medical [practitioner/facility] and therefore cannot be responsible for health-related problems. All group members are urged, however, to be under regular medical care. [Yourself/your organization] will provide, upon request, the names of physicians who have experienced treating patients with eating disorders.

5. If at any time during the course of group therapy the group leader has questions concerning a person's physical status, [yourself/your organization] may require a complete medical evaluation by a qualified physician as a condition of continued participation in the group. Failure to obtain a required medical examination will result in that person's termination from the group.

   Any group member required to undergo a medical evaluation will be required to sign a release form authorizing written and oral communication between [yourself/your organization] and the attending physician.

_____

Signature of Group Member

_____

Date

Handout 2

Feedback About the Group

1. What were your expectations concerning the group? Were these expectations met? Please explain.

2. Did you experience any change in your feelings about yourself in general during the group experience? If so, what were they? What did you learn about yourself?

3. To what extent were you able to reduce the input from your internal critic and replace it with healthier, more objective and compassionate self-statements?

4. Did your *attitudes* toward eating and your weight change at all during the course of the group? If so, how?

5. Did your *behavior* in regard to eating and your weight change at all during the course of the group? If so, how?

6. What comments do you have about the way in which the group functioned? Do you have any suggestions for improvements?

7. Do you have plans to continue the work on yourself that you began with the group? Please elaborate.

8. What feelings did you have about the group leader and his/her role in the group?

9. Any other comments?

Thank you!

Chapter 8

Rape Survivors Group

Julia Conyers-Boyd, M.Ed.

Introduction

Statistics show that one in three women has suffered the traumatic victimization of sexual assault at some point in her life. Although this number — provided by the National Crime Bureau and based on the women who actually report — may appear to be high, national law enforcement officials and mental health experts consider the estimate to be consertive. Many women who have been sexually assaulted *don't* report the crime. The social stigma that continues to plague women and taint them with the responsibility for sexual assault has historically discouraged them from speaking out about their abuse.

With the onset of the feminist movement, grassroots support groups were formed by and for women who had experienced abuse. Out of these support groups a viligant effort was begun by feminist therapists to reexamine current clinical practices for treating the victims of sexual assault. In the past, women had been revictimized in treatment by therapists and institutions that seemed to hold the women themselves responsible for the assault. Revisionist therapists have found that a blend of supportive and therapeutic techniques in the context of a group setting are the most helpful course of treatment for women who have been raped or otherwise assaulted.

This chapter will present informational concepts and techniques on how to design, plan, and facilitate a therapeutic support group for such women.

Selection and Screening

When at all possible, it's preferable to schedule individual interviews with prospective group members. One-on-one interviewing allows you and the prospective client to start building a relationship that will continue as the group progresses. This process also allows clients to sound you verbally and emotionally, and to share their expectations regarding the group experience.

The interview gives you the opportunity to ask questions that will help you assess the client's readiness to participate in a therapeutic support group. To form a clear picture of the prospective group member's emotional dynamics and coping style, you will need to gather several crucial pieces of information.

First, how much time has passed since the sexual assault? There are no hard-and-fast rules regarding ideal length of time between the assault and group treatment. Individuals who are in the very beginning stages of their crisis are prone to be more concerned with practical needs, such as reestablishing their daily routine. The emotional demands of the recently assaulted individual may also cause other group members to minimize their own needs. You should consider this if you have enough prospective clients to form more than one group.

You need to assess the individual's ability to benefit from a treatment program designed with a strong verbal and cognitive component. A psychotic individual would, for obvious reasons, be inappropriate for inclusion. Anyone who is actively abusing alcohol or drugs should also be referred to another treatment setting. However, if a substance abuser has received at least six months of prevention treatment, and agrees to continue with treatment while participating in the group, you can consider including her in the group for rape survivors.

Other important factors to consider in group member composition include age, ethnic background, individual sexual preference, and variables surrounding the sexual assault. For example, a thirty-five-year-old upwardly mobile white female who was raped at knifepoint by a stranger who broke into her home may have some difficulty relating to a twenty-year-old counterculture white prostitute who was raped by her pimp. It's important to have the group as homogenous as possible so that all group members can receive an equal measure of support.

Time and Duration

The group should run for an hour and a half, once a week, for 12 weeks.

Structure

Building trust among group members is a critical element in the format of a group for sexual assault survivors. Therefore a closed group structure is highly desirable. A closed group, as opposed to one where clients can drop in, provides a safe environment for women who will be disclosing personal and painful information. Consistency and trust are major issues for people whose expectations and sense of safety have been so grossly violated.

Agenda Setting

An agenda will allow you to lay a concrete foundation with which to support your group structure. For each week, the group agenda should be established in advance. You should make every attempt to adhere to it once the agenda is set. In particular, try to focus the group's attention on the weekly theme (trust, self-image, sexuality, guilt, and so on).

Each weekly group is divided into four parts: 1) check-in, to briefly establish how each member is feeling, 2) theme of the week, 3) sharing personal stories and reactions, and 4) closure, which includes a guided imagery exercise and a preview of the next week's agenda.

Goals

The goals of this group are to provide women who have been sexually assaulted with information about abuse, to provide a safe setting in which they can talk about their thoughts and feelings, and to reduce their sense of isolation. The group also validates the feelings that members experienced, including guilt, shame, anger, and powerlessness. Group members will work toward clarity about who was responsible for the assault and will focus on developing an increased sense of self-esteem.

Ground Rules

At the first session it's important to go over ground rules for the group. **Confidentiality** is always a priority in sexual assault groups. Go around the group and have each woman verbally commit to the rule that what's said in the group stays in the group. As a facilitator, you should also make this commitment, with one exception: you're bound by law to provide necessary intervention if you suspect that a client poses a danger to herself or someone else. **No drinking or drugs** up to four hours before or during group session. This rule should be strictly enforced. The only exception would be a group member who is taking medication prescribed by a physician. If a client is taking prescribed mood-altering medication, this information should be disclosed during the one-on-one interview. At that time, the client should sign a release form authorizing you to contact her physician for more specific information regarding the client's medical condition. **Attendance at every meeting is strongly encouraged.** Missed sessions are damaging in closed groups because group members form a close bond and learn to depend on each other for support. Request that clients call you if they're going to be absent or late, so that you can share this information with the rest of the group.

Starting the Group

Welcome group members to the session by introducing yourself and reviewing your experience with rape survivors. Then go around the group and have members give their first names: ask them to share one item (anything they wish) about themselves. Pass out a copy of the weekly group agenda. This is an optional step, but it allows group members to preview upcoming sessions. If you choose to include this step, ask clients if they have any questions about or reactions to the agenda. Cover housekeeping information (break times, bathroom location, and childcare). Explain the ground rules for the group: **confidentiality**, **no drinking or drugs**, and notifying the group about **missed sessions** or late arrival. Ask members individually to commit to the rules.

"I'm going to go around the group and ask you to verbally commit to the rules I just stated. Mary, do you agree to abide by the ground rules for the group?"

Main Concepts and Skills

A. Concept: Identifying and Defining Sexual Assault

"Sexual assault occurs on a continuum in such a way that it's not always immediately recognizable:

Sexual Assault Continuum

Suggestive Comments or Gestures	Obscene Phone Calls or Comments	Flashing; Voyeuristic Behavior	Unwelcome or Unsolicited Touch	Rape

"Sexual assault victims often have a difficult time identifying an assault as such if it doesn't culminate in rape.* Many times the victims do not recognize that the impact the assault had on their emotional lives is in itself what defines the action as an assault. Whether the offender is making obscene comments or has committed an actual rape, his behavior is a sexual assault when *you* experience it as hurtful or traumatic. It is your reaction that counts. It is your pain that defines an act as assaultive."

B. Concept: Impact of Sexual Assault

"While there isn't any definitive information suggesting that sexual assault permanently impairs an individual's life, clinical evidence reported by physicians and mental health professionals clearly shows that victims experience emotional trauma. Emotional and physical symptoms reported by victims are similar to those associated with Post-Traumatic Stress Disorder (PTSD) or other life traumas as described in the *Diagnostic and Statistical Manual of Mental Disorders III-Revised*. Emotional symptoms may include:

- Intrustive recollections (flashbacks)
- Recurrent dreams or nightmares
- Diminished affect or responsiveness
- Impaired memory function
- Feelings of detachment
- Loss of interest in activities that were once enjoyed
- Hypervigilance
- Depression
- Unreasonable fears
- An inability to experience intimacy
- A decrease in, or complete loss of, sexuality

Physical symptoms may include:
- Headaches
- Anorexia nervosa or bulimia
- Stomach problems
- Muscle tension
- Constipation
- Recurrent urinary tract infections
- Drug or alcohol abuse

---

*An assault may become confused in the victim's mind with other issues such as physical abuse, wife battering, or a problem with alcohol or drugs.

"All victims of trauma develop a set of coping mechanisms. Such coping behaviors as alcoholism, substance abuse, and eating disorders are readily identifiable; because these behaviors are more obvious then many of the more exclusively emotional symptoms, it's 'easier' to help the survivor validate the existence of a problem. Other forms of coping behaviors are less noticeable and less easily connected to the assault: emotional shutdown (not allowing yourself to experience emotions), dissociative behavior or 'spacing out' in stressful situations, amnesia in connection with the rape or assault, and unexplained or unreasonable anxiety around certain people or situations."

C. Concept: The Victim Is Not Responsible for Her Victimization

"Victims of sexual assault are not immune to cultural beliefs, myths, stereotypes, and images of women as sexual objects. It therefore becomes easy to fall into the trap of taking responsibility for the assault (for example, a woman who makes an effort to be sexually attractive is inviting assault).

"Knowing the offender (if he's an acquaintance, date, or partner) further increases your tendency to take responsibility. In such a situation, you may believe that there must have been something you could have done to prevent the assault. However, national crime reports and offender studies reveal that offenders rarely, if ever, consider the thoughts or feelings of their victims, no matter how well acquainted they may be. These same offender studies show that sexual assault victims have little or no control over the actions or behaviors of the offender. Often a sexual assault is the result of a well-thought-out plan on which your actions or decisions have no bearing whatsoever.

"Accepting the reality of not being responsible for the offender's behavior means that you have to give up your fantasy of control and accept on some level the feelings of having been helplessly victimized. It also means accepting the possibility of being helplessly victimized at some future date. This is a very painful and difficult reality to accept.

"It often feels preferable to remain in a state of denial surrounding the issue of your own helplessness, thus believing in some small way that you could have prevented the assault from happening. This position of denial allows you to take responsibility for the offender's behavior, and in a paradoxical way gives you a sense of control in a situation in which you have no control. You might say to yourself, 'I shouldn't have worn those tight jeans on that date with Marvin.' 'If only I hadn't gone to that party and had too much to drink!'

"You may believe that your decisions, both wise and unwise, are what determine your fate: that basically you are in complete control. And yet your decisions can only affect *your* actions, not someone else's. Maybe drinking too much at the party wasn't a wise decision, or walking home from the late movie wasn't a smart idea; but being sexually assaulted in conjunction with either of these events was not the result of any decision made by you. The sole responsibility for the sexual assault belongs to the man who assaulted you, no matter how you dressed, what you drank, or where you walked. That was *his* decision.

"Being sexually assaulted does not mean that you've done something wrong or bad. You are every bit as fine and good a person as you were before the assault. The offender chose to assault you: you must remind yourself, over and over again if necessary, that you are blameless for what he decided to do.

Everyone makes decisions all the time. Some of these decisions are wise, some are faulty. But women never deserve to be sexually assaulted, no matter what they've said, what they've worn or had to drink, or how they've walked. This blame-the-victim mentality is a mistaken idea that we've been taught to believe. But it's completely false: you are not to blame."

D. Concept: Being a Survivor

"Being a survivor is hard work emotionally and physically. You've endured a life-threatening trauma. The means by which one survives are not as important as the fact of survival itself.

There are two parts to survival. The first is surviving the rape itself — somehow making it through the experience alive, enduring the violation. But the second part is surviving all the feelings that the trauma sets off — fear, anger, depression, guilt. It takes a lot of courage to survive this flood of feelings.

"Living through a traumatic experience in which you had no control is a major challenge and ordeal, and will tax you physically, emotionally, and intellectually. The first step toward recovery is to recognize and validate the severity of your trauma."

E. Skill: Identifying Yourself as a Survivor

"One way of identifying and validating yourself as a survivor is to consciously look at the methods you've used for coping. You've probably changed your behavior in several ways since the assault. Perhaps you find yourself hyperalert in certain situations, or you are reluctant to drive alone at night, or you no longer go into unfamiliar environments alone. It's important to acknowledge and accept the specific coping responses that you've developed."

F. Concept: Offenders

"It would be nice if you could spot and identify rapists by the way they looked or acted. But the reality is that rapists and other sex offenders can look and act just like the men who don't sexually assault women. There are abundant myths, stereotypes, and images of who or what a sex offender is supposed to be. But the truth is that sex offenders come in all sizes, ages, and colors, from all walks of life: they can be bankers or crane operators, soldiers or barbers, teenagers or hardened criminals. The one common trait that all sex offenders seem to share is an ability to view women as objects and to act in ways that deny these women their individual humanity. Another common thread that links offenders is a tendency to blame their victim for the assault, thus refusing to take responsibility for their own actions and behavior."

G. Concept: Experiencing Uncomfortable Feelings

"There will be times when you feel as if you're on an emotional roller coaster, experiencing highs and lows for what may seem like no reason at all. These highs and lows are part of the healing process. Some feelings, such as anger, guilt, sadness, and fear, may stand out for you more than others. You may also notice feeling ashamed, withdrawn, unlovable, untouchable, asexual, and mistrustful. All of these feelings, however uncomfortable, are quite normal for a person who has experienced trauma. Give yourself permission to have these feelings: they are a perfectly healthy reaction. Experiencing them will be an important part of your recovery."

H. Skill: Dealing With Uncomfortable Feelings

"Feelings are normal — everyone has them. But some feelings may seem more acceptable than others. Below are descriptions of some of the feelings that tend to make people uncomfortable, along with ways to deal with these emotions. Above all, it's important for you to remember that feelings come and go; no feeling lasts forever."

Anger

"Feeling angry is a healthy emotional response in some situations. Often people don't feel comfortable with anger because there aren't many examples in their lives of how to express anger in healthy ways. Here are a few suggestions for healthy expressions of anger:

- Hit a pillow — go ahead, knock the stuffing out of it!

- Go to a safe, isolated place and scream — let it all out. You can sit in your car with all the windows rolled up and scream your head off — the car will be fairly soundproofed, and you can keep it locked.

- Perform a demanding physical task: chop wood, move furniture around, jump rope, play racketball, dig holes, run, dance, pull weeds. Any activity that requires putting your whole body into it is good.

- Write an angry letter using all the foul words you can think of and all the most elegant put-downs. Rip the letter up afterwards — put all your energy into ripping it into tiny little pieces and throw the pieces up into the air.

- In a situation in which it's not safe to act out your angry feelings, fantasize instead that you're bigger, stronger, and smarter than the situation, person, or event that's making you angry. Then imagine yourself picking it up and twirling it around in the air with one hand."

Guilt and Shame

"Guilt and shame are first cousins: generally wherever one is found, the other is close behind. If you're feeling guilty or ashamed, it might be helpful to examine the thoughts connected to your feelings. Thoughts about being wrong, bad, or immoral place you in the position of judging yourself. And when you're riding an emotional roller coaster, it's very likely that your judgment may be off. This may be a good time to talk to someone you trust about how you're feeling or thinking. In order to get a clearer perspective. You can also use questions as a way of expos any faultiness in the logic of your thinking. For example, you can ask yourself, 'Is this always true? Are there situations I can remember in which this hasn't been true? Are there nuances or shadings that I'm not considering? What other qualities about myself am I ignoring when I have this thought?' and so on. Try to reserve judgment on yourself for the time being, and focus blame where it belongs: on the person who sexually assaulted you."

Sadness

"Grief or sadnesss is a natural reaction to loss. Being sexually assaulted causes many losses: the loss of trust, stability, security, possibly your health, and the sense of freedom you had before the asssault occurred. You need time to grieve these losses. Allow yourself to be sad; don't try to chase your grief away. You won't feel sad forever, but for now you have the right to your feelings of grief. You've lost a lot."

Fear

"There may be times when you'll feel fearful. Check out your feelings about the situations in which you feel most frightened. Do you feel safest when you're alone or around others? Indoors or outdoors? In the city or the country? Feelings of fear are generally related to believing that you're not sufficiently in control of your environment. Do whatever you need to do for now to feel safe and in control. You may need to sleep with the light on, buy a dog, get a roommate, ask friends or family to accompany you to new or even familiar places, or even change your residence. Some of these things are much easier to do than others; and some may not be feasible for you. The important thing is to figure out what factors you *can* control, and then to exercise that control. There is no virtue in "toughing out" a situation that terrifies you. You need to nurture yourself now and respect your fears."

Withdrawal

"Give yourself permission to withdraw from others for a while. Spending time alone can allow you to collect your thoughts and experience your private feelings. Set aside a certain amount of time daily or weekly for your emotional healing. This takes the same discipline as a program of physical exercise, but it's harder to do because the process is invisible. You may feel foolish or selfish setting aside time just to sit in a comfortable chair or take a bubblebath — but this nurturing solitude is part of your recovery. Respect these times, and make sure that other people around you — spouse, partner, roommate, children — respect your solitude as well. Don't try to combine your "alone time" with other activities such as housework or chores. You might try setting aside 20 minutes a day for your withdrawal. If you find yourself needing more time than you've set aside for this process, it might be a good idea to consider seeing a therapist or joining another support group."

Worthlessness and Impaired Self-Esteem

"The sexual assault may cause you to doubt your ability to give or receive love. Because of societal misconceptions about women and rape, it's easy to see how you might now believe yourself to be unworthy of love and affection. This is a good time to challenge your beliefs. Use a sheet of paper to write down the names of everyone you love, including pets. Now write down the names of all the people or pets who you believe love you. What did you discover? If you need to challenge the results, call three people on the list and ask them if they love you. Go ahead and try it. Select two of the people or pets and give them a hug. What happens? What you will discover is that feelings and beliefs aren't facts: sometimes they need to be challenged."

Impaired Sexuality

"Sexual assault has nothing to do with sex or making love. But due to the nature of the violence and the way in which it's acted out, it's sometimes difficult to separate, emotionally and physically, the act of sex, or making love, from the assault. You may experience flashbacks or emotional detachment from your partner during lovemaking. If this occurs, it may be helpful to have your partner whisper his or her name or share a comforting phrase with you. For example, 'Sue, this (partner's name), and I'm here with you.' Or 'Betty, this is (partner's name); I'll keep you safe.' Certain parts of your body may be hypersensitive to touch after the assault; let your partner know what's comfortable or uncomfortable for you. Don't worry about expressing any new concerns to your partner as they come up. A loving partner will understand.

"You may not feel like being sexual for a while after the assault, and you may be unable to achieve an orgasm. Again, such changes are a normal part of the healing process. They're most likely temporary changes. Some women may need increased sexual affirmation as part of their healing. Everyone heals in a different way. Listen to your body, listen to your feelings. Respect your needs."

Mistrust

"You will probably experience a lot of confusion at first about whom to trust now that your trust has been so badly shaken. You may worry that you'll never trust anyone again, and that others may perceive you as distant and cold.

"You have the right to reserve your sense of trust for a while. After all, your trust has been violated. This is particularly true in cases of date or acquaintance rape by someone you've known and trusted in the past. Trusting is one of those tricky human emotions that is free and unconditional when first given; but once violated, it has to be re-earned. There may be a small number of people whom you continue to trust and believe in, but it's okay to expect others to earn the right to know you. It may be helpful to establish personal guidelines for how long you have to know someone before considering him or her a friend.

"For example, you might make the guideline, 'I will only invite very close friends to my home.' Or 'I will not share personal information about myself with people at the office.' Like all guidelines, these shouldn't be too rigid: allow some flexibility for exceptions. The purpose of the guidelines is not to have an inflexible rule to follow, but rather to provide yourself with a sense of structure and safety."

I. Concept: Recovery

"If you were to have open heart surgery, you could expect to spend up to six months or more recovering. Your whole daily personal program would be altered to accommodate the time needed for physical healing.

The emotional trauma of being sexually assaulted is like the physical trauma of surgery. Emotional and physical recovery takes time; it's not a process that can be rushed without negative consequences. The process of emotional recovery is marked by an array of physical symptoms. You may experience

- Needing more or less sleep

- Insomnia or waking at odd hours during the night

- Nightmares

- Decrease or increase in appetite

- Decrease in energy

- Impaired memory

- Lack of concentration

- Lack of interest in activities you once enjoyed

- Increase in physical illness, such as colds or flulike symptoms

- Irritability

- Jumpiness

- Flashbacks

- Mood swings

J. Skills: Recovery in Progress

"Emotional recovery, like physical recovery, occurs in stages. Here are some things to look for as you learn to recognize and cope with the emotional recovery process. Remember that the process takes time — up to six months or more, depending on your circumstances. You would not fault yourself for failing to recover faster if you'd had open heart surgery: emotional healing deserves the same respect and patience."

Sleep

"Sleep disruption is a common trait in emotional trauma. If you find that extra sleep is helpful, schedule it into your routine. Take naps, retire earlier in the evening. Your body and emotions are healing, and healing requires extra rest.

Early or odd-hour waking is your body's way of being alert as you try to re-establish your sleep patterns. If you find that you're waking early or at odd hours, wait a few minutes to see if you drift back to sleep. If you don't, do something restful (such as reading or listening to soft music) until you feel sleepy again. If the sleep disruption is causing severe problems in your regular routine, see your physician or refer to one of the many self-help books on techniques to fight insomnia."

Appetite

"You may notice an increase or decrease in your normal appetite. This is yet another of your body's ways of adjusting and healing. Try to establish a schedule for eating so that you're meeting basic nutritional needs. Make a date to have meals with a friend and fill two needs at the same time. If you are wasting away or eating way too much, you should consult a therapist or join a therapeutic support group for people with eating disorders to help you reestablish healthy eating habits."

Energy

"Emotional healing is hard work, and your body only has so much energy. You may notice a severe decline in your energy level. Three words of advice: *stop and rest*. You may say to yourself, 'But I used to be able to do twice this much!' Don't frustrate yourself by comparing past performance with the slower pace you need to take now. Take your time with everything. Spread chores over a longer period. If you work outside the home, request sick leave on the days when you need the extra rest. If your present job won't allow you to do this, consider taking a leave of absence or finding another job."

Memory

"Before the assault you may never have given much thought to your ability to remember minor details. But the trauma has heightened your sense of self-awareness, and any lapse in memory may now seem like a major flaw. It's natural to be distracted — and forgetful — during your recovery period. Your memory skills will regain strength with time — but for the present you can help yourself by writing things down that you want to remember. Like your energy, much of your memory and concentration are now being diverted to the process of emotional healing."

Concentration

"Daydreaming, or woolgathering, is your mind's way of taking a rest. When you find that you're unable to focus for periods of time, take a break. If possible, physically move away from the task at hand. If you find your mind drifting from what you're trying to get done and it's impossible to physically move away, give yourself five minutes to daydream; then gently bring yourself back by refocusing on your work."

Lack of Interest in Activities

"Everything may seem like a bother right now. Even activities that you once enjoyed may now seem like a chore Don't give up these activities, but scale them down into smaller doses. Instead of reading for an hour, try reading for ten minutes; take a short walk instead of a brisk run. Arrange to share an activity with a friend — something relaxing but entertaining. Be patient with your short attention span and diminished energy. Things will return to normal!"

Physical Illness

"Stress often mimics physical illness, so don't be surprised if you notice an increase in cold or flulike symptoms. Whatever the cause of these symptoms, rest is the answer. If you're unsure if an illness is caused by stress or the real McCoy, contact your physician. Take the time to pamper yourself, stay in bed, drink hot tea, eat your favorite comfort foods. Remember, healing is the goal."

Irritability

"Being edgy and irritable is a common sign of stress overload. When you find yourself snapping, yelling, or just getting plain frustrated with everyone, it's time to take a break. Have you been getting enough rest? Maybe it would be a good idea to talk to someone you trust about how you're feeling. You can also let the people around you — friends, family, co-workers — know that you're under a lot of stress now and you may sometimes react in ways that seem out of proportion or unfair. Don't expect people to read your mind about how much stress you're under! Most people will react to irritabilty by believing that they themselves have done something wrong. Your explanations will reassure them and will help you be more comfortable with your own behavior."

Flashbacks

"Flashbacks can come on without warning, interrupting your thoughts, concentration, sexual activities, relaxation, and work. For many trauma survivors, they are the most disruptive part of healing. Just when you thought you were getting better, an image, smell, or sensation will trigger a memory of the assault. As disturbing as they are, flashbacks are a normal part of the trauma experience. As fast as the flashbacks come, they will also go away. 'But I don't like them,' you protest. 'I want to forget about the assault — the flashbacks remind me of what happened.' It's natural not to like flashbacks. And you're right, they're very unpleasant. In ways that psychologists don't yet understand, flashbacks seem to be another one of the psyche's coping strategies. They decrease with time; they will eventually disappear. When flashbacks intrude on your consciousness, be ready with a set of positive affirmations to reassure you that you're safe. You can write these down on 3 by 5 cards that you keep with you at all times. Use the affirmations below, or make up your own:

- I'm in a safe place now.

- I was okay before the assault; I survived during the assault; I'm surviving now.

- I can survive my healing process one day at a time.

K. Concept: Getting Support

"Any type of recovery process is harder work without outside support. You don't have to be alone in your emotional recovery process. There are trained helping professionals throughout the United States who can provide you with support.

Perhaps you feel that you don't want anyone to know about what happened to you. Sharing the emotional pain of trauma isn't easy, but shouldering alone the burden of the pain is harder still. Remember that you didn't do anything wrong. It doesn't matter what the circumstances were surrounding the sexual assault. If you were hit by a car while crossing the street or were the victim of war, you would also need assistance to deal with your emotional trauma. As a victim of sexual assault, your pain is just as real, your need for help just as legitimate. Talking with a trained helping professional or taking part in a group will validate your experience and boost your emotional strength. You've already survived the hardest part of sexual assault and shown that you have the courage to continue living."

Main Interventions

Week 1

Introduction

See Starting the Group.

A. Concept: Identifying and Defining Sexual Assault

Intervention 1: Didactic Presentation (See Concepts and Skills section)

B. Concept: Impact of Sexual Assault

Intervention 1: Didactic Presentation (See Concepts and Skills section)
Intervention 2: Group Sharing of Personal Stories

Explain to group members that sharing the personal story of their victimization is a very difficult but crucial part of the group process. By openly exposing the details of their assault, the formal process of working through feelings of shame, guilt, hurt, and anger can begin. Letting go and sharing allows group members to receive support for placing the responsibility for the assault where it belongs — with the offender. Request that individuals give as many details as they can remember, such as where the assault took place, what was said to them by the offender, if others were nearby, the reactions of others to the assault, and whether the offender still poses a threat to them now. Allow individuals to take as much time as they need to tell their stories without interruption. Listen carefully to see if the group member uses language that places the blame for the assault on herself, so that you can later gently guide her back to recognizing that she had no control over the offender's actions.

The telling of stories is often a very emotional part of the group process. Be prepared to offer a great deal of nurturing and verbal support.

Intervention 3: Emotional Affirmation

Give verbal support to group members sharing their stories by using comforting language. For example, "Martha, we know this is hard for you, but you're in a safe place now. Everyone here understands the kind of pain you're feeling now. Everyone here wants to listen to what you have to say."

Intervention 4: Reframing

Attentive listening while group members recount their sexual victimization will give you an indication of how they've conceptualized their experience. Listen for linguistic clues suggesting that a client may be assuming some form of responsibility for the assault that wounded her.

Be especially attentive to "I let...I should have...If only I had...He didn't really mean to...I wasn't really hurt..." and other similar constructions.

Have the client reframe phrases that contain messages of culpability by bringing her focus back to the real cause of the assault: the offender himself. For example:

Connie:	It was stupid of me to wear that new off-the-shoulder red dress to the party on my date with Robert. But I wanted to look nice; it was my office party.
Therapist:	Connie, I hear several things in what you're saying. The party was a special occasion, and you wore your new dress to look special, not to invite Robert to assault you. There is never any legitimate excuse or rationale for sexual assault. Wanting to look nice isn't stupid, and wearing that new red dress didn't cause you to be raped.
Masha:	It was asking for trouble to go into that dark foyer.
Therapist:	You went in because you had to see _____. You weren't asking to be raped. It's the rapist who is responsible for assaulting you. That was his decision, and *he* is responsible for what he did to you.

Intervention 5: Socratic Dialogue

It's important to help group members pinpoint negative feelings they may have about themselves as a result of the sexual assault. By asking pointed questions and questioning the logic of their responses, you can help members of the group correct their negative self-talk and improve their self-esteem.

Jill:	I feel guilty all the time.
Therapist:	Are there times when you experience more guilt then others?
Jill:	Yes — whenever I'm around people I don't know very well.
Therapist:	What happens when you're around people you don't know very well?
Jill:	I get all nervous and jittery inside, and it's like they know what happened to me. And then I feel all guilty and bad, like I did something wrong.
Therapist:	Do you experience guilt at other times?
Jill:	Yeah, whenever I date a new guy.

Therapist:	How about other times?
Jill:	No, not really.
Therapist:	Jill, I'm curious. How does having nervous, anxious feelings about being around strangers, especially strange men, make you a bad, guilty person?
Jill:	I never thought about it like that. Maybe it's because I think they know about my assault.
Therapist:	How would they know about your victimization?
Jill:	Couldn't they tell by the way I acted?
Therapist:	They might be able to see that you're nervous, anxious, and shy, but they couldn't tell from your behavior that you've been sexually assaulted. Not unless they could read minds.
Jill:	I guess I sort of assume sometimes that people can see right through me.
Therapist:	They could only know about the assault if you told them. What do you experience when I say that, Jill?
Jill:	I feel sort of relieved.
Therapist:	Let me ask you something else. How would you begin to feel guilty and wrong if someone learned that you had been sexually assaulted?
Jill:	I think they'd kind of assume that I'd let it happen or acted in a way that brought it on. That's it. They'd think I'd brought it on myself.
Therapist:	Why would they think that? Why would they assume that you invited the rape?
Jill:	I don't know.
Therapist:	What would you think in their shoes?
Jill:	That the person must be in a lot of pain. That she had been incredibly hurt. I'd be really angry at the attacker.
Therapist:	Is it possible for you to allow that others might react to you just as sympathetically?

Intervention 6: Group Exercise — Visualization

Spend at least 15 minutes doing a simple guided imagery exercise with deep breathing to help bring group members back to the present.

"I want you to get comfortable. Close your eyes and listen to my voice for the next 15 minutes while we do some guided imagery. Take a deep breath through your nose and slowly let it escape through your mouth. We're going to do this three times, and on the third breath I want you to hold it in for one beat. Feel all the muscles in your body relax as you let out the last breath. Allow your mind to relax. You'll notice thoughts going by, but don't try to stop them. Just allow them to drift away. As the thoughts drift by, listen to the steady rhythm of your heartbeat and feel the warmth as your heart pumps life throughout your body. Imagine yourself in a warm, safe place. This is your place; it's safe, warm, and private. You can come to this place anytime you choose just by closing your eyes and listening to your heartbeat."

Closure

After this exercise, review the agenda for next week's session. This would be a good time to ask if group members have particular items they wish to include next week. Handouts (if any) should be provided at this time.

Your availability is an important factor. Provide the group with telephone numbers for reaching you or your co-therapist during the coming week. If you're not going to be available, give out the number for the local crisis hotline or the 24-hour Rape Crisis line.

Week 2

Check-in

Ask group members to give feedback about their thoughts, feelings, and events following last week's session. Make note of any absences that are unaccounted for, so that you can phone those individuals after the session.

If a member isn't present and has called to report in, be sure to pass this information on to the group.

Example

"Welcome back. Let's go around the group and do check-in on everyone's week since the last session. Before we start out, Jan called to say that she had an unexpected business trip, but she'll be returning to group next week. Who would like to start? (If no one volunteers, which is rare, it's permissible to call on someone.) Martha, how was your week?"

C. Concept: The Victim Is Not Responsible for Her Victimization

Intervention 1: Didactic Presentation (See Concepts and Skills section)

Intervention 2: Group Sharing — Reactions to the Issue of Responsibility

Intervention 4: Reframing

Beth:	I should have kicked and screamed.
Therapist:	Beth, this man held a knife to your throat, and you did what you needed to do to survive.
Sue:	If only I hadn't gone to that tavern alone, this wouldn't have happened to me. I was really dumb.
Therapist:	Sue, maybe going to the tavern alone at night wasn't a good idea. But you do have rights. And your going to a tavern alone at any time doesn't give someone the right to sexually assault you.

Intervention 2: Continued Sharing of Personal Stories

Intervention 3: Emotional Affirmation

Intervention 4: Reframing

Intervention 5: Socratic Dialogue

Open Discussion

There may be times when group members need to discuss issues apart from the focus of the weekly agenda. Allow time in each session for open discussion and feedback. For example: "Does anyone have a question or issue that they need time to discuss this week? Sharon, you mentioned having difficulty understanding your continued feelings of anger and rage. I would be glad to put aside some time this evening if you'd like to discuss this with the group."

Closure

Intervention 6: Group Exercise — Visualization
See Week 1.

Week 3

D. Concept: Being a Survivor

Intervention 1: Didactic Presentation (See Concepts and Skills section)

Intervention 2: Group Sharing — Reactions To Being a Survivor

Intervention 3: Emotional Affirmation

Validate each person's effort to survive the rape and its emotional aftermath as necessary and legitimate.

Connie:	I get so frustrated with myself for not standing up to that jerk. I'm tired of always letting other people push me around. I'm going to buy a gun, and the next time some guy tries to mess with me I'm going to blow him away.
Therapist:	Connie, I can sure appreciate your anger. It's tough being and feeling helpless. No one likes to be pushed around or hurt. And while a gun may help you feel safe, there's no guarantee that having it would be helpful. You did what you had to do to remain alive, and that's what's important. I'm aware that it's important to feel assertive and to believe that you can take care of yourself. But in order to be assertive you have to feel safe, and you weren't safe.
Linda:	I'm such a baby. When I'm alone I have to sleep with a night light. Isn't that silly?
Therapist:	Linda, it sounds as if that night light helps you feel comfortable and safe when you're alone. That doesn't seem at all silly to me.

E. Skills: Identifying Yourself as a Survivor

Intervention 1: Didactic Presentation (See Concepts and Skills section)

Intervention 6: Group Exercise — Writing Down Coping Styles

Have group members name different coping styles while you list them on the board. Give a few examples to get them started:

> *Preferring to be with people, rather than alone*
> *Getting angry when pushed too hard*
> *Being hyperalert in unfamiliar places*
> *Resisting sex or certain forms of sexual expression*
> *Going emotionally numb in threatening situations*
> *Resting more*
> *Loss of memory around certain events*
> *Not taking on new challenges*

Moving to a safer neighborhood
Installing new locks in apartment
Having someone walk the group member to her car
Eating to relieve depression
Burying herself in work

Open Discussion

See example from Week 2.

Closure

Intervention 6: Group Exercise — Visualization

Week 4

Check-in

See Week 2.

F. Concept: Offenders

Intervention 1: Didactic Presentation (See Concepts and Skills section)

Intervention 2: Group Sharing — Reactions to Offenders

Intervention 4: Reframing

   Example

Jill:	Bill put out this heavy macho image. You know, cowboy boots, a greasy hat that said "Jack Daniels."
Therapist:	A lot of men dress like that, Jill. Very few of them are rapists. You just can't tell from what a guy wears.
Sue:	I always pick the wrong guys to date.
Therapist:	Sue, how would you know that the guy you were dating would sexually assault you?

G. Concept: Experiencing Uncomfortable Feelings

Intervention 1: Didactic Presentation (See Concepts and Skills section)

Intervention 2: Group Sharing — Reactions to Feelings That Have Already Been Discussed

Open Discussion

Closure

Intervention 6: Group Exercise — Visualization

Week 5

Check-In

H. Skills: Dealing With Uncomfortable Feelings

Intervention 1: Didactic Presentation (See Concepts and Skills section)

Because this is a fairly long section covering many of the primary feelings that will be discussed, it may be wise to cover several feelings each week over the next three weeks. This will also allow more time for group sharing and processing.

Anger, Guilt and Shame, and Sadness (See Concepts and Skills section under these headings.)

Intervention 2: Group Sharing

Intervention 7: Exploring Feelings

Probe for a complete expression of the feeling. Facilitate a release of affect where appropriate.

Connie:	I feel this grief. Like my trust, my sense of being safe and okay in the world was taken away. It's like this hard, dead feeling inside of me. Like a rock in my chest.
Therapist:	If the rock could talk, Connie, what would it say?
Connie:	You're broken, you'll never be mended. (Starts to cry but stifles her sobs.)
Therapist:	Let it out, Connie. It's okay. It's safe here to feel how much your world changed when you were assaulted. To feel how much it hurts to lose the feeling of being safe and trusting.
Connie:	(crying) I used to feel so strong...

[later]

Therapist:	How do you feel now?
Connie:	A little better, but I still feel the rock. It's like anger now.
Therapist	Does the rock have more to say? Perhaps to the man who sexually assaulted you?
Connie:	You fuck. You took my freedom away. You made my life get small. (shouting) You made me sacred. You made me scared. You shouldn't be alive. You don't deserve to be alive and do this to people. God, I want revenge right now!

Intervention 8: Reality Testing

Here the therapist gives basic information and reassurance, acknowledges important needs, and may comfront maladaptive thoughts or coping patterns.

Therapist:	Connie, your strength never left you. It helped you to survive the sexual assault and talk about your feelings here. Every victim of sexual assault goes through a period of increased fear and lost trust. Gradually the worst of that passes, and what you later may be left with is a realistic awareness of danger situations and appropriate carefullness in those situations. Your sense of being free in the world, being safe or even invulnerable will never be quite the same. And that loss is a deep ache right now. I know. But the fear will lessen, your drive to do things and try things will gradually increase. And you will

do a lot of what you want to do — but with some increased awareness of your vulnerability.

Or another reality test intervention with Connie:

Therapist: Wanting revenge is normal and helps you put the blame where it belongs — on the man who assaulted you. You need justice. You made the decision to go to the police and name the man who raped you. You've acted on your need to justice in a healthy way.

Suppose Connie reported that in response to her grief and sadness, she was now isolating herself from people. In this situation, the therapist might need to gently confront Connie's coping response:

Therapist: The sadness and the anger make you want to pull back from people. It seems hard enough to cope with your own feelings, let alone the reactions of others. But if you withdraw from everybody, something happens that can affect you for weeks or months. You lose the support and nourishment that others can give you. And you may find yourself not only grieving the effects of the assault, but experiencing a kind of loneliness and isolation that can increase the sadness you feel.

Intervention 4: Reframing

As you did previously, deal with guilt and self-blame by insisting that responsibility rests with the offender.

Open Discussion

Closure

Intervention 6: Group Exercise — Visualization

Week 6

Check-in

H. Skill: Dealing With Uncomfortable Feelings (continued)

Fear, Withdrawal, Worthlessness and Impaired Self-Esteem (See Concepts and Skills section under these headings.)

Intervention 2: Group Sharing
Intervention 7: Exploring Feelings
Intervention 8: Reality Testing

Open Discussion

Closure

Intervention 6: Group Exercise — Visualization

Week 7

Check-in

H. Skills: Dealing With Uncomfortable Feelings (continued)

Impaired Sexuality and **Mistrust** (See Concepts and Skills section under these headings.)

Intervention 2: Group Sharing
Intervention 7: Exploring Feelings
Intervention 3: Emotional Affirmation

Give verbal support that while disturbing, these are normal reactions that gradually pass over time.

I. Concept: Recovery

Intervention 1: Didactic Presentation (See Concepts and Skills section)
Intervention 2: Group Sharing
Intervention 7: Exploring Feelings

Open Discussion

Closure

Intervention 6: Group Exercise — Visualization

Week 8

Check-in

J. Skill: Recovery in Progress

Areas to be covered are in the Concepts and Skills section. In order to cover all the areas mentioned, several will need to be presented at a time in each of the following weeks.

Sleep, Appetite, and **Energy**

Intervention 1: Didactic Presentation (See Concepts and Skills section)
Intervention 2: Group Sharing
Intervention 8: Reality Testing

Open Discussion

Closure

Intervention 6: Group Exercise — Visualization

Week 9

Check-in

J. Skill: Recovery in Progress (continued)

Memory, Concentration, Lack of Interest in Activities

Intervention 1: Didactic Presentation (See Concepts and Skills section)
Intervention 2: Group Sharing
Intervention 8: Reality Testing

Open Discussion

Closure

Intervention 6: Group Exercise — Visualization

Week 10

Check-in

J. Skill: Recovery in Progress (continued)

Physical Illness, Irritability

Intervention 1: Didactic Presentation
Intervention 2: Group Sharing
Intervention 8: Reality Testing

Open Discussion

Closure

Intervention 6: Group Exercise — Visualization

Week 11

Check-in

J. Skill: Recovery in Progress (continued)

Flashbacks

Intervention 1: Didactic Presentation
Intervention 2: Group Sharing
Intervention 8: Reality Testing

Open Discussion

This would be a good time to start preparing the group for the issues surrounding closure. Sexual assault survivors often have a difficult time dealing with closure. By beginning the process a week early, you provide the opportunity for group members to explore their thoughts and feelings about continuing their recovery after the group ends. This session will also be important for you as group facilitator in making notes on how clients have or have not progressed in the past several weeks. Your observations can be used in making follow-up recommendations or suggestions.

Intervention 2: Group Sharing

Intervention 7: Exploring Feelings

Intervention 3: Emotional Affirmation

Closure

Intervention 6: Group Exercise — Visualization

Week 12

Check-in

K. Concept: Getting Support

Intervention 1: Didactic Presentation

Intervention 2: Group Sharing

Intervention 9: Brainstorming Ideas on Resources for Continued Support

Open Discussion Regarding Final Group Closure

Give feedback about the progress of individuals in the group, along with constructive suggestions. For example:

Therapist: Sue, I've noticed over the past several weeks that you've really done a good job of sharing your personal insights about the anger you've been feeling. I wonder if you'd consider it worthwhile to continue with this issue in individual treatment.

Closure

Intervention 6: Group Exercise — Visualization

Criteria for Measuring Change

Change can best be measured by clients' reports of feeling less guilty, ashamed, and overwhelmed by symptoms of post-traumatic stress disorder (PTSD). If PTSD symptoms persist to a significant degree, then criteria for change may rest in the extent to which a group member has learned to accept the unpleasant but transient nature of PTSD reactions, and to implement healthy coping strategies.

Relapse Prevention

Relapse prevention involves encouraging group members to use their support system, to seek professional help when appropriate, and to remind themselves of one of the basic themes of the group: responsibility for the assault lies with the offender.

References

Adams, C., and Fay, J. *Free of the Shadows: Recovering From Sexual Violence.* Oakland, California: New Harbinger Publications, Inc., 1989.

Benedict, H. *Recovery: How to Survive Sexual Assault for Women, Men, Teenagers, and Their Friends and Family.* New York: Doubleday and Co., 1985.

Johnson, K.M. *If You Are Raped: What Every Woman Needs To Know.* Holmes Beach, Florida: Learning Publications, Inc., 1985.

Katz, J.H. *No Fairy Godmothers, No Magic Wants: The Healing Process After Rape.* Saratoga, California: R & E Publishers, 1984.

Ledray, L.E. *Recovering From Rape.* New York: Henry Holt and Co., 1986.

McEvoy, A.W., and Brookings, J.B. *If She Is Raped: A Book For Husbands, Fathers, and Male Friends.* Holmes Beach, Florida: Learning Publications, Inc., 1985.

NiCarthy, G. *Getting Free: A Handbook for Women in Abusive Relationships.* Seattle: Seal Press, 1982.

Warshaw, R. *I Never Called it Rape, The Ms. Report on Recognizing, Fighting and Surviving Date and Acquaintance Rape.* New York: Harper and Row Publishers, 1988.

Chapter 9

Brief Group Therapy With Adult Survivors of Incest

Margaret Schadler, Ph.D.

Introduction

Incest is taboo, yet it happens. Estimates of the frequency of incest and other forms of sexual molestation vary with the methods of sampling and assessment; but there is general agreement that it occurs frequently, is often denied, unreported, and unprosecuted. As the silence about incest is broken, those who have been molested in childhood and adolescence are seeking help, insisting on it.

The effects of molestation are often severe and enduring. They stem from the actual abusive acts and from living in an environment that enables it. Recovery is a long process. The brief form of therapy described here is not ideal, in that it *is* so brief and thus will leave many problems unresolved: but its brevity does make it practical. Such group therapy is intended to be used in conjunction with other forms of treatment, including individual therapy and self-help and support groups. The assumption underlying the treatment described here is that focus on the abuse will enable participants to work through enough of the trauma and the accompanying shame, guilt, and fear to be able to make use of other forms of treatment for continued healing.

Brief group therapy for incest survivors has been described in the literature. Herman and Schatow's (1984) approach appears to be more structured than the one presented here. Co-therapists worked with groups of five to seven women for ten sessions to achieve individually defined goals. Brief group approaches have also been presented by Cole and Barney (1987), Goodman and Nowak-Scibelli (1985), Sprei (1987), and Swink and Leveille (1986). All had female co-therapists and members and met for nine (Cole & Barney, 1987) to eighteen (Swink & Leveille, 1986) sessions. In contrast, Ganzarain and Buchele (1986) focused on countertransference issues arising with a long-term group for incest survivors. Only Singer (1989) described group treatment for male survivors, and this was long-term.

The similarities among the brief therapy groups are obvious. Group formats were relatively structured, limited in scope, and goal-oriented. Members were pre-screened in individual interviews; all but Sprei (1987) required concurrent participation in individual therapy. The selection criteria described later in this chapter were also used for all groups reviewed. These similarities suggest that certain group activities, such as talking about the incest and learning that others have had similar experiences, are important aspects of the healing process. Coping with recall and sharing is stressful, even for those who have individual therapists, and is not for everyone nor without risk. Structure and explicitly set goals (for example, as explained by Goodman & Nowak-Scibelli, 1985, and Herman & Schatzow, 1984) appear to facilitate progress during the few weeks of the groups' tenure. The time constraints obviously limit what can be accomplished, but Herman and Schatzow (1984) suggest that the time-limited format facilitates bonding and decreases resistance to sharing the emotion-laden material.

The decision to lead or co-lead a group for survivors of sexual molestation is not one to be undertaken lightly. The work, while rewarding, is stressful and demanding. Those who seek treatment might be described as having a "brittle" personality structure in that they may function relatively well in positive climates but respond disproportionately to stress. They may become extremely anxious, depressed, or enraged during the course of therapy. Dissociative experiences may occur. Multiple personality disorder is associated with severe chronic sexual abuse. Diagnostically, personality disorders, particularly with borderline and narcissistic traits, are common among those who have been severely abused. These are difficult populations. Ideally, any therapist who decides to undertake a survivors' group would be an experienced group therapist and would conduct the first group with an experienced co-therapist; consultation and supervision are recommended.

Selection and Screening

The work begins at the initial meeting, so selection of members who are likely to complete the treatment is important. As dropouts are likely, particularly if clients are not in concurrent individual therapy, you may wish to begin with one or two extra people.

Selection of group members is problematic. Survivor groups are stressful for participants and the people in their support systems. Sessions can arouse more thoughts and emotions than can be processed at the time. It's important for participants to have sufficient psychological and social resources to be able to cope with the experience and to benefit from it — yet these resources are often very limited for those who need them most.

Typical criteria for group membership include concurrent participation in individual therapy, so that members have other professional resources available to them in addition to the group. Alternatively, 12-step programs can provide useful and appropriate support; programs that are particularly relevant include Incest Survivors Anonymous, Al-Anon, CoDependents Anonymous, and Adult Children of Alcoholics. Participation in individual therapy or support groups tends to reduce the likelihood of leaving therapy.

Make a thorough inquiry about substance use and eating patterns. Exclude dividuals who have a history of substance abuse until they are sufficiently into recovery to be able to tolerate the stress of the therapy without relapse. If potential members are excluded for substance abuse or dependence, inform them of the basis for the exclusion and recommend reapplication when the problem is under control. This confrontation may help them face their addiction. Where substance abuse has been a problem in the past, active membership in AA or relevant support groups is particularly important.

Exclude individuals who are actively suicidal or psychotic to avoid burdening other members of the group. Screen carefully: incest survivors learned not to talk about family secrets, so they tend not to volunteer information. Inquire about suicidal ideation, intent, and previous suicide attempts. Ask about prior therapy and hospitalizations. Strong suicidal ideation sometimes develops during these groups; so it's particularly important to establish that members have good impulse control.

Select individuals who can set realistic goals that are suitable to a brief period of therapy. Some group therapists ask that participants demonstrate the capacity to talk about their abuse in the screening interview; however, individuals who can at least tolerate questions are usually able to overcome their difficulty talking about their experiences with relative speed.

Consider group composition. Any group can tolerate one or two people who have difficulty talking. But great diversity in level of functioning can be problematic, particularly in pacing the group. Diversity in age, education, ethnicity, sexual orientation, and income helps members decrease their sense of isolation and stigma. Avoid the most difficult composition, which is a homogeneous group with a single outsider, such as a group of 20- to 30-year-olds and one 60-year-old.

Time and Duration

The group therapy described here is designed for 12 sessions, plus an individual screening interview. Sessions are weekly and intended to last from 80 to 90 minutes.

Size

This therapy approach is intense and interactive; two therapists are recommended, preferably one male and one female. Group size is preferably seven to eight if there are co-leaders. Size can range from five to ten, with larger groups meeting for additional sessions; one therapist should work with small groups only.

Structure

The structure of the session is relatively simple. Each session begins with a member-initiated "check-in," in which all members briefly state how their week went, then describe their mood. The session continues with exploration of issues that arise in the check-in. These concerns take priority as long as the group is productive. Therapists will generally initiate topics during the middle third of the session rather than at the beginning. The session ends promptly at the designated time: state, "Our time is up." After a brief pause, stand and wait for clients to leave.

Homework is assigned infrequently and usually at the end of the session. When used, the assignment then serves as a lead-in to the therapist-initiated phase of the next session.

Therapists have two general functions. The first and most important is monitoring and commenting on group process, with the objective of facilitating productive group interaction. The second is working with individuals within the group structure to facilitate insight and conflict resolution. Make sure that anyone who looks distressed or who is behaving differently from usual has an opportunity to talk sometime during the session. Calling on individuals by name may be necessary at the outset.

Goals

Recovery from incest is a long process that cannot be accomplished during a brief episode of therapy. However, participants can make significant progress during the group if they set specific and realistic goals (see the section Starting the Group). There are three objectives for the group work described here. The first is learning to talk about the abuse and to identify the consequences in one's life. The second is beginning to overcome those consequences. The third is formulating individual plans for continuing the work started in the group.

Ground Rules

"The ground rules are simple. Come every week even when it's hard to do so. Sometimes there will be good reasons to be absent, but it is important to decide if the reasons are good enough. We will only meet 12 times, and every session is important for you, so do your best to rearrange your schedule so that you can come. If you must miss a session, call one of us and leave a message so that we can inform the rest of the group. Come on time and stay until the end of the session. Late entrances and early departures are disruptive

"Maintain confidentiality; membership in this group is confidential and so are the people's life stories. When you've heard things that are helpful to you and that you wish to share with others, do so — just do it in such a way that the privacy of others in the group is honored. Gossip hurts.

"Talk about your pain. Talking about things is the most difficult rule for incest survivors, who have usually grown up in secretive families. However, there really is nothing that can't be talked about, regardless of how difficult, painful, or unpleasant it feels. Some of you may be tempted to leave the group. Talk about this, too, and make your decision in the group; it's a decision that will affect all participants, not just you."

Starting the Group

Start with the group's focus and purpose; put the focus on the work rather than the abuse. "This is a therapy group for people who are working on issues related to their abuse and molestation as children and adolescents. The purpose is to provide you with a forum for talking about the things that happened to you and how those experiences affect you today as adults. Most importantly, it is an opportunity for you to make some changes in your thoughts, feelings, and, particularly, in ways you interact with other people."

Introduce yourself by name as a co-therapist. Ask the members to introduce themselves, perhaps telling a little about their work or school life and their current living situation. Provide each member with a written copy of the ground rules and other relevant information such as meeting times, therapists' or clinic phone numbers, emergency and hotline numbers. Review the written information briefly, giving particular attention to talking about group interactions. "Perhaps the most important rule that we have in this group concerns talking about our thoughts and feelings about other group members. Give other members your feedback. Following this rule is important to the success of the group and to coping with the effects of the abuse you experienced as a child. You didn't learn to talk about things as a child; probably you were expected to keep silent about the very things that you are now here to discuss. We hope that in this group you'll talk about your thoughts and feelings about other members as well as about the leaders, and you'll discover that doing so is helpful rather than destructive. Some examples: You may become angry with me or with one of the members of the group. If you do, say so. If you talk with a group member outside a session, let the group know — otherwise factions within the group can form and interfere with our work here."

Motives

Following the starting procedure presented earlier, return to the work of the group by asking members to talk about their motivation for joining. Cuing the group about the desirable level of disclosure may be useful. "Let's talk a bit about your reasons for joining the group. Before we start, think about what you might tell the others about how the abuse or incest in your life has affected you, your relationships, and your work. Share some things that are comfortable for you to talk about. We won't bother to go in order this time, but it's important for all of you to say a little about what brought you here; you can add some more information later on, when you feel ready to do so. Please say your name again when you start."

This part of the initial session sets the stage for dealing with the issues of isolation, distrust, and shame. Meeting others who have had similar experiences is reassuring. Joining a group of people who are working to deal with the consequences of their abuse offers hope and helps to normalize the experience. However, group members are likely to be quite anxious, which will tie the tongue for some and unleash it for others. It will be important here and in subsequent early sessions to help members modulate their disclosure and reveal neither so much that they will be unable to return and face the group the following week nor so little that they feel isolated from the other members.

As discussion progresses, use your interventions to encourage the sharing of experiences. Normalizing comments help (for example, "Uninvited memories and flashbacks are distressing and frequently lead people to seek therapy." Linking common experiences will help people bond ("So both of you have problems with intimacy."). Make sure that everyone says something, perhaps by asking people to identify themselves if they haven't spoken in this round ("Let's see, who have we missed?").

Goals

Exploring motives for joining the group can easily lead into a discussion of individual goals. When all members have had a chance to talk about their motives, listen for an opportunity to shift the discussion toward objectives. One way is to make a general process comment: "You've been talking about a variety of painful experiences, and it seems that you've realized that having been abused and molested as a child has really had a big impact on your lives. This group will meet only 12 times. To get the most out of the group, we've found that it's important for each person to set a couple of specific goals to achieve over the course of those 12 sessions. Each of you should share your goals with the others in the group so that you can each benefit from the group's support. Let's talk about what each of you might like to accomplish during this group."

Work with the group to identify goals, state them in action terms, then talk about what it would mean to accomplish them. Help members see how their goals interrelate. Watch for a snowball effect when one person states a particular goal and the others adopt it without consideration of their own individual needs. Some possible goals: telling significant others about having been abused or molested, confronting the abuser, improving sexual relations with one's partner, accepting one's childhood, dealing more positively with anger.

Main Concepts and Skills

A. Concept: The Therapeutic Window

"Talking about incest and listening to others' experiences are stressful. Each individual has a range of stress that can be usefully tolerated, called the therapeutic window [Cole & Barney, 1987]. Too much stress pushes one out of the window. There is a tendency to shut down and feel nothing or else to become flooded with feelings to the point where you can't think of anything else. Some people have nightmares, panic attacks, or even feel as if they are reexperiencing the abuse. Feeling shut down or flooded are extreme reactions that will keep you from making progress with your work. It isn't possible to avoid all the pain and still do the work needed to heal.You can learn to keep reactions inside your therapeutic window by limiting the input you receive and doing self-calming exercises. Your tolerance for experiencing distress emotions will probably increase as you work through your painful memories. Keep in mind that, although the memory is painful, you've already survived the actual experience. We will teach you some skills today that you can use to manage your distress. You may know and practice some of these already; if you have other techniques that work for you, perhaps you might share them with us."

B. Skill: A Safe Place

"When things get tough, it's important to have something good to think about. This something can be a mental lifeboat, a place in your imagination where you can go when you need to retreat, relax or reorganize. Take a moment and think of a place that feels safe to you. It can be a real place or one you've made up. Some people focus on a person, such as a friend, special teacher, or minister. Others want a stuffed toy or their old security blanket. You can be inside or outdoors. Picture the scene as it would be if you were there. Imagine what it looks like...sounds like ...smells like...feels like. Think of yourself being there. Is it warm? cool?... Are you sitting, walking? Let yourself feel comfortable...safe.

"Practice imagining your safe place and using it to calm yourself as often as you can. With practice you'll be able to bring it to your mind whenever you feel really stressed, fearful, or angry and need a few moments to regain control."

C. Skill: Requesting Time Out

"There will be times when your feelings are too intense, and you need time out. Let us know by saying something like, 'I need a minute,' or using a hand signal: for example, you can gesture with your palm open and out, pushing slightly outward at chest level. When you make your gesture, we'll stop so that you can take time out to get centered."

D. Transformational Experience: Talking About the Abuse

"Talking about your memories of the abuse you experienced is a painful but important part of the healing process. It lightens the burden you carry by reducing your feelings of shame and blame. Talking will help you understand what happened to you and why. It will not change what actually happened, but it will bring those events into perspective. Talking about the abuse is like studying history: what changes is not the past, but your understanding of the present, and the ways in which you'll deal with your future."

E. Concept: Shame Versus Guilt

"The terms shame and guilt are often used interchangeably or are confused, but there are important differences between them that warrant clarification. Shame is more pervasive and important than guilt in sexual abuse, particularly in cases of incest.

"Shame originates from the sense of being flawed, when only perfection is acceptable. It's usually early in a child's development that others let the child know that he or she doesn't measure up. Molestation, particularly incest, is surrounded by secrecy and silence and thus fosters shame in child victims, who are made to feel that they're involved in shameful behavior without having the opportunity to test this conclusion by discussing the incest with others. Exacerbating this, the perpetrator may deal with his own feelings of shame by projecting them onto the victim.

"Some shame may stem from having been used in an unacceptable or even degrading manner. Some is caused by the physical arousal or other forms of gratification experienced in the relationship: this may be the most difficult aspect of the abuse to admit to others and oneself.

"Guilt, on the other hand, comes from doing things that one believes to be wrong. For example, the perpetrator who tells the child, "This is our secret — it would kill your mother if she knew," obtains silence at the price of the child's feelings of guilt (derived from doing something with such potentially devastating consequences). Such feelings of guilt are alleviated as victims come to understand that they are not to blame for the abuse.

Shame, because it is associated with one's very being rather than mere actions, is more difficult to overcome than guilt. Overcoming shame is facilitated by acceptance and understanding from others, and by the abuse survivor eventually letting go of the need to be perfect."

F. Concept: Boundaries

"Boundaries, in this context, are the psychological lines drawn between people. Individuals with clear boundaries are able to set limits for themselves and others in relationship to them. Such limits are manifested in decision making and other aspects of individual functioning. Incestuous families tend to have poor boundaries in that members are intrusive and self-focused even in their concern for each other. They become skilled at anticipating the needs of others and expect others to anticipate theirs. They assume that they are the cause or the target of others' moods and thoughts. They rarely state their needs and wants and seem to believe that one does not need to do so. They often assume that if one asks for something, the other is obligated to provide it; they consequently feel hurt and rejected if their request is denied."

G. Concept: The Hot Seat

"Being the focus of an interaction in the group, particularly one that involves a therapist, can be an uncomfortable experience. In fact, many refer to it as 'being on the hot seat.' Feedback can feel like criticism or even punishment. In abusive families, being the center of attention is often a negative experience involving being belittled or even physically abused. Even praise might carry a penalty."

H. Concept: Delayed Distress

"You may experience a delayed reaction two or even three days after a group session during which other members have talked about their abuse experiences. You might feel depressed, frightened, or angry; you might experience flashbacks, nightmares, or recall other memories. Should you feel depressed or angry between sessions, think back to the previous session and review the topics discussed and your reactions to them. Understanding that the session was upsetting may make it easier for you to shift moods and let the feelings of distress go until the next group session. Write about your feelings in your journal, imagine your safe place, talk with someone you feel close to, or do something enjoyable to ease your distress. Then be sure to talk about your delayed reaction in the next group meeting."

I. Concept: Identification With the Family

"Survivors of incest and molestation tend to have complex and conflicting feelings about their families. If the incestuous parent was physically abusive and a step-relation rather than a biological parent, then the survivor's feelings about the abuser might be largely negative — for example, straight forward feelings of hate and anger. But relationships within the incestuous family, particularly between a child and an incestuous parent, are typically complex and conflicted. There is often intense love, family loyalty, and a need to see the family in an idealized fashion. Particularly in the case of incest, the parent may have given the child gifts, privileges, attention, and power. Furthermore, the victim may have experienced pleasure from the actual physical stimulation as well as gratification at being singled out for a 'special' relationship with the parent. As children increasingly come to realize that the incestuous relationship is not acceptable, their conflict increases."

J. Concept: Blaming the Victim

"Children who have been molested or abused typically believe that it was their fault. There are two reasons for this belief. First, others blame them. The perpetrator commonly blames the victim by saying such things as, 'You know you want this.' Colluding family members may also have blamed the victim of incest for seducing the perpetrator, for not telling, or for just being bad. The motivation of others for blaming the victim appears to be to minimize their guilt or shame by projecting it onto the victim. Perpetrators and their spouse or partner often see themselves as powerless and hapless victims of circumstances or uncontrollable urges; thus it's quite consistent with their self-perception to imagine the child to have been the instigator.

Secondly, victims have a stake in blaming themselves. Self-blame at least gives the illusion of power and control. In childhood and even into adulthood, holding yourself responsible on some level for the abuse allows you to avoid the painful conclusion that your abuser, was misusing and manipulating you. This illusion allows you to avoid the painful knowledge of your utter powerlessness as a child and the betrayal of your vulnerability by a close and trusted adult."

K. Concept: Betrayal

"All abuse is betrayal of the child. The betrayal in incest is threefold. Abusers betray children by selfishly using them to gratify their adult needs. Parents betray their children when they fail to protect them, particularly in the case of incest. The betrayal that is perhaps most difficult for the survivors to accept is that of their own bodies when they become aroused and respond pleasurably to the abuser's caresses. Touching and caressing can produce pleasant physiological sensations, even when the seducer is the parent. Some parents who commit incest rationalize that they are teaching their child about love and sexual skills. They use their knowledge about sexual response to induce pleasure in their young objects. The consequences of such pleasures can be devasting for survivors, who can feel overwhelmed by confusion and embedded shame and guilt. Incest survivors often report an inability to enjoy sex with their mates because they freeze, dissociate, or feel very guilty or afraid. Often these responses stem from having initially experienced pleasure in the early incestuous encounters — the memory of which is denied or repressed only to cause later difficulties."

L. Concept: Anger

"Anger is a normal emotion, one that is important to acknowledge and learn to express in ways that are acceptable to yourself and others. Adults who have been abused or molested as children are often (and with good reason) deeply angry. Some — particularly those who have been physically abused — acknowledge that they are always angry. Sarcasm and a short temper are also qualities that are sometimes found in survivors. However, others have coped by burying and denying their anger, or directing it against themselves. Some families forbid the expression of anger altogether, and other families make the expression of anger an occasion for trauma and fear. Be alert to feelings of anger in yourself and expressions of anger in others. Talk about the feelings, and give yourself permission to feel them."

M. Concept: Dissociation

"One common defense against distress is dissociation — that is, separating thoughts from physical sensations and emotions to the extent that you become unaware of what is going on around you. Dissociation is a common means of surviving severely stressful events such as sexual or physical abuse: most survivors know how to dissociate and do so automatically. Dissociation may have been necessary for your psychic survival when you were abused; for milder forms of distress, you can learn to use less drastic coping mechanisms, such as humor or relaxation exercises."

N. Skill: Taking Care of Yourself

"People who have suffered incest as children, like those who come from other types of dysfunctional families, tend to meet the needs of others at the expense of taking care of themselves. You then end up thinking that people take advantage of you, and they do — a lot. As children, you learned that you had to take care of others to get anything in return. People took advantage of you at times; sometimes you may have gotten special favors. Mostly people didn't do a very good job taking care of you. If you are like many survivors of incest, you have a lifelong wish to have someone take care of you the way a child should be cared for. No one will.

If it didn't happen in childhood, you won't be able to find others to fill that need for you as an adult. Rather, you have to learn to take care of yourself. As you do, you'll let go of the anger that you feel about no one taking care of you.

"What does it mean to take care of yourself? It means knowing what you want or need, and being able to ask for it assertively. It means negotiating and compromising rather than sacrificing. It means that you decide when you will help other people and when you will say 'no.' It means that you stop being a victim."

O. Skill: Assessing Choices

"'I have no choice' is a common phrase among survivors of abuse. Usually, if you say this, either you don't recognize the alternatives that are available or you consider them to be totally unacceptable. However, if you acknowledge those choices you've eliminating, you won't feel quite so helpless. You may choose to stay with a battering partner because the thought of being alone is so terrifying to you that it doesn't *seem* like an alternative. However, recognizing that an alternative, however unpalatable, *exists* will lend you a sense of control that may eventually lead to discovering other and better alternatives."

P. Skill: Reframing

"Reframing means reconceptualizing a situation or problem in a way that makes it more tolerable or allows you to see a possible solution. For example, perhaps you believe that your boss is demanding and has unreasonable expectations of you at work; but you're unable to leave because you don't think you can make enough money in another job. This leads to your feeling helpless and angry. Reframing the situation to see that you're well-paid in your current job because you agreed to work late to meet deadlines may make the hours more tolerable or the job easier to give up."

Q. Skill: Negotiating

"Negotiating is a matter of exchanging something that you want for something that another person wants so that you each get some of what you want and achieve a 'win-win' solution. It doesn't mean losing or giving up something you want for something someone else wants. Too often survivors tend to sacrifice their own wants and needs and then be angry or resentful."

R. Transformational Experience: Trust of Self

"Incest survivors have difficulty trusting either themselves or others. As you were betrayed by the very people whom you should have been able to trust, your capacity to trust became diminished. It will take time, practice, and feedback to correct the distortions in your beliefs about trust and make your judgments about trust more accurate."

S. Transformational Experience: Confronting the Abuser

"Confronting the abuser or other members of the family is often a goal set by survivors of incest and molestation. People who have been molested or abused may have a very strong wish to make everything all right, or a belief that somehow everything will be all right if they confront the abuser or tell other family members what happened. Oftentimes this doesn't work. It's important to examine both your wish to communicate and your knowledge of your family's dynamics. In fact, the outcome of such a confrontation is rarely what the person would wish, and it's usually disappointing and painful."

T. Concept: Effects on Sexual Relationships

"Incest and molestation survivors often have difficulty with sexual relationships, which may be what draws you to therapy. Common problems include promiscuity, confusion between sex and affection, or an inability to enjoy sex. Many survivors have flashbacks or will dissociate during sex. You may identify some of your partner's actions that seem abusive, or feel that your partner doesn't understand that you can't feel good about having sex while you're dealing with abuse issues in the group. Talking about these concerns in the group will be useful. Talking with your partner about your mutual needs and how to meet them can also be useful."

U. Concept: Avoiding Repetition of Abusive Relationships

"When children grow up being abused and unprotected, their expectations and boundaries are different from those who have been treated with respect. For you and others like you, abusers and abused are known entities; 'normies' may be experiences as threatening or boring. As a result, you may accept behavior that other people wouldn't. You may remain in jobs or relationships that have abusive elements; you may feel trapped and unable to leave a difficult situation. Alternatively, you may misjudge a situation, seeing it as abusive, because you easily feel victimized and hesitate to set limits. Experiencing limit setting and other self-protective acts in the group and/or practicing them in other situations can help reduce these tendencies."

Main Interventions

Three major interventions are used in this group therapy: didactic presentation, group exploration, and individual practice. Therapists' interventions in the form of process comments, interpretations, and confrontations are part of group exploration. Process comments serve to direct the group's attention to their interactions. Interpretations reframe an experience for an individual or group. Confrontations typically direct an individual's attention to his or her feelings or behavior. The challenge, particularly when the group contains individuals with little or no empathy, is to involve as many of the group in an intervention as possible. Thus one frequently used intervention is that of asking if others have had similar experiences or feelings.

The content of the group work is structured such that most of the first two weeks is concerned with preparatory activities; the next four weeks center on talking about childhood abuse; current issues stemming from an abusive childhood occupy weeks seven to ten; and termination take the final two sessions. Some flexibility in this structure is acceptable. Ideally you will be making continuous links between past abuse and its influence on current situations. The focus should shift, however, from the past in the first half of the therapy to acquiring more adaptive responses in the latter half. Begin to mention termination in the ninth and tenth sessions, then spend the final two sessions on this issue.

Week 1: Starting the Group

See the section on starting the group. Tell the group members what is expected of them and provide normative information about their possible reactions. Members may lack basic interpersonal skills and knowledge, such as how to protect themselves by gradually becoming more vulnerable as it becomes safe. Some will have fears, perhaps justifiably, about their ability and that of others to maintain control. The most likely results of those fears are that people will overcontrol and spontaneity will be lacking; use process comments to help the group become aware of their concerns and talk about them.

Week 2: Managing Strong Emotions

Check-in

All members briefly discuss how their week went and their current mood. When this procedure is introduced, inform the group that they can initiate the check-in without waiting for you to tell them to begin. Ask the members to be particularly attentive to thoughts and feelings they might have had about the group during the week. In the early weeks, members say their first names as they check in. Be attentive to posture and other subtle nonverbal cues of mood as well as shifts in descriptors. Group leaders do not check in.

Even those clients who may have been in individual therapy for a significant period of time may have intense reactions to group therapy. Experiences related in the group often trigger repressed memories. In this session, it's useful to teach some techniques for centering and comforting and to help the group anticipate and understand their reactions.

A. Concept: The Therapeutic Window

Intervention 1: Didactic Presentation (See Concepts and Skills section)

B. Skill: A Safe Place

Intervention 1: Didactic Presentation (See Concepts and Skills section)

Intervention 3: Individual Practice

It's important to make sure that every person can recall at least one place, person, or thing that is comforting. Ask the group to talk about their choices of a safe place and how they made a decision about what felt safe for them. Encourage each person to talk to the extent that they're able to recall and describe sufficient memories to have ready access to them. Have group members practice visualizing themselves in their safe places and shifting their focus to more pleasant thoughts. Use this technique at the end of each session to help the group relax and recover from the stress of the session.

C. Skill: Requesting Time out

Intervention 1: Didactic Presentation (See Concepts and Skills section)

Time out is adapted from Vannicelli (1989), who suggests enabling members to determine their own pace and to signal when they wish to stop for a moment and center. Time-out intervals won't be used often, but they give members the feeling that they are in control, which helps them to stay in control. Encourage use of time-out by responding quickly to either verbal or hand signs of distress (for example, "You seem to be having a hard time with this. Remember, we have a time-out signal that you can use."). Explore the use of the time-out signal (for example, "You signalled a time out; how did that work for you?").

Ending the Session

Take time at the end of each session for some relaxing and transitional activities. Intense sessions may require 15 to 20 minutes for transition. Focus on positive events and feelings. Visualizing safe places and asking each person to recall a good experience or describe his or her safe place are possibilities. Ask the group for their suggestions. A "check-out" in which group members each describe briefly their thoughts and feelings about the session may be useful.

Homework

Encourage clients to practice visualizing their safe place several times during the week. Encourage them to obtain a relaxation tape or take a workshop in relaxation techniques. Emphasize that learning to shift the focus of their mood is a skill that they can learn.

Weeks 3-6

Rather than force the introduction of the concepts and skills according to the order in which they're presented here, be prepared to cover a couple of topics as they arise in each session. Let the group get started and listen for a theme to emerge; then use your interventions to keep the group focused.

Check-in

At the beginning of the third and all subsequent sessions, greet the group briefly, then sit quietly until someone begins the check-in. Avoid more than brief eye-contact with any of the members until someone begins the check-in, since extended eye-contact is likely to be considered a signal for that person to start talking. Initiating the check-in is a means of actively taking control and thus taking care of oneself: let the group do it.

Be alert to members' comments during the check-in for stressors that can create problems either for the individual or for the group, particularly as it relates to abuse. Group members may come in and talk about a potentially or even obviously abusive situation occurring in their family. For example, Alice was furious one day because a welfare investigation had been initiated after her infant niece had been hospitalized with a fractured skull. The "accident" sounded as if it could have been abuse. Alice was angry because the child's parents were upset about being investigated. Some of the group began to sympathize with Alice and complain about the unfairness of Social Services. We intervened by wondering how people felt about the child involved. Some members then began to talk about their wish for just such an investigation when they were abused children. The next step was acknowledging both sides of the issue: protecting the child and the family's distress. The group then turned to a vital concern — their fear that they might abuse *th* marry someone who would.

Of course, if abuse or molestation is occurring, the issue of rep*or* addressed in group and worked through. This step is facilitated by *ma* pathetic link between group members and the abused child.

D. Transformational Experience: Talking About the Abuse

Intervention 1: Didactic Presentation (See Concepts and Skills sectio

Intervention 2: Group Exploration

In these early weeks, sharing experiences is a major focus. Encourage *me* to talk about their abuse in whatever detail they can tolerate. Let the grou*p* that they will determine their own pace and can stop talking anytime the*y* Use statements such as, "I wonder if that reminds anyone of their experienc*e* encourage broad participation. Also help clients connect with the present by as*k* what it's like to share their memories with the group. Encourage exploration of *cu* rent situations that remind them of the past. Too often, people don't see the *in* fluence of their past on present interactions.

Talking about the abuse serves several purposes. As individuals remember wh*at* happened to them and talk about it, they rewrite the script by adding an ending *in* which they survive and master the experience. Individuals also reduce the shame and guilt they feel as they find that they don't blame others as they tell their stories, nor do others blame them.

There are several important topics, embedded in the stories about abuse, that are important to explore. These include: reasons for submitting/participating; what happened when victims tried to tell people what was or had happened to them; feelings toward the perpetrator and toward other members of the family. Many will be angry at their mothers for failing to protect them: this is particularly common when the father is the perpetrator. Some may also feel intensely guilty if they believed that they supplanted one parent in the sexual relationship with the other. Explore these feelings and thoughts as they arise, helping members to look at the role of the various family members as well as their own.

E. Concept: Shame Versus Guilt

Intervention 1: Didactic Presentation (See Concepts and Skills section)

Intervention 2: Group Exploration

Shame is more difficult to ease than guilt. Shame is deeply ingrained, and people often feel that they have little control over the feelings, perhaps because shame is imposed by others. Encourage the group to share memories of how parents, teachers, and others shamed them. In doing so, focus on the "shamers": what did they say, what was their tone of voice, facial expression? Then move to the feelings of being shamed as individuals recall and share experiences. Why was the act so bad, so shameful? Often shame is used as a means of controlling behavior that embarrasses others, particularly parents. Use this idea to introduce the next concept.

F. Concept: Boundaries

Intervention 1: Didactic Presentation (See Concepts and Skills section)

Intervention 2: Group Exploration

Weak boundaries are pervasive in incestuous families. If the incestuous parent had been more able to see his or her child as an individual, rather than as a possession and a means of need gratification, the incest might not have occurred. Introduce this concept when it is first appropriate, then continue to use it throughout the therapy. Focus on helping group members to become more aware of their boundaries within the group.

G. Concept: The Hot Seat

Intervention 1: Didactic Presentation (See Concepts and Skills section)

Intervention 2: Group Exploration

Exploring the group's resistance to talking takes precedence over other issues in order to keep the group from dragging into repeated and painful silences. Be alert to behavior suggesting that participants are uncomfortable with the attention they're receiving. Particularly watch for indications of feeling criticized and shamed.

Explore past experiences of being the center of attention. Get sufficient detail from members so that they recall some of their feelings; these are usually fear, hurt, guilt, and shame. Ask them to compare their current experience of having the group's attention with that of being in the center of attention in their family; ask for similarities and differences. Be prepared to hear that you seem threatening, even abusive. Use the cues given you to ask about the feeling evoked (for example, "Some of you may be afraid I might humiliate you the way your dad did," or "...that we might laugh at you."). If someone confirms this, explore the fear further. Alternatively, ask about other current situations in their lives in which they have similar feelings. Realize that some employers and some partners can be verbally abusive, intend to and do succeed at humiliating people. Help the group to analyze these situations and to explore ways to cope with them.

This intervention can also help the group to identify current situations that evoke feelings similar to those from their abusive experiences; then to explore the similarities. Help them also to consider the possibility that being the focus of an interaction can be a neutral or even a positive experience.

H. Concept: Delayed Distress

Intervention 1: Didactic Presentation (See Concepts and Skills section)

Intervention 2: Group Exploration

Alert the group to the possibility of a delayed negative reaction toward the end of the first session, where members described their experiences of molestation and incest. Discuss ways in which they can cope with these responses to help decrease the intensity of the reaction.

Follow up the next week by asking members how they felt about the group and how their week went. Some will experience relief, others may have had distressful periods with flashbacks and additional memories. Be curious about how they coped with those times, whether or not they were able to remember their comforting techniques, and if the techniques worked. Wondering what else might help, or asking the group what has worked for them is also useful. It's important to recognize that group members are engaged in a painful struggle.

Returning to group after a painful session can be difficult. Help the group by anticipating this difficulty. A simple comment at the end of the first painful session will usual suffice.

I. Concept: Identification With the Family

Intervention 1: Didactic Presentation (See Concepts and Skills section)

Intervention 2: Group Exploration

The question: "Why didn't you leave (or tell)?" lacks understanding of family dynamics and identification; asking it results in defensiveness and increased feelings of shame. Questions such as "What gave you the courage to leave (or to stop the abuse) acknowledge the client's struggle and encourage exploration. The key to this intervention is to explore and understand family relationships and group members' feelings about their families, particularly their parents. Assume a neutral, curious stance. Look for feelings of love and hope as well as anger, hatred, and betrayal. This balanced, neutral approach will help the group acknowledge and integrate their complex responses.

J. Concept: Blaming the Victim

Intervention 1: Didactic Presentation (See Concepts and Skills section)

Intervention 2: Group Exploration

Self-blame arises in every group, usually sooner than later. Allow this to happen. If the concept is not obvious to all, explain it. Quick fixes won't work. Resist the temptation to reassure — "It wasn't your fault" — or to cut exploration short because members have reassured each other. Such reassurance may lead to intellectual acceptance and temporary relief; but emotionally, the victim remains unconvinced. Reassurance may actually backfire by either confirming the client's sense of powerlessness if the self-blame stems from a need for control, or deepening the shame if the client is struggling with memories of being aroused by or flirtatious with the abuser. Use your questions and process interventions to thoroughly explore all references to self-blame. Appropriate normalizing statements imbedded in your exploratory questions will also ease guilt, shame, and self-blame. If, for example, members suggest that they flirted with or encouraged their abuser, a statement such as, "Little girls (boys) commonly flirt with their fathers (mothers); most fathers are able to recognize and resist such advances in ways that build their daughter's self-esteem, rather than by reacting by seducing them. What do you think made your relationship with your father different?"

Acknowledge the prevalence and importance of self-blame among abuse victims. Don't be satisfied with the group's superficial disavowal: help them to identify and explore their emotionally based beliefs. Explore this theme in as much detail as possible as it recurs, looking at when, how, and why the notion of self-blame originated and was reinforced. Ask clients how they think they caused it to start. Help group members explore what they think they could have done to prevent or end the abuse. As individuals compare their rationales, they will tend to uncover contradictory and externally imposed explanations, which in turn will help them exonerate themselves.

Help the group to discover the purposes that self-blaming serves. It typically enables the victim to feel less helpless and more important by feeling like an active rather than passive participant. It may also help the individual maintain a personal myth about having a loving family. By the middle or latter part of therapy, when members have achieved some sense of accomplishment, self-blame can be confronted more openly; by this time, clients are more able to trade the notion of self-blame for the idea that they are responsible for their behavior as adults.

K. Concept: Betrayal

Intervention 1: Didactic Presentation (See Concepts and Skills section)

Intervention 2: Group Exploration

Arousal and pleasure in the incestuous relationship do occur and are difficult to address, particularly in short-term therapy. The dilemma is that some clients may remember being aroused but feel deeply ashamed of it. When they avoid talking about these feelings, they risk increasing their shame and isolation. Others in the group may have repressed such memories and are not ready to uncover them. Be alert to veiled references; encourage but don't insist on follow-up and exploration. It's vital to be as open, matter of fact, and therapeutically curious about the victim's memory of arousal as you are about any other reaction. You can state matter of factly that many victims could and did experience arousal and other pleasurable sensations during their abuse, which seems a terrible betrayal by one's body. Link such arousal to the parent's responsibility to protect the child. Such statements will begin to normalize the experience and open the door to the group for discussion.

L. Concept: Anger

Intervention 1: Didactic Presentation (See Concepts and Skills section)

Intervention 2: Group Exploration

Incest survivors often appear to be passive and without anger in the group; yet many describe episodes at home or work in which they explode into a rage.

There are specific techniques that clients can use for getting in touch with the anger associated with their abuse. Some writers (for example, Bass and Davis, 1988) assume that releasing this anger is cathartic. The interactive approach I'd like to suggest here is more subtle: it can help clients identify, name, and cope with their anger, but does not endorse "cathartic" rages. What is most important is that you do not ignore anger: it's a crucial component of treatment, and underlies the common fear among survivors of losing control.

Be particularly sensitive to nuances of facial expression, posture, and voice that signal anger, and confront it at every opportunity. The question "How are you feeling?" gives those who are aware of their feelings a chance to identify them. For whose who deny or cannot name their feelings, saying "You seem/sound/look angry" may help. If anger is denied, let it pass, perhaps with a nod or normalizing statement (for example, "People who have been sexually abused are often angry."). Note that anger is frequently taboo in abusive families ("Many children, especially in families where there is abuse, are never allowed to show anger in any way — so they learn to deny it.").

Make a point of questioning how anger was treated in different people's families. When group members are able to admit that their anger is a problem, pursue the issue in terms of how, when, where, provocations, consequences, and coping strategies.

Perhaps the most important part of dealing with anger is the therapists' implicit assumption, underlying their questions, comments, and matter-of-fact attitude, that anger is an acceptable emotion that can be understood and expressed just like other emotions. Be particularly sensitive to anger directed toward yourself and your co-therapist; address it with the attitude that this feeling and associated thoughts are valid and important to explore.

Anger management can be the focus of an entire group therapy (see the chapter on anger in this book). For the purposes of the survivor group, managing anger is limited to exploration, some modeling, and practice in talking about angry feelings and desired changes.

One note of caution: pursuing the angry affect in the face of denial may lead to escalation and the client's acknowledgment of anger. However, that individual is quite likely to attribute the emotion to being provoked by the therapist's questioning and may feel manipulated. This is not desirable; but the situation must be dealt with if it occurs. In the following dialogue, Mary Beth's tone and expression suggest that she's getting angry:

Therapist:	What are you feeling right now?
Mary Beth:	Nothing.
Therapist:	You seem a bit angry.
Mary Beth:	I'm not; there's no reason to be.
Therapist:	Sometimes there doesn't seem to be a reason; but feelings like anger can be triggered by very subtle cues, especially if something in the situation is similar to an old abusive situation.
Mary Beth:	Well, I'm not angry. I feel just fine.
Therapist:	Hmm. Well, your voice seems tense, and you're clenching your jaw.
Mary Beth:	You know, I wasn't angry, but you just keep pushing, insisting that I am. I probably am getting that way.
Therapist:	Uhuh.
Mary Beth:	You really are making me mad.
Co-therapist:	Let's stop and look at this interation. It's important because it's an excellent example of something that probably occurs often for many of you. As Mary Beth and Joanne [the therapist] worked together, Joanne noticed some cues that led her to think Mary Beth might be feeling some emotion — and she asked about it. When Mary Beth denied any feeling, Joanne pursued the point, and Mary Beth began to feel manipulated, perhaps even coerced. Does that seem accurate so far? Okay. This may seem similar to something that happens a lot in abusive families: a parent or older sibling confronts a child and keeps pushing him or her, and at the same time blames the child. Mary Beth, I wonder if that happened in your family. It did? Well, you're probably really sensitive to it. So now when you felt pushed, Mary Beth, you got mad and let Joanne know about it Right? Suppose this exchange had happened at work instead of here. Mary Beth, you've mentioned that your boss can be verbally abusive. What do you think would have happened if you'd had this interchange at work?

The advantage of the co-therapist making this intervention is that he or she is a neutral figure at this point. If the co-therapist does not begin, the involved therapist might invite the intervention: "Ann, can you help us out here?" The co-therapist, as illustrated above, engages the participants' attention, interprets the anger in a neutral way, then generalizes to other situations.

M. Concept: Dissociation

Intervention 1: Didactic Presentation (See Concepts and Skills section)

Intervention 2: Group Exploration

As people talk about their abuse experiences, monitor the group's responses. If the group is attentive and one story leads to another, the group is working; you can keep tabs on who is talking and on members' affect. If the silences lengthen and individuals seem withdrawn, check in with the group to see what is going on. Dissociation is a common defense for people who were abused as children. Dissociative behavior is particularly likely in the group when abusive experiences are the topic of discussion.

Look for initially pained expressions followed by blank looks and diminished affect among members of the group. Find a moment when most of the group look as if they have checked out and comment, "People seem quiet and look spaced-out. What are you thinking and feeling?" This question may produce evasive responses such as, "Oh, I was just listening." You have at least two directions in which you can go from here: with the speaker's feelings and with the reactions of the other members of the group.

The first time, check in with individual speakers to elicit their reactions when they stop talking and get no response from others. When feeling safe, they may indicate that they feel as if they're the only one who has ever had the experience they've been describing; they may indicate that they feel isolated or alone.

There are several options when clients express such feelings. If others in the group acknowledge that they've had similar experiences and begin to share them, you can remain silent and let the discussion continue; later you might point out the increased participation and its potential benefits, either by soliciting reactions or by merely calling attention to the situation. If the group is not reactive but remains silent or denies their identification with the speaker, you might briefly explain what you mean by a related experience, making broad connections so that clients can link their diverse experiences. For example, you might associate everyone's experience of disclosure about being molested with an individual client's story about coping with her mother's response to disclosure. You can increase the benefit that clients get from the group as well as increase their participation by coaching and encouraging everyone to actively recall related experiences and use the recollection to learn more about themselves and their coping strategies. Encouraging active group participation is particularly important in the early phases of this therapy.

Members of the group may have difficulty making links between their experiences and those of others if similarities aren't obvious. Survivors may lack empathy (LeRoi, 1986), which would facilitate connections from an emotional basis, and may not know how to frame their experience in a broader context (for example, this is about telling someone/wanting protection): this lack of skill may keep them from making a cognitive connection. Additionally, not connecting is a way of avoiding feelings of pain associated with the experience, thus resistance becomes a logical defense mechanism. Help the group see the ways in which a narrow focus is a means of avoiding pain; that may have been adaptive in childhood, but now interferes with therapy.

At some time, you may wish to work with the speaker for a few moments on the feelings associated with being the only one or with being alone, possibly linking these feelings to the abuse. Being alone then becomes the experience that brings the group back into the discussion.

Eventually, if dissociative responses continue, you may need to address them directly. Direct confrontation usually brings some acknowledgment and leads to a discussion of what group members are doing, how it feels, when and how they do it. Are they thinking about something else? Is this a response that's under their control, so that they can choose when to use it? The immediate objective is for the group to develop awareness of this defense, its advantages and disadvantages, and to increase their control of its use. It's important to help the group see this defense as one that may have been useful in childhood, and which can be very powerful; but that they have less need for this particular strategy now. You can encourage the use instead of less drastic but more active defenses, such as asking for time out.

Using the Process

Use process comments to help members become aware of what is happening in the group. The following example models inviting the group to reflect on reasons for an unexpected silence at the beginning of a session:

"It seems difficult for the group to get started on a topic today... [Keep the previous session in mind. Intensely emotional or intimate sessions, or sessions that deal with particularly difficult topics, are often followed by a session that starts slowly.] People were pretty open last week; perhaps you're feeling shy or cautious today and are waiting to see how the others react." This statement invites the group to focus either on last week's topic or on their feelings.

As members of the group become familiar with each other, shift the procedure so that clients become more active in initiating topics for discussion and directing group interactions. Two techniques will facilitate this shift. First, tell the group what you want to have occur, what you will do, and what you want then to do. For example, "I [Joanne and I] have been presenting topics and initiating discussions about them for the past few weeks. It's time to shift more responsibility to you from now on. We'd like group members to initiate the discussion as well as the check-in. This is your group, and you know what things are coming up for you and which are most important to you. This is also a good way to practice taking care of yourselves. Beginning now, we [co-therapists] will be less active and less directive. When we have something we want to introduce, we'll let you know." A second technique is to increase the time that you're willing to sit quietly and let group members begin talking. Rarely will any group remain silent for more than five minutes.

Sooner or later this shift in the procedure will arouse feelings, typically anger. Listen for inferences of abandonment, neglect, even abuse. There might be suggestions that you're not doing your job or that you're the experts and know what the group should be discussing. Deal with this issue by asking the group if others have similar thoughts; encourage elaboration of their concerns. Comment on the obvious emotions. Give clients sufficient opportunity to present their thoughts and express their feelings. You can then acknowledge the reality of the present situation, present some alternative interpretations, then link people's feelings to the past, including parental demands and expectations. Help the group to explore these similarities and links; eventually differences should also emerge.

> Therapist: (*after 5 to 7 minutes of silence following completion of a check-in in which several important themes were expressed*) It seems difficult for the group to get started today.
>
> Sally: You said that last week, too. If you want us to talk, you could start the discussion.

Therapist:	(*nodding*) Yes. You seem to have some strong feelings. Help me understand what's going on.
Sally:	We don't know what to talk about, so we don't say anything — then you jump on us because we aren't talking.
Therapist:	Do others feel the same way?
Ann:	It's really hard for us to know what we should talk about.
Mary:	Even when there's something bothering me, I don't know if I should bring it up. Maybe I'm the only one it's bothering, and everyone else will think it's a big waste of time.
Jan:	We don't have much time for this group, and you really are the one who knows what the most important things are for us to talk about. (*Other members nod and otherwise indicate their agreement.*)
Therapist:	Seems like people are feeling pretty frustrated and irritated with us. Time is short. We're the experts, we know what's important, but you're the ones who have to come up with the topics. Puts the pressure on you, then you feel like I'm criticizing you because you don't get started. (*Again, the group nods and grumbles.*) I can see your point, and we'll come back to that in a bit. First, though, I'd like for people to think back and see if you remember having similar thoughts and feelings as kids? (*The request triggers memories from several clients about times when their parents expected them to anticipate demands or to assume adult responsibilities. Their failures typically were met with derision, sometimes abuse.*) Your parents set you up with some unfair demands, then jumped on you when you blew it. (*Group agrees.*) Looks like I played right into an old script. (*Agreement again.*) So your anger is understandable. I also heard another feeling in you voices and saw it in your faces — fear. Fear that I would really scold you for wasting time or something. Is that what you parents did? (*When discussion of past abuse is completed, the therapist returns to the present.*) Back to our request about starting discussions and my comment about the difficulty in getting started. Let's look at these issues.

The group then explores the request, and several members are able to acknowledge that there are some issues that they have strong feelings about and want to explore. They also acknowledge that their reluctance to start lies in the fear that others will put them down. The final step in this particular session is to look at other places in their lives where they experience similar thoughts and feelings: you can encourage them to explore examples from work and with significant others.

Note that the process comment about the difficulty in getting started is used in two different examples: once with a link to the previous session and once without additional comment. Choice of approach depends on the stage of the therapy, previous sessions, and your objective. In linking the difficulty to the previous session, you give direction and invite a reaction to the linkage and events linked. This type of intervention is particularly useful in an early session. It provides some information about reactions to intimacy as well as inviting exploration. The unqualified observation is more provocative and is best used when the group appears to be having habitual difficulty in getting started. Exploring either the reaction to the comment or the actual difficulty itself are both possibilities.

Incest survivors have chronic low self-esteem. Group therapy can easily reinforce their sense of worthlessness because the focus tends to be on problems. It's important to build on clients' strengths and to reinforce them whenever possible. Help identify and acknowledge defenses, reinforce useful coping strategies, and facilitate modification of strategies for an adult environment (which, it's to be hoped, is more benign and neutral than that of their childhood).

Homework: Journal

"People often report that they're overwhelmed by memories once they start the process of recollection. You can gain some control by setting a limited time, say 30 to 60 minutes every day, preferably at the same time, during which you think and write about these difficult memories and experience your feelings about them. Get a special notebook and write in it every day. Don't let yourself think about the abuse at other times; that will be hard at the beginning but it will get easier. Follow each journal session with about 20 to 30 minutes of relaxation, deliberately shifting your mood and thoughts to something pleasant."

Work with the group for several sessions on keeping the journal, on honoring the times for writing, and on mood-shifting activities. Emphasize that these are important to establish as long-term habits that will continue beyond the duration of the group.

Weeks 7-10

In this phase of the therapy, the emphasis shifts from the past and talking about the abuse to the present. The focus is on exploring current situations; the objective is for clients to become more active and less victimized. As in the previous segment, the topics are determined by the group. However, concepts and skills listed below frequently arise and can be used as guidelines. Listen to clients' descriptions of their weeks, particularly with regard to their work and personal relationships. Also watch the interactions within the group, particularly in regard to taking care of others, intrusions on others, and self-neglect or martyrdom.

N. Skill: Taking Care of Yourself

Intervention 1: Didactic Presentation (See Concepts and Skills section)

Intervention 2: Group Exploration

Much of the focus of this group is on the expectation that participants will learn to take better care of themselves, ask for what they want, and meet their own needs rather than wishing for someone else to take care of them. Survivors tend not to expect help, yet they may feel quite hurt when it's not forthcoming. They have difficulty asking for help and discount its value once they have had to ask for it. These adults are sensitive to the needs and wishes of others and focus on them, often to the exclusion of their own needs. When asked how they feel about another's request, they tend to focus on the benefits for that person, disregarding the potential consequences for themselves. Later on, however, when they think about what they've given and lost, they become resentful and feel themselves to have been victimized.

For example, Ellen told the group that she would have to work overtime for a month, which meant that she would have to arrive late for group. When asked how they felt about Ellen's continuing with the group under these conditions, the members uniformly responded that it was okay with them; they could understand that she had to work. (They assumed that Ellen would lose her job if she refused the overtime. But when Ellen was asked if that were true, she said that she had requested the overtime.)

Members of the group need to learn to analyze what is being asked of them at any given time. Ellen, as well as the others, needed some help to realize that she was asking something of the group that had some cost for them. Only when we noted that Ellen's late entrance would routinely disrupt group process and could even delay the work of the group until her arrival did the group begin to consider the consequences for themselves. Even then individual members first considered the disruption in terms of its consequences for others in the group before they could get to the point where they acknowledged that their own needs were important, or that they might resent the disruption.

Members of a survivors' group are also likely to have problems identifying their needs; the group is a good place to practice this skill. You can help by asking, "What do you want from the group?" or "How can the group help you?" when a client presents a problem in group. It's particularly important to explore the less obvious implications of a request or demand so that everyone fully understands the request. Help members explore the consequences of getting or not getting what they and others want.

Once a need or wish is identified, it must then be transformed into a request that is sufficiently explicit to be fully understood. Again, it's useful to have group members practice making requests for group time, support, or suggestions.

O. Skill: Assessing Choices

Intervention 1: Didactic Presentation (See Concepts and Skills section)

Intervention 2: Group Exploration

People often insist that they have to stay with a partner because they have nowhere to go. Discussing alternatives — such as shelters for battered women — may help some to realize that they can leave and others that they do not want to do so.

P. Skill: Reframing

Intervention 1: Didactic Presentation (See Concepts and Skills section)

Intervention 2: Group Exploration

Intervention 3: Individual Practice

Q. Skill: Negotiating

Intervention 1: Didactic Presentation (See Concepts and Skills section)

Intervention 2: Group Exploration

The difference between compromise and sacrifice is an important distinction to make in helping members of the group learn to negotiate. Teach members to get what they want in return for what the other person wants in order to achieve a "win-win" solution. Too often survivors tend to sacrifice their needs and then feel angry. Requests for group time from two or more members at once presents a frequent opportunity for negotiation.

Set the stage as follows: "It seems that we have several requests for attention. How do you want to deal with this problem?" The first time the question arises, someone invariably offers to withdraw her request or to "wait until last, if there's time," and others usually follow suit. Respond, "[Name] is offering to sacrifice her time for others. Is this necessary?"; or even, "Six people wanted to talk, now all six have deferred their needs, and we're back where we started. What other alternatives are there?" It's to be hoped that someone in the group will suggest dividing the available time. "Will that work, will that give everyone enough time?" and "Who'll keep track of the time?" are questions that must be asked and answered. Avoid serving as the sole problem solver: ask questions until group members themselves come up with the answer. In the same way, avoid serving as the time keeper. There will be some temptation to get on with the clients' requests for time, but group processes that illustrate important concepts and skills take precedence over individual problems. Work this one through to a solution (if someone complains that doing so is a waste of time, explore that issue also).

Assertive negotiating may be a useful skill for clients when they're at work. Prior to entering a negotiation with an employer, clients may want to role-play the interaction with someone in the group. It's important to thoroughly assess the situation, and to understand that not getting one's way isn't a disaster. Help the group understand that the negotiation process is a matter of giving and receiving.

R. Transformational Experience: Trust of Self

Intervention 1: Didactic Presentation (See Concepts and Skills section)

Intervention 2: Group Exploration

Incest survivors have difficulty trusting either themselves or others. Cindy expressed her frustration and her dilemma at being told that she would have to trust her judgment in making some decision about interaction with her family. "How do I trust my judgment, when I've been told all my life that I don't know what I'm talking about?" The challenge is to respond to this type of statement in a way that supports her position.

> *Therapist:*   Cindy, you're in a tough spot. It really is difficult for you to have
> confidence in your ability to make decisions. Perhaps you can be kinder
> to yourself when you make mistakes than your father was and will give
> yourself lots of credit when things turn out okay.

The first statement serves both to acknowledge Cindy's difficulty and to reinforce her judgment by agreeing with her conclusion. Conversely, telling Cindy that she should trust her judgment or that she has good judgment would be disputing her belief, thereby confirming her fear that she actually cannot trust her judgment. The second statement suggests a strategy to help her overcome these self-doubts.

S. Transformational Experience: Confronting the Abuser

Intervention 1: Didactic Presentation (See Concepts and Skills section)

Intervention 2: Group Exploration

One or more group members will often set confrontation of the abuser as a personal goal. Some may have had such a confrontation prior to joining the group. Exploring the issues involved in such a confrontation can be a useful opportunity for clients to gain insight into their current feelings about their abuser and others who may have been involved. Explore what people wish to achieve. Encourage members to identify the worst, best, and most likely outcome should such a confrontation happen. Also explore how each group member would feel about others in the group confronting their abuser. Identifying each of these scenarios has value.

The most likely outcome is that the family members will respond in about the same way in which they have always responded. If the survivor was the family scapegoat, then scapegoating in some form is likely. If family members were non-responsive throughout the survivor's childhood, they are likely to continue to be so. This exercise can help clients identify each person's role in their family, including their own.

Another possible outcome of a confrontation is minimization by family members, dismissal, or even disbelief. A confrontator might be accused of lying, trying to break up the family, or making trouble. Given the dysfunctional nature of most families in which such a confrontation is likely to occur, the best possible outcome is not a likely scenario. However, defining this ideal at least allows clients to explore their wishes and fantasies surrounding disclosure. The wish can be a trap, in which the survivor is further wounded if a confrontation occurs without a high level of awareness on the part of the client. Revenge, vindication, and reparation are common but unrealistic desires. (In any case, they're desires more likely to be realized with the aid of a lawyer than a therapist.) Often a survivor's wish is for the abuser to beg forgiveness, to make amends, and for the survivor to be in control of the situation in which this occurs. Clients may also hope to be seen in a new light by the rest of the family, for fairness to prevail, and for the family to side with them against the abuser.

The value of this exploration in the group is the insight gained about the ways in which each person's family functions. Those clients who actually confront the abuser or the family may succeed in freeing themselves from false hopes, and thus may gain a sense of independence and strength. Few will find that their family is either supportive or repentant. Families are much more likely to resent the survivor for introducing an unpleasant issue. The actual decision about whether to confront or not is ideally made by each person, with support from the group for the eventual decision.

T. Concept: Effects on Sexual Relationships

Intervention 1: Didactic Presentation (See Concepts and Skills section)

Intervention 2: Group Exploration

Treat discussions about sex as matter-of-factly as any other subject. Explore what members want, and what they think their partners want. You may find that members don't talk about sex and appear to be unaware of their partner's feelings and needs. Survivors may tend to think that their partners are unreasonable and demanding when it comes to sex. Work with the group to show them that talking openly and being sympathetic about each other's needs can be helpful in easing the tension between partners.

Group members may never have told their partners that they were sexually abused or how they feel about certain sexual acts. Explore the possibility of clients talking with their partners about their partner's needs and how these can be met in ways that are acceptable to both people involved.

You may be tempted to encourage clients to disclose their abuse history to their partners. Resist the impulse. Partner's may be physically or sexually abusive; they may throw the information back in the victim's face at some later date. For the purposes of this therapy, stay with neutral exploration of the possible reasons for the secrecy. If appropriate, you can help the group explore what it's like to be intimately involved with someone you can't trust.

Groups for partners of adult victims of abuse may be helpful. Parents United and abuse hotlines may be a useful source of information about such groups in your area.

U. Concept: Avoiding Repetition of Abusive Relationships

Intervention 1: Didactic Presentation (See Concepts and Skills section)

Intervention 2: Group Exploration

Homework: An Unsent Letter to Your Abuser

"Write a letter to your abuser. Remind him of what happened and say everything that you ever wanted to say to him. Don't worry about the language you use or about the abuser's feelings — just get everything down on paper. This letter is likely to evoke some strong feelings — so protect yourself. Do this homework exercise when you have a couple of hours or more in a quiet place by yourself. When you finish, do your safe place and relaxation exercises; then do something pleasant for yourself. This letter is *not* to be sent; it is an activity for your recovery."

Homework: An Unsent Letter to the Unprotecting Parent(s)

Often survivors feel as much resentment and hurt toward the parent who did not protect you as toward the abuser himself. If the parent saw physical abuse or failed to believe the child who tried to tell about sexual abuse, the survivor's feelings may be conscious and acknowledged. However, writing this letter may arouse strong emotions and thoughts that might be distressing. Follow the same procedure used with the letter to the abuser. This letter is not to be sent."

Weeks 11-12: Termination

Intervention 1: Didactic Presentation (See Concepts and Skills section)

Intervention 2: Group Exploration

Termination usually evokes feelings of loss and abandonment in clients. They may ask if the group can be extended for a week or two, or say that they're not ready for the group to end. Alternatively, they may deny feelings or may emotionally withdraw. It's important to hold to the original schedule and assume the responsibility for the termination. Using "clinic policy" or other vague, institutional excuses for the ending date only avoids the issues of loss and feelings of betrayal that need to be processed.

Assume responsibility for sticking to the schedule. Attributing termination to agency policy or an administrative decision casts you in the victim's role, along with everyone else in the group. Part of the therapist's job in terminating any group is to model the adult's role of assuming responsibility for decisions — particularly important given the history of victimization among survivors of sexual abuse.

People use a variety of excuses to avoid facing the termination of any relationship; incest survivors are no exception. It will help forestall early departures if you talk about both the importance and difficulty of terminating. Do acknowledge the pressures of everyone's schedules (for example, "We'll be ending our work in a couple of weeks. You are busy people, and many of you have had to leave work early or make other sacrifices to come to the group. You may now find that those demands have increased, or that there's some cumulative pressure to do other things during the time allotted for our remaining group meetings. Do avoid the temptation to do something else or to give in to illness during the next two sessions. Saying good-by is hard, but it really is an important part of the work you've been doing here.").

Termination involves a review and brief reworking of the major issues addressed during the group. Have these in mind as you begin the termination process. Be on the alert for relapses, particularly in the eleventh session. If the group members plead for an extra session, explore their reasoning and feelings — but hold to the original contract. Yielding may be superficially gratifying, but the nonverbal message is that group members haven't yet accomplished what they should have or can't cope with the termination.

Some may deny either the ending (for example, "We can get together once a month for coffee.") or their feelings of loss ("We knew we were only going to meet 12 times when we started — why get upset now?"). Approach these and other defenses with your usual exploratory stance; be particularly alert to family-of-origin ways of saying good-by and dealing with feelings.

Anger is a likely reaction to termination, and it's important to anticipate this feeling and your possible reactions to it. Accept the anger, explore and interpret it, but also be willing to acknowledge that there is some realistic basis for anger in that most of the members will not have finished their work. Some may feel accepted for the first time; others may have come to see the group as a substitute for their family.

Watch for and be ready to interpret feelings related to victimization. This may, in fact, be your last opportunity to help group members work through their sense of helplessness and feelings of anger. What is important is your acknowledgment of their anger and your willingness to listen to them express their reasons for feeling angry or hurt. Your attitude should be one of openness to their feelings, wishes, and thoughts. In the end, however, you and they must honor the contract. End these final hours on time: this is your final statement on boundaries and consistency, two important concepts for your group to master.

Some acknowledgment that the final hour is different from the others is appropriate. Close the final hour with a brief recognition of the work done, acknowledgment that there is more to do, and best wishes for the future. Give permission for additional therapy without making is sound mandatory for survival.

Explore alternatives available in the area for survivors to continue their work. Also, indicate to clients that there is value in taking a "vacation" from treatment to allow the opportunity for consolidation of the gains from this work. Consider in advance whether you will feel most comfortable with a verbal farewell, handshake, or a hug, then take the lead so that the group isn't left with the question. One caution about hugging: difficulties about physical contact are inherent in this group, and there isn't the opportunity to process the meaning of the action after the group ends. Unless you are completely comfortable with such a gesture, don't hazard making it.

Relapse

Recovery from incest or other form of childhood abuse is a long and painful process, and relapses occur frequently. These take two forms: recurrence of the shame and self-blame and returning to old responses concerning the abuse. If the group has worked well together and developed a common sense of achievement, they may not welcome the idea that relapses are likely. From the onset, it's important to impart the notion that this group work is only part of recovery and growth. Individuals who continue to be isolated or secretive about their abuse are most likely to experience a relapse — so it's important for everyone to talk with people outside the group about their experiences. Some of the group may wish to exchange phone numbers in order to stay in touch. This idea should be explored toward the end of the group: it's important for individuals to be able to choose whether or not they wish to stay in touch.

The best way for adults who have been abused or molested as children to prevent relapses is to continue in therapy or support groups in which they can continue to work on their issues. There is currently a trend among 12-step groups for adult children of alcoholics to broaden their definition of the concept of dysfunctional families, without particular reference to alcoholism; such groups are good resources for sexual abuse survivors.

Daily logs or diaries are also good outlets. Encourage members to establish and maintain the habit of writing in their journals and letting their feelings surface as they do so.

Reading provides another avenue for staying in touch with feelings. *Outgrowing the Pain* by Elina Gil and the *The Courage to Heal* by Ellen Bass and Laura Davis are among the growing list of books that survivors have found helpful.

Resistance

Some group members will resist talking about their abuse, finding it too shameful or threatening to do so. The first step is to help talk about feelings that interfere with talking about their experiences. Many abused children were belittled and ridiculed as is discussed in the concept of the "hot seat"; they may feel initially threatened by being the center of attention in the group. Giving such individuals acceptable ways to withdraw when they wish (for example, saying they have talked enough for the time being) will usually help this problem. It may also be helpful for group members to talk about the feelings (frequently fear and shame) they have when they are the center of attention. Help group members to distinguish between situations that are actually or potentially abusive and ones that trigger old feelings without being threatening in themselves. After the group has overcome some initial resistance and explored a different issue, initiate some reflection on the feelings evoked during the discussion. Ask group members to explore whether they actually felt threatened or abused; if so, encourage them to identify the elements in the situation that evoked the feelings. As clients compare current and past experiences and learn to talk about their discomfort, they become more comfortable with doing so. If the therapist can accept these expressions of distrust and of feeling abused openly and nondefensively, group members eventually come to see that it is safe to talk.

You may be accused of being cold, uncaring, or unsupportive. The consequence of not talking about your personal histories and experiences is that clients may assume that therapists have not experienced abuse: you don't and can't understand them because you haven't been through it yourself. Use these accusations as an opportunity to permit clients to confront an authority aggressively and state their concerns. Then help them to explore their relationships with their parents and other authority figures in order to help them become more aware of what they experienced in the past, what they now want in an authority figure, and what triggers their feelings.

Informative feedback tends to be a trigger. Clients may interpret such feedback as criticism and may respond angrily or defensively, particularly when a key issue is involved. You may have to make repeated efforts to demonstrate that constructive feedback is useful and reflects caring feelings rather than destructive criticism.

Group members may say that they need more validation from you; they want encouragement and recognition that they are making progress. Provide this by nurturing the clients skills of self-evaluation and reflection. For instance, when group members have responded positively to a situation, ask them right away to reflect on their performance. You might ask the shy, quiet member of the group how she felt during a session in which she was actively participating and seemed to be relaxed or even enjoying herself. In other words, help to develop the ability to nurture and identify their progress and positive behavior.

Some individuals may deny progress or be self-derogating in some way. If this happens, confront the clients about their behavior immediately in a neutral but firm tone (for example, "Sally, it seems hard for you to give yourself credit when credit is due. What are your thoughts about this?").

Conclusion

Therapy group for adults who have been molested as children are demanding and stressful. They are also rewarding. Given a supportive and accepting environment, progress can be quite rapid as clients find others who have had similar experiences and begin to understand that they are not alone. Incest poses a particular challenge, as it tends to have deep and lasting effects on individuals. Group members must work through their hurt, anger, and distrust repeatedly; it's unlikely that these tasks will be completed for any individuals in the group by the time group therapy ends.

As a therapist, you are a vital element of the process of change. The model used here is one in which the co-therapists do not share their experiences with the group and may not have suffered abuse or molestation. In this model, the therapists monitor both group and individual progress, intervening when necessary and appropriate. Therapists in a survivor group must be willing to deal with accusations of being unsupportive, cold, or untrustworthy. The greater part of such accusations will be transference-based: even in brief treatment groups, therapists become targets for some of the anger that could never be safely directed at parents. Clients will express strong feelings of loss, betrayal, and hurt that they could not direct at their parents during their childhood.

Obviously, leading such a group will not be for everyone. You must be able to accept and absorb clients' intense and sometimes aggressive feelings. Your job is to help the group members understand what happened to them in the past so that they can accurately assess what is happening in the group. To the extent that you can facilitate this process, your clients' growth and recovery will proceed.

References

Bass, E., and Davis, L. *The Courage to Heal: A Guide for Women Survivors of Child Sexual Abuse*. New York: Harper and Row, 1988.

Bowker, L.H., and Maurer, L. "The effectiveness of counseling services utilized by battered women." *Women & Therapy, 5,* 65-82, 1986.

Cole, C.H., and Barney, E.E. "Safeguards and the therapeutic window: A group treatment strategy for adult incest survivors." *American Journal of Orthopsychiatry, 57,* 601-609, 1987.

Ganzarian, R., and Buchele, B. "Countertransference when incest is the problem." *International Journal of Group Psychotherapy, 35,* 549-566, 1986.

Gil, E. *Outgrowing the Pain.* Walnut Creek, California: Launch Press, 1984.

Goodman, B., and Nowak-Scibelli, D. "Group treatment for women incestuously abused as children." *International Journal of Group Psychotherapy, 35,* 531-544, 1985.

Herman, J., and Schatzow, E. "Time-limited group therapy for women with a history of incest." *International Journal of Group Psychotherapy, 35,* 605-616, 1984.

LeRoi, D. "Characteristics of adults abused as chilldren." Paper presented at the Conference on Child Abuse Assessment, Treatment, and Reporting. San Francisco, 1986.

Singer, K.I. "Group work with men who experienced incest in childhood." *American Journal of Orthopsychiatry, 59,* 468-472, 1989.

Sprei, J.E. "Group treatment of adult women incest survivors." In *Women's Therapy Groups: Paradigms of Feminist Treatment.* Edited by C.M. Brody. New York: Springer Publishing Co., 198-216, 1987.

Swink, K.K., and Leveille, A.E. "From victim to survivor: A new look at the issues and recovery process for adult incest survivors. *Women & Therapy, 5,* 119-141, 1986.

Vannicelli, M. *Group Psychotherapy with Adult Children of Alcoholics.* New York: Guilford Press, 1989.

Acknowledgment

Thanks to my co-therapists, colleagues, and supervisors. I'm particularly appreciative of Lowell Cooper, Chris DiMaio, Marvin James, Lynn Magnet, Randy Smith, Kim Storch, and Molly Stullman. Thanks also to the participants in the groups.

Chapter 10

Survivors of Toxic Parents

Marion Behrend, M.A., M.F.C.C.
& Mischelle Gerien, M.A.

Introduction

As the public has become better educated about child abuse and protective inter-vention, many people have realized that they themselves were abused as children. Perhaps these people remember that, as children, they always felt that they were bad: if only they could be better and do things right, they could please their par-ents. Naturally, they may not have had the inner strength to question the appro-priateness of their caretakers' behavior, even if violence, neglect, or sexual abuse were involved. Children see their own world, however filled with pain and suffer-ing, as normal; thus it is often only retrospectively that childhood abuse is iden-tified and dealt with on an emotional level.

Adult survivors of childhood abuse often have difficulties with close friendships and intimate relationships, and suffer from low self-esteem, depression, anxiety, phobias, and loneliness. This chapter provides instructions for leading a short-term focal therapy group; but this particular client population, unlike some others, will need and benefit from ongoing group therapy. Extended therapy will give clients the opportunity to work through the many different issues that the focal group will merely introduce, and sufficient time to assimilate the related concepts and skills. These clients need a safe, supportive, and nurturing environment in which they can move back and forth between uncovering and covering up their feelings. An ongo-ing group will provide the client with reality checks as well as with the experience of being re-parented. Charles L. Whitfield wrote in 1987, "Treatment of PTSD con-sists of long term group therapy with others who suffer from the condition and usually as needed shorter term individual counseling. Many of the treatment prin-ciples for healing our Child Within are helpful in treating PTSD [Post-Traumatic Stress Disorder]."

Selection and Screening

It's important to screen group members. The screening process gives the client an opportunity to meet the therapist and ask questions, and also allows the therapist to weed out those individuals who are not appropriate for the group.

There are several factors to be assessed:

- *Client's preparedness.* Clients must be able to talk about their current problems and a little about the childhood abuse they experienced.

- *Commitment to change.* Clients must be willing to look at the abuse and its effect on their present relationships and life situations.

- *Concurrent enrollment in individual therapy.* This is important, as many issues may be uncovered, and the group will not be able to give the individual as much attention as an individual therapist can. Particularly fragile and vulnerable clients may need to undergo individual therapy prior to entering group. If a group member has undergone long-term individual therapy and feels that he or she has grieved sufficiently (and is open to returning to individual therapy when the need arises), then this individual is a good candidate for the group.

   Clients with the following pathologies are inappropriate, as they may monopolize or disrupt the group: narcissistic-borderline, a bipolar who is not on medication, active psychotic, disoriented, volatile or aggressive, and alcoholics or drug addicts whose addictions are not under control (Yalom, 1985; Gil, 1988).

- *Abuse.* The individual must have experienced either physical or emotional abuse or neglect. Emotional abuse is an integral part of repeated sexual abuse; but if sexual abuse was the primary form of abuse, and there was no physical abuse, then the client should be referred to a group specifically geared toward dealing with sexual abuse, such as Incest Survivors or Adults Molested as Children. However, if repeated physical abuse was present along with sexual abuse, then the client belongs in the group for survivors of toxic parents.

Time and Duration

This group can be designed to be short term, from 10 to 12 weeks in length, if the primary goal is to educate and empower participants. Actual behavioral changes usually do not take place within such a short time-frame. Often clients will choose to remain in the group on a long-term basis to support their ongoing growth and change.

The group should meet one time per week for one and a half to two hours, depending on group size (more time will be needed for a larger group).

Structure

This group can be lead by either one or two group leaders. The advantage of two leaders is that while one interacts with a client, the other is available to monitor other group members. Whether you have a long- or short-term group, each individual must sign an agreement of confidentiality. When a new member joins, the therapist reads the agreement of confidentiality out loud and then has the client sign it in the presence of the other group members before the session may begin, thus creating a sense of safety for all.

For the short-term group, clients should make a commitment to participate for the entire duration of the group.

In a long-term, ongoing group, clients are to give at least three weeks' notice of their intention to leave the group, thus allowing other individuals in the group to prepare for their departure. When a new member joins the ongoing group, the existing group should have at least one week's notice of the impending arrival of the new group member. New members can be asked to commit to preferably six but not fewer than four sessions, thus reducing the incidence of group "shoppers."

The group should consist of four to not more than nine clients, as the process of sharing can sometimes be very emotional and time-consuming. With more than nine clients, some people may not get the opportunity to share.

Goals

Individual Goals

The primary goal for group members is to become aware of the real or feeling self versus the adaptive self, and to learn to live more in the real self. Members learn to move freely into their feelings with the assurance that they may distance themselves from these feelings again if and when they feel overwhelmed. It is *not* a goal for members to totally give up this useful survival mechanism, as life without it is much too frightening and also inappropriate.

When individuals slip back to the adaptive self, they will know that they possess the skills to return to the real or feeling self: this knowledge lends a feeling of empowerment to people who have come to see themselves as victims.

Group Goals

Survivors of toxic parents grew up in an environment in which their needs were unmet. The goal of the group leader is to create an environment in which group members can recognize their basic human needs and have them met unconditionally within the group. The group will be a source of reality checks and re-parenting.

Since awareness is a major step forward for this client population, no expectation of behavioral changes will be placed on clients within the context of the shorter-term group. Nonetheless, group members will be exposed to ways in which such changes can be effected when they are ready to change.

This group is primarily an adjunct to individual therapy, a place where awareness is built and support is given.

Starting the Group

When beginning the group, remember that these clients have felt out of place since childhood. This may be the first time they realize that there are actually other individuals who had similar childhood experiences. Because these individuals feel so out of place, it may be difficult for them to share their reasons for coming to the group.

Taking these factors into consideration, the therapists should first introduce themselves, give some personal background, and tell why they chose to lead a group for survivors of toxic parents. They should then inform group members about the structure and goals of the group.

At this point a therapist gives each group member a document that communicates an agreement of confidentiality. The therapist reads this agreement out loud; each client must sign it in the presence of the group, while the therapist signs as witness. This is the first step toward creating a safe environment.

The therapist can then define the different modalities of toxic parenting, including physical, emotional, and sexual abuse, as well as neglect. Sometimes, individuals
in the group may not realize that they were sexually abused until they hear these
definitions or learn about the experiences of other clients.

The therapist discusses the benefit of keeping a journal, especially while clients
are involved in group therapy. The purpose of the journal is to keep track of
thoughts and feelings that may surface during the clients' weeks of participation in
the group.

The therapist must remain sensitive to the transference that group members may
experience. In this process, the therapist is sometimes seen as the "good parent"
and at other times as the "bad parent." This transference will color many client-
therapist interactions.

Main Concepts and Skills

A. Concept: Defining Abuse

"Child abuse is an act of omission or commission that endangers or impairs a
child's physical or emotional health and development. Such acts include the following:

- *Physical abuse,* which is the intentional infliction of injury by another individual, no matter what the reason for this action may be. For example, in an
  attempt to teach a child not to play with fire, the adult places the child's
  hand in an open flame. Corporal punishment and willful cruelty are also considered physical abuse.

- *Emotional abuse and neglect,* which may be categorized together. Physical neglect of a child, such as abandonment or inadequate supervision, is also emotionally abusive. When a caretaker is cold, rejecting, and withholding, and
  seems unconcerned about the child's welfare, the child is deprived of nurturance and a sense of safety. Emotional abuse also occurs when a child is
  continuously being blamed and belittled, or when a parent willfully does
  nothing to protect the child from physical or sexual abuse within the family.
  Restraints or punishments such as tying a child up or locking the child in a
  closet are also forms of emotional abuse.

- *Sexual abuse,* including sexual molestation, incest, exhibitionism, inappropriately seductive behavior, and exploitation for prostitution or pornographic
  purposes. Any physical behavior that exploits a child for the purpose of adult
  sexual stimulation — even if this is a seemingly 'innocuous' activity, such as
  stroking — is sexually abusive." (Sexual abuse may be dealt with in this
  group if it was not the primary form of abuse.)

B. Concept: Awareness of Abuse

Clients need to become aware of how the abuse has affected them, realize that
they were not the cause of the abuse, and that their caretaker may also have been
abused as a child. The process of becoming aware is ongoing throughout the life of
the group. It is the therapist's job to make clients aware that what they experienced
was abusive; and to help them see how these experiences are affecting their lives
now. The more the therapist is able to point out abusive childhood experiences
shared within the group, the more group members will be able to recognize the

patterns of experience in other group members and finally in their own memories of childhood experience.

"Many adults who were abused, or observed a sibling being abused, feel that because they are out of the abusive situation, their life is now 'normal' and they can live 'happily ever after.' Unfortunately, this is misleading. The abused individual carries deep wounds. It's only by recognizing the source of these wounds, and working through the grief and pain of the abuse, that the wounds will finally be able to heal."

C. Concept: Family Systems

"Each person in the family plays an integral part in the entire system of the family. Understanding the dynamics of the family system in our individual families helps us let go of the blame that is often placed on us. Abused children frequently hear, 'It's your fault,' which causes them to feel and carry guilt, blame, and low self-worth into their adult lives. Parents who are not getting their needs met for various reasons will sometimes lash out at a child, casting that child into the role of scapegoat within the family system. It might be that all the children are abused at various times, or that one particular child gets singled out. The siblings not being punished are also deeply affected by the abuse. They feel guilt that they are not being abused, and helpless to stop the abuse they are witnessing. In turn, the abused child often lashes out at the weakest or youngest of the siblings.

"Sometimes one child may be singled out for special treatment by a parent. The message given to the family is that this child is 'special' or the 'favorite.' A frequent result is that this child is then often abused by the other parent or siblings. This specialness then becomes, in itself, emotionally abusive. The dynamic of triangling a child into the marital dyad is not uncommon in toxic families.

"In families of toxic parents, the family system is chaotic. Often there is no rhyme or reason to the parents' actions as to which child gets abused or when. The home is simply a 'war zone.' One day the parent may be cheerful, and no one is abused, even though the children failed to do their chores. On another day the parent may go on a tirade or rampage because someone forgot to bring in the newspaper from the driveway."

D. Concept: Boundaries, Rules, and Rituals in the Family

"As a survivor of toxic parents, you need to become aware of the part your dysfunctional family system played in hurting you as a child. You need to learn how the system prevented you from developing a strong, autonomous sense of self that would have made your adult life easier to handle, and would have spared you much of the guilt, anger, isolation, depression, and anxiety you have experienced. Throughout this session, I will be comparing and contrasting the functional family system with that of the chaotic, dysfunctional family.

"A functional family system has rules, rituals, and boundaries that function to provide stability, regularity, consistency, and continuity for the child. These, in turn, help a child develop a clear sense of self. Toxic families are so dysfunctional and chaotic that they are incapable of creating, much less maintaining, boundaries, rules, or rituals. The only rule in toxic families is that the children must keep the abuse a secret from outsiders. Sometimes this is an unspoken conspiracy of silence. In other toxic families, the children are explicitly warned by one or both parents to keep their mouths shut about what goes on in the home. These warnings often are backed up by threats such as, 'If you tell anyone I hit you, I'll really give you a beating'; or 'If you tell, your daddy will leave us all alone and we'll starve to death'; or 'If you tell, the police will put daddy in jail and put you in an orphanage.' Now that child abuse has become such an open issue, however, the rule of secrecy is slowly losing its power over the abused."

Boundaries and Rules

"'In healthy families, physical boundaries include the child's body and material possessions, such as toys and clothes.' (Farmer, 1989) Physical boundaries are established by family rules in the following way. A father might unintentionally hug his small daughter so tightly that she says, 'Daddy, I can't breathe. Stop it!' In a healthy family, he loosens his hold, explains that he didn't mean to hurt her, and in the future hugs her more gently. The rule established here, that daddy must be more gentle when hugging his daughter, lets her know that her physical boundaries will be consistently respected. Conversely, in a chaotic family the father might shove her away angrily because he has misinterpreted her words as a personal rejection. If his own unmet childhood need for acceptance supercedes his daughter's need for physical boundaries, he is also very apt to hold her too tightly or play with her too roughly in the future. As a result, she will be unlikely to develop a sense of what her own needs are or should be, much less learn how to get them met.

"In a healthy family, parents will also, for example, establish the rule that one sibling must ask permission before using another's toys. In a chaotic family, the parent might establish such a rule one day and refuse to enforce it the next. Thus such children learn that their rights of ownership are not respected, and that there are no solid boundaries between what belongs to them and what belongs to others. This blurring of personal boundaries eventually will extend to most family interactions and to the child's interactions with others outside the family.

"'Psychological boundaries are invisible yet very real. They include the sense of 'self' or 'me' as being separate from another person, and territorial boundaries — the immediate space around one's body.' (Farmer, 1989) Unless children are allowed to gain an awareness of their physical boundaries, they will not be able to develop psychological boundaries. Verbal abuse and name-calling violate psychological boundaries. A lack of physiological and psychological boundaries combines to further impede the child's development of a sense of self.

"In a functional family, whether family rules are spoken or unspoken, they are usually understood by all. Thus, if the father is appropriate in the way he touches or plays with his daughter, other family members will follow suit.

"Examples of other family rules include whether adults walk around the house naked and whether it's okay to close the door when a family member goes to the bathroom (Farmer, 1989). Boundaries change over time, as new family needs arise. For example, at puberty a girl may develop a strong sense of modesty that is respected by the rest of the family. In a dysfunctional family, she might be tormented by family members who walk in on her while she's dressing, thus destroying any sense of personal boundaries or limits she is trying to establish.

"Unlike those in healthy families, children in toxic families can never be sure what the family rules are or if they will be broken. The rules also seem to keep changing without warning. For example, in Jim's family sometimes it seemed to be okay to seek privacy by shutting his bedroom door. When his father was in a fighting mood, however, he was likely to barge into Jim's room and accuse him of trying to hide. Once he punched Jim in the face and called him a useless slob because his bed was unmade and his clothes weren't hung up. Such inconsistency makes home a dangerous place to be and makes the family a source of chaos and turbulence rather than a source of stability."

Rituals

"In a healthy family, there are rituals such as regular Sunday outings or take-out pizza and rented movies on Friday nights. 'There is a regularity to events. Routines and family rituals emphasize the continuity of the family unit.' (Farmer, 1989)

"In Joan's family, for example, she knew she could look forward to the ritual of fun holiday dinners at her uncle's. By contrast, Anita's father was so unpredictable that holiday dinners at his sister's were a dreaded event. On more than one occasion, her father flew into a rage over something minor and walked out in the middle of dinner, dragging a frightened, tearful Anita and her mother with him. Other times, holidays at her aunt's were happy, harmonious, and fun, with no mention ever being made of the previous unpleasant incidents.

"In toxic families, the lack of boundaries as well as the absence of consistent family rules and pleasurable family rituals prevent children from developing a sense of themselves as separate from other family members; nor do these children gain an awareness of their own needs, feelings, and limits. Instead, they soon learn that their survival depends upon denying their feelings, needs, and limits. In a family in which chaos is the rule and the unexpected is the only thing that can be counted on, a child's existence is dominated by the abusive parents' overriding compulsion to get their own needs met. Thus, the dysfunctional family system, which is really no system at all, may serve the parents but ignores the very legitimate needs of the child."

E. Concept: Roles in the Family

"Each family member has his or her own role in the family. There may be the child who takes on the role of *the caregiver* (cares for everyone except self), *the rebel* (is usually the 'bad' child who deflects the focus from other family members), *the perfectionist* (this is often the 'good' child), *the sick or fragile child* (the family revolves around this person, thus the tension is deflected from the marital dyad), or *the invisible child* (this is the child who stays in his or her room, away from the chaos or out of the house entirely). The role you adopted covered up your real self. It was an attempt to keep the pain out of your consciousness and to control your fears of further emotional abandonment. The role you took on as a child has been perpetuated into adult life, but it does not necessarily serve you well. It's time to learn to let go of that role and allow your true self to come forth.

"In some cases, it's possible that the roles you learned continue to serve you well; you may have learned to adapt them to new situations. In other cases, the roles may constrict you to the point that you have turned to an addiction such as drugs, alcohol, or food to control the pain of your denied feelings and needs.

"You may have learned conscious splitting. This is where an individual knowingly takes on another personality — and sometimes another name — in order to cope with a situation. An example is Alice, who has sexual difficulties stemming from childhood abuse. At times when she feels amorous, she tells her husband, 'I want you to know that Marilyn is coming into town.' Alice is then able to act and feel amorous toward her husband in the role of 'Marilyn'."

F. Concept: Intergenerational Process

"It has been found that individuals who were abused as children are at high risk of abusing their own offspring, thus perpetuating the cycle. Often the abusive parent was also abused as a child, but this doesn't mean that we are doomed to abuse our children. The fact that you have recognized that you were abused, and have chosen to seek help, is the precursor of change. Becoming aware of your behavior with people is the first step toward change. When you become aware that you are disciplining your child as your parents disciplined you, or speaking to your child as your parents spoke to you, realize that you also have the power to change your behavior."

G. Concept: How Dysfunctional Family Dynamics From the Past Affect Your Present Life

In beginning to understand their family system, the rules and rituals, the enmeshment of boundaries, and their own role in their family of origin, clients can also start to recognize how they are perpetuating the same system in their present lives. They will begin to see how they are responding with the old system's rules to people on the job, friends, significant others, children, siblings, and parents. This new-found awareness empowers clients to make changes in their lives. This sounds easy, but it is a long and difficult process requiring a great deal of positive reinforcement from the therapist and other group members. One example is a client who recognizes that he does not have clear boundaries with his boss and often feels that he is doing extra work that is not his responsibility. On examination, it emerges that this individual had assumed the role of caretaker in his own dysfunctional family of origin.

"When we feel used, unappreciated, overworked, always doing for others, we are probably failing to set limits for ourselves. Not setting limits is a signal that our boundaries are being crossed. An example would be a friend who always counts on you to house-sit when he goes out of town. Generally you don't mind, except that on this occasion you have plans and can't oblige. Your friend's response is such that you feel obliged to solve his problem, and thus find yourself in the role of caretaker again. You try to find another house-sitter or even cancel your own plans."

H. Concepts of Self: Real Self or Inner Child

"The real self or inner child is that part of us that is ultimately alive, energetic, creative, and instinctual. It is who we really are. Generally, people who have been abused do not have a clear sense of their real self. As these individuals grow up in the context of an abusive family, they learn to suppress or deny their inner child. They may also be unduly influenced by other authority figures and institutions, such as schools, religious training, and society as a whole, and tend to adapt to what they think is expected of them in a family or social setting.

"The inner child can be childlike in a mature way, able to play and have fun. Your inner child has a capacity to experience both painful and joyful feelings. It accepts those feelings without judgment or fear, and takes pleasure in receiving and being nurtured. Your inner child is attuned to your unconscious or instinctual self.

"Your real self is your spontaneity, honesty, and expressiveness. The decision to suppress these qualities, or to split off completely from your real self, only to let it emerge occasionally if at all, was a matter of survival for you. As a result of suppressing your real self is a painful feeling of emptiness.

"On the average, you may show your real self only 15 minutes a day. At those times, no matter if your feelings are painful, hurtful, or happy, you still feel alive.

"Finding your real self is an ongoing process that includes learning to identify your feelings. Because, as a child, you had to survive very traumatic conditions at home, you may have found that it was safer not to allow yourself to feel anything. Your authentic feelings probably would not have been understood or accepted by your parents. Also, had you allowed yourself to intensely feel the fear, sadness, or anger triggered by the traumatic events, you might not have been able to keep yourself out of harm's way. You were forced by circumstances to act quickly and instinctively for your survival, much as soldiers do in the heat of battle. Closing yourself off from emotions that could paralyze you became an automatic response. In the process, you may have lost the ability to know how you actually feel in various situations. Perhaps now you feel isolated, lonely, or alienated from other people and the world around you, wrapped in a cocoon of numbness that separates you from your real self and keeps you from responding in a real or natural way to people and events."

I. Concept: Shame Versus Guilt

"According to Charles L. Whitfield (1987), 'Shame is the uncomfortable or painful feeling that we experience when we realize that a part of us is defective, bad, incomplete, rotten, phony, inadequate or a failure.' When you feel guilt, you feel bad as a result of doing something wrong. You feel shame from *being* something wrong or bad. Thus guilt feels correctable and forgivable, while there seems to be no way out of shame.

"The real self feels shame and can express it to safe and supportive people, whereas the adaptive self suppresses feelings of shame and pretends not to have them. These shameful feelings may also be projected onto others in the form of anger, blame, contempt, control, resentment, withdrawal, or compulsive behavior.

"Shame is a universal human emotion. Both abused and nonabused individuals feel shame, but to different degrees. If shame is not worked through and released, it accumulates and becomes an emotional burden to the point where one falls victim to intense feelings of inadequacy and defectiveness.

"In growing up we often hear, 'Shame on you, you are so bad!' or 'You should be ashamed of yourself.' This shame is internalized and becomes a part of you. As a child you may feel guilty about a particular event — for instance, dropping and breaking your mother's vase — and you then use this mistake to convince yourself how bad or shameful you really are."

J. Concept: Post-Traumatic Stress Disorder

"Many individuals who were raised in toxic families are suffering to some degree from Post-Traumatic Stress Disorder (PTSD). In PTSD the following four conditions are present:

- *Identifiable Stressor.* When trauma is repeated and prolonged (longer than six months), is of human origin, and when those around the affected person deny the existence of the stressor, PTSD is more damaging and more difficult to overcome. All these are present in child abuse and do much to explain why the healing process is so difficult.

- *Flashbacks.* These include nightmares, bad dreams, and recurring intrusive memories of trauma with 'fight-or-flight' symptoms.

- *Psychic Numbing.* In order to survive, children often learn to block over-whelming feelings of physical or emotional pain. This psychic numbing provides some protection from events so destructive to the ego that it might not otherwise emerge intact. As a result of such survival mechanisms, you may have grown up with a limited ability to feel and respond emotionally. This split between self and experience requires the kind of active, supportive healing process that group therapy provides.

- *Other Symptoms.* You may experience hypervigilance, chronic depression, anxiety, poor concentration, procrastination, inability to stay on track in life, or difficulty with interpersonal relationships."

K. Skill: Learning About and Coping With Feelings

In a short-term group, the most that can be hoped for is the *recognition* of real feelings. You are only touching the tip of the iceberg. Group members must be assured and reassured that they will not be stripped of their survival mechanisms. The purpose of this group is to become aware of feelings. Group members will become *aware* of their real needs and feelings as the therapist labels these during the course of group therapy. Individuals often do not know the appropriate terminology for feelings, such as abandonment, engulfment or frozen rage. They often don't know what their needs are, and that they have a right to these needs, such as nurturance and being heard, accepted, and loved unconditionally. Such individuals need frequent reality checks to help them recognize the difference between adaptive behavior, which suppresses or denies real or genuine needs, and authentic behavior, which helps individuals get their needs met. The therapist must label feelings and needs throughout the duration of the group so that the group members will learn eventually to identify these feelings or needs for themselves. Deeper exploration of these feelings and needs can be made in individual therapy or in an ongoing group (not one that is time-limited).

"A group setting is a very safe place in which to explore these feelings and experience them as part of the grieving and healing process. You are not expected here to uncover these intense emotions and be with them all by yourself; nor are you expected to stay in those feelings to such an extent that you experience a degree of anxiety and fear that would be counterproductive to the healing process. One of the best ways we've found to treat the symptoms of PTSD is to facilitate your ability to uncover your feelings and then cover them up again. In group sessions, we'll help you swing back and forth between these two ends of the spectrum.

"The process of moving into your feelings and out of them again is accomplished partly by talking about how you're feeling as you recall childhood experiences and share them. If you reach a point while sharing a difficult memory at which you're beginning to feel overwhelmed by the emotion — whether it's anger or sadness or fear — one of the group leaders will be available to help you contain these feelings."

The group leader contains feelings by grounding clients: holding an individual's hand, sitting next to a group member and putting his or her arm around this person (if the client approves of touching), or leaning toward the client and giving verbal reassurance.

"Another way to cope with newly discovered feelings about your past is to simply back away from them on your own when you feel the need to do so. Your instincts often let you know when it's time to move out of your feelings to a safer emotional place. It's perfectly acceptable and appropriate to put the lid back on your feelings as soon as you want to.

"One way to move away from these feelings is to imagine having put them in a box; another way is to distract yourself by watching television (preferably a comedy), calling a friend, or participating in a physical activity such as exercise. Part of this group's process is to provide the permission and freedom that allow you to close yourself off from intense feelings. It's actually healthy, if you're experiencing some degree of PTSD, to move back and forth between feeling and suppressing those feelings.

"When you're writing in your journal about painful memories or experiences, and you find yourself in danger of being overwhelmed by them, it is sometimes helpful to put the lid back on. Tell yourself that you'll save the emotion that accompanies these unearthed memories until you get to group or see your therapist. You need to be where you feel safe, can be heard and nurtured, and your feelings can be contained.

"In group we will deal with this process of uncovering and covering feelings as and when they come up, not in any scheduled way."

L. Concept: Anger

Any individual for whom anger is an overriding issue is not appropriate for this group (see Selection and Screening section).

"As you become aware of your abuse and of your feelings about it, you begin the freeing process of grieving the lost childhood that the abuse deprived you of. Becoming aware of your anger and expressing it is part of that grieving process.

"Many of you are afraid to get in touch of your anger toward your parents for fear that it may get out of control and turn into rage. You basically have four choices about how you can deal with your anger:

1. Deny feeling angry and get depressed

2. Feel but not express the anger, risking physical or emotional illness

3. Numb the pain with drugs or alcohol

4. Express the pain and work it through with safe and supportive people

"Only the last choice allows you to experience your anger in a way that isn't harmful to you. The group will let you feel your anger in a safe way, and when you've felt and experienced enough, we'll help you place the lid back on your anger and put it away until the next time."

M. Skill: Empowerment Through the Release of Anger

"Survivors of toxic parents often feel helpless, isolated, out of control of their life situation, and doomed to never be 'normal' or happy. You need to realize that you can choose not to be a prisoner of your childhood.

"As a child, you didn't have a choice. Your parents were the only caretakers you had. You weren't aware of any other treatment, yet you may have felt that there was something seriously wrong with you or your family. As an adult, you have choices. You don't need to remain in a destructive relationship; you don't have to be degraded by fellow employees; you don't have to let others take advantage of you. Although it can be terribly frightening to leave the situation, leaving is one of your choices as an adult.

"Even so, for now you may choose to stay in a particular situation, even if you recognize it as abusive. This is your 'comfort zone.' You may hate your comfort zone — but the absence of abuse may actually feel strange, uncomfortable, and frightening for you. The unknown is usually frightening.

"By writing — in your journal, in the form of letters to your parents, confronting them with their abusive behavior — you break the secrecy and the denial about the abuse. Writing is an excellent release of anger. This writing is not done in the hope of resolving family problems or gaining apologies: such resolution may never happen. Your letters don't even have to be mailed; they are mainly an exercise for your own empowerment and the release of anger.

"Another way to cope with anger is to assertively protect your needs in daily life. When you don't take care of your needs, feelings of frustration and anger build up, often connected to the early feelings of helplessness you experienced in your toxic families.

"There are three things you need to do to assert your needs:

1. *State the problem.* Describe what happened or the thing that bothers you in nonblaming terms. Be objective and don't make the other person out to be bad or wrong. 'We're supposed to do our chores weekly but the bathroom hasn't been cleaned in three weeks,' or 'I've put in 11 hours of overtime for this week.'

2. *State your feelings.* Use 'I' messages, meaning that you describe the feeling as your own and don't blame the other person for having it. 'I feel very uncomfortable in the dirty bathroom, and frustrated and angry that it isn't cleaned weekly,' or 'I feel tired and overwhelmed with the amount of overtime I'm doing. It makes it hard to have an outside life.' Notice that the speaker doesn't give 'you' messages: 'You're making me angry with the lousy cleaning job,' or 'You're exhausting me and denying me an outside life.'

3. *State your needs.* Say exactly what you want changed. Be specific, and try to limit yourself to only one or two items. Try to stick to requests for behavior rather than attitude changes. It's a lot easier for a person to change what he does than what he thinks or believes. 'I'd like you to commit to the weekly cleaning and I think it would be helpful to make it into a scheduled routine — always doing it on a specific day.' Or 'I'd like to have an agreement with you that limits my overtime to no more than six hours per week.'"

N. Concept: Cognitive Distortions and Automatic Thoughts

"The term 'cognitive distortion' refers to our mistaken perceptions of events that happen to us and of the world in general. The interpretations and assumptions we make about events determine our emotional reactions. If we tend to interpret most of what happens to us in a negative way, we will inevitably have negative feelings. If we expect and focus on painful things in the future, if we are preoccupied with dangerous possibilities, we'll feel afraid. If we focus on loss or personal inadequacy, we'll tend to feel depressed. If we focus on how other people are responsible for our problems, we'll feel angry. Notice how the emotion is the product of the thought. We literally create our painful emotions with negative thoughts.

"If you were raised in an abusive family, your thought distortions are most likely the result of powerful parental programming of the most negative kind. Early parental messages are in large part responsible for your self-image as an adult. The only world children know is the world of their family and their parents. Even though what your parents told you may not have been accurate, as a child you didn't know any different, thus you grew up in a distorted world with a distorted view of yourself and life."

Your Critical Parent Voice

"The cognitive distortions and low self-esteem exhibited by adult children of toxic parents come about through the process of introjecting or internalizing your critical parent, thus making it an integral part of you. We call this your critical parent voice: it serves to perpetuate the verbal abuse that your toxic parent directed at you. Although there was little or no basis in fact for this verbal abuse, or for the negative attitudes your parents held about the world, constant repetition convinced you of their validity. You carry your critical parent voice inside you into adulthood, where it bombards you with a constant barrage of negative, self-critical thoughts that echo what you were told as a child.

"It's hardly surprising that children who are told angrily and often that they are stupid and worthless when they behave like normal children — for example, if they accidentally knock over a glass of milk or get dirty when they play outdoors — come to believe that they're stupid and worthless. The same result occurs when parents blame children for the parents' abusive or out-of-control behavior — for example, 'I have to beat you because you're such a bad child: you drive me to it!' or 'It's your fault that I drink because you make me crazy.' Even if children recognize on some level that this is neither logical nor true, constant repetition of the accusations damages their self-esteem so severely that eventually they accept the blame and perceive themselves as their toxic parents perceive them."

Automatic Thoughts

"In adulthood your internalized critical parent voice comes packaged in the form of automatic thoughts or negative self-messages. Automatic thoughts make up the internal dialogue with which we respond to whatever happens to us. They are called 'automatic' because they flash by so quickly and unconsciously that we aren't even aware of thinking them. Nevertheless, these thoughts have tremendous power to make us feel bad about ourselves and life in general, just as our abusive parent did. Because they act as a constant reinforcement of your early negative parental programming, automatic thoughts can trigger negative emotions such as self-hatred, fear, anger, and sadness, as well as hopelessness and helplessness, even when the event or situation does not warrant such responses.

"Automatic thoughts can

1. Increase your anxiety or depression.

2. Greatly affect your ability to cope by exaggerating your fears, thus making it more difficult to act in your own best interest.

3. Influence you to act in a way that perpetuates the abuse you suffered as a child, reinforcing your already low self-esteem."

Recognizing Automatic Thoughts

"The following characteristics of automatic thoughts will help you learn to recognize your own automatic thinking. The examples used will help you understand that these thoughts are actually coming from your introjected critical parent voice. Once you learn to identify the critical parent voice, you can talk back to it successfully, refuting its negative statements. Automatic thoughts

- Are almost always specific negative messages about yourself, such as: 'I'm no good,' 'I can't do anything right.' Clearly, these put-downs are coming straight from the internalized version of your critical parent, who told you that you were no good or couldn't do anything right whenever you made the slightest mistake as a child. For example, you may have cleaned your bedroom very thoroughly, but your parent invalidated all your good work by getting furious at you for one little streak on the window.

- Appear to you at the time to be completely logical and believable, no matter how extreme or irrational they are — such as, 'Everybody hates me,' when, in actuality, that is an impossibility. When you were a child, your toxic parent may have said, 'I hate you,' or behaved as if he or she did. And although your parent may not have really meant it, the fact that this statement came from your parent gave it authority. The voice of your internalized critical parent makes it easy to believe that 'everyone' indeed hates you.

- Often appear as 'should' or 'ought' imperatives, such as, 'I ought to accomplish more,' 'I should be a better mother.' The perfectionistic, highly critical parent who was never satisfied with your childhood accomplishments, however impressive they were, or the neglectful parent who simply ignored your achievements, are perpetuated through your internalized critical parent voice, making you feel inadequate as an adult.

- Feel more like facts than thoughts. Once again, your powerful critical parent voice has convinced you that your negative thoughts are true, and thus are facts — even when they are not. This is not surprising, considering the power your toxic parents had over you when you were a child.

- Often come in groups, one automatic thought starting a chain reaction of similar thoughts, all leading back to the same negative conclusions.

- Once started, are extremely difficult to stop. Often a toxic parent inflicts a torrent of abuse upon the child, who is powerless to stop it. That child grows up with an internal critical parent voice that perpetuates these abusive tirades.

- They invariably make you feel worse about what happens to you, never better.

"Because these thoughts flash through your mind so quickly, you probably aren't even aware of them. You must make a conscious, concerted effort to catch yourself in the act of thinking them."

O. Skills: Identifying and Responding to Cognitive Distortions

"Automatic thoughts fall into several categories that represent the types of cognitive distortions we fall prey to. The following lists those most common to adults from abusive families. This handout also includes logical comebacks to these thought distortions which will help you learn how to combat them."(The rest of this section can be zeroxed and used as a handout.)

Handout — Types of Cognitive Distortions

All-or-Nothing Thinking (Burns, 1981, pp. 31-32)

This refers to our tendency to see ourselves in extreme, black or white ways. In reality, few people or events are 100 percent good or bad. No one is a complete, unqualified success and no one is a total failure. If you try to force your experiences or yourself into impossible, absolute categories, you will end up confused, invalidated, and depressed because your perceptions do not conform to reality. Start looking for shades of gray, which is where most events or people fall in the continuum of life.

Example

You forget to put money in the parking meter and end up getting a ticket.

Typical Automatic Thoughts. "I blew it, as usual. I do the most stupid things. I'm just no good."

Logical Comebacks. "I goofed. Oh well, nobody's perfect. There is no reason to make a big deal out of it. I do lots of things right. Other people get parking tickets, too. This doesn't make me a bad, rotten person."

If you can't think of anything positive or logical to say to yourself at that moment, say, "Shut up, Mom (or Dad)!" referring to whomever was the most critical of you. Sometimes such an emphatic mental statement as "Shut up!" will stop that negative chain reaction in its tracks. This works equally well for all the types of distorted thinking.

Overgeneralization

You read a general conclusion about yourself or an event based on a single incident or piece of evidence. This comes from your actual childhood experience of repeated, unpleasant incidents such as undeserved spankings or the out-of-control behavior of an abusive parent. You grew up expecting any single unpleasant experience to occur again and again.

Example

You don't get a job you interviewed for.

Typical Automatic Thoughts. "I'll never get what I want." "I'll never get a job." "I'll never be a success." In short, any thoughts using "never," "always," "none," "nobody," "everybody."

Logical Comebacks. "Just because I didn't get this one job, doesn't mean I'll never get a job. Not getting this job doesn't make me a failure. I'll let the law of averages take care of me. If I interview for a number of jobs, I'm bound to get one."

The Dark Filter (Burns, 1981, p. 33)

You immediately filter out anything good, but let the negative aspect or detail of any event or situation slip through: you dwell on this negative detail in isolation. This comes from a parent who discounted or ignored the good things about you, picking out the one small error you made and then punishing you for it. This causes you to perceive the whole event and yourself in a negative way.

Example

Your boss gives you an evaluation and mentions an area in which you could improve. Instead of taking in all the good or neutral things he says, you dwell on the one criticism and use it to convince yourself that the whole evaluation was a disaster, and that you can't do anything right.

Typical Automatic Thoughts. "That was a terrible, devastating experience. He thinks I'm hopeless. I am hopeless. I'm a failure."

Logical Comebacks. Refuse to dwell on the negative details. Force yourself to write down all the positive things he said so that you can see more objectively what the evaluation represents. Say to yourself, "No need to blow this out of proportion. I refuse to dwell on it. I'm shifting my focus to the positive right this second! He said many good things about my work. I see the criticism as it truly is — one small aspect, not the whole evaluation. There's always room for improvement, so I'll deal with the evaluation on that basis, not as if it means that I'm hopelessly inept and ineffective in my job. If I were that bad, then he would have given me notice or fired me."

Disqualifying the Positive

This is similar to the dark filter, except that you perceive praise in such a way that you turn a positive into a negative. Because you've been conditioned to believe that you aren't a good or adequate person, but someone deserving only abuse and punishment, you cannot accept positive qualities in yourself even when others give you credit for having them.

Example

Someone compliments you on doing a great job on a certain task. You think he's saying it because he feels sorry for you, or that the good thing you did was an accident or fluke, or that if the person really knew you, he'd see you as the terrible, rotten person you really are.

Typical Automatic Thoughts. "He doesn't know the real me. If he only knew how incompetent I really am! Maybe I did okay this time, but I doubt that it will happen again."

Logical Comeback. "Guess I'm not really so bad after all. I think I'll let that praise nurture me and make me feel good. If I did a good job once, I can do it again. Hooray for me! I did do a good job and I'm proud of myself. I'm going to open myself up to more compliments and positive feedback. I like them and I deserve them!"

Emotional Reasoning

This is the belief that what you feel must be true. This comes from a childhood in which the abuse you received put you in a depressed or fearful frame of mind so much of the time that you began to perceive most of your experience from that emotional standpoint.

Example

You're at a party or social gathering and feel boring that evening. You then assume that because you feel that way you are that way.

Typical Automatic Thoughts. "If I feel it, it must be true."

Logical Comebacks. "Feelings aren't facts! I might be feeling boring because I'm bored. I'm too tired to be as sharp as usual, but that doesn't mean I'm a boring person."

Fortune-Telling

This is the distortion in which you make negative predictions about your future or the outcome of almost anything concerning you. Living with abusive parents taught you to expect the worst from them because it happened so often. You soon came to expect the worst from life. Those gloomy expectations continue to cloud your future, even when present evidence doesn't warrant it. Also, if something negative does happen, you tell yourself that you should have known about it.

Example

You and your spouse make an offer on a house you really want. You're so sure it won't be accepted that you wish you hadn't made the offer. You feel depressed, hopeless, and anxious.

Typical Automatic Thoughts. "I know it's useless to hope. They're probably turning it down at this very moment. I never get what I want and never will."

Logical Comebacks. "Nothing ventured, nothing gained. Even if they don't accept this offer, they might make a counteroffer. Besides, our chances are as good as anyone else's. If this deal falls through, there are certainly lots of other houses we might buy. After all, there's no guarantee it won't work out, just as there's no guarantee that it will."

Mind Reading

You assume that others are critical of you, looking down on you, rejecting you. You're so sure that your perception is right, you don't even bother to check it out. You feel all the pain of defeat, censure, or rejection without having the slightest idea whether it's really happening.

Example

A friend passes you on the street without saying "hello." You assume that she's ignoring you or is angry with you about something.

Typical Automatic Thoughts. 'She doesn't like me or she would have said something to me. She hates me. She thinks I'm not worth knowing."

Logical Comebacks. "Last time I saw her, things were great. Maybe she's got a lot on her mind and was so preoccupied she didn't see me. At any rate, I'm not going to make a big deal out of it without some real evidence."

Catastrophizing

This is the "what-if whammy." You expect disaster around every corner. You hear about an illness or problem and away you go with an endless list of terrible things that could happen to you and your loved ones.

Example

You notice a lump on your body.

Typical Automatic Thoughts. "Oh no, I've got cancer. My grandmother died of cancer. I'm sure to die."

Logical Comebacks. "How do you know it's malignant? Even if it is, you caught it early and can have it removed. Just make an appointment with the doctor right now and don't procrastinate."

P. Skill: Learning To Refute and Stop Automatic Thoughts and Cognitive Distortions

"In order to learn to turn around your negative or distorted thought patterns, you will have to practice the following techniques faithfully. You are unlearning some very powerful parental programming in this process; it will require patience and persistence on your part. Start by becoming aware of the situations that cause you to react in some ways outlined in the handout. Then, when one of those situations comes up, remind yourself that you are now going to put into practice what you are learning. The moment you notice yourself beginning to think in distorted ways and giving yourself those self-critical messages, stop. Just stop whatever you are doing at that moment if possible, take a deep breath, and let go of the old process. Slow down your thought processes by forcing yourself to become conscious of exactly what words you are using. Take it one thought at a time. That is, confront the first irrational thought in a very specific way, countering it with a calm, logical thought. This will lower your anxiety level and allow you to then contradict or talk back to the next thought that pops into your mind. Continue to talk back to every thought precipitated by the situation until you have run out of negative messages. You will find that when you're able to successfully talk back to these thoughts, you feel calmer and more in control. The more you practice this technique, the easier it will become.

"If you find yourself in a situation in which you cannot seem to summon up any positive comebacks, take the first opportunity you can find to sit down with paper and pencil and write all of the negative thoughts that are crossing your mind until you can't think of any more. Don't look at the list until several hours have passed. Then look it over again. You will find that some of those negative thoughts will seem ridiculously illogical. It will then be easier to think of logical comebacks and write them down. When developing comebacks, try to be *accurate* and *specific*. You aren't always screwing up, you missed a deadline twice in the last year. You aren't incompetent, you made a math error on your taxes. Also look for balancing positive realities. In spite of the missed deadline, you had a very positive evaluation from your boss. You made a mistake on your taxes, but at least you were able to do them yourself.

Force yourself to write logical comebacks even for those negative thoughts that you still believe to have some validity. Eventually you'll realize that looking at the event in a logical and positive way is helping you to get some perspective on it. You can demystify and defuse even the most fearful or convincing illogical thoughts in this way."

Q. Concept: Humor

Friedrich Nietzsche said, "The most acutely suffering animal on earth invented laughter" (Cousins, 1989).

As Norman Cousins notes, Swedish medical researchers' experiments demonstrated that "laughter helps the body to provide its own medications. A humor therapy program can improve the quality of life for patients with chronic problems. Laughter has an immediate symptom-relieving effect for these patients."

"It is a common fact that laughing makes us feel better. Sometimes we laugh so hard we have tears running down our face. The laughing response is the same as crying, except that laughing is generally brought on by what seems humorous to us. You may have noticed that when you watch a silly television program that causes you to laugh, you end up feeling better, especially if you were depressed. Being able to laugh is very healthy for you and is a great mood-alterer. Although what you experienced as a child is depressing, laughter about some of the more absurd aspects of your situations can lighten your perspective and lessen your grief."

"Norman Cousins says, 'It has always seemed to me that laughter is the human mind's way of dealing with the incongruous. Our train of thought will be running in one direction and then is derailed suddenly by running into absurdity. The sudden wreckage of logical flow demands release. Hence the physical reaction known as laughter.'" (Cousins, 1989)

R. Skill: Find Out What Makes You Laugh

"Finding out what makes you laugh and being able to turn to it when you're feeling particularly sad or depressed is a great medicine, and a great way to distance yourself from painful emotion when you need to. Throughout the process of this group, we will become aware of what makes us laugh so that we can turn to this in times of need."

S. Concept: Self-Nurturance

"In your families, you received very little to almost no nurturance. Nor did you have parents who modeled self-nurturance. Perhaps when you wanted to rest or relax you were told that you were lazy or selfish. When you asked for what you wanted, you may have been told that you were selfish.

"Things that give us peace of mind, that make us feel good, are nurturing to us. Some of us may like to listen to music or paint or draw. Some of us may like to dance or exercise. Some of us may like to take a walk on a beach or in a park. Some may want to lie in the grass or by a swimming pool. Some of us may like to take warm bubble baths, burn incense, or read a book. Some may like to garden.

"It is very important for you to find out what gives you nurturance and then to give yourself permission to do these things."

Main Interventions

Week 1

Introductions
See Starting the Group.

A. Concept: Defining Abuse

Intervention 1: Didactic Presentation (See Concepts and Skills section)

B. Concept: Awareness of Abuse

Intervention 1: Didactic Presentation (See Concepts and Skills section)

Homework

Group members are to keep a journal throughout the duration of the group. Encourage clients to write down memories of their abuse, what they did with their feelings at the time, and their feelings now as an adult remembering the past. They may also keep track of their feelings regarding daily events — at work, at home, with friends, or during contacts with their parent or guardian. This journal should be written as though the individual is explaining his or her situation to someone else: "Whenever I want to take a second portion of ice cream, I can hear my mother say, 'You're too fat, you don't need that ice cream; put it away.' I wish I could get her out of my head. It's my body. Every time I hear her voice, I eat twice as much, and then I feel guilty. Shit, it's a never-ending battle with my weight and my mother. I wish I could get her out of my head."

Once the group members feel stronger, encourage them to write their journal entries as though actually talking to the toxic parent, thus making the attribution more direct. This is more emotionally evocative, but also more threatening to most clients. An example of this dialogue might be as follows: "Every time I would have a second portion of ice cream, you would remind me that I'm overweight and I shouldn't eat it. This would make me want to eat it all the more. Why wouldn't you just leave me alone? You always had to tell me how to run my life. You told me what clothes to wear, who to be friends with. You never let me be myself. Maybe if you hadn't been so fat, and maybe if you had had more friends, you wouldn't have picked on me. I resent what you've done to me. My whole life, I've struggled to do what you told me and look what's happened — I'm unhappy and fat like you. I hate you."

Group members do not need to share what they've written in their journal unless they want to.

When making journal entries, clients shouldn't read over what they have written. The journal can be reviewed the week before the last group session for a short-term group, otherwise not for at least four months. The purpose of this is to let group members see a change from when they started the group to when they read the journal. The change will involve greater recognition of feelings, rather than denial or suppression of them.

Closing the Group — Centering and Hugs

Centering

"I would like us all just to sit back and take a deep breath. As you exhale, allow any tension, stress, sadness, anxiety, worry, fear, loneliness, and pain to just flow out of your body. With the next inhalation, take in peace, love, happiness, harmony, and contentment. With the next exhalation, just let go; and with the next intake of breath, take in peace of mind and readiness to drive home safely."

Hugs

For survivors of toxic parents, touching and being touched may be a major issue. Many have come to learn that touch is associated with pain. Others have shut down their senses because they have been touched by an anxious parent who may not have felt comfortable with touching. If an individual was emotionally abused, it may have been very uncomfortable for him or her to be touched by the abuser. The result was a shutting down of feelings.

The therapist must approach this subject with nurturance and reassurance, giving group members permission not to participate if it is extremely uncomfortable for them. The therapist needs to be comfortable with hugging and good at handling boundaries. If the therapist does not feel comfortable with this, then the process may be reduced to a simple handshake or a friendly statement: "See you next week."

The therapist might say, "Touching, such as hugging, is very important to emotional and physical well-being. As children, you may not always have gotten a lot of 'good' or safe touches, and as adults, you may also not often get 'good' or nurturing touches. It is very important that you get used to safe, nonthreatening and also nurturing touches. At the end of every group I like to close with a hug. If a hug is too uncomfortable for you, you don't need to participate; just let me know when you want a hug.

"See you next time and have a great week."

As group members leave and say goodbye, make contact with each one via a hug or a handshake, or make eye contact with a smile and say, "Have a good week." After a few weeks, you'll find that group members will also hug one another and will feel left out if you forget to hug one of them, or if others forget to hug someone they normally hug in the group.

Weeks 2 and 3

Check-in

Each group member, including the therapist, is to share one positive and one negative event that occurred during the week. If someone is in crisis, or needs to share something, he or she should make it known at this time. Such crises must be dealt with immediately.

C. Concept: Family Systems

Intervention 1: Didactic Presentation (See Concepts and Skills section)

D. Concept: Boundaries, Rules, and Rituals in the Family

Intervention 1: Didactic Presentation (See Concepts and Skills section)

Intervention 2: Group Discussion

This is the time when group members may begin to share some of their abusive childhood experiences. The therapist should be very supportive of these individuals. Others may not be ready to share, and must not be forced to do so.

Example

Therapist:	Were there any boundaries, rules, or rituals in your families?
Melanie:	Well, because my stepfather was in a wheelchair, there were no doors in the house, even the bathroom. I guess "no doors" wasn't exactly a rule, but it sure kept me from having any privacy.
Therapist:	Actually, it was a rule in a way, because it definitely affected your boundaries. As I explained, family rules function to set boundaries for children, but in your family the rule of "no doors" actually prevented

	you from developing any physical or psychological boundaries. Do you remember how it made you feel back then?
Melanie:	Exposed and vulnerable. It made me feel like I wasn't anybody at all, a nothing — except, of course, a punching bag for my mother when she got crazy. I used to envy the next-door neighbor's dog because he could crawl into his dog house and no one could get at him.
Therapist:	The dog house actually served as physical boundaries for him, and not even the humans could violate his boundaries by going in there. As a child you deserved to have boundaries that protected you, but you didn't. You didn't receive the love and care you deserved.
Melanie:	Is that why I feel so empty when I'm alone, and so unlovable?
Therapist:	Certainly. Not having any boundaries as a child led to those feelings. A lack of personal boundaries as a child keeps you from getting a sense of yourself as a being who is separate from others or as a worthwhile person. Therefore you end up feeling empty inside.
Tim:	That rule of secrecy you mentioned applied to my family. All of us kids learned early on to lie about our bruises to teachers and the other kids. Somehow we just knew better than to tell on our dad. Besides, we were too ashamed to tell.
Therapist:	The fact that you knew without having been told not to talk about the abuse meant that this was an unspoken or covert rule. How did that make you feel?
Tim:	I felt sorry for myself when I wasn't scared or furious.
Therapist:	Can you describe the self you felt sorry for?
Tim:	Well, it felt like I was a little, weak, pathetic creature, not a real person at all.
Therapist:	Like you were defenseless.
Tim:	Yes! Even when I was in my late teens and lifted weights and got very strong and muscular and could've flattened my dad, I still felt like a weak, worthless nothing.
Therapist:	By physically abusing you, your dad kept you from developing a strong sense of yourself as a child; and even as an adult, it's still very hard for you to think of yourself as strong.
Tim:	Right.
Therapist:	So even though there was a rule about keeping the abuse secret, there weren't any rules that said your dad couldn't hit you — consequently, there were no physical boundaries for you. That's a hard way to grow up. Were there any rituals in your family, Tim?
Tim:	If you mean like things the family did together on a regular basis, not really.
Melanie:	Heck, in my family my mom didn't even let me have birthdays. She ignored them completely. But then one of her favorite things was to tell me she wished I'd never been born.
Therapist:	That must have made you feel like you didn't have much of a right to exist. I can understand why your sense of self is so fragile.
Melanie:	Once, out of the blue though, on my sixteenth birthday, my mom gave me a car. I was absolutely thrilled. Then the next day she took it away from me for absolutely no reason at all. I was crushed.
Therapist:	That was a terrible thing to have happen to you. And it was part of your not being allowed any sense of what belonged to you, or any

sense of your rights in the family. Your mom's cruel capriciousness also taught you, for probably the millionth time, that all you could expect from her was the unexpected as well as the unpleasant.

Sophie: You know, I'll bet I'm not the only one in here who didn't have what you call family rituals. I remember looking around at other kids' families and noticing that there were things they all did together on a kind of regular basis. Like, my friend Felicia's folks made a point of the whole family going out to breakfast every Sunday after church. Sometimes they'd take me and I loved it. When I told my mom I wanted our family to go out to breakfast on Sundays, she just laughed and said, "What makes you think just because her family goes out to breakfast together, they're any better than we are? They're real phonies in my book."

Therapist: So your mom demeaned families who did nice things together as a way of convincing herself and you that family rituals were a lot of phony baloney. In a strange way, not having family rituals became kind of a ritual in your family, didn't it? Do you think it gave you a sense of continuity and family stability?

Sophie: It really confused me when she said things like that. It did give a kind of "them" against "us" feeling, but that's not very healthy, is it? At least it doesn't seem healthy. I still wished our family would go out to breakfast like Felicia's.

E. Concept: Roles in the Family

Intervention 1: Didactic Presentation (See Concepts and Skills section)
Intervention 2: Group Discussion

Example

Therapist: Would anyone like to share who, in your family, saw to it that you and your siblings were fed and got dressed for school? In other words, who was the caregiver in your family?

Faye: Usually my older sister did it. I remember her wearing one of mom's aprons. She was so young then, it came down to her ankles; and she used to have to stand on an old crate to reach the stove. But she managed to cook dinners for us a lot of the time. In the mornings, before school, she'd make my little brother and I get up and would help us dress, make sure we'd wash our face and hands and combed our hair. We hated it when she'd inspect our appearance, but it did make us feel like someone cared.

Therapist: Where was your mother throughout all this?

Faye: She was usually passed out drunk on the couch.

Therapist: What did you do when things were chaotic in the family?

Faye: I'd hole up in my bedroom, reading anything I could get my hands on. I even read the labels on stuff when I'd run out of books or magazines. My sister and brother teased me and called me a bookworm. They also said I was mom's favorite. I don't know why. I didn't get any special attention from her.

Therapist: Your role in the family was the invisible one. You stayed out of mom's way, and thus out of harm's way, as much as possible. As mom didn't have much interaction with you, you probably didn't get punished as much as your siblings. Thus they felt you were the favorite.

Faye: I hated that my sister always got punished and I didn't. She did so much that mom should have been grateful to her. I also remember my brother would get punished whenever I did something wrong. I would hide and watch him get punished. I was too afraid to say I did it. I feel so ashamed about that.

Therapist: It sounds like your brother was the scapegoat in the family. What's your relationship with your brother now?

Faye: It's actually quite good. I've told him how bad I feel that he always got punished instead of me, and he just brushes it off. I feel he needs to be in a group like this, but both he and my sister say, "Why do you have to dig up the past? Just forget it."

Therapist: Often people just want to forget the past — they feel that suppressing their feelings is an appropriate mechanism. The drawback with suppressing all the time and never getting rid of pent-up hurts is that we can end up with psychosomatic illnesses or project our anger onto innocent family members.

F. Concept: Intergenerational Process

Intervention 1: Didactic Presentation (See Concepts and Skills section)

G. Concept: How Dysfunctional Family Dynamics From the Past Affect Your Present Situation

Intervention 1: Didactic Presentation (See Concepts and Skills section)

Intervention 2: Group Discussion

  Example

Therapist: Let's look at some of your current roles and see if there's a connection between them and your childhood roles in the family.

Faye: Well, I guess all that reading had an effect, because as an ad copywriter I still create fantasy worlds; but because I'm so used to being the invisible child, I have a hard time presenting my ideas to others effectively. I've let co-workers take the credit for my ideas on occasion because I don't have the nerve to confront them.

Diane: I'm still a caretaker, because I'm actually taking care of my boyfriend by paying the bills and stuff when he's out of work, which is pretty often. I also cook for him and wash his clothes.

Therapist: You're both gaining an awareness about how we perpetuate our childhood roles as adults. Awareness is the first step to change. With awareness, you realize that you have choices. For instance, Faye, next time your co-worker tries to take credit for your work, you have the option to confront him. I realize that right now that may seem too scary for you to do; but when you're ready, I want you to know that the group and I are here to support your experiments with new behaviors.

Homework

Continue journal writing, focusing on family rules, boundaries, and roles.

Closing the Group — Centering and Hugs

Weeks 4 and 5

Check-in

Now is the time to start moving from the cognitive level to the level of feelings, which most clients will have suppressed or denied. The expression of feelings will be foreign and uncomfortable to many group members.

H. Concept: Real Self or Inner Child

Intervention 1: Didactic Presentation (See Concepts and Skills section)

I. Concept: Shame Versus Guilt

Intervention 1: Didactic Presentation (See Concepts and Skills section)

Intervention 3: Exercise — List-Making

Hand out paper and pencils.

Have group members do a short relaxation exercise before continuing. Everyone can sit quietly with eyes closed.

"I would like you to take a few deep breaths. With every exhalation, let go of any tension, stress, anxiety, or fears you might have been feeling in your body. With every inhalation, take in peace of mind, harmony, and contentment. Again, exhale [pause], letting go [pause], and inhale, feeling centered. When you're ready, open your eyes.

"I would now like you to make a list of adjectives or phrases that your caretaker would have used to describe you when you were a child (for example, stubborn, lazy, bad, unhelpful, selfish, a nuisance, dumb, a burden, and so on). [Give group members time to make notes.] Now I'd like you to make a list of adjectives or phrases you would use to describe yourself as a child (such as obedient, tried to do it right, sad, afraid, the scapegoat, the caretaker for my siblings, and so on). [Pause for writing.] Now make a list describing yourself as an adult. [Pause for writing.]

"Now I'd like you to make a list of how you'd like to be described (for example, creative, healthy, thoughtful, nurturing, strong, helpful, confident)."

Intervention 4: Group Sharing

Have individual group members share their answers for each of the four lists above. With your aid, and the help of other group members, have each client explore the possibility that he or she may already possess many of the qualities described by the list of ideal adjectives. You can draw from the examples below.

- *Creative.* The client may already express creativity in dress, work, or ways of thinking.

- *Healthy.* The fact that these individuals have recognized that they have some issues to deal with, and are seeking help, is a healthy step to recovery.

- *Thoughtful.* The client may have already expressed this quality during group or in anecdotes relating to a spouse or child.

- *Nurturing.* Many clients are very nurturing to other group members, but have trouble nurturing themselves or accepting nurturing from other members of the group.

- *Strong.* These people are already strong, or else they would not have survived.

- *Helpful.* These people are probably already helpful and were so as a child, but were never acknowledged as such. They now need to acknowledge their helpfulness to themselves.

- *Confident.* This is something that clients can work on in the group.

The therapist can also ask group members to share the difference between how they are now as opposed to how they were perceived by their caregivers. This is a good time for clients to do some reality checking in terms of who they are in reality versus the image of them promoted by their parents.

Homework

Continue journal writing, focusing on how clients perceive themselves and how others in daily life perceive them.

Closing the Group — Centering and Hugs

Week 6

Check-in

J. Concept: Post-Traumatic Stress Disorder

Intervention 1: Didactic Presentation (See Concepts and Skills section)

It is important to emphasize that many individuals who were raised in abusive families experience some degree of PTSD as adults. The PTSD model is helpful in explaining to such a group why their lives may not have proceeded in the orderly, happy way they would have liked. Learning that the reasons for one's behavior are a result of early childhood experience can be the first step toward relieving individuals of years of accumulated guilt and shame. It helps them separate themselves from their experience in such a way that their inner child or real self is free to emerge.

K. Skill: Learning About and Coping With Feelings

Intervention 1: Didactic Presentation (See Concepts and Skills section)

"As a result of the work you'll be doing in this group, you'll become more and more aware of suppressed events and feelings. As these are exposed, you can and should seek nurturing from within the group. You can also choose to suppress these feelings again, and let them out when you feel a little safer, always knowing that you have the choice to move back and forth between uncovering and covering up feelings."

Intervention 3: Exercise — Learning To Identify Feelings

Hand out paper and pencils. Have clients do a short relaxation exercise as in Weeks 4 and 5.

"To help you learn what you are really feeling, I would like to start by doing a word-association exercise.

As each word is spoken, write down the first emotion or feeling that comes to mind. Here are the words: night, family, mother, father, birthday, holiday, baby, sister, brother, friend, gift, dinnertime, home, parents, vacation, celebration, school, grandmother, grandfather, love, home, significant other, work, and marriage."

Have group members share their responses. Help them understand the difference between the vague sort of feelings they might be used to feeling and specific emotions felt in response to specific persons or events. Give clients permission to choose what, and whether or not, to share.

"If you find that your responses include such answers as 'nothing,' 'bad,' 'terrible,' 'I don't remember,' try doing the exercise again. This time choose one of the following responses: angry, sad, afraid, lonely, left out, abandoned, confused, jealous. If more than one response applies, write each response that does apply. If none applies, write 'none.' Don't be concerned if your responses aren't specific at first, as it often takes time to be comfortable with the process of uncovering your feelings about these people or events. Let's do this again."

Encourage discussion of the fears group members may have regarding confronting their feelings about the past, as well as about current issues. Point out the difference between the real self and adaptive self in terms of feelings; for example, the adaptive self may deny angry feelings toward someone for fear that expressing any resentment will trigger abandonment. Point out that once group members know their real feelings, they will be clearer about their needs. It's also important to emphasize that the ability to modulate their feelings in a balanced way is an ongoing process.

Some group members may feel uncomfortable with this exercise at first; it's inadvisable to push them beyond their capacity. Rather, it's sufficient at this point if they're aware that they may have been stifling their feelings, and that this habit accounts for their isolation, alienation, loneliness, or tendency to withdraw. Eventually, individuals in the group will feel safe enough to explore their new-found feelings more deeply. You can remind them that they are in a safe environment in which they have permission to express their feelings.

Since members of the group may be getting in touch with some overwhelming feelings, you must be available for individual clients to help them contain their feelings. Touching a hand or a shoulder, hugging a client or allowing him or her to cry are all appropriate ways of containment.

Homework

Group members are to record any feelings that come up during the week. These include feelings regarding childhood experiences, and also feelings regarding day-to-day events. Intense feelings are to be brought to group the next week, where group members can be free to feel or reexperience them in a contained environment.

Closing the Group — Centering and Hugs

Week 7

Check-in

L. Concept: Anger

Intervention 1: Didactic Presentation (See Concepts and Skills section)

M. Skill: Empowerment Through the Release of Anger

Intervention 1: Didactic Presentation (See Concepts and Skills section)

Clients need to learn that they have choices. Throughout the duration of the group meetings, you as the therapist must remain aware of, and make clients aware of, the range of their choices. If individual clients feel stuck, you can remind them, "You're in your 'comfort zone' now. This doesn't mean that you like this feeling — it means you know this feeling. When you change your behavior and experience new, positive feelings or interactions with people, you're outside your comfort zone. The more you explore being outside your comfort zone, the easier it becomes to let go of the old and accept the new."

Intervention 4: Group Sharing

Have group members refer back to the homework when they recorded their feelings about childhood experiences and day-to-day feelings. They should share any angry feelings that may have come up. Ask them if these angry feelings were

1. From their childhood

2. A result of abuse or neglect experienced or witnessed

3. From present-day situations

What feeling triggered the anger? Some examples would be hopelessness, inferiority, feeling out of control.

Now have clients look at what their choices were (in childhood there were probably few to none). As adults, clients may still not see any choices; so it's up to the therapist to point out some available options.

Example

Melanie:	Monday, my boss blamed me for a mistake I made in a letter I typed for him. His handwriting is so terrible, it's very hard to read; so I showed him what he'd given me to type from, so he could see it wasn't me being careless. He just said I should have checked with him before guessing wrong. I tried to explain that he was gone all morning and I couldn't reach him, and that I thought it was best to at least try getting the letter done instead of putting it off until he returned. He just cut me off in mid-sentence and gave me a list of all the people I had to get for him on the phone. I was so angry and upset I couldn't concentrate the rest of the afternoon, so I wrote about it in my journal.
Therapist:	Did your parents get angry at you for innocent mistakes, then refuse to hear your explanation?
Melanie:	Yes, lots of times.
Therapist:	When your boss did the same thing, did you feel powerless, like you were as a child?

Melanie: Definitely. Even though I knew the error was as much his fault as mine.

Therapist: Just as you felt as a child?

Melanie: Yes, and that feeling feels lousy.

Therapist: Do you see that your parents and your boss were being unfair, and that you are not a bad person?

Intervention 5: Individual Exercise

When feelings are bottled up and cannot be released, have the group member kneel down on the floor, sitting on his heels. The therapist is in the same position next to the client (about 1½ feet away from him), with the therapist's hand on the group member's back (if touching is all right with the client). The client is given a bataka or a rolled-up towel and directed to hit the floor in front of him. He is encouraged to breathe through his mouth and also to verbalize his feelings. The therapist may say the words for the client, "I hate you! How can you call yourself a mother? A mother is not supposed to hurt a child. You never cared about me!"

Intervention 1: Didactic Presentation (See Concepts and Skills section — Assertiveness Material)

Intervention 3: Exercise

Have group members privately list current issues and problem situations to which they react with anger. Encourage them to think of at least two situations that cause a relatively low level of anger, two in the moderate anger category, and two that evoke high anger. Now ask for a volunteer to describe a low-anger situation. Ask the group as a whole to help this member develop an assertiveness "script" that includes a description of the problem, "I" statements about feelings, and a specific statement of the client's need. Repeat this process with medium- and high-anger situations. Emphasize the importance of assertive communication for overcoming the feeling of powerlessness. Assertive problem solving not only reduces angry feelings, it very often results in positive change in very frustrating situations.

Homework

Continue journal writing.

Closing the Group — Centering and Hugs

Week 8

Check-in

N. Concept: Cognitive Distortions and Automatic Thoughts

Intervention 1: Didactic Presentation (See Concepts and Skills section)

Intervention 3: Exercise — Practice for Recognizing Automatic Thoughts

Ask group members to close their eyes for a few moments and think of a situation in their lives in which they felt inadequate. After asking members to share, you can then help zero in on their automatic thought process.

Example

Therapist:	All right, Karen, your example is a good one. You were at work and a new phone system had just been installed. You were trying to transfer a call to your boss and you lost the call. If you can't remember what you said to yourself when that happened, try to imagine what you might typically have thought to yourself.
Karen:	I know I was really frustrated and angry at myself for being so stupid. It's really a very easy system and this was the call my boss had been waiting for.
Therapist:	How did your body react?
Karen:	Well, my heart pounded, I had butterflies and a knot in my stomach, and I couldn't think straight.
Therapist:	Can you remember any similar situations from childhood that resulted in similar feelings of frustration, heart pounding, butterflies and a knot in your stomach?
Karen:	Yes, it reminds me of when it was my turn to cook. All the girls had to take turns cooking, and I hated to cook. I would invariably spill something in the process, and the food would either be overcooked or undercooked because I was always trying so hard to get it right. My father would always criticize and make fun of me. I can still hear him say, "I can't understand why you are so stupid!"
Therapist:	Do you see now where all those feelings of being stupid and frustrated and the physical reactions are coming from? Not only are you dealing with a situation at work, you're also responding to all those meals you had to cook. What do you think your chances would be of correcting your error in that state of mind?
Karen:	Not very good at all. I remember it was very hard for me to recover and put the call through correctly, even though I actually did know how to do it fairly well. My concentration was really lousy.
Therapist:	As Karen's story shows, automatic thoughts often originate in our childhood. They are self-critical messages to ourselves about ourselves, which affect how we feel and our ability to perform. They make us feel bad about ourselves and can make it very difficult for us to function well. Although you are away from your critical or abusive parent, you carry that person inside of you and continue to criticize yourself in your parent's absence. Once you catch yourself automatically criticizing yourself or being judgmental, you can then say, "Shut up, Dad! I can do this."

O. Skill: Identifying and Responding to Cognitive Distortions

Intervention 1: Didactic Presentation (See Concepts and Skills section)

Give clients the handout. Go through it with the group, discuss any confusion, and answer any questions about the different types of distortions. Remind group members that thought distortions result from parental programming that convinced them they were no good or were defective in some way; such thoughts are not reliable evidence the individual is actually defective or bad.

Intervention 2: Group Discussion

Go over the handout with the group again, concentrating now on "talking back" to these thoughts. Focus on making comebacks accurate and specific rather than global and generalized. Emphasize balancing positive realities that provide counter-weight to the critical parent's indictment. Ask group members to suggest additional logical comebacks. Then ask them how these logical, realistic, non-self-blaming comebacks make them feel. Emphasize to clients that when they stop negative self-messages in their tracks and replace them with calming, nurturing, positive self-talk, they will automatically feel better — calmer, clearer, more capable.

Intervention 6: Role-Play — Practicing Talking Back to Automatic Thoughts and Cognitive Distortions

Having the therapist play the role of the negative thinker is excellent practice for clients, as it is often easier to see another's distorted thinking as illogical.

Example

Therapist:	I'm out to dinner with friends and I'm telling a story about something funny that happened at work. I'm feeling kind of witty and am really getting into it, gesturing with my hands, when all of a sudden I knock over the glass of wine the person next to me was drinking. It goes all over the table, drips onto my friend's lap and onto the floor. My automatic thoughts are, "Oh no, I've done it again. I've made a total fool of myself in front of everyone. They'll think I'm completely stupid, awkward and socially undesirable. They know I'm a blithering idiot now. I'm just no good. I'm always doing stuff like that. No wonder everyone hates me. I'll never change. It's useless to try. I'll be doing dumb things like this for the rest of my life. I might as well stop trying to improve myself. I'm a loser and a failure.
	All right, group, who has the nerve to try to argue me out of my conviction that I'm the worst person who ever lived? [Laughter in reaction to the therapist's exaggeration.]
Melanie:	Well, for starters, just spilling a glass of wine does not literally make you a "total fool." It just makes you human because you accidentally knocked over the glass. Maybe the glass was too close to your plate or something. Who says it was all your fault you knocked it over anyway?
John:	Also, knocking over a glass of wine doesn't indicate that you're even partially stupid, much less completely stupid. Intelligence has nothing to do with it.
Therapist:	But I was right in saying, "I'm completely awkward and socially inept."
John:	"Completely" is a really all-or-nothing term and doesn't apply here; neither does "socially undesirable." Maybe if you'd *thrown* the glass of wine at someone...but you just accidentally knocked it over.
Therapist:	Okay, so I didn't do it on purpose, but I'm always doing stuff like that.
Sally:	Always? You mean every time you go out to dinner you knock over the wine?
Therapist:	No, just once in a while.
Sally:	Like once a month or what?
Therapist:	Well, actually, more like once a year.
Jerry:	So "always" was an overgeneralization that wasn't true!
Therapist:	But still, everyone probably thinks I'm a dope for knocking it over.
Susan:	That's mind reading and you don't have any idea of what the others are thinking. They are just likely to be thinking they're glad they didn't do it and would like to thank you for being the one to do it instead of

them! If you're going to try to read minds or tell fortunes, you may as well make it more or less positive.

Therapist: Why?

Susan: Because if it's at least sort of positive, you won't feel so bad.

Therapist: But even if I don't knock over glasses of wine all the time, I'll still do dumb things in public, no matter how hard I try; and I won't be able to change. Doing stuff like that makes me feel like a loser.

Judy: Now you're fortunetelling again and using emotional reasoning.

At this point, group members can switch and practice arguing each other out of their own illogical thinking. At the end of the practice session, reiterate, with the group's help, the following points:

1. Our automatic thoughts about ourselves have the power to affect how we feel about ourselves and lives in general.

2. Replacing negative, distorted, automatic thoughts with positive, logical ones makes us feel better about ourselves and the world in general.

3. Continuing to feed yourself negative self-messages will almost certainly guarantee negative outcomes, while reversing those messages gives you a much better chance at a better outcome in any situation.

4. We are entitled to the same benefit of the doubt as we give others.

Homework

"In order to catch your automatic thoughts, become very observant of yourself. Give yourself permission to be more self-absorbed than usual as you go through your day. Keep a small notebook handy, and whenever something happens that starts a chain of automatic thoughts, write them down immediately. It will take practice, but within a few days you'll be quite aware of that constant stream of silent self-talk."

Ask the group to come back the following week with at least three events that started the automatic thought process. Have them write the event on the left half of the page and their automatic thoughts on the right. If they can remember similar thoughts or situations from childhood, they should write those down as well.

Closing the Group — Centering and Hugs

Week 9

Check-in

P. Skill: Learning To Refute and Stop Automatic Thoughts and Cognitive Distortions

Intervention 2: Group Discussion

Go over the homework from Week 8 and discuss any problems or confusion with recognizing automatic thoughts. Ask each member to share at least one event and its accompanying automatic thoughts.

It's important again to mention the powerful effect automatic thoughts have on how people feel. This reinforces the concept that thoughts can create emotions and feelings, and will help clients to learn eventually how to control negative self-messages and improve their self-image and performance.

Intervention 6: Role-Play

Continue the role-plays in which a group member presents his or her automatic thoughts while other group members label the distortions and offer comebacks. Emphasize accurate and specific thinking with balancing positive realities.

Homework

* Ask group members to continue to list their automatic thoughts, adding a third column labeled "Logical Comebacks." They should write at least one positive comeback to counteract each negative self-message.

* Clients should continue journal writing.

* Ask group members to bring in a cartoon, joke, or funny anecdote for next week.

Closing the Group — Centering and Hugs

Week 10

Check-in

Go over the homework. By now the group members probably have a fairly clear idea about what automatic thoughts and logical comebacks are. Check for any questions or confusion.

This group will begin with the intervention and will conclude with the concept and skill to be explained at the end of the intervention.

Q. Concept: Humor

Intervention 7: Experiential Process

Have group members rate their mood, at the present time, on a scale of one to ten (one being very depressed and ten being very happy). Also have them rate their physical condition at the present time, on a scale of one to ten (one being in a lot of pain and ten being pain-free).

Now have clients share their cartoons, jokes, or anecdotes collected during the week. Remaining attuned to individuals' responses, ask particular group members to share their feelings and thoughts about the material.

This process is to be kept light, happy, and fun. Group members may remember and share other jokes or even personal incidents that are funny.

Now have group members rate their mood again on a scale from one to ten, and then rate their physical condition on the same scale. Note the difference in the "before" and "after" ratings.

Intervention 1: Didactic Presentation (See Concepts and Skills section)

R. Skill: Find Out What Makes You Laugh

Intervention 1: Didactic Presentation (See Concepts and Skills section)

S. Concept: Self-Nurturance

Intervention 1: Didactic Presentation (See Concepts and Skills section)

Intervention 3: Exercise — List-Making

Hand out paper and pencils. Have group members share self-nourishment activities. They should write these down for themselves and take them home to have at hand when needed.

Homework

Clients should watch a funny movie on television, at the theater, or on the VCR during the next week.

1. "Before seeing the movie, take an inventory of your body as to any physical complaints, and also of your mood, each on a scale of one to ten.

2. Watch the movie.

3. After the movie's over, rate yourself again and note if there is a difference between the two scores. Now rate the movie on a scale of one to ten, one being serious and ten being very funny.

4. If the movie wasn't very funny, then I would like you to do this exercise again on another day, this time trying to find a funnier movie.

5. Next week is our last session and I'm planning to bring some refreshments and make this a fun session to socialize and wind down. I'd like you to review your journal and take a look at how you've grown. We'll also discuss whether or not group members would like to continue in a support group, or if they plan to discontinue. For this last session, I would like you all to bring in a symbolic memento for each member of the group. This can be a flower, a seashell, a rock, a candle, a poem, a quote — whatever feels right to you. Be sure to bring a little token for each member of the group."

Closing — Centering and Hugs

Week 11

This week is the Re-Birthday Party and closing of the group. The group room should reflect a birthday party theme: a birthday cake, nonalcoholic beverages, balloons, and so on. The therapist may also choose to bring in some toys, such as drawing paraphernalia, clay or playdough, or small toys such as hand puppets, cars, stuffed animals, and blocks.

Check-in

Review homework, having group members share what they learned about what makes them feel better.

Allow time for group members to play with the toys and/or socialize — approximately 20 minutes — and allow time again at the end of the group session.

Reconvening, group members can share what they have learned about themselves and how they feel they have grown. The therapist reflects out loud about each person — where the individual was at the beginning of the group and how he or she has grown. Discuss the importance of ongoing therapy and a support group to aid clients in their continuing growth and to keep them from sliding back into their "comfort zones."

Then exchange presents. One person at a time gives each group member his or her memento and also makes a positive statement to that person. The recipient of the gift may only say "Thank you," as compliments are difficult for these clients to accept.

Allow group members to socialize before leaving.

Closing — Centering and Hugs

Ongoing Group

This particular client population needs an ongoing group in order to continue to grow. Growth is a gradual process. These individuals are having to learn new ways of looking at themselves and the world around them. They need frequent reality checks and re-parenting, which an ongoing therapy group can provide.

Possible Topics for Future Group Sessions

Fear of being abandoned	Fear of commitment
Fears in general	Self-image
Growing older	Body image
Weddings	Marriage
Birthdays	Divorce
Death	Holidays
Graduation	Illness
Issues around food and eating	Tears and crying
Money	Having fun
Family gatherings	Bedtime rituals
Whom can you trust?	Are you trustworthy?
Sexuality: homosexuality, heterosexuality	

Problems Specific to the Group

Noncooperative or Resistant Clients

It's crucial not to force this population to do anything they do not want to do. These are people who did not have choices as children. They are generally very obliging and feel extremely guilty when they do not follow through. The group must be a safe, supportive place in which clients can just be themselves.

Most of the group members will be open to any suggestion to improve their lives. Any noncooperation is in actuality resistance to change, which comes from a fear of failure and disappointment. Perhaps the most significant source or resistance is the fear of leaving one's comfort zone, even though the comfort zone may also be painful and nonnurturing.

There are some people who are so invested in maintaining their anger toward their abusive parents that they have difficulty letting go and accepting change.

These individuals will not do well in this group and must be referred to individual therapy before they will be ready for a group setting.

References

Bradshaw, J. *Bradshaw On: The Family*. Deerfield Beach, Florida: Health Communications, Inc., 1988.

Burns, D.D. *Feeling Good; the New Mood Therapy*. New York: Morrow, 1980.

_____. *Intimate Connections, The New Clinically Tested Programs for Overcoming Loneliness*. New York: Signet, 1985.

Cousins, N. *Head First the Biology of Hope*. New York: E.P. Dutton, 1989.

Farmer, S. *Adult Children of Abusive Parents*. Los Angeles: Lowell House, 1989.

Gil, E. *Treatment of Adult Survivors of Childhood Abuse.*. Walnut Creek, California: Launch Press, 1988.

Whitfield, C.L. *Healing the Child Within*. Deerfield Beach, Florida: Health Communications, Inc., 1987.

Yalom, I.D. *Theory and Practice of Group Psychotherapy, Third Edition*. New York: Basic Books, Inc., 1985.

Chapter 11

Group Therapy for Adult Incest Offenders and Adolescent Child Molesters

Brian R. Abbott, Ph.D.

Introduction

Group psychotherapy is considered a primary form of treatment for adult incest offenders (Knopp, 1984) and adolescent child molesters (National Adolescent Perpetrator Network, 1988; p. 29). This chapter presents the principles and methods of conducting an introductory psychoeducational group for adult incest offenders and adolescent child molesters. The psychoeducational group is viewed as a means to prepare the offenders to make better use of therapy and thus increase the efficacy of the therapeutic process.

The introductory psychoeducational group was developed from my clinical work with adolescent child molesters and adult incest offenders. At the initiation of sexual offender group therapy, I found that specific forms of resistance consistently emerged which impeded the offenders' ability to adequately make use of the group therapy process. These problems included: 1) fear of the actions being taken against them by the law enforcement and judicial systems; 2) having negative preconceived ideas about the nature of psychotherapy and their role as a client; 3) tremendous defensiveness manifested in outright denial of the offending behavior, or an individual client thinking that he's the only one who has committed the type of offending behavior that led to his referral for treatment. Entering a therapeutic group can heighten the anxiety associated with these issues and can prevent the offender from fully benefiting from or even participating in the group psychotherapy experience.

The psychoeducational group is a means to address these issues in a non-threatening manner and thus increase the likelihood of the offender maximizing the benefits provided by group therapy. Providing structure — for example, through psychoeducation — is an effective method for reducing the client's anxiety level to a more moderate level. This is a conducive to the client participating in and benefiting from the group process (Shapiro, 1978).

The psychoeducational group is usually run as part of a comprehensive treatment package consisting of individual therapy, group therapies, and self-help activities. A brief chronological outline of this package follows:

1. Individual therapy is a necessary adjunct throughout the entire program, with couple and family therapy occurring when appropriate.

2. Adult offenders first participate in an orientation group with their nonoffending partners and with adults molested as children. This group aims to facilitate the development of empathy and assumption of responsibility for the sexually offending behavior as prerequisites for further treatment. Adolescent offenders go straight into the psychoeducational group.

3. The psychoeducational group prepares offenders for ongoing therapy by helping them understand the impact of their behavior; identify the thoughts, feeling, and situations that led to the offending behavior; and assume personal responsibility for their offenses.

4. The first ongoing process group continues the focus on accepting full responsibility for the abusive behavior and to fully understand the factors that led to the occurrence of the sexual abuse.

5. The second group helps offenders develop adaptive ways to handle the stresses that contribute to their offenses. This includes working through the unresolved traumas or abuses of their own childhoods.

6. Parents of offending adolescents enter separate therapy groups to help them understand their own impact as parents on their sons' behavior, and to learn more effective parenting skills.

7. Skill groups follow, focusing on assertive communication, sexuality, and (for the adult offenders) parenting.

8. Throughout the treatment process, offenders participate in various self-help activities through a program called Parents United. These activities include, among others, sponsorship (where a veteran member of the program acts as a support person for a new member), four hours per month of volunteer work, and a speakers bureau where veteran members of the program go into the community with a therapist and give talks to educate the community about child sexual abuse.

For this chapter, the psychoeducational group has been modified for presentation as a group that is independent of other resources.

Screening and Selection

The screening and selection process is accomplished through a clinical interview of the offender, which usually takes 60 to 90 minutes.

Since the offender has usually been referred by the law enforcement, probation, or social services systems, it's helpful to obtain all available background information on the sexual offense, including the victim's statement of what occurred. Any additional information regarding the sexual offender's psychological and social functioning should always be requested prior to this interview.

Determining Appropriateness for Treatment

You must determine whether the offender fits the clinical criteria for outpatient treatment. The primary issue is to assess if a prospective group member is at minimal risk to reoffend while in treatment, and to assess any psychological problems that may preclude treatment of the offender in an outpatient setting. Generally speaking, the incest offender (as described by Groth, 1984, and Giarretto, 1989) and adolescent sexual offenders who fit the categories of the naive experimenter or undersocialized child exploiter (as described by O'Brien, 1985), are seen as being at minimal risk to reoffend while in outpatient treatment. Furthermore, these types of offenders typically have the psychological capacity and motivation to benefit from outpatient treatment.

In light of these issues, you will most frequently be confronted with having to differentially diagnose a fixated pedophile from an adult incest offender. Groth (1984) provides a comprehensive review of the clinical criteria and psychodynamics to assist in the differential assessment of these two types of offenders. Other types of adult sexual offenders who are inappropriate for the psychoeducational group are the rapist (Groth & Birnbaum, 1979) and the extrafamilial noncontact offender, who has neither a trusting nor a parental relationship to his child victim. Such offenders engage in sexually abusive behavior in which there is no actual hands-on contact with the victim — for example, exhibitionism, voyeurism, or obscene phone calls. It's possible and appropriate to treat an adult incest offender or an adolescent sexual offender if he exhibits this type of offense pattern toward a child with whom he has a trusting relationship.

When assessing adolescent sexual offenders, you will need to screen out those offenders who are considered adolescent rapists (Groth & Birnbaum, 1979) or sexual compulsives, disturbed impulsives, and peer-group-influenced offenders as defined by O'Brien (1985).

Once you've made a determination that the adult or adolescent sexual offender falls within acceptable offender type, there are several other factors that can affect whether or not a prospective sexual offender is conditionally accepted into the group. Exclude those offenders who suffer from mental retardation or have an IQ below 75, dementia, psychotic disorders (psychoactive substance-induced, schizophrenia, and delusional disorders), or multiple personality disorder, or who are antisocial, paranoid, or schizotypal.

When the offender is totally denying the sexual offense (in other words, saying "I did not do it"), he can be conditionally accepted into the group therapy for 90 days. During this time, the group clinicians, in conjunction with the therapist providing individual psychotherapy for the offender, evaluate his progress toward assuming some responsibility for the offending behavior. If, at the end of 90 days, the offender still denies the sexually offending behavior in total, he should be dropped from the group. Managing this offender in the psychoeducational group is fully discussed later in this chapter.

The offender with a substance abuse or dependence disorder can be conditionally accepted into treatment if one or both of the following contingencies are met:

- If needed, the offender completes detoxification or inpatient substance abuse treatment

- The offender is concurrently involved in a 12-step substance abuse program as prescribed by the group therapists; and the offender provides verification of his attendance at these meetings

Degree of Ability To Discuss the Sexual Offense

You need to determine the ability of the offender to discuss the sexual offense and to determine the types and the rigidity of his defenses related to exploring the offending behavior. More specifically, you're looking at content and process levels as they relate to the offender's degree of insight into the origins of the offending behavior, his levels of empathy for the victim, and his sense of responsibility for the offense.

You should assume a probing and confrontive approach in exploring these areas of inquiry while maintaining sensitivity to the effects of this type of questioning on the offender. The idea is for you to re-create in this interview a similar level of confrontation and probing that is to be found in the group. The end result is to obtain a sampling of the client's methods of dealing with this approach — not to have the offender admit fully to any aspect of the offending behavior. For example, the following is an excerpt from a screening interview:

Therapist:	Prior to the first time the sexual abuse happened, how long before that did you have thoughts of sexual involvement with your daughter?
Offender:	You mean did I — [pause, with irritated affect] was this premeditated? No, I didn't have any thoughts before it happened. It just happened all of a sudden.
Therapist:	So you want me to think that you walked into your daughter's bedroom that night and out of nowhere, with no thought, you began fondling her vagina.
Offender:	[with affect still irritated] Well, I can't really remember having any thoughts before I did that to her. You know I have a hard time remembering much about it.
Therapist:	So what you're saying is that you could have had some thoughts before the sexual abuse started but you can't really remember at this time.
Offender:	Yeah. I might have had some.
Therapist:	That's something you'll need to explore more in therapy. Okay, how about... [interview moves to different subject related to the offense].

The intent of the probing and confrontation is to assess the offender's coping strategies in reaction to these methods in order to determine the type of denial system he presents. This tactic is useful in helping to determine whether the offender can handle the group process without becoming unduly defensive or severely decompensating. This method of interviewing is crucial in determining the forms of denial the offender engages in.

There are types of denial which are not appropriately handled in the psychoeducational group. In fact, group participation for some offenders can further reinforce the denial as well as cause significant disruption in the group. The following types of denial, as defined by Salter (1988), would preclude an offender's involvement in the psychoeducational group:

1. *Admission with justification.* The offender will admit to the sexually abusive behavior but justify its occurrence. What is critical in understanding this form of denial is the characterological nature of the justification. The offender's justifications reflect his ego-syntonic beliefs that what is defined as sexually offending behavior is, in his opinion, appropriate sexual conduct. In fact, the offender does not perceive his actions as sexually abusive. Typically, this form of denial is seen in rapists and fixated pedophiles.

2. *Physical denial with or without family denial.* This is where the offender denies specific aspects of the offending behavior on a given day, time, or place. Typically, this offender will not deny the overall charges that he committed the sexual abuse but, rather, has a defense for each alleged instance of the sexual abuse. The offender presents an alibi which, in his perceptions, shows that he did not commit the offending behavior. In some cases the offender's family or friends will support his alibi and actively come to his defense.

3. *Psychological denial.* In this type of denial the offender makes an overall repudiation of the sexual abuse allegations (in other words, "I didn't do it."). The quality of his denial has an underlying theme of "I am not the sort of guy who would do something like this." This offender is not preoccupied with disputing the facts of the child's disclosure and may present vague responses to the report of sexual abuse made against him or may have no idea why it was made. Members of the offender's family may believe that he did not commit the sexual abuse; however, the elaborate stories which are typical of the physical denial pattern are not presented by family members. When this form of denial has been ongoing for three or more months after the initial disclosure of the sexual abuse, the psychoeducational group is not an appropriate choice for an initial group placement.

When faced with one of these forms of denial, the best course of action is to remove the offender from the group. If possible, have him placed in a process group which provides the appropriate therapeutic confrontation necessary to break through these forms of denial. Once an offender admits to some aspect of the sexual abuse, he can be placed back in the psychoeducational group.

Providing the Ground Rules for Entering the Group

When the offender is assessed as being appropriate for group therapy, and before entering treatment, he must read and sign an authorization regarding confidentiality. This form should emphasize that the treatment the offender will receive is being coordinated with other professionals who are supervising the offender and/or his family, such as the probation officer, social worker, or juvenile court. The authorization should also define what additional information can be released to the other professionals intervening with the offender and his family. Treatment should not begin until this document has been signed by the offender.

Many offenders may be ambivalent about signing this form. In answering any questions the offender has regarding the disclosure and authorization for release of confidential information, you should come from the position that the only information released is what is necessary for the other professionals to make intelligent decisions regarding the management of the offender's case.

Time and Duration

The psychoeducational group meets on a weekly basis for one and three-fourths hours per session. The group is seven weeks in length.

In some treatment settings, the lack of treatment personnel, or having a small and static number of offenders, may preclude having a psychoeducational group as a separate treatment entity. In these instances, you can implement selected parts of the psychoeducational group in the context of an ongoing sexual offender therapy group.

Structure

The number of clients in this group can vary from a minimum of 4 to a maximum of 30. A large number of clients can be involved in this group because there is a minimum amount of group process occurring.

The group is usually co-facilitated by a male-female team. While this is the preferred combination, other gender pairings of co-leaders can be used.

The group leaders take on the role of information providers and assist the group members in clarifying and applying concepts to their own personal situation. When group process interventions are used, they are usually brief.

In the adolescent sexual offender psychoeducational group, the parent or parents of the offender attend group meetings. The rationale of this approach is grounded in the experience that issues addressed in the group also apply to parents; clinically, the treatment program has seen better treatment outcomes for those adolescents whose parents participated in the group. As the parents come to understand the intent and methods of the treatment program, a spirit of cooperation between the treatment providers and the parents can be established. When this alliance is created, the parents can communicate to the adolescent the importance of participating and making progress in treatment. This results in a significant increase in the adolescent's and parents' motivations to complete the treatment goals of the program.

If the parents of an adolescent are not available to participate in the psychoeducational group, this does not preclude the adolescent's participation on his own. Invariably in these cases, the parent of one of the other offenders in group will strike up a relationship with this youth and act as a surrogate parent figure. When this paring occurs, the adolescent without a parent in group manifests higher levels of motivation to engage in and complete treatment than he would if this connection had not been established.

Goals

The primary goals of the psychoeducational group are

1. to provide a nonthreatening environment in which to confront the common forms of denial that are associated with the offending behavior,

2. to establish a basis for developing empathy in regard to the effects of the sexual abuse on the victim,

3. to understand the factors that led to the offending behavior, and to determine how to prevent it from recurring,

4. to establish an understanding of the expectations and goals of treatment.

Other general goals include attendance at all scheduled group sessions, arriving on time, maintaining good participation in all subgroup exercises, and completing all assigned homework.

Ground Rules

At the conclusion of the introduction, continue by establishing the ground rules of the group.

"Based on the information we present in the group, you will be expected to discuss the material further in the large group and in subgroups, and from time to time you will be required to complete homework assignments."

Review the following ground rules:

1. "Everything that is said in this room stays in this room. There is no reason to tell anyone who is not part of this group the identity of other members or things that other members say in group.

2. "You are expected to attend all sessions and to arrive when the group is scheduled to start. If you cannot attend or come on time to the group, you are expected to call and inform one of us of this fact. Provide a phone number where you can be contacted.

3. "Please respect other members' feelings. Do not cut others off when they are speaking. If you don't agree with what someone is saying, you can let that person know, in a respectful way, that you don't agree.

4. "We will take time to discuss topics that will apply to your case — however, this is not a time to debate or argue about the particulars of your case.

5. "Do not make fun of or put down other members or their cases for any reason at all.

6. "There is no eating, drinking, or smoking during group. Also, you are required to be sober and straight at all group sessions. If you need to use the restroom, please do so before or after the group.

7. "Pay attention during group, ask questions (especially if you do not understand something), and complete all assignments on time."

Starting the Group

At the initiation of session one, start with the following statement:

> Welcome to the offender psychoeducational group. In this group we will present and discuss different ideas regarding the sexually offending behavior that brings you here today. Before we go any further, I would like for each of you to introduce yourself. We will repeat this introduction whenever new people enter the group. In this introduction I'd like you to cover several things: first, tell us your first name; second, state briefly who you sexually abused, including that person's first name, how that person is related to you, and his or her age; and third, describe your status in the legal system and how long you've been in this group.[1] Below are sample introductions of an adult incest offender and the parent of an adolescent sexual offender:

---

1. When conducting the adolescent offender psychoeducational group, instruct parents to state their first names, indicate which offender they are affiliated with, and give a brief statement of why they're attending the group.

Offender: My name is George. I'm in this group because I molested my nine-year-old daughter, Marisol. My family is being supervised by Social Services and I am waiting to be arraigned by the criminal court. This is my first time in this group.

Parent: My name is Linda. I came to this group to support my son, Rod [points to him], who was accused of touching a neighbor boy who he was babysitting.

Main Concepts and Skills

The main concepts of the groups for adolescent sexual offenders and adult incest offenders are similar. When specific concepts of the groups differ between the two sexual offender populations, this distinction will be explained.

A. Concept: How the Criminal Justice System Works

"I'm sure many of you have fears about what the 'system' will do to you. Some of these fears are probably realistic; others may be unfounded. Whatever the case, we're going to begin with a description of how the criminal and social services systems operate. Hopefully, this will reduce your anxiety." The concepts discussed in this section are based on California law. This presentation may need to be adapted to reflect any differences in other jurisdictions.

The following information regarding the criminal justice system is only presented to the adolescent sexual offender group:

"After the police investigate your case, they can do several things: a) close the case; b) give your parents a notice-to-appear citation; or c) arrest you and place you in Juvenile Hall. In the case of b) and/or c), the Juvenile Probation Department gets involved.

"When a notice-to-appear citation is given, a copy of it goes to the Probation Department. It takes about 4 to 6 weeks before the probation officer will contact your family. You and your parents will meet with the probation officer to discuss the case. At this stage the probation officer can do one of several things: a) close the case or b) place you on informal supervision, for 6 to 12 months. When on informal supervision, you are expected to follow certain rules developed by the probation officer. If you fail to follow these rules, the probation officer can take the case to court. If you satisfactorily complete informal supervision, your case is closed. The third alternative, c), is when the probation officer files a petition with Juvenile Court charging you with certain crimes. When this occurs, it can take 4 to 8 weeks before the first court date comes up. The last possibility, d), is where the probation officer arrests you, places you in Juvenile Hall, and files the petition.

"When a petition is filed in Juvenile Court, you will go through at least two hearings. If you are in custody, three court hearings will take place.

"If you're in custody, the first court hearing is the detention hearing. This hearing should happen within 48 to 72 business hours after the arrest. In this hearing, the judge decides whether you are a danger to yourself or others insofar as you need to remain in custody.

"The second hearing is the jurisdictional hearing. In this hearing, the judge determines whether the petition is true. The judge makes a legal finding only, not a determination of guilt. Therefore, the judge only needs to be 51 percent certain that the crime happened, in order to uphold the petition. If there is a trial, it is held in front of the judge. There are no juries in Juvenile Court, and the general public is not allowed into the court room.

"The third hearing is called the disposition. At this stage the judge will decide how to handle the case. By law, the judge must provide the least restrictive alternative. This usually means that you will be given probation and court-ordered counseling. If the circumstances warrant it, you could be placed in a group home, the county ranch, or the Youth Authority, which is like a prison for adolescents.

"After you're processed in court, a new probation officer will be assigned to you. This probation officer has the job of making sure that you follow all conditions of your probation. Usually you'll have to meet with your probation officer once a month. Adolescent sexual offenders can spend up to two years on probation, or may remain on probation until they have successfully completed the treatment program."

Provide the following information about the criminal justice system only to adult incest offenders.

"As the police conduct the investigation of your case, they can arrest you; however, it's more common at the conclusion of the investigation for the case to be referred to the district attorney. The district attorney then decides whether legal charges should be filed.

"When legal charges are filed, the police can arrest you or ask that you surrender yourself to authorities. Whatever action is taken, the first court hearing is the arraignment. This is where the judge formally reads the charges against you and makes a decision about bail. The judge can set bail at a certain monetary amount or release you on your own recognizance (OR). When you are released or pay your bail, you'll be assigned a pretrial release officer. This person supervises you while you go through the court process. This officer is assigned because the judge usually sets other conditions of release, such as no contact with the victim.

"Your case then goes through a series of court hearings. These include:

- *"The preliminary hearing.* This determines if there is enough evidence to try the case in Superior Court. The judge needs to be reasonably certain that the crime happened before he or she can bind the case over to Superior Court.

- *"Pre-trial conference.* These are meetings between the judge, defense attorney, and district attorney, during which they prepare to take the case to trial. Usually part of this process in an attempt to resolve the case without having to go to trial.

- *"Trial or adjudication.* A trial takes place if you plead not guilty. An adjudication occurs when you plead guilty to the charges. A trial involves a jury that hears the evidence and the testimony of witnesses presented by the district attorney and defense attorney. After all the evidence is presented, the jury deliberates to determine your guilt or innocence. If you're found innocent, you are then free to leave the court.

- *"Sentencing hearing.* After you've pleaded guilty or been found guilty the judge will set a sentencing date. Before the sentencing date, you're interviewed by a probation officer, and the judge may also order a psychological evaluation. The probation officer will make a recommendation as to the sentence you should receive. The psychologist determines if you can be safely treated in the community. Usually the district attorney and the defense attorney write letters to the judge, making their recommendations for sentencing. Sometimes the defense attorney may present witnesses on your behalf at the sentencing hearing. Once the judge has received all the testimony and reports, he or she will pronounce your sentence.

"The types of sentences received can range from straight probation to work furlough to county jail time to state prison. Sometimes the judge may be undecided between state prison and a county jail sentence. In this case, he or she can send you to Vacaville State Prison for a 90-day evaluation to determine which sentence would be most appropriate. Most of the incest offenders who have gone through this evaluation are determined to be more appropriate for county jail or work furlough. When the case is being handled in the county, the judge usually orders counseling for the offender as well as other conditions of probation.

"When you're eventually released from prison, you will be assigned a parole officer. The length of your parole is determined by the maximum custody time you still have remaining upon your release from prison. The parole board grants you parole and usually sets specific conditions to be met while you're on parole. One of these conditions may be counseling. The parole officer's job is to ensure that you meet all the conditions of your parole."

B. Concept: How the Social Services System Works

In the adolescent sexual offender group, this section of material can be skipped if no one in the group is involved with social services.

"In intrafamilial sexual abuse cases, the family may be involved in both the criminal system and the social services system.

"Social services is charged with protecting the child victim. They usually become involved only in an intrafamilial sexual abuse case.

"In handling a child sexual abuse case, the social worker has several options. One is to close the case. Another is to informally supervise the case. This is where you agree to follow certain rules set by the social worker for 6 to 12 months. If you satisfactorily complete this period of supervision, the case is closed. The social worker can alternatively opt for formal court supervision.

"If the case goes to court, it becomes a civil matter. This basically means that you cannot go to jail. The social worker files a petition with the court stating that the child is in need of the court's protection and supervision. If the petition is upheld, the child becomes a ward of the court. This means that your legal custody is temporarily taken away. In some cases, the child may be placed in a foster home or children's shelter. In either case, you are expected to follow a service plan that has been developed by the social worker. Every 6 months the court reviews your progress. Social services and the court can stay involved in the case until it is determined that the child is no longer in need of protection.

"If the child victim is placed outside the home, the law states that there has to be a chance for the child to be reunified with his or her family within 12 months after placement. If the court determines at the end of this time that there is little chance for the child to return home safely, the court, by law, must begin a procedure called permanency planning. This is a process in which the court decides to place the child in a long-term foster home or to terminate parental rights and place the child up for adoption.

"The family is assigned a social worker who supervises the case and makes sure that the family follows the services plan ordered by the court.

"The treatment program's primary goal is to ensure community safety. This means that we have to work with the courts, social services, and the departments of probation and parole in our efforts to meet this goal. The treatment program makes reports only to the professional who is supervising or investigating your particular sexual abuse case. These reports reflect the therapist's impressions as to the progress you're making and whether you continue to be suitable for this type of treatment program. These reports are forwarded to the court for the judge's review. Your attorney will also get a copy of these reports.

"In cases where reunification of the family is possible, the treatment staff works closely with the supervising social worker or probation officer to decide when and how this reunification will occur."

C. Concept: What Makes Social Behavior Between Two People Abusive

"Sexual activity among teenagers or adults is a normal behavior. Many times when a sexual offense occurs the offender thinks that his sexual behavior is normal; or, even if he knows it's wrong, he believes that the sexual behavior is not harmful to the victim. In some situations, the victim may not overtly resist or protest against the offender's sexual behavior, which may reinforce the offender's ideas that what he is doing is not abusive. Some relevant concepts are defined below:

"Legal definitions. This is defined as the penal code sections you are charged with. In treatment, the legal charges are not as important as what you were thinking or feeling about your offending behavior.

"The age differences between yourself and the victim. Young children tend to trust and do what older people ask of them. In fact, many children perceive an adolescent to be an adult. Adolescents and adults can use their more sophisticated intellectual abilities to bribe or entice child victims into sexual behavior.

"The use of physical force or surprise. This form of coercion is more easily associated with abusive sexual behavior. This is where you use actual or threatened physical force, such as hitting, kicking, or a weapon, to coerce your victim. In some situations you may have been physically abusive toward the victim prior to the onset of the sexual abuse. Because of this, the victim submits to your sexual advances out of fear of being physically abused.

"The use of trust in the relationship. Most often this form of coercion is seen in incest cases involving parent-child or sibling incest. The offender manipulates the child's trust in order to bring about his or her cooperation or submission to the sexual abuse. Victims in this type of situation feel an extreme amount of guilt, as they tend to blame themselves, at least in part, for the abuse.

"Physical or mental handicap of the victim. This is where the victim, because of a physical or mental disability, cannot either consent to or refuse your initiation of sexual behavior."

D. Concept: Common Myths About Sexually Offending Behavior

"There are many myths about sexual abuse that serve to distort the seriousness of the offense or the offender's perception of the need for treatment.

"Myth 1: Sexual assault is a crime caused mostly by sexual issues or problems. This is not true. In part, sexual feelings do play a role in the commission of a sexual

offense. Sometimes the sexual offense may even reflect the offender's conflicts regarding his own sexual feelings. For the most part, however, sexual abuse occurs when other feelings, thoughts, and unresolved conflicts from childhood come together at a certain time, leading to the commission of the sexual abuse. In this way, sexual abuse can be seen as the expression of the offender maladaptively acting out conflicts and emotions that are not necessarily connected to sexual issues.

"*Myth 2: A teenager who is accused of committing a sexual assault is really only experimenting or curious.* Sexual experimentation or curiosity with another adolescent is defined as mutually consenting sexual relations between peers. But even if the sexual feelings the offender acts upon during the offense may be age-appropriate, the adolescent may still do so in an abusive way. Many times the idea that an adolescent who sexually offends is really only experimenting is a way for the offender or his family to dismiss the seriousness of the offending behavior. It's easier for the adolescent and his parents to view the sexual behavior as experimentation rather than abuse. This way of thinking is called *denial*.

"Denial is a common reaction when the sexual abuse is disclosed. The offender and his parents feel guilt, fear, and shame. Rather than face up to these feelings, it's easier to see the sexually offending behavior as normal or typical. Eventually, the offender and his parents need to see the sexual behavior for what it really is. They need to deal with it fully in order to minimize the risk of it happening again.

"*Myth 3: Once a sexual offender is caught by the law, this is enough to stop the sexually offending behavior from happening again.* How many of you knew your offending behavior was wrong or against the law when it was occurring?" Many of the offenders will answer this question affirmatively. "Clearly, many of you knew that the sexual abuse was wrong — however, this was not enough to keep you from doing it. The sexual offender is like the recovering alcoholic, who has to constantly be aware of the urges and stresses that can set off his drinking. Similarly, as you progress in treatment, you will find that the sexual abuse occurred because of your inability to handle your feelings, stresses in your life, and other problems. The treatment will focus on helping you identify the factors that led to your offending behavior, and develop ways to deal with these factors to minimize the probability that you might be sexually abusive again.

"I'm sure that many of you have a hard time accepting this idea. It may be difficult for you to accept yourself or feel better about yourself if you believe yourself capable of committing such an act again. But if you continue to deny to yourself that you could, in the future — maybe not today or next week but in six months, a year, or five years from now — you'll be at a greater risk to reoffend, because you will not have taken the opportunity to identify, and to learn to adaptively deal with, the factors that led to the occurrence of your offending behavior.

"*Myth 4: A person who sexually abuses someone must be 'crazy.'* For the purposes of this statement, crazy is defined as someone who is out of touch with reality. Many offenders consider this statement to be true and use this belief as either a rationalization that their behavior was not sexually abusive (for example, 'Sexual abusers are crazy, I am not crazy, therefore what I did was not sexually abusive') or, more commonly, as a self-punishing statement.

"Only a small number of offenders, maybe five to ten percent, are actually what we would call crazy. As you look around this group, you see individuals who, if seen on the street, would never be suspected of molesting a child. Sexual offenders come from all walks of life, rich and poor, and in all different colors. As we discussed in the earlier statement, sexual abuse occurs when certain factors build up over a period of time and are maladaptively acted out through the sexually offending behavior. Sexual abuse rarely occurs because of mental illness *per se*.

"*Myth 5: Most victims of sexual abuse do not know the offender who commits the abuse.* Most of the offenders in this group are related by blood to the victim or have a trusting relationship with the victim. This myth leads to another form of denial about the sexually offending behavior: it can lead the offender to feel as if he is the only person who ever sexually abused someone close to him. This can lead the offender to feel extremely guilty about his abusive behavior and thus increase his resistance to dealing with the problem.

"We know that approximately one out of three females and one out of every five males report having been sexually abused before their eighteenth birthday. Among those who are sexually abused, approximately 70 to 80 percent state they know the person who sexually abused them. As you can see, it's much more common for victims to be sexually abused by someone they know as opposed to a stranger. What we know from the offenders we work with here is that the offenders tend to use the victim's trust as a way of getting him or her to cooperate with the sexual advances."

E. Concept: Offense Patterns — How Are My Offense and My Family's Dynamics the Same as Those of Other Offenders?

"The legal system has a way of defining what is sexual abuse and what is not. I am sure that many of you felt shocked or disgusted when you read the legal charges the district attorney filed against you. I know that some of you would like to fight the charges just based on the way in which they're worded. As we discussed earlier, there are many factors other than sexual feelings which can lead one to commit sexually offending behavior. In treatment we look at your offenses differently than the legal system does. I'm going to explain to you some of the common traits of three types of sexual offenders. I want to stress that these descriptions are based on common patterns we see occurring many times, and that there are offense patterns other than the ones I'll talk about today.

"*The child molester.* This is the offender who chooses a young child as a victim. That child can be a family member — a brother, sister, daughter, niece, nephew, or cousin — or another child with whom the offender has a close or trusting relationship. Under these circumstances, the offender may only have to instruct the child about what to do, and the child will go along. In other instances, the offender may bribe, entice, or threaten the victim in some way to get his or her cooperation. Rarely do we ever see the child molester physically forcing or abusing the child in order to commit the offense."

Present the following material to the adult incest offender group.

"In the family in which incest occurs, we see some common patterns. Often the husband does not feel that he is getting his emotional needs met in his relationship with his wife. Mother and daughter may not be very close. The child and father may turn toward one another for support and affection. At this stage, no sexual abuse is occurring. As time goes on, the father begins seeing his child as another adult, and begins to express his closeness and affection in sexual ways. It is as if he relates to his daughter as an adult. This misperception is another form of denial on the part of the offender."

Present the following material to the adolescent sexual offenders.

"With the adolescent child molester, only about one out of five will molest a child who is a stranger. Usually this offender has some authority over the child as well as the child's trust.

"In many cases, the adolescent sexual offender has never been in trouble with the law, and his parents do not have major problems with him at home. A fair number of adolescents have major behavior problems at home and school. In most cases, the adolescent feels a lack of emotional closeness to his father. This may be due to his father being gone from the house, or his father may be uninvolved with the adolescent when at home. This breakdown in the father-son relationship is a major factor contributing to the adolescent's poor self-esteem. Sometimes the mother sees this problem, or she may be having problems in the marriage which result in her developing an overprotective attitude toward her son. The adolescent usually resents this overprotectiveness, but does not attempt to change it for fear of hurting his mother, or for fear that his mother may reject him. This can lead the adolescent to have hurt and angry feelings that he does not directly express to anyone.

"Many of these problems occur because one or both parents came from dysfunctional families. We see many parents who were sexually or physically abused or who feel emotionally abandoned by a parent or parents. Many times the parents model their parenting on their own parents' behavior. This happens frequently in our society.

"It's important to understand that these problems alone do not cause the adolescent to sexually offend. Again, it takes many factors for sexual abuse to occur.

"*The rapist.* The rapist is an offender who sexually abuses someone who is near his own age or older. Most often the victim is a stranger to the offender. This offender uses a lot of physical force, violence, or a weapon to coerce his victim. Because such people are at high risk to continue to act out in a sexually assaultive way even while in this type of treatment program, we do not accept them for treatment."

When conducting the adult incest offender group, add the following statement: "This type of offender illustrates an example of the difference between the legal system and treatment definitions of offenders. It's not uncommon for a stepfather who has intercourse with his stepdaughter to be legally charged with rape. From the treatment provider's point of view, this offender does not fit the psychological definition of a rapist that we discussed earlier. Instead, we would view this stepfather as an incest offender.

"*The noncontact offender.* The noncontact offender is an adult or adolescent who commits sexually offending behavior in which there is no hands-on contact with the victim. These types of offenses include peeping, exposing one's genitals to others, and making obscene phone calls. It's not uncommon for the noncontact offender to progress to hands-on contact with a victim. For instance, an offender may begin by peeping at a child when that child is bathing. As the offender engages in this behavior, he is thinking about engaging in sexual behavior with the child. After doing this for some time, the offender may act out what he is thinking. The family dynamics we discussed in regard to the child molester apply to this type of offender in our treatment program."

F. Concept: The Chain of Events Model

"The chain of event model is a way for you to understand the different thoughts, feelings, stresses, and unresolved childhood problems that came together and led to the commission of your offending behavior. As we go through this model, you may find that you will not be able to apply each aspect of it to your own situation. At this point, that's okay. We don't expect you to be able to fully apply this to your offense situation. What we do expect is that you understand what each part of the model means. As you progress in the treatment process, you'll have the opportunity to discuss this model further. Based on what you find out about the chain of events leading up to your offense, treatment will focus on ways to help you minimize the chances of committing another offense.

"The first link in the chain of events has to do with past hurts or abuses. These are some of the things that happened in your childhood which were upsetting to you and which you have not really talked about or which may still bother you to this day. Past hurts or abuses can include sexual or physical abuse as a child; witnessing physical violence in the family; having an alcoholic or drug-using parent; or having a parent or parents who used critical or demeaning language on a regular basis toward you. You may find yourself feeling troubled to this day when thinking about these event.

"The second link pertains to how these past hurts affected your thoughts and feelings about yourself and others. These are the negative feelings and thoughts you have about yourself and some of the fears or concerns which led you to have problems in relationships with others. What is important in understanding this concept is that these past hurts or abuses are events which led you to feel and think badly about yourself and other people. When you remember these events now, you have those bad feelings about yourself. For example, you may feel guilt, hurt, shame, embarrassment, or rejection. In addition, you may be aware that these past hurts also affect the way in which you get along with other people. You may have a hard time trusting others; you may feel that you are not able to make friends with your peers, so you avoid contact with them; or when you do have relationships with peers, either male or female, the relationship does not last long or is fraught with problems. You may tell yourself that you're worthless or unlovable, or that other people are cruel and untrustworthy. These and other similar negative thoughts maintain the bad feelings.

"The third link pertains to the high-risk situations that led to the sexual offenses. These are the times when you were feeling those bad feelings associated with past hurts or abuses, or thinking negative thoughts about yourself or others. These thoughts and feelings occurred each time you committed your sexual offense.

"You may have a hard time identifying those feelings in the present. Sometimes offenders experience them as tension, stress, or anxiety. Usually certain problems occur that set off the troubling feelings. These problems are usually with another person, such as your wife, parents, or a peer. In others cases, your feelings may be set off by a big stress in your life, such as a death, divorce, or being fired from a job. You begin to tell yourself once again that you're worthless or unlovable and begin to feel this same painful feelings.

"The fourth link pertains to the strategies used to cope with the negative thoughts and bad feelings which ultimately facilitated the sexual abuse. This link is difficult for offenders to understand, as they think it means that they planned out the sexual abuse. Usually this is not the case. What we find is that the offender handles the troubling thoughts and feelings in the high-risk situation in several different ways, which help lead toward the sexual abuse. For instance, a father may turn toward his daughter to get the love and acceptance he thinks he cannot get from his wife. An adolescent may associate with younger children because he thinks they accept him for who he is. Other offenders may also turn to drinking alcohol or using drugs as a way to cope with the high-risk situation. It's important to realize that the offender does not intend to commit a sexual offense when this process is happening, but that the combination of this and the false or distorted ways of thinking about the child, or the sexual thoughts that come up regarding the child, lead to the sexual offense being committed.

"The fifth link involves false or distorted ways of seeing or thinking about your offending behavior. These are the thoughts you had before, during, and after your sexually offending behavior which made your offense seem okay to you or did not make you feel so bad about it. This can include ideas such as: a) 'Since my victim didn't resist, he must have agreed to what we did.' b) 'I will only do this one time just to see what it's like.' c) 'I will never let this happen again.' d) 'This is a way to show love toward my daughter.' As you can see, these types of thoughts make the offender believe that what he is doing is not harmful or hurtful to the child. When the offender thinks this way, it makes it easier to act upon the sexual thoughts or ideas that he has toward the child."

G. Concept: Relapse Prevention

"Most of you probably think that you would never commit a sexual offense again. If you continue to think this way, then you probably will reoffend at a later time. As you find out more about your chain of events, you'll learn that the thoughts and feelings which contributed to your offending behavior are common. Under the right circumstances, these feelings and thoughts could recur. It may be years before this happens, or it may happen next week. The idea of relapse prevention is to help you develop healthy ways to cope with your chain of events, should you see all or part of it emerging later in your life."

H. Concept: Myths About the Victim

The following are common myths that offenders believe regarding how the victim is affected by the sexual abuse or how the victim perceives what occurs. These distorted ideas prevent the offender from genuinely understanding the effects of the sexually abusive behavior on the victim.

"*Myth 1: When a person does nothing to resist, like scream or fight back, it means that he or she does not really feel sexually abused.* This statement is false. Many victims of sexual abuse do not fight back. This may be due to many factors, such as fear of getting in trouble or making your parent angry, trusting that the offender will not hurt you, being threatened with physical force or some other negative consequence, or the offender using bribery.

"*Myth 2: Many victims invite abuse because of the way they act.* No matter how a person acts, there is no justification for forcing sexual behavior onto him or her. Sometimes children may act in a seductive manner which could be related to a phase in their development or might be a result of earlier sexual abuse. In this situation, it's your responsibility to take action by informing the child's parent, or if an adult incest offender, to discuss this issue with your wife, in order to deal with the situation adaptively. This misperception of blame is a way for the offender to rationalize his actions so that he does not have to feel so badly about himself for what he did.

"*Myth 3: When a child under the age of three is a victim of sexual abuse, he or she is too young to know what happened or to feel traumatized by it.* While a child under the age of three is not able to understand what sexual behavior is or means, that child does get the message that what's happening is a bad thing. The child then begins to think that 'this thing that makes me feel bad must have happened because I am a bad person.' This is the way a child's mind works. This can result in the child developing poor self-esteem, which can lead to significant emotional and behavioral problems for that child in the future.

"*Myth 4: Children make up stories or just lie about sexual abuse in order to get attention or get back at someone.* Young children do not have the sexual knowledge or the intelligence to make up such a story, let alone decide to get back at some one by fabricating such allegations. A child who consistently tells about sexual behavior in childlike words can be considered to be a reliable reporter of what happened.

"Because children have difficulty with remembering specific dates and times, it's normal to have reports that may incorrectly state the date or time of the offense. Also, because victims try to forget what happened to them, the story may not be that clear. A child may telescope several events into one event, too.

"Finally, in family-related cases, a child may report the abuse and later say that it didn't happen. Usually in these situations the victim is upset over the problems that have occurred in the family because of the disclosure — for example, no one in the family believes her, the offender is arrested, or the victim is removed from her family by the police. Under these circumstances, the victim retracts the statement alleging sexual abuse as a means of undoing the problems associated with the disclosure she made.

"*Myth 5: If a person felt sexually abused, she would surely report it right away.* The way in which the offender coerces the victim may prevent the child from reporting the sexual abuse. For instance, the offender could threaten the child with violence or getting in trouble. The child may feel to blame for the sexual abuse occurring, because the offender used bribery or enticement; it takes some time before the victim realizes that it was not his or her fault. In fact, if the sexual abuse occurred on several occasions or over a period of years, it's more common for the child to make a disclosure only after the abuse has stopped.

"*Myth 6: Victims always hate the person who sexually abuses them.* In the types of sexual abuse cases we deal with here, most of the offenders have a trusting relationship with their victim. In this situation, the victim has a lot of positive feelings for the offender. In fact, this adds to the trauma, because the victim is confused as to why someone who is so nice does something that is hurtful. The child victim may continue to want to have a relationship with the offender because of the positive aspects of their relationship. The offender may only see this side of the victim's feelings and may misperceive that the victim was not affected by the sexual abuse."

I. Concept: How Is My Victim (or Victims) Like Those of Other Offenders? [presented only in adolescent offender group]

"There are many characteristics common to the victims of adolescent sexual offenders. Here are some that occur most frequently.[2]

- "Three out of ten victims are male, seven out of ten are female.

- "Almost four out of ten victims are members of the offender's family, usually a sibling or cousin.

---

2. The information presented here can be adapted to more accurately reflect the victim characteristics that may be present in other treatment settings.

- "About five out of ten victims have some type of trusting relationship with the offender.

- "One out of ten victims is a stranger to the offender.

- "When the offender commits the sexual offense, he is more likely to talk the victim into it or use his authority over the victim to commit the offense rather than using violence.

- "Usually the offense goes on for two to six months and can happen anywhere from two to fifteen times.

- "The offender usually engages in such sexual behavior as touching the victim on the genitals, pretending to have sexual intercourse with the victim, or making the victim suck the offender's penis."

J. Concept: Common Reactions of Victims to Sexual Abuse

"Common emotional reactions of victims include:

- Shame

- Guilt

- Embarrassment

- Fear

- Confusion

- Helplessness

- Anxiety

- Sadness

- Anger

"Common behavioral reactions include:

- Difficulty sleeping

- Running away

- Poor school performance

- Bed wetting

- Thoughts of suicide or attempted or actual suicide

- Acting out aggressively

- Sexually abusing someone else

- Getting into trouble with the law

- Temper tantrums

- Withdrawal or isolation from others

- Drug or alcohol abuse

- Eating disorder, for example, refusing to eat, binging and purging
- Self-mutilation

"Common psychological reactions include:

- Impaired feelings of self-worth
- Confusion regarding sexuality
- Depression
- Fears about having a normal sexual life, of getting too emotionally close to others, or leaving the 'safety' of the home.
- Flashback memories of the sexual abuse
- Getting into other abusive relationships
- Getting into a relationship in which the partner sexually abuses their child
- Problems expressing feelings
- A need to control others
- Inappropriate adult behavior (on the part of a child)

"Common physical signs which are a direct result of sexual abuse include:

- Bleeding from the rectum or vagina
- Vaginal infections
- Poor personal hygiene
- Bruises and cuts"

"All victims do not experience every reaction listed above. There are other factors related to the offense which contribute to the types of reactions victims have. These factors include: the length of time over which the sexual abuse occurred, the type of sexual behaviors committed, and whether the offender used physical force in the offense. Even when the offender does not use physical force, or sexually abuses the victim for a short time, it doesn't mean that the victim will suffer less. Victims tend to react more negatively to the abuse when one or more of the following occur: a) when the abuse lasts more that one year, b) when the victim is sexually abused by a parent, c) when family members do not believe that the victim was sexually abused, and d) when the victim has to be placed outside of the home."

K. Concept: What Is Normal Sexual Behavior?

"It's common for offenders and their families to incorrectly define abusive behavior as typical or normal. This is most frequently seen with adolescent sexual offenders where the abuse is labeled as 'normal adolescent experimentation.' In other cases, offenders and parents may misinterpret attention-seeking behavior on the part of a child as sexual seductiveness.

"At about the age of three to five, children begin to notice that the opposite sex has different body parts. For instance, a male child sees that a female does not have a penis. When seeing a female, the child is curious, as is normal at this stage, and he wants to know what it feels like not to have a penis or maybe try to find if it is hidden someplace. During this stage the child's behavior is not sexual in nature but rather is a function of the child's natural curiosity. What happens is that many times adults misperceive such behavior as sexual. Similarly, it's common for children to touch their genitals because it feels good — not because the child is being sexual in adult terms or fantasizing about sex.

"It's common for a preteen or young teenage female to act in a seductive, flirty manner toward her father. The child is not attempting to be sexual with the father, but rather is looking for recognition that she is a developing young woman and is testing limits as to acceptable behavior with males.

"In sexual offense situations, we find that the offender misinterprets these normal forms of child development as the child wanting to engage in, or enticing the offender into, sexual acts. This type of thinking on the offender's part is a way for the offender to justify acting upon his own sexual urges toward the child.

"Children are not physically, intellectually, or emotionally prepared to engage in a sexual relationship with a parent or someone who is older than themselves. Furthermore, children do not have the knowledge or experience, unless they have been sexually abused, to make up stories that involve sexual behavior, such as describing an erect penis or what semen looks like.

"Healthy male adolescent sexual behavior can be defined as mutually consentual sexual behavior between two peers. Other definitions follow:

- "For younger adolescents (age twelve to fourteen), it's most common to see such behavior as kissing, touching of genitals or female's breasts, or 'dry humping.' The older the teenager becomes, the greater the likelihood for sexual intercourse. It's rare for an adolescent to engage in anal intercourse.

- "The adolescent has sexual fantasies regarding peer-age or older partners. It's common for adolescents to masturbate during these sexual fantasies. It's also common for adolescents to deny that they masturbate when they really do. This denial of masturbation occurs, in part, due to the idea that masturbation is wrong; or from false ideas that only boys who are homosexual or cannot "get a girl" are the ones who masturbate.

- "Adolescents usually learn about sex from classes in school, discussion among peers, and from watching television and non-X-rated movies. It's common for adolescents to have viewed some type of soft pornographic material such as *Playboy* or *Penthouse* magazines."

Only give the following information about adult male sexual development when conducting the adult incest offender group.

- "The adult goes through the same type of sexual experiences as described for the adolescent.

- "The adult more frequently engages in sexual intercourse than the adolescent.

- "It's normal for the adult male to have his highest level of sexual desire during his late teens and early twenties; whereas females experience their strongest levels of sexual desire in their early to mid-thirties."

The Role of Fantasy

"A sexual fantasy is a thought, no matter how short, about sexual involvement or activity. A sexual fantasy can occur with or without masturbation.

"An appropriate sexual fantasy involves a mutually consenting sexual relationship. It's not uncommon to have fantasies involving sexual partners that the person sees as being unattainable, such as a movie star; but even these fantasies involve mutually consenting sexual behavior. It's unhealthy to have a sexual fantasy involving sexual behavior being forced upon another person.

"It's unhealthy for adults or adolescents to have sexual fantasies involving young children. In fact, such fantasies or thoughts are one of the major factors that contribute to the occurrence of the sexually offending behavior. In the thoughts that lead up to the sexual abuse, the offender usually imagines that the victim is cooperating with the sexual behavior and is not being harmed by it. In a sense, the offender tricks himself into justifying the sexual behavior as appropriate."

There are major differences between consent and coercion.

"Consent usually involves the following elements:

- "One person does not have unequal power over the other. Power does not only apply to the physical size or strength of a person, but also to such factors as trust, intelligence, and authority.

- "Both people who are sexually involved like each other, and the sexual relationship is a means of expressing affection.

- "Privacy is honored between the two sexual partners. One person does not go around and brag about the sexual relationship or use it to shock or excite others. (This element of consent is not always honored in otherwise 'normal' relationships, such as when teenage boys may brag about sexual conquests among themselves, or when girls discuss their romantic exploits or sexual behavior.)

- "Both people who are sexually involved agree to have a sexual relationship. The consent must be clear and not based on what one person assumes the other to be thinking; nor does it rely exclusively on nonverbal communication such as body language.

"Coercion is defined as using some form of power over another person in order to have him or her submit to sexual behavior that the offender wants to engage in. The power takes away the ability of the victim to consent. Coercion can involve actual physical aggression as well as bribery, enticement, deception, or misuse of one's trust or authority in a relationship."

L. Skill: Discussing the Abuse in the Family

"When discussing the sexual abuse in intrafamilial cases, the primary concern should be how the victim will be affected by any discussion. It's important that any discussion of the sexual abuse does not further traumatize the victim.

"The nonoffending parent in the adult incest offender case and the parents of the adolescent sexual offender have the right to have their questions answered about the sexual abuse. These parties should show some sensitivity to the feelings of the offender, but should not allow the offender to avoid talking about the abuse. It's helpful to acknowledge to the offender his difficulty in talking about it, and to let him know that you need to discuss it with him. Talking about the abuse can help relieve the burden, for family members as well as the offender, of keeping the secret.

"In some situations, the details of the offending behavior may be important. The offender should understand that his partner or parents may feel a good deal of guilt over not realizing that the sexual abuse was occurring. Their need to discuss the sexual abuse, in many cases, is an attempt to determine whether they should feel guilty for not having recognized that the abuse was occurring.

"As part of the treatment process, the offender will be required to inform his spouse or parents of the factors that led to the occurrence of the offending behavior. This step helps improve the level of trust within the family and allows the partner or parents a means to monitor the offender to ensure that he is not slipping back into old patterns that could lead to a re-offense.

"Various feelings and fears prevent the discussion of sexual abuse within the family. Some of these include:

- "Fear on the part of the victim, the offender, or other family members of being rejected or abandoned

- "Embarrassment, shame, or guilt

- "Not wanting to pressure the offender more

- "Feeling sorry for the offender

- "Fear of punishments or verbal abuse inflicted by the parents"

Close with the following: "As you can see, there are some compelling reasons not to discuss the sexual abuse within the family. The question is, are these feelings or fears valid, or are they an attempt to avoid dealing directly with the sexual abuse? The only way to find this out is to talk about your feelings and concerns. In other words, you have to check them out. You have to tell your spouse or parents of your concern for feelings, and check to see whether your perceptions or fears are accurate."

M. Concept: Who Else Should Be Told?

"As a rule of thumb, the child molester should not be placed in a situation where he will be left unsupervised with children. Even when he can be supervised around children, the parents of the children should be informed of the offender's offense. This is necessary, as the parents of the children should have the right to decide if their children should be in such a situation. If you do not tell them and they find out another way, the parents may be quite upset and angry that you placed their child in a risky situation.

"Immediate family members should be told of the sexual abuse committed by the offender. It's a form of avoidance to think that the other children in the family do not know what occurred. Although the children may not know the exact details of what happened, they do sense that something is wrong. If they're not told of the problems in the family, the other children are left to imagine what these problems are. This can result in a child feeling highly anxious or thinking that he or she caused the problems that are being experienced by the family. It's important to tell the children in a way that is appropriate to their age and level of understanding. It's not necessary to go into great detail. For example, you might tell a six-year-old: 'Your brother was touched in bad ways by Uncle Hank, ways that made him feel sad and confused. He's going to a doctor now who will help him feel better; and we're looking out to make sure that Uncle Hank doesn't bother him again.'

"You might say to a twelve-year-old: 'Daddy did sexual things with your sister that he shouldn't have done. This is a very serious and painful situation for your sister, and for our whole family. Daddy is getting help to make sure that he never does anything like this again. But if he can't learn to change, we'll live apart from Daddy — because I have to protect you and your sister from being hurt by him in ways he might not be able to control. You sister is getting all the help that money can buy to help her get over her pain. She'll need a lot of understanding and love from all of us from now on — and this may mean that you'll need some extra love and understanding, too. Don't talk to Sally unless she wants to talk about what happened — but I'm available for you whenever you need to talk. And if you'd like to talk to someone besides me, that can arranged, too.'

"In the adult incest offender cases, the nonabused siblings may come to feel mad at the victim for causing the turmoil in the family. If this occurs, it may be necessary for the offender to sit down with the nonabused children to tell them what occurred and to remove the blame from the victim by assuming sole responsibility for the offending behavior.

"In adolescent offender cases, a parent may need to discuss the sexual abuse with a trusted friend in order to manage the stress associated with it. This is okay, even though the offender may not like it. It's important for parents to trust their own judgment and to realize that such support may be crucial to weathering this crisis.

"It should be left up to the parents to decide who is told about the sexual abuse in the extended family or outside of the family. In intrafamilial cases, the attitude of the victims toward discussing or not discussing the sexual abuse with others should be of primary consideration. For instance, the victim should not be put in the position of having to make up a story accounting for the hard times that others see the family going through. This only reinforces the sense of secrecy and badness that the victim is trying to work through in treatment."

Main Interventions

Week 1

Introduction

See Starting the Group.

A. Concept: How the Criminal Justice System Works

Intervention 1: Didactic Presentation (See Concepts and Skills section)

Intervention 2: Soliciting Information From Individuals

Call on participants to share their experiences going through particular parts of the criminal justice system.

B. Concept: How the Social Services System Works

Intervention 1: Didactic Presentation (See Concepts and Skills section)

Intervention 2: Soliciting Information From Individuals

Call on participants once again to share their experiences going through particular parts of the social services system.

Homework

Do this every day throughout the duration of the group.

"Once or several times a day you are to write down the details of any thoughts or fantasies that are related to your offenses. These thoughts or fantasies may be sexual, but may also include other feeling states — for example, anger, depression, pain. The details of the thoughts or fantasies should include what is happening, who is in the fantasy, what the thoughts and feelings are, and any other information you think is important. Include whether you masturbated or not. Also, you should record your feelings, thoughts, and what was happening around you before the start of the offense thoughts or fantasies. Finally, write down the time and day the thoughts or fantasies occurred. Here is an example.

> Sunday about 1 p.m. I was sitting in the living room feeling kind of bored. I had gotten into an argument earlier with my wife. I was thinking how unfair she was and how she is always on my case. I was feeling angry. Later I began having thoughts of my daughter. I thought about how nice it is to talk with her and how good it feels to play with her breasts and vagina. As I thought of this I began to beat off and I came. When I finished I felt better inside but also guilty for thinking about molesting her.

Week 2

Review of Homework

C. Concept: What Makes Sexual Behavior Between Two People Abusive

Intervention 1: Didactic Presentation (See Concepts and Skills section)

Intervention 2: Soliciting Information From Individuals

Write the concept at the top of a blackboard or flip chart. Ask the group to begin to define those things that they think make sexual behavior abusive. As group members respond, clarify answers that are unclear and write the main point of their responses on the board. If members fail to provide all the main ideas, continue to the next intervention.

Intervention 1: Didactic Presentation (See Concepts and Skills section)

D. Concept: Common Myths About Sexually Offending Behavior

Intervention 3: Group Discussion

Read each of the myths aloud (see Concepts and Skills section) and invite participants' reactions to each statement. Write down the comments that accurately reflect the reality. If the major issues aren't all raised, continue to the next.

Intervention 1: Didactic Presentation (See Concepts and Skills section)

E. Concept: Offense Patterns — How Are My Offense and My Family's Dynamics the Same as Those of Other Offenders?

Intervention 1: Didactic Presentation (See Concepts and Skills section)

Homework (for adult offenders)

"Read the article called *A Personal Account of a Father* (see Handout 1). After reading it, complete the questions at the end and we'll discuss them next week." Give each member a copy of the article and questions. Take a firm stand that homework is essential and must be completed.

Week 3

Review of Homework

Use the discussion of the homework to lead into the presentation of the next concept.

F. Concept: The Chain of Events Model

Intervention 1: Didactic Presentation (See Concepts and Skills section)

Intervention 4: Exercise — Chain of Events

The method in conducting this exercise varies between the two offender groups. The instructions for both are as follows.

Give each person a copy of the Chain of Events questions (Handout 2), and say: "Now that we have reviewed the chain of events model, we'd like you to apply it to your offense situation.

"There are questions about each link in the chain that you need to answer. These questions include:

1. "What are some of the past hurts or abuses that happened to you in your childhood that were upsetting, that you've not really talked about, or that still bother you?

2. "How have these past hurts or abuses affected your thoughts or feelings about yourself and others? What are the fears or concerns which lead you to have problems in relationships with others?

3. "What were the thoughts and feelings that were bothering you around the time, or just before, you committed each sexual offense.

4. "What were the coping strategies — behaviors, feelings, and thoughts — that helped you deal with the high-risk situations? How did these coping strategies lead you to act in sexually abusive ways?

5. "What were the false or distorted ways of seeing or thinking about your sexually offending behavior that made the offense seem okay to you or seem less bad?"

In the adult offenders' group, provide the following instructions:

"I want you to spend about ten minutes filling in, to the best of your knowledge, those parts of the chain of events that apply specifically to your offense. You have a sense of how this model applies based on the homework you completed. Don't be concerned whether your answers are correct. We'll discuss your answers in a few minutes. The idea of this exercise is to understand how the model is applied in order to help you use it in future therapy sessions. Okay, go ahead and start and I'll tell you when time is up."

For the adolescent group, provide a variation of the above directions as follows:

"We're going to break up into small groups, mixing parents and adolescents together. I'm going to count off around the group." Count one, two, three while pointing to each member of the group in turn.[3] Okay, now I want all number ones over here, the number twos over there, and the number threes here." Gesture to different parts of the room.

After the subgroups are formed, continue with the following directions: "You will have about 20 to 25 minutes to discuss how the chain of events model applies to your particular offense situation. I want each group to quickly choose one person to read aloud the different questions for the chain of events model. Go through them one at a time. Each person should give an example of that part of the chain of events that applies to his offense. For those parents in the groups, I would like you to give an example for each factor as you see it applying to your son. When we're done, we'll come back together as a large group and discuss what this experience was like. Okay, let's start. If you have any questions, raise your hand and one of us will come to your small group to answer it."

For both the adolescent and adult offender groups give the following instructions to conclude the exercise:

"All right, time is up. Let's get together as a large group again." Pause while the group gets back together. "What I would like to do is to have several of you share what was difficult about completing the exercise, and for some of you to share what you learned about your chain of events."

Help the members share their experiences related to the above two areas. Provide information to assist them in better understanding how to apply the chain of events to their offense situation.

G. Concept: Relapse Prevention

Intervention 1: Didactic Presentation (See Concepts and Skills section)

Intervention 4: Exercise — Relapse Prevention

Usually a group member will question the validity of this concept. It's important to interpret the offender's resistance to accepting this concept as a manifestation of the guilt he already feels about having committed the offense. Acknowledge that he could potentially do this again and it would only serve to intensify his guilt. After dispensing with this issue, continue by giving each member a copy of the Relapse Prevention Worksheet (Handout 3).

"Please look at the Relapse Prevention Worksheet. There are six questions which will help you develop a specific plan of action. This plan will help you develop ways to cope with the thoughts and feelings that could lead to a repetition of your offense. The questions are as follows: (Describe what you would do in order *not* to continue thinking of, or actually following through with, another sexual offense.)

---

3. The small groups should have no more than four persons. The size of the overall group will determine the range of numbers you will use to assign numbers to group members.

1. "What could I immediately do to deal with the ways of acting, the feelings, or the thoughts which could lead me to commit another sexual assault?

2. "Whom could I call or talk with to tell about my urges, feelings, or ways of acting?

3. "What do I want the person listed above to do?

4. "What can I do to stay away from opportunities that give me access to potential victims?

5. "What are some of the things I could do or say to handle the high-risk situations, feelings, and ways of acting that contributed to my offense?

6. "What are some true or realistic statements I need to make to myself to correct the distorted thinking which might lead to my committing another sexual offense?

"I would like you to jot down your responses to these questions.[4] We will give you about 25 minutes to do this. When you have completed this, we will discuss the exercise in the group."

Announce when time is up. Ask the group: "What are some of the responses that people came up with? Johnny, why don't you start."

Reinforce responses which show that the offender is seriously applying this concept to his current life circumstances. Help offenders think of more concrete steps to take in order to avoid a re-offense. At this stage, the offenders should be developing strategies for avoiding situations in which there is a potential for a re-offense to occur. They should also learn, when troubled by thoughts or feelings of a re-offense, to identify people with whom they can talk about their incendiary thoughts or feelings. For those offenders who cannot do, or who refuse to complete, this exercise, the leaders should express their concern over the offender's ability to control himself. It's also helpful to interpret out loud his inability to examine this issue as a way of setting the stage to reoffend; and to verbalize potential consequences of another offense.

Homework

"Describe in detail the things in your childhood which may have contributed to your offending behavior. You are to describe the incidents in detail, your feelings then and now, and how you see those events affecting your offending behavior."

Week 4

Review of Homework

H. Concept: Myths About the Victim

Intervention 3: Exercise — Group Discussion

---

4. The parents of the adolescent offenders are asked to imagine what actions their sons could take in order to prevent a reoffense from occurring.

Read each statement aloud (see Concepts and Skills section) and invite participants' responses. Most of the main points that debunk each myth will probably be raised in the discussion. If not, continue with the next intervention.

Intervention 1: Didactic Presentation (See Concepts and Skills section)

I. Concept: How Is My Victim (or Victims) Like Those of Other Offenders? [presented only in adolescent offender group]

Intervention 1: Didactic Presentation (See Concepts and Skills section)

Intervention 4: Exercise — Understanding the Victim

This is a small group exercise. The large group is divided into small groups according to the instructions given for the chain of events small group exercise. After clients assemble in the small groups, give each person a copy of the Readings From Victims of Sexual Abuse and questions (Handout 4).

Then state: "For the first passage, I would like one person to read the material that the victim wrote at one age. Then another person will read the material for the next age. Continue rotating the reading until this entire passage is complete.[5] Once you've complete the readings, answer the accompanying questions.

"There are 5 questions as follows:

1. "What are some of the short-term effects of sexual abuse on victims?

2. "What are some of the feelings the victims have regarding the sexual abuse committed against them? Also discuss your reaction to the victims' feelings.

3. "At whom are the victims' feelings directed?

4. "What do you think are the steps the victims need to take in order to get over their reactions to being sexually abused?

5. "If you were a victim of sexual abuse, you would feel, think, and react to being sexually abused in the following ways… (please write your answer in the first person — that is, 'I feel….' 'I think….')"

"In answering these questions, I want a member in the small group to read the question and then for the group to discuss it. Spend no more than five minutes on the question and then move on to the next one. As you discuss the questions, make sure that each of you writes down the answers you give in the small group. Continue doing this until you've answered and discussed all five questions. When you're done, we'll come back together as a large group to discuss the exercise. Okay, go ahead and start."

At the conclusion of the exercise, instruct group members to come back together in the large group. Facilitate a discussion of the questions, emphasizing how victims react to the sexual abuse in many different ways, both in the short and long term. In addition, elicit discussion regarding the members' reactions to doing this exercise. Usually offenders verbalize their difficulty in doing this exercise. Reframe this dif-

---

5. Usually the long passage plus one or two of the shorter passages can be completed in the time allowed. When reading the shorter passages, instruct one group member to read the entire excerpt to the small group.

ficulty as avoidance of facing the profound negative impact of the offending behavior on the victim.

Homework

"Write a detailed account of your offense. Use the following factors to organize your account.

- "How my offenses began and progressed until the time I was caught.

- "My fantasies and state of mind prior to, during, and after each sexual abuse incident.

- "How I was able to gain access to and coerce the victim to go along with the sexual behaviors I engaged in.

- "How I kept my sexually abusive behavior a secret and avoided being caught."

Week 5

Review of Homework

J. Concept: Common Reactions of Victims to Sexual Abuse

Intervention 2: Soliciting Information From Individuals

"Victims of sexual abuse are affected in different ways — on emotional, behavioral, psychological, and physical levels. The sexual abuse can have different short- and long-term effects on each of these levels. What are some of the emotional reactions that victims experience as a result of the sexual abuse?"

Write participants' responses on a blackboard or flip chart categories. Differentiate between short- and long-term effects (and those which are both).

Intervention 1: Didactic Presentation (See Concepts and Skills section)

Cover any reactions not listed by participants, and make concluding statements.

Intervention 3: Group Discussion

Write the following two questions on a blackboard or flip chart:

1. What are some of the negative behaviors, troubling feelings, and physical signs which my victim or victims may experience both in the short and long term?

2. What could it take and how could I (and we, if the parents are involved) help the victim or victims in overcoming the effects of being sexually abused?

Direct the group to break down into subgroups according to the instruction used during the chain of events transformational exercise. Once the members are in subgroups, instruct them as follows:

"Someone in the small group should read each question aloud. After the question is read, discuss your responses to it. When you've completed this exercise, we'll come together and discuss it further. Okay, go ahead and get started."

When the groups have completed the assignment or the time is up, ask the members to reconvene as a large group. Have them share their reactions to completing the exercise, as well as the content of their responses to the questions. In facilitating this discussion, follow these guidelines:

Acknowledge those responses that reflect the offender's difficulty in understanding how the victim was affected by the abuse. Many offenders will say they have no idea how their victims feel about the sexual abuse because they have no contact with them. Even when asked to imagine how the victim might feel, the offender may still state that he cannot imagine this. When you get this type of response, you can respond in either of two ways: 1) Point out that this inability may reflect the offender's guilt over the sexual abuse. To admit how his victim might be reacting to it would only make him feel worse. 2) This inability to understand how the victim feels is a major contributor to the offending behavior, as the offender might not have committed the offense in the first place if he realized the negative impact of his behavior. (This is an example of a false or dangerous way of thinking.)

Acknowledge the responses of group members that share sensitivity to the victim's reactions to the sexual abuse, or show that the offender is willing to appropriately assist the victim in the healing process. Emphasize that the healing process for the victim can be greatly facilitated by: the offender assuming personal responsibility for the offending behavior; the nonoffending parent(s) verbalizing their belief that the child was sexually abused; and, when indicated, the offender apologizing to the victim within the context of therapy sessions.

Week 6

K. Concept: What Is Normal Sexual Behavior?

Intervention 4: Exercise — Normal Sexual Behavior

Direct the group to break into subgroups per the instructions used in the chain of events small group exercise. Give each person a copy of the What Is Normal Sexual Behavior questions (Handout 5). Instruct: "Choose a person who will read the first three questions aloud in the group. These questions are as follows:

1. "What is considered normal sexual behavior on the part of an adolescent, adult, and a child?

2. "What is a sexual fantasy? What is an appropriate sexual fantasy as compared to one that is not normal?

3. "Explain the differences between consent and coercion."

Go through one question at a time. After the designated person reads the question, each member should share his reaction to it. "As you go along, write down your responses in the space provided on the worksheet. When I call time, we'll get back together as a group. You can start now."

After 20 minutes, call time. Instruct the small groups to stay together (there is one more exercise to complete in the small group) and to turn their chairs toward the front of the room. Elicit from the members their reactions to answering the questions as well as the specific content of their answers. Fill in any information that is not provided, using the following interventions.

Intervention 1: Didactic Presentation (See Concepts and Skills section)
Intervention 4: Exercise — Coercion and Abuse

Direct members to reconvene in their small groups to discuss the next three questions as follows:

1. What are the things that occurred in my offenses which involved coercion?

2. What are the things that occurred in my offenses which make the sexual behavior abusive?

3. What are some of the new ideas I've learned about coercion and abusive behavior in my sexual offense?

Instruct them to discuss the questions as per the previous exercise. Upon conclusion of the time limit, have the groups come together as a whole to discuss the exercise.

During the group discussion, there are most often two divergent responses. It's helpful to respond to these using the following guidelines:

1. Some offenders will be able to label the abusive or coercive aspects of the offending behavior. In these cases, acknowledge and praise the offenders who are able to report on the coercive or abusive aspects of their behavior. It's important to acknowledge how difficult it is for the offender to verbalize this, and that such recognition is a big step toward recovering from the sexually offending behavior.

2. Other offenders will continue to deny any coercive or abusive aspects of their behavior. Rather than being confrontive, interpret the offender's denial. Such an interpretation should come from a supportive frame of reference. Point out to the offender that his denial protects him from having to experience the painful feelings that would emerge if he were to acknowledge the abusive or coercive aspects of his offending behavior.

Offender: I guess I always thought what I did with Timmy was okay, because — you know — he always liked me so much. And he never yelled or anything; he never even told me to stop. But maybe he was afraid that his mother would send me away if she found out what was going on — I guess she would've. Or maybe he was afraid that he'd never get to ride the horses again, since I was his teacher and all. I never thought about that at the time.

Therapist: Your comments show the beginnings of empathy, Mike. This marks an important step in your recovery — and in making sure that you never commit a sex offense again.

Offender: Donna is sixteen going on forty. You'd have to see her before you could really understand. No red-blooded man could resist that kid — especially if she came on to him like she came on to me.

Therapist: Paul, I'd like the group to examine what you're saying and the words you're using. You say that your stepdaughter is sixteen going on forty. The reality is that she's sixteen. Try to think back to when you were sixteen, Paul, and what that felt like. And think about your relationship to your own stepfather. Were you intimidated by him at all? Were you scared of him? Did you look up to him? If he had asked you to do something you really didn't think was right, how likely would you be to go along with him anyway? You say that "No red-blooded man could resist that kid"— but the fact is that she *is* a kid, Paul. Maybe thinking about Donna as an adult makes it seem less horrible that you had sexual intercourse with her. Would anyone in the group like to comment?

Homework

"Write a detailed description of your sexual development. Write about

- The various ways in which you learned about sex

- The age at which you began having sexual feelings and thoughts, began mas-turbating, and had your first sexual experience

- Any negative sexual experiences

- Your general feelings and attitudes regarding sex"

Week 7

Review of Homework

L. Skill: Discussing the Abuse in the Family

Intervention 4: Exercise — Discussing the Abuse

Give each person a copy of the Discussing the Abuse in the Family outline con-sisting of the following three questions (Handout 6):

1. How often should the sexual abuse be discussed in the family, and how many of the details should be included?

2. What are some of the feelings or concerns which may stop me (or us) from discussing the sexual abuse in the family?

3. What are some of the limits that should be set on such things as being around situations or people where another offense could happen; and who should be told about what happened?

Then continue:

"Talking about the sexual abuse within the family is a difficult issue. Due to the shame and embarrassment associated with the abuse, most families would like to pretend that it doesn't exist. Some think that it's just more traumatizing to discuss the sexual abuse."

For the adult incest offender group, instruct the group to break down into sub-groups according to the directions used in the chain of events small group exercise. The method of dividing the adolescents and parents into subgroups is the same as that for the adults, except that the subgroups will not mix parents and adolescents together. Instead, each subgroup should be comprised of adults or adolescents and contain no more than four members. This type of division provides an interesting array of responses to the questions. The differences in responses will emerge when the large group processes the exercise.

After breaking into small groups, say:

"Someone in the small group should read each question aloud. After the question is read, each person should state his response to it. As you answer, write down your responses in the space provided. When the small groups have completed this exercise, we'll come together and discuss it further. Okay, go ahead and get started."

When the groups have completed the assignment or when the time is up, ask the members to reconvene as a large group. Ask them to share the content of their responses to the questions. Attempt to elicit from group members the major points which you're presenting through this exercise. Expand upon the responses given by group members when necessary, using the following intervention and closing statements:

Intervention 1: Didactic Presentation (See Concepts and Skills section)

With the adolescent sexual offender group, you can facilitate the following intervention:

Intervention 4: Exercise — Reality Testing

"Let's try this out in the group. How many of you parents would yell at your child or reject him if he talked to you about the sexual abuse? How many of you teens wouldn't be able to handle a discussion of the sexual abuse with your parents?"

Let the parents and adolescents respond to these questions. Usually the responses received are contrary to what the group members presented in the subgroup discussion. In this case, underscore the importance of false ideas leading one to make poor choices, and how it's important to check out what you are thinking about another person in order to determine whether your perception is accurate.

In some instances, an adolescent or parent will confirm the fear of a negative outcome in discussing the sexual abuse. In this situation, explore the reasons for this with the member who expresses it. Usually such statements are made out of anger or are an attempt to avoid dealing with the sexual abuse in a direct manner. You can respond to these statements by highlighting the underlying motive in making such a statement.

M. Concept: Who Else Should Be Told?

Intervention 1: Didactic Presentation (See Concepts and Skills section)

Review of Treatment Goals

When this group is run as part of a comprehensive treatment package, it is extended one week. Week 8 is then used to carefully review with participants the treatment process presented in the Introduction. During this session, a treatment agreement for the rest of the package is discussed and signed by each participant.

Criteria for Measuring Change

As stated earlier in this chapter, the psychoeducational group is intended to provide a preparatory group experience that introduces the sexual offender and the parents of the adolescent sexual offender to the methods of treatment that the offender will go through. The group is not structured to bring about significant behavior change (however, there have been experiences where the process of psychoeducation has helped in working through the denial of the sexual abuse that some offenders present during the early stages of treatment). Instead, the group is designed to plant seeds, in a nonthreatening manner, that will grow later in the treatment process.

The leaders determine whether a group member has adequately learned the material presented through the level of participation of the offender in the group. It's assumed that the offender who fully completes the assignments, attends the group regularly, takes notes on the material presented, and participates in the large and small group exercises is understanding the concepts that need to be learned in order to maximize the benefits of treatment. In some instance where the offender has made poor progress, he will be expected to complete the psychoeducational group over again.

Problems Specific to the Group

In conducting the psychoeducational group, there are several types of problem members who consistently emerge. There are those offenders who deny that the material is relevant to them, those who are withdrawn or uncooperative, and those who are disruptive or argumentative.

The Group Member in Denial ("I don't belong in this group")

These types of offenders or parents of adolescent sexual offenders may seem to be cooperative when judged by their participation in the group process. However, this person's responses to the issues discussed in the group consistently reflect the theme, "This does not apply to me." Psychologically, these individuals are avoiding and denying their painful feelings — shame, guilt, anger, embarrassment — associated with the sexually offending behavior. The issues discussed in the group begin to activate these feelings, and the individual goes on the defensive to suppress them.

In managing this form of resistance, it's most effective for the therapist to take a supportive role. The group leaders should respond by acknowledging the group member's feelings and thoughts. Then one of the leaders should interpret the underlying motive for the denial presented by the member. For example: "I'm hearing that you think the sexual abuse did not affect your victim. It seems to me that it would be too painful for you to admit the harm you caused your victim."

After making several of these types of supportive confrontations, and through the material presented in the group, this type of offender or parent of an adolescent sexual offender usually shows a positive change in the pattern of avoidance and denial.

The Argumentative Group Member

The argumentative member wants to contest the material presented by the group leaders. This person becomes problematic when this is the person's consistent style in group. He wants to argue about specific details with which he disagrees; the only basis for his arguments is his idiosyncratic way of thinking about and perceiving his environment and interpersonal relationships. In extreme cases, this type of consistent response pattern may be symptomatic of an underlying narcissistic or antisocial personality disorder. In other cases, the argumentative style of a member may reflect that person's primary way of avoiding the painful feelings that are activated by the group discussion (a neurotic defense pattern). The underlying dynamic for the member's argumentative behavior will determine the type of intervention that is made by the group leaders.

The member whose argumentativeness is a characterological trait requires firm limits and confrontation for his inappropriate behavior. The group leaders have to quickly intervene and let this member know that his argumentativeness is not appropriate in the discussion. For example:

> Joe, I find that you're splitting hairs over this subject and it's causing us to get off track. I want to stop the digression at this point and move on.

In some cases, confrontation and limit setting are futile, as the group member cannot modify his behavior to conform to the norms of the group. The group member may have to be prematurely discharged, in such circumstances, from the psychoeducational group. When this occurs, it may be appropriate to send the offender or the parents of the adolescent offender into an ongoing therapy group. A therapeutic group usually has better resources for managing this type of personality.

The group member who shows the neurotic form of argumentativeness is best handled by using the supportive approach described in the previous section. The group leader should interpret for the entire group the underlying dynamic that is contributing to the individual's argumentative response.

The Withdrawn Group Member

The withdrawn group member presents himself as being a nonparticipating member. This individual remains aloof from all or part of the group process. Several patterns of nonparticipation are seen:

- The member who remains completely aloof from any participation in group

- The person who remains quiet in the large group but is active in subgroup exercises

- The member who will not participate unless called upon

- The individual who does not complete homework assignments

The type of withdrawal can indicate what is motivating the person's nonparticipation.

A general consideration in addressing the four types of withdrawal is to determine if the member has some type of cognitive limitation or severe depressive disorder which precludes his ability to participate actively in the group. In the latter instance, the member will need to be precluded from the group until his mental status improves to the extent that he can participate in the group. When an offender has a cognitive limitation that affects his participation, it may be helpful to assign him a "buddy" in the group to help him complete the homework and discuss the material covered outside of the context of the group.

The initial intervention with the withdrawn member is for the group leader to specifically identify the type of withdrawal and to verbalize that problem behavior to the member. This is done in a supportive manner that places responsibility on the member to change this problem behavior. For example:

> Bill, I've noticed that you've really kept to yourself in the group and haven't said much during any of our discussions or exercises. I'm concerned that you're not getting much out of the group and I'm wondering what you have to do in order to begin participating more actively.

Through this process, the leader and member can establish some form of agreement regarding the person's more active participation. In other cases, it may come to light that the offender's lack of participation may reflect his anxiety about being in a group and/or be symptomatic of his poor self-esteem.

Shyness and low self-esteem are probably the most common reasons for nonparticipation in the group. It's helpful in this situation for the group leader to call upon such members directly to elicit a response. When the group member responds, he should be given verbal or nonverbal recognition for his contribution. Such positive reinforcement of the member's answers will increase the likelihood of his future participation.

The withdrawn member's lack of participation may reflect a passive-aggressive way of dealing with authority figures. The most effective way to deal with this member is to encourage his participation but not become involved in a power struggle. After encouraging him a few times, the leader then responds in a manner such at this:

> I can tell, John, that you don't want to participate in this group and I know I can't force you to. I do want to let you know that if you decide to continue not participating, I may have to terminate you from the group or have you repeat it. The choice is up to you.

It's crucial to enforce the consequence if this member decides to continue with his nonparticipatory behavior.

Relapse

Due to the preparatory nature of this group, relapse prevention is not an applicable concept. Relapse prevention as it relates to the sexually offending behavior is a standard and important aspect in treating the sexual offender. In the context of the psychoeducational group, however, relapse prevention is a concept that is introduced to the offender and more fully worked on later in sex offender therapy groups.

References

Ageton, S.S. *Sexual Assault Among Adolescents*. Lexington, Massachusetts: Lexington Books, 1983.

Broderick, C.B. "Adult sexual development." In *Handbook of Developmental Psychology*. Edited by B.B. Wolman and G. Stricker. Englewood Cliffs, New Jersey: Prentice Hall, 726-733, 1982.

Giarretto, H. "Community-based treatment of the incest family." *Psychiatric Clinics of North America, 12(2)*, 351-361, 1989.

_____. *Integrated Treatment of Child Sexual Abuse*. Palo Alto, California: Science and Behavior Books, 1982.

Groth, N.A. "The incest offender." In *Handbook of Clinical Intervention in Child Sexual Abuse* Edited by S.M. Sgroi. Lexington, Massachusetts: Lexington Books, 215-240, 1984.

_____, and Birnbaum, H.J. *Men Who Rape: The Psychology of the Offender*, New York: Pelum, 1979.

Jacobs, D.; Jacobs, C.E.; Weinstein, H.; and Mann, D. "Preparation for treatment of the disadvantaged patient: Effects on disposition and outcome." *American Journal of Orthopsychiatry*, 1972, 42, 666-674.

Knopp, F.H. *Retraining Adult Sexual Offenders: Methods and Models*, Syracuse, New York: Safer Society Press, 1984.

Marlatt, G.A. "Relapse prevention with sexual aggressives." In *Sexual Aggressors: Current Treatment Perspectives*. Edited by J.G. Greer and I.R. Stuart. New York: Van Nostrand and Reinhold, 1983.

_____, and Gordon, J.R. Relapse Prevention. New York: The Guilford Press, 1985.

Miller, P.Y., and Simon, W. "The development of sexuality in adolescents." In *Handbook of Adolescent Psychology*, Edited by J. Adelson. New York: John Wiley & Sons, 383-407, 1980.

"National Adolescent Perpetrator — Network, Preliminary Report by The National Task Force on Adolescent Perpetrators," *Journal of Juvenile and Family Court Judges*, Reno, Nevada: Council of Juvenile and Family Court Judges, 1988.

O'Brien, M. "Adolescent sexual offenders: An outpatient program's perspective on research perspectives." In *Adolescent Sexual Offenders: Issues in Research and Treatment*, Edited by E.M. Otey and G.D. Ryan. Rockville, Maryland: U.S. Department of Health and Human Services, 147-163, 1985.

Orne, M.T., and Wender, P.H. "Anticipatory socialization in psychotherapy: Method and rationale." *American Journal of Psychiatry*, 1968, *124*, 1202-1212.

Porter, F.; Blick, L.; and Sgroi, S.M. "Treatment of the sexually abused child." In *Handbook of Clinical Intervention in Child Sexual Abuse*. Edited by S.M. Sgroi. Lexington, Massachusetts: Lexington Books, 109-146, 1984.

Salter, A. *Treating Child Sex Offenders and Victims: A Practical Guide*. Newbury Park, California: Sage Publications, 1988.

Shapiro, J.L. *Methods of Group Psychotherapy and Encounter: A Tradition of Innovation*. Itasca, Illinois: F.E. Peacock Publishers, Inc., 1978.

Shepard-Look, D.L. "Sex differentiation and the development of sex roles." In *Handbook of Developmental Psychology*. Edited by B.B. Wolman and G. Stricker. Englewood Cliffs, New Jersey: Prentice Hall, 403-433, 1983.

Strupp, H. Bloxom, A. "Preparing lower-class patients for group psychotherapy: Development and evaluation of a role-induction film." *Journal of Consulting and Clinical Psychology*, 1973, *32*, 187-196.

Handout 1

A Personal Account of a Father

From: Giarretto, Hank. *Integrated Treatment of Child Sexual Abuse.* Palo Alto, California: Science and Behavior Books, 1982. (reprinted with permission of the author)

In the children's home where I grew up, I learned to hate: social workers, school, almost everything and everyone. Next I learned to destroy what I hated. I played some very sad and heavy games. It became easier to hate than to love. I stuffed inside myself any feelings of being hurt and didn't let myself hurt. I never let a tear come out of either eye, because guys I lived with at the home wouldn't have tolerated that. I learned not to discuss or share any emotion about being physically hurt or sad.

I didn't ever think I had a meaning or purpose or sense of flow about my life. I just pointed myself in a certain direction and tried to conquer and destroy. I had no sense of belonging to a family or to society. Once a priest came to the home and cornered me to get inside my thoughts. I wasn't a Catholic and didn't want him to know my thoughts. My faulty reasoning was that it would keep him from coming back. I was seventeen years old then but operating with a ten-year-old's reasoning. I wasn't close to males at any time in my life on any kind of feeling level. I didn't know how to deal with the fact that the males I know kept all their feelings repressed and pushed down. They couldn't do anything for me that I needed, so I just let them do their own thing.

I was ready to give but not receive, even when I was very young. I could give and give and give...but I didn't know how to let anyone else give. As a result, lots of people rejected me because I didn't accept anything from them. They needed to give, too, but I didn't let them. I learned not to attach myself to anything or anyone.

I liked being rejected because then I knew how to react. I knew my ground and what to do next each time that happened. I thought I knew what other people thought and that I could guess when they didn't want me around anymore. Then I'd say, "Okay, I don't have to be around anymore." And I'd hurry and detach myself, even if it was someone I really was drawn to. I learned that very young and kept that pattern as an adult. I learned to fantasize about relationships, about being close to people. Of course, it was always on my terms. At night lying down, I'd fantasize in a dream state about having relationships where people accepted me. The only place I could have relationships was in my dreams — not in real life.

As an adolescent, I had several girlfriends. I'd make each one reject me and make them go on to someone else. I kept repeating that pattern. I kept all of them from being able to harm me or get into my "garbage can." By garbage can I mean all my repressed or angry feelings that I kept stuffing inside myself and keeping a lid on.

What I learned in the children's home about stuffing feelings inside myself and denying them followed me into adulthood. I was very, very negative about everyone and everything. I was angry most of the time. That really affected my outlook on life. I didn't share my feelings with anyone. I didn't want to be touched or to be close to anyone, because they could reject me by surprise. I pushed people to reject me so that I could maintain control of any rejecting that resulted. I was used to being in a rejected state. Any other state was unfamiliar and left me feeling I didn't know what ground I was on. Being rejected was ground I knew, so I could handle that.

I kept my thoughts to myself in that garbage can I started filing as a boy. That can was never empty, because I kept filling it every day. I also held on to everything that I had ever put in there, so it got more and more full every day. I had a very low opinion of myself. I wasn't accomplishing much success or adding much to the world. I never tried suicide, but I often thought that if I snuffed out the light on my life that it would be better for the people around me.

I had very little self-control and let myself be very violent. I got frustrated a lot; and when I did, I wanted to throw or bang or destroy something. One time I got a bolt started right but couldn't make it fit back in my car. I threw my wrench neatly through the windshield and blew the glass apart. That just caused me more problems and more frustration. Another time, when I was in business for myself, I designed and drafted some drawings, which was $140 worth of work several years ago; I ruined it with one sweep of my knife. I did it because it didn't fit precisely the way I wanted. I did that even though it looked acceptable enough and the people I did it for had approved and accepted it. It wasn't what I wanted, so I destroyed it. And when I had to do it over, I got angry with the people and blamed them instead of myself. When I finished, I destroyed the plates because I didn't want any reminders around of that experience.

I was destructive to others and to myself. I didn't eat much or eat right. I'm six feet tall and was three hundred pounds and looked like a bloated hunk. Even if I got hungry at work, I wouldn't eat. I'd get the shakes and be nervous from hunger, but I'd use will power to deny that it was happening and try not to let it bother me.

I was a real loner. I thought I liked being alone. I wallowed in my garbage of thoughts by myself. I tried to keep thoughts straightened out in my head enough to satisfy myself. I didn't try to straighten out matters with anyone else. I avoided any place where there were crowds, like parks. I didn't want people staring at me, so I stared at them instead. I liked being the silent observer, so I'd sit in a corner and watch people. I'd try to figure out what was going on with them and try not to let them see what was going on with me. I watched football on TV and tried to be knowledgeable about it, because the guys at work related to that. I wanted to sound knowledgeable.

I deceived others about how much I drank. I thought it was manly to sit down and drink a case of beer. Sometimes, I'd follow the beer up with a quart or a couple of six-packs. I won approval from my fellow employees and other acquaintances by doing that. Right before I came to Parents United, I drank a fifth each day and drank all day long.

I convinced myself that drinking helped me cope with my wife's health problems. In reality, all it did was help me repress those problems. I kidded myself that if I lived alone, I could lick my drinking problem easily. When I drank, I could talk more easily, hold a conversation better (I thought), be a different person that I couldn't be when sober. When I was drunk, I related to other people's stories better and forgot some of my "garbage." Drinking helped me get into a comfortable "gray field." It made me feel more successful and stronger than I felt at any other time. In recent years, when I couldn't reach that level and just got sick, I felt helpless that booze couldn't do for me what it had done for me earlier in my life.

I became a Boy Scout leader. I learned about boys' problems and about counseling them. I didn't drink when I was with those boys, which was one weekend a month. I had to give up being a scout leader after I molested my stepdaughter. I couldn't risk that they'd find out about me. I still regret that so much and it still hurts. I can't take the chance, though, that someone would call them to say they had a child molester as a leader. I contribute to them now in a more direct way. Scouting seemed to me the one place where I really started to get in touch with myself. That happened on campouts when I had time to myself late in the evenings and would do some sober thinking.

I had met my first wife while I was still in the Marines. We lived together before marriage, then just took off one night and got married. We had two children. At first the marriage was very secure and we shared a lot of thoughts and feelings. I felt enlightened and enthused about the marriage. Then my drinking interfered. I became depressed and began visualizing us separated and divorced. That fantasy became a reality. I let both of my children go completely. That was very frightening then and still is today.

After my first wife and I became alienated from each other, I became aware of a warm feeling inside myself that I'll call love. I thought maybe I could be capable of love, but I didn't deal with it beyond being aware of it. Then I jumped out of my first marriage into my second one. I was single for only thirty days when I married my second wife. Our communication level was great before marriage but slipped right after we married. My drinking interfered, and she chose not to talk about some things anymore. I let my wife pay all the bills and take care of all the household needs, because I had no interest in the house or in my family. I was interested in one thing: drinking! I had a cocky, arrogant attitude at home. Everything had to be my way or no way at all. If I didn't like what my wife cooked for dinner, I didn't go to the table to eat. I didn't always win with my family; but at least when I lost, I knew where I stood. I knew the actions I would take about losing, because I was used to losing.

I didn't understand by wife. I was confused and I didn't know the reasons why I had married a woman with many physical illnesses. I resented her being sick because I hadn't asked to have those problems, and they were very hard to cope with. I was angry with my wife all of the time. Mostly because she was physically sick a lot of the time. One of the times was from a hysterectomy that caused her trouble afterwards. Our physical action certainly wasn't great. In sex, she made me feel like her partner didn't count. She seemed just to want to get herself taken care of. It took me longer to climax because of my heavy drinking, I think. My mind wanted to perform, but my body wouldn't. She didn't know how much I was drinking because I always denied it. It was at this point in my life that I began to get so close to my stepdaughter.

I never felt I was a natural, functioning part of my family. I was the strong arm, the heavy, in the relationship with my wife. I was the disciplinarian. My kids were used to my wife saying "Wait 'til your dad gets home." Sometimes I'd come unglued when I punished the kids: I'd lose control and I didn't know when to quit punishing. I wouldn't let things drop even after I had punished them. Whatever they had done wrong, I might bring it up over and over again for three weeks. I was mentally abusive about the way I did it, too, because I'd ride the hell out of one of my stepsons.

I acted differently to my stepdaughter. I let her get away with a lot of shit. The interaction between us was very different. She know how to twist me around to get what she needed, and I let her do that. I started to get close to my stepdaughter when I started helping her with her homework, and that's when I started molesting her. She started touching me first, and I really liked that. I started touching her back. It happened over a period of most of a year. I drove her to school and back every day, and that brought us even closer together. I was the one who took her clothes shopping for her gym clothes and uniforms that she needed for the private school she attended. My wife decided that it was more practical for me to be the one to shop with her since it was on my way home from work and since I was the one who picked her up from school.

I had set up in my own mind a plan, a fantasy, of making my wife reject and divorce me. That is what I wanted. I envisioned living alone in a trailer safe and sound, surrounded by my possessions and being only with myself. Then all of a sudden there was this young person loving me without question (my stepdaughter). She'd put her arms around me and depend on me to do things, which my wife did not do. She'd stand beside me while I watched football games just to be near me. She's pressured me in a nice way to do things I couldn't do on my own — like put on a swimsuit, which I was very self-conscious about. She'd make me feel it was okay to do. She had a special way of bringing me out of myself and she did it in a way no one else could. She got me to take her and other kids places — like a fair or somewhere — where there were those crowds I hated. She'd hold my hand and help me through those situations. I was still uncomfortable but at least I could bear it with her at my side.

We became very close. Then the touching became closer. One evening I was showing her how to operate a calculator, and she stated to rub my neck and shoulders. I returned her touches. This touching was the wrong message for me to give her.

The sexual abuse got progressively worse from that evening. I never had conscious intentions of having intercourse with her. I just wanted some self-gratification, I think. I don't really know. The amount I was drinking made me unable to get an erection or ejaculate, anyway. I had desire, but my body wouldn't respond physically. Because of that, I don't see how I could have done some of the things I was accused of doing. I remember touching her back and buttocks frequently and probably her private parts. (I say "probably" because my drinking made my memory hazy. I've accepted the responsibility of it, though. If it happened, then it did. All I can do about it is never do it again.)

My stepdaughter told my wife I was patting her on the butt. Moments before she told her mother, I was patting her on the butt and rubbing her back with her in my lap. She told her mother afterwards she didn't like that and didn't want that much closeness. At the time, I thought her idea of closeness and mine were the same because she'd often start rubbing my neck or back before I touched her.

I denied it and refused to admit I had been drinking. Immediately afterwards, I had a six-day drinking binge. During that time, I had a motorcycle accident but didn't get hurt badly. My wife has since told me that during those six days, I was extremely violent and ran all of my family out of our house. My wife told our relatives that I had molested my stepdaughter. Soon there were several people coming down on me for what I had done. I knew how to have enemies one at a time; but I couldn't handle this whole group.

My family left me. Then my wife called to tell me a police sergeant wanted to talk to me in a few days. I kept drinking until I got sicker and sicker and wasn't even high. On the third day, I contacted AA (Alcoholics Anonymous). I had listened to an employee of mine talk about it. My police interview was to be in two days, and I knew I needed help pulling myself together for it. AA sent a member over to my house. He didn't try to stop me from drinking. He said, "You said you wanted to kill yourself drinking. While you're doing that, I'd like to sit here and tell you a part of my life." I could really relate to him. Pretty soon he was making coffee with honey and orange juice with honey, and I was drinking it.

Guilt feelings started to surface. I confided to him that, in a rage, I had run off my family: I didn't tell him I had molested my stepdaughter, because I didn't think he or anyone else in AA would understand that. The AA people stayed with me for the next two days until my appointment with the sergeant. My wife and daughter had already seen the sergeant by that time. The sergeant cut some tapes about my case and had written a report. What he wrote was not the truth. He later admitted that the facts were a combination of my case and someone else's case.

I spent seven days in jail. I began feeling that I didn't want my family to reject me and that I wanted us all to be back together. I didn't know it at the time, but my wish would never come true. Two guys who were in jail with me for the same charge told me about all the frightening possibilities I was facing. I tried to deal with all the different people involved by myself: the public defender, the OR (own recognizance) program people, etc. A lady from the OR program was the one who told me about Parents United and its list of attorneys that I should consult. Since the public defender wanted me to plead guilty and told me to expect five to fifty years, I decided to try a private attorney.

At that point I had been sober several days. I thought I should be able to go on and live my own life and have this problem dealt with and over with. But I had no goals and no place to go. I didn't know whether I would work or go on welfare. I was very confused, and I'd stated crying inwardly over little things. I didn't want to be in jail, yet I wanted to be away from people. I was caught up in feeling guilty.

I contacted an attorney through Parents United, and a beautiful relationship developed with him. When he talked to me, I still had the shakes from days before and felt very uncertain of myself. I was going to be released on OR, but first I had to be arraigned. My attorney advised me to plead guilty, which switched my case from municipal to superior court. I was allowed to live in a Halfway House for alcoholics when I had been sober for nine days.

I went to several AA meetings that week. And I met Hank Giarretto and Ellie Breslin, who was to be my individual counselor at Parents United.

I did not know what to expect from the court system, and I was afraid. I had a woman judge in superior court, a woman counselor in Parents United, and a woman group leader. Women seemed to be in charge of my life at that point, and that was frightening. I also felt terror about not knowing what tomorrow would bring. The lawyer I had found through Parents United prepared me for what might happen in superior court. He spent time with me and put me at ease. Almost everything he prepared me for did happen. Now Parents United has a chart to offer members telling them about the court system and the possible sequence of events and explaining legal terminology like "arraignment" to those who have never been through the system. I'm one of the sources of that paper.

My case was postponed many times and dragged out for nine and one-half months. My attorney assured me that meant that the people in the court system were taking a thorough look at my case. The court system was not very humane. I felt I was locked up like an insane person. I do not think I should have been slapped into a brown uniform and forbidden to communicate with other prisoners. The system really did stink.

I was forced to have a Mentally Disordered Sex Offender Hearing, which scared the hell out of me. Someone else was going to make a value judgment about me, and they might see nothing else about me except that I was an alcoholic and child molester. The first doctor gave me a clean report. The other doctor decided I needed to see my mother. They gave me a clean report and stated that I was not mentally disordered. It was a frightening experience.

My sentencing was postponed four times, and each time was very frightening because it left me hanging, not knowing what was going to happen. Some Parents United members were in court with me. My shaking nerves may not have shown outside, but inside I was torn up. I didn't even hear my sentence when I finally got it; I just heard the woman judge say, "I am now sentencing Jim to five years." She paused before she said, "...probation," so I missed that word. I thought I was going to jail. I was also sentenced to do 500 hours of community service. The probation department allowed me to give all my community service time to Parents United work. That was really nice. Even as simple a thing as setting up chairs for the weekly meeting was a reward for me and let me contribute to the group and feel I belonged to that group.

I don't think being in jail would have helped me to grow at all. It would have made me clam up and not learn anything about myself or my problem. It probably would have taught me more about being a criminal. The adult probation department put my sentence up for modification now.

The week I came to Parents United and met Hank and Ellie (my individual counselor), emotions were cropping up from everywhere and driving me crazy. [When I met Dorothy Ross at CSATP, I resented her because she was an authority figure and I was the slave.] I felt I no longer had control over my body or mind, that these people could decree what I had to do.

I began individual counseling with Ellie, disliking her at first because she was trying to pry information out of me and get into my head and into my garbage can of stuffed feelings, I thought. I didn't think she could get in, though, because my garbage can was the long-lasting chrome kind, not just the galvanized kind that's easier to break through. She was making me deal with what I didn't want to deal with. By looking at the situation, though, I did start to deal with it. My wife and I went to the Parents United group session the second week I was out of jail. For a month I didn't say anything in those sessions in the orientation group. I didn't know what I was supposed to say. I didn't understand what purpose it served for all of these members to stir up the thoughts that made them feel bad. So my concept was that people in this group make everyone feel bad.

After finishing orientation, we went through the Couple's Communication Group. Two fantastic people led that group and let me be silent for a couple of weeks. Then they made me interact by throwing questions and statements to me. I was scared and told them so. One of them asked me if I could tell why I was so scared. I said, "Because no one else has ever felt the pain and guilt I'm feeling, and no one else could share it with me." I discovered that the other guys in the group felt exactly as I did. I talked to those guys and worked with them in the sessions. Things started opening up. Then my wife and I started to communicate. She told me she had filed for divorce. I didn't want to lose her and tried to hang on to her. I was afraid of being alone. Ellie recommended a book on loneliness. I was more aware of my loneliness than I had ever been in my life.

I underwent a big change after being a member for a while. For the first time, I wanted to take care of myself physically. I watched what I ate and drank. I took vitamins. I got enough sleep, brushed my teeth, kept my hair combed. I thought, "Hey, I ain't such a bad guy, but I'm going to be in a real bad place if I don't take care of myself." After taking care of what was physically wrong, I could deal with my emotional problems better. Ellie showed me a couple of meditation exercises in our counseling sessions that really put me in touch with my life. I'd sit quietly and count breaths. It taught me to let problems and feelings be there. It made me alert to the fact that I was hurting and crying.

After being in Parents United two months, I cried for the first time. I sat under a tree one day, and my whole life fell in on me. I felt very sad about who I was and what I had done. I still drive by that tree sometimes and remind myself that is where my life turned around. I felt relieved after crying and after talking to Hank and Ellie about my stepdaughter. I told them I couldn't remember doing all the things she said I had done, but I knew she had no reason to lie.

After that, I grew very rapidly in the program and kept seeing Ellie every week for counseling. I participated more in the groups and learned a lot about myself: What makes me tick, what I like and don't like, how I feel, whether I'm afraid. I got in contact with all the feelings I had suppressed for years. I learned that I could feel good if I wanted to feel good. I learned even from the things that went wrong. After I had been in Parents United for six months, I set goals for myself, and I have met all of them. My newest goal is to co-lead an Alcoholic Group for Parents United.

I have gotten more support from Parents United than from any other people in my life. I remember once one of the women members sat on one side of me and held my hand while my wife held my other hand. It helped me realize the kinds of love that aren't sexual at all but are just a way of caring about one another. But before that when any of the women members put their arms around me to give me a friendly hug, I would stiffen and pull away from them. What they did scared me and I'd think, "What do they want of me?" I hadn't realized yet that they just wanted to be my friend.

I learned to realize something else, too. Through Parents United, I learned to talk about incest outside of PU — like through the Speakers Bureau when I went on speaking engagements. I was surprised to realize that there were people out in the community who would relate to me personally and didn't think I was the most disgusting person in the world. I learned that they could talk about the problem. So all of a sudden I had a new worth I hadn't known I had.

I kept educating myself in many ways. Every time Ellie said a word I didn't understand, I looked it up in the dictionary. I read books that covered the topics she talked about. Now I have three shelves of paperbacks about self-esteem, humanistic psychology, etc. Being in Parents United made me look at myself, see how I had put it together, see how much garbage I was carrying. It's sad that I had to fall so near the bottom before I could get turned around, but now I'm on an uphill climb. I sometimes slip downhill, of course, but my worst day now doesn't compare with how bad my past days were.

This program saved my life. When I was first released from jail and lived in the Halfway House, I thought, "Why don't they just castrate me? They should just throw me in a box, close the lid, and throw dirt on it." They didn't. And what I learned is that human beings don't always destroy other human beings. That was really a revelation. That let me start thinking, "Maybe there is something worthwhile in me." I found the worthwhile parts, and now I can love life, and through that I can love other people.

I can't relive the past, but now that I know I have choices, I can choose not to live the same way I did. Now that I'm more aware of how and why I let my daughter twist me around to get what she wanted, I probably would never let myself slide into that situation again with anyone — the situation of letting someone control my behavior because they have some kind of hold on me. It's great to know I can be responsible for not getting back into the space where I would molest my stepdaughter.

I haven't lived in my make-believe world for a long time. Now I want to remember about the molestation. I want to find out where things went wrong. That knowledge may push me back down and make me take several steps backward in progress. Eventually, I'll look at more of what actually happened. When I do take that look, I'll have the wisdom that Alcoholics Anonymous taught me with its slogan: I know what I can change and what I can't. And I can accept things that I can't change.

Now I know how to let people into my life. I still have difficulty having a concept of God. But some higher power within me allows me to watch myself develop now and to watch what I do turn into accomplishments. Until after I molested my daughter, the only feelings I dealt with were anger and superiority over others.

My biggest concern now is love — whether I have enough of it and whether I'm giving enough of it. My main goal is to love everyone even if I can't like them. In my opinion, love means you keep trying to understand the other person and really listen to their words. I'm entering a new relationship with a woman, and I'm scared about it. I've never felt a natural or functional part of any family. I want to be able to do that now. I'm looking forward to marrying the beautiful woman so that we can share our lives. I want her to walk beside me — not under me. I do not want us to clip each other's wings. I want her to look ahead, behind, and to the side of me. She and I can enjoy the journey together.

Homework Assignment Questions for
A Personal Account by a Father

1. What were some of the offender's negative feelings and thoughts toward himself and others, based on his childhood upbringing?

2. How did his unresolved feelings and problems lead to him having difficulty in his relationship with women?

3. What are some of the behaviors, thoughts, and feelings he experienced that contributed to his sexually abusive behavior?

4. In what manner or ways did the offender see and feel about the victim that allowed him to act upon his impulse or urge to be sexual with her?

5. What are some of the ways in which the sexual abuse by the offender affected himself or his family?

6. What are some of the ways in which the offender takes responsibility for his sexually offending behavior?

7. In what ways did the offender's participation in all aspects of the treatment program help him?

Handout 2

Chain of Events Model

The chain of events model is a way for me to understand the different thoughts and feelings that made the sexual offense happen. Once I understand, I can learn other ways of handling my chain of events so that I can minimize the risk of acting in a similarly abusive way.

A. *Link 1:* What are some of the hurts and abuses that happened to you in your childhood that were upsetting, that you've not really talked about, or that still bother you?

B. *Link 2:* How have these past hurts and abuses affected your thoughts or feelings about yourself and others? What are the fears or concerns which led you to have problems in relationships with others?

C. *Link 3:* High-risk situations that led to the sexual abuse. What were the thoughts and feelings that were bothering you around the time of or just before you committed each sexual offense?

D. *Link 4:* What were the coping strategies — behaviors, feelings, and thoughts — that helped you deal with the high-risk situations? How did these coping strategies lead you to act in sexually abusive way?

E. *Link 5:* What were the false or distorted ways of seeing or thinking about your sexually offending behavior that made the offense seem okay or you seem less bad?

Handout 3

Relapse Prevention Worksheet

Purpose: At this time you are probably thinking that you have your sexually abusive behavior under control. "It will never happen again" or words like that are being said by you or your parents. While you really may not want the sexual abuse to happen again, you must take more active steps to prevent a re-offense.

Based on the discussion of the chain of events, this assignment helps you to develop a plan of action to deal adaptively and nonabusively with these situations, feelings, and thoughts.

Describe what you would do in order not to continue with thinking of, or actually following through on, another sexual offense.

1. What could I immediately do to deal with the ways of acting, the feelings, or the thoughts which could lead me to commit another sexual assault?

2. Whom could I call (list name and phone number) or talk with (give person's name) to tell about my urges, feelings, or way of acting?

3. What do I want the person listed above to do?

4. What can I do to stay away from opportunities which give me access to potential victims?

5. What are some of the things I could do or say to handle the high-risk situations, feelings, and ways of acting which contributed to my offense occurring?

6. What are some true or realistic statements I need to make to myself in order to correct the distorted ones which might lead to me committing another sexual offense?

Handout 4

Readings From Victims of Sexual Abuse

Letters to Myself

Dear Chris,

I'm only three. I was so scared and afraid when I was three. Daddy hurt me. I crawled into a corner in my room. It was so big. I cried and didn't know where Mommy was. Mommy, I need you. I need you to hold me. Mommy don't make me come out of the corner. I'm scared. Mommy you didn't help me. You just made me come out of the corner. I'm scared. Mommy don't leave me. Help me Mommy! I don't understand.

Dear Chris,

I'm five now. I liked rubbing myself down there. It felt good. Mommy sees me. Mommy why are you hitting me? Mommy stop hitting me. I won't do it again. Don't hurt me anymore. Please stop! Mommy stops. I'm scared of Mommy now too.

I'm so scared Mommy. I wet my bed. Grandma gives me a dolly. I stop wetting. I love my dolly. I feel safe with her. My dolly doesn't like my Mommy and Daddy. Sometimes I still wet. Mommy you take my dolly away. I get so scared because I'm alone. I don't have my dolly to take care of me. Mommy I was so afraid. It was dark. I didn't want to go down the stairs to the bathroom. Daddy might get me. Mommy, why can't you see how scared I am?

Daddy you hurt me. Why do you keep hurting me? I don't understand. I love you but you keep hurting me. Daddy it hurts. I don't like it. What have I done for you to hate me so? Stop hurting me, Daddy. I hate you Daddy!

I love my sister. She takes up for me sometimes. Mommy and Daddy take her away from me. I'm in this room. There are all of these children. I'm scared. Sister where are you? I do not talk. I am alone. Why did they take sister away? I must be bad.

Dear Chris,

I'm seven now. Mommy I hate you. You didn't believe me. Mommy, Daddy is hurting me down there. Mommy, help me. I'm mad at you Mommy.

I'm mad at my dolly. She doesn't take care of me anymore. I kill my dolly. I love you dolly. Why did I kill you? I'm all alone now.

Dear Chris,

I'm eight now. Hi, Grandma. I like you. I like it at your house. I love you, Grandma. Grandma, uncle hurt me down there. Grandma, yes he did. Please believe me. Grandma do not say that. There is no place that is safe now. I hate you Grandma. I'm not bad. I try to be a good girl. I must be bad...I hate myself.

Dear Chris,

I'm eleven now. I can't handle what's going on anymore. I just want to die. Dad you're still hurting me. I want to kill you. Dad I'm going to tell someone. You tell me don't you dare. I say I am. You put your hands around my throat. I wake up. I wanted to be dead? Why didn't I just die?

Dear Chris,

I'm thirteen now. I tell this man down the street what Daddy is doing to me. He is going to talk to my Daddy. Someone believes me! He talks to my Dad. Thursday night Daddy and that man both rape me. I tell Mom. She does nothing! Daddy and that man get me an abortion. Two years of Thursday nights go by. Now there is my Daddy and two men. They get me another abortion. I tell my Mom again. Nothing!

I am nothing. I hate everyone. I hate me. We move. No more Thursday nights.

Dear Chris,

I'm fifteen now. I have a friend. It feels good to have a friend. My first one. I love and trust her Mom. I tell her Mom what my Dad's doing to me. She says nothing. Help me I say!! She drives me home. I hate my friend. I hate myself. I never tell again.

Dear Chris,

I'm sixteen now. I have my first real boyfriend. I'm not scared of him. He is nice to me. He rapes me. I'm scared. A baby grows within me. I tell my Dad. I tell him I tell him I don't want to kill the baby. He makes that decision for me. My baby is dead. My father comes to rape me again. I say no more. He says if not, I'll tell everyone you killed your baby. It was I, or was it? I give up. I forget the rapes.

Dear Chris,

I'm nineteen now. I go out with this guy. I remember he is the guy who raped me when I was sixteen. I get scared! He rapes me again. I find a knife. I stab him. There is blood everywhere. I run. I'm home now. I'm going to forget all of these things. I love my Mommy and Daddy. I have had a really normal childhood. I do not feel. I do not remember.

Dear Chris,

I am now 34 years old. I have lived with the fantasy of having a really normal childhood for sixteen years. With the help of many adult women who were molested as children and a loving and caring woman, Leona, I am alive. I feel for all these years there has been this big black cloud that I needed to surround me. Bit by bit I've broken through that big black cloud. At first I only saw a bit of sunlight. Now the sunlight encircles me. I feel so warm. I do exist. I feel. I love myself.

I share "me" in hopes that this may help someone. I can think of no better way to turn what happened to me into a more positive thing than if by sharing "me" I help someone else.

—Chris Shultz[1] ©1982

* * *

Over the past six years, I have been molested by my brother and it messed me up pretty bad. I am writing this letter to tell everyone...especially my brother...how I feel.

I feel that I have been used, abused, and hurt a lot. I feel that because I have been molested by my brother I have bi-sexual feelings. I am just starting to accept the fact that I am bi-sexual...for a long time I was very ashamed about it.

I feel sorry for my brother because he had a rough life, too, and he has been abused himself. I hope that he starts working on getting his own life together. I hope that my brother can admit what he has done, so that he can get his problem out in the open and deal with it. I love my brother and don't want him to have this on his shoulders all his life.

Love,

David[2]

* * *

Molest Is

Molest is when a man touches a boy or girl
In the wrong place

It is the same like a woman touching a boy and a girl
In the wrong place

It is hardly any different
but a girl has more things to touch than boys.

Molest feels like all sorts of things.
It hurts
It tickles
and sometimes it can make you bleed.

Deena[2]

* * *

Mother and Son Secret

I am a man in my late 40s who was molested by my mother. The molest took many forms and occurred many times during my childhood and youth, culminating in an episode of intercourse which has seemed to me like a nightmare. She continued to invade my privacy as a young adult.

You may be wondering how this has affected me. It put me in a "double bind" and has caused me frequent periods of depression due to the conflict of anger, rage, hate, and compassion for both my parents. I was hooked into every secrecy and was made to feel responsible for "rescuing" my mother. She would tell me all her problems with my dad, not enough love or warmth. She ran him down and told me how loving and warm I was, all the things he wasn't. She manipulated and controlled the communication in the family. She had the power to have me beaten by my father and then to take care of my welts. She turned me against my father and I hate her for that. I hated being in this family triangle and having to be responsible for her happiness. There was tension all the time and I took every opportunity to get away from it — school, farm work, etc.

There were a few times as a child that I was horrified by my intense feelings of hostility and rage. I acted this out against my brother, putting him in the hospital once and another time almost killing him. Most of the time I stuffed down these feelings and pretended that I was a nice, sweet boy without a mean bone in my body, and eventually I convinced myself that I had no anger, either.

My mother says I am being "tacky" when I confront her with the incest and she refuses to talk about it. I am not going to tell my father because he is now 80 years old.

The damage for me has been distortion of reality, lies, deceit, dishonesty, hate, rage, destructiveness, guilt, shame, failure, self-rejection, and depression. The only way out for me is to accept that it happened and stop denying and pretending that it was just a nightmare. Parents United and Adults Molested as Children United has helped me to get in touch with my feelings that I have repressed for so long — and to finally accept the fact that I was a victim. I *am* a survivor.

—-A Male AMAC[2]

1. *Becoming Whole, Adults Molested as Children United*

2. *From DSU, We Love You*

Both publications are available from Giarretto Institute, 232 East Gish Road, San Jose, CA 95112.

Questions

Instructions: Based on the passages that you have read, please answer each of the five questions:

1. What are some of the short-term effects of sexual abuse on victims?

2. What are some of the feelings the victims have regarding the sexual abuse committed against them? Also discuss your reaction to victims' feelings.

3. Who are the victims' feelings directed at?

4. What do you think are the steps the victims need to take in order to get over their reactions to being sexually abused?

5. If you were a victim of sexual abuse, you would feel, think, and react to being sexually abused in the following ways: (Please write your answer in the first person — for example, "I feel...," "I think....")

Handout 5

What Is Normal Sexual Behavior?

In small groups you are to discuss and take notes on the following questions:

1. What is considered normal sexual behavior on the part of an adolescent, adult, and child?

2. What is a sexual fantasy? What is an appropriate sexual fantasy as compared with one which is not normal?

3. Explain the differences between consent (which means to agree, to give some-one permission) and coercion (which means to make someone do something by force; force can be physical or verbal).

Based on what you have learned about consent versus coercion and the difference between sexual abuse and typical adolescent sexual behavior, please write down your answers to the following questions:

1. What are the things that occurred in my offenses which involved coercion?

2. What are the things that occurred in my offenses which make the sexual behavior abusive?

3. What are some of the new ideas I've learned about coercion and abusive behavior in my sexual offense? (If parents are answering the questionnaire: What are some of the new ideas we've learned about coercion and abusive behavior in our child's sexual offense?)

Handout 6

Discussing the Abuse in the Family

1. How often should the sexual abuse be discussed in the family and how many of the details should be included?

2. What are some of the feelings or concerns which may stop me (or us) from discussing the sexual abuse in the family?

3. What are some of the limits that should be set on such things as being around situations or people where another offense could happen; and who should be told about what happened?

Chapter 12

Domestic Violence Offender Groups

by Alex Mackenzie, M.A.
& Jack Prendergast, M.A., M.F.C.C.

Introduction

What Is Abuse?

Abuse is any behavior that is intended to hurt, intimidate, or control another person or more than one person; or behavior, whether intentional or not, that has this effect. There is a prevalent belief in our society that men have the right to control other people. Men in our society also have a paucity of skills for getting what they need. For these reasons, men have a particularly problematic relationship to power and control. Because of the way in which these beliefs inform male socialization, it can be said that virtually all men are abusers on one level or another. In considering whether behavior is abusive, the question of what another person said or did is irrelevant. There are always alternative choices to abuse: each man must take responsibility for his own behavior at all times. If a person is unsure whether or not he has acted abusively, a good test is to ask that person's partner, who has been affected by the behavior in question.

Abusive behavior falls into four major categories:

- Physical — such as punching, kicking, slapping, burning, scratching, raping

- Verbal — such as shouting to intimidate, name-calling, "trashing," insulting

- Emotional — such as playing "mind games," using children for purposes of emotional manipulation, emotional blackmail

- Financial — such as neglecting financial responsibilities, spending joint money without prior agreement, appropriating credit cards or checkbooks, and not paying child support.

Failing to honor responsibilities in a relationship — such as not doing a fair share of housework or child care, or lying with an intent to deceive or defraud — can also constitute abuse.

Cycle of Abuse

Domestic violence tends to follow a particular pattern or cycle in which, over time, the abuse becomes both more frequent and severe. Many men, on entering the program, may experience a feeling of safety or security. If they have just been through a major abuse incident, joining the group may kick off what is termed "the honeymoon" or "hearts-and-flowers" period. Both the group member and his partner want to believe that the abuse won't happen again, are trying very hard to be "nice" to each other, and doing their best not to let things upset them.

Over time, however, the issues that the couple has been burying inevitably begin to surface again. The relationship then moves into the tension-building phase. This is the dominant phase for most abusive relationships. Like the hearts-and-flowers period, the third phase — the blowup — is relatively short in duration.

In a healthy relationship, tensions also arise day to day, but are acknowledged and discharged. The function of a domestic violence group is to teach men to avoid the explosive phase altogether. It's unrealistic to hope to maintain a relationship in the hearts-and-flowers phase; however, men can be taught skills that will allow them to acknowledge and discharge tensions in the manner of someone in a healthy relationship, without violent incident.

Social Context of Domestic Violence and Its Treatment

The work of facilitating domestic violence offenders' groups goes beyond "curing" the errant behavior of a group of individuals. Male violence is socially produced. A restructuring of the social order is needed to make a real and meaningful change in society that will affect the individuals within it. As such, these therapy groups are concerned not only with teaching skills to abusive men, resocializing them, encouraging psychological insight, and helping them to reorganize their relationships; but also with shaping the institutions that encourage sexism and violence, and moving society at large to be less abusive, more cooperative, and more flexible.

This work is revolutionary in this respect, and demands a great deal both of facilitators and group members. It's sometimes difficult to define the appropriate relationship between groups of this kind and other social institutions, including the criminal justice system, the psychotherapeutic community, community mental health services, and the larger progressive political community. Offenders' programs hold a special place in the constellation of services for victims of family violence; in that they nurture the offender, they have also at times been considered controversial. It is critical for therapists themselves to be observant of their own processes and principles, as these resonate within the support and treatment community.

We felt that it was important to collaborate on this chapter, co-writing it rather than assigning responsibility to one individual. Part of the etiology of male violence is the belief that men need to struggle with everything in isolation, rather than by cooperating. Facilitators in this work need to be very conscious of the pull exerted by our early socialization to reinforce the oppressive social order. We have co-facilitated groups together, and strongly recommend that men's groups of this nature have two facilitators. This models for group members cooperative behavior and conflict resolution. More subtly, they don't see another reinforcing example of one man taking on more than he can reasonably handle, heroically struggling alone. Male facilitation is important for several reasons:

- Nonviolent male behavior is modeled by the facilitators.

- The group creates a nonabusive male culture.

- Men in the group feel safe to talk about their feelings about men, women, masculinity, power, and control.

- Male facilitators in such an environment are bound to feel safer than women, who are the most frequent victims of the offender population.

An important part of this work is teaching men to take care of themselves appropriately. Batterers often feel incapable of taking care of themselves. This may lead to a sort of panic that they neutralize by exerting pressure on someone else — usually a spouse or partner — to appropriate this function. Since no one can successfully take on this role for another adult for any length of time, frustrations, anger, and a sense of betrayal can and often do occur on the part of the self-perceived "unnurtured" male. If this man cannot express such feelings in any other way, he may express them through violence or abuse.

Gay Domestic Violence

This chapter is about male violence as it applies to gay as well as straight relationships. Acknowledging and working with gay male domestic violence is complicated, as it is not always clear as in heterosexual relationships who the offender is and who the victim. Of course, each person in the relationship must take responsibility for his own abusive behavior. If presented with a gay man who is abusive in his relationship, and is also being abused, you should deal with the safety of the parties first, usually by separating them until the violence is contained. The exercises and interventions in this chapter have been used with gay and straight male offenders and are appropriate to both.

Although straight men in a group might benefit from the perspective of gay men, it makes most sense to see these populations of batterers in separate groups. Probation or diversion referrals for gay men are very rare, whereas about 50 percent of straight men in such groups are court-mandated. The police and courts intervene differently in cases of gay male domestic violence. This is an issue that needs continuing examination at the social and community levels.

Selection and Screening

Not all clients who present with domestic violence issues are appropriate for group treatment. The main tool for selection and screening should be a comprehensive intake procedure. Batterers' groups do not lend themselves to a "drop-in" format, as safety in the room is a fundamental concern. Please remember that the membership of this group is limited to men who are perpetrators of violence or abuse with their partners. Although child abuse, sexual abuse, or street violence may be a concurrent problem for members of the group, these issues should be treated separately as well. Refer these clients to appropriate treatment providers; and always adhere to legally mandated reporting procedures.

Therapists or counselors doing intakes with batterers should have experience with this population and feel confident in their ability to confront denial and minimization. At the same time, a warm and caring presence is necessary to help quell the fear and anxiety these men feel. The intake worker should have a keen eye for manipulation and inconsistency, and be willing to point these things out, setting the tone for honesty and accountability as treatment goals.

Red Flags

What are some of the "red flags," or indicators, that a client may not be appropriate for the group? A batterer capable of working in a group setting is not, by definition, mentally ill. The typical batterer is functioning normally in his everyday life; his use of force and violence is a traditional male mode of expression and problem solving. Very often these men are shocked at being arrested or threatened with divorce, as they have seen their fathers exhibit these same behaviors unchallenged. Such men are workable clients.

Sometimes men will come to treatment, however, displaying psychotic, sociopathic, or sadistic behaviors. These men need help above and beyond the group setting. They should be referred to treatment with professionals qualified to deal with these pathologies.

Another red flag first encountered by the intake worker is high lethality. Ritualized abuse, the use of weapons, rape, and a history of serious injury to the partner are all indicators that interventions other than, or in addition to, group treatment may be called for. It is important for all intake workers to seek supervision or consultation if they are unclear about a client's appropriateness for group treatment based upon lethal potential.

Untreated substance abuse should be confronted and satisfactorily addressed before a man can gain entry to a batterers' group. A man who presents as a drug or alcohol abuser will have little chance of success in changing his battering behavior without concurrent substance abuse treatment. Intake workers should refer these men to treatment providers, and require written proof of compliance, before placing them in a group. Men are informed at intake that if the group facilitators at any time assess that drug or alcohol abuse is inhibiting an individual's participation, he will not be allowed to continue in the group.

Unclear motivation can also serve as a red flag for admission to a group. While minimization of their abuse is the norm for batterers, some men take no responsibility for their behavior, blaming their partner and the system, or flat-out denying the action itself in spite of overwhelming evidence. Sometimes a man is required to come to counseling by a judge or under threat of divorce and, predictably, his motivation is limited to escaping a jail sentence or retaining his partner. These men should be seen individually rather than in a group setting until they gain internal motivation and display some accountability.

Language or cultural barriers can make it difficult for a man to work in a group setting. In these situations, every attempt should be made to refer men to a group in which their language is spoken or to a therapist or counselor familiar with the culture-specific needs of the client.

Lastly, the intake worker needs to be aware that a few men will attempt to use treatment as a means to "prove" their nonviolence. This scenario usually presents itself in child custody disputes, whereby a man attempts to smooth over a history of violence or abusiveness by entering a group and thus look better in court. The worker should make it clear from the start that behavior cannot be predicted and that while the individual may be welcome in treatment, no claims concerning his safety will be substantiated by the treatment provider.

Time and Duration

Battering behavior is not easy to change. Clients should expect to spend a minimum of six months in weekly two-hour group sessions. For the purposes of this chapter, the group format is described as a twenty-four-week program; however, clients should not be terminated until they have demonstrated a mastery of the techniques and concepts taught in the group. One strategy for achieving this is to encourage group members who are not ready to leave the group to reenroll in twelve-week increments. This maintains more stability of membership and allows each man to stay in treatment until he is able to demonstrate a cessation of his battering behavior.

Issues will surface in the course of group treatment requiring help that the group alone cannot give. Often in such cases clients have not dealt with their own abuse issues as victims in their families of origin. Depression or suicidal ideation may surface for men who have lost their partners or families because of their abusive behavior. Men should be encouraged to deal with these types of issues in individual treatment that is concurrent with their participation in the group. Resistance to treatment should be gently confronted; remind men that they have an opportunity now to solve problems that will otherwise plague them for the rest of their lives.

Finally, it should be recognized that people learn and change at different rates; some acknowledgment of this fact should be built into any program. Rather than a standard schedule for change, a program should have specific termination criteria: men should be able to continue in group until they successfully meet those criteria. Batterers have spent a lifetime learning these behaviors: they cannot be expected to unlearn them quickly. Clients should be encouraged to stay with the process and not to expect quick and easy solutions.

Structure

Group Size

An ideal group for batterers would contain between eight and ten men, with two facilitators. Because of the volatile nature of some clients, dual facilitation is highly recommended to provide safety for both clients and facilitators, as well as a role model for male cooperation. Dual facilitation also ensures leadership continuity in cases of illness, vacation, or leaves of absence.

Batterers' groups suffer from a fairly high dropout rate for a variety of reasons. Sometimes a violent incident will inspire a man to seek help, but his interest may wane as the incident loses its vividness for him. Issues raised in the group may be painful for the man to deal with, making it hard for him to return to the group every week. There is also the case of men who are in treatment only to get their partner to come home. When this fails, the man's motivation for treatment usually evaporates. Lastly, general life issues, such as money or scheduling problems, can cause a man to drop out unexpectedly.

For these reasons, it is often best to start a group with an excessive number of men, about 12 or 13, knowing that you'll probably end up with an ideal number after a few weeks. Adding men to the group once it has begun is not recommended, as this changes the group dynamics with each addition, and undermines feelings within the group of trust and safety.

Group Structure

In recent years, law enforcement agencies have been mandated to hold men accountable for their abusive behavior. Such men have been arrested in increasing numbers for domestic violence. Mandated counseling is often a condition of probation for the first-time offender, with jail as the option for noncompliance.

The court-referred client presents difficult issues for the group and its facilitators. The motivation for such a client is sometimes limited to avoidance of punishment, and he may be in heavy denial about his behavior. For these reasons, it's important to make it clear from the outset of treatment that attendance alone does not constitute fulfillment of the court-mandated counseling requirement. On the contrary, every client is expected to own responsibility for his violence, be willing to apply behavioral techniques to stop his violent behavior, and to gain a thorough understanding of the skills and concepts presented in the group. Court-mandated clients have not fulfilled their term of rehabilitation until they meet these requirements.

Clients who are court-referred may be effectively mixed with self-referred clients, as their issues and behaviors are essentially the same. The reality is that the self-referred clients were either responsible enough or lucky enough to seek help before they were arrested. Unfortunately, poor and minority men are more likely to be arrested for this offense than white middle- or upper-class men. These race and class issues should be explored in the group, as the stress and the anger that accompany poverty and discrimination are often contributing factors to a man's violent behavior.

Goals

The primary goal of the batterers' group is to stop the domestic violence and ensure the safety of the victim. For this reason, the initial intervention is the teaching of behavioral techniques, such as the time-out, designed to remove the client from his environment before he is at risk for violent behavior. Although behavioral techniques can help the client stop his battering behavior in the short term, lasting change involves a multifaceted approach challenging many of the fundamental assumptions of male culture. Domestic violence can be seen as an expression of the pain, rage, and helplessness that men may actually feel in relation to power and control issues within the family. An important facet of any batterers' group should be the presentation of nonviolent alternatives for expressing these feelings. The use of "feeling statements" is an example of one such technique. The client must be willing to give up his impulse to control his partner, exert his will, or simply vent his frustrations through violence.

In addition to the collective goal of stopping violent behavior, it's helpful in the course of the group to have members set individual short-term goals. These goals can be regarded as stepping stones toward the larger goal; they should be realistic and reflect a measurable behavior. For example, while it is not realistic for a man to resolve never to feel angry again, it is possible for him to strive to take a time-out whenever he feels angry with his partner.

The group is also a good place for men to gain empathy for and an understanding of their partner's predicament. Specific exercises are designed to help men own and identify their own prior and present experiences of victimization, whether in their family of origin, in society in general, or at the hands of other men. This can lead to an empathy for the mixture of love and fear felt by partners.

Some programs include a mandatory partner contract designed to educate the victim about the counseling services, shelters, and legal remedies available. It is important that the victim as well as the perpetrator be warned that participation in the group in no way guarantees a cure for the problem of battering. Victims should be cautioned that the decision to stay in a relationship with a batterer in treatment involves risk, and that support is available for her in the community if she decides to leave.

Ground Rules

Because these clients tend to be manipulative and to test limits, a firm set of ground rules for the group is recommended. Fundamentally, no violence or verbal abuse of any kind should be tolerated in sessions, and weapons of any kind should not be allowed in the room. A tight attendance and lateness policy should be in place to underscore the commitment and responsibility necessary to be successful in treatment. No drug or alcohol use should be tolerated. Anyone with a substance abuse problem should be required to seek treatment. All fees should be kept up-to-date. Any client who chooses to drop out of the group is asked to come and tell the group why, rather than simply to "disappear."

Lastly, clients are expected to report any episodes of violence or abuse of any kind to the group. All clients must agree to maintain confidentiality outside of the group. Any client who cannot or will not honor the ground rules will be terminated from the group.

Group Process

Once the membership has made a commitment to the group and its rules and expectations, the work of the group begins. Initially, the educational and behavioral content tends to dominate, as the men must quickly learn tools to avoid further violent incidents. Once the men have been able to demonstrate an understanding of and an ability to utilize these tools, the focus shifts to "process." The task of this phase is to integrate the tools and concepts with the real-life experiences of the men in the group, who can begin to analyse their patterns of success and failure.

In all sessions, the men should engage in a short "check-in." The check-in should consist of two parts: "How are you feeling right now?", and "Have there been any incidents of violence or avoidance of violence since our last session?"

To end each session, it's helpful to have a closing or "check-out" ritual. This should include a "safety check," giving each man a moment to look ahead to the week's activities and anticipate any stressers or situations that might be setups for potentially violent incidents. For example, a client might be attending a company party with his wife. In the past, the boss has flirted with the batterer's wife, which has in turn aroused his violent jealousy. The group can offer support and advice as to how he can deal with this situation differently than he has in the past.

Another helpful component of the closing segment is "appreciation and criticism." Each man is given the opportunity to appreciate or criticize (appropriately, without trashing) another man in the group for something he said that evening. This serves to give men practice in direct expression, as well as allowing for support and feedback for the work they are doing.

Facilitators should model the check-in and check-out procedures in the initial group session. The men will need help and support in identifying their feelings in the check-in: a large "feeling chart," with lists of feelings, both positive and negative, should be posted in each group room as a helping tool. Men should not be allowed to make the traditional "I'm okay" response when asked how they feel;

instead, they should be guided toward more descriptive expressions. The men should continually be validated for displaying a willingness to talk in the check-in about violent or potentially violent incidents so that information is not driven "underground."

In the check-outs, men should be reminded to be specific in their appreciations and criticisms. They should be practicing direct expression, looking each other in the eyes, and beginning sentences with "you" rather than speaking in the third person. Generalizations such as "I appreciate the whole group" should be discouraged. Ask group members to pick out one man, and to appreciate or criticize him for something he did or said that evening. Facilitators themselves should be open to feedback or criticism from group members if it is presented appropriately — in other words, with the same consideration afforded other members of the group.

As the weeks go on, the men's depth of feeling for each other will increase. This is fueled by the process the men are experiencing, and is contained by the safety of the group. Ideally, new norms are being created in the group — a willingness to confront as well as appreciate each other, the expression of honesty and vulnerability, and, most importantly, an ethic of nonviolence. Of course, every group learns at its own pace; a strict "recipe" format for these groups is unrealistic. Outlined in broad terms, however, the groups do follow a predictable growth pattern, and the skills and concepts that must be learned build on each other in a systematic way. It's important that the group be allowed to move at its own speed, and that each skill and concept be learned and integrated before the group proceeds.

Starting the Group

In starting a batterers' group, it's important to establish the group's purpose right away. The collective self-esteem of these men is very low, which is a primary reason for their behavior: it's therefore especially important to be nonjudgmental, empathic, and caring. Because most of the men will be new to therapy and group situations, unifying rituals are a good way to establish common ground by including all men in the group process.

Begin with an introduction of yourselves and the purpose of the group. For example, "Welcome to [name of agency]. My name is_____, and I will be your facilitator, along with_____. I'm sure that some of you may be feeling nervous. I want to assure you that although we'll be doing serious work together in the next 24 weeks, the task we've come together to do is possible. We've set up ground rules to make this work both possible and safe."

Introduce the ground rules of the group. It's helpful to provide a handout, which the clients sign and retain.

Ground Rules

1. No weapons may be brought to the group.

2. Men must not have used drugs or alcohol for 24 hours prior to the group meeting.

3. No verbal trashing of partners or other group members is allowed.

4. Members must arrive on time for each group session.

5. No more than three absences will be tolerated in any 24-week period.

6. Fees must be kept up to date.

7. No violence of any kind will be tolerated within the group. Members will be terminated if any such event occurs.

Next, have the men introduce themselves and tell about the incidents of abuse that convinced them they needed to get help for their violent behavior. These vignettes will allow the men to establish their membership in the group, as well as end the isolation they feel by realizing that everyone in the room shares the same problem.

As the room fills with stories, an air of seriousness pervades, allowing the men to put down their defenses and false bravado. Often a man will break down and cry as he confesses to things that he may not have shared previously with anyone.

The facilitators' role in the initial session is to provide support and containment. They should remind clients that their negative behaviors do not define them as bad people. Group members should be given credit for seeking help and be given support and approval for appropriate displays of emotion. Additionally, facilitators should keep a close watch on the clock to allow each man in the room sufficient time to share his personal story. Discourage blaming, woman-bashing, denial, and minimization. Your goal should be to establish a group norm of honesty and accountability.

Main Concepts and Skills

A. Skill: Self-Reporting

"In order to tell about the incidents that brought you here (or that happened since last week), you will be narrating factually through the incident, telling how it started, what you were saying, how you were feeling, specifically what you did, how it stopped, and what the consequences were. This is not the place to talk extensively about your partners, nor will it be appropriate here for you to blame them. Instead, you should focus on taking responsibility and reporting your feelings and behavior. This takes some getting used to, but I'll be available to help you focus your story if you get off course."

B. Skill: Time-out

"The time-out is the cornerstone of domestic violence intervention. Most importantly, it provides a guaranteed method for stopping the violence now. It also serves as a catalyst for beginning to talk about your resistance to changing abusive, controlling, or violent behavior: it's an intervention that puts the responsibility for changing on you.

"Here's how the time-out works: when you're beginning to feel angry, you say out loud to yourself and your partner, 'I'm beginning to feel angry. I'm going to take a time-out. I'll be back in one hour and check in.' You then leave the physical location for one hour (no longer and no shorter), you don't drink or drive or use drugs, and you come back to check in. If at that time both of you want to talk about what happened, you can do so; if not, you don't. If you find yourself getting angry again, you take another time-out.

"The time-out is a specific tool, which is to be used exactly as presented. If you don't say exactly, 'I'm beginning to feel angry; I'm going to take a time-out, I'll be back in one hour and check in,' you may be doing something helpful, but you're not taking a time-out. Each word is there for a reason and, as simplistic as it looks, the formula works as an elegant, profound intervention for domestic violence. It teaches you where your authority **really** rests: with yourself and your determination of your physical proximity to upsetting situations. Rather than controlling the situation, you learn to leave it without behaving abusively. This marks the point where you begin to take care of yourself, which is a crucial element for change.

"Saying the phrase, 'I'm beginning to feel angry,' is a way of learning to identify and express feelings, rather than acting them out or controlling circumstances and other people in an attempt to *avoid* feeling them. This phrase emphasizes the skill of talking about yourself and your internal state, rather than focusing on what is wrong with the other person that "causes" you to feel angry or uncomfortable.

"It's important to emphasize the word 'beginning' in this phrase. The time-out is to be taken when you first notice warning signs of anger — I'll explain more about warning signs next week — rather than after you are already in a blinding rage and have already done something abusive.

" 'I'm going to take a time-out' is your statement about what you are going to do to respond to your feeling, rather than manipulating or controlling your partner so that she will do something to change it. The word 'going' is important, in that it indicates to both of you that the time-out is not negotiable, not open for discussion, and that it is happening *now*. Although it may seem a minute point, choosing 'going' over 'think I need' in this phrase can make the difference between getting out the door and not getting out at all — which can be a life-and-death difference."

" 'I'll be back and check in in one hour,' is your statement to both of you about what will happen after the time-out. As such, it keeps the time-out from becoming an abusive gambit in itself. That is, your partner knows that you aren't leaving forever, or going to go out and get drunk and come back with a weapon. When you come back in one hour, this serves to build trust in your partner, as well as yourself, that you can and will do as you say and live up to your word. This is important, because many men have eroded their partners' and their own trust in themselves by repeatedly breaking their promises not to be violent or abusive."

C. Skill: Recognition of Warning Signs

"Men are not trained to be particularly attentive to, or aware of, their feelings. During the time-out presentation, some of you may have felt confused about how to tell when you are beginning to feel angry.

"In order to learn more about what happens when you're beginning to feel angry, I'm going to ask you to visualize what happened just prior to the incidents that brought you here. This will help give you a sense of what your warning signs are.

"Close your eyes, sit up straight in the chair, with both feet on the floor. Take a deep breath and let it out. Now, try to remember the day of the incident. Think of what was going on then. What pressures were you under? What made you feel tense or uptight? What was worrying you? How were you talking to people? Was there anything unusual about your tone of voice, your language, your posture, your position with respect to them? Notice anything unusual in your behavior. Were you pacing, clenching, holding tension in your body? Take another deep breath, and as you let it out, notice any tension in your body now. Where are you holding tension?

"Now move up to a couple of hours before the incident. What thoughts are running through your mind? Are you arguing with your partner or anyone else? What is the subject of the argument? What about it snags you? How are you talking to people now? Again, notice your tone, language, posture, and position with respect to other people. What's going on in your body now?

"Go back to an hour before the incident — what are you feeling? Check in with your body again. Notice anything unusual? What do you see? What do you hear? What are you doing? Who is around? What are you thinking? Have you used any drugs or alcohol today? Are you talking? What are you saying?"

Continue in this manner, asking clients to check in at half-an-hour, fifteen minutes, five minutes, one minute, fifteen seconds, five seconds, and the moment of the first instance of abuse.

"Now, open your eyes and return to the room. Tell me what you noticed. I'll write your responses on the board."

D. Concept: Cycle of Violence

Note: This didactic segment lends itself very well to a visual aid which can be drawn on the blackboard or can be xeroxed and serve as a permanent poster. (See the diagram on the next page.) Men locate themselves with respect to their progress through the cycle.

Use the diagram as per this example:

"Tony has suggested that since things are going well between himself and his partner now, he might not need this group any longer. This is a good time to talk about the Cycle of Violence. Let's look at the diagram on the wall.

"At the top of the diagram is the position we call the "volcano." This is the eruption of your unmanaged anger into a violent or abusive incident.

"From about one o'clock to three o'clock on the diagram, the couple is in what we call the "honeymoon" or "hearts-and-flowers" phase. In this stage, the man may feel remorseful and affectionate toward his partner. The partner may like this behavior and try to maintain it by responding affectionately. By the time a man finds his way into a domestic violence offenders' program, his partner is familiar with this cycle, and probably doesn't believe him when he promises that he won't be violent again. She doesn't really want the candy or flowers he offers: she wants him to do something real about changing. Nonetheless, both partners' denial may rally during this time, allowing them to believe that the battering partner is sufficiently sorry not to do it again. This creates a very dangerous, false sense of security.

"The next phase is located from four o'clock on, very near the volcano itself. This is called the "tension-building" phase. This is where most relationships spend most of their time, and entails the day-to-day tensions that inevitably arise in a relationship: disagreements about money, parenting, how to spend time, and negotiating the vicissitudes of intimacy. Research has shown that, over time, the cycle moves faster and faster, and incidents become increasingly violent. It is not the goal of the group to get couples back up into the hearts-and-flowers part of the cycle — that would be unrealistic. Rather, the group's charter is to give a man the tools to **manage** tension, releasing it as it comes up, without being abusive. Gradual release of tension in this way renders the volcano completely inactive."

E. Concept: Emotional Funnel

The Feelings List and the Emotional Funnel diagram are recommended for use as displays in the room where the group meets. They should also be distributed as handouts.

Cycle of Violence

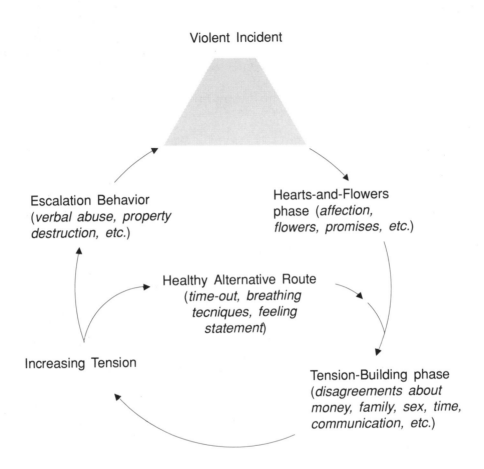

Violent Incident

Escalation Behavior (*verbal abuse, property destruction, etc.*)

Hearts-and-Flowers phase (*affection, flowers, promises, etc.*)

Healthy Alternative Route (*time-out, breathing tecniques, feeling statement*)

Increasing Tension

Tension-Building phase (*disagreements about money, family, sex, time, communication, etc.*)

Feelings List

Happy	Sad	Angry	Afraid	Hurt	Ashamed
comfortable	down	mad	vulnerable	crushed	embarrassed
glad	unhappy	incensed	insecure	wronged	humiliated
elated	heart-broken	frustrated	terrified	misunder-stood	mortified
delighted	dejected	furious	alarmed	wounded	guilty
thrilled	discouraged	enraged	nervous	provoked	exposed
ecstatic	miserable	annoyed	uncertain	abandoned	contrite
cheerful	depressed	irritated	threatened	ignored	disgraced
pleased	despondent	exasperated	hesitant	invalidated	belittled
satisfied	melancholy	righteous	panic-stricken		conscience-stricken
relieved			worried		haunted

Emotional Funnel

**Anger, Violence,
Rage, Action**

"I'm going to talk to you about some of the origins of anger, and I'll offer you the alternative of experiencing your original feelings, rather than turning them into anger or rage.

"Men are taught not to experience or express certain kinds of feelings — specifically those feelings associated with helplessness, or with being a victim. Rather, men are taught to feel indifferent or to become angry, but they aren't even supposed to feel angry for long. Instead, men are supposed to take action to change whatever is causing their uncomfortable feelings.

"Can anyone describe a situation in which you were angry, and what about it specifically snagged you?" (Wait for description; help the volunteer focus on specifics.) "Now, can you name the emotion you felt or feel when faced with such a situation? Other group members, how do you think you might feel? Let's use words from the Feelings List. Can you identify with words from some of the other columns besides the list of anger words? [Wait] If this happened to me, I might feel wounded or helpless. Would anyone else feel that way? What other feeling words apply?

"You can see that I'm stressing the more vulnerable responses in the picture I'm drawing here. Those words that describe anger characterize someone else's behavior, or what action we might take to avoid the feeling of going further down in the funnel. At the bottom of the funnel, I've written Anger, Violence, Rage, Action. Feelings of powerlessness, fear, and humiliation come up for people many times during a day, filling the top end of the funnel, weighing down the other feelings that are already contained within. As you fail to express or discharge these feelings, they get pushed further down into lower levels of the emotional funnel, changing from fear, sadness, and hurt to anger, aggression, and violence.

"What does it mean to say 'I'm humiliated' rather than 'I'm pissed off'? What kind of person says those kinds of things? What do you give up by moving upward in this diagram? What do you lose by not moving up? How do you feel when you are at the receiving end of anger, rage, and violence? When someone else tells you that he or she feels vulnerable, how do you tend to react? Do you laugh at that person? Or do you tend to be kinder in the way you listen? How do you think your partner might react if you were to express your own feelings of vulnerability?

F. Skill: Three-Breath Technique

"When you notice that you're acting emotionally, or experiencing any early warning sign at all, take a deep breath. Notice where any tension or other unusual physical sensations are occurring (heat, chills, tingling, and so on). Ask yourself as you exhale, 'Am I feeling angry?' Then take another deep breath and ask, 'Am I feeling afraid?' as you exhale. Finally, take another deep breath, still being aware of your physical sensations, and ask yourself as you exhale, 'Am I feeling sad?'

"Don't stop the exercise after getting one 'yes' answer — it's important to check in about all three feelings. If you identify fear or sadness accompanying the anger, this may give you some very important information about the more vulnerable feelings that the anger is covering. You'll also learn to interpret your physical sensations as reactions to or precursors of emotions."

G. Skill: Feeling Statement

The following is recommended as a permanent poster in the room where the group meets. You can also use it as a handout:

The Feeling Statement

I feel_____

when you _____

(because I_____).

I would like_____.

"One of the reasons men choose to behave violently is because they don't have the skills to talk about their feelings. Instead of talking about your feelings, you act to change the circumstances that stimulated them, or else you act out to make someone else experience your feelings. For example, a man who feels that his partner has hurt him or made him feel powerless may make her suffer in the same way by hurting or controlling her.

"The purpose of expressing feelings is to describe and clarify for yourself, your partner, or others your internal emotional state. In doing this, you'll explain what meanings and "weights" outside influences have for you. Understanding your own feelings and those of other people, and being understood, are basic human needs: this understanding is the fundamental building block of intimacy.

"Still, as men, you'll find yourselves in many ways, and for a variety of reasons, resisting talking about your feelings. Men are taught that feelings are unimportant, dangerous, or irrational. Men believe that angry feelings will frighten their partners, and that softer feelings are women's domain. Men also fear what other people's reactions will be to their feelings, imagining (not necessarily incorrectly) that their feelings may seem burdensome or be perceived as manipulative. The fact is, however, that talking **directly** about your feelings is the *least* burdensome or manipulative way you can manage them. You are offering your partner a gift which may be accepted or not.

"Feelings are not descriptions or judgments about outside events or thoughts about what might be going on. A good test of whether a statement is really a feeling is to see if the 'I feel' part of what you are saying could be restated as 'I think.' 'I feel that you...' is not a feeling statement. A description of your inner state — your gut reaction — such as 'I feel afraid when you...' — does qualify. Another good test is to see if the feeling expressed is similar to any of the words on the Feelings List.

"Now, focus on the Feeling Statement diagram. I would like to try to help group members practice expressing some feelings. Like the time-out, the feeling statement is a powerful tool, and should be used exactly as diagrammed. When using the feeling statement, say, 'I feel,' and fill in the blank with a feeling such as one of those on the Feelings List. Next, say 'When you,' and describe as specifically as possible the behavior you're responding to. This means not using words like always or never, since you're responding to one specific thing. This also means that you're not characterizing your partner in general, but sticking to the particular behavior. If it seems to be helpful, you can add 'because I' (this is in parentheses because it's optional): fill in the blank by describing your interpretation of what you're feeling, what it is about you that makes this behavior have its particular effect. Finally, say, 'I would like,' and fill in the blank with a specific desire, bearing in mind that this is about communicating a wish, not about getting the listener to fulfill it.

"Watch out for some of these stumbling blocks:

- Saying 'I feel that you...,' which characterizes the other person's behavior rather than describing your own internal state.

- Justifying. Feelings need no justification: they are just your feelings. Giving too much power to your partner's behavior is one way of justifying your feelings rather than just expressing them.

- Overly long or complicated statements about your feelings provide another avenue for escaping them. This goes hand in hand with justifying.

- Blaming. No matter what another person has said or done, you are responsible for your own feelings. This is a key concept in learning how to manage what you feel.

- Expecting your partner to do something in response to your feeling is again giving too much control to your partner and directing attention away from your experience of the feeling itself.

"Would anyone be willing to try to think of a feeling statement they could have used in the past instead of controlling or hurting someone?"

H. Skill: Goal Setting

Goals are necessary for members to determine their progress and success; setting goals is the first step toward reaching them.

"Tonight, we're going to work on setting goals. This will give you a means of measuring your progress and success in the group. This exercise will also have the benefit of giving you a chance to help and be helped by another man, confronting the false assumption that men have to do everything by themselves without outside help."

In setting goals, it's important to ask the following questions:
(Use these questions as a handout.)

- How will you be able to tell that you've accomplished what you set out to do here?

- What will your life be like when you have accomplished your goal? How will you be able to describe yourself?

- What will you gain by making the change you've chosen?

- What will you lose?

- How will you feel?

"What makes a good goal? Some characteristics of a good goal are that it

- Contains a statement about *yourself*, not anyone else.

- Contains a statement about *behavior*, not about emotions or circumstances you'll be in — not "I won't be so angry," but rather, "I'll take three practice time-outs per week."

- Is specific in describing what your behavior will be. Use numbers and specific responses to specific situations — *not* "I'll pitch in more around the house," but rather, "I'll cook dinner if I get home first, and will always do the dishes on the days my partner cooks."

- Is a statement of what you will do, not what you will try to do; it shouldn't depend on others — *not* "I will try to get along better with my partner," but rather, "I will use feeling statements at least three times a day when I'm tempted to be verbally abusive."

"I'd like to call your special attention to the questions, "What will you lose?" and "How will you feel?" You may tend toward saying that you have everything to gain, nothing to lose, and that you'll feel great. If it was really that simple, wouldn't you have already made this change? The fact is that by giving up controlling behavior, you are giving up power and control over areas of your lives in which you are heavily invested. If a man makes a commitment to stop using financial coercion to manipulate his wife's treatment of their child, he is giving up his level of control over something very important. This is *not* to say that you shouldn't make this commitment; but if the commitment is to succeed, you must make the pledge consciously, without denial about any negative aspects of the outcome. Making changes like this doesn't necessarily feel good. In fact, it can feel unaccustomed, weird, uncomfortable, unnatural, and frightening. It's a bit like writing with the opposite hand from the one you usually write with."

I. Concept: Responsibility

"Men taking responsibility for violent or abusive behavior is the key to change. Violent behavior is a choice, and men must acknowledge it as such in order to make a different choice.

"Who has some examples of things you say when you're avoiding responsibility? How about things you say when you're taking full responsibility for yourself? I'll write these down and we can talk about them after we've come up with a list."

If clients have difficulties coming up with examples, suggest the following:

Taking Responsibility	Avoiding Responsibility
I have been violent.	She/he provoked me.
I control my own actions.	My hand just flew out at her/him.
I'll tell you exactly what I did.	If she/he wouldn't..., then I wouldn't be violent.
I choose not to be violent again.	I'll try not to be violent.
I accept the consequences of my actions.	
I need a time-out.	

After the exercise, continue. "Some common ways in which men avoid responsibility are by minimizing what they did, denying it altogether, forgetting or simply omitting parts of it, justifying themselves, abstracting or intellectualizing their actions, and blaming someone else for their behavior. It's important to understand these defenses: you can help each other by confronting instances when some of you avoid responsibility. Let's come up with some examples of when you have used these defenses in the past."

J. Concept: Gender Roles and Male Socialization

"What we're trying to do here is unlearn male violence. As part of this process, it's important to look at the ways in which we become oppressed by our own rigid adherence to narrowly defined gender roles, where these roles come from, and how they relate to domestic violence.

"What does it mean to be human? What positive qualities do we start with prior to being molded by society? Let's brainstorm about this. If you're having a hard time thinking about it, think of the kind of person you would like to be involved with as a friend or partner." (List the group's results of brainstorming.)

"You've come up with some good examples of desirable human characteristics: intelligent, strong, caring, trusting, cooperative, trustworthy, attractive, loving, sensitive, generous, responsible, and honest. What qualities come to mind when you think of what it takes to be a man? I'll write down this second list." (Write down adjectives suggested by the group.)

"You've come up with some telling examples: strong, brave, macho, fearless, stubborn, isolated, competitive, violent, hardass, and 'has to be right.' What do you notice about these two lists?" (If necessary, continue.) "Some of the things I've noticed are that

1. The terms you used to describe men are quite different from the terms you used to describe the people you would like to be involved with. What does that mean for your partner in terms of being involved with you? How desirable is it to be involved with a 'he-man'?

2. Some of the characteristics of 'he-men,' by virtue of the language we use, cut men off from talking about their vulnerable feelings — and cut them off from comfort as well. Having to appear fearless, for example, means that you can't acknowledge your fear and can't ask for help. Needing to be right all the time means that you can't ever back down from a position, even when you can see how wrong you are.

3. Many positive qualities are left off from list 2, which means that, somehow, male socialization cuts us off from these positive human qualities. This affects the quality of our lives and relationships profoundly, and hurts the people we love. Which kind of father would you want — one from list 1 or list 2?

4. One of the lists is less constricting and would meet your human needs better. Which one? Why would anyone choose the other list?"

(Continue the discussion.) "How does this happen? How and why do we allow ourselves to be constricted in this way? As a man, what is the result of being seen by other men as having some of the 'softer,' positive human characteristics such as being gentle, emotional, caring, loving? What happened when you were a boy when someone stepped outside the male sex-role stereotype?

"As children, you probably saw other boys beaten up, cast out, and labeled as queer, sissy, or girlish when they exhibited those softer characteristics. Perhaps that happened to you. Can you remember the first time when you wanted comfort from someone, and received the message that this was an inappropriate thing for boys to want? How many times did an adult say to you, 'Be a big boy now — boys don't cry'?

"How can men claim a broader, more flexible gender role and keep their positive male characteristics? How can we allow ourselves to experience a greater range of feelings? Is it worth it? We need to grapple with this, because it's in this spirit that we are able to develop closer relationships: by learning to take care of our human needs, and no longer hurting the people we love."

K. Skill: Empathic Listening

"Empathic listening is a way of hearing what another person is trying to tell you. The way it works is that you put aside your own agenda and focus entirely on helping yourself and the speaker clarify the specific facts and feelings that he or she is trying to communicate. To check your understanding, you ask questions and paraphrase what the speaker has said.

"Questioning as part of empathic listening requires that you not try to build an argument against what the speaker is saying, that you're not strategizing about your own agenda or trying to manipulate in any way: the goal is simply to try to enhance your understanding. Paraphrasing means saying back in your own words the information you're getting from the speaker.

"Empathic listening is a good way to neutralize an escalating conflict. If your partner knows that you're really attempting to listen to her, there's no need to shout, talk faster, or talk in hurtful terms. This allows you to be more flexible, and fosters a safe environment in which neither of you has to compete to be heard and understood.

"Some behaviors that get in the way of active listening are

- *Judging* — 'You've got a lot of nerve saying that!'

- *Analysing* — 'The reason you're depressed is that you just have too much time on your hands!'

- *Debating* — 'What you really mean is…'

- *Advising* — 'The best thing for you would be to put the kids in daycare.'

L. Concept: The Abusive Behavior Package

"Abusive, violent, and controlling behaviors are all part of a package. The same underlying beliefs that give you permission to give your partner the silent treatment, withhold child support, or take away the car keys are what ultimately make you believe you can, need to, or have permission to hit her, or worse. These behaviors all reflect your relationship to issues of control. You can't give up one of these behaviors in the long term without making a commitment to giving up all of them."

M. Concept: Victim and Victimizer

"Some important things to highlight from this discussion are that men who have been violent have eroded their partner's trust, which will be in a slow process of repair long after the violence has stopped. Long after a person has experienced an incident of violence, she will remember it, and is likely to have trouble trusting the person who victimized her. You should be aware of this in terms of your partner, who has been victimized by you.

"We've also talked about male defenses against pain. As boys, you learned how to numb or deny your pain. As an adult, this can leave you desensitized to the pain you inflict on others. As men, you're not supposed to experience yourselves as victims: you've learned to master your pain by identifying with the abuser — becoming the one who abuses.

"You also need to look at the effect on your children. By becoming aware of how you have been hurt and are hurting, and of the patterns of violence you learned as children, you can stop these violent behaviors from being passed down to your children."

N. Concept: Family of Origin

"We are going to look at your relationships with our parents from the standpoint of how they affected your current understanding of violence, power, and control. If you look at the board, you see what I have written."

My name is _____

My son's name is _____

Things I like are _____

Things I don't like are _____

Something I believe strongly in is _____

What I think and feel about my son is _____

What I think he thinks and feels about me is _____

What I want him to know about being a man is _____

What I want him to know about women is _____

I discipline him when_____

The way I discipline him is_____

What I've wanted to say, but have never said to him, is _____

"What we're going to do in this session is have each member, in turn, speak in his father's voice, introducing himself by his father's name (or that of your nearest male relative or father-equivalent), filling in the blanks as your father would have when you were between the ages of 12 and 17."

"When all the members of the group have done the exercise, we will run through it again, this time speaking as your mothers might have done."

O. Concept: Dependency and Isolation

"Who did you turn to when you needed emotional support as a child? Who soothed you when you had a skinned knee? Most likely, a lot of you will identify your mother as this person, or will describe a special relationship with another female relative. Whom do you turn to now for emotional support? Many of you have few if any other people to turn to besides your partner. If you can name other friends, what kinds of things can you talk with them about? Can you, for example, talk about your violence problem? Can you talk about deep insecurities? In most cases, the answer will be 'No.'

"Let's look at how dependent this makes you, and at the problem it poses. A basic human need, whether acknowledged or not, is the need to be heard and understood with respect to your feelings. For many of you, your partner is the only person with whom you have developed a relationship in which your feelings are acknowledged. When your partner, for whatever reason, isn't able to take care of that need, you feel disappointed and frightened; and, perhaps unconsciously, you mobilize some controlling or manipulative behavior in reaction. Your partner may respond by gratifying you; but at least some of the time, she doesn't or can't or won't. Your partner may, in fact, be overwhelmed by your needs or repelled by your controlling or manipulative behavior.

"As this happens, your fears increase, and you escalate your attempts to control. You become jealous if your partner turns her attention to anyone else; you may express that directly, or may continue to escalate your controlling behavior.

"The bottom line is that these needs are just too much for one person to satisfy. It is too much to expect from your partner; but where does this leave you?

"Let's talk about this further. How can you become less isolated? How can you spread this dependency around? Whom else can you build relationships with? It's easy to respond by saying that you could form more open relationships with other men — even men in this group, but it's also important to challenge yourself to consider what kinds of thoughts would get in the way of such relationships. What prevents men from being close to one another?"

P. Concept: The Package — Homophobia, Racism, and Sexism

"In this exercise, we are going to work on building some appreciation of how homophobia, racism, and sexism are inseparable and oppress us all. This is a huge topic, and could lend itself to a well-spent, long term of study; we're just going to get a small start.

"In the exercise on male socialization, you learned that the ways in which we rigidly cling to and enforce oppressive gender roles ultimately oppresses all of us. Now we're going to look at oppression more broadly by understanding how homophobia, racism, and sexism are part of one package, inseparable because of their common roots in fear.

"People fear being 'less than' or being victimized. To prove that they are 'better than,' and immune to victimization, they oppress gay people, women, poor people, and people of other races. Some of you may claim not to be homophobic, racist, classist, or sexist; but all of us are stopped by some of these issues from establishing close relationships or trusting other people. The impulse is to protect yourself from identifying with these groups and, hence, subjecting yourself to the oppression that goes with being gay, nonwhite, poor, or female. Denying your prejudices prevents you from looking at them and working to free yourself from them; and also prevents other people from trusting you. Acknowledging your fears, and listening to gay people's experiences of homophobia, women's experiences of sexism, and other people's experiences of racism, is a way to learn and change.

Homophobia

"Homophobia is the fear of homosexuality, and also reflects a fear of being gay or being perceived as gay. Each of us, even the most stereotypically masculine male (maybe especially the most stereotypically masculine), has feared the consequences of acting outside the prescribed male gender role. Because of this fear, and because we have few accepted outlets for the display of love and affection between heterosexual men in our culture, people oppress gay men (and gay women, too). Sometimes the oppression takes the relatively subtle form of creating stereotypes in your mind about what gay people are like, so that you can easily differentiate yourself from someone who is gay. This can take the form of such unconscious thought as, 'Since I don't lisp and like opera, I'm not subject to the kind of treatment gay men get.' Sometimes the oppression is less subtle, and includes such things as employment and housing discrimination, harassment, and physical abuse. And this oppression doesn't affect just gays: it stops us all from having close relationships with members of the same sex, because we fear being gay or being perceived as gay. It locks us in the male gender role through fear that nonmacho behavior will leave any man subject to oppression. By isolating you and increasing your dependency on your partner, it also makes you more prone to violence.

"Think of a time when you were with a best buddy or a loved male family member and felt affectionate toward him. How did you express your affection? How did he respond? What stopped you both from being more expressive? What stopped you at that point is homophobia. It is important that we look at this and how it affects our lives and relationships."

Racism

"Racism is another way in which people attempt to feel different and better than other people and to protect themselves from the oppression those people experience.

"Systematic mistreatment of people of color generates misinformation and ignorance that ultimately sanction racist attitudes, beliefs, and assumptions. These, in turn, become the justification for further mistreatment. It is a vicious cycle.

"There is much to be learned when people are willing, and feel safe enough, to share some of their experiences of racism and its effects. There are some ground rules that help people feel safer about this: for instance, when someone says your behavior is racist, listen — don't argue with them. What other ideas do you have about how to foster communication about racism and prejudice?"

Sexism

"When you believe that your sex is superior to the other one, you are being sexist. The term sexism also refers to the oppression that follows such beliefs.

"At this point, I want to take a minute to acknowledge that this is hard work talking about and looking at issues of sexism, homophobia, and racism. Let's consider how sexism is similar to racism and homophobia, as well as the ways in which it is different.

"In its roots, sexism is conceptually very similar to racism and homophobia, but the stereotypes that accompany sexism may be different. There is also less perspective on this topic in a domestic violence group, since there are no women here. Sexism is also the oldest prejudice, as it has been around since the days of Adam and Eve [or, if you prefer: "since the first men and women roamed the earth."].

"What are some stereotypes you know about that are applied to women? What 'rules of sexism' are used to oppress women? Some examples might include the following:

- All women want to get married and have children; women who don't want children are unnatural.

- A woman should put her husband's and children's needs before her own.

- Women should doubt their own thinking when a man asserts what he believes to be true.

- Feminine women do not act powerful.

- Women do nothing of lasting value: their work disappears.

- Women are weak, confused, and hysterical.

- All women secretly want to be overpowered by a man.

"How have stereotypes affected your attitudes about important women in your life? How have stereotypes affected your behavior toward women?"

Closing Thoughts

"You don't have to be straight to be homophobic — some gays also use stereotypes of out-of-gender role behavior to feel different from 'butch dykes' or 'queers' to make themselves immune to anti-gay violence or discrimination. You don't have to be white to be racist, middle or upper class to be classist, or male to be sexist.

"Also, things don't divide up so evenly along racial or sexual lines of orientation. Many of us are racially mixed, and many more of us than we might realize fall somewhere other than completely heterosexual on the Kinsey scale. Some of us now live in a different class than the one into which we were born. This causes conflicts about racism, sexism, class identity, and homophobia within each of us, as well as in society."

Q. Concept: Sex

"What attitudes prevail about women and sex? Women may be forced into a rigid role in which they are treated as a 'whore' or a frigid madonna or snow queen. Some women feel pressured to pretend that they don't crave sex or, in order to gratify their partner, that they're enjoying it when they're not. Many women fear that they will be thought unfeminine or overly aggressive if they take the initiative in sexual encounters or communicate their sexual preferences to their partner. Yet these same women may feel that it is their duty to supply sex on demand for their partner, and fear the criticism or withdrawal of affection that may accompany a refusal. Do you think that these conditions get in the way of women enjoying sex? Given the effect on them, how does it affect your enjoyment of sex?

"What are the conditions that apply for men during sex? Where did you learn the 'rules' about what is and isn't acceptable sexual practice? Why do we continue to enforce and live by these rules? Can you imagine sex being improved by not adhering to them? What is it like to live with the requirements of always being strong, always ready for sex, always taking the initiative, and having permission to always get what you want?"

Main Interventions

Domestic violence offender program counseling does not lend itself to a weekly formula, since self-reporting and the group's response of supportive confrontation is such an important aspect of the treatment. The group facilitators continuously strive to strike a balance between making space for productive group process and problem solving about reported incidents and presenting the needed didactic and structured experiences.

Certain exercises do take precedence, and some naturally follow from others. For example, the time-out exercise comes at the beginning of the program, and is naturally followed by "Recognition of Warning Signs," which answers the question, "When do I take a time-out?" Some lectures or exercises, however, are best presented when they correspond to an identifiable theme in the presentation of one or more group members. The "Cycle of Violence," for example, is most useful when one or more members are saying that they have nothing to worry about because they are getting along well with their partners.

Self-reporting is part of the session every week. In some weeks, because of the amount of time needed to process the reports of group members, there will be inadequate time to cover even one skill or concept fully. In other weeks, there will be ample time to cover two concepts or skills, in addition to leaving some time for open process.

Different exercises, discussions, and lectures have a different emotional impact on the group; this needs to be taken into consideration as well. In the beginning sessions, when clients are reporting the incidents that brought them into the group and are being held responsible, the mood can be serious and depressed. After a few weeks, when the group is becoming more united and the men are enjoying the group and each other, a discussion such as "Types of Abuse" can bring back a more serious mood again. In each group, it is ideal to have time to process the feelings brought up by the exercises; but this is not always possible, since the priority is always to teach the skills that will stop violent behavior.

Because each session will vary depending on the business at hand, the week-by-week schedule below is only an example: many variations of this schedule are possible within a 24-week format.

Week 1

Check-in

See Starting the Group.

A. Skill: Self-Reporting

Intervention 1: Didactic Presentation (See Concepts and Skills section)

Intervention 2: Discussion

Members are prompted to be very specific in their descriptions of their own behavior. Use very concrete questions, such as, "You say that you hit her. What were you feeling just before you did that? Which hand did you hit your partner with? Was it open or closed? What did your partner's face look like? Where were the children? What were you doing with your other hand? Were you wearing that ring? How are you feeling right now?" Attempts to deflect or talk about the partner's behavior are confronted: "It's hard for you to focus on your behavior; but your partner isn't here, and we are interested in talking about is you, how you felt and feel, and what you might do differently in the future."

The group's reactions are important. One common defense mechanism among group members is to cultivate safety by creating distance from the experience of other group members. That is, while some members may say that they relate to another member's story, others may want to focus on differences, especially ways in which the other member is "worse." This is important to interpret.

> *Example*
>
> Facilitator: Who will begin by telling us about the incident that brought you here?
> Joe: Sure, I'll go.
> Facilitator: Thanks Joe. What I'd like you to do is tell me as specifically as possible about the incident, focusing on what you were feeling and doing before the incident, what you actually did, what you felt during the incident, how and why you stopped, how you felt afterward, and what the consequences were. We'll be helping you to stay focused.

Joe:	Okay, right. Well, first, you've got to understand about my wife. See, she's always hurting herself and...
Facilitator:	(interrupting) Okay, Joe. Here's one way I'll need to help you focus: We're not going to be talking or understanding about your wife. This is about you, your feelings, and your behavior. If you'd like to tell us about what you were feeling before the incident, we'd like to hear that.
Joe:	Hmmm. Okay, well, I just don't want to seem like such a bad guy... So anyway, we were arguing about something, she was all in my face and I told her to leave — I just said, "Get out of here." So she just kept on and I could feel myself getting pissed.
Facilitator:	How did you know you were getting pissed?
Joe:	I can always feel the tension in my face.
Facilitator:	Good, that's an important warning sign for you. So you could feel yourself getting pissed, then what happened?
Joe:	Well, my hand just flew out and hit her. I don't know what happened, but I didn't hit her very hard, and the next thing I knew, she's flying across the room, slamming into the wall. I think she has hollow bones or something. [There's laughter from the group.]
Facilitator:	Joe, I'm going to have to help you some more here. First of all, your hand didn't just fly out and hit her. Who's in control of your hands?
Joe:	Well, I am of course, but...
Facilitator:	(again interrupting) Good. I'll invite you to stop there, and take responsibility for what happened. What happened is that you hit her, and you need to say that and acknowledge your responsibility for it.
Joe:	Well, I...
Facilitator:	Joe, did you hit her or not?
Joe:	Yes, I hit her.
Facilitator:	Good. You just took partial responsibility, and that's an important step. Now, I want to help you go the rest of the way. You hit her, and you blame her for flying against the wall. Do you really think she has hollow bones?
Joe:	No, I know she doesn't.
Facilitator:	I know that you know. Why did she fly across the room and hit the wall?
Joe:	Because I hit her that hard.
Facilitator:	Good. Thanks Joe. Then what happened?
Joe:	Nothing much. The little idiot called the police, they came and arrested me, cost me $300 plus what this program costs.
Facilitator:	Again, Joe, I'm going to apply the rules here. We're not going to be trashing our partners here. You may be mad at her for calling the police, but we're not going to collude with you abusing her in here by referring to her as the "little idiot." And I'd add that she didn't cost you $300 — that's just a way of deflecting. You cost yourself $300, plus a lot more. Whatever she is, whatever she does, you're responsible for your behavior, and for the consequences. We're going to tell the truth about that in here.

The discussion continues in this admittedly painstaking way until Joe has reached the end of his report. The facilitator then asks Joe what it was like for him to tell the story, and how he is feeling now. Then group members can give Joe feedback about how it was for them to hear it, sticking as closely as possible to their emotional experience.

Note: Due to the critical group-formative nature of this initial exercise, only men who are present at this first group should be allowed to attend the rest of the groups in the cycle. Men who miss the first week should be asked to enroll in a future cycle.

If there's time, add the material below.

B. Skill: Time-out

Intervention 1: Didactic Presentation (See Concepts and Skills section)

Intervention 2: Discussion

When the time-out is presented, men invariably have reasons why it would not work for them, or why they wouldn't want to do it. These reasons that surface are the very entrenched ideas these men have about their rights and needs for power and control.

The facilitator should ask the men to practice saying the words to the time-out during the session, and afterward should ask them to specify when they should have taken the time-out. By trouble-shooting in advance, it is possible to iron out any problems that might come up when taking a real time-out.

The times when men initially say that they would take a time-out are typically too late. Tell them that the key operative in the time-out phrase, "I'm beginning to feel angry," is "beginning." Especially at the beginning of a domestic violence offenders' program, clients need to play it very safe, taking time-outs when the danger level is low. The time to take a time-out is not the second before a man hits his partner, but when he first notices his muscles tightening or his voice rising.

Explore with the group whether members believe that the time-out could work for them. It's common for men to react as if they're being asked to back down from a fight. Taking a time-out may feel like backing down. Men's presented reactions can vary from "I wouldn't go out in the rain" to "It's my house, she should leave" to "But what if she says something that really gets my goat as I'm going out the door?" What is underlying all such reactions is the fact that the time-out forces men to let go of the power struggle, at least temporarily letting the partner win. It's important in your discussion to raise this phenomenon to a conscious level and get members' commitments to practicing the time-out anyway.

The time-out is reviewed in some form nearly every week, either as part of a didactic presentation or during the discussion of self-reported incidents.

Check-out

See Group Process section.

Week 2

Check-in

Review Time-out

Intervention 2: Discussion

Explore how and whether group members successfully used the time-out or practiced it with their partners

Check-out

Week 3

Check-in
C. Skill: Recognition of Warning Signs

Intervention 3: Guided Visualization (See Concepts and Skills section)

Intervention 2: Discussion

Group members report on what they noticed, and their warning signs are written on the board or flip chart in categories. Use the examples below if group members are having trouble getting started:

Sensory

Tension in arms, shoulders, chest
Heat sensations or chills
Seeing red
Ringing in ears
Faster heartbeat and breathing
Shallow breathing

Thoughts

Specific words ("You bitch," "shit")
"This is not fair."
"Somebody's gotta do something."
"I'll fix you."

Actions

Pacing
Stalking
Being in partner's personal space
Shouting
Being very quiet

Individuals in the group will relate to the warning signs of the other men. As a group, they will come up with many more than if they had done this exercise individually. When the exercise is completed and all the warning signs are noted, the men should be encouraged to write down those that are most important to them and to keep these for reference.

It's important to take time to process the feelings brought up by this exercise, as it takes men back to their original incident, stimulating fear, shame, and guilt. By this time in their therapy, the men have had time to rally their defenses, distancing themselves from the incident, telling themselves that they are getting help and that things are better now. This exercise — appropriately — debunks that notion.

Occasionally, a man may report a lapse in memory or consciousness during an incident of abuse. For example, at one moment he was arguing at the top of the stairs, and the next thing he knew, his partner was on the floor on the landing below with a broken arm: the man doesn't remember what happened in between.

Such cases are sometimes difficult to assess. It's possible that the man indeed experienced dissociation or has a multiple personality. This is the case more often than many clinicians realize, since many offenders were victims of serious abuse as children. The lapse may also be a function of the man's denial — or may be an outright lie.

In any case, identifying the warning signs that precede a "blackout" will be helpful to someone who has experienced such incidents in order to avert them in the future.

Review Time-out

Intervention 2: Discussion

Review the concept of a time-out. Explore what, if anything, is getting in the way of practicing time-outs.

Check-out

Week 4

Check-in

D. Concept: Cycle of Violence

Intervention 1: Didactic Presentation (See Concepts and Skills section)
Intervention 2: Discussion

Have members identify their particular behaviors that correspond to the different points of the cycle.

Check-out

Week 5

Check-in

E. Concept: Emotional Funnel

Intervention 1: Didactic Presentation (See Concepts and Skills section)
Intervention 2: Discussion

Check-out

Week 6

Check-in

F. Skill: Three-Breath Technique

This technique is best taught when a man in the group has been asked how he feels or how he felt when something happened, and is unable to identify his feelings. The facilitator then describes the three-breath technique and asks the man to try it.

Intervention 1: Didactic Presentation (See Concepts and Skills section)
Intervention 3: Guided Visualization
Intervention 2: Discussion

G. Skill: Feeling Statement

Intervention 1: Didactic Presentation (See Concepts and Skills section)
Intervention 2: Discussion

The facilitator should encourage the expression of feelings in the group. For many men, the difficulty isn't merely one of learning to give expression to feelings, but goes much deeper, involving a lack of training in even recognizing a feeling when it comes up. Before men can express their feelings, they must learn to acknowledge and experience them. Explore these difficulties with the group.

Check-out

Week 7

Check-in

H. Skill: Goal Setting

Intervention 1: Didactic Presentation (See Concepts and Skills section)
Intervention 2: Discussion

The group is divided into dyads, and one copy of the handout is passed out to each member (see Concepts and Skills section). Each dyad establishes and writes two goals (on the form) for each member. While the group is working, the facilitators should check in with each dyad, giving assistance when needed.

When the dyads are finished, each man reads at least one of his goals aloud to the group (some members may want to set some private goals). This provides group members with some alternative suggestions for goals, and establishes a basis for supporting each other by checking in about their progress.

Review Time-out

Intervention 2: Discussion

Explore what, if anything, is getting in the way of using time-outs and taking practice time-outs.

Check-out

Week 8

Check-in

I. Concept: Responsibility

Intervention 1: Didactic Presentation (See Concepts and Skills section)
Intervention 2: Discussion

The presentation and discussion of this concept works best when it is raised in the context of a man's avoiding responsibility as he reports an incident. The more group members can participate in this intervention, the better. Part of what you hope to accomplish if you're doing your best work is to teach men to organize a social system — for which the group serves as a laboratory — to confront abuse in a way that supportively holds men accountable for their behavior. That is, men in the group are at once creating a tool — the group culture or environment — and a result. This means that they both assume greater ownership in the concept and learn how to create relationships, institutions, and a society in which abuse is no longer the norm.

This concept can be referred to throughout the course of the group by the facilitator — or preferably by group members — any time a man is avoiding responsibility.

Check-out

Week 9

Check-in

Review Feeling Statement

Intervention 2: Discussion

Ask group members to discuss their understanding of the use of the feeling statement.

Intervention 4: Role-Play

Use a group member's reported incident to practice using feeling statements.

Intervention 5: Moderated Group Process

Use moderated group process to practice using the feeling statement with current feelings in the group.

J. Concept: Gender Roles and Male Socialization

Intervention 1: Didactic Presentation (See Concepts and Skills section)

Intervention 2: Discussion

Men like answering the questions about what men are supposed to be like. The object of this exercise is not to demean men — so it is fine if there are some positive qualities on this list, too.

In an articulate, verbal group, after making the list of positive human qualities, the facilitator can simply ask what the men notice about these two lists. If, in the facilitator's judgment, the men wouldn't be able to respond, or if the group doesn't come up with a complete list, the facilitator can continue with the didactic material.

Check-out

Week 10

Check-in
Review Goal Setting

Intervention 2: Discussion

Review by having group members check in with each other about their progress in working toward their chosen goals. This can be done by the group as a whole, or in dyads.

Review Time-out

Intervention 2: Discussion

Again, it is important to check in about actual time-outs and practice ones, identifying and confronting resistance and problems.

Check-out

Week 11

Check-in
K. Skill: Empathic Listening

Intervention 1: Didactic Presentation (See Concepts and Skills section)

Intervention 2: Discussion

Have a group member describe how empathic listening might have worked for him during an incident.

Intervention 4: Role-Play

Next, set up a role-play in which two group members have a disagreement. One is the speaker, and the other is the listener. The speaker begins by making a provocative statement about the disagreement, and the listener, coached by the facilitator, only uses active listening skills. This is a good skill to present when there is a real disagreement in the group.

L. Concept: The Abusive Behavior Package

Intervention 1: Didactic Presentation (See Concepts and Skills section)

Intervention 2: Discussion

The purpose of this exercise is to expand the definition of abuse to include all behavior that has the effect of controlling or hurting someone else; or behavior that has this intention.

Start the discussion by asking that clients report on the kinds of abuse that they have perpetrated or by which they've been victimized. Then write the following column headings on the board or flip chart: Physical, Emotional, Verbal, and Financial. As the men mention instances of abuse, the facilitator writes them under the appropriate column (some instances may fit under more than one category).

The important thing is to get as large a list as possible. Discuss the men's feelings about contemplating so many types of abusive behavior.

Check-out

Week 12

Check-in

M. Concept: Victim and Victimizer

Intervention 2: Discussion

The facilitator divides the group into dyads, and instructs them to take turns discussing a time or incident in which each man was a victim of violence. The speaker is to stick to this topic, describing exactly what happened and what it was like; and the listener is to participate only by asking questions that will clarify what happened and what the speaker's emotional experience was.

This discussion should be given about five to ten minutes. The facilitators should move between dyads, helping and coaching as needed. After the allotted time is up, the roles within dyads should switch. When all the men have had a chance to do this exercise, they should be given another topic to discuss: they can tell about an incident from the same period when they themselves were violent.

After group members have had a chance to discuss this topic, the group should be reconstituted as a whole. A more open conversation should be initiated around what the exercise was like emotionally, what the men learned about their violence and its roots, and what the consequences of violence are.

Intervention 1: Didactic Presentation (See Concepts and Skills section)

Check-out

Week 13

Check-in

N. Concept: Family of Origin

Intervention 1: Didactic Presentation (See Concepts and Skills section)

Intervention 2: Discussion

Note: This may require more than one week. Group members gain more insight into the roots of their violence and the origins of their assumptions about power and control. This exercise is, of necessity, somewhat superficial — men, particularly if they have never been in therapy before, have a lot to say on this subject. However, the exercise can still be powerful by stimulating the curiosity of group members about how they continue to be affected by their upbringing. In addition, this can be a healing way to experience anger and forgiveness, concluding with empathy for their parents.

After the final speaker answers the last question, the facilitator asks him to speak in his own voice again, specifically to talk for a minute about what the exercise was like for him, and what he learned about his current relationship to power, control, and violence.

Check-out

Week 14

Check-in

O. Concept: Dependency and Isolation

Intervention 1: Didactic Presentation (See Concepts and Skills section)

Intervention 2: Discussion

Ask the group to discuss their reactions to the didactic material, and how they could respond to the problem.

Review Time-out

Intervention 2: Discussion

Again, discuss resistance to, and problems with, taking real and practice time-outs.

Check-out

Week 15

Check-in

P. Concept: The package — Homophobia, Racism, and Sexism

Intervention 1: Didactic Presentation (See Concepts and Skills section)

Intervention 2: Discussion

Discuss each of the three issues below separately, following the relevant didactic presentation.

1. Have the men discuss how homophobia may have gotten in the way of their relationships with other men.

2. Many domestic violence offenders' groups are multiracial. The balance of the group will depend on a number of social factors, including police response to domestic violence in the various cultural communities in your area, what services are available, and whether the court racially discriminates in terms of who gets diversion programs versus jail terms.

Dealing with racism directly in the group makes it safer for everyone, and is especially important when the group is led by Caucasian facilitators. Racism should always be dealt with — both as part of this exercise and whenever it crops up in the group process.

The facilitator might open the discussion by drawing on the board the diagram on the next page and asking for the men's reactions.

3. Next ask if men feel safe enough to share more of their feelings of anger, fear, or isolation in the group; ask what would make the group safer. There should be consensus about safety before proceeding. It's important that men not be railroaded into saying that they feel safe enough if they really don't.

When agreement is reached, some questions for discussion include:

- How have you been hurt by racism?

- What stereotypes about your race make it hard for you to believe that you can stop acting violently?

- From where and whom did you learn about racism?

- What fears and beliefs did those people have?

- What fears and attitudes have kept you from getting closer to people of your own or other races?

- What have you noticed about your own or other men's racism in this group?

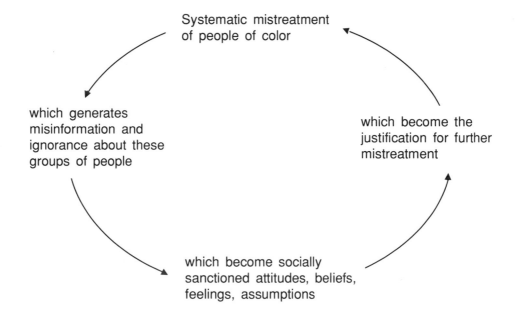

Intervention 4: Role-Play

After the initial didactic presentation on sexism, set up a role-play in groups of three clients: one group member plays the part of a husband confronting his wife about not having dinner ready for him. The other client plays the wife, and must follow the rules described in the didactic section. Another group member plays the woman's conscience, chastising her when she fails to follow the socially imposed rules for female behavior.

After the role-play, the men should discuss what feelings the wife and husband had, and what they sacrificed through rigid adherence to the rules.

At this point, the facilitator should ask the group how men and women learn these rules, and why they keep following and enforcing them. "What attitudes do we have and what behaviors do we practice that reinforce sexism?"

Check-out

Week 16

Check-in
Review Goal Setting

Intervention 2: Discussion

Have group members check in with each other about their progress in working toward their chosen goals. This can be done by the group as a whole or in dyads.

Review Feeling Statement

Intervention 2: Discussion

Have a group member or group members review the concept of the feeling statement, including how and why to use it.

Intervention 5: Moderated Group Process

Process feelings in the room by coaching members in using the feeling statement.

Check-out

Week 17

Check-in
Review Time-out

Intervention 2: Discussion

Any remaining blocks to taking the time-out should be discussed at this point. If members are still having a problem with this, they should be confronted directly.

Review Feeling Statement

Intervention 2: Discussion

Review the feeling statement, and discuss incidents where it could have been, or was, used.

Check-out

Week 18

Check-in
Q. Concept: Sex

Intervention 1: Didactic Presentation (See Concepts and Skills section)
Intervention 3: Role-Play

Select a group of four clients: one client plays the man, a second plays his partner, and the third and fourth, respectively, speak for traditional male and female expectations about acceptable sexual practice. Interrupting to keep the dialogue on target, have the female partner express her sexual needs or preferences or take the initiative prior to a sexual encounter. The clients representing expectations should react to what she's said. Then the male partner responds, in effect taking sides either with the woman or with traditional expectations. This exercise allows clients to recognize that they have a choice when it comes to their attitudes about acceptable sexual practice; that there is a whole range of possible responses. When the argument is talked out, have the male and female partners switch roles. Repeat with another group of four if time allows.

Check-out

Week 19

Check-in

Review Empathic Listening

Intervention 2: Discussion
Review the skill of empathic listening by having a group member explain how it works, and how he has used it. Instruct other group members to give him feedback.

Intervention 5: Moderated Group Process
Coach group members in using empathic listening as a way of hearing each other's expressions of their feelings.

Check-out

Week 20

Check-in

Review

Write all concepts and skills headings on the board. Group members have the opportunity to ask for clarification of any items.

Check-out

Week 21

Check-in

Review

Self- and peer review: group members review how they have changed individually, and how the group has changed over the past 20 weeks. This is an opportunity to discuss any feelings about these changes. The facilitators should keep the discussion focused on feelings and specific behavior changes on the part of the men. For example, it's fine to talk about the disappointment associated with the fact that their partners may not have changed, but it's unproductive to spend a lot of time talking in detail about what things about the partner or the relationship have not changed.

Example

Jose:	Well, for me, this group has been just great. I've learned some great new tools to be intimate, but I can't use them all because Bill just isn't that interested in talking. Yesterday, I fired off a couple of good feeling statements and he just looked up from the carburetor he was cleaning and said, "So? What kind of a reply do you want from me?" I think he should come to this group now?
Facilitator:	Sounds like you're disappointed about the limitations of this work.
Jose:	No, I think it's been great, but he has to change now.
Maurice:	Sorry, but we've observed that our partners don't have to change.
Jose:	I know, I know. Yeah, I guess I am disappointed.
Facilitator:	Sounds like you've been doing some good work yourself in your relationship, though. Would you like to say any more about your disappointment?
Jose:	Well, I would, but I don't know what to say. I guess I'm disappointed because when we were up against my limitations in the relationship, I came here. Now we're up against his, and we're stuck.
Facilitator:	You're stuck?
Jose:	Yeah. Like we can't go any further.
Max:	I know what he's talking about. It's like we got a taste in here of what closeness can be like, and now we have to go back to our partners every night where there isn't the same level of closeness as in here. It's sad.
Facilitator:	This is a big change we're noticing about you, Max. You're sad instead of angry.
Max:	Great. Thanks a lot.
Facilitator:	It doesn't seem like such a great trade-off to you?
Max:	As a matter of fact, no.
Facilitator:	Sounds like you're mad at me... Can you say more?
Max:	No, I'm not mad at you. It's just... I don't know. [pause]
Maurice:	Maybe I can help. This is scary, too. Maybe I have to leave my partner to get the kind of closeness I want.
Jose:	Yes! That's right. It's scary alright. Here is this person who I've idolized and abused in the same week, who has put up with me for five years, and now I'm wondering if I still want to be with him.
Facilitator:	Max, is that what was up for you, too?
Max:	Yeah. I think so.
Facilitator:	So, although we see some changes we feel proud of and happy about, there is a sad, scary side to those changes, too. How about some things that we haven't changed that we still need to?

Check-out

Week 22

Check-in

Review Goal Setting

Intervention 2: Discussion

Revisit goals by having group members check in with each other about their progress in working toward their chosen goals; have them set and commit to new goals to achieve after they leave the group. Staying free of violence is a life-long process, and clients will have to continue practicing some interventions for the rest of their lives. Explore their feelings about this. Some men might be encouraged to make reenrollment a goal; others might be ready for individual therapy or some other type of group therapy. Some may prefer to commit to doing practice time-outs. Unlike the earlier goal-setting exercise, this one is more effective if done by the group as a whole.

Check-out

Week 23

Check-in

Review Empathic Listening

Review Feeling Statement

Intervention 5: Moderated Open Process

Reinforce skills and process termination by focusing communication using these two techniques. Discuss clients' feelings about leaving the group and each other.

Check-out

Week 24

Check-in

Review Empathic Listening

Review Feeling Statement

Intervention 5: Moderated Open Process

In this session, the facilitator adds that before the end of the group, clients must offer each other individual expressions of appreciation, preferably something a client will miss about that individual.

Check-out

Criteria for Measuring Change

Unfortunately, no one can predict with absolute certainty whether or not a batterer will re-offend. What is most important is that clients and partners understand clearly that a "cure" for battering is not available. With this in mind, let us look at some ways in which facilitators can assess the likelihood of change for individuals in the group.

One way that change can be assessed is through the use of measurable criteria for program completion. Basic criteria should include a demonstrated knowledge of the skills and concepts taught in the group, group participation, and a cessation of the violent behavior. In assessing the men for these criteria, it's generally true that the more concrete and quantifiable the means of assessment, the more accurate will be the results. For example, if you want to verify a man's willingness to practice time-outs, you would be better served by having him phone in two practice time-outs per week to a phone machine in your office, rather than relying on his self-report of weekly practice.

Another helpful tool for assessing change is the "partner contract." The facilitator can get a very clear picture of a man's progress in stopping his abusive behavior by talking to the partner, after obtaining a signed release of information from the client. Batterers do not exist in a void. The absent victims deserve support, education, and protection while their partners are in treatment, and their voices need to be heard. An unfortunate reality is that a man may come to group from week to week reporting great success and transformation while continuing his battering behavior behind closed doors. Facilitators need a complete picture of the abuse in order to provide the best treatment possible for their clients.

While re-offenses are disheartening for client and facilitator alike, it is important to keep in mind the larger picture, that, in fact, batterers' groups help reduce the violence visited by men on their partners. Facilitators are increasingly supported in their work by a legal system, which has begun holding men accountable for their violent behavior. The most effective tools to ensure high success rates with clients are a well-constructed program and an open flow of information between all parties involved, including partners and, in the case of court-referred clients, probation officers.

Problems Specific to the Group

Working with this population raises problems for facilitators that should be examined closely before undertaking this work. Motivation is always an issue for batterers. Clients who are in treatment under court-mandate or who are participating as a last resort to save a failing relationship may be in denial about their problem. These clients are generally more interested in their goal (not going to jail, not losing their wife) than in owning and changing their violent behavior. They can be a drain on a group's energy, as the facilitators continually confront those clients' blaming, denial, and accompanying anger. One way in which these clients can deal with such issues before entering group treatment is through short-term individual counseling. In these sessions, men can be given an opportunity to vent their rage and frustration and to own responsibility for their violence. This counseling can continue until you feel that the client is ready to participate in a group.

Transference and counter-transference present special problems with this client population. Potential group leaders should realize that they will be dealing with high levels of rage that will test their capacity for empathy and caring. Some facilitators will find the things these men have done to be so abhorrent that they don't seem deserving of caring and forgiveness. If a facilitator has unresolved personal issues with abuse and violence, it will probably be difficult for him to work with these men.

These clients are used to controlling and asserting power through force. You, as facilitator, will be challenged to set limits for, and to confront, men who may never have been confronted before. The ability to keep your own feelings in check and not get "hooked" by the client's inevitable attempts to control and manipulate you are essential qualities for doing this work.

Clients may see you as part of the system; and they may feel that you are invading their private space, namely the realm of their family. They may feel that you are challenging their authority to lord over these families as men have for centuries. The fact is, you will be doing these things and, as a result, you may not be seen as the loving, caring professional you know yourself to be. You will need to ask yourself whether you can be comfortable with such clients before entering this exhausting, exacting, and exciting work.

Relapse Prevention

As stated earlier in this chapter, there are no "cures" for abusive behavior. It's important to convey to both client and partner that any decisions made about their future relationship should be made with this fact in mind. However, men who do re-offend should be encouraged to seek treatment; remind men in the final weeks of group therapy that changing violent or abusive behavior is a lifelong commitment that requires continuous work.

Resistance

Male domestic violence offenders are resistant to changing a status quo that gives them power and control over their partners. Paradoxically, they may resist by denying their own behavior while looking down on other men who exhibit the same objective behaviors. Working with such resistance is the cornerstone of domestic violence work.

References

Adler, R., and Towne, N. *Looking Out, Looking In*. New York: Holt, Rinehart and Winston, 1987.

Caesar, P., and Hamberger, L.K. *Treating Men Who Batter*. New York: Springer Publishing Co., 1989.

Gondolf, E.W., and Russell, D.M. *Man to Man A Guide for Men in Abusive Relationships*. Bradenton, Florida: Human Services Institute, 1987.

Hartnett, T. "Curriculum of Sixteen Week Ending Violence Group and Group Exercise Handbook" (Unpublished), 1988.

Holzman, L., and Polk, H. "Introduction." In *History is the Cure*. New York: Practice Press, 1985.

Sonkin, D.J., Del Martin, L., and Walker, E.D. *The Male Batterer: A Treatment Approach*. New York: Springer Publishing Co., 1985.

Sonkin, D.J., and Durphy, M. *Learning to Live Without Violence*. San Francisco: Volcano Press, 1982.

Yalom, I.D. *The Theory and Practice of Group Psychotherapy.* New York: Basic Books, 1985.

Chapter 13

Beginning Group Therapy With Addicted Populations

Peter D. Rogers, Ph.D.

Introduction

The succinct term, addicts, will be used throughout this chapter to describe all persons with chemical dependency problems, regardless of their drug of choice. *Alcohol* is considered a drug just like heroin, cocaine, or marijuana. All addicts in recovery are faced with a variety of problems. This chapter will describe how to go about the difficult business of helping this most challenging population begin the process of recovery.

The initial stage of recovery frequently requires a medically supervised detoxification process, a safe way of "coming down" or "off" the addict's drug of choice. The cessation of drug or alcohol use is an *event*. While this may be a dramatic or traumatic event, it is only the beginning of the actual recovery *process*. Group psychotherapy is the treatment of choice for addicts. A group has the ability to provide support, structure, and reinforcement for abstinence. One-on-one therapy, while often a useful adjunct, does not provide the therapeutic impact of a savvy peer group. No single person can match the power of a group of addicts confronting the denial system of another newly recovering addict; and *denial* is the main component of what Alcoholics Anonymous (A.A.) calls the disease of addiction.

Group therapy for addicted people must provide more than simply a place to *process* (Yalom, 1985). For addicts, process, like love, is never enough. What *is* required is a unique blend of skill-building, problem solving, and support.

Twelve-Step Programs

In any discussion of substance abuse groups, it's essential to give serious consideration to Alcoholics Anonymous (A.A.), Narcotics Anonymous (N.A.), Cocaine Anonymous (C.A.), or similar 12-step meetings. In fact, it's probably a good idea for all group leaders dealing with substance abusers to attend a few 12-step meetings themselves.

A.A. began in 1935 with "Bill W." and "Dr. Bob, " two alcoholics who talked to each other instead of drinking. From this humble start, the contemporary self-help movement has grown to international proportions. Hundreds of thousands of 12-step meetings occur daily all over the world. No matter what the addiction — whether alcohol, narcotics, gambling, or even compulsive sexuality (S.L.A.A., or Sex and Love Addicts Anonymous), 12-step programs offer a well-trod road to recovery.

No one can match A.A. for availability. There's a meeting somewhere, literally 24 hours around the clock. This includes holidays such as Christmas and New Years, when 24-hour "alcathons" take place.

A.A. meetings, however, do not serve the crucial need for inducting the addict into the group therapy "frame of mind." For example, A.A. actively discourages "crosstalk," or feedback, which is an important therapeutic ingredient of group psychotherapy.

Many addicts have a problem with A.A.'s "higher power." Spirituality, in any form, is often not a comfortable realm for addicts, who may have been turned off by religious trainings at an early age. There is now a movement called the *Secular Organization for Sobriety* (S.O.S.) to fill this gap. S.O.S. provides 12-step group meetings in which no reference is made to a deity.

Many people have been helped by 12-step programs. These are the fortunate ones. Regular attendance at meetings greatly increases the addict's chances for recovery. Many others, who sadly comprise the majority, are made uncomfortable by such meetings and are unable to profit from this ubiquitous, low-cost form of group therapy. Nonetheless, *all* addicts should be strongly encouraged to try out several meetings before rejecting this extremely valuable form of help. Many group therapists do, in fact, routinely *require* members to attend A.A. meetings.

The Disease Model

A.A. is committed to the controversial concept of addiction as a *disease*. This means viewing alcoholism as a *physical illness* and not as a secondary sign or symptom of some underlying mental or emotional disorder. The disease model requires that you accept the idea that the chemically dependent person's metabolic and physiologic response to alcohol is entirely different from the rest of the population (often referred to as "Normies").

The major impact of the disease model is that it absolves the addict from personal responsibility for problematic behaviors. Alcoholics, for example, may come to see their drinking as the result of a physiological addiction. They are passive victims. Recovery involves accepting the fact, but responding actively by using increased vigilance and restraint to monitor and modify behavioral patterns.

There has been much heated discussion about this issue in the field of substance abuse. One thing is clear: as a *metaphor*, the disease model has a great deal of value. Using the disease metaphor, alcoholics are no longer seen as "weak-willed, morally bankrupt degenerates." Instead, they can now be viewed as people suffering from a treatable condition. Recovery is possible.

The Choice Model (an Alternative Point of View)

In recent years, a third approach has emerged as an alternative to the moral and disease models of addiction. From a social-learning perspective, addictive behaviors are seen as "bad habits." Habits can be analyzed and modified. The habituated person can learn to make new choices.

There is no argument about the fact that excessive indulgence in a habit can lead to disease "end-states." Cirrhosis of the liver in alcoholics, or lung cancer in smokers, is often the end result of addictive behavior. This does not mean, however, that the *behavior* is a disease, or that it is caused by an underlying *physiological* disorder.

An interesting example is provided by heavy smokers who continue to indulge their habit despite the irrefutable evidence of harmful consequences. There is also a high relapse rate among those who try to quit. This raises the question of whether the smoking habit itself qualifies as a disease.

The *choice model* circumvents the problem of blame. Individuals are not considered responsible for the development of the problem. Whether or not the addictive behavior is genetic or even environmentally based is considered irrelevant. Addicts are seen as people who can compensate for their problems by assuming responsibility for changing their behavior, even in the face of setbacks or relapses. Reverend Jesse Jackson summed it up best when he said, "You are not responsible for being down, but you are responsible for getting up." This is the basic idea to get across to the group in explaining this model: You have a choice.

Selection and Screening

If you have the opportunity to use selection and screening in filling your group, your work as its leader will be much easier. (Most therapists working in county agencies or HMOs are not afforded this luxury.)

There are a variety of options to consider before starting a group with an addicted population. By controlling the rules for inclusion in the group, you can significantly predetermine the therapeutic course and potential outcome. A group that is gender-restricted (such as a men's group) will address different issues than one that is mixed. Groups that are restricted to a single "drug of choice" (such as cocaine) will function differently than polydrug groups.

If possible, you should individually interview each applicant. Ideally, it's preferable to have clients who are personally motivated rather than court-referred, and who have a commitment to being clean and sober. Group therapy doesn't work as well if the client is participating only to save a marriage or a job. These factors may serve to motivate the client's enrollment in a group, but they are poor prognostic indicators.

Other factors to keep in mind when selecting for group membership are

- *Recidivism.* Consider the number of previous treatment attempts or failures.

- *Insight.* This refers to the client's understanding of the addiction process.

- *Type of addiction.* Alcoholics and cocaine abusers, for instance, don't usually make congenial groupmates. This is not simply due to the nature of the drugs (in this case, downers versus uppers) but because the concomitant lifestyles of the drug users are often quite different (alcohol is legal, cocaine is not).

The assumption in this chapter is that you are leading a group that includes both men and women, and group members who are using a variety of drugs. For the purposes of this chapter, I'm also assuming that participation of all group members is voluntary rather than court-mandated.

Time and Duration

Groups with addicted populations are usually held weekly for a period of an hour and a half. The ideal duration for a beginners' group is ten weeks. If you can safely guide your group over the rapids and shoals of this turbulent part of the recovery process, the odds for your clients' success are greatly increased.

Structure

Addicts are people who lead very unstructured lives. It is therefore crucial to provide a group setting that gives them the security of consistency. Under no circumstances should you change the meeting time or place. It's also essential to begin and end the meeting *on time*.

Begin each session with a check-in. This usually includes following up on the previous week's material. End each session with a homework assignment. You should encourage group members to do the homework, since this will solidify the recovery process. However, don't badger people who are slow to comply. Remember, this population is known for being rebellious and "deviant."

Ask group members to make a strong commitment to attend every session. Experience will teach you that, realistically, these groups always have some relapse and dropout problems. It is therefore acceptable to start the group with up to twelve members, knowing that you will end up with the ideal group size of eight to ten participants.

Using a co-therapist (preferably one of the opposite sex) can be very helpful. However, for economic reasons, this is rarely a viable option. The assumption in this chapter is that you will be working alone.

Goals

In the long run, the only acceptable goal for addicted populations is to be "clean and sober." In fact, each client is required to make this commitment to the group.

One short-range goal involves demonstrating the ability to use alternative coping skills. It's not enough to "just say no." Addicts need to learn to say "yes" to a variety of new coping skills if they are to have a chance of remaining clean and sober.

Another short-range goal is to avoid "slippery places and people." This refers to places where relapses (slips) might occur, and to people who are not supportive of sobriety.

Ground Rules

- **No alcohol or drug use**. The use of caffeine and nicotine, while not encouraged, is still allowed. The same approach is used in A.A.

- **No "war stories."** These may serve some purpose in providing a bonding experience, but are generally a waste of the group's time.

- **Confidentiality**. There is a high value placed on honesty and self-disclosure in these groups. Confidentiality is therefore a basic requirement. This is especially true where use of illegal substances, such as cocaine or heroin, is discussed freely.

  Nonetheless, it's important for you to warn the group about the conditions for mandatory reporting. For example, in cases of child abuse, confidentiality is not as important as the need to protect the child in question. Reporting, in such cases, is your legal obligation.

- **Commitment**. Group members are required to maintain regular attendance. There is some slack given, in the form of occasional excused absences for illness or unavoidable conflicting business. This means that the client must call prior to the meeting. "Unexcused" absences (when the client has failed to call beforehand) become topics for group discussion and confrontation.

- **Feedback**. Feedback is a valuable contribution from group members, but only *one person must speak at a time*. Clients are usually encouraged to spend more time listening than talking in the group.

Starting the Group

Since this is the first session, the check-in takes the form of an introduction. Begin by introducing yourself. Include any relevant experience, education, or background that qualifies you as the group leader. If you are in recovery yourself, this is a good time to make that fact known.

Next, go around the room. Ask group members to give their first name, drug of choice, and length of time they've been "clean and sober." This usually ranges from a couple of days to a couple of weeks — but don't be surprised if someone says, "a couple of hours." Everyone gets his or her turn: you must *provide the structure*. The group is already beginning to learn that this will be a safe environment, a place where everyone will be treated fairly.

This is the time to introduce the basic framework of the group, including the rules listed above. Leave plenty of time for questions and discussion. It's important that no ambiguity exists. Addicts are always looking for "loopholes."

There is bound to be someone who wants to try to return to "social drinking" or "recreational" drug use. This fantasy is a dangerous illusion for the addict.

Defer all such questions until the person has achieved 90 days of being clean and sober. At that time, the addict will be able to look at the issue with a clear mind. Most people will value their sobriety and will not want to take the risk. There's really no point in discussing this issue with someone who is technically still "under the influence."

Group members should be encouraged to help each other over the rough spots. Let them know that it's acceptable to exchange telephone numbers and call other group members for support during the week.

Main Concepts and Skills

A. Concept: Making a Choice

The basic idea is that using or abusing alcohol and drugs is a matter of choice. No matter what the genetic predisposition or environmental stressors, choice is still possible.

There are, in fact, two levels of choice. First, there is basic choice to be "clean and sober." This is a *long-term* choice, a healthy decision to live a life free of chemical dependency. Such a choice is the basis for the addict's recovery.

This basic choice, however, must be supported by an infrastructure of smaller, everyday choices. Recovery literally takes place "one day at a time." This incremental approach leads to an examination of the *environmental cues* that might touch off problems. The emphasis is on how to make early choices involving "slippery places and people."

Pass out copies of the handout, *Five Days in the Life of an Addict*.

"It would be wonderful if all drug addicts could have such a productive 'week.' Then they could really enjoy the weekend! In reality, these five 'days' (or stages of recovery) are usually spread out over many years.

"The first 'day' portrays the addict as a helpless *victim*. You may be a victim of 'genetic inheritance' or a 'dysfunctional family.' You can't help it — it's not your fault.

"The second stage of addiction is *denial*. The problem is there, but you don't want to see it.

"The third stage is the beginning of the recovery process. You see the problem for what it is, and recognize it *as a habit*. You *accept responsibility*, and are now able to respond in a more adaptive way.

"The fourth stage represents the validation of your recognition of the problem, and your decision to *act responsibly*.

"Finally, the fifth day demonstrates your ability to make new choices and open up a whole new world of possibilities."

Five Days is useful as a metaphor for talking about the recovery process. It sets the tone and mood for the difficult days ahead. This leads naturally into a discussion of specific day-to-day (even hour-by-hour) choices that must be made by the addict.

Tell the group: "It's *easy* to decide 'not to drink.' But this long-term decision must be supported by a myriad of short-term decisions. The early recovery process is actually based on "mini-decisions" during every hour of the day.

"After the first few drinks, or several 'lines' or 'tokes,' your ability to make sensible choices is severely impaired. In recovery, addicts need to learn to make *early* choices about *slippery places and people*."

B. Concept: Understanding Addiction — Physiological and Psychological Addiction

Physiological addiction is defined by two criteria. You can explain these concepts to the group as follows:

- *"Tolerance.* This occurs when the body gets used to a drug. More and more of the same drug is required simply to achieve the same effect. With heroin, for example, after a week of continuous use an addict must triple (or even quadruple) his or her dose just to get the same 'high.' This is similar to the alcoholic's ability to tolerate amounts of alcohol that would 'waste' an ordinary person.

- *"Withdrawal Syndrome.* This is basically a *rebound* phenomenon. When the body gets used to an altered chemical state (such as dependence on a drug), it responds strongly when that drug is no longer administered. In withdrawal, the body may respond in the opposite way to its usual response to the drug. For example, heroin use promotes constipation, but cessation of its use will cause diarrhea. For the alcoholic, who usually gets a profound effect from alcohol, *delirium tremens* (D.T.s) and seizures are potentially life threatening."

Follow these definitions by describing the notions of *psychological addiction* and *denial*.

Five Days in the Life of an Addict

(A modified version of *Autobiography* by Portia Nelson)

Day One

I walk down the street
    There is a deep hole in the sidewalk.
    I fall in.
    I feel lost...I feel helpless.
    It isn't my fault!
    I'm not responsible.
It takes forever to find a way out.

Day Two

I walk down the same street.
    There is a deep hole in the sidewalk.
    I pretend I don't see it.
    I fall in again.
    I can't believe I'm back in the same place.
    But it *isn't my fault.*
    I *don't* feel responsible.
It still takes a long time to get out.

Day Three

I walk down the same street.
    There is a deep hole in the sidewalk.
    I see it is there.
    I still fall in...it's a habit.
    But, my eyes are open, I know where I am.
    It *is* my fault.
    I *am* responsible.
I get out very quickly.

Day Four

I walk down the same street.
    There is a deep hole in the sidewalk.
    I walk around it.

Day Five

I walk down a different street.

Psychological addiction is characterized by a pattern of compulsive behavior (continued use or abuse) in the presence of clear signs of negative consequences. Several citations for Driving Under the Influence (D.U.I.s), and the loss of job, family, or friends will not deter the committed addict from using his or her drug of choice. Psychological addiction is not limited to substance abuse, as witnessed by the proliferation of 12-step groups: *O.A.* (Overeaters Anonymous), *G.A.* (Gamblers Anonymous), and even *S.L.A.A.*

Understanding *denial* is the key to understanding the addicted person. On this point there is general agreement among all theorists and practitioners in the addiction field. All addicts typically adopt a defensive posture based on rationalization and denial, which enables them to avoid seeing the disastrous results of their behavior. This characterological style prevents them from recognizing or admitting to themselves that they have a serious problem.

Most theorists agree on the necessity for identifying the addict's use of denial as an ego defense. Although there is some disagreement about how to go about breaking through this denial system, there is no doubt that such a breakthrough represents the essential first step in the recovery process. A.A. has dealt with this issue in an elegantly simple way. Their first step in the addict's recovery process is an admission of "powerlessness" in the face of the addict's drug of choice (see A.A.'s *The Twelve Steps* at the end of this chapter).

Three Broad Categories of Drugs and Drug Use

↑

Uppers

"Up" drugs are characterized by increased central nervous system (CNS) activity. They are vasoconstrictors and depress appetite.

Cocaine (Regular, "Free-base" [Crack])

Methamphetamine ("Speed," "Whites," "Crank," "X-Tops," "Chrystal," "Ice")

Diet Pills (especially *Preludin*)

Ritalin ("Pellets")

Caffeine ("Java")

Nicotine ("Coffin-nails")

Sugar (not generally considered a drug, but it has similar effects!)

Chart 1

Your discussion of this section should include the following information: "Free-base" is a process for altering regular cocaine (which is snorted by "doing lines") to a smokable form, commonly called "crack." The original method involved ether as a chemical reagent. This volatile substance accounted for Richard Pryor going up in flames. Baking soda is now more commonly used as a safe reagent. "Ice" is a new form of smokable methamphetamine, which has dangerous long-term effects. *Ritalin* was once used to counteract hyperactivity in kids. It produced a paradoxical calmness. "Pellets" are *Ritalin* that has been crushed, "cooked," and injected intravenously. The danger here is that the talc covering can form emboli in the blood system.

↓

Downers

"Downer" drugs are characterized by their ability to depress central nervous system (CNS) activity. They are, in general, soporifics and vasodilators.

Alcohol (ETOH)

Sedative-hypnotics: Barbiturates ("Reds," *Seconal*, Phenobarb, *Nembutal, Tuinal*, et al.)

Nonbarbiturate, Sedative-hypnotic: *Qaalude* ("Ludes")

Benzodiazipines: *Valium, Librium, Xanax*, etc.

Opiates: Heroin, ("Tar," "China White," "Chiva") *Darvon-napsalate*, Opium, Codeine, *Talwin, Demerol, Methadone [Dolophine]*, Fentanyl [*not* China White]

Chart 2

Your discussion of this section should emphasize the fact that, of all the drugs listed above, alcohol is the one that is a major cause of death in this country. Alcohol, in excess, has a harmful effect on all body systems. As a side note, alcohol and Chloral Hydrate, when combined, were known as "knock-out drops" or a "Mickey Finn." This can lead in to a discussion of the dangers of mixing drugs that are synergistic (in other words, they have a multiplying effect). The danger of mixing alcohol and barbiturates was demonstrated by Dorothy Killgalen's unfortunate death. Similarly, mixing heroin and cocaine ("Speedball") caused John Belushi's death. Fentanyl, a powerful synthetic form of heroin (falsely advertised as "China White") has been responsible for many deaths by overdose. It's also important to note that the benzodiazipines are physiologically addicting. They can cross the placental barrier and result in addicted newborns.

←——→

Sideways Drugs

"Sideways" drugs are characterized by their ability to alter consciousness. They are primarily known as hallucinogens and psychedelics, but also as "psychotomimetics" (for their ability to mimic psychotic states).

LSD (D-Lysergic Acid): "Acid," "Fry," "Window Pane," "Owsley," etc. Also DOM, STP, DMT

Mescaline: Peyote, Cactus, "Buttons"

Psylocybin: "Shrooms," Magic Mushrooms

Marijuana: "Pot," "Grass," THC, also "Hash"

PCP (Phencyclidine): "Dust," Angel Dust, "Sherms"

MDMA: "Adam," "XTC," (not MDA)

Designer Drugs: such as MPTP

Chart 3

Your discussion of this section should begin with the dangers of abusing mind-altering drugs. However, some of these drugs do have legitimate uses. Marijuana has been used to offset the effects of chemotherapy in cancer victims. It also can reduce intraocular pressure caused by glaucoma. Mescaline is legally used in religious ceremonies of the Native American Church, and PCP is a common tranquilizer for large animals. Designer drugs are produced by street "psychopharmacologists" to circumvent the law, which regulates drugs by molecular formulae. Changing the molecular structure of a drug slightly can produce a "legal" version with the same effect (such as "Eve," which followed the banned "Adam"). Sometimes, however, (MPTP is an example), these experiments go tragically awry. In an effort to produce yet another synthetic heroin, MPTP yielded a drug that caused irreversible Parkinsonian symptoms in its users.

Psychoactive Drugs	Effects	
	Average Dose	**Large Dose**
Alcohol Beer Wine Hard Liquors	*Depressant* Relaxation, lowered inhibitions, reduced intensity of physical sensations, digestive upsets, body heat loss, reduced muscular coordination	Loss of body control, passing out (also causing physical injuries), susceptibility to pneumonia, cessation of breathing
Sedative Hypnotics Barbituates, i.e., Phenobarbital, Nembutal, Seconal, Tranquilizers, i.e., Valium, Milltown, Librium Quaaludes	*Depressant* Relaxation, lowered inhibitions, reduced intensity of physical sensations, drowsiness, body heat loss, reduced muscular coordination in speech movement and manual dexterity	Passing out, loss of body control, stupor, severe depression of respiration. (Effects are exaggerated when used in combination with alcohol — synergistic effect)
Opiates and Opioids Opium, Morphine, Heroin, Codeine, Dilaudids, Percodan, Darvon, Methadone	*Depressant* Supression of pain, lowered blood pressure and respiratory rate, constipation, disruption of menstral cycle, hallucinations.	Coma, respiratory depression, death
Stimulants Amphetamines, i.e., Dexadrine, Methamphetamines (Speed), Ritalin, Cocaine, Diet Pills, MDA	*Stimulation of Central Nervous System* Increased blood pressure and pulse rate, appetite loss, increased alertness, dilated and dried out bronchi, restlessness	Temporary psychosis, irritability, convulsions, palpitations. (Not generally true for caffeine)
Psychodelis LSD, Mescaline, Psilocybin	*Alteration of Mental Process* Distored perceptions, hallucinations, confusion, vomiting	Psychosis, hallucinations, vomiting, anxiety, panic, stupor
PCP	Sedation, altered mental processes	With PCP: Aggressive behavior, catatonia, convulsions, come, high blood pressure
Hashish, Marijuana		Distored perception, anxiety, panic
Other (Inhalants): A. Organic solvents: glue, paint, gasoline, kerosene, aerosol	Exhiliration and lightheadedness, excitement, reduced muscle coordination, lowered inhibitions	Mental confusion, loss of body control, slurred speech, double vision, hallucinations, memory loss, coma, collapsing of lungs
B. Nitrous Oxide, Amyl Nitrite, Butyl Nitrite	Dizziness, flushing of the face, lightheadedness, increased heart rate, decreased blood pressure, headache, nausea	Confusion, weakness, fainting, loss of body control, coma

Chart 4   *Short- and Long-term Effects of Drug Use*

Psycho Active Drugs	Development of Tolerance	Prolonged Use of Large Amounts	Withdrawal Symptoms After Prolonged Use
Alcohol Beer Wine Hard Liquors	Moderate	Liver damage, ulcers, chronic diarrhea, amnesia, vomiting, brain damage, internal bleeding, debilitation	Convulsions, hallucinations, loss of memory, uncontrolled muscle spasms, psychosis
Sedative Hypnotics Barbiturates, i.e., Phenobarbital, Nembutal, Seconal, Tranquilizers, i.e., Valium, Milltown, Librium, Quaaludes.	Moderate	Amnesia, confusion, drowsiness, personality changes	Uncontrolled muscle spasm, a series of possibly fatal convulsions, hallucinations
Opiates and Opioids Opium, Morphine, Heroin, Codeine, Dilaudids, Percodan, Darvon, Methadone	High	Depressed sexual drive, lethargy, general physical debilitation	Severe back pains, stomach cramps, sleeplessness, nausea, diarrhea, sweating
Stimulants Amphetamines, i.e., Dexadrine, Methamphetamines (Speed), Ritalin, Cocaine, Diet Pills, MDA	High	Psychosis, insomnia, paranoia, nervous system damage. (Not generally true for caffeine)	Severe depression both physical and mental. (Not true for caffeine)
Psychedelis LSD, Mescaline, Psilocybin PCP Hashish, Marijuana	Moderate Mild	Psychosis, continued hallucinations, mental disruption Controversial	Occasional flashback phenomena, depression No true withdrawal symptoms except possible depression
Other (Inhalants): A. Organic solvents: glue, paint, gasoline, kerosene, aerosol	Moderate	Heart, liver, lung, blood cells, and brain damage; amnesia, confusion and personality changes	Irritability, sleeplessness, hallucinations, depressions, and (rarely) delirium tremens
B. Nitrous Oxide, Amyl Nitrate, Butyl Nitrate	Mild to Moderate	Confusion personality changes, blood abnormalities with the Nitrates	No true withdrawal yet observed

Chart 5

C. Skill: Surviving the Weekend Without Alcohol or Drugs

The basic strategy for surviving the weekend is to keep busy and avoid slippery places. To begin with, it's helpful to get suggestions from the group on how to keep busy. Keep adding your own ideas as a supplement. The following is a representative sampling of possible activities:

Go to the beach
Go for a ride
Visit friends
Bake a cake
Play cards
Play Frisbee
Wash your car
Help a neighbor
Read a book
Build a snowman
Plant a tree
Have a picnic
Rent a video
Watch the sunset
Climb Squaw Peak
Call a friend
Play racquetball
Play tennis
Listen to music
Play handball or golf
Go roller-skating
Practice Tai-Chi
Play ping-pong
Go shopping
Recycle newspapers and glass
Go to a garage sale
Dye Easter eggs
Go fishing
Trim the Christmas tree
Visit a nudist colony
    (use sun screen)

Take a hike
Crochet
Fly a kite
Do crossword puzzles
Watch the ballgame on TV
Make a barbecue
Work in the garden
Go to a concert
Go swimming or ice skating
Make love
Take kids to the zoo
Go to the movies
Write a letter
Take a nap
Go jogging
Do aerobics
Sleep late on Sunday
Tune the car
Write a poem
Get or give a massage
Learn to tap dance
Knit a sweater
Watch Shakespeare-in-the-Park
Buy a new hat
Have a garage sale
Practice archery
Lift weights
Go rowing
Light Hanukkah candles
Go skiing, sky diving, wind surfing

Go to a museum, an aquarium,
    a church or synagogue
Go horseback riding, hang gliding, dancing
Play soccer, baseball, basketball, football, cricket
Play bridge, cribbage, poker, whist
Attend a workshop
(In California) "clear" your crystals, or take a hot-tub
Practice playing the guitar (or your instrument of choice)

The other part of successfully surviving the weekend is dealing with *denial*. As noted earlier, this refers to the addict's characterological inability to recognize the negative consequences of his or her behavior. At this point in the recovery process, denial is often manifested by overconfidence or cockiness in the face of early success with sobriety. Addicts may begin to delude themselves that they can "handle" such situations as going to a bar to meet old friends or — even worse — having "just one beer."

D. Skill: Relaxation Training

It's possible to learn how to relax without using alcohol or drugs.

You can introduce the topic of relaxation training to the group by saying, "To begin with, it's important to learn to breathe. In order to live, you have to breathe. In order to live well, you have to breathe well. Your best teacher is the nearest baby. Watch as the baby, at rest, fills his or her belly with air, like a balloon."

Instruct group members to put their left hand on their abdomen (belly), and right hand on their chest. Scan the room. At least one member will be "out of sync." Gently get everybody together.

Now instruct the group: "Inhale slowly, through your nose. Fill your abdomen, push the air into your belly. Notice your left hand being pushed up. Your right hand should move only slightly, and at the same time as your left one.

"Exhale through your mouth, making a relaxed, quiet, 'whooshing' sound." Instruct them to relax the mouth, tongue, and jaw. Then have the group take long, slow, deep breaths that raise and lower the abdomen."

The next step is to demonstrate a technique for systematic relaxation of all the muscles in the body. The following exercise is specifically designed to be useful for addicted populations. It is neither too short nor too long, and will be readily accepted by the group.

Instruct the group to *begin at the bottom*:

"Extend your legs, and point your toes forward; now point your toes toward your head. Notice the tension in your calves. Hold it, hold it, and let go, and *relax*.

"Next, tighten your thighs and buttocks, hold it, hold it, and relax. *Sigh*. Now tighten your stomach muscles; hold, and *relax*. Finally, arch your back (don't do this if you have back problems), and tighten the muscles of your back. Hold, and *relax*.

"Now, tighten your hands (make a fist), forearms, biceps: demonstrate the "Charles Atlas" pose. Hold, and *relax*. Hunch your neck and shoulders (like a turtle), hold, let go. Now roll your neck around, slowly. First one way, and then in the other direction. *Breathe*."

Finally, ask the group to focus on the face. "Begin by tightening your chin, mouth, lips, nose, eyes, forehead, scalp, and ears. *Make an ugly face*. Hold it, and relax."

Lastly, ask the group to take a deep breath and compress their lips. "Now relax and blow out, making a horsey sound." This is usually followed by relaxed laughter.

Instruct the group members to close their eyes, *relax*, and "enjoy the trip." You will then read out loud the following hypnotic induction. The *underlined* words should be gently stressed for maximum effect. Pause, as indicated by the commas. Notice the suggestions at the beginning to *see, feel, hear,* and *smell* ("smells *green*" is deliberately confusing in order to distract the critical faculties of the analytical mind). With each repetition of *down*, you are deepening the trance. Entering a "clearing" is a deliberate metaphor, reinforced by allowing the mind to clear at the stream. "And you can remember..." induces a post-hypnotic effect of relaxation. Finally, the induction begins and ends, in the chair, with a feeling of *support*.

First Visualization Exercise

"Feel yourself sitting in your chair — notice the <u>support</u>, underneath and behind you. <u>Now</u>, imagine yourself standing up and walking around. <u>See</u> yourself walking out the door, down the hallway, and outside to the parking lot.

"You can <u>feel</u> the concrete, under your feet, and <u>hear</u> the noise of traffic. Walk on down the street. Notice that there are trees in the distance. You're approaching a place where the city ends and the forest begins. You walk down the street until you come to the trees: you can <u>see</u> a path in the forest. Follow the path, and keep walking. Notice the difference, as you walk. The ground is softer, and more yielding to your weight. There are trees to your left, and to your right. Sometimes the trees grow closer together, and the forest is darker; sometimes they grow further apart, and the forest is lighter.

"As you're walking down the path, it feels as if you're going <u>downhill</u>. You go <u>down</u>, through the trees, until you see light at the end of the path. It's light now, and you're out of the woods. You've come into a <u>clearing</u>, a quiet meadow in the middle of the forest. Here the sun is always shining, and the grass <u>smells</u> green. Walk around, explore, then find your perfect spot. When you've found it, sit <u>down</u>. Sit all the way <u>down</u>.

"<u>Relax</u>, stretch out, and lie <u>down</u> in the sweet-smelling grass. Feel yourself sinking, <u>deeper and deeper</u>, feeling more and more relaxed: the warm sun on your body, every muscle getting <u>softer and softer</u>. And when you're really relaxed, it's time to stretch your legs and arms.

"As you're stretching, just like a cat in the sun, you notice a gentle sound off to the side of the meadow. It's the sound of running water, and you follow the sound until you find the stream that borders the meadow. It's a clear mountain stream, and you can sit on the bank and watch the water flow. Put your feet in the stream, and <u>feel</u> the cool, clear water.

"Sometimes, thoughts come to you mind that you don't like. Let them come. And <u>let them go</u>. Put those thoughts on a leaf, and let them float on the water. Watch those thoughts flow <u>down, down</u> the stream, <u>down</u> to the river, fed by the stream, and finally <u>down</u> to the sea. And you know that the water always flows <u>down, down</u> to the sea. The water has been doing that for all of time, and it always will.

"Sit for a while. And let your mind become <u>clear</u> and cool as the stream. It's very relaxing and refreshing to sit here, by the stream. Your whole body is relaxed, your mind is cool and <u>clear</u>. And you can come here any time you like, to find peace, comfort, and relaxation, and a sense of well-being.

"When you feel really <u>clear, relaxed, and confident</u>, then you can begin to <u>come back</u>. <u>Come back</u> to the meadow, and <u>remember</u> your perfect spot. And <u>you can remember</u> the relaxation, the sense of perfect peace, and strength. Continue to walk through the meadow and find the path back. Walking slightly <u>uphill</u> through the trees. Notice how sometimes the trees grow closer together, and it gets darker, and sometimes they grow further apart, and it gets lighter.

"And you follow the path all the way <u>back</u> to the edge of the forest, where the pavement begins. You walk <u>back</u> along the streets, <u>back</u> to the parking lot. <u>Come back</u> to this building, walk down the hall, back to this room. And now you're sitting in your chair. Feel the <u>support</u> underneath and behind you. And now, take your time, and <u>come all the way back</u>. Take a deep breath, slowly open your eyes, and <u>come back to this room</u>."

You can finish this session by giving the group a handout on relaxation, to facilitate practice at home.

Second Visualization Exercise (to be used the week following the first visualization)

Use the first visualization exercise up to the point of reaching the meadow. Instruct the group as follows:

"... And as you return to the meadow you notice a path on the <u>other</u> side. This path winds uphill, and you decide to find out where it leads. It's not easy going, this path. It's hard to climb uphill. And the terrain <u>begins to change</u>. Instead of grass there are bushes, and large rocks. It really takes an effort to climb up, but <u>you can do it — you can make it</u> all the way up to the top.

"As you look up you can see that the trail ends, in front of a cave. It's a warm, dry cave. As you reach the top, and sit down to rest in front of the cave, you notice a flashlight. Turn it on. And with the light on, go inside the cave and look around. <u>You can safely explore</u> the cave. And now, you notice, <u>way, way in the back</u> of the cave, there's a chest, an old wooden chest, with leather and brass fittings. Go all the way to the back of the cave. You see the chest and you know that there's something inside, inside the chest, just for you.

"Open the chest and look inside. Use the flashlight to look inside. And now <u>you have a choice</u>. <u>You can choose</u>: to either take what's in the chest with you, or to leave it behind. Whatever <u>you choose,</u> it's time to turn around and leave the cave. Come outside, turn off the flashlight, and put it down. The flashlight will be there whenever <u>you choose</u> to return to the cave.

"Now climb back down the hill. Notice that the going is <u>easier now</u>, coming down the path. And soon you're back in the clearing, the peaceful meadow, where the sun is always shining, and grass smells green. You can take a moment to feel the comfort and relaxation of being in your special place. It feels so good to be here, and <u>you can remember</u> the feeling of peace. And remember <u>the choice</u> you made.

"Now it's time to find the path that leads back to our room...."

Finish the trip as you did last week, by reminding clients of the chair that supports them in this room.

Once again, the underlined words are to be gently emphasized. This trip offers many possibilities: the possibility of trying something new; the possibility of taking a difficult path and successfully reaching the goal; and, most importantly, the possibility of making new choices.

E. Concept: Stress and Addiction

"Knowing how stress affects addiction can have a major influence on your life. Let's find out a little about the stresses you've been facing, and how they may have affected your drug or alcohol use. During the past year, did you have a *major* change in any of the following areas? (This can be a major change in either direction, for example, a lot more or a lot less. Even "good" changes induce stress.)

- Sleeping habits (such as through a change in job shift)

- Eating habits (loss or gain of a lot of weight)

- Type or amount of recreation

- Social or church activities

- Number of family get-togethers

- Number of arguments with spouse

Relaxation Handout

Remember to breathe naturally (like a baby) into your diaphragm: in through your nose, out through pursed lips. Do this in between exercises.

Relaxation begins by (paradoxically) increasing the tension first, then "letting go." Tense each muscle group for five seconds. Notice the contrast between the feelings of tension and of relaxation.

Remember to begin "at the bottom":

1. Lift your legs. Point your toes away from you, then toward your face. Feel the tension in your calves. Tighten your thighs and buttocks, hold, and relax.

2. Arch your back (omit this if you have back problems), tightening muscles; take a deep breath into your chest. Hold, and relax. Tighten your stomach, hold, and relax.

3. Make a fist, tighten your forearms and biceps (make a Charles Atlas pose): hold, and relax. Hunch your neck and shoulders (like a turtle): hold, let go, and roll your neck around.

4. Finally, make an ugly face. Tighten your chin, mouth, lips, nose, eyes, forehead and scalp. Hold, then relax.

5. Let your lips go loose and blow air through them. (Make a "horsey" sound).

To practice the visualization, remember to

1. Walk along the street to the woods.

2. Find the path through the trees to the clearing.

3. Relax in your "perfect spot."

4. Go to the stream and let your thoughts go, down the stream, to the river, and down to the sea.

- Different personal habits (clothes, associates)

- Trouble with your boss

- In-law troubles

- Sexual difficulties

"During the past two years, did any of these things happen to you?

- Death of a close friend, family member, or spouse

- Major personal injury or illness

- Major change in health or behavior of a family member

- Major business reorganization; change in working hours, conditions, or responsibilities

- Being fired or retiring from work

- Marriage

- Marital separation or reconciliation with spouse

- Divorce or termination of a long-term relationship

- Change in living conditions or residence

- Son or daughter moving away from home

- Detention in jail or another institution

- Getting traffic tickets or being cited for D.U.I.

- Outstanding personal achievement (book gets published, win the lottery)

- Spouse beginning or ending job

- Pregnancy

- Changing to a new school or line of work

- Beginning or ending formal education

- Taking on a new mortgage (over $10,000)

- Taking out a major loan (car or major appliance)

- Foreclosure on a mortgage or loan

- Vacation

(Adapted from the "Schedule of Recent Experiences" by Thomas Holmes, M.D.)

F. Concept: Family Roles in Addiction

It's helpful for addicts to put their lives in perspective. Learning the role that families have in the addiction process often helps the addict realize that he or she is not alone.

Explain to the group that children in alcoholic families often assume one or more or the following roles:

The Family Hero

"This is usually the oldest child in the family, a 'parentified' child who is overly responsible and rarely misbehaves. Often encouraged to take on adult tasks such as cooking, cleaning, and babysitting, the family hero is deprived of his or her own childhood. This child is well organized, good in school, and often a class leader. Family heroes like order and structure. They learn early on to rely only on themselves, making it difficult to develop intimacy or trusting relationships."

The Scapegoat

"These children often do poorly in school and display delinquent behavior in order to distract attention from the family secret (alcoholism or drug abuse). The scapegoat will often resort to sexual 'acting out' (females may even get themselves pregnant) or use a variety of drugs in their attempt to 'save' the family. These kids will have to learn to *talk* about their feelings, rather than acting them out."

The Lost Child

"This child tends to be nonverbal and to withdraw to avoid attention. The lost child is often literally forgotten by other family members. Regardless of ability, this child will be only an average achiever in school. Similarly, the lost child will make few if any friends, and will be detached from social circles. Issues involving trust in others will be a problem."

The Mascot

"Often the family clown, this child laughs harder (and cries harder) than anyone else. The mascot's job is to make others feel better by diverting attention from pain by making jokes or trying to smooth things over. By staying focused on others, children in this role are able to avoid focusing on their own pain."

G. Skill: Assertiveness

Addicts may use and abuse alcohol and drugs in an attempt to deal with everyday stress. This behavior often *does* provide temporary relief, by numbing or masking feelings. Unfortunately for the addict, this "solution" makes for more problems in the long run.

Many therapists working with addicts believe that a good deal of drug abuse and alcoholism could be eliminated through teaching people to be more assertive. The reasoning is that assertive behavior — standing up for your legitimate rights and saying "no" when you don't want to do something — can reduce stress and thus reduce the need for the short-term fix of alcohol or drugs.

Explain to the group that there are three basic styles of interpersonal behavior: passive, aggressive, and assertive.

Passive

"The passive style of interaction is characterized by letting others push you around. Passive people do not stand up for themselves, and usually do what they are told, regardless of how they feel about it. When using this style, you will rarely experience direct rejection. On the other hand, you will feel that others are taking advantage of you, and will carry around a load of resentment and anger."

Aggressive

"The aggressive style is typified by fighting, accusing, and threatening behavior. In general, the person using this style steps on others without regard for their feelings, in the manner of a bully. This style has its advantages, since aggressive people often get what they want. On the "down" side, other people may avoid your company."

Assertive

"Finally, the assertive style allows you to stand up for yourself, express your feelings, and get what you want. You can have all this without feeling guilty or being inconsiderate of other people's feelings. You can be direct in asking for what you want or saying what you *don't* want. For example, you can say, 'No thank you, I don't want a drink.'"

Continue by explaining to the group that the key to being assertive is making *assertive statements*.

"An assertive statement has three basic components that relate to the situation at hand:

1. Your perception of the situation ('I think...')

2. Your feelings about the situation ('I feel...')

3. What you want in this situation ('I want...')

H. Skill: Dealing With Relapse

Remember — having a "slip" is the norm for this population. Picking up the pieces and continuing the recovery process as gracefully as possible is the way to success.

Say to the group that some things to be careful about include the following:

Negative physical or emotional states

"Don't allow yourself to become overly hungry, tired, depressed, or angry. If you feel bad enough, drinking or drug use will seem like an attractive solution." As a helpful reminder, write the following on the blackboard. First write the *HALT* vertically, then fill in the rest horizontally:

H *ungry*
A *ngry*
L *onely*
T *ired*

"These are the primary things to watch out for. These are the main causes of relapse. The solution is obvious. *Take care of yourself.* If you're hungry, eat something. If you're angry, deal with it by being assertive. If you're lonely, call a friend, or go to an A.A. meeting. If tired, take a nap. Be good to yourself *without using drugs or alcohol.*"

Thinking about drinking (or using drugs)

"Some reflection or fantasizing about drinking or drug use is normal and natural during the early stages of recovery. However, if you find yourself dwelling on such thoughts, you may be heading for a relapse. Carry a notebook around with you and make a note of every alcohol- or drug-related thought, along with what you were doing at the time. You may begin to see a pattern in the circumstances that trigger such thoughts."

Dishonesty

"Dishonesty may begin with little lies to friends and family. When you start lying to yourself, making rationalizations or excuses for not doing things you know you should, *be careful*. A relapse may be just around the corner."

Expecting too much

"Many people in recovery think that once they've stopped 'using,' everything will be fine. Unfortunately, you'll continue to have problems, just like before. This does not mean that you should return to drug abuse. Problems are part of being human. When you're clean and sober, you're better equipped to deal with them."

Feeling "cocky" (too self-assured)

"A really subtle trap in early recovery is feeling cavalier or overly self-assured. 'I've got it made,' you may find yourself thinking after a period of abstinence. Having made a good beginning is great! However, *recovery is a long-term process*. The recovering addict is 'at risk' for the rest of his or her life."

Letting go of healthy activities

"It's all too easy to stop doing the things that are good for you. These might include exercise, relaxation and meditation, or attending A.A. meetings. Fighting your impulse to procrastinate or just drop out might mean the difference between winning and losing your struggle with addiction. Your healthy activities are part of your support system: treat them as vital aspects of your survival, as important as food and shelter."

I. Skill: Preventing Relapse

One helpful way to prevent relapse is to develop a "map" that allows the addict to avoid the "holes in the sidewalk."

You can begin discussion by saying:

"Once you're in the middle of a 'run,' there's *no choice*. After the first couple of drinks or a couple of 'lines,' you have no choice but to continue until your body tells you to stop. And your own body's signals are unique.

"Choice is only possible during periods of sobriety. These are the only times when addicts are truly responsible for their choices, being capable of responding in new and different ways. The trick is to learn to recognize the *triggers* that will inevitably result in a relapse.

"A simple solution is not to take the first drink or the first 'line.' This will work every time. But 'Just say no' is a simplistic solution that fails to take all the temptations of modern life into consideration. There is danger everywhere. One client counted 28 places to buy liquor between our meeting place and her home, which was one and a half miles away. Some cars seem to 'automatically' stop at liquor stores; cocaine is increasingly plentiful. In some places, it's hard to go into a bathroom without finding someone doing a 'line.'"

Main Interventions

Week 1

Introduction

See Starting the Group.

A. Concept: Making a Choice

Intervention 1: Didactic Presentation

Hand out *Five Days in the Life of an Addict* (see Concepts and Skills section) and discuss specific choices that an addict can make.

Intervention 2: Group Sharing

Ask group members to discuss situations in which they were aware (or unaware at the time) of having made a choice that led to drinking or using drugs. Some examples might be 1) went to a party with old drinking buddies; 2) slept with an old girlfriend with whom coke was always the third member of a *menage a trois;* 3) accepted an invitation to a family reunion during which the client expected to be criticized; 4) spent the evening alone instead of seeking needed support.

It's important to reexamine all these situations to find the point at which a new choice could be made. Remember, the earlier the choice is made, the easier it is to change habitual behavior.

Homework

For homework this week, simply suggest (with a smile) that the group "watch out for holes in the sidewalk."

Week 2

Check-in

This is a very important component of the ongoing structure of the group. Basic ingredients include:

1. Querying group members about how their last week went and whether they encountered any problems

2. Asking for questions regarding the material presented in group last week

3. Doing a follow-up on the previous week's homework assignment.

Always leave plenty of time for clients' responses. The important thing here is for group members to feel comfortable sharing their concerns. But you should nonetheless discourage "war stories." Encourage group interaction by asking other members how they would respond in a similar situation. This sets the tone for future group work.

There are times when this process is so productive that it may take up the entire session. Be flexible. There's plenty of time in the ten weeks to present the didactic and structured material. However, it's best to cover the material in the *order* suggested by this outline.

If you're running late this week, omit the drug overview, saving it for a later date. It's more important to leave enough time to do a thorough job on *surviving the weekend*.

B. Concept: Understanding Addiction — Physiological and Psychological Addiction

Intervention 3: Group Exercise — Haight-Ashbury Drug Rap

The first step is to provide an overview of "Drugs of Abuse," a pamphlet put out in the early 1970s by STASH (Student Association for the Study of Hallucinogens). This is usually introduced as "The Haight-Ashbury Drug Rap," since that's where the style originated.

This exercise is designed to be fun, and is best done with audience participation. As the categories are drawn on the blackboard, people shout out names of drugs. These are recorded in the appropriate spaces, with additional commentary from the group leader.

To begin, divide the blackboard into three equal sections. At the top, label each section as follows:

$$\uparrow \qquad \downarrow \qquad \longleftrightarrow$$

"There are three basic types of drugs: Then turn to the group and ask ingenuously," any questions so far?"

The three basic types of drugs are; Uppers, stimulants; Downers, which are depressants; and Sideways, which are drugs that can work both ways (such as psychedelics or hallucinogens)." (Refer to charts 1, 2, and 3 in the Concepts and Skills section.)

Next, discuss the specific short- and long-term effects of these drugs, including tolerance and withdrawal effects. (See charts 4 and 5 in the Concepts and Skills section.)

In doing this exercise, it's important to maintain a neutral and nonjudgmental attitude. Drugs are neither good nor bad — it's the *abuse* that's a problem. The bottom line of this session must make the basic point that all of these drugs, while useful in some situations, are not necessary. In fact, there is nothing that any of these drugs can do that cannot be accomplished in their absence. Nondrug alternatives, however, such as relaxation techniques and meditation, *do* take longer and involve more effort.

Intervention 2: Group Sharing

Explore with the group how denial has had an impact on each person's drug or alcohol abuse. Remember that when it comes to the issue of denial, group therapy is the most potent solution for this population. From the addict's point of view, the so-called experts can only preach what they've learned from books. Group members, who have "really been there," can confront the addict based on their own experience with substance abuse. Such statements as, "I only drink beer (two six-packs a day)" or "I only drink wine with dinner (well, one of those big 1.5 liter bottles)" are met with howls of laughter among a group of recovering alcoholics. "Yes, brother, you're one of us." The group can bring a sobering dose of reality to even the most recalcitrant of addicts.

C. Skill: Surviving the Weekend Without Alcohol or Drugs

Intervention 3: Group Exercise

Gather suggestions from the group for keeping busy, and write each one of them on a blackboard until it is completely filled. (See example in the Concepts and Skills section.)

It should be acknowledged that many, if not most, of the activities you'll list may carry some association with drinking or using drugs. The bottom line, however, is that none of theses activities *requires* the use of alcohol or drugs. Of course, the addict won't be able to comfortably attend a wine-tasting party, but that's pretty much the only limitation on the weekend activity.

After the list is made, go around the room and solicit individual plans for the weekend.

Intervention 3: Group Exercise — Handling
Potential Problems

Not only do group members need to plan safe weekend activities: they also need to plan to handle potential problems and problematic activities. It's best to use real-life situations as ways to talk about potential problems, and to formulate well-planned strategies to deal with them.

Raise a typical problem situation, such as going to a party, and ask members to suggest strategies for dealing with such "slippery places."

One potential solution is for clients to take their own nonalcoholic beverages to the party. Holding a glass of gingerale (or bubbly water with a twist) is usually adequate protection against being offered an alcoholic drink. It's unlikely that anyone will ask that the contents of the glass be identified. Having their own transportation is helpful, too, in that clients won't be stuck if the urge to drink at the party becomes overwhelming.

What if group members find themselves in a situation in which their drug of choice is available? What if the drug is offered in an act of hospitality or friendship? Allow clients to brainstorm various strategies. You might add that one of best responses is, "I'd love to, but my doctor told me that it's not good for me."

Below is a sample dialogue from an addiction group meeting:

Therapist:	OK, Bob, what are you doing this weekend?
Bob:	I don't know, I guess I'll just hang out.
Therapist:	Uh oh, that sounds like trouble. You know you need to keep busy in the early stages of recovery.
Bob:	Yeah, maybe I'll go to a barbecue at my brother's house.
Therapist:	Sounds okay — but don't your brother and his friends drink a lot of beer?
Bob:	Yeah, but I'll just tell them that I don't want any.
Therapist:	Uh huh, do you think they'll buy that?
Bob:	I don't know. They all know I love beer. I guess they might rag me about not drinking.
Therapist:	Group, any suggestions for Bob?
Amanda:	Well, you could take a six-pack of one of those nonalcoholic beers. I hear they taste pretty good.
Gil:	Or, you could just tell 'em that you're an alcoholic, and can't drink any more.

Bob:	I don't think I'm ready to do that yet.
Gil:	Well, you could go to an A.A. meeting first and practice saying it...
Amanda:	Yeah, that's a good idea. Or you could just take a six-pack of Diet Coke, and say you're on a diet. [Laughter: Bob has a big "beer gut."]
Therapist:	Whatever you do, don't get stuck at the barbecue. If people start pressuring you to have a beer, make sure you have a way out. Either take your own car, or have a supportive friend along who can bail you out.

Don't forget to bring up the issue of denial at this point. The addict needs some-one on whom to rely for honest feedback. A.A. members can use their "sponsor"; others can use the group as a reality check.

End the session by saying, "Remember — your *friends*, the people who care about you, will be glad that you've stopped drinking or using drugs. The people who *aren't* glad obviously aren't your friends. And, yes, there will be many people who will be made uncomfortable by your decision to be 'clean and sober.' Good luck this weekend."

Homework

Ask the group to notice the slippery places and people in their lives, and to try out some of the alternatives suggested by the group if the need arises.

Week 3

Check-in

It's very important to follow up on the previous session by asking about the weekend. Go around the room getting reports from each group member. Applaud successes. If someone has had a slip, gently ask, "What happened?" Ask the group to help with suggestions. If one of the causes of the slip was a need to relax, you have a natural segue to the topic of the day.

For many substance abusers, drinking or drug use began as an attempted *solution* to a problem, such as how to relax. This session offers the addict a *different solution*, and an alternative to chemical dependency.

D. Skill: Relaxation Training

Intervention 3: Group Exercise (See Concepts and Skills section)

Begin by reading the deep-breathing and progressive muscle relaxation script. Then lead the hypnotic induction — the visualization about the walk to the meadow.

The exercise is followed by a "debriefing." Go around the room and ask clients to share what the experience was like for them. Ask for specific information about the trees in the forest. You'll hear a variety of descriptions of trees — redwoods, birch, pine, eucalyptus. Emphasize these differences: everyone has a *unique path* to recovery.

The entire group will now have shared a common experience, which will help build group cohesion. At the same time, clients are beginning to learn the valuable skills of relaxation and visualization.

Homework

Ask group members to practice the relaxation exercise, using the handout, three or four times during the week, and to "return to the meadow" at least once before the next session.

Week 4

Check-in

How was the week? What sorts of experiences did people have with the relaxation technique? How about the visualization exercise? By now a familiar pattern is emerging for clients. The consistency of the group format is reassuring to the addict. Structure means safety and helps build trust.

D. Skill: Relaxation Training (continued)

Intervention 3: Group Exercise

This session builds on the previous one. Repeat the relaxation exercise verbatim. *Repetition enhances skill-building.* Once again, lead the group to the meadow and stream. Tell the group, "And now you're *feeling so good* that you're ready for an adventure — a new experience."

Using that comment as a segue, you can proceed with phase two of the visualization exercise (see Concepts and Skill section for the script for phase two).

This visualization "seeds" the work that the group will do in the weeks to come. Individuals will explore scary places inside themselves, and perhaps will go "way, way back." It will be *safe to remember*, because you've built a sense of support in the room.

Intervention 2: Group Sharing

Now it's time to go around the room and share the experience. Not everyone will have gone into the cave during the visualization. Some people will have seen the chest and chosen not to open it. Others will have opened it, only to find it empty. The number of group members who will admit to having opened the chest, and who will talk about its contents, is a diagnostic indicator of the trust level in the group.

It is crucial at this stage of group development that you respond carefully and respectfully to each person's offering. Don't allow group members to make frivolous interpretations or take "cheap shots" at another member's confidences.

For clients who have chosen not to enter the cave, you can say: "I support your choice not to enter the cave at this time. You can go back there anytime you like, to check it out." Emphasize the importance of the good feelings in the meadow, and the accomplishment of their successful climb to the top of the hill.

Use a similar strategy for those who chose not to open the chest. Underline the fact that they made a choice. This situation can call to mind Pandora's box, and can therefore feel threatening to clients who know the myth.

It helps to remind the group that when Pandora looked at the bottom of the box after all the world's troubles were released from it, she found a precious gift: *hope*.

Where the opened box in the visualization was empty for individuals, remind them that this exercise is open-ended. "Many people don't find what they're looking for *at first*. But you can go back as often as you like. It's your box, and *you will* find something of value there *when the time is right for you*." Another option is to use the empty box as a repository in which to store some things for safekeeping. You might pose the question, "What would you like to put in the box, to keep safe there, during your recovery?"

Whatever is found in the box is to be valued. This is a simple matter when the image involves a pirate treasure chest filled with gold and jewels. You can tell the group, "We all have within ourselves a source of wealth."

Sometimes people are embarrassed to report finding drugs in the chest. One client in a group of mine saw an ice chest full of cold beer. If a similar situation comes up, it's important to emphasize the choice made during the visualization, rather than passing judgment on anyone's fantasy. Usually if people imagine drugs or booze in the chest, they choose to turn around and leave it behind. "You've made the choice to turn your back on drugs and start a new life. Drugs will always be around, but you can always choose to turn your back on them."

If someone finds drugs or alcohol during the visualization, and chooses to take them, this is usually an indicator of a poor prognosis. "Perhaps you're not ready to stop using *right now*. The choice to turn your back on drugs is available *at any time in the future*. As the people in A.A. say — and they're right — *today* is the first day of the rest of your life."

People find the damnedest things in that old chest. Tim, a Silicon Valley technician, found a samurai sword during the visualization. This was interpreted in our group as a symbol of honor and integrity. When last seen, he was sporting a four-year "chip" from A.A. Inez, a flight attendant, found a blue crystal in the box, radiating a cool light. She has been clean and sober for over three years.

Sometimes there are unpleasant things in the box. An occasional pile of bones — certainly a disconcerting image for the client — might prompt you to say, "We all have a few skeletons in the closet." Or you might comment, "Sometimes we have to let our addiction die before we can be reborn into a clean and sober life."

This kind of sharing — taking a risk in a group — builds trust when it is carefully and sensitively handled. Taking special care in the beginning sets the stage for future painful revelations.

Homework

Once again, ask the group to practice the relaxation *at least once* during the upcoming week, using the handout as a guide. Daily practice is the ideal, but you need to be realistic with this population. For people who are having trouble, suggest that they listen to a prerecorded relaxation tape that includes music. Adventurous clients may return to the cave for a second peek.

Week 5

Check-in

More people will report success with relaxation this week. Some others will have had an interesting experience with their visualization involving the chest. Follow the protocol outlined for the previous session.

E. Concept: Stress and Addiction

Intervention 3: Group Exercise

Hand out paper and pencils. Let the group know that this is not a quiz. As you read the list of stressful events from the Concepts and Skills section, ask the group to note how many of the experiences apply to their recent lives. They should tally up one point for each item checked.

Remind the group that *all change* can be stressful, even "good" change. Point out that a changed lifestyle that is drug- and alcohol-free will unfortunately bring increased stress as well — although this is different in nature from the stresses of an addicted lifestyle.

Ask the group how many points they got. Since this is only a partial list, you can solicit ideas about additional stressful events. These can be added to you master list for future groups.

Intervention 2: Group Sharing

The Schedule of Recent Experiences exercise will usually lead the group to discuss past painful personal events. Ask individuals, "How did you deal with that?" Often you'll hear such responses as, "I stayed stoned for a month after that happened"; or "I went immediately to the bar and stayed until closing time." At this point in the recovery process, it's appropriate to respond to this sort of admission with nonjudgmental acceptance. Remember, *sharing* in the group builds trust.

An all-too-common response to stressful events is for the addict to resort to chemical solutions. After all, these do provide temporary relief from the emotional pain brought on by stress.

This is a good time for you to encourage the group to do some brainstorming for alternative ways in which to cope with stressful events. Group members might suggest going to church or synagogue, prayer, A.A. meetings, relying on family support, meditation, or getting a good lawyer or tax accountant. Other suggested solutions might involve the group's newly acquired relaxation skill. If no one else suggests it, point out that a walk in the woods or on the beach often provides a new perspective and some relief from painful emotions.

At the end of this session, remind the group, when all else fails, to remember the "Serenity Prayer" promulgated by A.A.:

> God grant me the *serenity* to accept the things I cannot change, the *courage* to change the things that I can, and the *wisdom* to know the difference.

Homework

Have group members continue their relaxation regimen. For new homework this week, suggest a simple exercise using the serenity prayer. Ask the group to look at a couple of events in their lives in terms of 1) something to be accepted or 2) something that can be changed. Emphasize the value of knowing the difference.

Week 6

Check-in

At the beginning of this session, many members will spontaneously report that they've noticed all sorts of stressful things going on in their lives, things that they hadn't noticed before. Since much of this stress will involve family issues, you'll have the perfect lead-in for this week's discussion topic: roles in an alcoholic family.

F. Concept: Family Roles in Addiction

Intervention 1: Didactic Presentation (See Concepts and Skills section)

Intervention 2: Group Sharing

The group discussion in this session usually focuses on personal revelations. Group members share what role they believe they played in their family of origin. Let the group know that roles can change over time. When there is only one child, he or she may be required to play more than one role. Children can also switch roles over the course of years. This session capitalizes on the trust the group has built over previous sessions.

Homework

Ask group members to continue their relaxation exercises. In addition, assign them the task of discovering their role in their family of origin.

Calling siblings or talking to parents will help clients gain perspective on what they were like as children. Since denial often plays such a large role in dysfunctional families, clients will have to check the opinions of family members carefully against their own recollections. It might also be useful to seek out the perspectives of child-hood friends and friends of the family.

Week 7

Check-in

Ask group members what they found out from their investigations. For many of them, their insights will have come as a revelation. Take as much time as necessary in this process. There is a real benefit for group members to know that they are not alone in the odd or unhappy role they were forced to play in their families.

This is a golden opportunity to ask group members who are working the "fifth step" of A.A. (see The Twelve Steps at the end of this chapter) to do some sharing.

Check in about the relaxation regimen, and suggest that members set up a definite schedule for their relaxation exercises.

G. Skill: Assertiveness

Intervention 3: Group Exercise

Hand out paper and pencils. This exercise is a way to ascertain the groups' current level of assertiveness. Read the following five scenarios (adapted from Davis et al., *The Relaxation and Stress Reduction Workbook*, 1988), and have group members write down what they would *actually* do in each situation:

1. You're at a convenience store, and have just brought some Seven-Up. When you're just *outside* the store, you realize that your change is a dollar short.

2. In this situation, you are a person who likes his steak rare. You go to a restaurant and order a steak — rare, of course. The waiter eventually brings you the steak, and it's medium-well.

3. You've got the car and have promised to give a friend a lift to your A.A. meeting. When you arrive, your friend isn't ready. He keeps 'putzing around' for half an hour. At this rate, you're going to be late for the meeting.

4. You leave the house to go to the movies. You're carrying ten dollars cash, but you've left your credit cards, automatic teller card, and checkbook at home. On the way, you stop at a gas station and ask the attendant for *five dollars* worth of gas (the movie will cost five dollars also). A few minutes later the attendant returns and says, "I've filled up your tank. That'll be $9.50."

5. You're buying a sweater in a clothing store. You take it to the cashier. While you wait for the clerk to finish with the customer ahead of you, another customer comes in. The clerk then proceeds to help the new customer, instead of you.

After each scenario, ask, "What would *you* do?" Instruct group members to write their answers down. When they're finished, ask people to put the paper aside. Now proceed with the following interventions.

Intervention 1: Didactic Presentation: (See Concepts and Skills section)

As you discuss the three interpersonal styles of behavior — passive, aggressive, and assertiveness — include how assertiveness affects addiction.

Intervention 3: Group Exercise

Now, go back to the assertiveness "quiz." Read out each situation again and go around the room asking for individual responses. Note out loud which answers fall into the passive or aggressive style.

Some people will passively accept the loss of a dollar in situation 1, and will continue to feel irritated all day. There's always someone who ends up passively eating an overdone steak (*and then won't leave a tip!*). Similarly, many others will hang around (with their guts churning inside), while their disorganized friend looks for his socks, his shoes, his shirt, his tie...

Many people respond in an aggressive way to situation 4. Maybe it's just the accumulation of frustrating scenarios up to this point: anyway, many people end up yelling at or threatening the gas station attendant. Others, of course, pay up and passively go home, missing the movie. Finally, situation 5 is a toss-up, depending largely on how much of a hurry you're in. Still, most people will assertively (politely, but firmly) remind the clerk that they were next.

In a recent group of mine, one client reported seeing a bumper sticker that seems to sum it up best: "SHIT HAPPENS." Being assertive is a way to reduce stress in the context of inevitable frustrations. Assertive behavior won't always get you what you want, but it's probably your best bet. The most important point to emphasize is that the passive and aggressive styles increase stress, and often lead to alcohol and/or drug abuse.

Intervention 4: Dyadic Exercise

You can follow up the assertiveness quiz by having group members form into dyads. The pairs will take turns making *assertive statements* (see Concepts and Skills section) concerning a variety of current issues in their lives. Remember the three elements of assertive statements: "I think...," "I feel...," "I want...." Have the member of the dyad who is listening give feedback noting whether all three elements of an assertive statement are present.

Suggested areas of concern might include the following:

- Doing the dishes

- Finances

- Taking out the garbage

- Sexuality

- Respect

Homework

Ask group members to be assertive during the week in a situation in which they would usually act otherwise. Specifically focus on situations in which they might be tempted to drink or use drugs — for example, saying "no" when offered a joint during a coffee break, or refusing to join the guys who are going out for a couple of beers after work. Mention the importance of continuing with the relaxation exercises.

Week 8

Check-in

Ask group members to share what new experiences they had last week doing the assertiveness assignment. Sometimes people will report feeling great after standing up for themselves for the first time in years. Others may take this opportunity to sheepishly announce that they have had a "slip."

Remember, nearly two-thirds of all relapses occur in the first 90 days of recovery (Marlatt & Gordon, 1985). This well-documented phenomenon occurs across all addictions, regardless of treatment modality.

It's a helpful strategy to "reframe" a relapse as a slip in the recovery *process* and perhaps an inevitable part of that process. For the lucky few, recovery, once begun, proceeds smoothly — "all downhill and shady." The vast majority of recovering addicts, however, have a rockier road to travel.

Every group therapy program should have a built-in mechanism that allows people who perceive themselves as failures to continue in treatment. Group members who have had a slip should be welcomed back like the proverbial prodigal son. Commend them for their courage in admitting to having had a slip. Praise these clients for having cut short a potentially disastrous course of events (a full-blown relapse).

There is, of course, a limit. Group members who continually have slips are obviously not committed to recovery. Worse, they can become a drain on the group's energy. A helpful rule is, "Three slips and you're *out*."

This naturally leads into a group discussion of the potential causes of relapse.

H. Concept: Dealing With Relapse

Intervention 1: Didactic Presentation (See Concepts and Skills section)

Intervention 2: Group Sharing

It's always helpful when you can encourage the group to share their hard-earned wisdom. Most group members will have had some personal experience with relapse. Minimize the war stories, and maximize the helpful advice. (This is called "separating the wheat from the chaff.")

Like so many other journeys, the road to relapse is usually paved with good intentions. Relapses occur when addicts have a "lapse" of attention, and don't follow their program. This might mean not attending their customary A.A. meetings, failing to exercise, or not using their support system. A support system can entail nothing more than a list of telephone numbers or friends to visit in person. Making human contact with others who are committed to sobriety can be an excellent alternative to drinking or using drugs.

Homework

Ask the group to watch out for potential relapse triggers and other "holes in the sidewalk" during the next week. Ask clients to maintain their relaxation regimen.

Week 9

Check-in

In many ways, relapse prevention is the most important component of the entire program. By now, the group has done a good job of identifying the various *slippery places and people* that will put them at risk. Remind the group that drinking or drug use is a matter of choice. Having a relapse is *also* a matter of choice. Therefore, it's important to pay attention to the "choice junctures" that occur in their lives.

I. Skill: Preventing Relapse

Intervention 1: Didactic Presentation (See Concepts and Skills section)

It's difficult, but not impossible, to avoid drinking or using drugs. One solution is to make a *map*.

Intervention 3: Group Exercise

Have group members draw simple maps of their usual routes to and from work, school, shopping, and so on. Using a different colored pen or pencil, they should mark the areas to avoid, such as liquor stores, addicted friends' houses, parks where addicts hang out — the danger zones will be different, depending on your client population and geographical location. Next, have clients figure out how to avoid these places and still get to where they need to go.

Unfortunately, the map may highlight as perilous many favorite places and people. Explain to the group that an addict's social structure is often unconsciously designed around supporting the addiction. Toxic friends and even family members may have to be rejected right along with alcohol and drugs, especially in the early stages of recovery.

The map will indicate all the client's "choice junctures." Explain to group members: "You don't have to turn off the freeway in the direction of your drug connection — take another exit instead. On your way home, when you find yourself in the liquor store, you can choose to buy a soda or a lottery ticket rather than booze. If you're on your way to a party that will involve heavy drinking or drug use, you can choose to turn around and go home. Choices are not easy. And some of your choices, even though they'll speed your recovery, may also bring you sadness and pain."

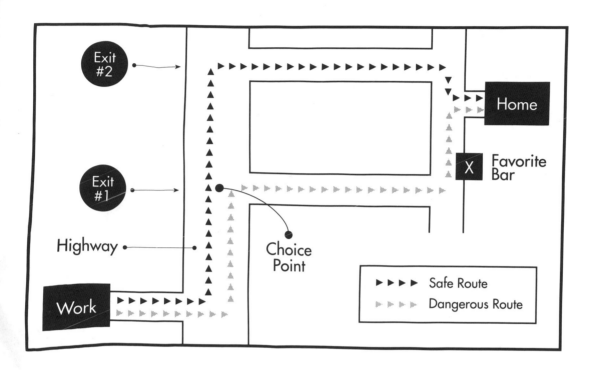

The group can use this opportunity to discuss the difficulty of staying clean and sober. Urge clients to be optimistic — the odds are beginning to turn in their favor.

Below is an example of a dialogue that might take place at this point in the group:

Therapist:	Okay, now we're getting down to the bottom line. You all know, by now, that you have the ability to choose. Whether you choose to drink [use drugs] or not is up to you. Let's disuss your maps for success.
Douglas:	I've drawn my map, but I'm still concerned about staying straight.
Therapist:	Okay, let's look at your map.
Douglas:	Well, the problem is right here [points to diagram]. You see, on Friday, when I get off from work, I have to pass this bar where all my friends are relaxing and having a good time.
Therapist:	I can see how that would be a problem for you. Any suggestions from the group?
Terry:	I've had the same problem myself. I hated it when I had to go home without some brew. And I could picture my drinking friends in that bar having a good old time. Finally, I decided to go one more exit on the freeway. It takes a little longer, but the extra gas costs a lot less than the booze.
Therapist:	That's great. Really helpful. Any other feedback?
Dana:	I used to have trouble with my map, too. My connection's house was in a direct line between my house and where I used to work. My "higher

power" solved that problem for me: I lost my job by being late too many mornings! [Laughter] My new job is in a different direction.

Therapist: Well, that's one way of solving the problem. Most people will be able to work out alternate routes for themselves that avoid their danger zones.

Homework

Ask group members to make additional maps showing their potential relapse points. These can involve other places and situations than those explored in the first map. The more specific the maps are, the better. Again, remind clients to continue their relaxation regimen.

Week 10

Check-in

Follow up on the relapse maps. This exercise will provide clients with guidance for a lasting recovery.

Graduation Celebration

It's useful to use a graduation ceremony to mark the official end of this phase of treatment. Our culture is notably lacking in transitional rituals. Handing out a "diploma" enhances the specialness of the event. You can easily create a diploma, such as the sample at the end of this chapter, on a Macintosh-type computer.

In this final session, you should stress the following concepts:

Enjoying sobriety

Instead of "white-knuckling it," recovering addicts should try to relax and feel good about not drinking or using drugs.

Continuing plans

Ask the group, "What will you do now to *maintain* your sobriety?" One alternative that you can make available is a long-term follow-up group. Another alternative is for clients to utilize a 12-step group for support. Tell clients to keep looking until they find a comfortable "home group" for themselves.

Clean and sober friends

Finding and maintaining a clean and sober support system is probably the single most important factor in a successful recovery. A good place to find these people is at 12-step meetings.

Keep in touch

Encourage group members to exchange telephone numbers and to use them when slippery situations arise.

Finally, end the meeting with some nonalcoholic refreshments. Coffee and cake, or sparkling apple cider, provide a sweet finish to this group experience.

Criteria for Change

In the case of addiction groups, there is only one criterion for change: the client must be *clean and sober* and remain so for the duration of the group.

Resistance

A good part of the group work is accomplished by the *modeling* of other members. At times, *the group leader who does least, does best*. Depending on you client population, the words of a group leader (often a licensed therapist with advanced degrees but no actual substance abuse experience) may have far less clout than those of a streetwise recovering addict.

There are other times, however, when the group leader must make a stand. This is especially true when confronting denial. Sometimes the group will collude with an errant group member, replicating a dysfunctional family. Here, the therapist must step in firmly to break up an unhealthy process. By confronting the relapsed member and the group simultaneously, the therapist demonstrates a willingness to "take the heat" and bring up painful issues.

Confrontation of Denial

Synanon and similar groups that routinely practiced "hard" confrontation have earned their place in the history of substance abuse group therapy. Although there is some value in breaking down the character armour of the hard-core addict (in the hope of rebuilding a better structure), this confrontational approach is rarely useful in the average therapy setting. On the other hand, confrontation *is* required to counteract denial. When an addict continues to "use," or will not admit to a drug's negative impact, confrontation is necessary. Involvement of the entire group, rather than just the group leader, is optimally effective.

Antabuse

The therapeutic application of Antabuse (disulfiram) was discovered accidently. Certain workers in the rubber industry, where disulfiram was used as an antioxidant, were getting sick after lunch. Eventually, heavy lunch-time beer drinking combined with exposure to disulfiram was discovered to be the cause of extreme flushing and vomiting.

Antabuse does not have any effects on the body *per se*. In fact, a double-blind study (Christensen, Ronsted, & Vaag, 1984) found that the control group reported more side effects than the group receiving the antabuse. The drug does, however, affect the body's ability to metabolize alcohol.

In other words, if a client takes Antabuse *and drinks*, he or she will get very sick, very quick. While such clients probably *won't* die, they'll probably *wish* they would.

Antabuse, administered under the supervision of a qualified M.D., can be a useful adjunct to ongoing group therapy. The drug can provide added insurance to maintaining sobriety for alcoholics in difficult situations. The client may *want* to drink, but won't want to face the unpleasant physical consequences.

You can describe the situation as being analogous to a broken leg. "When someone has a broken leg, using a crutch (Antabuse) can be a necessary part of the recovery process. When the leg (alcoholic) is well enough to support itself, then it's great to throw the crutch away — perhaps to serve as fuel for a ceremonial bonfire!"

Serendipity

When life gives lemons, make lemonade. Capitalize on chance events. When all the women in the group fail to show up for a particular meeting, use the opportunity to explore "men's only" issues.

References

Bratter, T.E., and Forrest, G.G., *Alcoholism and Substance Abuse, Strategies for Clinical Intervention.* New York: The Free Press, 1985.

Christensen, J.K.; Ronsted, P.; and Vaag, U.H., "Side effects after disulfram, comparison of disulfram and placebo in a double-blind multicentre study." Acta psychiatr. Scand., 1984, *69*, 265-273.

Davis, M.; Eshelman, E.R.; and McKay, M. *The Relaxation and Stress Reduction Workbook.* 3rd Edition, Oakland, California: New Harbinger Publications, 1988.

Hester, R.K., and Miller, R.W. , eds. *Handbook of Alcoholism Treatment Approaches: Effective Alternatives.* New York: Pergamon Press, 1989.

Marlatt, G.A., and Gordon, J.R., eds. *Relapse Prevention, Maintenance Strategies in the Treatment of Addictive Behaviors.* New York: Guilford Press, 1985.

McKay, M.; Rogers, P.D.; McKay., J. *When Anger Hurts: Quieting the Storm Within.* Oakland, CA: New Harbinger Publications, Inc., 1989.

Spitz, H.I., and Rosecan, J.S., eds. *Cocaine Abuse, New Directions in Treatment and Research.* New York: Brunner/Mazel Inc., 1987.

Yalom, I.D. *Theory and Practice of Group Psychotherapy.* 3rd Edition. New York: Basic Books, 1985.

The Twelve Steps

1. We admitted we were powerless over alcohol — that our lives had become unmanageable.

2. Came to believe that a Power greater than ourselves could restore us to sanity.

3. Made a decision to turn our will and our lives over to the care of God *as we understood Him.*

4. Made a searching and fearless moral inventory of ourselves.

5. Admitted to God, to ourselves and to another human being the exact nature of our wrongs.

6. Were entirely ready to have God remove all these defects of character.

7. Humbly asked him to remove our shortcomings.

8. Made a list of all persons we had harmed, and became willing to make amends to them all.

9. Made direct amends to such people wherever possible, except when to do so would injure them or others.

10. Continued to take personal inventory and when we were wrong promptly admitted it.

11. Sought through prayer and meditation to improve our conscious contact with God, *as we understood Him*, praying only for knowledge of His will for us and the power to carry that out.

12. Having had a spiritual awakening as a result of these steps, we tried to carry this message to alcoholics, and to practice these principles in all our affairs.

YOU ARE A SURVIVOR!

GOOD LUCK ON YOUR RECOVERY

Chapter 14

Parenting Groups

Kim Paleg, Ph.D.

Introduction

Being a parent is perhaps the hardest task facing adults today. And yet it's a task for which adults have little or no training. More and more parents are recognizing that child-rearing methods that apparently worked in the past are no longer successful. Neither repressive nor permissive strategies work. Children need structure, but it must be nonattacking and nonabusive.

Adler (1933) developed the concept of "social interest." He saw children as having an innate striving for connection. How this striving manifests itself depends on the child's understanding of the social context which, in turn, is influenced by parents.

Dreikurs (1964) applied Adler's concepts to the task of child-rearing, describing all children's behavior as being directed toward the goal of belonging. Misbehavior implies faulty beliefs about the means of achieving that goal.

Others (Dinkmeyer & McKay, 1982, 1983; Nelson, 1981) have developed parenting training programs based on Dreikurs' principles.

Selection and Screening

In running parenting groups, it's preferable to have both members of the parenting couple participate. Obviously this isn't always possible. Often one of the parents isn't interested in learning new parenting skills; sometimes the family has only one parent.

You should run separate groups for parents of teens and for those with younger children. Often parents of eleven- and twelve-year-olds ("pre-teens") are dealing with teen issues, and parents may benefit from participating in the parenting group for older children. Where to draw the line is a judgment call.

Meet with each applicant during the screening phase and assess for aggressive or disruptive potential. Carefully evaluate parents who have been referred by the courts as a result of child abuse allegations. Such applicants may be hostile and disruptive. Similarly, parents of kids who are involved in the juvenile justice system because of their misbehavior may have problems beyond the scope of this chapter.

Time and Duration

The group should run for an hour and a half, once a week, for eight weeks.

Structure

Since each new skill presented builds on previously learned skills, it's important that participants attend all sessions, and that new participants not join part way through the series.

If possible, run the group with a co-therapist, preferably one of the opposite sex. Fathers are usually far outnumbered in parenting groups, and are more likely to actively participate when there's a male leader. Co-therapists can also model communication, problem solving, and other more specific parenting skills for the group.

The optimal size for the group is between eight and sixteen parents.

By the time parents have sought a parenting group, they are usually feeling helpless and sometimes desperate. Most are already quite committed to learning anything that will improve their situation at home.

Goals

The group is aimed at helping parents elicit more appropriate behaviors from their children. If the group is successful, individuals will begin to feel better about themselves as parents, and to worry less about their children. Parents will begin to understand their children's behaviors from a new perspective. All behavior, whether manifested by a child or an adult, can be seen as an attempt to belong, to find a place in the world at large or, for children, in the smaller world of the family.

Parents will begin to recognize the systemic nature of families: that the most effective way to facilitate changes in their children's behavior is for the parents to make changes in their own behavior.

Behavioral goals of the group include learning and practicing specific skills in such areas as communication, problem solving, and limit setting. These skills can be used to develop specific strategies to help parents deal with the problems they bring to the group.

Ground Rules

There are several ground rules that must be established at the beginning of the group. One of the most important is that you describe the limits of confidentiality. Occasionally you may discover in the course of the group that a parent's disciplinary methods are abusive, and you will be obligated to report this to the appropriate authorities. Be sure that you are familiar with the current child-abuse reporting laws of your state.

Other ground rules include one person talking at a time (while ensuring that each person gets the opportunity to speak). Group meetings should begin and end on time, and participants are expected to arrive promptly and attend all sessions. There should be no aggressive or attacking criticism allowed, particularly criticism by parents of their children.

Description of Group Process

Each meeting consists of three parts: first, a brief check-in with each parent that includes a follow-up on specific strategies attempted during the week; second, a short review of the contents of the previous week, followed by the introduction of new concepts or skills, including their relevance to participants and the planning of specific strategies.

In the first meeting, the check-in is replaced by introductory exercises. Introduce yourself and describe the function of the group and the ground rules before having parents introduce themselves. You might say something like

"Hi. My name is Kim and this is Jerry. We'll be running this group together and we'd like to start by telling you something about the group. As you know, we'll be meeting for eight weeks, during which time you'll have the opportunity to learn and practice many new skills.

"There are a few guidelines that usually help groups run more smoothly. To get the most benefit from the eight sessions, we'd like to begin and end promptly, and hope that each of you will make it a priority to come to every meeting. While Jerry and I will try to ensure that everyone gets a chance to speak, it helps if only one person talks at a time. We'd also like to keep aggressive or attacking criticism out of the group. Being a parent is hard enough on your self-esteem, and believe it or not, so is being a kid today."

Jerry might continue at this point with:

"You'll be able to teach the concepts and skills described in the sessions to any and all of your friends and acquaintances. However, it's important that material relating to any specific parent or child remain confidential. Can we have agreement on this?" Make sure you get an affirmative response from everyone. "The only possible exception to this rule is if Kim or I feel that someone in the group or at your home is abusive, being abused, or suicidal. Under those circumstances, we would have to contact the appropriate authorities. Are there any questions about anything we've said so far?

"Each week we'll be learning some new skills that we hope you'll take home and practice. Some of you may have very specific problems with one or more children that you'd like to resolve. You'll have the opportunity to develop, with the group's help, some strategies to address those problems.

"So, let's continue with some introductions from each of you."

Starting the Group

Most of the participants will feel somewhat anxious about being in the group. Although the meeting where the initial screening took place may have relieved some of this anxiety, being in the group at all implies a perceived lack of success as a parent. In this frame of mind, parents feel isolated and focus on the negative traits and behaviors of their children. The introductory exercise helps parents see their problems with their children's behavior in the context of the problems of others, and refocuses parents on their children's more positive and promising qualities.

The exercise is in two parts. First, have each person say his or her name, the names of the other family members involved (including the ages of the children), and give a brief statement summarizing any significant parenting problems. The second time around, have members describe a behavior or incident that best illustrates what they like most about their problem child or children.

Main Concepts and Skills

A. Concept: Three Styles of Parenting

"There are three major styles of parenting: authoritarian, permissive, and one that emphasizes mutual respect."

Authoritarian

"Authoritarian parents exert strict control with rigid rules and regulations. What their children want is rarely considered. The children obey out of fear of punishment and/or with considerable resentment. Their orientation toward rules and limits is to do whatever they can get away with."

Permissive

"Permissive parents basically allow their children to do whatever they want. Some hate to see their children unhappy; others simply want their children to have all the advantages they themselves never had. These parents often feel out of control and defeated. Their children's attitude is to do whatever they want, because someone else will always pick up the pieces or take the heat."

Mutual Respect

"The key to more effective parenting is mutual respect. For children to learn respect and responsibility, they must be treated with respect and given responsibility for appropriate aspects of their lives. Children's feelings, opinions, needs, and desires must be treated as equal in worth to those of adults; that is, listened to and considered. Equality as individuals doesn't imply equal decision-making power in every area. But often simply listening to a child's feelings or desires and validating them, as one would do for a friend, can defuse a potential battle. Mutual respect combines kindness and firmness, nurturing and limit setting."

B. Concept: How Do Children Change?

"Family systems theory describes the family as so interdependent that altering any part of the system can result in the entire system changing. Accordingly, the most effective way to elicit different, more appropriate behaviors from your children is to act differently yourselves. Yelling at Tommy for forgetting his homework doesn't help him remember, but making his afternoon play activities contingent on his remembering might."

C. Concept: All Children Want To Belong

"All behavior, whether manifested by a child or an adult, can be seen as an attempt to belong, to find a place in the world at large or in the smaller world of the home. For children, a sense of belonging can result from feeling like an active participant in the family and a valued contributor to the household. In authoritarian households, children receive rewards only when their behavior conforms to their parents' rigid demands. In permissive homes, children receive rewards without having had to do anything for them. In neither case is the child's potential contribution looked upon."

Discouraged Children Misbehave

"When children don't feel able to participate in or contribute to the family in any valuable or constructive way, they become discouraged. They still want to belong, so they attempt to find other ways to reach this goal. Faulty beliefs about how to do this result in misbehavior."

Four Mistaken Beliefs

"Discouraged children develop four mistaken beliefs about how to achieve the goal of belonging.

- The first mistaken belief is that they can belong and feel worthy only by receiving complete parental attention. For these children, negative attention (scolding, yelling) is better than no attention at all. Their goal is simply to receive attention.

- The second mistaken belief among children is that they can belong and feel worthy only by being powerful and by subjugating a parent. Interactions with these children are characterized by power struggles ('You can't make me!' 'Oh, can't I? We'll see about that.'). The goal resulting from this belief is power.

- The third (less frequently occurring) belief among children is that they're totally unlovable. They feel so hurt themselves that their goal becomes one of hurting back, taking revenge.

- The fourth faulty belief among children is that they lack the resources to be competent. They see anything short of perfection as being worthless. Thus, they display their inadequacy in order to avoid the pressure of others' expectations."

D. Skill: Diagnosing Your Child's Misbehavior

"Your child's mistaken goals can be most easily identified from two observations: 1) how you feel in response to your child's behavior, and 2) what happens when you respond to the behavior. These are important cues from which you'll be able to diagnose which one of the mistaken beliefs is at the root of your child's misbehavior."

Attention

"When your child's goal is attention, the overriding feeling you'll experience is irritation. When you respond by scolding (giving some attention), the child stops misbehaving temporarily. But the same behavior, or something equally irritating, soon starts again. Tommy may play quietly as long as you are watching, but will become an impossible, whining nuisance as soon as you attempt to read the paper or talk on the phone. When you tell him to go away, the goal of getting attention is temporarily met, and Tommy will go away — temporarily. But before long he's back, pestering you again."

Power

"When your child's goal is power, the feeling you'll experience is anger and a desire to control. When you attempt to set a limit, a power struggle ensues. When Tommy says his newly learned curse word, and you forbid him to use such language in the house, it will suddenly become his favorite word. The more you attempt to prevent his saying the word, the more attached to it he becomes."

Revenge

"When your child's goal is revenge, the feeling you'll experience is one of deep hurt and a desire to hurt back. Punishing your child results in further escalations of vengeful behavior. If you yell at Tommy and spank him for hitting his baby sister, he may try next time to tip her out of her crib."

Avoiding Expectations Through Inadequacy

"When your child's goal is to display inadequacy to avoid the pressure of expectations (yours and his own), your overriding feelings will be despair and helplessness. When you attempt to help improve the child's performance, he or she becomes even more discouraged. When Tommy complains that he's too dumb to do his homework, your assertions to the contrary only spur him to further statements of his inadequacy."

E. Skill: Increasing Positive Behavior

"Rewarding a behavior will increase its chances of being repeated. Of the many things that are rewarding for children, one of the most powerful is parental attention. This can be positive (a smile or caress) or negative (a sharp word, a slap).

"Parents will sometimes ask why they should reward children for 'what they should be doing anyway.' It's useless to argue about whether or not the child *should* be behaving in the desired way and therefore 'deserves' a reward. Rather, a more useful question is whether the child *is* behaving in the desired way. The answer is presumably no (or else the parents wouldn't be discussing the issue in a parenting group). Reinforcement works. Parents have the choice of using it or continuing to struggle with the problem behavior. Parents and children alike will benefit from knowing that their contributions to the family (even those that are considered ordinary responsibilities) are appreciated.

"It's important to be very specific about which behaviors you want to encourage. 'I want him to set the table when asked' is more specific than 'I want him to do what I tell him.'

"Identifying appropriate reinforcements for your child requires consideration of such factors as the child's age and the difficulty or magnitude of the behavior change being encouraged. With older children the reinforcements can include future activities (a movie, a trip to the zoo), whereas with younger children the reinforcements must be more immediate. Rewards must also be proportionate to the task at hand. A new bicycle may be an appropriate reinforcement for a semester of hard work at school, but it would be an inappropriate reward for making the bed five mornings in a row.

"Timing is crucial. For the most part, whichever behavior directly precedes the reinforcement is the one that will be reinforced. Thus, the more immediate the reward, the greater its impact. When Tommy mows the lawn without being asked, an immediate expression of appreciation is a more effective reinforcement than mentioning it a day or two later. When he's to be rewarded with a trip to the zoo, telling him immediately is more effective than telling him on the day of the trip."

F. Skill: Other Ways To Increase the Positive and Decrease the Negative

Shaping

"Most of you don't want to sit around waiting for your children to randomly exhibit a desired behavior so that you can then reinforce it. Instead, you can 'shape' your children's behavior. Begin by reinforcing behavior even if it is only somewhat close to the desired behavior, and then gradually reinforce only those behaviors that are closer to the desired behavior."

Reinforcing an Incompatible Behavior

"If there's a particular behavior that you want to eliminate, teach another behavior that's incompatible. In other words, teach something pleasant that cannot physically occur if the other behavior is going on. Then consistently reward the new behavior."

Reinforcing Anything But Unwanted Behaviors

"Discourage a particularly undesirable behavior by reinforcing every other behavior. Later, reinforce only those behaviors that you'd like to see repeated."

G. Skill: A Misbehaving Child Is Still a Worthwhile Child

"It's important to separate the child from his or her behavior. The key concept for this group is that the intrinsic worth of children is not dependent on how they behave. All children misbehave at times. When the message they receive is that they are 'bad' when they behave badly, then they are liable at these times to become discouraged, and their rate of misbehavior is likely to increase. When they are told that it's simply their behavior that's unacceptable, their self-worth is not affected. Instead of calling Tommy a lazy slob, you could tell him how disappointed you were that he didn't mow the lawn when asked."

H. Skill: Encouraging Your Child

"Encouraging children involves helping them see their strengths and the value of their contributions, no matter how small. Encouragement can be nonverbal and implied rather than specific.

"Treat your child *as if* he or she were responsible. This will go a long way toward encouraging the child to behave in accordance with that expectation. 'Never do for a child what she can do for herself' is a good rule of thumb for encouraging autonomy. Of course, it's essential to know the appropriate expectations for children of different ages. If your expectations exceed your child's capacities, this can be a setup for feelings of failure and discouragement.

"When appropriate, ask your children for their advice or opinions, and encourage them to participate in decision making.

"Show your children a different, more positive perception of themselves, based on past experience. When Tommy speaks disparagingly about himself, don't invalidate his feelings. Instead, remind him of the occasions when he displayed very different, positive characteristics."

I. Skill: Children Need To Be Heard

"Many children will escalate their misbehavior when they feel that they haven't been heard. They hope that if they scream louder or kick harder or even sulk more dramatically, someone will finally understand what they're trying to express. Unfortunately, these escalations usually elicit just the opposite reaction: an attempt to silence the child and/or stop the behavior. The child ends up feeling even less acknowledged or understood.

"Listen to and acknowledge the feelings your child is expressing. To do this adequately, you have to give your complete attention. As children develop the skill of verbalizing their feelings, they will need to act them out less. Giving your child's feelings a name will model this process. When Jenny tells you how much she hates the girl who only yesterday was her best friend, a response of 'Gee, you sound really mad at her' will let her know that you're listening and understanding."

Acknowledging Negative Feelings

"It's difficult to acknowledge your child's angry or painful feelings. But you don't have to agree with feelings to acknowledge them. The key is respect, not blanket agreement. 'I understand you're disappointed at not being included in the decision' doesn't imply that you agree that he should have been included.

"Instead of trying to solve your children's problems for them, ask the children for solutions. Encourage them to use their own resources. 'What do you think you could do about it?' gives the encouraging message that you trust their ability to solve their own problems.

"Don't make children feel guilty for negative feelings. Tell them 'Everyone gets angry at times. Getting angry is fine. Yelling, screaming, and hitting aren't.'"

Expressing Your Own Feelings

"Sometimes you can engage cooperation by expressing how you feel about your child's behavior. Children don't usually want their parents to be unhappy."

I-Statements. "Make *I*-statements rather than *you*-statements. *You*-statements ('You make me so angry') tend to impart blame and are usually heard as an attack. The object of the *you*-statement then gets defensive and often attacks back. *I*-statements acknowledge that the speaker owns the feeling or problem without blaming or attacking.

"An *I*-statement usually begins 'I feel....' and continues 'and I want.....' Be careful not to turn *I*-statements into hidden *you*-statements: 'I feel that *you* are.....'"

J. Skill: Solving Problems

"The most useful model of problem solving includes the following fours steps:

1. *Define the problem in specific terms*. This is the most important step, because if you don't accurately define the problem, you can't find an accurate solution.

2. *Brainstorm alternatives*. Be respectful of all alternatives, yours and your child's. List them before evaluating them.

3. *Eliminate alternatives*. Go through the list and eliminate alternatives that either you or your child don't want. Remaining alternatives must be acceptable to both of you. If none are left, either more alternatives must be created (step 2), or you must both reevaluate the alternatives that have been eliminated.

4. *Develop a plan to put the chosen alternative into practice, and evaluate its success.* If the first plan doesn't work, repeat steps 3 and 4."

K. Concept: Punishment Doesn't Work

"Punishment doesn't work for many reasons. It doesn't help children learn to be mature, responsible, or independent. It demonstrates to children that the best way to get what they want is coercion.

"Punishment does stop the undesired behavior temporarily. But usually the punishment is so unrelated to the crime — and the child is so angry and resentful for being punished — that the intended message about acting appropriately and responsibly goes unnoticed.

"Sometimes the punishment actually leaves a message that is totally contradictory to the one you want to convey. You can't expect a child to learn not to fight with siblings, for instance, if you punish him or her by spanking.

"The attention given during punishment can actually serve as reinforcement for the misbehavior, especially if the goal of the behavior was attention. When the behavior recurs, it's easy to assume that the punishment wasn't strong enough; but the use of stronger measures will only meet with a similar lack of success."

L. Skill: Give Your Child Choices

"For children to learn to act responsibly, they must learn that they have choices. Wherever possible, give your child a choice about what you want him or her to do. The choice can concern when the task is done, how the task is done, or with whom the task is done (but not whether the task is done). Children feel more in control of their lives — and therefore better about themselves — when they have choices. Given choices, they are less likely to engage in power struggles or to misbehave in order to feel worthwhile."

M. Skill: Setting Consequences

"Children must also learn that their choices have consequences. There are two kinds of consequences, natural and logical. Natural consequences occur without any kind of intervention from you. If Jenny forgets to take her lunch to school, the natural consequence is that she'll be hungry at lunch time. In the mistaken belief that they are being helpful, many parents would jump in their cars and deliver the forgotten lunch. In fact, this response prevents Jenny from experiencing the consequences of her actions. She doesn't learn to remember to take her lunch (to prevent being hungry). She doesn't have to learn the lesson offered by the situation. If she forgets her lunch, someone will always bring it to her. Despite all your nagging, threats, and punishment, the message that is retained is that remembering to take lunch to school is unnecessary. A healthy child won't suffer serious harm from missing lunch for a day or two, but the experience of being hungry as a direct result of his or her own choice (to remember or not remember) will have a profound learning impact on the child.

"Logical consequences are those that require your intervention. If a friend borrows something and returns it in significantly worse condition, chances are that you won't lend anything else to that friend. To withhold your property from a person who doesn't respect it is a logical consequence of that lack of respect. If the item were ruined, it would be logical to ask that it be replaced or repaired at the other person's expense. No consequences would automatically present themselves to your friend without your intervention (refusal to lend next time, or request for payment): this is a *logical* rather than a *natural* consequence.

"Many parents tire of cajoling, nagging, and threatening their children to get ready to be taken to school in the morning. Instead, parents could calmly announce what time they'll be leaving: those children who aren't ready might need to dress in the car, skip breakfast, or (if safety permits) walk. Under these circumstances, children would learn that they can either be ready on time or suffer some potential hardships — and that the choice is theirs.

"There are several key issues to consider in designing logical consequences.

1. Make sure that the consequence is *related* to the behavior in question.

2. Once a consequence is designed, *follow through* with it. If what you say is going to happen doesn't, the message is that your child shouldn't believe what you say. Consistency is essential.

3. Present the consequence *without anger* or blame. Children are able to learn from consequences when choices are presented respectfully with the message that the children themselves are fully capable of making the best choice. The consequence of the choice they make must be presented neutrally. In this way there is no one to blame for the result — it's simply the consequence of their choice. This is what differentiates consequences from punishment. If you present the consequences with anger or glee, or indulge in 'I told you so,' the lesson will again be lost in the child's anger and resentment.

"It may help to try and see yourself simply as an agent of your child's decisions and choices. Keeping this in mind, it may be easier to enforce consequences without anger."

N. Skill: Using Time Out

"*Time out* means just that: time away from whatever is going on. Usually this means that a child will go to his or her room for a specified amount of time (a few minutes for a young child is enough). This is not punishment; the child can go to the bedroom and play with whatever toys he or she chooses. It's a time for the child to reflect.

"Time out can be useful in two ways. You can present it as one of two alternatives to your child, and let the decision be his or hers. You can also present time out as a logical consequence of behaving inappropriately around others. In both cases, the choice is essentially the child's."

O. Skill: Putting It All Together

"Determining what response is most appropriate for a particular situation involves the question 'Whose problem is it?' The answer depends on the answer to another question: 'Whose rights are being affected?' If your child wants to sleep in his T-shirt and shorts instead of his pajamas for a night, is it really worth a fight? Are your rights really being violated? If your child doesn't want to finish everything on her dinner plate, are your rights affected? What if your teenager wants to shave his head and wear a mohawk, spray-painted hot pink? This is a difficult issue, especially for those of you who desire some measure of control over your children's lives.

"Some of you may want your children to be just like you—in behavior, tastes, and opinions. You may feel personally affronted when they differentiate themselves in these areas. However, children must develop a sense of their separateness in order to become autonomous and independent. This separateness is usually manifested by flaunting differences in just those areas that are dear to parents: dress, hairstyle, political opinions. Treating children with respect means accepting their differences and allowing them to make their own decisions, *providing their health or safety isn't at risk.*

"Try to let go of issues that are ultimately your child's responsibility. Telling your teenager that she can't wear makeup when she goes out may simply teach her to be sneaky, waiting until she's out of the house to put the makeup on. Your opposition may even enhance the attraction of the behavior you're trying to stop.

"Depending on the answer to the question, 'Whose problem is it?' there are certain steps to take in responding appropriately."

1. *The Child's Problem.* "When the child owns the problem, the appropriate responses are

    a. to listen and validate the child's feelings

    b. to encourage problem solving'

"Don't be pushy in offering help — after all, it's their problem."

2. *The Parent's Problem.* "When your rights are being affected, then it *is* your problem and your responsibility to take action. When you lie awake at night worrying about the safety of your child who consistently breaks curfew, then your rights are being violated. The appropriate steps are to

    a. express your feelings in an *I*-statement

    b. engage your child in problem solving

    c. determine consequences

3. *When Ownership of the Problem Is Unclear.* "Sometimes it's difficult to distinguish who owns the problem, because both persons' rights are affected. If your teenager is unhappy over the break-up of a relationship, it's his or her problem. But if he or she behaves aggressively at home as a result of the unhappiness, it may become your problem as well.

    "In these cases, start with the child's problem. When that is resolved, your problem might get resolved in the process. So the appropriate responses are to

    a. listen and validate feelings

    b. encourage problem solving

"If that doesn't resolve the problem for you, go on to

    c. express your feelings in an *I*-statement

    d. engage your child in problem solving

    e. set consequences

"The steps you choose in dealing with different situations will reflect your own values. If your fifteen-year-old is skipping school, some of you may decide that your child owns the problem, and allow him or her to repeat the year. Others may choose to set some logical consequences ('I'm happy to support you while you're attending school. I'm not willing to support you if you're just playing around. If you choose not to attend school, you'll have to find a job or somewhere else to live.')."

P. Concept: Have Fun

"When the conflict level in a family is high, the enjoyment level is low. It's hard to have fun in an atmosphere of tension and resentment, where every interaction becomes a power struggle. It's important, therefore, while working on decreasing the conflict, to try and increase the frequency of pleasurable activities.

"Special alone time with each child can be incorporated into bedtime rituals (reading a story, reviewing the day).

"Set aside a 'family day' each week for the entire family to do something fun together. Ensure that the whole family participates in planning this event, and that everyone shares in the preparatory activities."

Main Interventions

Week 1

Introduction

See Starting the Group.

A. Concept: Three Styles of Parenting

Intervention 1: Didactic Presentation (See Concepts and Skills section)

Intervention 2: Role-plays

   Example 1

Parents can role-play interactions which they perceive as typical of the parenting styles just described. Most will recognize their own styles as being either authoritarian or permissive.

James:	*(role-playing a ten-year-old)* Mom, can I watch TV?
Pamela:	*(role-playing James' mother)* Have you finished your homework yet?
James:	Not quite, but —
Pamela:	No but! Get in your room and finish it right now.
James:	But why can't I just watch one program?
Pamela:	Because I said so. And if I hear one more peep out of you, you'll be very sorry. Now go!

   Example 2

Catherine:	*(role-playing a fifteen-year-old)* Dad, Jenny's having a party at her house on Saturday. May I go?
Fred:	*(role-playing Catherine's father)* Well, I don't know. Who's going to be there?
Catherine:	Everyone's going to be there. Don't be so stuffy, it's just a party.
Fred:	Well, I'd like to think that Jenny's parents were going to be there.
Catherine:	Jesus! What do you think, we're all babies? Don't you trust me? No one else's parents give them such trouble about a simple party.

Fred: Okay, okay! Go! Just leave me alone!

B. Concept: How Do Children Change?

Intervention 1: Didactic Presentation (See Concepts and Skills section)

Intervention 3: Group Discussion

   Example

"What do you think about the idea that if you want your kids to change, you have to change first?"

Note to therapists: No matter how bad things have been at home, they will improve if parents follow the guidelines presented in the context of this group. However, at this point we can safely predict that things may get worse before they get better. Children will be suspicious at first when their parents begin responding to them differently. They may interpret unfamiliar signs of respect as sarcasm and reject invitations to talk or solve problems. Even though children might be unhappy with things as they are, their situation is at least predictable and they can therefore feel comfortable and familiar with it. When faced with unfamiliar, unpredictable behavior from their parents, children will attempt to elicit the old, familiar responses: they'll increase their levels of acting up or acting out to provoke their parents' old controlling behaviors. It will feel to parents as if things are getting worse. But if they can remember and anticipate this reaction, they will be able to persevere with the skills they're learning, and eventually things will improve.

Week 2

Check-in

Solicit reactions to the previous meeting.

C. Concept: All Children Want To Belong

Intervention 1: Didactic Presentation (See Concepts and Skills section)

D. Skill: Diagnosing Your Child's Misbehavior

Intervention 1: Didactic Presentation (See Concepts and Skills section)

Most parents will easily be able to identify their child's mistaken goal in any particular interaction. Although the goal may differ from time to time, one will probably — though not always — be more in evidence than the others. The two most common goals are attention and power. Avoiding others' expectations through displays of inadequacy is also frequently seen, while revenge is rare as a general theme.

Intervention 4: Soliciting Examples From Parents

   Example

"Think about your own children for a minute. What are the goals of their misbehavior, and what are the cues that enable you to recognize those goals?"

Gloria: Paul's goal is definitely attention. He constantly bugs me when we're home alone — for something to eat, something to drink, to answer his

	questions, to tell me he's bored. It drives me crazy. And he'll go away for about two minutes when I yell at him...and then we'll start again.
Therapist:	And the cues?
Gloria:	Well, I guess that I feel frustrated, and that when I yell at him, he goes away — temporarily. I suppose I gave him the attention he wanted at that point.

Homework

Observe (a) your feelings and (b) what happens when you intervene, to practice diagnosing your children's misbehavior.

Week 3

Check-in

Include success and problems with homework.

E. Skill: Increasing Positive Behavior

Intervention 1: Didactic Presentation (See Concepts and Skills section)

Parents sometimes complain that reinforcement sounds like bribery. This concern arises from the belief that bribery is always bad. In fact, people are always making agreements about appropriate rewards for desired behaviors. Bosses pay salaries only if their employees turn up for work and perform adequately. There is nothing inherently wrong with a clear agreement between parents and their children. Preferably, however, reinforcements are unsolicited responses to desired behavior. They are aimed less at increasing the contents of the child's money box than increasing the child's pride in his or her accomplishments and, therefore, self-esteem.

Intervention 4: Soliciting Examples From Parents

Example 1

"What have you found to be effective reinforcement with your own kids?"

Julie:	Certainly attention, just like you said. Sometimes when Justin comes home from school and starts to tell me about his day, I'm tired and sort of only half-listen. Usually he disappears after a few sentences. And it's true, when I really pay attention to him, he's much more enthusiastic about talking to me.
Chris:	The only thing that seems to work with Robert these days is supplementing his pocket money.
Margaret:	I agree with Julie. My daughter's teacher began giving the kids stickers every time they got their homework right. My daughter suddenly became much more conscientious about doing her homework. I guess getting the stickers was like being noticed — getting attention.

Example 2

"What about negative attention?"

Gloria:	When we're home alone and Paul bugs me. Yelling at him to go away and play gives him attention. That's why he's back again after two minutes.

F. Skill: Other Ways To Increase the Positive and Decrease the Negative

Intervention 1: Didactic Presentation (See Concepts and Skills section)

Intervention 5: Case Presentation With Problem Solving

Example 1

"Let's take a specific case and see how with shaping we might increase positive behavior."

Claire:	I'd really love my four-year-old Ben to get himself dressed in the morning. None of my nagging or badgering has helped.
Therapist:	Okay. What specifically does getting dressed entail?
Claire:	Well, putting on his underpants, a T-shirt, jeans or sweatpants, socks and shoes. And maybe a sweater. I'm happy to lay them out for him the night before, but it's a pain to have to dress him and he's old enough to be able to do it himself.
Therapist:	So what might the first step be?
Darryl:	Reward even a small step toward getting himself ready.
Therapist:	Good. Claire, what small step could you reward, and how could you reward it?
Claire:	Well, usually he lifts up his feet one at a time to step into his underpants, and then again to get into his jeans. I don't have to ask him to do that. Maybe I could make a fuss over that as a first step.
Therapist:	Okay. What could the next step be?
Claire:	Maybe seeing if he could pull them up by himself once I've helped him step into them.
Therapist:	So once the foot lifting is well established, you'd begin reinforcing him only for doing the next step: both lifting his feet and then pulling up the pants. What next?
Claire:	I guess the same thing with pulling on his T-shirt. When he's got the underpants routine, I could add the step of his lifting up his arms for me, and then add pulling the shirt down over his head. I think I'm getting the picture.
Darryl:	Won't it take forever at that pace?
Therapist:	It won't happen in one day, it's true, but it *will* happen. And it'll be a lot faster than the pace at which he's currently going, with the nagging and badgering.

Example 2

"What about another example to see how reinforcing incompatible behavior might work to decrease negative behavior?"

Pamela:	Great! My two kids are a nightmare in the car. I hate having to drive them anywhere because they're so rowdy.
Therapist:	What specifically do they do in the car?
Pamela:	Fight. Actually, they do that everywhere. It's just that in the confines of the car, it's intolerable. And it's not just fighting, it's fighting at the top of their lungs.
Therapist:	How are you currently reinforcing that behavior?
Pamela:	I guess I've been giving them lots of attention for it.

Therapist:	So the first step would be to stop reinforcing the fighting. Okay. What behavior would be incompatible with fighting?
Dave:	What about singing? If they were singing, they couldn't be fighting.
Therapist:	Great Idea! Pamela, do the kids know any songs?
Pamela:	It's weird, but I don't really know. I suppose I could find out. And if they don't, I could teach them some. I used to play the guitar, so I'm sure I have a collection of songbooks somewhere. Maybe I'll even pull out my guitar again!
Therapist:	And then, of course, you'd have to reinforce their singing. But what if they sing at the top of their lungs?
Pamela:	That'd be fine — it's the loud fighting that's so distracting.

Example 3

"Let's explore an example of how reinforcing anything but unwanted behavior can decrease that behavior."

Peter:	My daughter Penny tears up my books and magazines whenever she can get her hands on them. Sometimes it seems as if she does it deliberately to provoke me — she looks straight at me then toddles right over to the bookcase.
Therapist:	What's her goal and how are you currently reinforcing it?
Peter:	Well, it drives me crazy and it hasn't stopped, so I guess it's attention...and I really give it to her, going on and on about how books are for reading, not tearing up etc., etc.
Therapist:	So what's the first step?
Peter:	Stop reinforcing the tearing...but what can I do when she tears the books?
Therapist:	Good question — any suggestions?
Peter:	I guess I could temporarily move the books from the bottom shelf of the bookcase so she couldn't get at them at all. Or make sure that they're ones that I don't care much about.
Therapist:	Both those suggestions seem reasonable. So what's the next step?
Margaret:	Finding other things to reinforce — I suppose things like playing with other toys, talking, running around. Maybe even little things like smiling?
Therapist:	Yes. The task is to pay close attention in order to observe all the other things that Penny does — and to reinforce them. Once again, it's important to be specific with the behaviors you choose to reinforce, and to reward them promptly. Once she's stopped tearing books, you can decide which of all the alternative behaviors you want to continue reinforcing, and which not.

Homework

Choose one specific behavior and attempt to either increase or decrease its frequency, using the reinforcement skills learned this session.

Week 4

Check-in

Include success and problems with homework.

G. Skill: A Misbehaving Child Is Still a Worthwhile Child

Intervention 1: Didactic Presentation (See Concepts and Skills section)

Intervention 4: Soliciting Examples From Parents

Example 1

"Let's say your child just set the table for you — how might you respond to him?"

Fred:	My automatic response would be to say, "Good boy!" — but I realize that's just the opposite of what you're talking about.
Therapist:	You're right. "Good boy" suggests that his worth as a person results from setting the table. What really has resulted from him setting the table?
Fred:	He's really helped me out. Maybe a better response would be: "Thanks for setting the table, it's a real help."

Example 2

"What about when your daughter mows the lawn?"

James:	To not imply that her worth depends on her behavior, I would say something like "You did a great job mowing the lawn. I really appreciate it."
Therapist:	Good. Why is it better to say "great job" than "good girl?"
James:	Because "great job" is simply a comment on the behavior, not on the person.

H. Skill: Encouraging Your Child

Intervention 1: Didactic Presentation (See Concepts and Skills section)

Many parents think that encouragement means pushing their children to greater heights of achievement. It's important to stress that, in fact, it refers to helping children feel better about themselves, their role in the family, and the value of their contributions.

Intervention 4: Soliciting Examples From Parents

Example 1

"What's an example of a behavior that suggests discouragement?"

Dave:	Molly won't practice her guitar anymore. Ever since her younger sister started playing, Molly seems to have just given up.
Therapist:	Okay, how have you tried to encourage her to continue practicing?
Dave:	First we reminded her of how much her lessons were costing us. I know, I know, that didn't work. Then we tried telling her that if she didn't practice, Judy would soon be as good as her. That was even worse. She just about stopped altogether. So we gave up saying anything to her about it.
Therapist:	You got discouraged, too. Sounds like Molly saw herself as unable to compete with her sister. To avoid your expectations, she demonstrated her inadequacy. How might you be encouraging in a way that makes Molly feel good about herself?
Dave:	I could remind her how much we enjoyed the times when she played to us, how special it was to share her enjoyment of music. [Show your

children a different perception of themselves, based on your experience of them.]

Example 2

"What are other examples suggesting discouragement?"

Gloria: My older son used to just drag around the house all the time with a face as long as a horse. He wasn't interested in anything we suggested doing; didn't really even want to talk to us. He must have been discouraged, because I felt discouraged, and all our attempts to cheer him up failed miserably.

Therapist: How did you try to encourage him?

Gloria: A million different ways that didn't work. Then recently, my husband and I decided to buy a new car. We asked Robbie if he'd be responsible for doing some research and coming up with a few recommendations. We simply told him what our price ceiling was, and a few other requirements. He loved it! He seemed like a new person! I guess it fits with your suggestions about treating him as if he were responsible. [Treat your children as if they're competent. Where appropriate, ask their advice, opinions, and encourage problem solving.]

Intervention 2: Role-plays

Parents can practice being encouraging by role-playing in parent-child dyads. First, the parent can make an automatic response, and get feedback from the "child" about how it feels to hear that response. Then the response can be amended to be truly encouraging.

Example

Julie: (role-playing a child) I can't do this math. I'm so stupid!

Ted: (role-playing Julie's father) No you're not — don't say that!

Julie: I am so. I can never get it right. I can't get anything right.

Ted: If you tried harder instead of just complaining, you'd do better.

Therapist: Julie, how did it feel to have Ted respond that way?

Julie: Horrible. I felt like he didn't understand or care how I was feeling. That he just wanted me to do well so he wouldn't be embarrassed by having a stupid child. Then I got angry.

Therapist: Okay, Ted, try giving a more encouraging response.

Ted: Math is a tough subject. I had difficulty with it when I was in school, too. But I remember when we couldn't find what was wrong with the heater and you worked it out on your own. That doesn't sound like stupid to me. And last night when I forgot where my keys were, you remembered where I'd left them. That doesn't spell stupid either. [Show your children a different perception of themselves, based on your experience.]

Julie: Well, maybe if you would give me a hand getting started, I might be able to do it.

Ted: Okay. Let's look at problem number one. What do you think the first step might be? [Never do for children what they can do for themselves.]

Homework

Practice responding to your children in ways that separate their worth as people from their behavior. Also practice encouraging your children, whether or not they seem discouraged.

Week 5

Check-in

Include success and problems with homework.

I. Skill: Children Need To Be Heard

Intervention 1: Didactic Presentation (See Concepts and Skills section)

Intervention 2: Role-plays

Role-plays of parent-child dyads can be used to practice listening to and validating feelings without blaming (using *I* messages).

Example 1

Chris:	*(role-playing an eight-year-old)* I hate Mommy!
Bill:	*(role-playing parent)* You do not — you love Mommy! [an invalidating response]
Chris:	I don't — I hate her! I hate her! I hate her!
Therapist:	Now try really listening to Chris' feelings.
Bill:	You're really furious at her? [listening]
Chris:	Yes! She wouldn't let me play on the swing while you were out.
Bill:	And I know how much you really like playing on the swing. No wonder you're angry! [validating]
Chris:	Yes. [pause] Maybe tomorrow it won't rain and Mommy will let me swing.

Example 2

Margaret:	*(role-playing parent)* Kate, how many times do I have to tell you to do the dishes when you get home from school? Why don't you listen? [blaming]
Kate:	*(role-playing fourteen-year-old)* All right! All right! [under her breath] Bitch!
Therapist:	Okay, now try again, using an *I*-statement.
Margaret:	Kate, when I come home from work I'm tired. When I see the dishes not done, I feel even more tired and disappointed at the thought of having to do extra work. [*I*-statement]
Kate:	Sorry, Mom, I was on the phone with Angie all afternoon. I'll do them now.

J. Skill: Solving Problems

Intervention 1: Didactic Presentation (See Concepts and Skills section)

Intervention 2: Role-plays

Example 1: Define the Problem

Tony:	*(role-playing parent)* Darryl, when I see your dog staring hungrily at her empty bowl, I get upset that she's not being taken care of properly.
Darryl:	*(role-playing child)* Okay, okay, I'll feed her now.
Tony:	I'm sure she'll appreciate it. Darryl, I'm concerned that it's so hard for you to remember to feed her and that she isn't getting the kind of care that she deserves. Do you see it as a problem?
Darryl:	Not really — she always gets fed in the end.

Tony:	Yes, but often only because I remind you. And sometimes she's waited hours past her usual feeding time.
Darryl:	Well, I guess that's true sometimes.
Tony:	So we have a problem: Goldie isn't getting fed on time.

Example 2: Brainstorm Alternatives

Tony:	What can we do about it? Let's brainstorm. I'll write our suggestions down. Let's not evaluate them, just list them.
Darryl:	(teasing) Well, you could feed her for me!
Tony:	(writing it down) That's one idea. I have one, too — that we find Goldie a home where she'll be better cared for.
Darryl:	I could get her a huge bucket and fill it with food and let her eat out of it all week.
Tony:	If you forget to feed her in the morning, you won't watch TV or do any other fun thing that you have planned when you get home from school that day.
Darryl:	Maybe I could feed her in the afternoon instead of in the morning? I'd be less rushed then, and I could take her for a walk, too.

Example 3: Eliminate Alternatives

Tony:	If neither of us has any more suggestions, let's go through our list and evaluate. I'll read out each suggestion, and if either of us doesn't want it, then I'll cross it out. The first one is, I could feed Goldie for you. I'm not willing to keep that as an alternative. She's not my dog, so I don't want that responsibility. [crosses it off the list] The next one is, we find Goldie a home where she'll be better cared for.
Darryl:	No! I don't want that!
Tony:	Okay. You could fill a big bucket with food and let her eat out of it all week. I don't think you'd like it if I left a big bowl of oatmeal on the table for you to eat out of all week.
Darryl:	Yuck! Okay, cross that off.
Tony:	If you forget to feed her in the morning, you don't watch TV or do any other fun thing planned for that day.
Darryl:	I guess that would be okay. But I like my next suggestion better.
Tony:	That you feed her in the afternoon when you get home from school? That would be okay with me, too. So we have two possible solutions.

Example 4: Develop a Plan

Tony:	Which would work best?
Darryl:	I want to try feeding her in the afternoon when I get home from school. If I still forget, then I won't watch TV or do whatever else I planned for that day.
Tony:	Okay. That sounds good to me. When shall we start, and when should we evaluate how it's working?
Darryl:	Tomorrow. If I haven't fed her by the time you get home, I won't watch TV. Let's do it for a week and talk about it again.
Tony:	Great. I'm really glad you were willing to solve this problem with me. I know how much you love Goldie. [Reinforce the problem-solving behavior that you'd like to see.]

Homework

Practice the four problem-solving steps.

Week 6

Check-in

Include success and problems with homework.

K. Concept: Punishment Doesn't Work

Intervention 4: Soliciting Examples From Parents

Example

"How many of you have tried punishment as a way of getting your children to cooperate? Everyone? Well, who's found it to be really effective? [Usually no one.] Let's hear from some of you who haven't found it to work very well."

Pamela:	When Brian talks back to me, I've tried slapping his face, sending him to his room, and grounding him. Nothing seems to work. Once I extended his grounding to six months before I realized how ridiculous that was. Half the time he's still muttering under his breath, and I leave because I'm afraid I'll really blow my stack.
Margaret:	I have that trouble, too. I send Sue to her room, she slams the door, yells something I can't quite hear, and I'm ready to kill her.

Intervention 1: Didactic Presentation (See Concepts and Skills section)

It's important not to argue with parents about whether their children "deserve" to be punished for their misbehavior. The key issue is whether punishment works to teach responsibility and cooperation.

L. Skill: Give Your Child Choices

Intervention 1: Didactic Presentation (See Concepts and Skills section)

Intervention 2: Role-plays

Role-plays in parent-child dyads can give parents the opportunity to practice avoiding power struggles by offering choices.

Example 1

Claire:	(role-playing parent) Peter, it's time for your bath.
Peter:	No! I don't want a bath!
Claire:	Come on — you love baths.
Peter:	I hate baths! I'm not having one.
Therapist:	Now try giving Peter a choice.
Claire:	Peter, would you like your bath before or after dinner?
Peter:	After.
Claire:	Okay. Would you like your boats or your ducks in the bath with you?
Peter:	My ducks.

Sometimes the situation is more difficult and requires perseverance in giving choices.

Example 2

Pamela:	*(role-playing parent)* Gloria, I know you're angry, but it's not okay for you to scream at me like that. You can either talk to me quietly or go to your room till you calm down.
Gloria:	*(still screaming)* I hate you! I wish I had another mother!
Pamela:	I see you've decided to go to your room till you calm down. Do you want to go there yourself or do you want me to carry you?
Gloria:	I won't go!
Pamela:	I see you've decided to have me carry you. Would you like me to come and tell you when ten minutes is up, or shall I set the timer?
Gloria:	Set the timer.

M. Skill: Setting Consequences

Intervention 1: Didactic Presentation (See Concepts and Skills section)

The key points to stress are that logical consequences must be 1) *related* to the misbehavior, 2) *consistent* (with respect to follow-through), and 3) *presented without anger*.

Intervention 5: Case Presentation With Problem Solving

Example

"Let's practice setting consequences. What's a problem we can use?"

Peter:	How about when Andrew fights with other kids at the playground?
Therapist:	Okay. Are there natural consequences that would teach Andrew about his behavior?
Judy:	Well, if the other kids don't like fighting, they might stop playing with him.
Peter:	But I don't like him hitting people.
Therapist:	That's a good point, Peter. Sometimes there are natural consequences that might work, but it's inappropriate for some reason to use them. In this case, someone might get hurt. What about logical consequences. What are the logical consequences of not knowing how to behave properly on a playground?
Peter:	Not being allowed to go to the playground?
Therapist:	Okay. What would you say to Andrew?
Judy:	Well, I'd want to give him a choice first. I might say: People aren't for hitting. You can play with the other kids in the playground and work out your conflicts without hitting, or you can play alone at home. It's your choice.
Therapist:	And then if he hits?
Peter:	You blew it! Let's go. Now!
Therapist:	What about the rule of no anger? The idea is not to punish, but to let Andrew learn something about his choices and their consequences.
Peter:	Okay. What about: I guess you've decided to play alone at home.
Therapist:	Good. Now, what if Andrew throws a temper tantrum, screaming that he doesn't want to go home?

Gloria: That's when I get so embarrassed I want to disappear. Sometimes I just drop the issue to avoid the scene.

Therapist: And what would Andrew learn?

Gloria: That he can do what he wants.

Therapist: And even more, that you don't mean what you say. It's difficult when your children misbehave in public. It's hard not to feel that they're reflections of you. But if you want to teach them responsibility, it's important to persevere and follow through with the consequence that's been set. What are some things that could be said at that point?

Judy: Maybe to acknowledge that he doesn't like it much, but to remind him that it was his choice.

Dave: And to continue giving him choices. You could ask him if he would like to walk to the car or have you carry him.

Peter: What about the next time? We usually go almost every day.

Therapist: There's no reason not to give him another chance the next day. Remind him of his choices, and maybe encourage him by telling him that you're sure he can make the best choice for himself.

Peter: And if he hits again, go home again? I guess when I look at it like that, it makes it easier not to feel angry at him — or guilty about depriving him of the playground.

Homework

Practice developing and setting logical consequences (or letting natural consequences have their impact) as alternatives to punishment.

Week 7

Check-in

Include success and problems with homework.

N. Skill: Using Time Out

Intervention 1: Didactic Presentation (See Concepts and Skills section)

Intervention 3: Group Discussion

Parents can benefit from a brief discussion of when *time out* would be an appropriate alternative to their current disciplinary methods.

O. Skill: Putting It All Together

Intervention 1: Didactic Presentation (See Concepts and Skills section)

Parents sometimes have difficulty determining whose rights are being affected in a particular situation, and therefore who owns the problem. Differentiating between what parents would like versus what their rights are is often helpful.

Intervention 5: Case Presentation With Problem Solving

  Example 1: The Child's Problem

"Let's do some problem solving. Who'd like to present a situation?"

Chris:	My sixteen-year-old son, Jeffery, just found out that he failed three of his subjects at school. He's been told that he either has to go to summer school or repeat the year. He's furious, says the teachers are discriminating against him, and wants me to somehow intervene.
Therapist:	Whose problem is it?
Chris:	I feel like it's my problem. I know he didn't work hard enough last semester, didn't do his homework, skipped some classes, but I hate to see him fall behind. All his friends have passed and will be going on ahead.
Therapist:	Are your rights being affected by the situation?
Chris:	I guess not...no.
Therapist:	So who owns the problem?
Chris:	Jeffrey.
Therapist:	So what are the appropriate steps in responding to a problem that your son owns?
Chris:	Acknowledge his feelings, and encourage problem solving.
Therapist:	Good. How could you do that? What feelings is he expressing?
Chris:	He's furious, and I'm sure he's really disappointed as well.
Therapist:	So what might you say?
Fred:	How about: "I can imagine how disappointing it must be to have failed. And a tough choice to either give up your summer or miss out on being with your friends next year."
Therapist:	That's an excellent example. There's no blame or "I told you so" implied. Simply an acknowledgment that he feels pretty awful.
Chris:	But what about when he comes to me telling me I have to do something?
Claire:	What if you were to say what Fred suggested, but follow it with: "I know that you'll make the best decision for yourself, and I'm certainly willing to help you in the process." [encourage problem solving]
Fred:	He must know on some level that he didn't do the necessary work and that's why he failed. You could always add, "I'm not willing to intervene at school," if he pushes.
Therapist:	And continue to acknowledge his feelings, for example, frustration at your unwillingness to intervene. It's difficult to know that you're not helping Jeffrey in the way he wants to be helped. But it's essential to remember that, in fact, you're helping him much more by teaching him to be responsible for his choices and their consequences.

Example 2: The Parent's Problem
"Let's take another example."

Pamela:	My fifteen-year-old daughter, Sherry, consistently breaks curfew — not by much, but even after twenty minutes I'm worried and can't sleep.
Therapist:	Whose problem is it?
Pamela:	Well, I think I have the right to not have to lie awake and worry about her safety. It seems to me that whenever there's an issue of safety, my rights are involved.
Therapist:	Yes. So if it's your problem, what's the first step?
Pamela:	Express my feelings. I've done a ton of that. Just about every time she's late I tell her how pissed off I am that she's so thoughtless and irresponsible. She doesn't care — just gets furious at me.

Therapist:	Can you see how, although you started with an *I*-statement, you turned it into a blaming *you*-statement? What do you really feel when Sherry's late? Is there something underneath the anger?
Pamela:	Yes, I'm scared stiff.... Okay, I see. So I should say "Sherry, I get really scared when you don't come home on time. I can't sleep so I just lie awake worrying"?
Therapist:	That'll probably feel less like an attack to Sherry, and it might make her more open to the next step — engaging in problem solving. What could you say to get her cooperation?
Dave:	What about, "Since I don't want to continue worrying about you at night, let's see if we can come up with a solution that would work for us both"?
Pamela:	She'd probably say that I should just stop worrying.
Therapist:	Well, that's one suggestion, and it should be listed along with all the others the two of you come up with. You can always eliminate the unacceptable alternatives in step 3 of the problem-solving procedure. But you may come up with something that you're both willing to try.
Pamela:	I could suggest that she call me if she's going to be late — but I'm afraid that she'd call every time, and I still wouldn't know when to expect her.
Therapist:	So if you can't come up with a mutually acceptable solution, or if the solution you agree on doesn't work, what's next?
Margaret:	Setting consequences.
Therapist:	Are there natural consequences that would be appropriate here?
Margaret:	No. Nothing automatically happens when Sherry's late. I'd want to set some logical consequences, like if she's not home by curfew this time, then she doesn't get to go next time. Her choice.
Therapist:	Okay. So the message is that if you want to be trusted to be responsible and go out at night, then you have to behave like a responsible, trustworthy person. That means respecting agreements. If Sherry chooses to be irresponsible this Saturday night, then next Saturday night she'll have to be treated accordingly and stay home. The following Saturday she could try again.

Example 3: When Ownership of the Problem Is Unclear

"We've explored situations in which the problem belongs to the child and those in which it belongs to the parent. What about a situation in which it's hard to tell who owns the problem?"

James:	Brian is my step-son, nine years old. Most of the time he's just a great kid. But every time he comes home from spending the weekend with his dad, he treats me with such contempt I could kill him.
Therapist:	What exactly does he do?
James:	He ignores my existence. He doesn't talk to me and doesn't respond when I talk to him or ask him questions about the weekend.
Therapist:	Sounds like Brian has a hard time when he leaves his dad. Seeing you must remind him of just how much he misses him.
James:	That's what my wife says. I know it's true, and I guess that's his part of the problem. But I have the right to be treated with respect.
Therapist:	Yes, you do. In situations in which both the child and parent own part of the problem, what's the best response?
Ted:	Start with the child's problem. That means acknowledging Brian's feelings. We had the same problem, but it was my wife who was getting the silent

	treatment from my son. She told him that she knew he had a mother whom he missed and loved very much. She also told him that she imagined he would be sad coming home and seeing her because it smashed his dream of his mom and dad getting back together. That seemed to do the trick with Pete. Could you say something similar to Brian?
James:	I suppose so. Maybe I could tell him at a time when we're getting along okay.
Therapist:	That's a good idea. And the second part of addressing the child's problem is encouraging problem solving. In this case, perhaps it would help to ask Brian if there's something that would make it easier for him when he gets home. If that all works, great. But what if it doesn't?
Gloria:	Deal with the parent's problem: express feelings, problem solve, and set consequences. Something like "When I talk to you and you don't respond, my feelings get hurt," followed by "What do you think we could do about it?"
Ted:	In our case, my wife greeted Pete when he first got home, but then gave him an hour or so without trying to interact with him, so that he could adjust to being back with us. Pete actually came up with that suggestion!
Therapist:	And if problem solving doesn't work?
James:	Set consequences. I'd be willing to offer him the choice of talking with me politely, or if he needs time to adjust, doing it in his room. I guess that fits under *time out*.

Homework

Practice using the skills of determining who owns the problem and responding accordingly.

Week 8

Check-in

Include success and problems with homework.

P. Concept: Have Fun

Intervention 1: Didactic Presentation (See Concepts and Skills section)

Most of this last session should be spent planning strategies with parents which address specific problems or concerns.

Intervention 5: Case Presentation With Problem Solving

Criteria for Measuring Change

There is one main behavioral criterion for measuring change. This is to demonstrate in the group (for instance, in role-plays and case presentations) the concepts and skills being taught: the ability to listen, make *I*-statements, solve problems, determine whose rights are being affected by particular behaviors, and create appropriate consequences. Parents' reports of their children responding in new and positive ways also will indicate successful use of the parenting tools.

Problems Specific to the Group

The most common problem is that of the dominating participant. Parents who continue to speak without letting others contribute will have to be gently silenced ("Let's hear from some others," "I'm glad you feel comfortable enough in the group to participate so freely; I'd like to encourage some of the others to speak up, too," "I know Johnny is a problem, but we need to give everyone a chance to deal with their children's problems as well"). Parents who speak very little can be encouraged by ensuring that everyone has the opportunity to participate in role-plays and other activities.

Sometimes it becomes apparent after a few sessions that a participant has more severe problems than can be appropriately dealt with in the group. Meeting privately with the parent(s) and recommending (and, if desired, making a referral to) either individual or family therapy may be necessary.

Similarly, sometimes the children's problems presented by the parents may be beyond the scope of the group and require more individualized attention. For example, if a parent suspects drug abuse or serious depression, an appropriate referral is essential.

Relapse Prevention

As with all new skills, parenting skills require practice. And time. Parents are going to make mistakes. At times of peak stress, they're going to forget the skills. One of the tools to prevent relapse is to encourage parents to take time before responding. It's better to not respond immediately than to respond inappropriately.

Another very effective strategy is to have parents exchange a list of their names and phone numbers. When parents feel stuck, they can call someone from the class for help in solving problems more objectively.

Resistance

Resistance is not usually a big problem if there are no parents who are participating as a result of a court mandate. The occasional parent who comes to the group hoping to find a brand-new punishment strategy usually doesn't return after the first session.

The major challenges arise in the form of resistance to the idea of giving up control: *Why can't I tell my fifteen-year-old daughter she can't wear makeup?* The best answer is that, of course, the parent *can* tell her. But does it work? Is the parent's life easier when he or she tries to enforce what is ultimately the daughter's choice? The fact is, the strategies that parents have been using haven't been working, or the parents wouldn't be in the group. The strategies presented here work. It's the parent's choice.

References

Ansbacher, H.L., and Ansbacher, R. R., eds. Alfred A. *Superiority and Social Interest.* New York: W.W. Norton & Co. Inc., 1979.

Bayard, R.T., and Bayard, J. *How to Deal with Your Acting-Up Teenager.* New York: M. Evans & Co., Inc., 1981.

Dinkmeyer, D., and McKay, G.D. *The Parent's Guide: Systematic Training for Effective Parenting of Teens.* Circle Pines, Minnesota: American Guidance Service, 1983.

_____ . *The Parent's Handbook: Systematic Training for Effective Parenting.* Circle Pines, Minnesota: American Guidance Service, 1982.

Dreikurs, R. *Children: The Challenge.* New York: Hawthorn Books, 1964.

Faber, A., and Mazlish, E. *How to Talk So Kids Will Listen and Listen So Kids Will Talk.* New York: Avon Books, 1980.

Fleming, D. *How to Stop the Battle with Your Teenager.* New York: Prentice Hall Press, 1989.

Nelson, J. *Positive Discipline.* New York: Ballantine Books, 1981.

Pryor, K. *Don't Shoot the Dog!* New York: Bantam Books, 1984.

Samalin, N. *Loving Your Child Is Not Enough.* New York: Penguin Books, 1987.

York, P.; York, D; and Wachtel, T. *Tough Love.* New York: Bantam Books, 1982.

Biographies

Chapter 1
Co-Dependency Groups

Ani Amerslav, M.A., M.F.C.C. is a psychotherapist in private practice in the San Francisco Bay Area. She is an adjunct faculty member at John F. Kennedy University in Orinda, California. She also is a clinical supervisor at Haight-Ashbury Psychological Services in San Francisco. She specializes in all phases of chemical dependency issues, working with incest survivors, and doing dream interpretations. She received her B.S. from the University of Minnesota and her M.A. from the University of San Francisco. In addition to her deep interest in Jungian psychology, she is certified in Reality Therapy.

Chapter 2
Shyness Groups

Lynne Henderson, M.S., M.F.C.C., is Director of the Palo Alto Shyness Clinic and is in private practice in Menlo Park, California. She specializes in shyness and social phobia. She received her bachelor's degree from the University of Pittsburgh, Pennsylvania, and her master's degree from San Jose State University, California. She is a Ph.D. candidate at Pacific Graduate School of Psychology (PGSP), California, where she has been chair of the student council and has received the Beacon of Light Award for outstanding service to the PGSP community. She is also a predoctoral fellow at Cowell Student Health Service at Stanford University. She is a member of the American Psychological Association, the California State Psychological Association, and the American Association of Behavior Therapists.

Chapter 3
The Agoraphobia Treatment Group

Edmund J. Bourne, Ph.D., is a psychologist in private practice in Campbell, California. He specializes in the treatment of panic attacks, agoraphobia, and other anxiety disorders. He received his doctorate from the University of Chicago and did postdoctoral research at Michael Reese Medical Center in Chicago. He has taught at several colleges and universities and is the recipient of national awards from the National Institute of Mental Health and the Association for the Advancement of Science. Dr. Bourne is the author of *The Anxiety & Phobia Workbook*.

Chapter 4
Cognitive-Behavioral Group Treatment for Depression

Jeanne Miranda, Ph.D., is Assistant Clinical Professor at the University of California, San Francisco, and San Francisco General Hospital. She specializes in the treatment of depression in disadvantaged medical patients. She received her Ph.D. from the University of Kansas, and is the Director of the Depression Clinic at San Francisco General Hospital. Dr. Miranda has written numerous articles on depression and somatization in medical patients.

Janice Schreckengost, Ph.D., is a Post-doctoral Fellow in Clinical Psychology at the University of California, San Francisco, and San Francisco General Hospital. She received her Ph.D. from the University of Illinois at Chicago. She has specialized in the treatment of depression during a two-year fellowship at UCSF, working in the Depression Clinic at San Francisco General Hospital. She is a published author in the area of community psychology.

Linda Heine, M.S., R.N., is a Clinical Nurse Specialist at the Department of Psychiatry at Highland Hospital, Oakland, California. She received her M.S. from the University of California, San Francisco, and training in the Depression Clinic at San Francisco General Hospital. She is a member of Sigma Theta Tau.

Chapter 5
Anger Control Groups

Matthew McKay, Ph.D., is Co-Director of Brief Therapy Associates and Haight-Ashbury Psychological Services in San Francisco. In private practice, he specializes in the cognitive-behavioral treatment of phobia, depression, and anger. He received his Ph.D. from the California School of Professional Psychology in Berkeley. Dr. McKay's other publications include: *The Relaxation & Stress Reduction Workbook, Thoughts & Feelings: The Art of Cognative Stress Intervention, Messages: The Communication Skills Book, The Divorce Book, Self-Esteem, When Anger Hurts,* and *Prisoners of Belief.*

Chapter 6
Assertiveness Groups

Martha Davis, Ph.D., is a psychologist in the Department of Psychiatry at Kaiser-Permanente Medical Center in Santa Clara, California. In addition to her brief-therapy work with individuals and couples, she leads co-dependancy groups, and occasionally conducts assertiveness training, stress management, and relaxation workshops, as well as cognitive and behavior modification groups. She received her doctorate in Social Clinical Psychology from the Wright Institute Graduate School in Berkeley, California. She is a member of the California Psychological Association and serves on the Board of Directors of Haight-Asbury Psychological Services. Dr. Davis is a co-author of *The Relaxation & Stress Reduction Workbook, Thoughts Feelings: The Art of Cognitive Stress Intervention,* and *Messages: The Communication Skills Book.* She is author of the *Leader's Guide to the Relaxation & Stress Reduction Workbook,* and *Relax: The Stress Reduction System.*

Chapter 7
Groups for Eating Disorders

Stephen S. Zimmer, C.S.W., is in private practice in New York City and specializes in the treatment of people with eating disorders. He received his M.S.W. from Hunter College School of Social Work, New York City. He is a co-founder of the Center for the Study of Anorexia and Bulimia in New York City and is the Director of group therapy at the center.

Chapter 8
Rape Survivors Group

Julia Conyers-Boyd, M.Ed., is a psychotherapist at Group Health Cooperative, Seattle, and in private practice. She specializes in sexual and domestic assault, cross-cultural counseling, and depression in women. She received her Master's degree from Pacific Luthern University, Washington, and is currently in a Doctorate at Seattle University. Ms. Conyers-Boyd's other publications include "Whose Reality; Personal Reflections and Comments on the Color Purple as It Relates to the Lives of Black Women," in *Sexual Coercion & Assault: Issues and Perspectives*, May/June 1986; and "Ethnic and Cultural Diversity: Keys to Power in Diversity and Complexity," in *Feminist Therapy*, 1990. Reprint of this article was also included in the *Black Women's Health Book, Speaking for Ourselves*.

Chapter 9
Brief Group Therapy With Adult Survivors of Incest

Margaret Schadler, Ph.D., is a psychologist at Kaiser Permanente Medical Center in Oakland, California, and in private practice in San Francisco. She received her Ph.D. from the University of Colorado in Boulder and has additional training in clinical psychology from the California School of Professional Psychology in Berkeley. She was a faculty member in the Department of Psychology at the University of Kansas before moving to California. Dr. Schadler is the co-author of a number of chapters and articles, and has made several presentations on family violence and on treating adult victims of abuse, incest, and violence.

Chapter 10
Survivors of Toxic Parents

Marion Behrend, M.A., M.F.C.C., is a counselor and hypnotherapist in private practice in Woodland Hills, California, specializing in treating adult survivors of physical and emotional abuse. She recieved her Master of Arts degree from the Azusa Pacific University satellite program at the California Family Study Center, and has worked for Bridge: A Way Across, in Burbank, California. She has also presented child abuse prevention programs in the Los Angeles Unified Schools, and was instrumental in developing the first SPEAK (Survivors of Physical and Emotional Abuse as Kids) groups for Parents Anonymous.

Mischelle Gerien, M.A., is an M.F.C.C. intern in private practice in Woodland Hills, California, specializing in treating adult survivors of physical and emotional abuse. She recieved her Master of Arts degree from California State University, Northridge, and interned for one year at the Valley Trauma Center in Northridge, California. For three years, she worked as co-therapist/trainee for one of the first SPEAK groups for Parents Anonymous. She has been a published writer for over 25 years, specializing in writing for and about adolescents.

Chapter 11
Group Therapy for Adult Incest Offenders and Adolescent Child Molesters

Brian R. Abbott, Ph.D., is the Director of Clinical and Training Services at the Giarretto Institute in San Jose, California. He specializes in research, assessment, and treatment of adolescent sexual offenders and adult incest offenders. He received his Ph.D. from the California Institute of Intergal Studies and his M.S.W. from the University of Hawaii at Manoa. He is a lecturer in the area of assessment and treatment of sexual offenders as well as the primary trainer for the Giarretto Institute's international training program.

Chapter 12
Domestic Violence Offender Groups

Alex MacKenzie, M.A., is an Employee Assistance Counselor and Organizational Development Consultant for the city and county of San Francisco. He received his Masters degree in Social Clinical Psychology from New College of California, San Francisco. He is a member of the Victims Services Advisory Committee to the Board of Supervisors in San Francisco.

Jack Prendergast, M.A., M.F.C.C., is a counselor working with groups and individuals at Men Overcoming Violence in San Francisco. He is a graduate of Notre Dame University, Indiana, and recieved his Masters degree in Clinical Psychology from Antioch University in San Francisco. Mr. Prendergast is a frequent guest on radio and television, addressing issues relating to counseling men in violent relationships.

Chapter 13
Beginning Group Therapy With Addicted Populations

Peter D. Rogers, Ph.D., is a licensed clinical psycholgist working in the Alcohol and Drug Treatment program at Kaiser Permanente Hospital in Redwood City, California. He received his doctoral degree from Adelphi University, New York. For the past 15 years, he has specialized in group psychotherapy with alcoholics and drug addicts. His professional background includes several years as Clinical Supervisor at the Haight-Ashbury Drug Detoxification and Rehabilitation Project, Clinical Director of the Contra Costa County Methadone Detoxification Program, and Consultant to the Social Security Administration on disabled alcoholics and drug addicts. Dr. Rogers is the co-author of *The Divorce Book* and *When Anger Hurts*.

Chapter 14
Parenting Groups

Kim Paleg, Ph.D., is the Clinical Coordinator at Haight-Ashbury Psychological Services in San Francisco. In private practice, she specializes in couple and family psychotherapy. She received her Ph.D. from the California Graduate School of Marital and Family Therapy in San Rafael, California (now the California Gradute School of Family Psychology). Dr. Paleg's other publications include "Spouse Abuse," a chapter that appears in the book *When Anger Hurts*.

Some Other New Harbinger Self-Help Titles

The Headache & Neck Pain Workbook, $14.95
Perimenopause, $13.95
The Self-Forgiveness Handbook, $12.95
A Woman's Guide to Overcoming Sexual Fear and Pain, $14.95
Mind Over Malignancy, $12.95
Treating Panic Disorder and Agoraphobia, $44.95
Scarred Soul, $13.95
The Angry Heart, $13.95
Don't Take It Personally, $12.95
Becoming a Wise Parent For Your Grown Child, $12.95
Clear Your Past, Change Your Future, $12.95
Preparing for Surgery, $17.95
Coming Out Everyday, $13.95
Ten Things Every Parent Needs to Know, $12.95
The Power of Two, $12.95
It's Not OK Anymore, $13.95
The Daily Relaxer, $12.95
The Body Image Workbook, $17.95
Living with ADD, $17.95
Taking the Anxiety Out of Taking Tests, $12.95
The Taking Charge of Menopause Workbook, $17.95
Living with Angina, $12.95
PMS: Women Tell Women How to Control Premenstrual Syndrome, $13.95
Five Weeks to Healing Stress: The Wellness Option, $17.95
Choosing to Live: How to Defeat Suicide Through Cognitive Therapy, $12.95
Why Children Misbehave and What to Do About It, $14.95
Illuminating the Heart, $13.95
When Anger Hurts Your Kids, $12.95
The Addiction Workbook, $17.95
The Mother's Survival Guide to Recovery, $12.95
The Chronic Pain Control Workbook, Second Edition, $17.95
Fibromyalgia & Chronic Myofascial Pain Syndrome, $19.95
Diagnosis and Treatment of Sociopaths, $44.95
Flying Without Fear, $12.95
Kid Cooperation: How to Stop Yelling, Nagging & Pleading and Get Kids to Cooperate, $12.95
The Stop Smoking Workbook: Your Guide to Healthy Quitting, $17.95
Conquering Carpal Tunnel Syndrome and Other Repetitive Strain Injuries, $17.95
The Tao of Conversation, $12.95
Wellness at Work: Building Resilience for Job Stress, $17.95
What Your Doctor Can't Tell You About Cosmetic Surgery, $13.95
An End to Panic: Breakthrough Techniques for Overcoming Panic Disorder, $17.95
Living Without Procrastination: How to Stop Postponing Your Life, $12.95
Goodbye Mother, Hello Woman: Reweaving the Daughter Mother Relationship, $14.95
Letting Go of Anger: The 10 Most Common Anger Styles and What to Do About Them, $12.95
Messages: The Communication Skills Workbook, Second Edition, $13.95
Coping With Chronic Fatigue Syndrome: Nine Things You Can Do, $12.95
The Anxiety & Phobia Workbook, Second Edition, $17.95
Thueson's Guide to Over-the-Counter Drugs, $13.95
Natural Women's Health: A Guide to Healthy Living for Women of Any Age, $13.95
I'd Rather Be Married: Finding Your Future Spouse, $13.95
The Relaxation & Stress Reduction Workbook, Fourth Edition, $17.95
Living Without Depression & Manic Depression: A Workbook for Maintaining Mood Stability, $17.95
Coping With Schizophrenia: A Guide For Families, $13.95
Visualization for Change, Second Edition, $13.95
Postpartum Survival Guide, $13.95
Angry All the Time: An Emergency Guide to Anger Control, $12.95
Couple Skills: Making Your Relationship Work, $13.95
Self-Esteem, Second Edition, $13.95
I Can't Get Over It, A Handbook for Trauma Survivors, Second Edition, $15.95
Dying of Embarrassment: Help for Social Anxiety and Social Phobia, $12.95
The Depression Workbook: Living With Depression and Manic Depression, $17.95
Men & Grief: A Guide for Men Surviving the Death of a Loved One, $13.95
When the Bough Breaks: A Helping Guide for Parents of Sexually Abused Children, $11.95
When Once Is Not Enough: Help for Obsessive Compulsives, $13.95
The Three Minute Meditator, Third Edition, $12.95
Beyond Grief: A Guide for Recovering from the Death of a Loved One, $13.95
The Divorce Book, $13.95
Hypnosis for Change: A Manual of Proven Techniques, Third Edition, $13.95
When Anger Hurts, $13.95

Call **toll free, 1-800-748-6273,** to order. Have your Visa or Mastercard number ready. Or send a check for the titles you want to New Harbinger Publications, Inc., 5674 Shattuck Ave., Oakland, CA 94609. Include $3.80 for the first book and 75¢ for each additional book, to cover shipping and handling. (California residents please include appropriate sales tax.) Allow four to six weeks for delivery.

Prices subject to change without notice.